KEYBOARD SCAN CODES

The following keyboard scan codes may be retrieved either by calling INT 16h or by calling INT 21h for keyboard input a second time (the first keyboard read returns 0). All codes are in hexadecimal:

FUNCTION KEYS

Key	Normal	With Shift	With Ctrl	With Alt
F1	3B	54	5E	68
F2	3C	55	5F	69
F3	3D	56	60	6A
F4	3E	57	61	6B
F5	3F	58	62	6C
F6	40	59	63	6D
F7	41	5A	64	6E
F8	42	5B	65	6F
F9	43	5C	66	70
F10	44	5D	67	71
F11	85	87	89	8B
F12	86	88	8A	8C

Key	Alone	With Ctrl Key
Home	47	77
End	4F	75
PgUp	49	84
PgDn	51	76
PrtSc	37	72
Left arrow	4B	73
Rt arrow	4D	74
Up arrow	48	8D
Dn arrow	50	91
Ins	52	92
Del	53	93
Back tab	0F	94
Gray +	4E	90
Gray −	4A	8E

Assembly Language for Intel®-Based Computers

Fifth Edition

KIP R. IRVINE

Florida International University
School of Computing and Information Sciences

PEARSON
Prentice Hall

Pearson Education, Inc.
Upper Saddle River, NJ 07458

Library of Congress Cataloging-in-Publication Data

Irvine, Kip R.
   Assembly language for intel-based computers/Kip R. Irvine.—5th ed.
      p. cm.
   Includes index.
   ISBN 0-13-238310-1
   1. IBM Personal Computer—Programming.   2. Assembler language (Computer program language)   I. Title.
   QA76.8.I77 2006
   005.265—dc22   2006012500

Vice President and Editorial Director, ECS: *Marcia J. Horton*
Executive Editor: *Tracy Dunkelberger*
Associate Editor: *Carole Snyder*
Editorial Assistant: *Christianna Lee*
Executive Managing Editor: *Vince O'Brien*
Managing Editor: *Camille Trentacoste*
Production Editor: *Karen Ettinger*
Director of Creative Services: *Paul Belfanti*
Creative Director: *Juan Lopez*
Managing Editor, AV Management and Production: *Patricia Burns*
Art Editor: *Gregory Dulles*
Manufacturing Manager, ESM: *Alexis Heydt-Long*
Manufacturing Buyer: *Lisa McDowell*
Executive Marketing Manager: *Robin O'Brien*
Marketing Assistant: *Mack Patterson*

© 2007, 2003, 1999 Pearson Education, Inc.
Pearson Prentice Hall
Pearson Education, Inc.
Upper Saddle River, New Jersey 07458

The author and publisher of this book have used their best efforts in preparing this book. These efforts include the development, research, and testing of the theories and programs to determine their effectiveness. The author and publisher make no warranty of any kind, expressed or implied, with regard to these programs or the documentation contained in this book. The author and publisher shall not be liable in any event for incidental or consequential damages in connection with, or arising out of, the furnishing, performance, or use of these programs.

Printed in the United States of America
All other trademarks or product names are the property of their respective owners.

TRADEMARK INFORMATION
IA-32, Pentium, and Intel 386 are trademarks of Intel Corporation.
TASM and Turbo Debugger are trademarks of Borland International.
Microsoft Assembler (MASM),Windows NT, Windows Me, Windows 95, Windows 98, Windows 2000, Windows XP, MS-Windows, PowerPoint, Win32, DEBUG, WinDbg, MS-DOS, Visual Studio, Visual C++, and CodeView are registered trademarks of Microsoft Corporation.
Autocad is a trademark of Autodesk.
PartitionMagic is a trademark of Symantec.

10 9 8 7 6 5 4 3 2 1

ISBN 0-13-238310-1

Pearson Education Ltd., *London*
Pearson Education Australia Pty. Ltd., *Sydney*
Pearson Education Singapore, Pte. Ltd.
Pearson Education North Asia Ltd., *Hong Kong*
Pearson Education Canada, Inc., *Toronto*
Pearson Educación de Mexico, S.A. de C.V.
Pearson Education—Japan, *Tokyo*
Pearson Education—Malaysia, Pte. Ltd.
Pearson Education, Inc., *Upper Saddle River, New Jersey*

To Jack and Candy Irvine

CONTENTS

17 Floating-Point Processing and Instruction Encoding   562

Preface

Assembly Language for Intel-Based Computers, Fifth Edition, teaches assembly language programming and architecture for Intel IA-32 processors. It is an appropriate text for the following types of college courses:

- Assembly Language Programming
- Fundamentals of Computer Systems
- Fundamentals of Computer Architecture

Students use Intel or AMD processors and program with **Microsoft Macro Assembler (MASM) 8.0,** running on any of the following MS-Windows platforms: Windows 95, 98, Millenium, NT, 2000, and XP.

Although this book was originally designed as a programming textbook for college students, it has evolved over the last 15 years into much more. Many universities use the book for their introductory computer architecture courses. As a testament to its popularity, the fourth edition was translated into Korean, Chinese, French, Russian, and Polish.

Emphasis of Topics   This edition includes topics that lead naturally into subsequent courses in computer architecture, operating systems, and compiler writing:

- Virtual machine concept
- Elementary boolean operations
- Instruction execution cycle
- Memory access and handshaking
- Interrupts and polling
- Pipelining and superscalar concepts
- Hardware-based I/O
- Floating-point binary representation

Other topics relate specifically to Intel IA-32 architecture:

- IA-32 protected memory and paging
- Memory segmentation in real-address mode
- 16-bit interrupt handling
- MS-DOS and BIOS system calls (interrupts)
- IA-32 Floating-Point Unit architecture and programming
- IA-32 Instruction encoding

Certain examples presented in the book lend themselves to courses that occur later in a computer science curriculum:

- Searching and sorting algorithms
- High-level language structures
- Finite-state machines
- Code optimization examples

Improvements in the Fifth Edition   A number of improvements and new information have been added in this edition, listed in the following table by chapter number:

Chapter	Improvements
2	Improved explanation of the instruction execution cycle.
5	An expanded link library with additional subroutines to write rich user interfaces, calculate program timings, generate pseudorandom integers, and parse integer strings. The documentation of the library has greatly improved.
6	Improved explanation of conditional jump encoding and relative jump ranges.
7	Two-operand and three-operand IMUL instructions are added. Performance comparisons are shown for differing approaches to integer multiplication.
8	Completely redesigned so that low-level details of stack frames (activation records) are explained first before introducing MASM's high-level INVOKE and PROC directives.
10	Improved documentation of the book's macro library.
11	New topic: Dynamic memory allocation in MS-Windows applications. Improved coverage of file handling and error reporting in MS-Windows applications.
12	Improved coverage of calling C and C++ functions from assembly language.
17	Introduction to the IA-32 floating-point instruction set. Floating-point data types. IA-32 Instruction encoding and decoding.

Still a Programming Book   This book is still focused on its original mission: to teach students how to write and debug programs at the machine level. It will never replace a complete book on computer architecture, but it does give students the first-hand experience of writing software in an environment that teaches them how a computer works. Our premise is that students retain knowledge better when theory is combined with experience. In an engineering course, students construct prototypes; in a computer architecture course, students should write machine-level programs. In both cases, they have a memorable experience that gives them the confidence to work in any OS/machine-oriented environment.

Real Mode and Protected Mode   This edition emphasizes 32-bit protected mode, but it still has three chapters devoted to real-mode programming. For example, there is an entire chapter on BIOS programming for the keyboard, video display (including graphics), and mouse. Another chapter covers MS-DOS programming using interrupts (system calls). Students can benefit from programming directly to hardware and the BIOS.

The examples in the first half of the book are nearly all presented as 32-bit text-oriented applications running in protected mode using the flat memory model. This approach is wonderfully simple because it avoids the complications of segment-offset addressing. Specially marked paragraphs and popup boxes point out occasional differences between protected mode and real mode programming. Most differences are abstracted by the book's parallel link libraries for real mode and protected mode programming.

Link Libraries   We supply two versions of the link library that students use for basic input-output, simulations, timing, and other useful stuff. The 32-bit version (*Irvine32.lib*) runs in protected mode, sending its output to the Win32 console. The 16-bit version (*Irvine16.lib*) runs in real-address mode. Full source code for the libraries is supplied on the book's Web site. The link libraries are available only for convenience, not to prevent students from learning how to program input-output themselves. Students are encouraged to create their own libraries.

Included Software and Examples   All the example programs were tested with Microsoft Macro Assembler Version 8.0. The 32-bit C++ applications in Chapter 12 were tested with Microsoft Visual C++ .NET. The real-address mode programs in Chapter 12 (linking to C++) were assembled with Borland Turbo Assembler (TASM).

Web Site Information   Updates and corrections to this book may be found at the book's Web site, http://www.asmirvine.com, including additional programming projects for instructors to assign at the ends of chapters. If for some reason you cannot access this site, information about the book and a link to its current Web site can be found at **www.prenhall.com** by searching for the book title or for the author name "Kip Irvine."

Overall Goals

The following goals of this book are designed to broaden the student's interest and knowledge in topics related to assembly language:

- Intel IA-32 processor architecture and programming
- Real-address mode and protected mode programming
- Assembly language directives, macros, operators, and program structure
- Programming methodology, showing how to use assembly language to create system-level software tools and application programs
- Computer hardware manipulation
- Interaction between assembly language programs, the operating system, and other application programs

One of our goals is to help students approach programming problems with a machine-level mind set. It is important to think of the CPU as an interactive tool, and to learn to monitor its operation as directly as possible. A debugger is a programmer's best friend, not only for catching errors, but as an educational tool that teaches about the CPU and operating system. We encourage students to look beneath the surface of high-level languages and to realize that most programming languages are designed to be portable and, therefore, independent of their host machines.

In addition to the short examples, this book contains hundreds of ready-to-run programs that demonstrate instructions or ideas as they are presented in the text. Reference materials, such as guides to MS-DOS interrupts and instruction mnemonics, are available at the end of the book.

Required Background   The reader should already be able to program confidently in at least one other programming language, preferably Java, C, or C++. One chapter covers C++ interfacing, so it is very helpful to have a compiler on hand. I have used this book in the classroom with majors in both computer science and management information systems, and it has been used elsewhere in engineering courses.

Features

Complete Program Listings   A companion CD-ROM contains all the source code from the examples in this book. Additional listings are available on the book's Web page. An extensive link library is supplied with the book, containing more than 30 procedures that simplify user input-output, numeric processing, disk and file handling, and string handling. In the beginning stages of the course, students can use this library to enhance their programs. Later, they can create their own procedures and add them to the library.

Programming Logic   Two chapters emphasize boolean logic and bit-level manipulation. A conscious attempt is made to relate high-level programming logic to the low-level details of the machine. This approach helps students to create more efficient implementations and to better understand how compilers generate object code.

Hardware and Operating System Concepts   The first two chapters introduce basic hardware and data representation concepts, including binary numbers, CPU architecture, status flags, and memory mapping. A survey of the computer's hardware and a historical perspective of the Intel processor family helps students to better understand their target computer system.

Structured Programming Approach   Beginning with Chapter 5, procedures and functional decomposition are emphasized. Students are given more complex programming exercises, requiring them to focus on design before starting to write code.

Disk Storage Concepts   Students learn the fundamental principles behind the disk storage system on MS-Windows–based systems from hardware and software points of view.

Creating Link Libraries   Students are free to add their own procedures to the book's link library and create new libraries. They learn to use a toolbox approach to programming and to write code that is useful in more than one program.

Macros and Structures   A chapter is devoted to creating structures, unions, and macros, which are esential in assembly language and systems programming. Conditional macros with advanced operators serve to make the macros more professional.

Interfacing to High-Level Languages   A chapter is devoted to interfacing assembly language to C and C++. This is an important job skill for students who are likely to find jobs programming in high-level languages. They can learn to optimize their code and see examples of how C++ compilers optimize code.

Instructional Aids   All the program listings are available on disk and on the Web. Instructors are provided a test bank, answers to review questions, solutions to programming exercises, and a Microsoft PowerPoint slide presentation for each chapter.

Summary of Chapters

Chapters 1 to 8 contain a basic foundation of assembly language and should be covered in sequence. After that, you have a fair amount of freedom. The following chapter dependency graph shows how later chapters depend on knowledge gained from other chapters. Chapter 10 was split into two parts for this graph because no other chapter depends on one's knowing how to create macros:

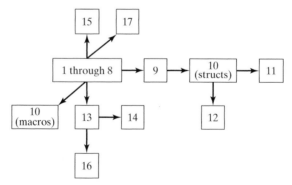

1. **Basic Concepts:** Applications of assembly language, basic concepts, machine language, and data representation.
2. **IA-32 Processor Architecture:** Basic microcomputer design, instruction execution cycle, IA-32 processor architecture, IA-32 memory management, components of a microcomputer, and the input-output system.
3. **Assembly Language Fundamentals:** Introduction to assembly language, linking and debugging, and defining constants and variables.

4. **Data Transfers, Addressing, and Arithmetic:** Simple data transfer and arithmetic instructions, assemble-link-execute cycle, operators, directives, expressions, JMP and LOOP instructions, and indirect addressing.

5. **Procedures:** Linking to an external library, description of the book's link library, stack operations, defining and using procedures, flowcharts, and top-down structured design.

6. **Conditional Processing:** Boolean and comparison instructions, conditional jumps and loops, high-level logic structures, and finite state machines.

7. **Integer Arithmetic:** Shift and rotate instructions with useful applications, multiplication and division, extended addition and subtraction, and ASCII and packed decimal arithmetic.

8. **Advanced Procedures:** Stack parameters, local variables, advanced PROC and INVOKE directives, and recursion.

9. **Strings and Arrays:** String primitives, manipulating arrays of characters and integers, two-dimensional arrays, sorting, and searching.

10. **Structures and Macros:** Structures, macros, conditional assembly directives, and defining repeat blocks.

11. **MS-Windows Programming:** Protected mode memory management concepts, using the Microsoft Windows API to display text and colors, and dynamic memory allocation.

12. **High-Level Language Interface:** Parameter passing conventions, inline assembly code, and linking assembly language modules to C and C++ programs.

13. **16-Bit MS-DOS Programming:** Calling MS-DOS interrupts for console and file input-output.

14. **Disk Fundamentals:** Disk storage systems, sectors, clusters, directories, file allocation tables, handling MS-DOS error codes, and drive and directory manipulation.

15. **BIOS-Level Programming:** Keyboard input, video text, graphics, and mouse programming.

16. **Expert MS-DOS Programming:** Custom-designed segments, runtime program structure, and Interrupt handling. Hardware control using I/O ports.

17. **Floating-Point Processing and Instruction Encoding:** Floating-point binary representation and floating-point arithmetic. Learning to program the IA-32 Floating-Point Unit. Understanding the encoding of IA-32 machine instructions.

> **Appendix A:** MASM Reference
> **Appendix B:** The IA-32 Instruction Set
> **Appendix C:** BIOS and MS-DOS Interrupts
> **Appendix D:** Answers to Review Questions

Reference Materials

Web Site The author maintains an active Web site at **www.asmirvine.com**.

Help File Help file (in Windows Help Format) by Gerald Cahill of Antelope Valley College. Documents the book's link libraries, as well as Win32 data structures.

Assembly Language Workbook An interactive workbook is included on the book's Web site, covering such important topics as number conversions, addressing modes, register usage, Debug programming, and floating-point binary numbers. The content pages are HTML documents, making it easy for students and instructors to add their own customized content. This workbook is also available on the book's Web site.

Debugging Tools Tutorials on using Microsoft CodeView, Microsoft Visual Studio, and Microsoft Windows Debugger (WinDbg).

BIOS and MS-DOS Interrupts Appendix C contains a brief listing of the most-often-used INT 10h (video), INT 16h (keyboard), and INT 21h (MS-DOS) functions.

Instruction Set Appendix B lists most nonprivileged instructions for the IA-32 processor family.

For each instruction, we describe its effect, show its syntax, and show which flags are affected.

PowerPoint Presentations   A complete set of Microsoft PowerPoint presentations written by the author.

Acknowledgments

Special thanks are due to Tracy Dunkleberger, Executive Editor for Computer Science at Prentice Hall, who provided friendly, helpful guidance during the writing of the fifth edition. Karen Ettinger did a terrific job as production editor, constantly keeping track of numerous minute details. Camille Trentacoste was the book's managing editor.

Fifth Edition

I offer my special thanks and gratitude to the following professors who boosted my morale, gave me great pedagogical tips, and tirelessly examined the entire book. They have been a huge influence on the development of this book, in some cases across multiple editions:

- **Gerald Cahill**, Antelope Valley College
- **James Brink**, Pacific Lutheran University
- **William Barrett**, San Jose State University

Many thanks to **Scott Blackledge** and **John Taylor**, both professional programmers, who proofread most of the manuscript and flagged numerous errors. Several people reviewed individual chapters:

- Jerry Joyce, Keene State College
- Tianzheng Wu, Mount Mercy College
- Ron Davis, Kennedy-King College
- David Topham, Ohlone College
- Harvey Nice, DePaul University

Fourth Edition

The following people were tremendously helpful in creating the fourth edition:

- Gerald Cahill, Antelope Valley College
- James Brink, Pacific Lutheran University
- Maria Kolatis, County College of Morris
- Tom Joyce, Chief Engineer at Premier Heart, LLC
- Jeff Wothke, Purdue Calumet University
- Tim Downey, Florida International University

The following individuals provided valuable proofreading help in the fourth edition:

- Andres Altamirano, Miami
- Courtney Amor, Los Angeles
- Scott Blackledge, Platform Solutions, Inc.
- Ronald Davis, Kennedy-King College
- Ata Elahi, Southern Connecticut State University
- Jose Gonzalez, Miami
- Leroy Highsmith, Southern Connecticut State University
- Sajid Iqbal, Faran Institute of Technology
- Charles Jones, Maryville College
- Vincent Kayes, Mount St. Mary College
- Eric Kobrin, Miami
- Pablo Maurin, Miami
- Barry Meaker, Design Engineer, Boeing Corporation
- Ian Merkel, Miami
- Sylvia Miner, Miami

- M. Nawaz, OPSTEC College of Computer Science
- Kam Ng, Chinese University of Hong Kong
- Hien Nguyen, Miami
- Ernie Philipp, Northern Virginia Community College
- Boyd Stephens, UGMO Research, LLC
- John Taylor, England
- Zachary Taylor, Columbia College
- Virginia Welsh, Community College of Baltimore County
- Robert Workman, Southern Connecticut State University
- Tianzheng Wu, Mount Mercy College
- Matthew Zukoski, Lehigh University

1

Basic Concepts

1.1 Welcome to Assembly Language

Assembly Language for Intel-Based Computers focuses on programming microprocessors compatible with the Intel IA-32 processor family on the MS-Windows platform. You can use an Intel or AMD 32-bit/64-bit processor to run all programs in this book.

The IA-32 family began with the Intel 80386, continuing to (and including) the Pentium 4. Microsoft MASM (*Macro Assembler*) 8.0 is our assembler of choice, running under MS-Windows. There are other good assemblers for Intel-based computers, including TASM (*Turbo Assembler*), NASM (*Netwide Assembler*), and the GNU assembler. Of these, TASM has the most similar syntax to MASM, and you could (with some help from your instructor) assemble and run most of the programs in this book. The other assemblers, NASM and GNU, have a somewhat different syntax.

Assembly language is the oldest programming language, and of all languages, bears the closest resemblance to native machine language. It provides direct access to computer hardware, requiring you to understand much about your computer's architecture and operating system.

Educational Value   Why read this book? Perhaps you're taking a college course whose name is similar to one of these:

- Microcomputer Assembly Language
- Assembly Language Programming
- Introduction to Computer Architecture
- Fundamentals of Computer Systems
- Embedded Systems Programming

These are names of courses at colleges and universities using previous editions of this book. This book covers basic principles about computer architecture, machine language, and low-level programming. You will learn enough assembly language to test your knowledge on today's most widely used microprocessor family. You won't be learning to program a "toy" computer using a simulated assembler; MASM is an industrial-strength assembler, used by practicing professionals. You will learn the architecture of the Intel IA-32 processor family from a programmer's point of view.

If you doubt the value of low-level programming and studying details of computer software and hardware, take note of the following quote from a leading computer scientist, Donald Knuth, in discussing his famous book series, *The Art of Computer Programming:*

> Some people [say] that having machine language, at all, was the great mistake that I made. I really don't think you can write a book for serious computer programmers unless you are able to discuss low-level detail.[1]

Visit this book's Web site to get lots of supplemental information, tutorials, and exercises at **www.asmirvine.com**

1.1.1   Good Questions to Ask

What Background Should I Have?   Before reading this book, you should have completed a college-level introductory computer programming course. You will better understand high-level programming constructs such as IF statements, loops, and arrays when implemented in assembly language.

What Are Assemblers and Linkers?   An *assembler* is a utility program that converts source code programs from assembly language into machine language. A *linker* is a utility program that combines individual files created by an assembler into a single executable program. A related utility, called a *debugger*, lets you to step through a program while it's running and examine registers and memory.

What Hardware and Software Do I Need?   You need a computer with Intel386, Intel486, Pentium, or compatible processor. AMD processors, for example, work very well with this book. MASM (the assembler) is compatible with all 32-bit versions of Microsoft Windows, beginning with Windows 95. A few of the advanced programs relating to direct hardware access and disk sector programming must be run under MS-DOS, Windows 95/98/Me, because of tight security restrictions imposed by Windows NT/2000/XP.

In addition, you will need the following:

- ***Editor:*** Use a text editor or programmer's editor to create assembly language source files. The CD-ROM accompanying this book contains Microsoft Visual C++ 2005 Express. It has an excellent text editor in its integrated development environment.
- ***32-Bit Debugger:*** Strictly speaking, you don't need a debugger, but you will probably want one. The debugger supplied with Visual C++ 2005 Express is excellent.

What Types of Programs Will I Create? This book shows how to create two general classes of programs:

- *16-Bit Real-Address Mode:* 16-bit real-address mode programs run under MS-DOS and in he console window under MS-Windows. Also known as *real mode* programs, they use a segmented memory model required of programs written for the Intel 8086 and 8088 processors. There are notes throughout the book with tips about programming in real-address mode, and two chapters are exclusively devoted to color and graphics programming in real mode.
- *32-Bit Protected Mode:* 32-bit protected mode programs run under all 32-bit versions of Microsoft Windows. They are usually easier to write and understand than real mode programs.

What Do I Get with This Book? Besides a lot of printed paper, you get a CD-ROM attached to the book containing Visual C++ 2005 Express. You will be able to download the Microsoft Assembler from the Microsoft Web site. See www.asmirvine.com for details on how to obtain the assembler.

The book's Web site (*www.asmirvine.com*) has the following:

- *Online Help File* detailing the book's library procedures and essential Windows API structures, by Gerald Cahill.
- *Assembly Language Workbook,* a collection of tutorials by the author.
- *Irvine32 and Irvine16 link libraries* for real-address mode and protected mode programming, with complete source code.
- *Example programs* with all source code from the book.
- *Corrections* to the book and example programs. Hopefully not too many!
- *Tutorials* on installing the assembler.
- *Articles* on advanced topics not included in the printed book for lack of space.
- *Discussion Group*, which over 500 members have joined.

What Will I Learn? This book should make you better informed about computer architecture, programming, and computer science. Here's what you will learn:

- Basic principles of computer architecture as applied to the Intel IA-32 processor family.
- Basic boolean logic and how it applies to programming and computer hardware.
- How IA-32 processors manage memory, using real mode, protected mode, and virtual mode.
- How high-level language compilers (such as C++) translate statements from their language into assembly language and native machine code.
- How high-level languages implement arithmetic expressions, loops, and logical structures at the machine level.
- Data representation, including signed and unsigned integers, real numbers, and character data.
- How to debug programs at the machine level. The need for this skill is vital when you work in languages such as C and C++, which provide access to low-level data and hardware.
- How application programs communicate with the computer's operating system via interrupt handlers, system calls, and common memory areas.
- How to interface assembly language code to C++ programs.
- How to create assembly language application programs.

How Does Assembly Language Relate to Machine Language? *Machine language* is a numeric language specifically understood by a computer's processor (the CPU). IA-32–compatible processors understand a common machine language. *Assembly language* consists of statements written with short mnemonics such as ADD, MOV, SUB, and CALL. Assembly language has a *one-to-one* relationship with machine language: Each assembly language instruction corresponds to a single machine-language instruction.

How Do C++ and Java Relate to Assembly Language?

High-level languages such as C++ and Java have a *one-to-many* relationship with assembly language and machine language. A single statement in C++ expands into multiple assembly language or machine instructions. We can show how C++ statements expand into machine code. Most people cannot read raw machine code, so we will use its closest relative, assembly language. The following C++ statement carries out two arithmetic operations and assigns the result to a variable. Assume X and Y are integers:

```
int Y;
int X = (Y + 4) * 3;
```

Following is the statement's translation to assembly language. The translation requires multiple statements because assembly language works at a detailed level:

```
mov   eax,Y        ; move Y to the EAX register
add   eax,4        ; add 4 to the EAX register
mov   ebx,3        ; move 3 to the EBX register
imul  ebx          ; multiply EAX by EBX
mov   X,eax        ; move EAX to X
```

(*Registers* are named storage locations in the CPU that hold intermediate results of operations.)

The point in this example is not to claim that C++ is superior to assembly language or vice versa, but to show their relationship.

> **We? Who's that?** Throughout this book, you're going to see constant references to *we*. Authors of textbooks and academic articles often use *we* as a formal reference to themselves. It just seems too informal to say, "I will now show you how to" do such-and-such. If it helps, think of *we* as a reference to the author, his reviewers (who really helped him a lot), his publisher (Prentice Hall), and his students (thousands).

Is Assembly Language Portable?

An important distinction between high-level languages and assembly language has to do with portability. A language whose source programs can be compiled and run on a wide variety of computer systems is said to be *portable*. A C++ program, for example, should compile and run on just about any computer, unless it makes specific references to library functions existing under a single operating system. A major feature of the Java language is that compiled programs run on nearly any computer system.

Assembly language is not portable because it is designed for a specific processor family. There are a number of different assembly languages widely used today, each based on a processor family. Some well-known processor families are Motorola 68x00, Intel IA-32, SUN Sparc, Vax, and IBM-370. The instructions in assembly language may directly match the computer's architecture or they may be translated during execution by a program inside the processor known as a *microcode interpreter*.

Why Learn Assembly Language?

Why not just read a good book on computer hardware and architecture and avoid learning assembly language programming?

- If you study computer engineering, you may likely be asked to write *embedded* programs. They are short programs stored in a small amount of memory in single-purpose devices such as telephones, automobile fuel and ignition systems, air-conditioning control systems, security systems, data acquisition instruments, video cards, sound cards, hard drives, modems, and printers. Assembly language is ideal for writing embedded programs because of its economical use of memory.

- Real-time applications such as simulations and hardware monitoring require precise timing and responses. High-level languages do not give programmers exact control over machine code generated by compilers. Assembly language permits you to precisely specify a program's executable code.

- Computer game consoles require their software to be highly optimized for small code size and fast execution. Game programmers are experts at writing code that takes full advantage of hardware features in a target system. They use assembly language as their tool of choice because it permits direct access to computer hardware, and code can be hand optimized for speed.

- Assembly language helps you to gain an overall understanding of the interaction between computer hardware, operating systems, and application programs. Using assembly language, you can apply and test theoretical information you are given in computer architecture and operating systems courses.

- Application programmers occasionally find that limitations in high-level languages prevent them from efficiently performing low-level tasks such as bitwise manipulation and data encryption. They will often call subroutines written in assembly language to accomplish their goal.

- Hardware manufacturers create device drivers for the equipment they sell. *Device drivers* are programs that translate general operating system commands into specific references to hardware details. Printer manufacturers, for example, create a different MS-Windows device driver for each model they sell. The same is true for Mac OS, Linux, and other operating systems.

Are There Rules in Assembly Language?   Most rules in assembly language are based on physical limitations of the target processor and its machine language. The CPU, for example, requires two instruction operands to be the same size. Assembly language has fewer rules than C++ or Java because the latter use syntax rules to reduce unintended logic errors at the expense of low-level data access. Assembly language programmers can easily bypass restrictions characteristic of high-level languages. Java, for example, does not permit access to specific memory addresses. One can work around the restriction by calling a C subroutine using JNI (Java Native Interface) classes, but the resulting program can be awkward to maintain. Assembly language, on the other hand, can access any memory address. The price for such freedom is high: Assembly language programmers spend a lot of time debugging!

1.1.2   Assembly Language Applications

In the early days of programming, most applications were written partially or entirely in assembly language. They had to fit in a small area of memory and run as efficiently as possible on slow processors. As memory became more plentiful and processors dramatically increased in speed, programs became more complex. Programmers switched to high-level languages such as C, FORTRAN, and COBOL that contained a certain amount of structuring capability. More recently, object-oriented languages such as C++, C#, and Java have made it possible to write complex programs containing millions of lines of code.

It is rare to see large application programs coded completely in assembly language because they would take too much time to write and maintain. Instead, assembly language is used to optimize certain sections of application programs for speed and to access computer hardware. Table 1-1 compares the adaptability of assembly language to high-level languages in relation to various types of applications.

Table 1-1   Comparison of Assembly Language to High-Level Languages.

Type of Application	High-Level Languages	Assembly Language
Business application software, written for single platform, medium to large size.	Formal structures make it easy to organize and maintain large sections of code.	Minimal formal structure, so one must be imposed by programmers who have varying levels of experience. This leads to difficulties maintaining existing code.
Hardware device driver.	Language may not provide for direct hardware access. Even if it does, awkward coding techniques may be required, resulting in maintenance difficulties.	Hardware access is straightforward and simple. Easy to maintain when programs are short and well documented.
Business application written for multiple platforms (different operating systems).	Usually portable. The source code can be recompiled on each target operating system with minimal changes.	Must be recoded separately for each platform, using an assembler with a different syntax. Difficult to maintain.
Embedded systems and computer games requiring direct hardware access.	Produces too much executable code, and may not run efficiently.	Ideal, because the executable code is small and runs quickly.

C++ has the unique quality of offering a compromise between high-level structure and low-level details. Direct hardware access is possible but completely nonportable. Most C++ compilers have the ability to generate assembly language source code, which the programmer can customize and refine before assembling into executable code.

1.1.3   Section Review

1. How do assemblers and linkers work together?
2. How will studying assembly language enhance your understanding of operating systems?
3. What is meant by a *one-to-many relationship* when comparing a high-level language to machine language?
4. Explain the concept of *portability* as it applies to programming languages.
5. Is the assembly language for the Intel 80x86 processor family the same as those for computer systems such as the Vax or Motorola 68x00?
6. Give an example of an *embedded systems* application.
7. What is a device driver?
8. Do you suppose type checking on pointer variables is stronger (stricter) in assembly language or in C++?
9. Name two types of applications that would be better suited to assembly language than a high-level language.
10. Why would a high-level language not be an ideal tool for writing a program to directly access a particular brand of printer?
11. Why is assembly language not usually used when writing large application programs?
12. *Challenge:* Translate the following C++ expression to assembly language, using the example presented earlier in this chapter as a guide: X = (Y * 4) + 3.

1.2   Virtual Machine Concept

A most effective way to explain how a computer's hardware and software are related is called the *virtual machine concept*. Our explanation of this model is derived from Andrew Tanenbaum's book, *Structured Computer Organization*.[2] To explain this concept, let us begin with the most basic function of a computer, executing programs.

A computer can usually execute programs written in its native *machine language*. Each instruction in this language is simple enough to be executed using a relatively small number of electronic circuits. For simplicity, we will call this language **L0**.

Programmers would have a difficult time writing programs in L0 because it is enormously detailed and consists purely of numbers. If a new language, **L1**, could be constructed that was easier to use, programs could be written in L1. There are two ways to achieve this:

- *Interpretation:* As the L1 program is running, each of its instructions could be decoded and executed by a program written in language L0. The L1 program begins running immediately, but each instruction has to be decoded before it can execute.
- *Translation:* The entire L1 program could be converted into an L0 program by an L0 program specifically designed for this purpose. Then the resulting L0 program could be executed directly on the computer hardware.

Virtual Machines   Rather than using only languages, it is easier to think in terms of a hypothetical computer, or *virtual machine*, at each level. The virtual machine **VM1**, as we will call it, can execute commands written in language L1. The virtual machine **VM0** can execute commands written in language L0:

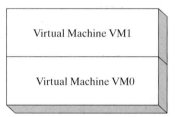

Each virtual machine can be constructed of either hardware or software. People can write programs for virtual machine VM1, and if it is practical to implement VM1 as an actual computer, programs can be executed directly on the hardware. Or programs written in VM1 can be interpreted/translated and executed on machine VM0.

Machine VM1 cannot be radically different from VM0 because the translation or interpretation would be too time-consuming. What if the language VM1 supports is still not programmer-friendly enough to be used for useful applications? Then another virtual machine, VM2, can be designed that is more easily understood. This process can be repeated until a virtual machine VM*n* can be designed to support a powerful, easy-to-use language.

The Java programming language is based on the virtual machine concept. A program written in the Java language is translated by a Java compiler into *Java byte code*. The latter is a low-level language quickly executed at run time by a program known as a *Java virtual machine (JVM)*. The JVM has been implemented on many different computer systems, making Java programs relatively system independent.

Specific Machines   Let us relate this to actual computers and languages, using names such as **Level 1** for VM1 and **Level 0** for VM0, shown in Figure 1–1. A computer's digital logic hardware represents machine Level 0, and Level 1 is implemented by an interpreter hardwired into the processor called *microarchitecture*. Above this is Level 2, called the *instruction set architecture*. This is the first level at which users can typically write programs, although the programs consist of binary numbers.

Microarchitecture (Level 1)   Computer chip manufacturers don't generally make it possible for average users to write microinstructions. The specific microarchitecture commands are often a proprietary secret. It might require three or four microcode instructions to carry out a primitive operation such as fetching a number from memory and incrementing it by 1.

FIGURE 1–1   Virtual Machine Levels 0 through 5.

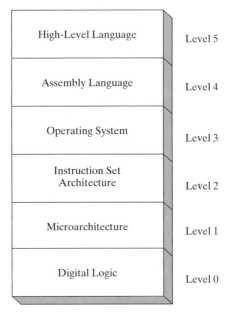

Instruction Set Architecture (Level 2)   Computer chip manufacturers design into the processor an *instruction set* to carry out basic operations, such as move, add, or multiply. This set of instructions is also referred to as *conventional machine language*, or simply *machine language*. Each machine-language instruction is executed by several microinstructions.

Operating System (Level 3)   As computers evolved, additional virtual machines were created to enable programmers to be more productive. A Level 3 machine understands interactive commands by users to load and execute programs, display directories, and so forth. This is known as the computer's *operating system*. The operating system software is translated into machine code running on a Level 2 machine.[3]

Assembly Language (Level 4)   Above the operating system level, programming languages provide the translation layers to make large-scale software development practical. Assembly language, which appears at Level 4, uses short mnemonics such as ADD, SUB, and MOV, which are easily translated to the instruction set architecture level (Level 2). Other assembly language statements, such as Interrupt calls, are executed directly by the operating system (Level 3). Assembly language programs are translated (*assembled*) in their entirety into machine language before they begin to execute.

High-Level Languages (Level 5)   At Level 5 are high-level programming languages such as C++, C#, Visual Basic, and Java. Programs in these languages contain powerful statements that translate into multiple instructions at Level 4. Internally, compilers translate Level 5 programs into Level 4 programs, which are in turn translated into Level 4 code. The latter are assembled into conventional machine language.

> The Intel IA-32 processor architecture supports multiple virtual machines. Its *virtual-86* operating mode emulates the architecture of the Intel 8086/8088 processor, used in the original IBM Personal Computer. The Pentium can run multiple instances of the virtual-86 machine at the same time, so that independent programs running on each virtual machine seem to have complete control of their host computer.

1.2.1   History of PC Assemblers

There is no official standard assembly language for Intel processors. What has emerged over the years is a *de facto* standard, established by Microsoft's popular MASM Version 5 assembler. Borland International established itself as a major competitor in the early 1990s with TASM (Turbo Assembler). TASM added many enhancements, producing what was called *Ideal Mode*, and Borland also provided a *MASM compatibility mode,* which matched the syntax of MASM Version 5.

Microsoft released MASM 6.0 in 1992, which was a major upgrade with many new features. Since then, Microsoft has released a number of upgrades to keep up with the ever-expanding Pentium family instruction set. MASM assembler syntax has not fundamentally changed since Version 6.0. Borland released 32-bit TASM 5.0 in 1996, which matches the current MASM syntax. There are other popular assemblers, all of which vary from MASM's syntax to a greater or lesser degree. To name a few, these include NASM (Netwide Assembler) for both Windows and Linux: MASM32, a shell built on top of MASM; Asm86; and GNU assembler, distributed by the Free Software Foundation.

1.2.2   Section Review

1. In your own words, describe the *virtual machine* concept.
2. Why don't programmers write application programs in machine language?
3. (*True/False*): When an interpreted program written in language L1 runs, each of its instructions is decoded and executed by a program written in language L0.
4. Explain the technique of translation when dealing with languages at different virtual machine levels.
5. How does the Intel IA-32 processor architecture contain an example of a virtual machine?
6. What software permits compiled Java programs to run on almost any computer?
7. Name the six virtual machine levels named in this section, from lowest to highest.
8. Why don't programmers write applications in microcode?
9. Conventional machine language is used at which level of the virtual machine shown in Figure 1–1?
10. Statements at the assembly language level of a virtual machine are translated into statements at which other level(s)?

1.3   Data Representation

Before discussing computer organization and assembly language, let us clarify binary, hexadecimal, decimal, and character-based storage concepts. Assembly language programmers deal with data at the physical level, so they must be adept at examining memory and registers. Often, binary numbers are used to describe the contents of computer memory; at other times, decimal and hexadecimal numbers are used. Programmers develop a certain fluency with number formats and can quickly translate numbers from one format to another.

Each numbering format, or system, has a *base*, or maximum number of symbols that can be assigned to a single digit. Table 1-2 shows the possible digits for the numbering systems used most commonly in computer literature. In the last row of the table, hexadecimal numbers use the digits 0 through 9 and continue with the letters A through F to represent decimal values 10 through 15. It is quite common to use hexadecimal numbers when showing the contents of computer memory and machine-level instructions.

Table 1-2   Binary, Octal, Decimal, and Hexadecimal Digits.

System	Base	Possible Digits
Binary	2	0 1
Octal	8	0 1 2 3 4 5 6 7
Decimal	10	0 1 2 3 4 5 6 7 8 9
Hexadecimal	16	0 1 2 3 4 5 6 7 8 9 A B C D E F

1.3.1 Binary Numbers

A computer stores instructions and data in memory as collections of electronic charges. Representing these entities with numbers requires a system geared to the concepts of *on* and *off* or *true* and *false*. *Binary numbers* are base 2 numbers in which each binary digit (called a *bit*) is either a 0 or a 1. *Bits* are numbered starting at zero on the right side and increasing toward the left. The bit on the left is called the *most significant bit* (MSB), and the bit on the right is the *least significant bit* (LSB). The MSB and LSB bit numbers of a 16-bit binary number are shown in the following figure:

```
MSB                          LSB
1 0 1 1 0 0 1 0 1 0 0 1 1 1 0 0
15                             0
```

Binary integers can be signed or unsigned. A signed integer is positive or negative. An unsigned integer is by default positive. Zero is considered positive. Using special encoding schemes, one can represent real numbers in binary, but we will defer the discussion of these for a later chapter. For now, let's begin with unsigned binary integers.

Unsigned Binary Integers

Starting with the least significant bit, each bit in an unsigned binary integer represents an increasing power of 2. The following figure contains an 8-bit binary number, showing how powers of two increase from right to left:

```
1   1   1   1   1   1   1   1
2^7 2^6 2^5 2^4 2^3 2^2 2^1 2^0
```

Table 1-3 lists the decimal values of 2^0 through 2^{15}.

Table 1-3   Binary Bit Position Values.

2^n	Decimal Value	2^n	Decimal Value
2^0	1	2^8	256
2^1	2	2^9	512
2^2	4	2^{10}	1024
2^3	8	2^{11}	2048
2^4	16	2^{12}	4096
2^5	32	2^{13}	8192
2^6	64	2^{14}	16384
2^7	128	2^{15}	32768

Translating Unsigned Binary Integers to Decimal

Weighted positional notation represents a convenient way to calculate the decimal value of an unsigned binary integer having n digits:

$$dec = (D_{n-1} \times 2^{n-1}) + (D_{n-2} \times 2^{n-2}) + \cdots + (D_1 \times 2^1) + (D_0 \times 2^0)$$

D indicates a binary digit. For example, binary 00001001 is equal to 9. We calculate this value by leaving out terms equal to zero:

$$(1 \times 2^3) + (1 \times 2^0) = 9$$

The same calculation is shown by the following figure:

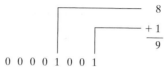

$$
\begin{array}{r}
8 \\
+\ 1 \\
\hline
9
\end{array}
$$

0 0 0 0 1 0 0 1

Translating Unsigned Decimal Integers to Binary

To translate an unsigned decimal integer into binary, repeatedly divide the integer by 2, saving each remainder as a binary digit. The following table shows the steps required to translate decimal 37 to binary. The remainder digits, starting from the top row, are the binary digits D_0, D_1, D_2, D_3, D_4, and D_5:

Division	Quotient	Remainder
37 / 2	18	1
18 / 2	9	0
9 / 2	4	1
4 / 2	2	0
2 / 2	1	0
1 / 2	0	1

Collecting the binary digits in the remainder column in reverse order produces binary 100101. Because Intel computer storage always consists of binary numbers whose lengths are multiples of 8, we fill the remaining two digit positions on the left with zeros, producing 00100101.

1.3.2 Binary Addition

When adding two binary integers, proceed bit by bit, starting with the low-order pair of bits (on the right) and add each subsequent pair of bits. There are four ways to add two binary digits, as shown here:

0 + 0 = 0	0 + 1 = 1
1 + 0 = 1	1 + 1 = 10

When adding 1 to 1, the result is 10 binary (think of it as the decimal value 2). The extra digit generates a carry to the next-highest bit position. In the following figure, we add binary 00000100 to 00000111:

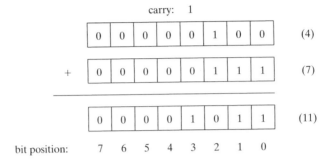

Beginning with the lowest bit in each number (bit position 0), we add $0 + 1$, producing a 1 in the bottom row. The same happens in the next highest bit (position 1). In bit position 2, we add $1 + 1$, generating a sum of zero and a carry of 1. In bit position 3, we add the carry bit to $0 + 0$, producing 1. The rest of the bits are zeros. You can verify the addition by adding the decimal equivalents shown on the right side of the figure $(4 + 7 = 11)$.

1.3.3   Integer Storage Sizes

The basic storage unit for all data in an IA-32–based computer is a *byte*, containing 8 bits. Other storage sizes are *word* (2 bytes), *doubleword* (4 bytes), and *quadword* (8 bytes). In the following figure, the number of bits is shown for each size:

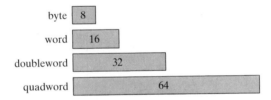

Table 1-4 shows the range of possible values for each type of unsigned integer.

Table 1-4   Ranges of Unsigned Integers.

Storage Type	Range (Low–High)	Powers of 2
Unsigned byte	0 to 255	0 to $(2^8 - 1)$
Unsigned word	0 to 65,535	0 to $(2^{16} - 1)$
Unsigned doubleword	0 to 4,294,967,295	0 to $(2^{32} - 1)$
Unsigned quadword	0 to 18,446,744,073,709,551,615	0 to $(2^{64} - 1)$

Large Measurements   A number of large measurements are used when referring to both memory and disk space:[4]

- One *kilobyte* is equal to 2^{10}, or 1024 bytes.
- One *megabyte* (MB) is equal to 2^{20}, or 1,048,576 bytes.
- One *gigabyte* (GB) is equal to 2^{30}, or 1024^3, or 1,073,741,824 bytes.

- One *terabyte* (TB) is equal to 2^{40}, or 1024^4, or 1,099,511,627,776 bytes.
- One *petabyte* is equal to 2^{50}, or 1,125,899,906,842,624 bytes.
- One *exabyte* is equal to 2^{60}, or 1,152,921,504,606,846,976 bytes.
- One *zettabyte* is equal to 2^{70} bytes.
- One *yottabyte* is equal to 2^{80} bytes.

1.3.4 Hexadecimal Integers

Large binary numbers are cumbersome to read, so hexadecimal digits offer a convenient way to represent binary data. Each digit in a hexadecimal integer represents four binary bits, and two hexadecimal digits together represent a byte. A single hexadecimal digit represents decimal 0 to 15, so letters A to F represent decimal values in the range 10 through 15. Table 1-5 shows how each sequence of four binary bits translates into a decimal or hexadecimal value.

Table 1-5   Binary, Decimal, and Hexadecimal Equivalents.

Binary	Decimal	Hexadecimal	Binary	Decimal	Hexadecimal
0000	0	0	1000	8	8
0001	1	1	1001	9	9
0010	2	2	1010	10	A
0011	3	3	1011	11	B
0100	4	4	1100	12	C
0101	5	5	1101	13	D
0110	6	6	1110	14	E
0111	7	7	1111	15	F

The following example shows how binary 0001011010100011110010100 is equivalent to hexadecimal 16A794:

1	6	A	7	9	4
0001	0110	1010	0111	1001	0100

Converting Unsigned Hexadecimal to Decimal

In hexadecimal, each digit position represents a power of 16. This is helpful when calculating the decimal value of a hexadecimal integer. Suppose we number the digits in a four-digit hexadecimal integer with subscripts as $D_3D_2D_1D_0$. The following formula calculates the number's decimal value:

$$dec = (D_3 \times 16^3) + (D_2 \times 16^2) + (D_1 \times 16^1) + (D_0 \times 16^0)$$

The formula can be generalized for any *n*-digit hexadecimal number:

$$dec = (D_{n-1} \times 16^{n-1}) + (D_{n-2} \times 16^{n-2}) + \cdots + (D_1 \times 16^1) + (D_0 \times 16^0)$$

For example, hexadecimal 1234 is equal to $(1 \times 16^3) + (2 \times 16^2) + (3 \times 16^1) + (4 \times 16^0)$, or decimal 4660. Similarly, hexadecimal 3BA4 is equal to $(3 \times 16^3) + (11 \times 16^2) + (10 \times 16^1) + (4 \times 16^0)$, or decimal 15,268. The following figure shows this last calculation:

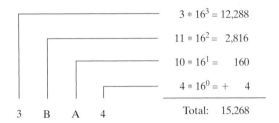

Table 1-6 lists the powers of 16 from 16^0 to 16^7.

TABLE 1-6   Powers of 16 in Decimal.

16^n	Decimal Value	16^n	Decimal Value
16^0	1	16^4	65,536
16^1	16	16^5	1,048,576
16^2	256	16^6	16,777,216
16^3	4096	16^7	268,435,456

Converting Unsigned Decimal to Hexadecimal

To convert an unsigned decimal integer to hexadecimal, repeatedly divide the decimal value by 16 and retain each remainder as a hexadecimal digit. For example, the following table lists the steps when converting decimal 422 to hexadecimal:

Division	Quotient	Remainder
422 / 16	26	6
26 / 16	1	A
1 / 16	0	1

When one collects the digits from the remainder column in reverse order, the hexadecimal representation is **1A6**. The same algorithm was used for binary numbers in Section 1.3.1.

1.3.5   Signed Integers

Signed binary integers are positive or negative. On Intel-based computers, the most significant bit (MSB) indicates the sign: 0 is positive and 1 is negative. The following figure shows examples of 8-bit negative and positive integers:

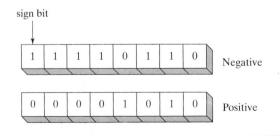

Two's-Complement Notation

Negative integers use *two's-complement* representation, using the mathematical principle that the two's complement of an integer is its additive inverse. (If you add a number to its *additive inverse*, the sum is zero.)

Two's-complement representation is useful to processor designers because it removes the need for separate digital circuits to handle both addition and subtraction. For example, if presented with the expression $A - B$, the processor can simply convert it to an addition expression: $A + (-B)$.

The two's complement of a binary integer is formed by inverting (complementing) its bits and adding 1. Using the 8-bit binary value 00000001, for example, its two's complement turns out to be 11111111, as can be seen as follows:

Starting value	00000001
Step 1: Reverse the bits	11111110
Step 2: Add 1 to the value from Step 1	11111110 +00000001
Sum: Two's-complement representation	11111111

11111111 is the two's-complement representation of -1. The two's-complement operation is reversible, so the two's complement of 11111111 is 00000001.

Two's Complement of Hexadecimal   To form the two's complement of a hexadecimal integer, reverse all bits and add 1. An easy way to reverse the bits of a hexadecimal digit is to subtract the digit from 15. Here are several examples of hexadecimal integers converted to their two's complements:

```
6A3D --> 95C2 + 1 --> 95C3
95C3 --> 6A3C + 1 --> 6A3D
21F0 --> DE0F + 1 --> DE10
DE10 --> 21EF + 1 --> 21F0
```

Converting Signed Binary to Decimal   To calculate the decimal equivalent of a signed binary integer, do one of the following:

- If the highest bit is a 1, the number is stored in two's-complement notation. Form its two's complement a second time to get its positive equivalent. Then convert this new number to decimal as if it were an unsigned binary integer.
- If the highest bit is a 0, you can convert it to decimal as if it were an unsigned binary integer.

For example, signed binary 11110000 has a 1 in the highest bit, indicating that it is a negative integer. First we form its two's complement, then we convert the result to decimal. Here are the steps in the process:

Starting value	11110000
Step 1: Reverse the bits	00001111
Step 2: Add 1 to the value from Step 1	00001111 + 1
Step 3: Form the two's complement	00010000
Step 4: Convert to decimal	16

Because the original integer (11110000) was negative, we infer its decimal value was **−16**.

Converting Signed Decimal to Binary   To determine the binary representation of a signed decimal integer, do the following:

1. Convert the absolute value of the decimal integer to binary.
2. If the original decimal integer was negative, form the two's complement of the binary number from the previous step.

For example, −43 decimal is translated to binary as follows:

1. The binary representation of unsigned 43 is 00101011.
2. Because the original value was negative, we form the two's complement of 00101011, which is 11010101. This is the representation of −43 decimal.

Converting Signed Decimal to Hexadecimal   To convert a signed decimal integer to hexadecimal, do the following:

1. Convert the absolute value of the decimal integer to hexadecimal.
2. If the decimal integer was negative, form the two's complement of the hexadecimal number from the previous step.

Converting Signed Hexadecimal to Decimal   To convert a signed hexadecimal integer to decimal, do the following:

1. If the hexadecimal integer is negative, form its two's complement; otherwise, retain the integer as is.
2. Using the integer from the previous step, convert it to decimal. If the original value was negative, attach a minus sign to the beginning of the decimal integer.

> You can tell whether a hexadecimal integer is positive or negative by inspecting its most significant (highest) digit. If the digit is ≥ 8, the number is negative; if the digit is ≤ 7, the number is positive. For example, hexadecimal 8A20 is negative and 7FD9 is positive.

Maximum and Minimum Values

A signed integer of n bits uses only $n - 1$ bits to represent the number's magnitude. Table 1-7 shows the minimum and maximum values for signed bytes, words, doublewords, and quadwords.

Table 1-7   Storage Sizes and Ranges of Signed Integers.

Storage Type	Range (Low–High)	Powers of 2
Signed byte	−128 to +127	-2^7 to $(2^7 - 1)$
Signed word	−32,768 to +32,767	-2^{15} to $(2^{15} - 1)$
Signed doubleword	−2,147,483,648 to 2,147,483,647	-2^{31} to $(2^{31} - 1)$
Signed quadword	−9,223,372,036,854,775,808 to +9,223,372,036,854,775,807	-2^{63} to $(2^{63} - 1)$

1.3.6 Character Storage

If computers can store only binary data, how do they represent characters? A *character set* is required, a mapping of characters to integers. Until a few years ago, character sets used only 8 bits. Even now, when running in character mode (such as MS-DOS), IBM-compatible microcomputers use the *ASCII* (pronounced "askey") character set. ASCII is an acronym for *American Standard Code for Information Interchange*. In ASCII, a unique 7-bit integer is assigned to each character. Because ASCII codes use only the lower 7 bits of every byte, the extra bit is used on various computers to create a proprietary character set. On IBM-compatible microcomputers, for example, values 128 through 255 represent graphics symbols and Greek characters.

ANSI Character Set American National Standards Institute (ANSI) defines an 8-bit character set used to represent up to 256 characters. The first 128 characters correspond to the letters and symbols on a standard U.S. keyboard. The second 128 characters represent special characters such as letters in international alphabets, accents, currency symbols, and fractions. MS-Windows Me, 98, and 95 use the ANSI character set. To increase the number of available characters, MS-Windows switches between character tables known as *code pages*.

Unicode Standard There has been a need for some time to represent a wide variety of international languages in computer software and to avoid the clutter of hundreds of diverse coding schemes in existence. As a result, the *Unicode* standard was created as a universal way of defining characters and symbols. It defines codes for characters, symbols, and punctuation used in all major languages, as well as European alphabetic scripts, Middle Eastern right-to-left scripts, and many scripts of Asia.[5] Three encoding forms are available in Unicode, permitting data to be transmitted in byte, word, or doubleword formats:

- **UTF-8** is used in HTML, and has the same byte values as ASCII (American Standard Code for Information Interchange). It can be incorporated into a variable-length encoding system for all Unicode characters.
- **UTF-16** is used in environments that balance efficient access to characters with economical use of storage. Windows NT, 2000, and XP, for example, use UTF-16 encoding. Each character is encoded in 16 bits.
- **UTF-32** is used in environments where space is no concern and fixed-width characters are required. Each character is encoded in 32 bits.

You can copy a smaller Unicode value (byte, for example) into a larger one (word or doubleword) without losing any data.

ASCII Strings A sequence of one or more characters is called a *string*. More specifically, an *ASCII string* is stored in memory as a succession of bytes containing ASCII codes. For example, the numeric codes for the string "ABC123" are 41h, 42h, 43h, 31h, 32h, and 33h. A *null-terminated* string is a string of characters followed by a single byte containing zero. The C and C++ languages use null-terminated strings, and many MS-DOS and MS-Windows functions require strings to be in this format.

Using the ASCII Table A table on the inside back cover of this book lists ASCII codes used when running in MS-DOS mode. To find the hexadecimal ASCII code of a character, look along the top row of the table and find the column containing the character you want to translate. The most significant digit of the hexadecimal value is in the second row at the top of the table; the least significant digit is in the second column from the left. For example, to find the ASCII code of the letter **a**, find the column containing the **a** and look in the second row: The first hexadecimal digit is 6. Next, look to the left along the row containing **a** and note that the second column contains the digit 1. Therefore, the ASCII code of **a** is 61 hexadecimal. This is shown as follows in simplified form:

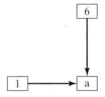

ASCII Control Characters Character codes in the range 0 through 31 are called *ASCII control characters*. If a program writes these codes to standard output (as in C++), the control characters will carry out predefined actions. Table 1-8 lists the most commonly used characters in this range.

Table 1-8   ASCII Control Characters.

ASCII Code (Decimal)	Description
8	Backspace (moves one column to the left)
9	Horizontal tab (skips forward *n* columns)
10	Line feed (moves to next output line)
12	Form feed (moves to next printer page)
13	Carriage return (moves to leftmost output column)
27	Escape character

Terminology for Numeric Data Representation   It is important to use precise terminology when describing the way numbers and characters are represented in memory and on the display screen. Decimal 65, for example, is stored in memory as a single binary byte as 01000001. A debugging program would probably display the byte as "41," which is the number's hexadecimal representation. If the byte were copied to video memory, the letter **"A"** would appear on the screen. Why? Because 01000001 is the ASCII code for the letter **A**. Because a number's interpretation can depend on the context in which it appears, we assign a specific name to each type of data representation to clarify future discussions:

• A *binary integer* is an integer stored in memory in its raw format, ready to be used in a calculation. Binary integers are stored in multiples of 8 bits (8, 16, 32, 48, or 64).

• An *ASCII digit string* is a string of ASCII characters, such as "123" or "65," which is made to look like a number. This is simply a representation of the number and can be in any of the formats shown for the decimal number 65 in Table 1-9:

Table 1-9   Types of Numeric Strings.

Format	Value
ASCII binary	"01000001"
ASCII decimal	"65"
ASCII hexadecimal	"41"
ASCII octal	"101"

1.3.7   Section Review

1. Explain the term LSB.

2. Explain the term MSB.

3. What is the decimal representation of each of the following unsigned binary integers?
   a. 11111000
   b. 11001010
   c. 11110000

4. What is the decimal representation of each of the following unsigned binary integers?
   a. 00110101
   b. 10010110
   c. 11001100

5. What is the sum of each pair of binary integers?
   a. 00001111 + 00000010

    b. 11010101 + 01101011

    c. 00001111 + 00001111

6. What is the sum of each pair of binary integers?

    a. 10101111 + 11011011

    b. 10010111 + 11111111

    c. 01110101 + 10101100

7. How many bytes are in each of the following data types?

    a. word

    b. doubleword

    c. quadword

8. How many bits are in each of the following data types?

    a. word

    b. doubleword

    c. quadword

9. What is the minimum number of binary bits needed to represent each of the following unsigned decimal integers?

    a. 65

    b. 256

    c. 32768

10. What is the minimum number of binary bits needed to represent each of the following unsigned decimal integers?

    a. 4095

    b. 65534

    c. 2134657

11. What is the hexadecimal representation of each of the following binary numbers?

    a. 1100 1111 0101 0111

    b. 0101 1100 1010 1101

    c. 1001 0011 1110 1011

12. What is the hexadecimal representation of each of the following binary numbers?

    a. 0011 0101 1101 1010

    b. 1100 1110 1010 0011

    c. 1111 1110 1101 1011

13. What is the binary representation of the following hexadecimal numbers?

    a. E5B6AED7

    b. B697C7A1

    c. 234B6D92

14. What is the binary representation of the following hexadecimal numbers?

    a. 0126F9D4

    b. 6ACDFA95

    c. F69BDC2A

15. What is the unsigned decimal representation of each hexadecimal integer?

    a. 3A

    b. 1BF

    c. 4096

16. What is the unsigned decimal representation of each hexadecimal integer?

    a. 62

b. 1C9

c. 6A5B

17. What is the 16-bit hexadecimal representation of each signed decimal integer?

    a. −26

    b. −452

18. What is the 16-bit hexadecimal representation of each signed decimal integer?

    a. −32

    b. −62

19. The following 16-bit hexadecimal numbers represent signed integers. Convert to decimal.

    a. 7CAB

    b. C123

20. The following 16-bit hexadecimal numbers represent signed integers. Convert to decimal.

    a. 7F9B

    b. 8230

21. What is the decimal representation of the following signed binary numbers?

    a. 10110101

    b. 00101010

    c. 11110000

22. What is the decimal representation of the following signed binary numbers?

    a. 10000000

    b. 11001100

    c. 10110111

23. What is the 8-bit binary (two's-complement) representation of each of the following signed decimal integers?

    a. −5

    b. −36

    c. −16

24. What is the 8-bit binary (two's-complement) representation of each of the following signed decimal integers?

    a. −72

    b. −98

    c. −26

25. What are the hexadecimal and decimal representations of the ASCII character capital X?

26. What are the hexadecimal and decimal representations of the ASCII character capital M?

27. Why was Unicode invented?

28. *Challenge:* What is the largest value you can represent using a 256-bit *unsigned* integer?

29. *Challenge:* What is the largest positive value you can represent using a 256-bit *signed* integer?

1.4 Boolean Operations

Boolean algebra defines a set of operations on the values **true** and **false.** It was invented by George Boole, a mid–nineteenth-century mathematician who designed the first model of a computer (named the *Analytical Engine*[6]). When early digital computers were invented, it was clear that Boole's algebra could be used to describe the design of digital circuits. At the same time, boolean expressions are used in programming to express logical operations.

Boolean Expression   A boolean expression involves a boolean operator and one or more operands. Each boolean expression implies a value of true or false. The set of operators includes the folllowing:

• NOT: notated as ¬ or ~ or '

- AND: notated as ∧ or •
- OR: notated as ∨ or +

The NOT operator is unary, and the other operators are binary. The operands of a boolean expression can also be boolean expressions. The following are examples:

Expression	Description
¬X	NOT X
X ∧ Y	X AND Y
X ∨ Y	X OR Y
¬X ∨ Y	(NOT X) OR Y
¬(X ∧ Y)	NOT (X AND Y)
X ∧ ¬Y	X AND (NOT Y)

NOT   The NOT operation reverses a boolean value. It can be written in mathematical notation as ¬X, where X is a variable (or expression) holding a value of true (T) or false (F). The following truth table shows all the possible outcomes of NOT using a variable **X**. Inputs are on the left side and outputs (shaded) are on the right side:

X	¬X
F	T
T	F

A truth table can use 0 for false and 1 for true.

AND   The Boolean AND operation requires two operands, and can be expressed using the notation X ∧ Y. The following truth table shows all the possible outcomes (shaded) for the values of X and Y:

X	Y	X ∧ Y
F	F	F
F	T	F
T	F	F
T	T	T

The output is true only when both inputs are true. This corresponds to the logical AND used in compound boolean expressions in C++ and Java.

OR   The Boolean OR operation requires two operands, and is often expressed using the notation **X ∨ Y**. The following truth table shows all the possible outcomes (shaded) for the values of X and Y:

X	Y	X ∨ Y
F	F	F
F	T	T
T	F	T
T	T	T

The output is false only when both inputs are false. This truth table corresponds to the logical OR used in compound boolean expressions in C++ and Java.

Operator Precedence   In a boolean expression involving more than one operator, precedence is important. As shown in the following table, the NOT operator has the highest precedence, followed by AND and OR. To avoid ambiguity, use parentheses to force the initial evaluation of an expression:

Expression	Order of Operations
$\neg X \vee Y$	NOT, then OR
$\neg(X \vee Y)$	OR, then NOT
$X \vee (Y \wedge Z)$	AND, then OR

1.4.1   Truth Tables for Boolean Functions

A *boolean function* receives boolean inputs and produces a boolean output. A truth table can be constructed for any boolean function, showing all possible inputs and outputs. The following are truth tables representing boolean functions having two inputs named X and Y. The shaded column on the right is the function's output:

Example 1: $\neg X \vee Y$

X	$\neg X$	Y	$\neg X \vee Y$
F	T	F	T
F	T	T	T
T	F	F	F
T	F	T	T

Example 2: $X \wedge \neg Y$

X	Y	$\neg Y$	$X \wedge \neg Y$
F	F	T	F
F	T	F	F
T	F	T	T
T	T	F	F

Example 3: $(Y \wedge S) \vee (X \wedge \neg S)$

X	Y	S	Y∧S	¬S	X∧¬S	$(Y \wedge S) \vee (X \wedge \neg S)$
F	F	F	F	T	F	F
F	T	F	F	T	F	F
T	F	F	F	T	T	T
T	T	F	F	T	T	T
F	F	T	F	F	F	F
F	T	T	T	F	F	T
T	F	T	F	F	F	F
T	T	T	T	F	F	T

This boolean function describes a *multiplexer,* a digital component that uses a selector bit (S) to select one of two outputs (X or Y). If S = false, the function output (Z) is the same as X. If S = true, the function output is the same as Y. Here is a block diagram of a multiplexer:

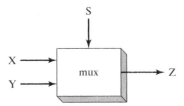

1.4.2   Section Review

1. Describe the following boolean expression: $\neg X \vee Y$.
2. Describe the following boolean expression: $(X \wedge Y)$.
3. What is the value of the boolean expression $(T \wedge F) \vee T$?
4. What is the value of the boolean expression $\neg(F \vee T)$?
5. What is the value of the boolean expression $\neg F \vee \neg T$?
6. Create a truth table to show all possible inputs and outputs for the boolean function described by $\neg(A \vee B)$.
7. Create a truth table to show all possible inputs and outputs for the boolean function described by $(\neg A \wedge \neg B)$.
8. *Challenge:* If a boolean function has four inputs, how many rows would be required for its truth table?
9. *Challenge:* How many selector bits would be required for a four-input multiplexer?

1.5   Chapter Summary

This book focuses on programming microprocessors compatible with the Intel IA-32 processor family, using the MS-Windows platform.

We cover basic principles about computer architecture, machine language, and low-level programming. You will learn enough assembly language to test your knowledge on today's most widely used microprocessor family.

Before reading this book, you should have completed a single college course or equivalent in computer programming.

An assembler is a program that converts source-code programs from assembly language into machine language. A companion program, called a linker, combines individual files created by an assembler into a single executable program. A third program, called a debugger, provides a way for a programmer to trace the execution of a program and examine the contents of memory.

You will create two basic types of programs: 16-bit real-address mode programs and 32-bit protected mode programs.

You will learn the following concepts from this book: basic computer architecture applied to Intel IA-32 processors; elementary boolean logic; how IA-32 processors manage memory; how high-level language compilers translate statements from their language into assembly language and native machine code; how high-level languages implement arithmetic expressions, loops, and logical structures at the machine level; and the data representation of signed and unsigned integers, real numbers, and character data.

Assembly language has a *one-to-one* relationship with machine language, in which a single assembly language instruction corresponds to one machine language instruction. Assembly language is not portable because it is tied to a specific processor family.

Languages are tools you apply to individual applications or parts of applications. Some applications, such as device drivers and hardware interface routines, are more suited to assembly language. Other applications, such as multiplatform business applications, are suited to high-level languages.

The *virtual machine* concept is an effective way of showing how each layer in a computer architecture represents an abstraction of a machine. Layers can be constructed of hardware or software, and programs written at any layer can be translated or interpreted by the next-lowest layer. The virtual machine concept can be related to real-world computer layers, including digital logic, microarchitecture, instruction set architecture, operating system, assembly language, and high-level languages.

Binary and hexadecimal numbers are essential notational tools for programmers working at the machine level. For this reason, you must understand how to manipulate and translate between number systems and how character representations are created by computers.

The following boolean operators were presented in this chapter: NOT, AND, and OR. A boolean expression combines a boolean operator with one or more operands. A truth table is an effective way to show all possible inputs and outputs of a boolean function.

End Notes

1. Donald Knuth, *MMIX, A RISC Computer for the New Millennium,* Transcript of a lecture given at the Massachusetts Institute of Technology, December 30, 1999.

2. Andrew S. Tanenbaum, *Structured Computer Organization,* 5th Ed., Prentice Hall, 2005.

3. Its source code might have been written in C or assembly language, but once compiled, the operating system is simply a Level 2 program that interprets Level 3 commands.

4. Source: www.webopedia.com.

5. Read about the Unicode Standard at http://www.unicode.org.

6. You can see a working model of Boole's Analytical Engine in the London Science Museum.

2

IA-32 PROCESSOR ARCHITECTURE

2.1 General Concepts

This chapter describes the architecture of the Intel IA-32 processor family and its host computer system from a programmer's point of view. Included in this group are all Intel-compatible processors, such as the AMD Athlon and Opteron processors. Assembly language is a great tool for learning how a computer works, and it requires you to have a working knowledge of computer hardware. To that end, the concepts and details in this chapter will help you to understand the assembly language code you write.

We strike a balance between concepts applying to all microcomputer systems and specifics about IA-32 processors. You may work on various processors in the future, so we expose you to broad concepts. To avoid giving you a superficial understanding of machine architecture, we focus on specifics of the IA-32 family, which will give you a solid grounding when programming in assembly language.

> If you want to learn more about IA-32's architecture, read Intel's *IA-32 Intel Architecture Software Developer's Manual, Volume 1: Basic Architecture*. It's a free download from the Intel Web site (www.intel.com).

2.1.1   Basic Microcomputer Design

Figure 2–1 shows the basic design of a hypothetical microcomputer. The *central processor unit* (CPU), where calculations and logic operations take place, contains a limited number of storage locations named *registers*, a high-frequency clock, a control unit, and an arithmetic logic unit.

- The *clock* synchronizes the internal operations of the CPU with other system components.
- The *control unit* (CU) coordinates the sequencing of steps involved in executing machine instructions.
- The *arithmetic logic unit* (ALU) performs arithmetic operations such as addition and subtraction and logical operations such as AND, OR, and NOT.

The CPU is attached to the rest of the computer via pins attached to the CPU socket in the computer's motherboard. Most pins connect to the data bus, the control bus, and the address bus.

The *memory storage unit* is where instructions and data are held while a computer program is running. The storage unit receives requests for data from the CPU, transfers data from random access memory (RAM) to the CPU, and transfers data from the CPU into memory.

A *bus* is a group of parallel wires that transfer data from one part of the computer to another. A computer's system bus usually consists of three separate buses: the data bus, the control bus, and the address bus. The *data bus* transfers instructions and data between the CPU and memory. The *control bus* uses binary signals to synchronize actions of all devices attached to the system bus. The *address bus* holds the addresses of instructions and data when the currently executing instruction transfers data between the CPU and memory. Many personal computers use the PCI (*Peripheral Component Interconnect*) bus developed by Intel Corporation. In addition, many computers have a *PCI Express* graphics slot, which is significantly faster than the older AGP graphics slot.

FIGURE 2–1   Block Diagram of a Microcomputer.

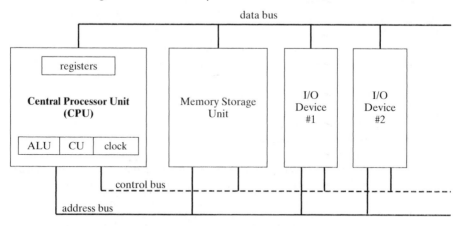

Clock   Each operation involving the CPU and the system bus is synchronized by an internal clock pulsing at a constant rate. The basic unit of time for machine instructions is a *machine cycle* (or *clock cycle*). The length of a clock cycle is the time required for one complete clock pulse. In the following figure, a clock cycle is depicted as the time between one falling edge and the next:

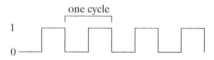

The duration of a clock cycle is the reciprocal of the clock's speed, measured in oscillations per second. A clock that oscillates 1 billion times per second (1 GHz), for example, produces a clock cycle with a duration of one billionth of a second (1 nanosecond).

A machine instruction requires at least one clock cycle to execute, and a few require in excess of 50 clocks (the multiply instruction on the 8088 processor, for example). Instructions requiring memory access often have empty clock cycles called *wait states* because of the differences in the speeds of the CPU, the system bus, and memory circuits. (Recent research suggests that in the near future we may abandon the synchronized computing model in favor of a type of asynchronous operation that would not require a system clock.)

2.1.2   Instruction Execution Cycle

The execution of a single machine instruction can be divided into a sequence of individual operations called the *instruction execution cycle*. Before executing, a program is loaded into memory. The *instruction pointer* contains the address of the next instruction. The *instruction queue* holds a group of instructions about to be executed. Executing a machine instruction requires three basic steps: *fetch, decode,* and *execute.* Two more steps are required when the instruction uses a memory operand: *fetch operand* and *store output operand.* Each of the steps is described as follows:

- *Fetch:* The control unit fetches the instruction from the instruction queue and increments the instruction pointer (IP). The instruction pointer is also known as the *program counter.*
- *Decode:* The control unit decodes the instruction's function to determine what the instruction will do. The instruction's input operands are passed to the arithmetic logic unit (ALU), and signals are sent to the ALU indicating the operation to be performed.
- *Fetch operands:* If the instruction uses an input operand located in memory, the control unit uses a *read* operation to retrieve the operand and copy it into internal registers. Internal registers are not visible to user programs.
- *Execute:* The ALU executes the instruction using the named registers and internal registers as operands and sends the output to named registers and/or memory. The ALU updates status flags providing information about the processor state.
- *Store output operand:* If the output operand is in memory, the control unit uses a write operation to store the data.

The sequence of steps can be expressed neatly in pseudocode:

```
loop
     fetch next instruction
     advance the instruction pointer (IP)
     decode the instruction
     if memory operand needed, read value from memory
     execute the instruction
     if result is memory operand, write result to memory
continue loop
```

The Pentium processor's basic design, shown in Figure 2–2, helps to show relationships between components that interact during the instruction execution cycle. You can see, for example, the path that data takes as it is transfered from memory to the data cache, registers, and ALU. Similarly, the diagram shows how the ALU and registers can read directly from the data cache. The instruction pointer references the code cache, an area where instructions are kept before being executed. The instruction decoder reads from the code cache and sends its output to the control unit.

Multi-Stage Pipeline

Each step in the instruction cycle requires at least one tick of the system clock, called a *clock cycle.* The processor does not have to wait until all steps are completed before beginning the next instruction.

FIGURE 2–2   Simplified Pentium CPU Block Diagram.

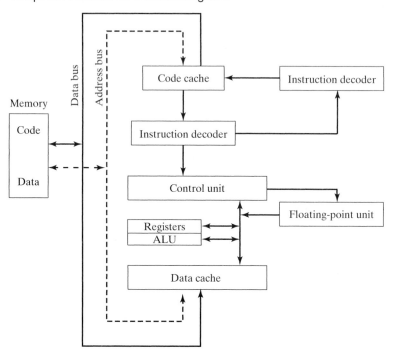

It can execute steps in parallel, a technique known as *pipelining*. The Intel486 processor, for example, has a six-stage execution cycle. In the following sequence, each stage is associated with a part of the processor that executes the stage:

1. *Bus Interface Unit* (BIU): accesses memory and provides input-output.
2. *Code Prefetch Unit:* receives machine instructions from the BIU and inserts them into a holding area named the *instruction queue.*
3. *Instruction Decode Unit:* decodes machine instructions from the prefetch queue and translates them into microcode.
4. *Execution Unit:* executes the microcode instructions produced by the instruction decode unit.
5. *Segment Unit:* translates logical addresses to linear addresses and performs protection checks.
6. *Paging Unit:* translates linear addresses into physical addresses, performs page protection checks, and keeps a list of recently accessed pages.

Example   Suppose each execution stage in the processor requires a single clock cycle. Figure 2–3 uses a grid to represent a six-stage *non-pipelined* processor, the type used by Intel prior to the Intel486. When instruction I-1 finishes stage S6, instruction I-2 begins. Twelve clock cycles are required to execute the two instructions. In other words, for k execution stages, n instructions require $(n * k)$ cycles to process.

Pipelining   The processor described in Figure 2–3 wastes CPU resources because each stage is used only one-sixth of the time. If, on the other hand, a processor supports pipelining, as in Figure 2–4, a new instruction can enter stage S1 during the second clock cycle. Meanwhile, the first instruction has entered stage S2, enabling overlapped execution of the instructions. Figure 2–4 shows two instructions, I-1 and I-2, progressing through the pipeline. I-2 enters stage S1 as soon as I-1 has moved to stage S2. Only seven clock cycles are required to execute the two instructions. When the pipeline is full, six stages are in continuous use. In general, for k execution stages, n instructions require

$k + (n - 1)$ cycles to process. Whereas the non-pipelined processor we showed earlier required 12 cycles to process two instructions, the pipelined processor can process seven instructions in the same amount of time.

Figure 2–3 Six-Stage Non-Pipelined Instruction Execution.

Stages

Cycles	S1	S2	S3	S4	S5	S6
1	I-1					
2		I-1				
3			I-1			
4				I-1		
5					I-1	
6						I-1
7	I-2					
8		I-2				
9			I-2			
10				I-2		
11					I-2	
12						I-2

Figure 2–4 Six-Stage Pipelined Execution.

Stages

Cycles	S1	S2	S3	S4	S5	S6
1	I-1					
2	I-2	I-1				
3		I-2	I-1			
4			I-2	I-1		
5				I-2	I-1	
6					I-2	I-1
7						I-2

Superscalar Architecture

A *superscalar*, or *multi-core* processor has two or more execution pipelines, making it possible for two instructions to be in the execution stage at the same time. To better understand why a superscalar processor would be useful, let's consider the preceding pipelined example, in which we assumed that the execution stage (S4) required a single clock cycle. That was an overly simplistic approach. What would happen if stage S4 required two clock cycles? Then a bottleneck would occur, shown in Figure 2–5. Instruction I-2 cannot enter stage S4 until I-2 has completed the stage, so I-2 has to wait one more cycle before entering stage S4. As more instructions enter the pipeline, wasted cycles occur (shaded in gray). In general, for k stages (where one stage requires two cycles), n instructions require $(k + 2n - 1)$ cycles to process.

Figure 2–5 Pipelined Execution Using a Single Pipeline.

Stages

Cycles	S1	S2	S3	S4 (exe)	S5	S6
1	I-1					
2	I-2	I-1				
3	I-3	I-2	I-1			
4		I-3	I-2	I-1		
5			I-3	I-1		
6				I-2	I-1	
7				I-2		I-1
8				I-3	I-2	
9				I-3		I-2
10					I-3	
11						I-3

A superscalar processor permits multiple instructions to be in the execution stage at the same time. For n pipelines, n instructions can execute during the same clock cycle. The Intel Pentium, with two pipelines, was the first superscalar processor in the IA-32 family. The Pentium Pro processor was the first to use three pipelines.

Figure 2–6 shows an execution scheme with two pipelines in a six-stage pipeline. We assume stage S4 requires two cycles. Odd-numbered instructions enter the *u-pipeline* and even-numbered instructions enter the *v-pipeline*. Wasted cycles are removed, so n instructions can be executed in $(k + n)$ cycles, where k indicates the number of stages.

FIGURE 2–6   Superscalar 6-Stage Pipelined Processor.

Stages
⌐— S4 —⌐

Cycles	S1	S2	S3	u	v	S5	S6
1	I-1						
2	I-2	I-1					
3	I-3	I-2	I-1				
4	I-4	I-3	I-2	I-1			
5		I-4	I-3	I-1	I-2		
6			I-4	I-3	I-2	I-1	
7				I-3	I-4	I-2	I-1
8					I-4	I-3	I-2
9						I-4	I-3
10							I-4

2.1.3   Reading from Memory

Program throughput is often dependent on the speed of memory access. CPU clock speed might be several gigahertz, whereas access to memory occurs over a system bus running at a sluggish 33 MHz. The CPU is forced to wait one or more clock cycles until operands have been fetched from memory before instructions can execute. The wasted clock cycles are called *wait states*.

Several steps are required when reading instructions or data from memory, controlled by the processor's internal clock. Figure 2–7 shows the processor clock (CLK) rising and falling at regular time intervals. In the figure, a clock cycle begins as the clock signal changes from high to low. The changes are called *trailing edges,* and they indicate the time taken by the transition between states.

The following is a simplified description of what happens during each clock cycle during a memory read:

Cycle 1: The address bits of the memory operand are placed on the *address bus* (ADDR).

Cycle 2: The *read line* (RD) is set low (0) to notify memory that a value is to be read.

Cycle 3: The CPU waits one cycle to give memory time to respond. During this cycle, the memory controller places the operand on the *data bus* (DATA).

Cycle 4: The read line goes to 1, signaling the CPU to read the data on the data bus.

Cache Memory   Because conventional memory is so much slower than the CPU, computers use high-speed *cache memory* to hold the most recently used instructions and data. The first time a program reads a block of data, it leaves a copy in the cache. If the program needs to read the same data a second time, it looks for the data in cache. A *cache hit* indicates the data is in cache; a *cache miss* indicates the data is not in cache and must be read from conventional memory.

In general, cache memory has a noticeable effect on improving access to data, particularly when the cache is large. IA-32 processors have two types of cache memory: *Level 1 cache* is smaller, faster, and more expensive. *Level 2 cache,* once outside the processor, is now integrated into the chip.

FIGURE 2–7   Memory Read Cycle.

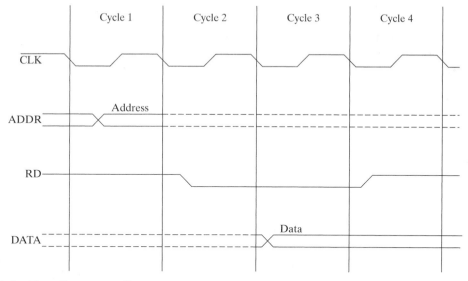

2.1.4   How Programs Run

Load and Execute Process

The following steps describe, in sequence, what happens when a computer user runs a program at a command prompt:

- The operating system (OS) searches for the program's filename in the current disk directory. If it cannot find the name there, it searches a predetermined list of directories (called *paths*) for the filename. If the OS fails to find the program filename, it issues an error message.
- If the program file is found, the OS retrieves basic information about the program's file from the disk directory, including the file size and its physical location on the disk drive.
- The OS determines the next available location in memory and loads the program file into memory. It allocates a block of memory to the program and enters information about the program's size and location into a table (sometimes called a *descriptor table*). Additionally, the OS may adjust the values of pointers within the program so they contain addresses of program data.
- The OS executes a branching instruction that causes the CPU to begin execution of the program's first machine instruction. As soon as the program begins running, it is called a *process*. The OS assigns the process an identification number (*process ID*), which is used to keep track of it while running.
- The *process* runs by itself. It is the OS's job to track the execution of the process and to respond to requests for system resources. Examples of resources are memory, disk files, and input-output devices.
- When the process ends, its handle is removed and the memory it used is released so it can be used by other programs.

> If you're using Windows 2000 or XP, press *Ctrl-Alt-Delete* and click on the *Task Manager* button. There are tabs labeled *Applications* and *Processes*. Applications are the names of complete programs currently running, such as Windows Explorer or Microsoft Visual C++. When you click on the *Processes* tab, you see 30 or 40 names listed, often some you might not recognize. Each of those processes is a small program running independent of all the others. Note that each has a PID (process ID), and you can continuously track the amount of CPU time and memory it uses. Most processes run in the background. You can shut down a process somehow left running in memory by mistake. Of course, if you shut down the wrong process, your computer may stop running, and you'll have to reboot.

Multitasking

A *multitasking* operating system is able to run multiple tasks at the same time. A *task* is defined as either a program (a process) or a thread of execution. A process has its own memory area and may contain multiple threads. A thread shares its memory with other threads belonging to the same process. Game programs, for example, often use individual threads to simultaneously control multiple graphic objects. Web browsers use separate threads to simultaneously load graphic images and respond to user input.

Most modern operating systems simultaneously execute tasks that communicate with hardware, display user interfaces, perform background file processing, and so on. A CPU can really execute only one instruction at a time, so a component of the operating system named the *scheduler* allocates a slice of CPU time (called a *time slice*) to each task. During a single time slice, the CPU executes a block of instructions, stopping when the time slice has ended.

By rapidly switching tasks, the processor creates the illusion they are running simultaneously. One type of scheduling used by the OS is called *round-robin scheduling*. In Figure 2–8, nine tasks are active. Suppose the *scheduler* arbitrarily assigns 100 milliseconds to each task, and switching between tasks takes 8 milliseconds. One full circuit of the task list requires 964 milliseconds $(9 \times 100) + (10 \times 8)$ to complete.

Figure 2–8   Round-Robin Scheduler.

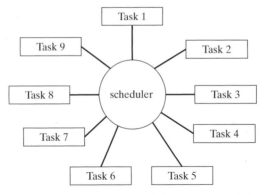

A multitasking OS runs on a processor that supports *task switching*. The processor saves the state of each task before switching to a new one. A task's *state* consists of the contents of the processor registers, program counter, and status flags, along with references to the task's memory segments. A multitasking OS will usually assign varying priorities to tasks, giving them relatively larger or smaller time slices. A *preemptive* multitasking OS (such as Windows XP or Linux) permits a higher-priority task to interrupt a lower-priority one, leading to better system stability. Suppose an application program is locked in loop and has stopped responding to input. The keyboard handler (a high-priority OS task) can respond to the user's Ctrl-Alt-Del command and shut down the buggy application program.

2.1.5 Section Review

1. The central processor unit (CPU) contains registers and what other basic elements?
2. The central processor unit is connected to the rest of the computer system using what three buses?
3. Why does memory access take more machine cycles than register access?
4. What are the three basic steps in the instruction execution cycle?
5. Which two additional steps are required in the instruction execution cycle when a memory operand is used?
6. During which stage of the instruction execution cycle is the program counter incremented?

7. Define *pipelined execution.*

8. In a five-stage non-pipelined processor, how many clock cycles would it take to execute two instructions?

9. In a five-stage single-pipelined processor, how many clock cycles would it take to execute eight instructions?

10. What is a *superscalar processor?*

11. Suppose a five-stage dual-pipelined processor has one stage that requires two clock cycles to execute, and there are two pipelines for that stage. How many clock cycles would be required to execute 10 instructions?

12. When a program runs, what information does the OS read from the filename's disk directory entry?

13. After a program has been loaded into memory, how does it begin execution?

14. Define *multitasking.*

15. What is the function of the OS scheduler?

16. When the processor switches from one task to another, what values in the first task's state must be preserved?

17. What is the duration of a single clock cycle in a 3-GHz processor?

2.2   IA-32 Processor Architecture

As we said, IA-32 refers to a family of processors beginning with the Intel386 and continuing up to the latest 32-bit processor, the Pentium 4. Numerous improvements to the internal architecture of the Intel processors have been made along the way, such as pipelining, superscalar, branch prediction, and hyperthreading. In terms of programming, the visible changes are instruction set extensions for multimedia processing and graphics calculations.

2.2.1   Modes of Operation

IA-32 processors have three primary modes of operation: protected mode, real-address mode, and system management mode. Another mode, named virtual-8086, is a special case of protected mode. Here are short descriptions of each:

Protected Mode   Protected mode is the native state of the processor, in which all instructions and features are available. Programs are given separate memory areas named *segments*, and the processor prevents programs from referencing memory outside their assigned segments.

Virtual-8086 Mode   While in protected mode, the processor can directly execute real-address mode software such as MS-DOS programs in a safe multitasking environment. In other words, if an MS-DOS program crashes or attempts to write data into the system memory area, it will not affect other programs running at the same time. Windows XP can execute multiple separate virtual-8086 sessions at the same time.

Real-Address Mode   Real-address mode implements the programming environment of the Intel 8086 processor with a few extra features, such as the ability to switch into other modes. This mode is available in Windows 98, and can be used to run an MS-DOS program that requires direct access to system memory and hardware devices. Programs running in real-address mode can cause the operating system to crash (stop responding to commands).

System Management Mode   System Management mode (SMM) provides an operating system with a mechanism for implementing functions such as power management and system security. These functions are usually implemented by computer manufacturers who customize the processor for a particular system setup.

2.2.2 Basic Execution Environment

Address Space

IA-32 processors can access 4GB of memory in protected mode, a limit based on the size of a 32-bit unsigned binary integer address. Real-address mode programs have a 1 MB memory range. If the processor is in protected mode and running multiple programs in virtual-8086 mode, each program has its own 1 MB memory area.

Basic Program Execution Registers

Registers are high-speed storage locations directly inside the CPU, designed to be accessed at much higher speed than conventional memory. When a processing loop is optimized for speed, for example, loop counters are held in registers rather than variables. Figure 2–9 shows the *basic program execution registers*. There are eight general-purpose registers, six segment registers, a processor status flags register (EFLAGS), and an instruction pointer (EIP).

Figure 2–9   IA-32 Basic Program Execution Registers.

32-bit General-Purpose Registers

EAX	EBP
EBX	ESP
ECX	ESI
EDX	EDI

16-bit Segment Registers

EFLAGS		CS	ES
		SS	FS
EIP		DS	GS

General-Purpose Registers   The *general-purpose registers* are primarily used for arithmetic and data movement. As shown in the following figure, each register can be addressed as either a single 32-bit value or two 16-bit values:

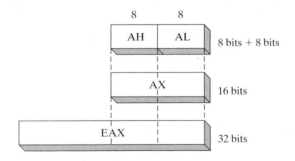

Portions of some registers can be addressed as 8-bit values. For example, the 32-bit EAX register has a 16-bit lower half named AX. The AX register, in turn, has an 8-bit upper half named AH and an 8-bit lower half named AL. The same overlapping relationship exists for the EAX, EBX, ECX, and EDX registers:

32-Bit	16-Bit	8-Bit (High)	8-Bit (Low)
EAX	AX	AH	AL
EBX	BX	BH	BL
ECX	CX	CH	CL
EDX	DX	DH	DL

The remaining general-purpose registers only have specific names for their lower 16 bits. The 16-bit registers shown here are generally used when writing real-address mode programs:

32-Bit	16-Bit
ESI	SI
EDI	DI
EBP	BP
ESP	SP

Specialized Uses   Some general-purpose registers have specialized uses:
- EAX is automatically used by multiplication and division instructions. It is often called the *extended accumulator* register.
- The CPU automatically uses ECX as a loop counter.
- ESP addresses data on the stack (a system memory structure). It is rarely used for ordinary arithmetic or data transfer. It is often called the *extended stack pointer* register.
- ESI and EDI are used by high-speed memory transfer instructions. They are sometimes called the *extended source index* and *extended destination index* registers.
- EBP is used by high-level languages to reference function parameters and local variables on the stack. It should not be used for ordinary arithmetic or data transfer except at an advanced level of programming. It is often called the *extended frame pointer* register.

Segment Registers   In real-address mode, segment registers indicate base addresses of preassigned memory areas named *segments*. In protected mode, segment registers hold pointers to segment descriptor tables. Some segments hold program instructions (code), others hold variables (data), and another segment named the *stack segment* holds local function variables and function parameters.

Instruction Pointer   The EIP, or *instruction pointer*, register contains the address of the next instruction to be executed. Certain machine instructions manipulate EIP, causing the program to branch to a new location.

EFLAGS Register   The EFLAGS (or just *Flags*) register consists of individual binary bits that control the operation of the CPU or reflect the outcome of some CPU operation. Some instructions test and manipulate individual processor flags.

A flag is *set* when it equals 1; it is *clear* (or reset) when it equals 0.

Control Flags. Control flags control the CPU's operation. For example, they can cause the CPU to break after every instruction executes, interrupt when airthmetic overflow is detected, enter virtual-8086 mode, and enter protected mode.

Programs can set individual bits in the EFLAGS register to control the CPU's operation. Examples are the *Direction* and *Interrupt* flags.

Status Flags. The Status flags reflect the outcomes of arithmetic and logical operations performed by the CPU. They are the Overflow, Sign, Zero, Auxiliary Carry, Parity, and Carry flags. Their abbreviations are shown immediately after their names:

- The **Carry** flag (CF) is set when the result of an *unsigned* arithmetic operation is too large to fit into the destination.
- The **Overflow** flag (OF) is set when the result of a *signed* arithmetic operation is too large or too small to fit into the destination.
- The **Sign** flag (SF) is set when the result of an arithmetic or logical operation generates a negative result.
- The **Zero** flag (ZF) is set when the result of an arithmetic or logical operation generates a result of zero.
- The **Auxiliary Carry** flag (AC) is set when an arithmetic operation causes a carry from bit 3 to bit 4 in an 8-bit operand.
- The **Parity** flag (PF) is set if the least-significant byte in the result contains an even number of 1 bits. Otherwise, PF is clear. In general, it is used for error checking when there is a possibility that data might be altered or corrupted.

System Registers

IA-32 processors have a number of important system registers. MS-Windows only permit access to these registers by programs running at the highest privilege level (level 0). The operating system kernel is such a program. The registers are as follows:

- **IDTR (Interrupt Descriptor Table Register):** This register contains the address of the Interrupt Descriptor Table, which provides a way to handle interrupts (system routines designed to respond to events such as the keyboard and mouse).
- **GDTR (Global Descriptor Table Register):** The GDTR register contains the address of the Global Descriptor Table, a table containing pointers to task state segments and local program descriptor tables.
- **LDTR (Local Descriptor Table Register):** The LDTR register contains pointers to the code, data, and stack of currently running programs.
- **Task Register:** The task register contains the address of the TSS (task state segment) for the currently executing task.
- **Debug Registers:** The debug registers let programs set breakpoints when debugging programs.
- **Control registers CR0, CR2, CR3, CR4:** The control registers contain status flags and data fields that control system-level operations such as task switching, paging, and enabling cache memory. (Register CR1 is not used.)
- **Model-Specific Registers:** The model-specific registers are used for such operating system tasks as performance monitoring and checking the machine architecture. Their use varies among different IA-32 processors.

We will discuss GDTR and LDTR in the context of protected mode memory management in Chapter 11. Application programs cannot access system registers. Because this book concentrates on application programs in assembly language, we will not use the system registers.

2.2.3 Floating-Point Unit

The IA-32 *floating-point unit* (FPU) performs high-speed floating-point arithmetic. At one time a separate coprocessor chip was required for this. From the Intel486 onward, the FPU has been integrated into the main processor chip. There are eight floating-point data registers in the FPU, named ST(0), ST(1), ST(2), ST(3), ST(4), ST(5), ST(6), and ST(7). The remaining control and pointer registers are shown in Figure 2–10.

Figure 2–10   Floating-Point Unit Registers.

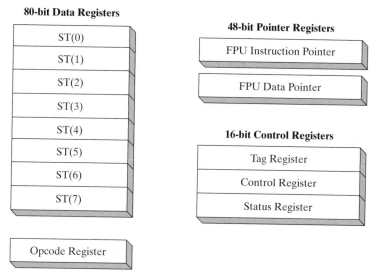

Other Registers

In passing, we will mention two other sets of registers used for advanced multimedia programming in the Pentium processor series:

- Eight 64-bit registers for use with the MMX instruction set
- Eight 128-bit XMM registers used for single-instruction, multiple-data (SIMD) operations

2.2.4   Intel Microprocessor History

Let's take a short trip down memory lane, starting when the IBM-PC was first released, when PC's had 64K of RAM and no hard drives.

Intel 8086   The Intel 8086 processor (1978) marks the beginning of the modern Intel architecture family. The primary innovations of the 8086 over earlier processors were that it had 16-bit registers and a 16-bit data bus and used a segmented memory model permitting programs to address up to 1MB of RAM. Greater access to memory made it possible to write complex business applications. The IBM-PC (1980) contained an Intel 8088 processor, which was identical to the 8086, except it had an 8-bit data bus that made it slightly less expensive to produce. Today, the Intel 8088 is used in low-cost microcontrollers.

Downward Compatibility. Each processor introduced into the Intel family since the 8086 has been downward-compatible with earlier processors. This approach enables older software to run on newer computers without modification. Newer software eventually appeared, requiring features of more advanced processors.

Intel 80286   The Intel 80286 processor, first used in the IBM-PC/AT computer, set a new standard of speed and power. It was the first Intel processor to run in protected mode. The 80286 addresses up to 16MB of RAM using a 24-bit address bus.

IA-32 Processor Family

The Intel386 processor introduced 32-bit data registers and a 32-bit address bus and external data path. As such, it was the first member of the IA-32 family. IA-32 processors can address virtual memory larger than the computer's physical memory. Each program is assigned a 4GB linear address space.

Intel486   Continuing the IA-32 family, the Intel486 processor features an instruction set microarchitecture using pipelining techniques that permit multiple instructions to be processed at the same time.

Pentium   The Pentium processor added many performance improvements, including a superscalar design with two parallel execution pipelines. Two instructions could be decoded and executed simultaneously. The Pentium used a 32-bit address bus and a 64-bit internal data path, and introduced MMX technology to the IA-32 family.

P6 Processor Family

The P6 family of processors was introduced in 1995, based on a new micro-architecture design that improved execution speed. It also extended the basic IA-32 architecture. The P6 family includes the Pentium Pro, Pentium II, and Pentium III. The Pentium Pro introduced advanced techniques to improve the way instructions were executed. The Pentium II added MMX technology to the P6 family. The Pentium III introduced SIMD (streaming extensions) to the IA-32 family, with specialized 128-bit registers designed to move large amounts of data quickly.

Pentium 4 and Xeon Family

The Pentium 4 processor and Xeon processors use the Intel *NetBurst* micro-architecture, which permits the processor to operate at higher speeds than previous IA-32 processors. It is optimized for high-performance multimedia applications. More advanced Pentium 4's use *hyperthreading* technology, which executes multhreaded applications in parallel on a multi-core processor.

CISC and RISC

The Intel 8086 processor was the first in a line of processors using a *Complex Instruction Set Computer* (CISC) design. The instruction set is large, and includes a wide variety of memory-addressing, shifting, arithmetic, data movement, and logical operations. Complex instruction sets permit compiled programs to contain a relatively small number of instructions. A major disadvantage to CISC design is that complex instructions require a relatively long time to decode and execute. An interpreter inside the CPU written in a language called *microcode* decodes and executes each machine instruction. Once Intel released the 8086, it became necessary for all subsequent Intel processors to be compatible with the first one. Customers did not want to throw away their existing software every time a new processor was released.

A completely different approach to microprocessor design is called *Reduced Instruction Set* (RISC). A RISC consists of a relatively small number of short, simple instructions that execute relatively quickly. Rather than using a microcode interpreter to decode and execute machine instructions, a RISC processor directly decodes and executes instructions using hardware. High-speed engineering and graphics workstations have been built using RISC processors for many years. Unfortunately, the systems have been expensive because the processors were produced in small quantities.

Because of the huge popularity of IBM-PC–compatible computers, Intel was able to lower the price of its processors and dominate the microprocessor market. At the same time, Intel recognized many advantages to the RISC approach and found a way to use RISC-like features (such as pipelining and superscalar) in the Pentium series. The IA-32 instruction set continues to be complex and constantly expanding.

2.2.5   Section Review

1. What are the IA-32 processor's three basic modes of operation?
2. Name all eight 32-bit general-purpose registers.

3. Name all six segment registers.

4. What special purpose does the ECX register serve?

5. Besides the stack pointer (ESP), what other register points to variables on the stack?

6. Name at least four CPU status flags.

7. Which flag is set when the result of an *unsigned* arithmetic operation is too large to fit into the destination?

8. Which flag is set when the result of a *signed* arithmetic operation is either too large or too small to fit into the destination?

9. Which flag is set when an arithmetic or logical operation generates a negative result?

10. Which part of the CPU performs floating-point arithmetic?

11. How many bits long are the FPU data registers?

12. Which Intel processor was the first member of the IA-32 family?

13. Which Intel processor first introduced superscalar execution?

14. Which Intel processor first used MMX technology?

15. Describe the CISC design approach.

16. Describe the RISC design approach.

2.3 IA-32 Memory Management

IA-32 processors manage memory according to the basic modes of operation discussed in Section 2.2.1. Protected mode is the simplest and most powerful; the others are usually used when programs must directly access system hardware.

In *real-address* mode, only 1MB of memory can be addressed, from hexadecimal 00000 to FFFFF. The processor can run only one program at a time, but it can momentarily interrupt that program to process requests (called *interrupts*) from peripherals. Application programs are permitted to read and modify any area of RAM (random-access memory), and they can read but not modify any area of ROM (read-only memory). The MS-DOS operating system runs in real-address mode, and Windows 95 and 98 can be booted into this mode.

In *protected* mode, the processor can run multiple programs at the same time. It assigns each process (running program) a total of 4GB of memory. Each program can be assigned its own reserved memory area, and programs are prevented from accidentally accessing each other's code and data. MS-Windows and Linux run in protected mode.

In *virtual-8086* mode, the computer runs in protected mode and creates a virtual 8086 machine with its own 1MB address space that simulates an 80 × 86 computer running in real-address mode. Windows NT and 2000, for example, create a virtual 8086 machine when you open a *Command* window. You can run many such windows at the same time, and each is protected from the actions of the others. Some MS-DOS programs that make direct references to computer hardware will not run in this mode under Windows NT, 2000, and XP.

In Sections 2.3.1 and 2.3.2 we will explain details of both real-address mode and protected mode. If you want to study this subject in more detail, a good source is the three-volume *IA-32 Intel Architecture Software Developer's Manual*. You can read or download it from Intel's Web site (www.intel.com).

2.3.1 Real-Address Mode

In real-address mode, the IA-32 processor can access 1,048,576 bytes of memory (1MB) using 20-bit addresses in the range 0 to FFFFF hexadecimal. Intel engineers had to solve a basic problem: The 16-bit registers in the 8086 processor could not hold 20-bit addresses. They came up with a scheme known as *segmented memory*. All of memory is divided into 64-kilobyte units called *segments*, shown in Figure 2–11. An analogy is a large building, in which *segments* represent the building's floors. A person can ride the elevator to a particular floor, get off, and begin following the room numbers to locate a room. The *offset* of a room can be thought of as the distance from the elevator to the room.

Again in Figure 2–11, each segment begins at an address having a zero for its last hexadecimal digit. Because the last digit is always zero, it is omitted when representing segment values. A segment value of C000, for example, refers to the segment at address C0000. The same figure shows an expansion of the segment at 80000. To reach a byte in this segment, add a 16-bit offset (0 to FFFF) to the segment's base location. The address 8000:0250, for example, represents an offset of 250 inside the segment beginning at address 80000. The linear address is 80250h.

FIGURE 2–11   Segmented Memory Map, Real-Address Mode.

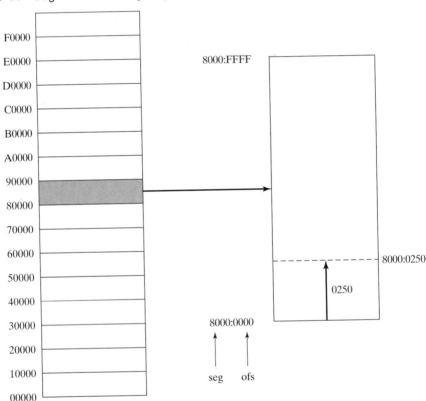

20-Bit Linear Address Calculation   An *address* refers to a single location in memory, and each memory byte has a distinct address. In real-address mode, the *linear* (or *absolute*) address is 20 bits, ranging from 0 to FFFFF hexadecimal. Programs cannot use linear addresses directly, so addresses are expressed using two 16-bit integers. A *segment-offset* address includes the following:

• A 16-bit **segment** value, placed in one of the segment registers (CS, DS, ES, SS).
• A 16-bit **offset** value.

The CPU automatically converts a segment-offset address to a 20-bit linear address. Suppose a variable's hexadecimal segment-offset address is 08F1:0100. The CPU multiplies the segment value by 16 (10 hexadecimal) and adds the product to the variable's offset:

```
08F1h * 10h = 08F10h          (adjusted segment value)
```

```
Adjusted Segment value:        0  8  F  1  0
Add the offset:                   0  1  0  0
Linear address:                0  9  0  1  0
```

A typical program has three segments: code, data, and stack. Three segment registers, CS, DS, and SS, contain the segments' base locations:

- CS contains the 16-bit **code** segment address.
- DS contains the 16-bit **data** segment address.
- SS contains the 16-bit **stack** segment address.
- ES, FS, and GS can point to alternate data segments.

2.3.2   Protected Mode

Protected mode is the more powerful "native" processor mode. When running in protected mode, a program can address 4GB of memory, with addresses 0 to FFFFFFFF hexadecimal. In the context of the Microsoft Assembler, the **flat** memory model (see the .MODEL directive) is appropriate for protected mode programming. The flat model is easy to use because it requires only a single 32-bit integer to hold the address of an instruction or variable. The CPU performs address calculation and translation in the background, all of which are transparent to application programmers. Segment registers (CS, DS, SS, ES, FS, GS) point to *segment descriptor tables,* which the operating system uses to keep track of locations of individual program segments. A typical protected-mode program has three segments: code, data, and stack, using the CS, DS, and SS segment registers:

- CS references the descriptor table for the code segment.
- DS references the descriptor table for the data segment.
- SS references the descriptor table for the stack segment.

Flat Segmentation Model

In the flat segmentation model, all segments are mapped to the entire 32-bit physical address space of the computer. At least two segments are required, one for code and one for data. Each segment is defined by a *segment descriptor*, a 64-bit integer stored in a table known as the *global descriptor table* (GDT). Figure 2–12 shows a segment descriptor whose *base address* field points to the first available location in memory (00000000). The *segment limit* field can optionally indicate the amount of physical memory in the system. In this figure, the segment limit is 0040. The *access* field contains bits that determine how the segment can be used.

> Suppose a computer had 256MB of RAM. The segment limit field would contain 10000 hex because its value is implicitly multiplied by 1000 hex, producing 10000000 hex (256MB).

Multi-Segment Model

In the multi-segment model, each task or program is given its own table of segment descriptors, called a *local descriptor table* (LDT). Each descriptor points to a segment, which can be distinct from all segments used by other processes. Each segment has its own address space. In Figure 2–13, each entry in the LDT points to a different segment in memory. Each segment descriptor specifies the exact size of its segment. For example, the segment beginning at 3000 has size 2000 hexadecimal, which is computed as (0002 * 1000 hexadecimal). The segment beginning at 8000 has size A000 hexadecimal.

Paging

IA-32 processors support *paging*, a feature that permits segments to be divided into 4,096-byte blocks of memory called *pages*. Paging permits the total memory used by all programs running at the same time to be much larger than the computer's physical memory. The complete collection of pages mapped by the operating system is called *virtual memory*. Operating systems have utility programs named *virtual memory managers.*

FIGURE 2–12   Flat Segmentation Model.

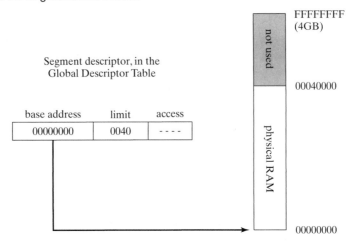

FIGURE 2–13   Multi-Segment Model.

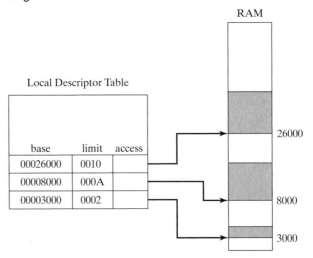

Paging is an important solution to a vexing problem faced by software and hardware designers. A program must be loaded into main memory before it can run, but memory is expensive. Users want to be able to load numerous programs into memory and switch among them at will. Disk storage, on the other hand, is cheap and plentiful. Paging provides the illusion that memory is almost unlimited in size. Disk access is much slower than main memory access, so the more a program relies on paging, the slower it runs.

When a task is running, parts of it can be stored on disk if they are not currently in use. Parts of the task are *paged* (swapped) to disk. Other actively executing pages remain in memory. When the processor begins to execute code that has been paged out of memory it issues a *page fault*, causing the page or pages containing the required code or data to be loaded back into memory. To see how this works, find a computer with somewhat limited memory and run many large applications at the same time. You should notice a delay when switching from one program to another because the OS must transfer paged portions of each program into memory from disk. A computer runs faster when more memory is installed because large application files and programs can be kept entirely in memory, reducing the amount of paging.

2.3.3   Section Review

1. What is the range of addressable memory in protected mode?
2. What is the range of addressable memory in real-address mode?
3. The two ways of describing an address in real-address mode are segment-offset and _____.
4. In real-address mode, convert the following hexadecimal segment-offset address to a linear address: 0950:0100.
5. In real-address mode, convert the following hexadecimal segment-offset address to a linear address: 0CD1:02E0.
6. In MASM's flat memory model, how many bits hold the address of an instruction or variable?
7. In protected mode, which register references the descriptor for the stack segment?
8. In protected mode, which table contains pointers to memory segments used by a single program?
9. In the flat segmentation model, which table contains pointers to at least two segments?
10. What is the main advantage to using the paging feature of IA-32 processors?
11. *Challenge:* Can you think of a reason why MS-DOS was not designed to support protected-mode programming?
12. *Challenge:* In real-address mode, demonstrate two segment-offset addresses that point to the same linear address.

2.4   Components of an IA-32 Microcomputer

This chapter introduces you to the architecture of IA-32 processors from several points of view. First, the hardware (physical parts of the computer) can be viewed on the *macro* level, looking at peripherals. Then we can look at the internal details of the Intel processor, called the *central processing unit* (CPU). Finally, we look at the software architecture, which is the way the memory is organized, and how the operating system interacts with the hardware.

2.4.1   Motherboard

The heart of a microcomputer is its *motherboard*, a flat circuit board onto which are placed the computer's CPU, supporting processors (*chipset*), main memory, input-output connectors, power supply connectors, and expansion slots. The various components are connected to each other by a *bus*, a set of wires etched directly on the motherboard. Dozens of motherboards are available on the PC market, varying in expansion capabilities, integrated components, and speed. The following components have traditionally been found on PC motherboards:

- A CPU socket. Sockets are different shapes and sizes, depending on the type of processor they support.
- Memory slots (SIMM or DIMM) holding small plug-in memory boards
- BIOS (*basic input-output system*) computer chips, holding system software
- CMOS RAM, with a small circular battery to keep it powered
- Connectors for mass-storage devices such as hard drives and CD-ROMs
- USB connectors for external devices
- Keyboard and mouse ports
- PCI bus connectors for sound cards, graphics cards, data acquisition boards, and other input-output devices

The following components are optional:

- Integrated sound processor

- Parallel and serial device connectors
- Integrated network adapter
- AGP bus connector for a high-speed video card

Following are some important support processors in a typical IA-32 system:

- The *Floating-Point Unit* (FPU) handles floating-point and extended integer calculations.
- The 8284/82C284 *Clock Generator*, known simply as the *clock,* oscillates at a constant speed. The clock generator synchronizes the CPU and the rest of the computer.
- The 8259A *Programmable Interrupt Controller* (PIC) handles external interrupts from hardware devices, such as the keyboard, system clock, and disk drives. These devices interrupt the CPU and make it process their requests immediately.
- The 8253 *Programmable Interval Timer/Counter* interrupts the system 18.2 times per second, updates the system date and clock, and controls the speaker. It is also responsible for constantly refreshing memory because RAM memory chips can remember their data for only a few milliseconds.
- The 8255 *Programmable Parallel Port* transfers data to and from the computer using the IEEE Parallel Port interface. This port is commonly used for printers, but it can be used with other input-output devices as well.

PCI and PCI Express Bus Architectures

The **PCI** (*Peripheral Component Interconnect*) bus provides a connecting bridge between the CPU and other system devices such as hard drives, memory, video controllers, sound cards, and network controllers. More recently, the *PCI Express* bus provides two-way serial connections between devices, memory, and the processor. It carries data in packets, similar to networks, in separate "lanes." It is widely supported by graphics controllers, and can transfer data at about 4GB per second.

Motherboard Chipset

Most motherboards contain an integrated set of microprocessors and controllers called a *chipset.* The chipset largely determines the capabilities of the computer. The names listed here are by Intel, but many motherboards use compatible chipsets from other manufacturers:

- The Intel 8237 Direct Memory Access (DMA) controller transfers data between external devices and RAM, without requiring any work by the CPU.
- The Intel 8259A Interrupt Controller handles requests from the hardware to interrupt the CPU.
- The 8254 Timer Counter handles the system clock, which ticks 18.2 times per second, the memory refresh timer, and the time-of-day clock.
- Microprocessor local bus to PCI bridge.
- System memory controller and cache controller.
- PCI bus to ISA bus bridge.
- Intel 8042 keyboard and mouse microcontroller.

2.4.2　Video Output

The video adapter controls the display of text and graphics on IBM-compatibles. It has two components: the video controller and video display memory. All graphics and text displayed on the monitor are written into video display RAM, where it is then sent to the monitor by the video controller. The video controller is itself a special-purpose microprocessor, relieving the primary CPU of the job of controlling video hardware.

Cathode-ray tube (CRT) video monitors use a technique called *raster scanning* to display images. A beam of electrons illuminates phosphorus dots on the screen called *pixels.* Starting at the top of the screen, the gun fires electrons from the left side to the right in a horizontal row, briefly turns off, and returns to the left side of the screen to begin a new row. *Horizontal retrace* refers to the time period when the gun is off between rows. When the last row is drawn, the gun turns off (called the *vertical retrace*) and moves to the upper left corner of the screen to start over.

A direct digital liquid crystal display (LCD) monitor receives a digital bit stream directly from the video controller and does not require raster scanning. Digital displays generally display sharper text than analog displays.

2.4.3   Memory

Several basic types of memory are used in Intel-based systems: read-only memory (ROM), erasable programmable read-only memory (EPROM), dynamic random-access memory (DRAM), static RAM (SRAM), video RAM (VRAM), and complimentary metal oxide semiconductor (CMOS) RAM:

- **ROM** is permanently burned into a chip and cannot be erased.
- **EPROM** can be erased slowly with ultraviolet light and reprogrammed.
- **DRAM**, commonly known as main memory, is where programs and data are kept when a program is running. It is inexpensive, but must be refreshed within less than 1 millisecond or it loses its contents. Some systems use ECC (error checking and correcting) memory.
- **SRAM** is used primarily for expensive, high-speed cache memory. It does not have to be refreshed. CPU cache memory is comprised of SRAM.
- **VRAM** holds video data. It is dual ported, allowing one port to continuously refresh the display while another port writes data to the display.
- **CMOS RAM** on the system motherboard stores system setup information. It is refreshed by a battery, so its contents are retained when the computer's power is off.

2.4.4   Input-Output Ports and Device Interfaces

Universal Serial Bus (USB)   The Universal Serial Bus port provides intelligent, high-speed connection between a computer and USB-supported devices. USB Version 2.0 supports data transfer speeds of 480 megabits per second. You can connect single-function units (mice, printers) or compound devices having more than one peripheral sharing the same port. A USB hub, shown in Figure 2–14, is a compound device connected to several other devices, including other USB hubs.

FIGURE 2–14   USB Hub Configuration.

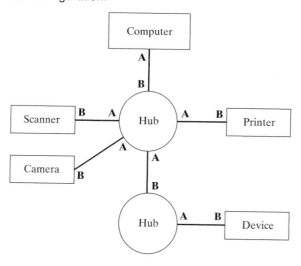

When a device is attached to the computer via USB, the computer queries (enumerates) the device to get its name, device type, and the type of device driver it supports. The computer can suspend power to individual devices, putting them in a suspended state.[1]

Parallel Port Printers have traditionally been connected to computers using *parallel ports*. The term *parallel* indicates that the bits in a data byte or word travel simultaneously from the computer to the device. Data is transferred at high speed (1MB per second) over short distances, usually no more than 10 feet. DOS automatically recognizes three parallel ports: LPT1, LPT2, and LPT3. Parallel ports can be *bidirectional*, allowing the computer to both send data to and receive information from a device. Although many printers now use USB connectors, parallel ports are useful for high-speed connections to laboratory instruments and custom hardware devices.

IDE Known as *intelligent drive electronics* or *integrated drive electronics*, IDE interfaces connect computers to mass-storage devices such as hard drives, DVDs, and CD-ROMs. IDE devices are almost always located inside the computer's system unit. Most IDE devices today are actually parallel ATA (*advanced technology attachment*) devices, in which the drive controller is located on the drive itself. Devices with built-in controller logic relieve the computer CPU of controlling internal drive logic. A related interface is SATA (serial ATA), which provides higher data transfer rates than parallel ATA.

FireWire FireWire is a high-speed external bus standard supporting data transfer speeds up to 800MB per second. A large number of devices can be attached to a single FireWire bus, and data can be delivered at a guaranteed rate (*isochronous* data transfer).

Serial Port An *RS-232 serial port* sends binary bits one at a time, more slowly than parallel and USB ports, but with the ability to send over larger distances. The highest data transfer rate is 19,200 bits per second. Laboratory acquisition devices often use serial interfaces, as does the telephone modem. The 16550 UART (*Universal Asynchronous Receiver Transmitter*) chip controls serial data transfer.

2.4.5 Section Review

1. Describe SRAM and its most common use.
2. Which Intel processor was behind the creation of the PCI bus?
3. In the motherboard chipset, what task does the Intel 8259A perform?
4. Where is the memory used by the video display located?
5. Describe raster scanning on a CRT video monitor.
6. Name four types of RAM mentioned in this chapter.
7. Which type of RAM is used for Level 2 cache memory?
8. What advantages does a USB device offer over a standard serial or parallel device?
9. What are the names of the two types of USB connectors?
10. Which processor chip controls the serial port?

2.5 Input-Output System

> Want to write computer games? Usually memory and I/O intensive, they push computer performance to the max. Programmers who excel at game programming often know a lot about video and sound hardware, and optimize their code for hardware features.

2.5.1 How It All Works

Application programs routinely read input from keyboard and disk files and write output to the screen and to files. I/O need not be accomplished by directly accessing hardware—instead, you can call functions provided by the operating system. I/O is available at different access levels, similar to the virtual machine concept shown in Chapter 1. There are three primary levels:

- **HLL language functions:** A high-level programming language such as C++ or Java contains functions to perform input-output. These functions are portable because they work on a variety of different computer systems and are not dependent on any one operating system.

- **Operating system:** Programmers can call operating system functions from a library known as the API (application programming interface). The operating system provides high-level operations such as writing strings to files, reading strings from the keyboard, and allocating blocks of memory.
- **BIOS:** The Basic Input-Output System is a collection of low-level subroutines that communicate directly with hardware devices. The BIOS is installed by the computer's manufacturer and is tailored to fit the computer's hardware. Operating systems typically communicate with the BIOS.

Device Drivers   What happens if a new device is installed in a computer unknown to the BIOS? When the operating system boots, it loads a device driver program containing functions that communicate with the device. A device driver works much like the BIOS, providing input-output functions tailored to a particular device or family of devices. An example is CDROM.SYS, which enables MS-DOS to read CD-ROM drives.

We can put the I/O hierarchy into perspective by showing what happens when an application program displays a string of characters on the screen in (Figure 2–15). The following steps are involved:

1. A statement in the application program calls an HLL library function that writes the string to standard output.
2. The library function (Level 3) calls an operating system function, passing a string pointer.
3. The operating system function (Level 2) uses a loop to call a BIOS subroutine, passing it the ASCII code and color of each character. The operating system calls another BIOS subroutine to advance the cursor to the next position on the screen.
4. The BIOS subroutine (Level 1) receives a character, maps it to a particular system font, and sends the character to a hardware port attached to the video controller card.
5. The video controller card (Level 0) generates timed hardware signals to the video display that control the raster scanning and displaying of pixels.

FIGURE 2–15   Access Levels for Input-Output Operations.

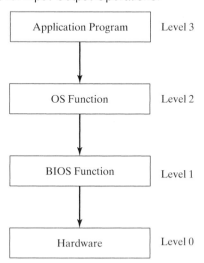

Programming at Multiple Levels   Assembly language programs have power and flexibility in the area of input-output programming. They can choose from the following access levels (Figure 2–16):

- Level 3: Call library functions to perform generic text I/O and file-based I/O. We supply such a library with this book, for instance.
- Level 2: Call operating system functions to perform generic text I/O and file-based I/O. If the OS uses a graphical user interface, it has functions to display graphics in a device-independent way.

• Level 1: Call BIOS functions to control device-specific features such as color, graphics, sound, keyboard input, and low-level disk I/O.

• Level 0: Send and receive data from hardware points, having absolute control over specific devices.

Figure 2–16 Assembly Language Access Levels.

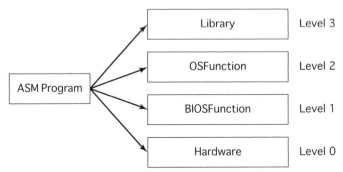

What are the tradeoffs? Control versus portability is the primary one. Level 2 (OS) works on any computer running the same operating system. If an I/O device lacks certain capabilities, the OS will do its best to approximate the intended result. Level 2 is not particularly fast because each I/O call must go through several layers before it executes.

Level 1 (BIOS) works on all systems having a standard BIOS, but will not produce the same result on all systems. For example, two computers might have video displays with different resolution capabilities. A programmer at Level 1 would have to write code to detect the user's hardware setup and adjust the output format to match. Level 1 runs faster than Level 2 because it is only one level above the hardware.

Level 0 (hardware) works with generic devices such as serial ports and with specific I/O devices produced by known manufacturers. Programs using this level must extend their coding logic to handle variations in I/O devices. Real-mode game programs are prime examples because they usually take control of the computer. Programs at this level execute as quickly as the hardware will permit.

Suppose, for example, you wanted to play a WAV file using an audio controller device. At the OS level, you would not have to know what type of device was installed, and you would not be concerned with nonstandard features the card might have. At the BIOS level, you would query the sound card (using its installed device driver software) and find out whether it belonged to a certain class of sound cards having known features. At the hardware level, you would fine tune the program for certain brands of audio cards, taking advantage of each card's special features.

Finally, not all operating systems permit user programs to directly access system hardware. Such access is reserved for the operating system itself and specialized device driver programs. This is the case with Windows NT, 2000, and XP, in which vital system resources are shielded from application programs. MS-DOS, on the other hand, has no such restrictions.

2.5.2 Section Review

1. Of the three levels of input/output in a computer system, which is the most universal and portable?

2. What characteristics distinguish BIOS-level input/output?

3. Why are device drivers necessary, given that the BIOS already has code that communicates with the computer's hardware?

4. In the example regarding displaying a string of characters, which level exists between the operating system and the video controller card?

5.   At which level(s) can an assembly language program manipulate input/output?

6.   Why do game programs often send their sound output directly to the sound card's hardware ports?

7.   *Challenge:* Is it likely that the BIOS for a computer running MS-Windows would be different from that used by a computer running Linux?

2.6   Chapter Summary

The central processor unit (CPU) is where calculations and logic processing occur. It contains a limited number of storage locations called *registers*, a high-frequency clock to synchronize its operations, a control unit, and the arithmetic logic unit. The memory storage unit is where instructions and data are held while a computer program is running. A *bus* is a series of parallel wires that transmit data among various parts of the computer.

The execution of a single machine instruction can be divided into a sequence of individual operations called the *instruction execution cycle*. The three primary operations are fetch, decode, and execute. Each step in the instruction cycle takes at least one tick of the system clock, called a *clock cycle*. The *load and execute* sequence describes how a program is located by the operating system, loaded into memory, and executed by the operating system.

Pipelined execution greatly improves the throughput of multiple instructions in a CPU by permitting the overlapped execution of multi-stage instructions. A *superscalar* processor is a pipelined processor with multiple execution pipelines. Such a processor is particularly useful when one of the execution stages requires multiple clock cycles.

A *multitasking* operating system can run multiple tasks at the same time. It runs on a processor that supports *task switching*, the ability to save the current task state and transfer control to a different task.

IA-32 processors have three basic modes of operation: *protected* mode, *real-address* mode, and *system management* mode. In addition, *virtual-8086* mode is a special case of protected mode.

Registers are named locations within the CPU that can be accessed much more quickly than conventional memory. Following are brief descriptions of register types:

• The *general-purpose* registers are primarily used for arithmetic, data movement, and logical operations.
• The *segment registers* are used as base locations for preassigned memory areas called segments.
• The EIP (*instruction pointer*) register contains the address of the next instruction to be executed.
• The EFLAGS (*extended flags*) register consists of individual binary bits that control the operation of the CPU and reflect the outcome of ALU operations.

The IA-32 has a floating-point unit (FPU) expressly used for the execution of high-speed floating-point instructions.

The Intel 8086 processor marked the beginning of the modern Intel architecture family. The Intel386 processor, the first of the IA-32 family, featured 32-bit registers and a 32-bit address bus and external data path. The P6 processor family (Pentium Pro onward) is based on a new micro-architecture design that improves execution speed.

The earliest Intel processors for the IBM Personal Computer were based on the *complex instruction set* (CISC) approach. The Intel instruction set includes powerful ways to address data and instructions that are relatively high level complex operations. A completely different approach to microprocessor design is the *reduced instruction set* (RISC). A RISC machine language consists of a relatively small number of short, simple instructions that can be executed quickly by the processor.

In real-address mode, only 1MB of memory can be addressed, using hexadecimal addresses 00000 to FFFFF. In protected mode, the processor can run multiple programs at the same time. It assigns each process (running program) a total of 4GB of virtual memory. In virtual-8086 mode, the computer runs in protected mode and creates a virtual 8086 machine with its own 1MB address space that simulates an 80×86 computer running in real-address mode.

In the flat segmentation model, all segments are mapped to the entire physical address space of the computer. In the multi-segment model, each task is given its own table of segment descriptors, called a local descriptor table (LDT). The IA-32 supports a feature called *paging*, which permits a segment to be divided into 4096-byte blocks of memory called pages. Paging permits the total memory used by all programs running at the same time to be much larger than the computer's actual (physical) memory.

The heart of any microcomputer is its motherboard, holding the computer's CPU, supporting processors, main memory, input-output connectors, power supply connectors, and expansion slots. The PCI (Peripheral Component Interconnect) bus provides a convenient upgrade path for Pentium processors. Most motherboards contain an integrated set of several microprocessors and controllers, called a chipset. The chipset largely determines the capabilities of the computer.

The video adapter controls the display of text and graphics on IBM-compatibles. It has two components: the video controller and video display memory.

Several basic types of memory are used in PCs: ROM, EPROM, Dynamic RAM (DRAM), Static RAM (SRAM), Video RAM (VRAM), and CMOS RAM.

The Universal Serial Bus (USB) port provides an intelligent, high-speed connection between a computer and USB-supported devices. A parallel port transmits 8 or 16 data bits simultaneously from one device to another. An RS-232 serial port sends binary bits one at a time, resulting in slower speeds than the parallel and USB ports.

Input-output is accomplished via different access levels, similar to the virtual machine concept. The operating system is at the highest level. The BIOS (Basic Input-Output System) is a collection of functions that communicate directly with hardware devices. Programs can also directly access input-output devices.

End Note

1. For more information, see Jack G. Ganssle, *An Introduction to USB Development*, Embedded Systems Programming. Available at www.embedded.com/2000/0003/0003ia2.htm.

Assembly Language Fundamentals

3.1 Basic Elements of Assembly Language

There is an element of truth in saying "*Assembly language is simple.*" It was designed to run in little memory and consists of mainly low-level, simple operations. Then why does it have the reputation of being difficult to learn? After all, how hard can it be to move data between registers and do a calculation? Here's a proof of concept—a simple program in assembly language that adds two numbers and displays the result:

```
main PROC
        mov     eax,5           ; move 5 to the EAX register
        add     eax,6           ; add 6 to the EAX register
        call    WriteInt        ; display value in EAX
        exit                    ; quit
main ENDP
```

We simplified things a bit by calling a library subroutine named **WriteInt**, which itself contains a fair amount of code. But in general, assembly language is not hard to learn if you're happy writing short programs that do practically nothing.

Details, Details Becoming a skilled assembly language programmer requires a love of details. Build a foundation of basic information and gradually fill in the details until you have something solid. Chapter 1 introduced number concepts and virtual machines. Chapter 2 introduced hardware basics. Now you're ready to begin programming. If you were a cook, we would show you around the kitchen and explain how to use mixers, grinders, knives, stoves, and saucepans. Similarly, we will identify the ingredients of assembly language, mix them together, and cook up a few tasty programs.

3.1.1   Integer Constants

An *integer constant* (or integer literal) is made up of an optional leading sign, one or more digits, and an optional suffix character (called a *radix*) indicating the number's base:

```
[{+|-}] digits [radix]
```

> Microsoft syntax notation is used throughout this chapter. Elements within square brackets [..] are optional and elements within braces {..} require a choice of one of the enclosed elements (separated by the | character). Elements in *italics* denote items that have known definitions or descriptions.

Radix may be one of the following (uppercase or lowercase):

h	Hexadecimal		r	Encoded real
q/o	Octal		t	Decimal *(alternate)*
d	Decimal		y	Binary *(alternate)*
b	Binary			

If no radix is given, the integer constant is assumed to be decimal. Here are some examples using different radixes:

26	Decimal	42o	Octal
26d	Decimal	1Ah	Hexadecimal
11010011b	Binary	0A3h	Hexadecimal
42q	Octal		

A hexadecimal constant beginning with a letter must have a leading zero to prevent the assembler from interpreting it as an identifier.

3.1.2   Integer Expressions

An *integer expression* is a mathematical expression involving integer values and arithmetic operators. The expression must evaluate to an integer, which can be stored in 32 bits (0 through FFFFFFFFh). The arithmetic operators are listed in Table 3-1 according to their precedence order, from highest (1) to lowest (4).

Table 3-1   Arithmetic Operators.

Operator	Name	Precedence Level
( )	Parentheses	1
+, −	Unary plus, minus	2
*, /	Multiply, divide	3
MOD	Modulus	3
+, −	Add, subtract	4

Precedence refers to the implied order of operations when an expression contains two or more operators. The order of operations is shown for the following expressions:

```
4 + 5 * 2              Multiply, add
12 - 1 MOD  5          Modulus, subtract
-5 + 2                 Unary minus, add
(4 + 2) * 6            Add, multiply
```

The following are examples of valid expressions and their values:

Expression	Value
16 / 5	3
−(3 + 4) * (6 − 1)	−35
−3 + 4 * 6 − 1	20
25 mod 3	1

> Use parentheses in expressions to clarify the order of operations so you don't have to remember precedence rules.

3.1.3   Real Number Constants

Real number constants are represented as decimal reals or encoded (hexadecimal) reals. A *decimal real* contains an optional sign followed by an integer, a decimal point, an optional integer that expresses a fraction, and an optional exponent:

```
[sign]integer.[integer][exponent]
```

Following are the syntax for the sign and exponent:

```
sign       {+,-}
exponent   E[{+,-}]integer
```

Following are examples of valid real number constants:

```
2.
+3.0
-44.2E+05
26.E5
```

At least one digit and a decimal point are required.

Encoded Reals An encoded real represents a real number in hexadecimal, using the IEEE floating-point format for short reals (see Chapter 17). The binary representation of decimal +1.0, for example, is

    0011 1111 1000 0000 0000 0000 0000 0000

The same value would be encoded as a short real in assembly language as

    3F800000r

3.1.4 Character Constants

A *character constant* is a single character enclosed in single or double quotes. MASM stores the value in memory as the character's binary ASCII code. Examples are

    'A'
    "d"

A complete list of ASCII codes is printed on the inside back cover of this book.

3.1.5 String Constants

A *string constant* is a sequence of characters (including spaces) enclosed in single or double quotes:

    'ABC'
    'X'
    "Goodnight, Gracie"
    '4096'

Embedded quotes are permitted when used in the manner shown by the following examples:

    "This isn't a test"
    'Say "Goodnight," Gracie'

3.1.6 Reserved Words

Reserved words have special meaning in MASM and can only be used in their correct context. There are different types of reserved words:

- Instruction mnemonics, such as MOV, ADD, and MUL.
- Directives, which tell MASM how to assemble programs.
- Attributes, which provide size and usage information for variables and operands. Examples are BYTE and WORD.
- Operators, used in constant expressions.
- Predefined symbols, such as @data, which return constant integer values at assembly time.

A complete list of MASM reserved words can be found in Appendix A.

3.1.7 Identifiers

An *identifier* is a programmer-chosen name. It might identify a variable, a constant, a procedure, or a code label. Keep the following in mind when creating identifiers:

- They may contain between 1 and 247 characters.
- They are not case sensitive.
- The first character must be a letter (A..Z, a..z), underscore (_), @ , ?, or $. Subsequent characters may also be digits.
- An identifier cannot be the same as an assembler reserved word.

> You can make all keywords and identifiers case sensitive by adding the –Cp command line switch when running the assembler.

The @ symbol is used extensively by the assembler as a prefix for predefined symbols, so avoid it in your own identifiers. Make identifier names descriptive and easy to understand. Here are some valid identifiers:

```
var1                    Count                   $first
_main                   MAX                     open_file
@@myfile                xVal                    _12345
```

3.1.8 Directives

A *directive* is a command embedded in the source code that is recognized and acted upon by the assembler. Directives do not execute at run time, whereas instructions do. Directives can define variables, macros, and procedures. They can assign names to memory segments and perform many other housekeeping tasks related to the assembler. In MASM, directives are case insensitive. It recognizes **.data**, **.DATA**, and **.Data** as equivalent.

The following example helps to show that directives do not execute at run time. The DWORD directive tells the assembler to reserve space in the program for a doubleword variable. The MOV instruction executes at run time, copying the contents of **myVar** to the EAX register:

```
myVar  DWORD 26                     ; DWORD directive
mov    eax,myVar                    ; MOV instruction
```

Each assembler has a different set of directives. TASM (Borland) and NASM (Netwide Assembler), for example, share a common subset of directives with MASM. The GNU assembler, on the other hand, has almost no directives in common with MASM.

Defining Segments   One important function of assembler directives is to define program sections, or *segments*. The .DATA directive identifies the area of a program containing variables:

```
.data
```

The .CODE directive identifies the area of a program containing instructions:

```
.code
```

The .STACK directive identifies the area of a program holding the runtime stack, setting its size:

```
.stack 100h
```

Appendix A is a useful reference for MASM directives and operators.

3.1.9 Instructions

An *instruction* is a statement that becomes executable when a program is assembled. Instructions are translated by the assembler into machine language bytes, which are loaded and executed by the CPU at run time. An instruction contains four basic parts:

- Label (optional)
- Instruction mnemonic (required)
- Operand(s) (usually required)
- Comment (optional)

This is the basic syntax:

```
[label:] mnemonic operand(s) [;comment]
```

Let's explore each part separately, beginning with the *label* field.

Label

A *label* is an identifier that acts as a place marker for instructions and data. A label placed just before an instruction implies the instruction's address. Similarly, a label placed just before a variable implies the variable's address.

Data Labels   A data label identifies the location of a variable, providing a convenient way to reference the variable in code. The following, for example, defines a variable named count:

```
count  DWORD 100
```

The assembler assigns a numeric address to each label. It is possible to define multiple data items following a label. In the following example, array defines the location of the first number (1024). The other numbers following in memory immediately afterward:

```
array  DWORD 1024, 2048
       DWORD 4096, 8192
```

Variables will be explained in Section 3.4.2, and the MOV instruction will be explained in Section 4.1.4.

Code Labels   A label in the code area of a program (where instructions are located) must end with a colon (:) character. In this context, labels are used as targets of jumping and looping instructions. For example, the following JMP (jump) instruction transfers control to the location marked by the label named **target**, creating a loop:

```
target:
     mov   ax,bx
     ...
     jmp   target
```

A code label can share the same line with an instruction, or it can be on a line by itself:

```
L1:  mov   ax,bx
L2:
```

A data label cannot end with a colon. Label names are created using the rules for identifiers discussed in Section 3.1.7. Data label names must be unique within the same source file; code labels must only be unique within the same procedure.

Instruction Mnemonic

An *instruction mnemonic* is a short word that identifies an instruction. In English, a *mnemonic* is a device that assists memory. Similarly, assembly language instruction mnemonics such as mov, add, and sub provide hints about the type of operation they perform:

```
          mov    Move (assign) one value to another
          add    Add two values
          sub    Subtract one value from another
          mul    Multiply two values
          jmp    Jump to a new location
          call   Call a procedure
```

Operands   Assembly language instructions can have between zero and three operands, each of which can be a register, memory operand, constant expression, or I/O port. We discussed register names in Chapter 2, and we discussed constant expressions in Section 3.1.2. A *memory operand* is specified by the name of a variable or by one or more registers containing the address of a variable. A variable name implies the address of the variable and instructs the computer to reference the contents of memory at the given address. The the following table contains several sample operands:

Example	Operand Type
96	Constant (*immediate value*)
2 + 4	Constant expression
eax	Register
count	Memory

Following are examples of assembly language instructions having varying numbers of operands. The STC instruction, for example, has no operands:

```
        stc                             ; set Carry flag
```

The INC instruction has one operand:

```
        inc   eax                       ; add 1 to EAX
```

The MOV instruction has two operands:

```
        mov count,ebx                   ; move EBX to count
```

In a two-operand instruction, the first is called the *destination* or *target*. The second operand is the *source*. In general, the contents of the destination operand are modified by the instruction. In a MOV instruction, for example, data is copied from the source to the destination.

Comments

Comments are an important way for the writer of a program to communicate information about how the program works to a person reading the source code. The following information is typically included at the top of a program listing:

- Description of the program's purpose
- Names of persons who created and/or revised the program
- Program creation and revision dates
- Technical notes about the program's implementation

Comments can be specified in two ways:

- Single-line comments, beginning with a semicolon character (;). All characters following the semicolon on the same line are ignored by the assembler.
- Block comments, beginning with the COMMENT directive and a user-specified symbol. All subsequent lines of text are ignored by the assembler until the same user-specified symbol appears. For example,

```
    COMMENT   !
        This line is a comment.
        This line is also a comment.
    !
```

We can also use any other symbol:

```
    COMMENT &
        This line is a comment.
        This line is also a comment.
    &
```

3.1.10   The NOP (No Operation) Instruction

The safest instruction you can write is called NOP (no operation). It takes up 1 byte of program storage and doesn't do any work. It is sometimes used by compilers and assemblers to align code to even-address boundaries. In the following example, the first MOV instruction generates three machine code bytes. The NOP instruction aligns the address of the third instruction to a doubleword boundary (even multiple of 4):

```
    00000000  66 8B  C3mov ax,bx
    00000003  90     nop                         ; align next instruction
    00000004  8B D1  mov edx,ecx
```

IA-32 processors are designed to load code and data more quickly from even doubleword addresses.

3.1.11 Section Review

1. Identify valid suffix characters used in integer constants.
2. *(Yes/No):* Is A5h a valid hexadecimal constant?
3. *(Yes/No):* Does the multiply sign (*) have a higher precedence than the divide sign (/) in integer expressions?
4. Write a constant expression that divides 10 by 3 and returns the integer remainder.
5. Show an example of a valid real number constant with an exponent.
6. *(Yes/No):* Must string constants be enclosed in single quotes?
7. Reserved words can be instruction mnemonics, attributes, operators, predefined symbols, and _____.
8. What is the maximum length of an identifier?
9. *(True/False):* An identifier cannot begin with a numeric digit.
10. *(True/False):* Assembly language identifiers are (by default) case insensitive.
11. *(True/False):* Assembler directives execute at run time.
12. *(True/False):* Assembler directives can be written in any combination of uppercase and lowercase letters.
13. Name the four basic parts of an assembly-language instruction.
14. *(True/False):* MOV is an example of an instruction mnemonic.
15. *(True/False):* A code label is followed by a colon (:), but a data label does not have a colon.
16. Show an example of a block comment.
17. Why would it not be a good idea to use numeric addresses when writing instructions that access variables?

3.2 Example: Adding Three Integers

We now introduce a short assembly language program that adds and subtracts integers. Registers are used to hold the intermediate data, and we call a library subroutine to display the contents of the registers on the screen. Here is the program source code:

```
TITLE Add and Subtract              (AddSub.asm)

; This program adds and subtracts 32-bit integers.

INCLUDE Irvine32.inc
.code
main PROC

        mov     eax,10000h              ; EAX = 10000h
        add     eax,40000h              ; EAX = 50000h
        sub     eax,20000h              ; EAX = 30000h
        call    DumpRegs                ; display registers

        exit
main ENDP
END main
```

Let's go through the program line by line. In each case, the program code appears before its explanation:

```
TITLE Add and Subtract              (AddSub.asm)
```

The TITLE directive marks the entire line as a comment. You can put anything you want on this line.

```
; This program adds and subtracts 32-bit integers.
```

All text to the right of a semicolon is ignored by the assembler, so we use it for comments.

```
INCLUDE Irvine32.inc
```

The INCLUDE directive copies necessary definitions and setup information from a text file named *Irvine32.inc*, located in the assembler's INCLUDE directory. (The file is described in Chapter 5.)

```
.code
```

The **.code** directive marks the beginning of the *code segment*, where all executable statements in a program are located.

```
main PROC
```

The PROC directive identifies the beginning of a procedure. The name chosen for the only procedure in our program is **main**.

```
mov   eax,10000h                        ; EAX = 10000h
```

The MOV instruction moves (copies) the integer 10000h to the EAX register. The first operand (EAX) is called the *destination operand,* and the second operand is called the *source operand.*

```
add   eax,40000h                        ; EAX = 50000h
```

The ADD instruction adds 40000h to the EAX register.

```
sub   eax,20000h                        ; EAX = 30000h
```

The SUB instruction subtracts 20000h from the EAX register.

```
call DumpRegs                          ; display registers
```

The CALL statement calls a procedure that displays the current values of the CPU registers. This can be a useful way to verify that a program is working correctly.

```
      exit
main ENDP
```

The **exit** statement (indirectly) calls a predefined MS-Windows function that halts the program. The ENDP directive marks the end of the **main** procedure. Note that **exit** is not a MASM keyword; instead, it's a command defined in *Irvine32.inc* that provides a simple way to end a program.

```
END main
```

The END directive marks the last line of the program to be assembled. It identifies the name of the program's *startup* procedure (the procedure that starts the program execution).

Program Output   The following is a snapshot of the the program's output, generated by the call to DumpRegs:

```
EAX=00030000   EBX=7FFDF000   ECX=00000101   EDX=FFFFFFFF
ESI=00000000   EDI=00000000   EBP=0012FFF0   ESP=0012FFC4
EIP=00401024   EFL=00000206   CF=0   SF=0   ZF=0   OF=0   AF=0   PF=1
```

The first two rows of output show the hexadecimal values of the 32-bit general-purpose registers. EAX equals 00030000h, the value produced by the ADD and SUB instructions in the program. The third row shows the values of the EIP (extended instruction pointer) and EFL (extended flags) registers, as well as the values of the Carry, Sign, Zero, Overflow, Auxiliary Carry, and Parity flags.

Segments   Programs are organized around segments, which are usually named code, data, and stack. The *code* segment contains all of a program's executable instructions. Ordinarily, the code segment contains one or more procedures, with one designated as the *startup* procedure. In the

AddSub program, the startup procedure is **main**. Another segment, the *stack* segment, holds procedure parameters and local variables. The *data* segment holds variables.

Coding Styles   Because assembly language is case insensitive, there is no fixed style rule regarding capitalization of source code. In the interest of readability, you should be consistent in your approach to capitalization, as well as the naming of identifiers. Following are some approaches to capitalization you may want to adopt:

- Use lowercase for keywords, mixed case for identifiers, and all capitals for constants. This approach follows the general model of C, C++, and Java.
- Capitalize everything. This approach was used in pre-1970 software when many computer terminals did not support lowercase letters. It has the advantage of overcoming the effects of poor-quality printers and less-than-perfect eyesight, but seems a bit old-fashioned.
- Use capital letters for assembler reserved words, including instruction mnemonics, and register names. This approach makes it easy to distinguish between identifiers and reserved words.
- Capitalize assembly language directives and operators, use mixed case for identifiers, and lowercase for everything else. This approach is used in this book, except that lowercase is used for the .code, .stack, .model, and .data directives.

3.2.1   Alternative Version of AddSub

The **AddSub** program used the *Irvine32.inc* file, which hides a few details. Eventually you will understand everthing in that file, but we're just getting started in assembly language. If you prefer full disclosure of information from the start, here is a version of AddSub that does not depend on include files. A bold font is used to highlight the portions of the program that are different from the previous version:

```
TITLE Add and Subtract                      (AddSubAlt.asm)

; This program adds and subtracts 32-bit integers.

.386
.model flat,stdcall
.stack 4096
ExitProcess PROTO, dwExitCode:DWORD
DumpRegs PROTO

.code
main PROC

        mov    eax,10000h            ; EAX = 10000h
        add    eax,40000h            ; EAX = 50000h
        sub    eax,20000h            ; EAX = 30000h
        call   DumpRegs

        INVOKE ExitProcess,0
main ENDP
END main
```

Let's discuss the lines that have changed. As before, we show each line of code followed by its explanation:

```
.386
```

The .386 directive identifies the minimum CPU required for this program (Intel386).

```
.model flat,stdcall
```

The .MODEL directive instructs the assembler to generate code for a protected mode program, and STDCALL enables the calling of MS-Windows functions.

```
ExitProcess PROTO, dwExitCode:DWORD
DumpRegs PROTO
```

Two PROTO directives declare prototypes for procedures used by this program: **ExitProcess** is an MS-Windows function that halts the current program (called a *process*), and **DumpRegs** is a procedure from the Irvine32 link library that displays registers.

```
INVOKE ExitProcess,0
```

The program ends by calling the **ExitProcess** function, passing it a return code of zero. INVOKE is an assembler directive that calls a procedure or function.

3.2.2   Program Template

Assembly language programs have a simple structure, with small variations. When you begin a new program, it helps to start with an empty shell program with all basic elements in place. You can avoid redundant typing by filling in the missing parts and saving the file under a new name. The following protected-mode program (*Template.asm*) can easily be customized. Note that comments have been inserted, marking the points where your own code should be added:

```
TITLE Program Template          (Template.asm)

; Program Description:
; Author:
; Creation Date:
; Revisions:
; Date:              Modified by:

INCLUDE Irvine32.inc
.data
      ; (insert variables here)

.code
main PROC
      ; (insert executable instructions here)

      exit
main ENDP

      ; (insert additional procedures here)
END main
```

Use Comments   Several comment fields have been inserted at the beginning of the program. It's a very good idea to include a program description, the name of the program's author, creation date, and information about subsequent modifications.

Documentation of this kind is useful to anyone who reads the program listing (including you, months or years from now). Many programmers have discovered, years after writing a program, that they must become reacquainted with their own code before they can modify it. If you're taking a programming course, your instructor may insist on additional information.

3.2.3   Section Review

1. In the AddSub program (Section 3.2), what is the meaning of the INCLUDE directive?
2. In the AddSub program, what does the .CODE directive identify?
3. What are the names of the segments in the AddSub program?

4. In the AddSub program, how are the CPU registers displayed?

5. In the AddSub program, which statement halts the program?

6. Which directive begins a procedure?

7. Which directive ends a procedure?

8. What is the purpose of the identifier in the END statement?

9. What does the PROTO directive do?

3.3   Assembling, Linking, and Running Programs

In earlier chapters we saw examples of simple machine-language programs, so it is clear that a source program written in assembly language cannot be executed directly on its target computer. It must be translated, or *assembled* into executable code. In fact, an assembler is very similar to a *compiler*, the type of program you would use to translate a C++ or Java program into executable code.

The assembler produces a file containing machine language called an *object file*. This file isn't quite ready to execute. It must be passed to another program called a *linker*, which in turn produces an *executable file*. This file is ready to execute from the MS-DOS/Windows command prompt.

3.3.1   The Assemble-Link-Execute Cycle

The process of editing, assembling, linking, and executing assembly language programs is summarized in Figure 3–1. Following is a detailed description of each step.

Step 1: A programmer uses a **text editor** to create an ASCII text file named the *source file*.

Step 2: The **assembler** reads the source file and produces an *object file*, a machine-language translation of the program. Optionally, it produces a *listing file*. If any errors occur, the programmer must return to Step 1 and fix the program.

Step 3: The **linker** reads the object file and checks to see if the program contains any calls to procedures in a link library. The **linker** copies any required procedures from the link library, combines them with the object file, and produces the *executable file*. Optionally, the linker can produce a *map file*.

Step 4: The operating system **loader** utility reads the executable file into memory and branches the CPU to the program's starting address, and the program begins to execute.

Figure 3–1   Assemble-Link-Execute Cycle.

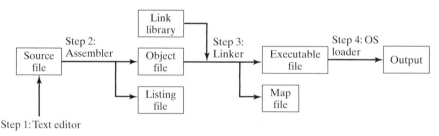

See the book's Web site (www.asmirvine.com) for detailed instructions on assembling, linking, and running assembly language programs using Microsoft Visual C++ 2005 Express.

Listing File

A *listing* file contains a copy of the program's source code, suitable for printing, with line numbers, offset addresses, translated machine code, and a symbol table. Let's look at the listing file for the **AddSub** program we created in Section 3.2:

```
Microsoft (R) Macro Assembler Version 8.00
Add and Subtract (AddSub.asm)                    Page 1 - 1

TITLE Add and Subtract               (AddSub.asm)

; This program adds and subtracts 32-bit integers.

INCLUDE Irvine32.inc
C    ; Include file for Irvine32.lib (Irvine32.inc)
C    INCLUDE SmallWin.inc

00000000        .code
00000000        main PROC

00000000  B8 00010000      mov eax,10000h   ; EAX = 10000h
00000005  05 00040000      add eax,40000h   ; EAX = 50000h
0000000A  2D 00020000      sub eax,20000h   ; EAX = 30000h
0000000F  E8 00000000E     call DumpRegs

                  exit
0000001B        main ENDP
                  END main
```

```
Structures and Unions: (omitted)

Segments and Groups:

N a m e          Size    Length   Align   Combine Class
FLAT . . . . . . .GROUP
STACK. . . . . . .32 Bit  00001000  DWord   Stack    'STACK'
_DATA. . . . . . .32 Bit  00000000  DWord   Public   'DATA'
_TEXT. . . . . . .32 Bit  0000001B  DWord   Public   'CODE'

Procedures, parameters and locals (list abbreviated):

N a m e              Type Value Attr
CloseHandle. . . . P Near 00000000 FLAT   Length=00000000   External STDCALL
ClrScr . . . . . . P Near 00000000 FLAT   Length=00000000   External STDCALL
.
.

main . . . . . . . P Near 00000000 _TEXT Length=0000001B  Public STDCALL

Symbols (list abbreviated):

N a m e                            Type   Value       Attr
@CodeSize  . . . . . . . . . . . Number 00000000h
@DataSize  . . . . . . . . . . . Number 00000000h
@Interface . . . . . . . . . . . Number 00000003h
@Model . . . . . . . . . . . . . Number 00000007h
@code  . . . . . . . . . . . . . Text              _TEXT
@data  . . . . . . . . . . . . . Text              FLAT
@fardata?  . . . . . . . . . . . Text              FLAT
@fardata . . . . . . . . . . . . Text              FLAT
@stack . . . . . . . . . . . . . Text              FLAT
.
.
```

```
exit . . . . . . . . . . . . . . Text    INVOKE ExitProcess,0
       0 Warnings
       0 Errors
```

Files Created or Updated by the Linker

Map File   A *map* file contains information (in plain text) about a program's segments, including the following:

- The module name, used as the base name of the EXE file produced by the linker
- The timestamp from the program file header (not from the file system)
- A list of segment groups containing each group's start address, length, group name, and class
- A list of public symbols containing each symbol's address, symbol name, flat address, and module where it is defined
- The program's entry point address

Program Database File   When MASM assembles a program with the debugging option (–Zi) , it reates a *program database file* with a pdb filename extension. During the link step, the linker reads and updates the pdb file. When you run the program using a debugger, it displays the program's source code, data, runtime stack, and other information.

3.3.2 Section Review

1. What types of files are produced by the assembler?
2. *(True/False):* The linker extracts assembled procedures from the link library and inserts them in the executable program.
3. *(True/False):* When a program's source code is modified, it must be assembled and linked again before it can be executed with the changes.
4. Which operating system component reads and executes programs?
5. What types of files are produced by the linker?

3.4 Defining Data

3.4.1 Intrinsic Data Types

MASM defines intrinsic data types, each of which describes a set of values that can be assigned to variables and expressions of the given type. The essential characteristic of each type is its size in bits: 8, 16, 32, 48, 64, and 80. Other characteristices (such as signed, pointer, or floating-point) are optional and are mainly for the benefit of programmers who want to be reminded about the type of data held in the variable. A variable declared as DWORD, for example, logically holds an unsigned 32-bit integer. In fact, it could hold a signed 32-bit integer, a 32-bit single precision real, or a 32-bit pointer. The assembler is not case sensitive, so a directive such as DWORD can be written as **dword**, **Dword**, **dWord**, and so on.

In Table 3-2, all data types pertain to integers except the last three. In those, the notation IEEE refers to standard real number formats published by the IEEE Computer Society.

3.4.2 Data Definition Statement

A *data definition statement* sets aside storage in memory for a variable, with an optional name. Data definition statements create variables based on intrinsic data types (Table 3-2). A data definition has the following syntax:

```
[name] directive initializer [,initializer]...
```

Table 3-2   Intrinsic Data Types.

Type	Usage
BYTE	8-bit unsigned integer
SBYTE	8-bit signed integer
WORD	16-bit unsigned integer (can also be a Near pointer in real-address mode)
SWORD	16-bit signed integer
DWORD	32-bit unsigned integer (can also be a Near pointer in protected mode)
SDWORD	32-bit signed integer
FWORD	48-bit integer (Far pointer in protected mode)
QWORD	64-bit integer
TBYTE	80-bit (10-byte) integer
REAL4	32-bit (4-byte) IEEE short real
REAL8	64-bit (8-byte) IEEE long real
REAL10	80-bit (10-byte) IEEE extended real

Name The optional name assigned to a variable must conform to the rules for identifiers (Section 3.1.7).

Directive The directive in a data definition statement can be BYTE, WORD, DWORD, SBYTE, SWORD, or any of the types listed in Table 3-2. In addition, it can be any of the legacy data definition directives shown in Table 3-3, supported also by the NASM and TASM assemblers.

Table 3-3   Legacy Data Directives.

Directive	Usage
DB	8-bit integer
DW	16-bit integer
DD	32-bit integer or real
DQ	64-bit integer or real
DT	define 80-bit tenbyte

Initializer At least one *initializer* is required in a data definition, even if it is zero. Additional initializers, if any, are separated by commas. For integer data types, *initializer* is an integer constant or expression matching the size of the variable's type, such as BYTE or WORD. If you prefer to leave the variable uninitialized (assigned a random value), the **?** symbol can be used as the initializer. All initializers, regardless of their format, are converted to binary data by the assembler. Initializers such as 00110010b, 32h, and 50d all end up being having the same binary value.

3.4.3 Defining BYTE and SBYTE Data

The BYTE (define byte) and SBYTE (define signed byte) directives allocate storage for one or more unsigned or signed values. Each initializer must fit into 8 bits of storage. For example,

```
value1 BYTE   'A'            ; character constant
value2 BYTE    0             ; smallest unsigned byte
value3 BYTE   255            ; largest unsigned byte
value4 SBYTE –128            ; smallest signed byte
value5 SBYTE +127            ; largest signed byte
```

A question mark (?) initializer leaves the variable uninitialized, implying it will be assigned a value at runtime:

```
value6 BYTE ?
```

The optional name is a label marking the variable's offset from the beginning of its enclosing segment. For example, if **value1** is located at offset 0000 in the data segment and consumes 1 byte of storage, **value2** is automatically located at offset 0001:

```
value1 BYTE 10h
value2 BYTE 20h
```

The DB legacy directive can also define an 8-bit variable, signed or unsigned:

```
val1 DB 255                  ; unsigned byte
val2 DB –128                 ; signed byte
```

Multiple Initializers

If multiple initializers are used in the same data definition, its label refers only to the offset of the first initializer. In the following example, assume **list** is located at offset 0000. If so, the value 10 is at offset 0000, 20 is at offset 0001, 30 is at offset 0002, and 40 is at offset 0003:

```
list BYTE 10,20,30,40
```

The following illustration shows **list** as a sequence of bytes, each with its own offset:

Offset	Value
0000:	10
0001:	20
0002:	30
0003:	40

Not all data definitions require labels. To continue the array of bytes begun with **list**, for example, we can define additional bytes on the next lines:

```
list BYTE 10,20,30,40
     BYTE 50,60,70,80
     BYTE 81,82,83,84
```

Within a single data definition, its initializers can use different radixes. Character and string constants can be freely mixed. In the following example, **list1** and **list2** have the same contents:

```
list1 BYTE 10, 32, 41h, 00100010b
list2 BYTE 0Ah, 20h, 'A', 22h
```

Defining Strings

To define a string of characters, enclose them in single or double quotation marks. The most common type of string ends with a null byte (containing 0). Called a *null-terminated* string, strings of this type are used in C, C++, and Java programs:

```
greeting1 BYTE "Good afternoon",0
greeting2 BYTE 'Good night',0
```

Each character uses a byte of storage. Strings are an exception to the rule that byte values must be separated by commas. Without that exception, **greeting1** would have to be defined as

```
greeting1 BYTE 'G','o','o','d'....etc.
```

which would be exceedingly tedious. A string can be spread across multiple lines without having to supply a label for each line:

```
greeting1 BYTE "Welcome to the Encryption Demo program "
    BYTE "created by Kip Irvine.",0dh,0ah
    BYTE "If you wish to modify this program, please "
    BYTE "send me a copy.",0dh,0ah,0
```

The hexadecimal codes 0Dh and 0Ah are alternately called CR/LF (carrriage-return line-feed) or *end-of-line characters*. When written to standard output, they move the cursor to the left column of the line following the current line.

The line continuation character (\) concatenates two source code lines into a single statement. It must be the last character on the line. The following statements are equivalent:

```
greeting1 BYTE "Welcome to the Encryption Demo program "
```

and

```
greeting1 \
BYTE "Welcome to the Encryption Demo program "
```

DUP Operator

The DUP operator allocates storage for multiple data items, using a constant expression as a counter. It is particularly useful when allocating space for a string or array, and can be used with initialized or uninitialized data:

```
BYTE 20 DUP(0)          ; 20 bytes, all equal to zero
BYTE 20 DUP(?)          ; 20 bytes, uninitialized
BYTE  4 DUP("STACK")    ; 20 bytes: "STACKSTACKSTACKSTACK"
```

3.4.4   Defining WORD and SWORD Data

The WORD (define word) and SWORD (*define signed word*) directives create storage for one or more 16-bit integers:

```
word1  WORD   65535      ; largest unsigned value
word2  SWORD  -32768     ; smallest signed value
word3  WORD   ?          ; uninitialized, unsigned
```

The legacy DW directive can also be used:

```
val1  DW  65535                    ; unsigned
val2  DW  -32768                   ; signed
```

Array of Words   Create an array of words by listing the elements or using the DUP operator. The following array contains a list of values:

```
myList  WORD  1,2,3,4,5
```

Following is a diagram of the array in memory, assuming **myList** starts at offset 0000. The addresses increment by 2 because each value occupies 2 bytes:

Offset	Value
0000:	1
0002:	2
0004:	3
0006:	4
0008:	5

The DUP operator provides a convenient way to initialize multiple words:

```
array WORD 5 DUP(?)                ; 5 values, uninitialized
```

3.4.5   Defining DWORD and SDWORD Data

The DWORD (define doubleword) and SDWORD (define signed doubleword) directives allocate storage for one or more 32-bit integers:

```
val1 DWORD    12345678h            ; unsigned
val2 SDWORD  -2147483648           ; signed
val3 DWORD    20 DUP(?)            ; unsigned array
```

The legacy DD directive can also be used:

```
val1 DD 12345678h                  ; unsigned
val2 DD -2147483648                ; signed
```

Array of Doublewords   Create an array of doublewords by explicitly initializing each element, or use the DUP operator. Here is an array containing specific unsigned values:

```
myList DWORD 1,2,3,4,5
```

The following is a diagram of the array in memory, assuming **myList** starts at offset 0000. The offsets increment by 4:

Offset	Value
0000:	1
0004:	2
0008:	3
000C:	4
0010:	5

3.4.6 Defining QWORD Data

The QWORD (define quadword) directive allocates storage for 64-bit (8-byte) values:

```
quad1 QWORD 1234567812345678h
```

The legacy DQ directive can also be used:

```
quad1 DQ 1234567812345678h
```

3.4.7 Defining TBYTE Data

The TBYTE (define tenbyte) directive creates storage for 80-bit integers. This data type is primarily for the storage of binary-coded decimal numbers. Manipulating these values requires special instructions in the floating-point instruction set:

```
val1 TBYTE 1000000000123456789Ah
```

The legacy DT directive can also be used:

```
val1 DT 1000000000123456789Ah
```

3.4.8 Defining Real Number Data

REAL4 defines a 4-byte single-precision real variable. REAL8 defines an 8-byte double-precision real, and REAL10 defines a 10-byte double extended-precision real. Each requires one or more real constant initializers:

```
rVal1      REAL4 -1.2
rVal2      REAL8  3.2E-260
rVal3      REAL10 4.6E+4096
ShortArray REAL4  20 DUP(0.0)
```

The following table describes each of the standard real types in terms of their minimum number of significant digits and approximate range:

Data Type	Significant Digits	Approximate Range
Short real	6	1.18×10^{-38} to 3.40×10^{38}
Long real	15	2.23×10^{-308} to 1.79×10^{308}
Extended-precision real	19	3.37×10^{-4932} to 1.18×10^{4932}

The legacy DD, DQ, and DT directives can define real numbers:

```
rVal1 DD -1.2         ; short real
rVal2 DQ  3.2E-260    ; long real
rVal3 DT  4.6E+4096   ; extended-precision real
```

3.4.9 Little Endian Order

Intel processors store and retrieve data from memory using *little endian* order. The least significant byte is stored at the first memory address allocated for the data. The remaining bytes are stored in the next consecutive memory positions. Consider the doubleword 12345678h. If placed in memory at offset 0000, 78h would be stored in the first byte, 56h would be stored in the second byte, and the remaining bytes would be at offsets 0003 and 0004:

0000:	78
0001:	56
0002:	34
0003:	12

Little endian

Some other computer systems use *big endian* order (high to low). The following figure shows an example of 12345678h stored in big endian order at offset 0:

0000:	12
0001:	34
0002:	56
0003:	78

Big endian

3.4.10   Adding Variables to the AddSub Program

Using the **AddSub** program from Section 3.2, we will can add a data segment containing several doubleword variables. The revised program is named **AddSub2**:

```
TITLE Add and Subtract, Version 2        (AddSub2.asm)

; This program adds and subtracts 32-bit unsigned
; integers and stores the sum in a variable.

INCLUDE Irvine32.inc
.data
val1  DWORD 10000h
val2  DWORD 40000h
val3  DWORD 20000h
finalVal DWORD ?

.code
main PROC
      mov   eax,val1          ; start with 10000h
      add   eax,val2          ; add 40000h
      sub   eax,val3          ; subtract 20000h
      mov   finalVal,eax      ; store the result (30000h)
      call  DumpRegs          ; display the registers
      exit
main ENDP
END main
```

How does it work? First, the integer in **val1** is moved to EAX:

```
mov  eax,val1                 ; start with 10000h
```

Next, **val2** is added to EAX:

```
add  eax,val2                 ; add 40000h
```

Next, **val3** is subtracted from EAX:

```
sub  eax,val3                      ; subtract 20000h
```

EAX is copied to **finalVal**:

```
mov  finalVal,eax                  ; store the result (30000h)
```

3.4.11 Declaring Uninitialized Data

The .DATA? directive declares uninitialized data. When definiting a large block of uninitialized data, the .DATA? directive reduces the size of a compiled program. For example, the following code is declared efficiently:

```
.data
smallArray DWORD 10 DUP(0)         ; 40 bytes
.data?
bigArray DWORD 5000 DUP(?)         ; 20,000 bytes, not initialized
```

The following code, on the other hand, produces a compiled program 20,000 bytes larger:

```
.data
smallArray DWORD 10 DUP(0)         ; 40 bytes
bigArray DWORD 5000 DUP(?)         ; 20,000 bytes
```

Mixing Code and Data   The assembler lets you switch back and forth between code and data in your programs. You might, for example, want to declare a variable used only within a localized area of a program. The following example inserts a variable named **temp** between two code statements:

```
.code
mov eax,ebx
.data
temp DWORD ?
.code
mov temp,eax
. . .
```

Although **temp** appears to interrupts the flow of executable instructions, MASM places **temp** in the data segment, separate from the segment holding compiled code.

3.4.12 Section Review

1. Create an uninitialized data declaration for a 16-bit signed integer.
2. Create an uninitialized data declaration for an 8-bit unsigned integer.
3. Create an uninitialized data declaration for an 8-bit signed integer.
4. Create an uninitialized data declaration for a 64-bit integer.
5. Which data type can hold a 32-bit signed integer?
6. Declare a 32-bit signed integer variable and initialize it with the smallest possible negative decimal value. (*Hint:* Refer to integer ranges in Chapter 1.)
7. Declare an unsigned 16-bit integer variable named **wArray** that uses three initializers.
8. Declare a string variable containing the name of your favorite color. Initialize it as a null-terminated string.
9. Declare an uninitialized array of 50 unsigned doublewords named **dArray**.
10. Declare a string variable containing the word "TEST" repeated 500 times.
11. Declare an array of 20 unsigned bytes named **bArray** and initialize all elements to zero.
12. Show the order of individual bytes in memory (lowest to highest) for the following doubleword variable:

```
val1 DWORD 87654321h
```

3.5 Symbolic Constants

A *symbolic constant* (or *symbol definition*) is created by associating an identifier (a symbol) with an integer expression or some text. Symbols do not reserve storage. They are used only by the assembler when scanning a program, and they cannot change at run time. The following table summarizes their differences:

	Symbol	Variable
Uses storage?	No	Yes
Value changes at run time?	No	Yes

We will show how to use the equal-sign directive (=) to create symbols representing integer expressions. We will use the EQU and TEXTEQU directives to create symbols representing arbitrary text.

3.5.1 Equal-Sign Directive

The *equal-sign* directive associates a symbol name with an integer expression (see Section 3.1.2). The syntax is

```
name = expression
```

Ordinarily, *expression* is a 32-bit integer value. When a program is assembled, all occurrences of *name* are replaced by *expression* during the assembler's preprocessor step. For example, if the assembler reads the lines

```
COUNT = 500
mov  ax,COUNT
```

it generates and assembles the following statement:

```
mov  ax,500
```

Why Use Symbols?   We might have skipped the COUNT symbol entirely and simply coded the MOV instruction with the literal 500, but experience has shown that programs are easier to read and maintain if symbols are used. Suppose COUNT were used 10 times throughout a program. At a later time, it could be increased to 600 by altering only a single line of code:

```
COUNT = 600
```

When the program using COUNT is reassembled, all instances of COUNT are automatically replaced by 600. Without this symbol, the programmer would have to manually find and replace every 500 with 600 in the program's source code. What if one occurrence of 500 were not actually related to all of the others? Then a bug would be caused by changing it to 600.

Keyboard Definitions   Programs often define symbols for important keyboard characters. For example, 27 is the ASCII code for the Esc key:

```
Esc_key = 27
```

Later in the same program, a statement is more self-describing if it uses the symbol rather than an immediate value. Use

```
mov  al,Esc_key                    ; good style
```

rather than

```
mov  al,27                         ; poor style
```

Using the DUP Operator   Section 3.4.3 showed how to use the DUP operator to create storage for arrays and strings. The counter used by DUP should be a symbolic constant, to simplify program maintenance. In the next example, if COUNT has been defined, it can be used in the following data definition:

```
array DWORD COUNT DUP(0)
```

Redefinitions   A symbol defined with = can be redefined within the same program. The following example shows how the assembler evaluates COUNT as it changes value:

```
COUNT = 5
mov al,COUNT                          ; AL = 5
COUNT = 10
mov al,COUNT                          ; AL = 10
COUNT = 100
mov al,COUNT                          ; AL = 100
```

The changing value of a symbol such as COUNT has nothing to do with the runtime execution order of statements. Instead, the symbol changes value according to the assembler's sequential processing of the source code.

3.5.2   Calculating the Sizes of Arrays and Strings

When using an array, we would usually like to know its size. The following example uses a constant named **ListSize** to declare the size of **list**:

```
list BYTE 10,20,30,40
ListSize = 4
```

Manually calculating array sizes is not a good idea when the array may later change size. If we were to add more bytes to **list**, **ListSize** would have to be corrected. A better way to handle this situation would be to let the assembler automatically calculate **ListSize**. The $ operator (*current location counter*) returns the offset associated with the current program statement. In the following example, **ListSize** is calculated by subtracting the offset of **list** from the current location counter ($):

```
list BYTE 10,20,30,40
ListSize = ($ - list)
```

ListSize must follow immediately after **list**. The following, for example, produces too large a value for **ListSize** because the storage used by **var2** affects the distance between the current location counter and the offset of **list**:

```
list BYTE 10,20,30,40
var2 BYTE 20 DUP(?)
ListSize = ($ - list)
```

Rather than calculating the length of a string manually, let the assembler do it:

```
myString  BYTE "This is a long string, containing"
          BYTE "any number of characters"
myString_len = ($ – myString)
```

Arrays of Words and DoubleWords   When calculating the number of elements in an array containing 16-bit words, divide the difference in offsets by 2:

```
list  WORD  1000h,2000h,3000h,4000h
ListSize = ($ – list) / 2
```

Similarly, each element of an array of doublewords is 4 bytes long, so its overall length must be divided by four to produce the number of array elements:

```
list  DWORD  10000000h,20000000h,30000000h,40000000h
ListSize = ($ –list) / 4
```

3.5.3 EQU Directive

The EQU directive associates a symbolic name with an integer expression or some arbitrary text. There are three formats:

```
name EQU expression
name EQU symbol
name EQU <text>
```

In the first format, *expression* must be a valid integer expression (see Section 3.1.2). In the second format, *symbol* is an existing symbol name, already defined with = or EQU. In the third format, any text may appear within the brackets <. . .>. When the assembler encounters *name* later in the program, it substitutes the integer value or text for the symbol.

EQU can be useful when defining a value that does not evaluate to an integer. A real number constant, for example, can be defined using EQU:

```
PI EQU <3.1416>
```

Example The following example associates a symbol with a character string. Then a variable can be created using the symbol:

```
pressKey EQU <"Press any key to continue...",0>
.
.
.data
prompt BYTE    pressKey
```

Example Suppose we would like to define a symbol that counts the number of cells in a 10-by-10 integer matrix. We will define symbols two different ways, first as an integer expression and second as a text expression. The two symbols are then used in data definitions:

```
matrix1   EQU    10 * 10
matrix2   EQU    <10 * 10>
.data
M1 WORD matrix1
M2 WORD matrix2
```

The assembler produces different data definitions for **M1** and **M2**. The integer expression in **matrix1** is evaluated and assigned to **M1**. On the other hand, the text in **matrix2** is copied directly into the data definition for **M2**:

```
M1 WORD    100
M2 WORD    10 * 10
```

No Redefinition Unlike the = directive, a symbol defined with EQU cannot be redefined in the same source code file. This restriction prevents an existing symbol from being inadvertently assigned a new value.

3.5.4 TEXTEQU Directive

The TEXTEQU directive, similar to EQU, creates what is known as a *text macro*. There are three different formats: the first assigns text, the second assigns the contents of an existing text macro, and the third assigns a constant integer expression:

```
name TEXTEQU <text>
name TEXTEQU textmacro
name TEXTEQU %constExpr
```

For example, the **prompt1** variable uses the **continueMsg** text macro:

```
continueMsg TEXTEQU <"Do you wish to continue (Y/N)?">
```

```
.data
prompt1 BYTE continueMsg
```

Text macros can build on each other. In the next example, **count** is set to the value of an integer expression involving **rowSize**. Then the symbol **move** is defined as **mov**. Finally, **setupAL** is built from **move** and **count**:

```
rowSize = 5
count    TEXTEQU  %(rowSize * 2)
move     TEXTEQU  <mov>
setupAL  TEXTEQU  <move al,count>
```

Therefore, the statement

```
setupAL
```

would be assembled as

```
mov al,10
```

A symbol defined by TEXTEQU can be redefined at any time.

3.5.5   Section Review

1. Declare a symbolic constant using the equal-sign directive that contains the ASCII code (08h) for the Backspace key.
2. Declare a symbolic constant named **SecondsInDay** using the equal-sign directive and assign it an arithmetic expression that calculates the number of seconds in a 24-hour period.
3. Write a statement that causes the assembler to calculate the number of bytes in the following array, and assign the value to a symbolic constant named **ArraySize**:

    ```
    myArray WORD 20 DUP(?)
    ```

4. Show how to calculate the number of elements in the following array, and assign the value to a symbolic constant named **ArraySize**:

    ```
    myArray DWORD 30 DUP(?)
    ```

5. Use a TEXTEQU expression to redefine "PROC" as "PROCEDURE."
6. Use TEXTEQU to create a symbol named **Sample** for a string constant, and then use the symbol when defining a string variable named **MyString**.
7. Use TEXTEQU to assign the symbol **SetupESI** to the following line of code:

    ```
    mov esi,OFFSET myArray
    ```

3.6   Real-Address Mode Programming (Optional)

Programs designed for MS-DOS must be 16-bit applications running in real-address mode. Real-address mode applications use 16-bit segments and follow the segmented addressing scheme described in Section 2.3.1. If you're using an IA-32 processor, you can still use the 32-bit general-purpose registers for data.

3.6.1   Basic Changes

There are a few changes you must make to the 32-bit programs presented in this chapter to transform them into real-address mode programs:

• The INCLUDE directive references a different library:

```
INCLUDE Irvine16.inc
```

- Two additional instructions are inserted at the beginning of the startup procedure (main). They initialize the DS register to the starting location of the data segment, identified by the predefined MASM constant **@data**:

```
mov ax,@data
mov ds,ax
```

- See the book's Web site (www.asmirvine.com) for instructions on assembling 16-bit programs.
- Offsets (addresses) of data and code labels are 16 bits.

> You cannot move @data directly into DS and ES because the MOV instruction does not permit a constant to be moved directly to a segment register.

The AddSub2 Program

Here is a listing of the *AddSub2.asm* program, revised to run in real-address mode. New lines are marked by comments:

```
TITLE Add and Subtract, Version 2    (AddSub2.asm)

; This program adds and subtracts 32-bit integers
; and stores the sum in a variable.
; Target: real-address mode.

INCLUDE Irvine16.inc                 ; changed *
.data
val1     DWORD 10000h
val2     DWORD 40000h
val3     DWORD 20000h
finalVal DWORD ?

.code
main PROC
        mov ax,@data                 ; new *
        mov ds,ax                    ; new *

        mov eax,val1                 ; get first value
        add eax,val2                 ; add second value
        sub eax,val3                 ; subtract third value
        mov finalVal,eax             ; store the result
        call DumpRegs                ; display registers

        exit
main ENDP
END main
```

3.7   Chapter Summary

An integer expression is a mathematical expression involving integer constants, symbolic constants, and arithmetic operators. *Precedence* refers to the implied order of operations when an expression contains two or more operators.

A *character constant* is a single character enclosed in quotes. The assembler converts a character to a byte containing the character's binary ASCII code. A *string constant* is a sequence of characters enclosed in quotes, optionally ending with a null byte.

Assembly language has a set of *reserved words* with special meanings that may only be used in the correct context. An *identifier* is a programmer-chosen name identifying a variable, a symbolic constant, a procedure, or a code label. Identifiers cannot be reserved words.

A *directive* is a command embedded in the source code and interpreted by the assembler. An *instruction* is a source code statement that is executed by the processor at run time. An *instruction mnemonic* is a short keyword that identifies the operation carried out by an instruction. A *label* is an identifier that acts as a place marker for instructions or data.

Operands are values passed to instructions. An assembly language instruction can have between zero and three operands, each of which can be a register, memory operand, constant expression, or I/O port number.

Programs contain *logical segments* named code, data, and stack. The code segment contains executable instructions. The stack segment holds procedure parameters, local variables, and return addresses. The data segment holds variables.

A *source file* contains assembly language statements. A *listing file* contains a copy of the program's source code, suitable for printing, with line numbers, offset addresses, translated machine code, and a symbol table. A *map file* contains information about a program's segments. A source file is created with a text editor. An *assembler* is a program that reads the source file, producing both object and listing files. The *linker* is a program that reads one or more object files and produces an executable file. The latter is executed by the operating system loader.

MASM recognizes intrinsic data types, each of which describes a set of values that can be assigned to variables and expressions of the given type:

- BYTE and SBYTE define 8-bit variables.
- WORD and SWORD define 16-bit variables.
- DWORD and SDWORD define 32-bit variables.
- QWORD and TBYTE define 8-byte and 10-byte variables, respectively.
- REAL4, REAL8, and REAL10 define 4-byte, 8-byte, and 10-byte real number variables, respectively.

A data definition statement sets aside storage in memory for a variable, and may optionally assign it a name. If multiple initializers are used in the same data definition, its label refers only to the offset of the first initializer. To create a string data definition, enclose a sequence of characters in quotes. The DUP operator generates a repeated storage allocation, using a constant expression as a counter. The current location counter operator ($) is used in address-calculation expressions.

Intel processors store and retrieve data from memory using *little endian* order: The least significant byte of a variable is stored at its starting address.

A *symbolic constant* (or symbol definition) associates an identifier with an integer or text expression. Three directives create symbolic constants:

- The equal-sign directive (=) associates a symbol name with an integer expression.
- The EQU and TEXTEQU directives associate a symbolic name with an integer expression or some arbitrary text.

You can convert almost any program from 32-bit protected mode to 16-bit real-address mode. This book is supplied with two link libraries containing the same procedure names for both types of programs.

3.8   Programming Exercises

The following exercises can be done in protected mode or real-address mode.

1.   Subtracting Three Integers

Using the **AddSub** program from Section 3.2 as a reference, write a program that subtracts three integers using only 16-bit registers. Insert a **call DumpRegs** statement to display the register values.

2. Data Definitions

Write a program that contains a definition of each data type listed in Section 3.4. Initialize each variable to a value that is consistent with its data type.

3. Symbolic Integer Constants

Write a program that defines symbolic constants for all of the days of the week. Create an array variable that uses the symbols as initializers.

4. Symbolic Text Constants

Write a program that defines symbolic names for several string literals (characters between quotes). Use each symbolic name in a variable definition.

4

DATA TRANSFERS, ADDRESSING, AND ARITHMETIC

4.1 Data Transfer Instructions

4.1.1 Introduction

This chapter introduces a great many details, highlighting a fundamental difference between assembly language and high-level languages: In assembly language, one must be aware of data storage and machine-specific details. High-level language compilers such as C++ and Java perform strict type checking on variables and assignment statements. Compilers do this to help programmers avoid logic errors relating to mismatched data. Assemblers, on the other hand, provide enormous freedom when declaring and moving data. They perform little error checking, and supply a wide variety of operators and address expressions. What price must you pay for this freedom? You must master a significant number of details before writing meaningful programs.

If you take the time to thoroughly learn the material presented in this chapter, the rest of the reading in this book will be easier to understand. As the example programs become more complicated, you must rely on mastery of fundamental tools presented in this chapter.

4.1.2   Operand Types

Three types of instruction operands are presented in this chapter: *immediate*, *register*, and *memory*. Of these, only the third is slightly complicated. Table 4-1 lists a simple notation for operands freely adapted from the Intel IA-32 manuals. We will use it from this point on to describe the syntax of individual Intel instructions.

Table 4-1   Instruction Operand Notation.

Operand	Description
r8	8-bit general-purpose register: AH, AL, BH, BL, CH, CL, DH, DL
r16	16-bit general-purpose register: AX, BX, CX, DX, SI, DI, SP, BP
r32	32-bit general-purpose register: EAX, EBX, ECX, EDX, ESI, EDI, ESP, EBP
reg	Any general-purpose register
sreg	16-bit segment register: CS, DS, SS, ES, FS, GS
imm	8-, 16-, or 32-bit immediate value
imm8	8-bit immediate byte value
imm16	16-bit immediate word value
imm32	32-bit immediate doubleword value
r/m8	8-bit operand, which can be an 8-bit general register or memory byte
r/m16	16-bit operand, which can be a 16-bit general register or memory word
r/m32	32-bit operand, which can be a 32-bit general register or memory doubleword
mem	An 8-, 16-, or 32-bit memory operand

4.1.3   Direct Memory Operands

Section 3.4 explained that variable names are references to offsets within the data segment. For example, the following declaration indicates that a byte containing the number 10h has been allocated in the data segment:

```
.data
var1 BYTE 10h
```

Program code contains instructions that dereference (look up) memory operands using their addresses. Suppose **var1** were located at offset 10400h. An assembly language instruction moving it to the AL register would be

```
mov  AL,var1
```

MASM would assemble it into the following machine instruction:

```
A0 00010400
```

The first byte in the machine instruction is the op code. The remaining part is the 32-bit hexadecimal address of **var1**. Although it might be possible to write programs using only numeric addresses, symbolic names such as **var1** make it easier to reference memory.

Alternative Notation. Some programmers prefer to use the following notation with direct operands because the brackets imply a dereference operation:

```
mov  al,[var1]
```

MASM permits this notation, so you can use it in your own programs if you want. Because so many programs (including those from Microsoft) are printed without the brackets, we will only use them in this book when an arithmetic expression is involved:

```
mov  al,[var1 + 5]
```

(This is called a direct-offset operand, a subject discussed at length in Section 4.1.8.)

4.1.4   MOV Instruction

The MOV instruction copies data from a source operand to a destination operand. Known as a *data transfer* instruction, it is used in virtually every program. Its basic format shows that the first operand is the destination and the second operand is the source:

```
MOV destination,source
```

The destination operand's contents change, but the source operand is unchanged. The right to left movement of data is similar to the assignent statement in C++ or Java:

```
dest = source;
```

(In nearly all assembly language instructions, the left-hand operand is the destination and the right-hand operand is the source.)

MOV is very flexible in its use of operands, as long as the following rules are observed:

• Both operands must be the same size.
• Both operands cannot be memory operands.
• CS, EIP, and IP cannot be destination operands.
• An immediate value cannot be moved to a segment register.

Here is a list of the general variants of MOV, excluding segment registers:

```
MOV reg,reg
MOV mem,reg
MOV reg,mem
MOV mem,imm
MOV reg,imm
```

Segment registers should not be directly modified by programs running in protected mode. The following options are available when running in real mode, with the exception that CS cannot be a target operand:

```
MOV r/m16,sreg
MOV sreg,r/m16
```

Memory to Memory   A single MOV instruction cannot be used to move data directly from one memory location to another. Instead, you can move the source operand's value to a register before moving its value to a memory operand:

```
.data
var1 WORD ?
```

```
var2 WORD ?
.code
mov  ax,var1
mov  var2,ax
```

You must consider the minimum number of bytes required by an integer constant when copying it to a variable or register. For unsigned integer constants, refer to Table 1-4 in Chapter 1. For signed integer constants, refer to Table 1-7.

4.1.5   Zero/Sign Extension of Integers

Copying Smaller Values to Larger Ones

Although MOV cannot directly copy data from a smaller operand to a larger one, programmers can create workarounds. Suppose **count** (unsigned, 16-bits) must be moved to ECX (32 bits). We can set ECX to zero and move **count** to CX:

```
.data
count WORD 1
.code
mov ecx,0
mov cx,count
```

What happens if we try the same approach with a signed integer equal to −16?

```
.data
signedVal SWORD -16                ; FFF0h (-16)
.code
mov ecx,0
mov cx,signedVal                   ; ECX = 0000FFF0h (+65520)
```

The value in ECX (+65520) is completely different from −16. On the other hand, if we had filled ECX first with FFFFFFFFh and then copied **signedVal** to CX, the final value would have been correct:

```
mov ecx,0FFFFFFFFh
mov cx,signedVal                   ; ECX = FFFFFFF0h (-16)
```

This presents a problem when dealing with signed integers: we don't want to have to check their values to see whether they are positive or negative before deciding how to fill destination operands. Fortunately, the engineers at Intel noticed this problem when designing the Intel386 processor and introduced the MOVZX and MOVSX instructions to deal with both unsigned and signed integers.

MOVZX Instruction

The MOVZX instruction (*move with zero-extend*) copies the contents of a source operand into a destination operand and zero-extends the value to 16 or 32 bits. This instruction is only used with unsigned integers. There are three variants:

```
MOVZX   r32,r/m8
MOVZX   r32,r/m16
MOVZX   r16,r/m8
```

(Operand notation was explained in Table 4-1.) In each of the three variants, the first operand (a register) is the destination and the second is the source. The following instruction moves binary 10001111 to AX:

```
movzx ax,10001111b
```

Figure 4–1 shows how the source operand is zero-extended into the 16-bit destination.

FIGURE 4–1   Diagram of MOVZX ax, 8Fh.

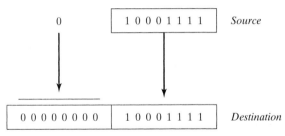

The following examples use registers for all operands, showing all the size variations:

```
mov     bx,0A69Bh
movzx   eax,bx                          ; EAX = 0000A69Bh
movzx   edx,bl                          ; EDX = 0000009Bh
movzx   cx,bl                           ; CX  = 009Bh
```

The following examples use memory operands for the source and produce the same results:

```
.data
byte1 BYTE 9Bh
word1 WORD 0A69Bh
.code
movzx   eax,word1                       ; EAX = 0000A69Bh
movzx   edx,byte1                       ; EDX = 0000009Bh
movzx   cx,byte1                        ; CX  = 009Bh
```

> If you want to run and test examples from this chapter in real-address mode, use INCLUDE with Irvine16.lib and insert the following lines at the beginning of the main procedure:
>
> ```
> mov ax,@data
> mov ds,ax
> ```

MOVSX Instruction

The MOVSX instruction (move with sign-extend) copies the contents of a source operand into a destination operand and sign-extends the value to 16 or 32 bits. This instruction is only used with signed integers. There are three variants:

```
MOVSX r32,r/m8
MOVSX r32,r/m16
MOVSX r16,r/m8
```

An operand is sign-extended by taking the smaller operand's highest bit and repeating (replicating) the bit throughout the extended bits in the destination operand. Suppose the 8-bit value 10001111b is moved to a 16-bit destination:

```
movsx ax,10001111b
```

The lowest 8 bits are copied as is (Figure 4–2). The highest bit of the source is copied into each of the upper 8 bit positions of the destination.

Here are a few more examples that use a variety of register sizes:

```
mov     bx,0A69Bh
movsx   eax,bx                          ; EAX = FFFFA69Bh
movsx   edx,bl                          ; EDX = FFFFFF9Bh
movsx   cx,bl                           ; CX  = FF9Bh
```

Figure 4–2   Diagram of MOVSX ax,10001111b.

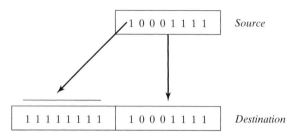

4.1.6   LAHF and SAHF Instructions

The LAHF (load status flags into AH) instruction copies the low byte of the EFLAGS register into AH. The following flags are copied: Sign, Zero, Auxiliary Carry, Parity, and Carry. Using this instruction, you can easily save a copy of the flags in a variable for safekeeping:

```
.data
saveflags BYTE ?
.code
lahf                              ; load flags into AH
mov   saveflags,ah                ; save them in a variable
```

The SAHF (store AH into status flags) instruction copies AH into the low byte of the EFLAGS register. For example, you can retrieve the values of flags saved earlier in a variable:

```
mov   ah,saveflags                ; load saved flags into AH
sahf                              ; copy into Flags register
```

4.1.7   XCHG Instruction

The XCHG (exchange data) instruction exchanges the contents of two operands. There are three variants:

```
XCHG reg,reg
XCHG reg,mem
XCHG mem,reg
```

The rules for operands in the XCHG instruction are the same as those for the MOV instruction (Section 4.1.4), except that XCHG does not accept immediate operands. In array sorting applications, XCHG provides a simple way to exchange two array elements. Here are a few examples using XCHG:

```
xchg   ax,bx                      ; exchange 16-bit regs
xchg   ah,al                      ; exchange 8-bit regs
xchg   var1,bx                    ; exchange 16-bit mem op with BX
xchg   eax,ebx                    ; exchange 32-bit regs
```

To exchange two memory operands, use a register as a temporary container and combine MOV with XCHG:

```
mov   ax,val1
xchg  ax,val2
mov   val1,ax
```

4.1.8   Direct-Offset Operands

You can add a displacement to the name of a variable, creating a direct-offset operand. This lets you access memory locations that may not have explicit labels. Let's begin with an array of bytes named **arrayB**:

```
arrayB  BYTE 10h,20h,30h,40h,50h
```

If we use MOV with **arrayB** as the source operand, we automatically move the first byte in the array:

```
mov  al,arrayB                       ; AL = 10h
```

We can access the second byte in the array by adding 1 to the offset of **arrayB**:

```
mov  al,[arrayB+1]                   ; AL = 20h
```

The third byte is accessed by adding 2:

```
mov  al,[arrayB+2]                   ; AL = 30h
```

An expression such as **arrayB + 1** produces what is called an *effective address* by adding a constant to the variable's offset. Surrounding an effective address with brackets indicates the expression is dereferenced to obtain the contents of memory at the address. The brackets are not required by MASM, so the following statements are equivalent:

```
mov  al,[arrayB+2]
mov  al,arrayB+1
```

Range Checking   MASM has no built-in range checking for effective addresses. If we execute the following statement, the assembler just retrieves a byte of memory outside the array. The result is a sneaky logic bug, so be extra careful when checking array references:

```
mov  al,[arrayB+20]                  ; AL = ??
```

Word and Doubleword Arrays   In an array of 16-bit words, the offset of each array element is 2 bytes beyond the previous one. That is why we add 2 to **ArrayW** in the next example to reach the second element:

```
.data
arrayW WORD 100h,200h,300h
.code
mov  ax,arrayW                       ; AX = 100h
mov  ax,[arrayW+2]                   ; AX = 200h
```

Similarly, the second element in a doubleword array is 4 bytes beyond the first one:

```
.data
arrayD DWORD 10000h,20000h
.code
mov  eax,arrayD                      ; EAX = 10000h
mov  eax,[arrayD+4]                  ; EAX = 20000h
```

4.1.9   Example Program (Moves)

The following program demonstrates most of the data transfer examples from Section 4.1:

```
TITLE Data Transfer Examples              (Moves.asm)

INCLUDE Irvine32.inc
.data
val1 WORD 1000h
val2 WORD 2000h
array BYTE 10h,20h,30h,40h,50h
array WORD 100h,200h,300h
array DWORD 10000h,20000h

.code
main PROC

;   MOVZX
        mov    bx,0A69Bh
```

```
            movzx  eax,bx                    ; EAX = 0000A69Bh
            movzx  edx,bl                    ; EDX = 0000009Bh
            movzx  cx,bl                     ; CX  = 009Bh

        ; MOVSX
            mov    bx,0A69Bh
            movsx  eax,bx                     ; EAX = FFFFA69Bh
            movsx  edx,bl                     ; EDX = FFFFFF9Bh
            mov    bl,7Bh
            movsx  cx,bl                      ; CX  = 007Bh

        ; Memory-to-memory exchange:
            mov    ax,val1                    ; AX = 1000h
            xchg   ax,val2                    ; AX=2000h, val2=1000h
            mov    val1,ax                    ; val1 = 2000h

        ; Direct-Offset Addressing (byte array):
            mov    al,arrayB                  ; AL = 10h
            mov    al,[arrayB+1]              ; AL = 20h
            mov    al,[arrayB+2]              ; AL = 30h

        ; Direct-Offset Addressing (word array):
            mov    ax,arrayW                  ; AX = 100h
            mov    ax,[arrayW+2]              ; AX = 200h

        ; Direct-Offset Addressing (doubleword array):
            mov    eax,arrayD                 ; EAX = 10000h
            mov    eax,[arrayD+4]             ; EAX = 20000h
            mov    eax,[arrayD+TYPE arrayD]   ; EAX = 20000h

            exit
    main ENDP
    END main
```

This program generates no screen output, but you can (and should) run it using a debugger. Please refer to tutorials on the book's Web site showing how to use the Microsoft Visual Studio debugger. Section 5.3 explains how to display integers using a function library supplied with this book.

4.1.10   Section Review

1. What are the three basic types of operands?

2. *(True/False):* The destination operand of a MOV instruction cannot be a segment register.

3. *(True/False):* In a MOV instruction, the second operand is known as the *destination* operand.

4. *(True/False):* The EIP register cannot be the destination operand of a MOV instruction.

5. In the operation notation used by Intel, what does *r/m32* indicate?

6. In the operation notation used by Intel, what does *imm16* indicate?

Use the following variable definitions for the remaining questions in this section:

```
    .data
    var1 SBYTE -4,-2,3,1
    var2 WORD 1000h,2000h,3000h,4000h
    var3 SWORD -16,-42
    var4 DWORD 1,2,3,4,5
```

7. For each of the following statements, state whether or not the instruction is valid:

    a. mov ax,var1
    b. mov ax,var2
    c. mov eax,var3

```
d. mov var2,var3
e. movzx ax,var2
f. movzx var2,al
g. mov ds,ax
h. mov ds,1000h
```

8. What will be the hexadecimal value of the destination operand after each of the following instructions execute in sequence?

```
mov    al,var1              ; a.
mov    ah,[var1+3]          ; b.
```

9. What will be the value of the destination operand after each of the following instructions execute in sequence?

```
mov    ax,var2             ; a.
mov    ax,[var2+4]         ; b.
mov    ax,var3             ; c.
mov    ax,[var3-2]         ; d.
```

10. What will be the value of the destination operand after each of the following instructions execute in sequence?

```
mov     edx,var4           ; a.
movzx   edx,var2           ; b.
mov     edx,[var4+4]       ; c.
movsx   edx,var1           ; d.
```

4.2   Addition and Subtraction

Arithmetic is a fairly big subject in assembly language, so we will approach it in steps. Here we focus on integer addition and subtraction. Chapter 7 introduces integer multiplication and division. Chapter 17 shows how to do floating-point arithmetic with a completely different instruction set. Let's begin with INC (increment), DEC (decrement), ADD, SUB, and NEG (negate). The question of how status flags (Carry, Sign, Zero, etc.) are affected by these instructions is important, and will be discussed in Section 4.2.6.

4.2.1   INC and DEC Instructions
The INC (increment) and DEC (decrement) instructions, respectively, add 1 and subtract 1 from a single operand. The syntax is

```
INC reg/mem
DEC reg/mem
```

Following are some examples:

```
.data
myWord WORD 1000h
.code
inc    myWord              ; 1001h
mov    bx,myWord
dec    bx                  ; 1000h
```

The Overflow, Sign, Zero, Auxiliary Carry, and Parity flags are changed according to the value of the destination operand. They do not affect the Carry flag (which is something of a surprise).

4.2.2   ADD Instruction
The ADD instruction adds a source operand to a destination operand of the same size. The syntax is

```
ADD dest,source
```

Source is unchanged by the operation, and the sum is stored in the destination operand. The set of possible operands is the same as for the MOV instruction (Section 4.1.4). Here is a short code example that adds two 32-bit integers:

```
.data
var1 DWORD 10000h
var2 DWORD 20000h
.code
mov  eax,var1          ; EAX = 10000h
add  eax,var2          ; EAX = 30000h
```

Flags   The Carry, Zero, Sign, Overflow, Auxiliary Carry, and Parity flags are changed according to the value of the destination operand.

4.2.3   SUB Instruction

The SUB instruction subtracts a source operand from a destination operand. The set of possible operands is the same as for the ADD and MOV instructions (see Section 4.1.4). The syntax is

```
SUB dest,source
```

Here is a short code example that subtracts two 32-bit integers:

```
.data
var1 DWORD 30000h
var2 DWORD 10000h
.code
mov  eax,var1          ; EAX = 30000h
sub  eax,var2          ; EAX = 20000h
```

A simple way of performing subtraction without having to create new digital circuts is to negate and then add. For example, $4 - 1$ can be interpreted as $4 + (-1)$. Two's-complement notation is used for negative numbers, so -1 is represented by 11111111:

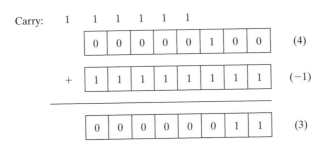

Flags   The Carry, Zero, Sign, Overflow, Auxiliary Carry, and Parity flags are changed according to the value of the destination operand.

4.2.4   NEG Instruction

The NEG (negate) instruction reverses the sign of a number by converting the number to its two's complement. The following operands are permitted:

```
NEG reg
NEG mem
```

(Recall that the two's complement of a number can be found by reversing all the bits in the destination operand and adding 1.)

Flags The Carry, Zero, Sign, Overflow, Auxiliary Carry, and Parity flags are changed according to the value of the destination operand.

4.2.5 Implementing Arithmetic Expressions

Armed with the ADD, SUB, and NEG instructions, you have the means to implement arithmetic expressions involving addition, subtraction, and negation in assembly language. In other words, one can simulate what a C++ compiler might do when reading an expression such as

```
Rval = -Xval + (Yval - Zval);
```

The following signed 32-bit variables will be used:

```
Rval SDWORD ?
Xval SDWORD 26
Yval SDWORD 30
Zval SDWORD 40
```

When translating an expression, evaluate each term separately and combine the terms at the end. First, we negate a copy of **Xval**:

```
; first term: -Xval
mov   eax,Xval
neg   eax                         ; EAX = -26
```

Then **Yval** is copied to a register and **Zval** is subtracted:

```
; second term: (Yval - Zval)
     mov   ebx,Yval
     sub   ebx,Zval               ; EBX = -10
```

Finally, the two terms (in EAX and EBX) are added:

```
; add the terms and store:
     add   eax,ebx
     mov   Rval,eax               ; -36
```

4.2.6 Flags Affected by Addition and Subtraction

When executing arithmetic instructions, we often want to know something about the result. Is it negative, positive, or zero? Is it too large or too small to fit into the destination operand? Answers to such questions can help us detect calculation errors that might otherwise cause erratic program behavior. We use the values of CPU status flags to check the outcome of arithmetic operations. We also use status flag values to activate conditional branching instructions, the basic tools of program logic. Here's a quick overview of the status flags. We will go into more detail later:

- The Carry flag indicates unsigned integer overflow. For example, if an instruction has an 8-bit destination operand but the instruction generates a result larger than 11111111 binary, the Carry flag is set.
- The Overflow flag indicates signed integer overflow. For example, if an instruction has a 16-bit destination operand but it generates a negative result smaller than $-32,768$ decimal, the Overflow flag is set.
- The Zero flag indicates that an operation produced zero. For example, if an operand is subtracted from another of equal value, the Zero flag is set.
- The Sign flag indicates that an operation produced a negative result. If the most significant bit of the destination operand is set, the Sign flag is set.
- The Parity flag counts the number of 1 bits in the least significant byte of the destination operand.

• The Auxiliary Carry flag is set when a 1 bit carries out of position 3 in the least significant byte of the destination operand.

To display CPU status flag values in programs, call **DumpRegs** from the book's link library.

Unsigned Operations: Zero, Carry, and Auxiliary Carry

The Zero flag is set when result of an arithmetic operation is zero. The following examples show the state of the destination register and Zero flag after executing the SUB, INC, and DEC instructions:

```
mov   ecx,1
sub   ecx,1  ; ECX = 0, ZF = 1
mov   eax,0FFFFFFFFh
inc   eax                          ; EAX = 0, ZF = 1
inc   eax                          ; EAX = 1, ZF = 0
dec   eax                          ; EAX = 0, ZF = 1
```

Addition and the Carry Flag   The Carry flag's operation is easiest to explain if we consider addition and subtraction separately. When adding two unsigned integers, the Carry flag is a copy of the carry out of the MSB (most significant bit) of the destination operand. Intuitively, we can say CF = 1 when the sum exceeds the storage size of its destination operand. In the next example, ADD sets the Carry flag because the sum (100h) is too large for AL:

```
mov   al,0FFh
add   al,1                         ; AL = 00, CF = 1
```

The following figure shows what happens at the bit level when 1 is added to 0FFh. The carry out of the highest bit position of AL is copied into the Carry flag:

On the other hand, if 1 is added to 00FFh in AX, the sum easily fits into 16 bits and the Carry flag is clear:

```
mov   ax,00FFh
add   ax,1                         ; AX = 0100h, CF = 0
```

But adding 1 to FFFFh in the AX register generates a Carry out of the high bit position of AX:

```
mov   ax,0FFFFh
add   ax,1                         ; AX = 0000, CF = 1
```

Subtraction and the Carry Flag   A subtract operation sets the Carry flag when a larger unsigned integer is subtracted from a smaller one. It's easiest to consider subtraction's effect on the Carry flag from a hardware point of view. Let's assume, for a moment, that the CPU can negate a positive unsigned integer by forming its two's complement:

1. The source operand is negated and added to the destination.
2. The carry out of MSB is inverted and copied to the Carry flag.

Let's subtract 2 from 1, as 8-bit operands. After negating 2, we add the integers:

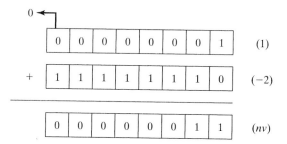

The sum (255) is not valid. The carry out of bit 7 is inverted and placed in the Carry flag, so CF = 1. Here is the corresponding assembly code:

```
mov   al,1
sub   al,2                        ; AL = FFh, CF = 1
```

> The INC and DEC instructions do not affect the Carry flag. Applying NEG to a nonzero operand always sets the Carry flag.

Auxiliary Carry   The Auxiliary Carry (AC) flag indicates a carry or borrow out of bit 3 in the destination operand. It is primarily used in binary coded decimal (BCD) arithmetic (Section 7.6), but can be used in other contexts. Suppose we add 1 to 0Fh. The sum (10h) contains a 1 in bit position 4 that was carried out of bit position 3:

```
mov   al,0Fh
add   al,1                        ; AC = 1
```

Here is the arithmetic:

```
    0 0 0 0 1 1 1 1
  + 0 0 0 0 0 0 0 1
  -------------------
    0 0 0 1 0 0 0 0
```

Parity   The Parity (PF) flag is set when the least significant byte of the destination has an even number of 1 bits. The following ADD and SUB instructions alter the parity of AL:

```
mov   al,10001100b
add   al,00000010b                ; AL = 10001110, PF = 1
sub   al,10000000b                ; AL = 00001110, PF = 0
```

After the ADD, AL contains binary 10001110 (four 0 bits and four 1 bits), and PF = 1. After the SUB, AL contains an odd number of 1 bits, so PF = 0.

Signed Operations: Sign and Overflow Flags

Sign Flag   The Sign flag is set when the result of a signed arithmetic operation is negative. The next example subtracts a larger integer (5) from a smaller one (4):

```
mov   eax,4
sub   eax,5                        ; EAX = -1, SF = 1
```

From a mechanical point of view, the Sign flag is a copy of the destination operand's high bit. The next example shows the hexadecimal values of BL when a negative result is generated:

```
mov   bl,1                        ; BL = 01h
sub   bl,2                        ; BL = FFh (-1)
```

Overflow Flag   The Overflow flag is set when the result of a signed arithmetic operation overflows or underflows the destination operand. For example, from Chapter 1 we know that the largest possible integer signed byte value is +127; adding 1 to it causes overflow:

```
mov   al,+127
add   al,1                        ; OF = 1
```

Similarly, the smallest possible negative integer byte value is −128. Subtracting 1 from it causes underflow. The destination operand value does not hold a valid arithmetic result, and the Overflow flag is set:

```
mov   al,-128
sub   al,1                        ; OF = 1
```

The Addition Test   There is a very easy way to tell whether signed overflow has occurred when adding two operands. Overflow occurs when

- Two positive operands generate a negative sum
- Two negative operands generate a positive sum

Overflow never occurs when the signs of two addition operands are different.

How the Hardware Detects Overflow   The CPU uses an interesting mechanism to determine the state of the Overflow flag after an addition or subtraction operation. The bit carried out of the MSB (most significant bit) of an operand is exclusive-ORed with the the bit carried into into the MSB. The resulting value is placed in the Overflow flag. For example, adding the 8-bit binary integers 10000000 and 11111110 produces no carry into bit 7 (MSB), but there is a carry from bit 7 into the Carry flag:

In other words, 1 XOR 0 produces OF = 1.

NEG Instruction   The NEG instruction produces an invalid result if the destination operand cannot be stored correctly. For example, if we move −128 to AL and try to negate it, the correct value (+128) will not fit into AL. The Overflow flag is set, indicating that AL contains an invalid value:

```
mov   al,-128             ; AL = 10000000b
neg   al                  ; AL = 10000000b, OF = 1
```

On the other hand, if +127 is negated, the result is valid and the Overflow flag is clear:

```
mov   al,+127             ; AL = 01111111b
neg   al                  ; AL = 10000001b, OF = 0
```

> How does the CPU know whether an arithmetic operation is signed or unsigned? We can only give what seems a dumb answer: It doesn't! The CPU sets all status flags after an arithmetic operation using a set of boolean rules, regardless of which flags are relevant. You (the programmer) decide which flags to interpret and which to ignore, based on your knowledge of the type of operation performed.

4.2.7 Example Program (AddSub3)

The following program implements various arithmetic expressions using the ADD, SUB, INC, DEC, and NEG instructions, and shows how certain status flags are affected:

```
TITLE Addition and Subtraction        (AddSub3.asm)
```

```
        INCLUDE Irvine32.inc
        .data
        Rval    SDWORD ?
        Xval    SDWORD 26
        Yval    SDWORD 30
        Zval    SDWORD 40

        .code
        main PROC
            ; INC and DEC
            mov     ax,1000h
            inc     ax                  ; 1001h
            dec     ax                  ; 1000h

            ; Expression: Rval = -Xval + (Yval - Zval)
            mov     eax,Xval
            neg     eax                 ; -26
            mov     ebx,Yval
            sub     ebx,Zval            ; -10
            add     eax,ebx
            mov     Rval,eax            ; -36

            ; Zero flag example:
            mov     cx,1
            sub     cx,1                ; ZF = 1
            mov     ax,0FFFFh
            inc     ax                  ; ZF = 1

            ; Sign flag example:
            mov     cx,0
            sub     cx,1                ; SF = 1
            mov     ax,7FFFh
            add     ax,2                ; SF = 1

            ; Carry flag example:
            mov     al,0FFh
            add     al,1                ; CF = 1,   AL = 00

            ; Overflow flag example:
            mov     al,+127
            add     al,1                ; OF = 1
            mov     al,-128
            sub     al,1                ; OF = 1

            exit
        main ENDP
        END main
```

4.2.8 Section Review

Use the following data for the next several questions:

```
        .data
        val1 BYTE   10h
        val2 WORD   8000h
        val3 DWORD  0FFFFh
        val4 WORD   7FFFh
```

1. Write an instruction that increments **val2**.

2. Write an instruction that subtracts **val3** from EAX.

3. Write instructions that subtract **val4** from **val2**.

4. If **val2** is incremented by 1 using the ADD instruction, what will be the values of the Carry and Sign flags?

5. If **val4** is incremented by 1 using the ADD instruction, what will be the values of the Overflow and Sign flags?

6. Where indicated, write down the values of the Carry, Sign, Zero, and Overflow flags after each instruction has executed:

```
mov   ax,7FF0h
add   al,10h      ; a. CF =      SF =      ZF =      OF =
add   ah,1        ; b. CF =      SF =      ZF =      OF =
add   ax,2        ; c. CF =      SF =      ZF =      OF =
```

7. Implement the following expression in assembly language: AX = (−val2 + BX) − val4.

8. *(Yes/No):* Is it possible to set the Overflow flag if you add a positive integer to a negative integer?

9. *(Yes/No):* Will the Overflow flag be set if you add a negative integer to a negative integer and produce a positive result?

10. *(Yes/No):* Is it possible for the NEG instruction to set the Overflow flag?

11. *(Yes/No):* Is it possible for both the Sign and Zero flags to be set at the same time?

12. Write a sequence of two instructions that set both the Carry and Overflow flags at the same time.

13. Write a sequence of instructions showing how the Zero flag could be used to indicate unsigned overflow after executing INC and DEC instructions.

14. In our discusstion of the Carry flag we subtracted unsigned 2 from 1 by negating the 2 and adding it to 1. The Carry flag was the inversion of the carry out of the MSB of the sum. Demonstrate this process by subtracting 3 from 4 and show how the Carry flag value is produced.

4.3   Data-Related Operators and Directives

Operators and directives are not executable instructions; instead, they are interpreted by the assembler. You can use a number of MASM directives to get information about the addresses and size characteristics of data:

• The OFFSET operator returns the distance of a variable from the beginning of its enclosing segment.
• The PTR operator lets you override a variable's default size.
• The TYPE operator returns the size (in bytes) of an operand or of each element in an array.
• The LENGTHOF operator returns the number of elements in an array.
• The SIZEOF operator returns the number of bytes used by an array initializer.

In addition, the LABEL directive provides a way to redefine the same variable with different size attributes. The operators and directives in this chapter represent only a small subset of the operators supported by MASM. You may want to view the complete list in Appendix D.

MASM continues to support the legacy directives LENGTH (rather than LENGTHOF) and SIZE (rather than SIZEOF).

4.3.1   OFFSET Operator

The OFFSET operator returns the offset of a data label. The offset represents the distance, in bytes, of the label from the beginning of the data segment. To illustrate, the following figure shows a variable named **myByte** inside the data segment:

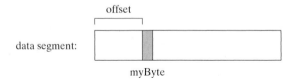

In protected mode, offsets are 32 bits. In real-address mode, offsets are 16 bits.

OFFSET Example

In the next example, we declare three different types of variables:

```
.data
bVal  BYTE  ?
wVal  WORD  ?
dVal  DWORD ?
dVal2 DWORD ?
```

If **bVal** were located at offset 00404000 (hexadecimal), the OFFSET operator would return the following values:

```
mov  esi,OFFSET bVal          ; ESI = 00404000
mov  esi,OFFSET wVal          ; ESI = 00404001
mov  esi,OFFSET dVal          ; ESI = 00404003
mov  esi,OFFSET dVal2         ; ESI = 00404007
```

OFFSET can also be applied to a direct-offset operand. Suppose **myArray** contains five 16-bit words. The following MOV instruction obtains the offset of **myArray**, adds 4, and moves the sum to ESI:

```
.data
myArray WORD 1,2,3,4,5
.code
mov  esi,OFFSET myArray + 4
```

4.3.2   ALIGN Directive

The ALIGN directive aligns a variable on a byte, word, doubleword, or paragraph boundary. The syntax is

ALIGN *bound*

Bound can be 1, 2, 4, or 16. A value of 1 aligns the next variable on a 1-byte boundary (the default). If bound is 2, the next variable is aligned on an even-numbered address. If bound is 4, the next address is a multiple of 4. If bound is 16, the next address is a multiple of 16, a paragraph boundary. The assembler can insert one or more empty bytes before the variable to fix the alignment. Why bother aligning data? Because the CPU can process data stored at even-numbered addresses more quickly than those at odd-numbered addresses.

In the following revision of an example from Section 4.3.1, **bVal** is arbitrarily located at offset 00404000. Inserting the ALIGN 2 directive before **wVal** causes it to be assigned an even-numbered offset:

```
bVal  BYTE  ?                 ; 00404000
ALIGN 2
wVal  WORD  ?                 ; 00404002
bVal2 BYTE  ?                 ; 00404004
ALIGN 4
dVal  DWORD ?                 ; 00404008
dVal2 DWORD ?                 ; 0040400C
```

Note that **dVal** would have been at offset 00404005, but the ALIGN 4 directive bumped it up to offset 00404008.

4.3.3   PTR Operator

You can use the PTR operator to override the declared size of an operand. This is only necessary when you're trying to access the variable using a size attribute that's different from the one used to declare the variable.

Suppose, for example, that you would like to move the lower 16 bits of a doubleword variable named **myDouble** into AX. The assembler will not permit the following move because the operand sizes do not match:

```
.data
myDouble  DWORD  12345678h
.code
mov  ax,myDouble                        ; error
```

But the WORD PTR operator makes it possible to move the low-order word (5678h) to AX:

```
mov  ax,WORD PTR myDouble
```

Why wasn't 1234h moved into AX? Intel uses the *little endian* storage format (Section 3.4.9), in which the low-order byte is stored at the variable's starting address. In the following figure, the memory layout of **myDouble** is shown three ways: first as a doubleword, then as two words (5678h, 1234h), and finally as four bytes (78h, 56h, 34h, 12h):

doubleword	word	byte	offset	
12345678	5678	78	0000	myDouble
		56	0001	myDouble + 1
	1234	34	0002	myDouble + 2
		12	0003	myDouble + 3

The CPU can access memory in any of these three ways, independent of the way a variable was defined. For example, if **myDouble** begins at offset 0000, the 16-bit value stored at that address is 5678h. We could also retrieve 1234h, the word at location **myDouble+2,** using the following statement:

```
mov  ax,WORD PTR [myDouble+2]            ; 1234h
```

Similarly, we could use the BYTE PTR operator to move a single byte from **myDouble** to BL:

```
mov  bl,BYTE PTR myDouble                ; 78h
```

Note that PTR must be used in combination with one of the standard assembler data types, BYTE, SBYTE, WORD, SWORD, DWORD, SDWORD, FWORD, QWORD, or TBYTE.

Moving Smaller Values into Larger Destinations We might want to move two smaller values from memory to a larger destination operand. In the next example, the first word is copied to the lower half of EAX and the second word is copied to the upper half. The DWORD PTR operator makes this possible:

```
.data
wordList WORD 5678h,1234h
.code
mov  eax,DWORD PTR wordList              ; EAX = 12345678h
```

4.3.4 TYPE Operator

The TYPE operator returns the size, in bytes, of a single element of a variable. For example, the TYPE of a byte equals 1, the TYPE of a word equals 2, the TYPE of a doubleword is 4, and the TYPE of a quadword is 8. Here are examples of each:

```
.data
var1 BYTE  ?
var2 WORD  ?
var3 DWORD ?
var4 QWORD ?
```

The following table shows the value of each TYPE expression:

Expression	Value
TYPE var1	1
TYPE var2	2
TYPE var3	4
TYPE var4	8

4.3.5   LENGTHOF Operator

The LENGTHOF operator counts the number of elements in an array, defined by the values appearing on the same line as its label. We will use the following data as an example:

```
.data
byte1    BYTE   10,20,30
array1   WORD   30 DUP(?),0,0
array2   WORD   5 DUP(3 DUP(?))
array3   DWORD  1,2,3,4
digitStr BYTE   "12345678",0
```

When nested DUP operators are used in an array definition, LENGTHOF returns the product of the two counters. The following table lists the values returned by each LENGTHOF expression:

Expression	Value
LENGTHOF byte1	3
LENGTHOF array1	30 + 2
LENGTHOF array2	5 * 3
LENGTHOF array3	4
LENGTHOF digitStr	9

If you declare an array that spans multiple program lines, LENGTHOF only regards the data from the first line as part of the array. In the following example, LENGTHOF myArray returns the value 5:

```
myArray BYTE 10,20,30,40,50
        BYTE 60,70,80,90,100
```

Alternatively, you can end the first line with a comma and continue the list of initializers onto the next line. In the following example, LENGTHOF myArray returns the value 10:

```
myArray BYTE 10,20,30,40,50,
        60,70,80,90,100
```

4.3.6   SIZEOF Operator

The SIZEOF operator returns a value that is equivalent to multiplying LENGTHOF by TYPE. For example, **intArray** has TYPE = 2 and LENGTHOF = 32. Therefore, SIZEOF **intArray** equals 64:

```
.data
intArray WORD 32 DUP(0)
.code
mov  eax,SIZEOF intArray          ; EAX = 64
```

4.3.7   LABEL Directive

The LABEL directive lets you insert a label and give it a size attribute without allocating any storage. All standard size attributes can be used with LABEL, such as BYTE, WORD, DWORD, QWORD or

TBYTE. A common use of LABEL is to provide an alternative name and size attribute for the variable declared next in the data segment. In the following example, we declare a label just before **val32** named **val16** and give it a WORD attribute:

```
.data
val16 LABEL WORD
val32 DWORD 12345678h
.code
mov   ax,val16            ; AX = 5678h
mov   dx,[val16+2]        ; DX = 1234h
```

val16 is an alias for the same storage location named **val32**. The LABEL directive itself allocates no storage.

Sometimes we need to construct a larger integer from two smaller integers. In the next example, a 32-bit value is loaded into EAX from two 16-bit variables:

```
.data
LongValue LABEL DWORD
val1   WORD   5678h
val2   WORD   1234h
.code
mov eax,LongValue         ; EAX = 12345678h
```

4.3.8 Section Review

1. *(True/False):* In 32-bit protected mode, the OFFSET operator returns a 16-bit value.

2. *(True/False):* The PTR operator returns the 32-bit address of a variable.

3. *(True/False):* The TYPE operator returns a value of 4 for doubleword operands.

4. *(True/False):* The LENGTHOF operator returns the number of bytes in an operand.

5. *(True/False):* The SIZEOF operator returns the number of bytes in an operand.

Use the following data definitions for the next seven exercises:

```
.data
myBytes BYTE 10h,20h,30h,40h
myWords WORD 3 DUP(?),2000h
myString BYTE "ABCDE"
```

6. Insert a directive in the given data that aligns **myBytes** to an even-numbered address.

7. What will be the value of EAX after each of the following instructions execute?

```
mov   eax,TYPE myBytes        ; a.
mov   eax,LENGTHOF myBytes     ; b.
mov   eax,SIZEOF myBytes       ; c.
mov   eax,TYPE myWords         ; d.
mov   eax,LENGTHOF myWords     ; e.
mov   eax,SIZEOF myWords       ; f.
mov   eax,SIZEOF myString      ; g.
```

8. Write a single instruction that moves the first two bytes in **myBytes** to the DX register. The resulting value will be 2010h.

9. Write an instruction that moves the second byte in **myWords** to the AL register.

10. Write an instruction that moves all four bytes in **myBytes** to the EAX register.

11. Insert a LABEL directive in the given data that permits **myWords** to be moved directly to a 32-bit register.

12. Insert a LABEL directive in the given data that permits **myBytes** to be moved directly to a 16-bit register.

4.4   Indirect Addressing

Direct addressing is impractical for array processing. We would rarely provide a unique label for each array element. We would not want to use constant offsets to address more than a few array elements. The only practical way to handle an array is to use a register as a pointer (called *indirect addressing*) and manipulate the register's value. When an operand uses indirecting addressing, it is called an *indirect operand*.

4.4.1   Indirect Operands

Protected Mode   An indirect operand can be any 32-bit general-purpose register (EAX, EBX, ECX, EDX, ESI, EDI, EBP, and ESP) surrounded by brackets. The register is assumed to contain the offset of some data. In the next example, ESI contains the offset of **val1**. The MOV instruction uses the indirect operand as the source, the offset in ESI is dereferenced, and a byte is moved to AL:

```
.data
val1 BYTE 10h
.code
mov  esi,OFFSET val1
mov  al,[esi]                    ; AL = 10h
```

If the destination operand uses indirect addressing, a new value is placed in memory at the location pointed to by the register:

```
mov  [esi],bl
```

Real-Address Mode   In real-address mode, a 16-bit register holds the offset of a variable. If the register is used as an indirect operand, it may only be SI, DI, BX, or BP. We usually avoid BP because it addresses the stack rather than the data segment. In the next example, SI references **val1**:

```
.data
val1 BYTE 10h
.code
main PROC
     startup
     mov  si,OFFSET val1
     mov  al,[si]                ; AL = 10h
```

General Protection Fault   In protected mode, if the effective address points to an area outside your program's data segment, the CPU executes a *general protection (GP) fault*. This happens even when an instruction does not modify memory. For example, if ESI were uninitialized, the following instruction would probably generate a general protection fault:

```
mov  ax,[esi]
```

Always initialize registers before using them as indirect operands. The same applies to high-level language programming with subscripts and pointers. General protection faults do not occur in real-address mode, which makes uninitialized indirect operands difficult to detect.

Using PTR with Indirect Operands   The size of an operand may not be clear from the context of an instruction. The following instruction causes the assembler to generate an "operand must have size" error message:

```
inc [esi]                       ; error
```

The assembler does not know whether ESI points to a byte, word, doubleword, or some other size. The PTR operator makes the operand size clear:

```
inc BYTE PTR [esi]
```

4.4.2 Arrays

Indirect operands are particularly useful when dealing with arrays because an indirect operand's value can be modified at runtime. Similar to array subscript, indirect operands can point to different array elements. In the next example, **arrayB** contains 3 bytes. We can increment ESI and make it point to each byte, in order:

```
.data
arrayB  BYTE 10h,20h,30h
.code
mov  esi,OFFSET arrayB
mov  al,[esi]                    ; AL = 10h
inc  esi
mov  al,[esi]                    ; AL = 20h
inc  esi
mov  al,[esi]                    ; AL = 30h
```

If we use an array of 16-bit integers, we add 2 to ESI to address each subsequent array element:

```
.data
arrayW  WORD 1000h,2000h,3000h
.code
mov  esi,OFFSET arrayW
mov  ax,[esi]                    ; AX = 1000h
add  esi,2
mov  ax,[esi]                    ; AX = 2000h
add  esi,2
mov  ax,[esi]                    ; AX = 3000h
```

Suppose **arrayW** is located at offset 10200h. The following illustration shows ESI in relation to the array data:

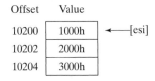

Offset	Value
10200	1000h ◄——[esi]
10202	2000h
10204	3000h

Example: Adding 32-Bit Integers   The following program excerpt adds three doublewords. A displacement of 4 must be added for each subsequent array value because doublewords are 4 bytes long:

```
.data
arrayD DWORD 10000h,20000h,30000h
.code
mov  esi,OFFSET arrayD
mov  eax,[esi]; first number
add  esi,4
add  eax,[esi]; second number
add  esi,4
add  eax,[esi]; third number
```

If **arrayD** were located at offset 10200h, the following illustration would show ESI in relation to the array data:

Offset	Value
10200	10000h ◄— [esi]
10204	20000h ◄— [esi] + 4
10208	30000h ◄— [esi] + 8

4.4.3   Indexed Operands

An *indexed operand* adds a constant to a register to generate an effective address. Any of the 32-bit general-purpose registers may be used as index registers. There are different notational forms permitted by MASM (the brackets are part of the notation):

```
constant[reg]
[constant + reg]
```

The first notational form combines the name of a variable with a register. The variable name is a constant that represents the variable's offset. Here are examples that show both notational forms:

arrayB[esi]	[arrayB + esi]
arrayD[ebx]	[arrayD + ebx]

Indexed operands are ideally suited to array processing. The index register should be initialized to zero before accessing the first array element:

```
.data
arrayB BYTE 10h,20h,30h
.code
mov  esi,0
mov  al,[arrayB + esi]          ; AL = 10h
```

The last stateme nt adds ESI to the offset of **arrayB**. The address generated by the expression **[arrayB + ESI]** is dereferenced and the byte in memory is copied to AL.

Adding Displacements   The second type of indexed addressing combines a register with a constant offset. The index register holds the base address of an array or structure, and the constant identifies offsets of various array elements. The following example shows how to do this with an array of 16-bit words:

```
.data
arrayW  WORD 1000h,2000h,3000h
.code
mov  esi,OFFSET arrayW
mov  ax,[esi]                    ; AX = 1000h
mov  ax,[esi+2]                  ; AX = 2000h
mov  ax,[esi+4]                  ; AX = 3000h
```

Using 16-Bit Registers   It is usual to use 16-bit registers as indexed operands in real-address mode. In that case, you are limited to using SI, DI, BX, or BP:

```
mov  al,arrayB[si]
mov  ax,arrayW[di]
mov  eax,arrayD[bx]
```

As is the case with indirect operands, avoid using BP except when addressing data on the stack.

Scale Factors in Indexed Operands

Indexed operands must take into account the size of each array element when calculating offsets. Using an array of doublewords, for example, we multiply the subscript (3) by 4 (the size of a doubleword) to generate the offset of the array element containing 400h:

```
.data
arrayD  DWORD 100h, 200h, 300h, 400h
.code
mov  esi,3 * TYPE arrayD         ; offset of arrayD[3]
mov  eax,arrayD[esi]             ; EAX = 400h
```

Intel designers wanted to make a common operation easier for compiler writers, so they provided a way for offsets to be calculated, using a *scale factor*. The scale factor is the size of the array component (word = 2, doubleword = 4, or quadword = 8). Let's revise our previous example by setting ESI to the array subscript (3) and multiplying ESI by the scale factor (4) for doublewords:

```
.data
arrayD  DWORD 1,2,3,4
.code
mov  esi,3                        ; subscript
mov  eax,arrayD[esi*4]            ; EAX = 400h
```

The TYPE operator can make the indexing more flexible should arrayD be redefined as another type in the future:

```
mov  esi,3                        ; subscript
mov  eax,arrayD[esi*TYPE arrayD]  ; EAX = 400h
```

4.4.4 Pointers

A variable containing the address of another variable is called a *pointer*. Pointers are a great tool for manipulating arrays and data structures, and they make dynamic memory allocation possible. Intel-based programs use two basic types of pointers, NEAR and FAR. Their sizes are affected by the processor's current mode (16-bit real or 32-bit protected), as shown in Table 4-2:

Table 4-2   Pointer Types in 16- and 32-Bit Modes.

	16-Bit Mode	**32-Bit Mode**
NEAR pointer	16-bit offset from the beginning of the data segment	32-bit offset from the beginning of the data segment
FAR pointer	32-bit segment-offset address	48-bit segment selector-offset address

The protected-mode programs in this book use near pointers, so they are stored in doubleword variables. Here are two examples: **ptrB** contains the offset of **arrayB**, and **ptrW** contains the offset of **arrayW**:

```
arrayB BYTE   10h,20h,30h,40h
arrayW WORD   1000h,2000h,3000h
ptrB   DWORD  arrayB
ptrW   DWORD  arrayW
```

Optionally, you can use the OFFSET operator to make the relationship clearer:

```
ptrB   DWORD OFFSET arrayB
ptrW   DWORD OFFSET arrayW
```

> High-level languages purposely hide physical details about pointers because their implementations vary among different machine architectures. In assembly language, because we deal with a single implementation, we examine and use pointers at the physical level. This approach helps to remove some of the mystery surrounding pointers.

Using the TYPEDEF Operator

The TYPEDEF operator lets you create a user-defined type that has all the status of a built-in type when defining variables. TYPEDEF is ideal for creating pointer variables. For example, the following declaration creates a new data type PBYTE that is a pointer to bytes:

```
PBYTE TYPEDEF PTR BYTE
```

This declaration would usually be placed near the beginning of a program, before the data segment. Then, variables could be defined using PBYTE:

```
.data
arrayB BYTE 10h,20h,30h,40h
ptr1    PBYTE ?                          ; uninitialized
ptr2    PBYTE arrayB                     ; points to an array
```

Example Program: Pointers   The following program (*pointers.asm*) uses TYPEDEF to create three pointer types (PBYTE, PWORD, PDWORD). It creates several pointers, assigns several array offsets, and dereferences the pointers:

```
TITLE Pointers                          (Pointers.asm)

INCLUDE Irvine32.inc

; Create user-defined types.
PBYTE   TYPEDEF PTR BYTE                 ; pointer to bytes
PWORD   TYPEDEF PTR WORD                 ; pointer to words
PDWORD  TYPEDEF PTR DWORD                ; pointer to doublewords

.data
arrayB BYTE  10h,20h,30h
arrayW WORD  1,2,3
arrayD DWORD 4,5,6

; Create some pointer variables.
ptr1 PBYTE  arrayB
ptr2 PWORD  arrayW
ptr3 PDWORD arrayD

.code
main PROC
; Use the pointers to access data.
     mov   esi,ptr1
     mov   al,[esi]                      ; 10h
     mov   esi,ptr2
     mov   ax,[esi]                      ; 1
     mov   esi,ptr3
     mov   eax,[esi]                     ; 4
     exit
main ENDP
END main
```

4.4.5   Section Review

1. *(True/False):* Any 16-bit general-purpose register can be used as an indirect operand.
2. *(True/False):* Any 32-bit general-purpose register can be used as an indirect operand.
3. *(True/False):* The BX register is usually reserved for addressing the stack.
4. *(True/False):* A general-protection fault occurs in real-address mode when an array subscript is out of range.
5. *(True/False):* The following instruction is invalid: inc [esi]
6. *(True/False):* The following is an indexed operand: array[esi]

Use the following data definitions for the remaining questions in this section:

```
myBytes   BYTE 10h,20h,30h,40h
myWords   WORD 8Ah,3Bh,72h,44h,66h
myDoubles DWORD 1,2,3,4,5
myPointer DWORD myDoubles
```

7.   Fill in the requested register values on the right side of the following instruction sequence:

```
mov   esi,OFFSET myBytes
mov   al,[esi]                          ; a. AL =
mov   al,[esi+3]                        ; b. AL =
mov   esi,OFFSET myWords + 2
mov   ax,[esi]                          ; c. AX =
mov   edi,8
mov   edx,[myDoubles + edi]             ; d. EDX =
mov   edx,myDoubles[edi]                ; e. EDX =
mov   ebx,myPointer
mov   eax,[ebx + 4]                     ; f. EAX =
```

8.   Fill in the requested register values on the right side of the following instruction sequence:

```
mov   esi,OFFSET myBytes
mov   ax,WORD PTR [esi]                 ; a. AX =
mov   eax,DWORD PTR myWords             ; b. EAX =
mov   esi,myPointer
mov   ax,WORD PTR [esi+2]               ; c. AX =
mov   ax,WORD PTR [esi+6]               ; d. AX =
mov   ax,WORD PTR [esi-4]               ; e. AX =
```

4.5   JMP and LOOP Instructions

By default, the CPU loads and executes programs sequentially. But the current instruction might be *conditional*, meaning that it transfers control to a new location in the program based on the values of CPU status flags (Zero, Sign, Carry, etc.) Assembly language programs use conditional instructions to implement high-level statements such as IF statements and loops. Each of the conditional statements involves a possible transfer of control (jump) to a different memory address. A *transfer of control*, or *branch*, is a way of altering the order in which statements are executed. There are two basic types of transfers:

  • **Unconditional Transfer:** The program transfers (branches) to a new location in all cases; a new address is loaded into the instruction pointer, causing execution to continue at the new address. The JMP instruction is a good example.
  • **Conditional Transfer:** The program branches if a certain condition is true. A wide variety of conditional transfer instructions can be combined to create conditional logic structures. The CPU interprets true/false conditions based on the contents of the ECX and Flags registers.

4.5.1   JMP Instruction

The JMP instruction causes an unconditional transfer to a destination, identified by a code label that is translated by the assembler into an offset. The syntax is

```
JMP destination
```

When the CPU executes an unconditional transfer, the offset of *destination* (from the start of the code segment) is moved into the instruction pointer, causing execution to continue at the new location. Under normal circumstances, you can only jump to a label inside the current procedure.

Creating a Loop   The JMP instruction provides an easy way to create a loop by jumping to a label at the top of the loop:

```
top:
    .

    .
    jmp top                         ; repeat the endless loop
```

JMP is unconditional, so the loop will continue endlessly unless another way is found to exit the loop.

4.5.2 LOOP Instruction

The LOOP instruction repeats a block of statements a specific number of times. ECX is automatically used as a counter and is decremented each time the loop repeats. Its syntax is

```
LOOP destination
```

The execution of the LOOP instruction involves two steps: First, it subtracts 1 from ECX. Next, it compares ECX to zero. If ECX is not equal to zero, a jump is taken to the label identified by *destination*. Otherwise, if ECX equals zero, no jump takes place, and control passes to the instruction following the loop.

> In real-address mode, CX is the default loop counter for the LOOP instruction. On the other hand, the LOOPD instruction uses ECX as the loop counter, and the LOOPW instruction uses CX as the loop counter.

In the following example, we add 1 to AX each time the loop repeats. When the loop ends, AX = 5 and ECX = 0:

```
        mov    ax,0
        mov    ecx,5
    L1:
        inc    ax
        loop L1
```

A common programming error is to inadvertently initialize ECX to zero before beginning a loop. If this happens, the LOOP instruction decrements ECX to FFFFFFFFh, and the loop repeats 4,294,967,296 times! If CX is the loop counter (in real-address mode), it repeats 65,536 times.

The loop destination must be within −128 to +127 bytes of the current location counter. Machine instructions have an average size of about 3 bytes, so a loop might contain, on average, a maximum of 42 instructions. Following is an example of an error message generated by MASM because the target label of a LOOP instruction was too far away:

```
error A2075: jump destination too far : by 14 byte(s)
```

If you modify ECX inside the loop, the LOOP instruction may not work properly. In the following example, ECX is incremented within the loop. It never reaches zero, and the loop never stops:

```
    top:
        .
        .
        inc    ecx
        loop top
```

If you run out of registers and need ECX for another purpose, save it in a variable at the beginning of the loop and restore it just before the loop instruction:

```
    .data
    count DWORD ?
    .code
        mov    ecx,100            ; set loop count
    top:
        mov    count,ecx          ; save the count
        .
        mov    ecx,20             ; modify ECX
        .
        mov    ecx,count          ; restore loop count
        loop   top
```

Nested Loops   When creating a loop inside another loop, special consideration must be given to the outer loop counter in ECX. You can save it in a variable:

```
.data
count DWORD ?
.code
    mov    ecx,100              ; set outer loop count
L1:
    mov    count,ecx            ; save outer loop count
    mov    ecx,20               ; set inner loop count
L2:
    .
    .
    loop   L2                   ; repeat the inner loop

    mov    ecx,count            ; restore outer loop count
    loop   L1                   ; repeat the outer loop
```

As a general rule, avoid nesting loops more than two levels deep. Otherwise, managing the loop counters becomes too much trouble. If the algorithm you're using requires deep loop nesting, move some of the inner loops into subroutines.

4.5.3 Summing an Integer Array

There's hardly any task more common in beginning programming than calculating the sum of the elements in an array. In assembly language, you would follow these steps:

1. Assign the array's address to a register that will serve as an indexed operand.
2. Set ECX to the number of elements in the array (use CX in 16-bit mode).
3. Assign zero to the register that accumulates the sum.
4. Create a label to mark the beginning of the loop.
5. In the loop body, use indirect addressing to add a single array element to the register holding the sum.
6. Set the index register forward to the next array element.
7. Use a LOOP instruction to repeat the loop from the beginning label.

Steps 1 through 3 may be performed in any order. Here's a short program that does the job:

```
TITLE Summing an Array           (SumArray.asm)

INCLUDE Irvine32.inc
.data
intarray WORD 100h,200h,300h,400h

.code
main PROC
    mov    edi,OFFSET intarray        ; address of intarray
    mov    ecx,LENGTHOF intarray      ; loop counter
    mov    ax,0                       ; zero the accumulator
L1:
    add    ax,[edi]                   ; add an integer
    add    edi,TYPE intarray          ; point to next integer
    loop   L1                         ; repeat until ECX = 0

    exit
main ENDP
END main
```

4.5.4 Copying a String

Programs often have to copy large blocks of data from one location to another. The data may be arrays or strings, but they can contain any type of objects. Let's see how this can be done in assembly language, using a loop that copies a string. Indexed addressing works well for this type of operation because the same index register references both strings. The target string must have enough available space to receive the copied characters, including the null byte at the end:

```
TITLE Copying a String                      (CopyStr.asm)

INCLUDE Irvine32.inc
.data
source  BYTE  "This is the source string",0
target  BYTE  SIZEOF source DUP(0)

.code
main PROC
      mov    esi,0                  ; index register
      mov    ecx,SIZEOF source      ; loop counter
L1:
      mov    al,source[esi]         ; get a character from source
      mov    target[esi],al         ; store it in the target
      inc    esi                    ; move to next character
      loop   L1                     ; repeat for entire string

      exit
main ENDP
END main
```

The MOV instruction cannot have two memory operands, so each character is moved from the source string to AL, then from AL to the target string.

> When programming in C++ or Java, beginning programmers often do not realize how often background copy operations take place. In Java, for example, if you exceed the existing capacity of an ArrayList when adding a new element, the runtime system allocates a block of new storage, copies the existing data to a new location, and deletes the old data. (The same is true when using a C++ vector.) If a large number of copy operations take place, they have a significant effect on a program's execution speed.

4.5.5 Section Review

1. *(True/False):* A JMP instruction can only jump to a label inside the current procedure, unless the label has been designated global.

2. *(True/False):* JMP is a conditional transfer instruction.

3. If ECX is initialized to zero before beginning a loop, how many times will the LOOP instruction repeat? (Assume ECX is not modified by any other instructions inside the loop.)

4. *(True/False):* The LOOP instruction first checks to see whether ECX is greater than zero; then it decrements ECX and jumps to the destination label.

5. *(True/False):* The LOOP instruction does the following: It decrements ECX; then, if ECX is greater than zero, the instruction jumps to the destination label.

6. In real-address mode, which register is used as the counter by the LOOP instruction?

7. In real-address mode, which register is used as the counter by the LOOPD instruction?

8. *(True/False):* The target of a LOOP instruction must be within 256 bytes of the current location.

9. *(Challenge):* What will be the final value of EAX in this example?

```
      mov    eax,0
      mov    ecx,10                 ; outer loop counter
L1:
      mov    eax,3
      mov    ecx,5                  ; inner loop counter
```

```
     L2:
          add     eax,5
          loop    L2                          ; repeat inner loop
          loop    L1                          ; repeat outer loop
```

10. Revise the code from the preceding question so the outer loop counter is not erased when the inner loop starts.

4.6 Chapter Summary

MOV, a data transfer instruction, copies a source operand to a destination operand. The MOVZX instruction zero-extends a smaller operand into a larger one. The MOVSX instruction sign-extends a smaller operand into a larger register. The XCHG instruction exchanges the contents of two operands. At least one operand must be a register.

Operand Types   The following types of operands are presented in this chapter:

- A *direct* operand is the name of a variable, and represents the variable's address.
- A *direct-offset* operand adds a displacement to the name of a variable, generating a new offset. This new offset can be used to access data in memory.
- An *indirect* operand is a register containing the address of data. By surrounding the register with brackets (as in [esi]), a program dereferences the address and retrieves the memory data.
- An *indexed* operand combines a constant with an indirect operand. The constant and register value are added, and the resulting offset is dereferenced. For example, [array + esi] and array[esi] are indexed operands.

The following arithmetic instructions are important:

- The INC instruction adds 1 to an operand.
- The DEC instruction subtracts 1 from an operand.
- The ADD instruction adds a source operand to a destination operand.
- The SUB instruction subtracts a source operand from a destination operand.
- The NEG instruction reverses the sign of an operand.

When converting simple arithmetic expressions to assembly language, use standard operator precedence rules to select which expressions to evaluate first.

Status Flags   The following CPU status flags are affected by arithmetic operations:

- The Sign flag is set when the outcome of an arithmetic operation is negative.
- The Carry flag is set when the result of an unsigned arithmetic operation is too large for the destination operand.
- The Auxiliary Carry flag is set when a carry or borrow occurs in bit position 3 of the destination operand.
- The Zero flag is set when the outcome of an arithmetic operation is zero.
- The Overflow flag is set when the result of an signed arithmetic operation is too large for the destination operand. In a byte operation, for example, the CPU detects overflow by exclusive-ORing the carry out of bit 6 with the carry out of bit 7.

Operators   The following operators are common in assembly language:

- The OFFSET operator returns the distance of a variable from the beginning of its enclosing segment.
- The PTR operator overrides a variable's declared size.
- The TYPE operator returns the size (in bytes) of a single variable or of a single element in an array.
- The LENGTHOF operator returns the number of elements in an array.
- The SIZEOF operator returns the number bytes used by an array initializer.
- The TYPEDEF operator creates a user-defined type.

Loops   The JMP instruction unconditionally branches to another location. The LOOP instruction is used in counting-type loops. In 32-bit mode, LOOP uses ECX as the counter; in 16-bit mode, CX is the counter. In both 16- and 32-bit modes, LOOPD (loop double) uses ECX as the counter.

4.7   Programming Exercises

The following exercises can be done in protected mode or real-address mode.

1.   Carry Flag

Write a program that uses addition and subtraction to set and clear the Carry flag. After each instruction, insert the **call DumpRegs** statement to display the registers and flags. Using comments, explain how (and why) the Carry flag was affected by each instruction.

2.   INC and DEC

Write a short program demonstrating that the INC and DEC instructions do not affect the Carry flag.

3.   Zero and Sign Flags

Write a program that uses addition and subtraction to set and clear the Zero and Sign flags. After each addition or subtraction instruction, insert the **call DumpRegs** statement (see Section 3.2) to display the registers and flags. Using comments, explain how (and why) the Zero and Sign flags were affected by each instruction.

4.   Overflow Flag

Write a program that uses addition and subtraction to set and clear the Overflow flag. After each addition or subtraction instruction, insert the **call DumpRegs** statement (see Section 3.2) to display the registers and flags. Using comments, explain how (and why) the Overflow flag was affected by each instruction. Include an ADD instruction that sets both the Carry and Overflow flags.

5.   Direct-Offset Addressing

Insert the following variables in your program:

```
.data
Uarray WORD 1000h,2000h,3000h,4000h
Sarray SWORD -1,-2,-3,-4
```

Write instructions that use direct-offset addressing to move the four values in **Uarray** to the EAX, EBX, ECX, and EDX registers. When you follow this with a **call DumpRegs** statement (see Section 3.2), the following register values should display:

```
EAX=00001000   EBX=00002000   ECX=00003000   EDX=00004000
```

Next, write instructions that use direct-offset addressing to move the four values in **Sarray** to the EAX, EBX, ECX, and EDX registers. When you follow this with a **call DumpRegs** statement, the following register values should display:

```
EAX=FFFFFFFF   EBX=FFFFFFFE   ECX=FFFFFFFD   EDX=FFFFFFFC
```

6.   Fibonacci Numbers

Write a program that uses a loop to calculate the first 12 values in the *Fibonacci* number sequence, {1, 1, 2, 3, 5, 8, 13,...}. Place each value in the EAX register and display it with a **call DumpRegs** statement (see Section 3.2) inside the loop.

7.   Arithmetic Expression

Write a program that implements the following arithmetic expression:

```
EAX = -val2 + 7 - val3 + val1
```

Use the following data definitions:

```
val1 SDWORD 8
val2 SDWORD -15
val3 SDWORD 20
```

In comments next to each instruction, write the hexadecimal value of EAX. Insert a **call DumpRegs** statement at the end of the program.

8. Copy a String Backwards

Write a program using the LOOP instruction with indirect addressing that copies a string from **source** to **target**, reversing the character order in the process. Use the following variables:

```
source  BYTE "This is the source string",0
target  BYTE  SIZEOF source DUP('#')
```

Insert the following statements immediately after the loop to display the hexadecimal contents of the target string:

```
mov   esi,OFFSET target     ; offset of variable
mov   ebx,1                 ; byte format
mov   ecx,SIZEOF target     ; counter
call  DumpMem
```

If your program works correctly, it will display the following sequence of hexadecimal bytes:

```
67 6E 69 72 74 73 20 65 63 72 75 6F 73 20 65 68
74 20 73 69 20 73 69 68 54
```

(The DumpMem procedure is explained in Section 5.3.2.)

5

Procedures

5.1 Introduction

We can think of several good reasons for you to read this chapter:

- You want to know how input-output works in assembly language.
- You need to learn about the *runtime stack*, the fundamental mechanism for calling and returning from subroutines.
- You will learn how to divide large programs into modular subroutines.
- You will learn about *flowcharts*, which are graphing tools that portray program logic.
- Your instructor might give you a test.

5.2 Linking to an External Library

If you spend the time, you can write detailed code for input-output in assembly language. It's a lot like assembling your car's engine every time you go for a ride. Interesting work, but time consuming. In Chapter 11 you will get a chance to see how input-output is handled in MS-Windows protected mode. It is great fun, and a new world opens up when you see the available tools. For now, however, input-output should be easy while you are learning assembly language basics. Section 5.3 shows how to call procedures from the book's link libraries, named **Irvine32.lib** and **Irvine16.lib**. The complete library source code is available on the book's CD-ROM, and is regularly updated on the book's Web site (*www.asmirvine.com*).

The Irvine32 library is for programs written in 32-bit protected mode. It contains procedures that link to the MS-Windows API when they generate input-output. The Irvine16 library is for programs written in 16-bit real-address mode. It contains procedures that execute MS-DOS Interrupts when they generate input-output.

5.2.1 Background Information

A *link library* is a file containing procedures (subroutines) that have been assembled into machine code. A link library begins as one or more source files, which are assembled into object files. The object files are inserted into a specially formatted file recognized by the linker utility. Suppose a program displays a string in the console window by calling a procedure named **WriteString**. The program source must contain a PROTO directive identifying the WriteString procedure:

```
WriteString PROTO
```

Next, a CALL instruction executes **Writestring**:

```
call WriteString
```

When the program is assembled, the assembler leaves the target address of the CALL instruction blank, knowing that it will be filled in by the linker. The linker looks for **WriteString** in the link library and copies the appropriate machine instructions from the library into the program's executable file. In addition, it inserts **Writestring's** address into the CALL instruction. If a procedure you're calling is not in the link library, the linker issues an error message and does not generate an executable file.

Linker Command Options   The linker utility combines a program's object file with one or more object files and link libraries. The following command, for example, links hello.obj to the irvine32.lib and kernel32.lib libraries:

```
link hello.obj irvine32.lib kernel32.lib
```

Linking 32-Bit Programs   Let's go into more detail regarding linking 32-bit programs. The kernel32.lib file, part of the Microsoft Windows Platform *Software Development Kit*, contains linking information for system functions located in a file named kernel32.dll. The latter is a fundamental part of MS-Windows, and is called a *dynamic link library*. It contains executable functions that perform character-based input-output. The following figure shows how kernel32.lib is a bridge to kernel32.dll:

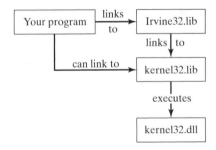

In Chapters 1 through 10, our programs link to Irvine32.lib. Chapter 11 shows how to link programs directly to kernel32.lib.

5.2.2 Section Review

1. *(True/False):* A link library consists of assembly language source code.

2. Use the PROTO directive to declare a procedure named **MyProc** in an external link library.

3.   Write a CALL statement that calls a procedure named **MyProc** in an external link library.

4.   What is the name of the 32-bit link library supplied with this book?

5.   Which library contains functions called from **Irvine32.lib**?

6.   What type of file is **kernel32.dll**?

7.   What name is used for the replaceable filename parameter in the **make32.bat** file?

5.3   The Book's Link Library

5.3.1   Overview

Table 5-1 contains a list of the more commonly used procedures in the Irvine32 and Irvine16 libraries supplied on the book's CD-ROM. Although the Irvine16 is for programs running in 16-bit mode (real-address mode), it uses 32-bit registers. Most procedures documented in this section exist in both libraries. Procedures found only in the Irvine32 library are marked by * at the end of their descriptions.

Console Window   The *console window* (or *command window*) is a text-only window created by MS-Windows when a command prompt is displayed. You can display it by clicking on Start and Run and typing in **cmd** (for Windows 2000 and Windows XP) or **command** (for Windows 95 and 98). In Windows 2000 and Windows XP, you can resize the console window buffer by right-clicking on the system menu in the window's upper-left corner. You can also select various font sizes and colors. In Windows 95 and 98, you can set the number of rows to one of several defaults. In all versions of Windows and MS-DOS, the console window defaults to 25 rows by 80 columns. You can change the number of lines using the **mode** command. The following, typed at the command prompt, sets the console window to 40 columns by 30 lines:

```
mode con cols=40 lines=30
```

Table 5-1   Procedures in the Link Library.

Procedure	Description
CloseFile	Closes a disk file that was previously opened.*
Clrscr	Clears the console window and locates the cursor at the upper left corner.
CreateOutputFile	Creates a new disk file for writing in output mode.*
Crlf	Writes an end-of-line sequence to the console window.
Delay	Pauses the program execution for a specified *n*-millisecond interval.
DumpMem	Writes a block of memory to the console window in hexadecimal.
DumpRegs	Displays the EAX, EBX, ECX, EDX, ESI, EDI, EBP, ESP, EFLAGS, and EIP registers in hexadecimal. Also displays the most common CPU status flags.
GetCommandTail	Copies the program's command-line arguments (called the *command tail*) into an array of bytes.
GetMaxXY	Gets the number of columns and rows in the console window's buffer.
GetMseconds	Returns the number of milliseconds elapsed since midnight.
GetTextColor	Returns the active foreground and background text colors in the console window.*
Gotoxy	Locates the cursor at a specific row and column in the console window.
IsDigit	Sets the Zero flag if the AL register contains the ASCII code for a decimal digit (0–9).
MsgBox	Displays a popup message box.*

Table 5-1   *(Continued)*

Procedure	Description
MsgBoxAsk	Display a yes/no question in a popup message box.*
OpenInputFile	Opens an existing disk file for input.*
ParseDecimal32	Converts an unsigned decimal integer string to 32-bit binary.
ParseDecimal32	Converts a signed decimal integer string to 32-bit binary.
Random32	Generates a 32-bit pseudorandom integer in the range 0 to FFFFFFFFh.
Randomize	Seeds the random number generator with a unique value.
RandomRange	Generates a pseudorandom integer within a specified range.
ReadChar	Waits for a single character to be typed at the keyboard and returns the character.
ReadDec	Reads an unsigned 32-bit decimal integer from the keyboard, terminated by the Enter key.
ReadFromFile	Reads an input disk file into a buffer.*
ReadHex	Reads a 32-bit hexadecimal integer from the keyboard, terminated by the Enter key.
ReadInt	Reads a 32-bit signed decimal integer from the keyboard, terminated by the Enter key.
ReadKey	Reads a character from the keyboard's input buffer without waiting for input.
ReadString	Reads a string from the keyboard, terminated by the Enter key.
SetTextColor	Sets the foreground and background colors of all subsequent text output to the console.
StrLength	Returns the length of a string.
WaitMsg	Displays a message and waits for a key to be pressed.
WriteBin	Writes an unsigned 32-bit integer to the console window in ASCII binary format.
WriteBinB	Writes a binary integer to the console window in byte, word, or doubleword format.
WriteChar	Writes a single character to the console window.
WriteDec	Writes an unsigned 32-bit integer to the console window in decimal format.
WriteHex	Writes a 32-bit integer to the console window in hexadecimal format.
WriteHexB	Writes a byte, word, or doubleword integer to the console window in hexadecimal format.
WriteInt	Writes a signed 32-bit integer to the console window in decimal format.
WriteString	Writes a null-terminated string to the console window.
WriteToFile	Writes a buffer to an output file.*
WriteWindowsMsg	Displays a string containing the most recent error generated by MS-Windows.*

* Procedure not available in the Irvine16 library.

Redirecting Standard Input-Output

The Irvine32 and Irvine16 libraries both write output to the console window, but the Irvine16 library has one additional feature: *redirection of standard input-output*. Its output can be redirected at the DOS or Windows command prompt to write to a disk file rather than the console window. Here's how it works: Suppose a program named *sample.exe* writes to standard output; then we can use the following command (at the DOS prompt) to redirect its output to a file named *output.txt:*

```
sample > output.txt
```

Similarly, if the same program reads input from the keyboard (*standard input*), we can tell it to read its input from a file named *input.txt:*

```
sample < input.txt
```

We can redirect both input and output with a single command:

```
sample < input.txt > output.txt
```

We can send the standard output from *prog1.exe* to the standard input of *prog2.exe* using the pipe (|) symbol:

```
prog1 | prog2
```

We can send the standard output from *prog1.exe* to the standard input of *prog2.exe*, and send the output of *prog2.exe* to a file named *output.txt:*

```
prog1 | prog2 > output.txt
```

Prog1.exe can read input from *input.txt*, send its output to *prog2.exe*, which in turn can send its output to *output.txt:*

```
prog1 < input.txt | prog2 > output.txt
```

The filenames input.txt and output.txt are completely arbitrary, so you can choose any filenames you want.

5.3.2   Individual Procedure Descriptions

CloseFile   (*Irvine32 only*) The CloseFile procedure closes a file that was previously opened. The file is identified by a 32-bit integer *handle*, which is passed in EAX. If the file is closed successfully, the value returned in EAX will be nonzero. Sample call:

```
mov   eax,fileHandle
call CloseFile
```

Clrscr   The Clrscr procedure clears the console window. This procedure is typically called at the beginning and end of a program. If you call it at other times, you may need to pause the program by calling WaitMsg. Doing this allows the user to view information already on the screen before it is erased. Sample call:

```
call WaitMsg                         ; "Press any key..."
call Clrscr
```

Crlf   The Crlf procedure advances the cursor to the beginning of the next line in the console window. It writes a string containing the values 0Dh and 0Ah. Sample call:

```
call Crlf
```

CreateOutputFile   The CreateOutputFile procedure creates a disk file and opens it in output mode. Pass the offset of a file name in EDX. When the procedure returns, if the file was created successfully, EAX contains a valid file handle (32-bit integer). Otherwise, EAX equals INVALID_HANDLE_VALUE (a predefined constant). Sample call:

```
.data
filename BYTE "newfile.txt",0
handle DWORD ?
.code
mov   edx,OFFSET filename
call CreateOutputFile
cmp   eax,INVALID_HANDLE_VALUE
je    file_error                     ; display error message
mov   handle,eax                     ; save the file handle
```

Note: The foregoing sample code compares the value in EAX to a predefined constant. If they are equal, the JE instruction jumps to a label named **file_error**. The CMP and JE instructions will be described in Chapter 6. We provide this error-handling code for future reference.

Delay The Delay procedure pauses the program for a specified number of milliseconds. Before calling Delay, set EAX to the desired interval. Sample call:

```
mov   eax,1000                        ; 1 second
call Delay
```

(The Irvine16.lib version does not work under Windows NT, 2000, or XP.)

DumpMem The DumpMem procedure writes a range of memory to the console window in hexadecimal. Pass it the starting address in ESI, the number of units in ECX, and the unit size in EBX (1 = byte, 2 = word, 4 = doubleword). The following sample call displays an array of 11 doublewords in hexadecimal:

```
.data
array DWORD 1,2,3,4,5,6,7,8,9,0Ah,0Bh
.code
main PROC
      mov   esi,OFFSET array            ; starting OFFSET
      mov   ecx,LENGTHOF array          ; number of units
      mov   ebx,TYPE array              ; doubleword format
      call  DumpMem
```

The following output is produced:

```
00000001  00000002  00000003  00000004  00000005  00000006  00000007
00000008  00000009  0000000A  0000000B
```

DumpRegs The DumpRegs procedure displays the EAX, EBX, ECX, EDX, ESI, EDI, EBP, ESP, EIP, and EFL (EFLAGS) registers in hexadecimal. It also displays the values of the Carry, Sign, Zero, Overflow, Auxiliary Carry, and Parity flags. Sample call:

```
call DumpRegs
```

Sample output:

```
EAX=00000613  EBX=00000000  ECX=000000FF  EDX=00000000
ESI=00000000  EDI=00000100  EBP=0000091E  ESP=000000F6
EIP=00401026  EFL=00000286  CF=0  SF=1  ZF=0  OF=0  AF=0  PF=1
```

The displayed value of EIP is the offset of the instruction following the call to DumpRegs. DumpRegs can be useful when debugging programs because it displays a snapshot of the CPU. It has no input parameters and no return value.

GetCommandTail The GetCommandTail procedure copies the program's command line into a null-terminated string. If the command line was found to be empty, the Carry flag is set; otherwise, the Carry flag is cleared. This procedure is useful because it permits the user of a program to pass information on the command line. Suppose a program named **Encrypt** reads an input file named **file1.txt** and produces an output file named **file2.txt**. The user can pass both filenames on the command line when running the program:

```
Encrypt file1.txt file2.txt
```

When it starts up, the Encrypt program can call GetCommandTail and retrieve the two filenames. When calling Get_Commandtail, EDX must contain the offset of an array of at least 129 bytes. Sample call:

```
.data
cmdTail BYTE 129 DUP(0)                       ; empty buffer
```

```
    .code
    mov  edx,OFFSET cmdTail
    call GetCommandTail                    ; fills the buffer
```

GetMaxXY   *(Irvine32 only)* The GetMaxXY procedure returns the size of the console window's buffer. If the console window buffer is larger than the visible window size, scroll bars appear automatically. GetMaxXY has no input parameters. When it returns, the DL register contains the number of buffer columns and DH contains the number of buffer rows. The possible range of each value can be no greater than 255, which may be smaller than the actual window buffer size. Sample call:

```
    .data
    rows BYTE ?
    cols BYTE ?
    .code
    call GetMaxXY
    mov  rows,dh
    mov  cols,dl
```

GetMseconds   The GetMseconds procedure returns the number of milliseconds elapsed since midnight in the EAX register. You can use it to measure the time between events. No input parameters are required. The following example calls GetMseconds, storing its return value. After the loop executes, we call GetMseconds a second time and subtract the two time values. The difference is the approximate duration of the loop:

```
    .data
    startTime DWORD ?
    .code
    call GetMseconds
    mov  startTime,eax
    L1:
      ; (loop body)
    loop L1
    call GetMseconds
    sub  eax,startTime              ; EAX = loop time, in milliseconds
```

GetTextColor   The GetTextColor procedure returns the current foreground and background colors of the console window (Irvine32 only). It has no input parameters. It returns the background color in the upper four bits of AL and the foreground color in the lower four bits. Sample call:

```
    .data
    color BYTE ?
    .code
    call GetTextColor
    mov  color,AL
```

Gotoxy   The Gotoxy procedure locates the cursor at a given row and column on the screen. By default, the console window's X-coordinate range is 0 to 79 and the Y-coordinate range is 0 to 24. When you call Gotoxy, pass the Y-coordinate (row) in DH and the X-coordinate (column) in DL. Sample call:

```
    mov  dh,10                      ; row 10
    mov  dl,20                      ; column 20
    call Gotoxy                     ; locate cursor
```

The user may have resized the console window, so you can call GetMaxXY to find out the current number of rows and columns.

IsDigit   The IsDigit procedure determines whether the character in AL is a valid decimal digit. When calling it, pass an ASCII character in AL. The procedure sets the Zero flag if AL contains a valid decimal digit; otherwise, the Zero flag is clear. Sample call:

```
mov   AL,somechar
call  IsDigit
jz    digit_found
```

(The JZ instruction, covered in Section 6.3.2, jumps to a label when the Zero flag is set.)

MsgBox   *(Irvine32 only)* The MsgBox procedure displays a graphical popup message box with an optional caption. Pass it the offset of a string in EDX, which will appear in the inside the box. Optionally, pass the offset of a string for the box's title in EBX. To leave the title blank, set EBX to zero. Sample call:

```
.data
caption db "Dialog Title", 0
HelloMsg BYTE "This is a pop-up message box.", 0dh,0ah
         BYTE "Click OK to continue...", 0
.code
mov   ebx,OFFSET caption
mov   edx,OFFSET HelloMsg
call  MsgBox
```

Sample output:

MsgBoxAsk   *(Irvine32 only)* The MsgBoxAsk procedure displays a graphical popup message box with Yes and No buttons. Pass it the offset of a question string in EDX, which will appear in the inside the box. Optionally, pass the offset of a string for the box's title in EBX. To leave the title blank, set EBX to zero. MsgBoxAsk returns an integer in EAX that tells you which button was selected by the user: IDYES (equal to 6) or IDNO (equal to 7). Sample call:

```
.data
caption BYTE "Survey Completed",0
question BYTE "Thank you for completing the survey."
  BYTE 0dh,0ah
  BYTE "Would you like to receive the results?",0
results BYTE "The results will be sent via email.",0dh,0ah,0
.code
mov   ebx,OFFSET caption
mov   edx,OFFSET question
call  MsgBoxAsk
;(check return value in EAX)
```

Sample output:

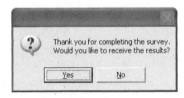

OpenInputFile   *(Irvine32 only)* The OpenInputFile procedure opens an existing file for input. Pass it the offset of a filename in EDX. When it returns, if the file was opened successfully, EAX contains a valid file handle. Otherwise, EAX equals INVALID_HANDLE_VALUE (a predefined constant). Sample call:

```
.data
filename BYTE "myfile.txt",0
handle DWORD ?
.code
mov  edx,OFFSET filename
call OpenInputFile
cmp  eax,INVALID_HANDLE_VALUE
je   file_error                     ; display error message
mov  handle,eax                     ; save the file handle
```

Note: The foregoing sample code compares the value in EAX to a predefined constant. If they are equal, the JE instruction jumps to a label named **file_error**. The CMP and JE instructions will be described in Chapter 6. We provide this error-handling code for future reference.

ParseDecimal32   The ParseDecimal32 procedure converts an unsigned decimal integer string to 32-bit binary. All valid digits occurring before a non-numeric character are converted. Leading spaces are ignored. Pass it the offset of a string in EDX and the string's length in ECX. The binary value is returned in EAX. Sample call:

```
.data
buffer BYTE "8193"
bufSize = ($ - buffer)
.code
mov  edx,OFFSET buffer
mov  ecx,bufSize
call ParseDecimal32                 ; returns EAX
```

See the description of the **ReadDec** procedure for details about how the Carry flag is affected.

ParseInteger32   The ParseInteger32 procedure converts a signed decimal integer string to 32-bit binary. All valid digits occurring before a non-numeric character are converted. Leading spaces are ignored. Pass it the offset of a string in EDX and the string's length in ECX. The binary value is returned in EAX. Sample call:

```
.data
buffer BYTE "-8193"
bufSize = ($ - buffer)
.code
mov  edx,OFFSET buffer
mov  ecx,bufSize
call ParseInteger32                 ; returns EAX
```

The string may contain an optional leading plus or minus sign, followed only by decimal digits. The Overflow flag is set and an error message is displayed on the console if the value cannot be represented as a 32-bit signed integer (range: $-2,147,483,648$ to $+2,147,483,647$).

Random32   The Random32 procedure generates and returns a 32-bit random integer in EAX. When called repeatedly, Random32 generates a simulated random sequence in which each number is called a *pseudorandom integer.*[1] The numbers are created using a simple function having an input called a *seed*. The function uses the seed in a formula that generates the random value. Subsequent random values are generated using each previously generated random value as their seeds. From this point forward, the term *random* will imply pseudorandom. Sample call:

```
.data
randVal DWORD ?
.code
call Random32
mov  randVal,eax
```

Random32 is also available in the Irvine16 library, returning its value in EAX.

Randomize   The Randomize procedure initializes the starting seed value of the Random32 and RandomRange procedures. The seed equals the time of day, accurate to 1/100 of a second. Each time you run a program that calls Random32 and RandomRange, the generated sequence will be different, and any sequence of random numbers will also be unique. You need only call Randomize once at the beginning of a program. In the following example, we produce 10 random integers:

```
      call   Randomize
      mov    ecx,10
L1:   call   Random32

      ; use or display random value in EAX here...

      loop   L1
```

RandomRange   The RandomRange procedure produces a random integer within the range of 0 to $n - 1$, where n is an input parameter passed in the EAX register. The random integer is returned in EAX. The following example generates a single random integer between 0 and 4999 and places it in EAX:

```
.data
randVal DWORD ?
.code
mov  eax,5000
call RandomRange
mov  randVal,eax
```

ReadChar   The ReadChar procedure reads a single character from the keyboard and returns the character in the AL register. The character is not echoed in the console window. Sample call:

```
.data
char BYTE ?
.code
call ReadChar
mov  char,al
```

If the user presses an extended key such as a function key, cursor arrow key, Ins, or Del, the procedure sets AL to zero, and AH contains a keyboard scan code. A list of scan codes is shown on the page facing the book's inside front cover. The upper half of EAX is not preserved.

ReadDec   The ReadDec procedure reads a 32-bit unsigned decimal integer from the keyboard and returns the value in EAX. Leading spaces are ignored. The return value is calculated from all valid digits found until a nondigit character is encountered. For example, if the user enters 123ABC, the value returned in EAX is 123. Sample call:

```
.data
intVal DWORD ?
.code
call ReadDec
mov  intVal,eax
```

ReadDec affects the Carry flag in the following ways:

- If the integer is blank, EAX = 0 and CF = 1
- If the integer contains only spaces, EAX = 0 and CF = 1
- If the integer is larger than $2^{32}-1$, EAX = 0 and CF = 1
- Otherwise, EAX = converted integer and CF = 0

ReadFromFile   (*Irvine32 only*) The ReadFromFile procedure reads an input file into a buffer. Pass it an open file handle in EAX, the offset of a buffer in EDX, and the maximum number of bytes to read in ECX. When the procedure returns, if CF = 0, EAX contains a count of the number of bytes read from the file. If CF = 1, EAX contains the system error code explaining what went wrong. (Call WriteWindowsMsg to get a text representation of the message.) Sample call:

```
.data
BUFFER_SIZE = 5000
.data
buffer BYTE BUFFER_SIZE DUP(?)
bytesRead DWORD ?
.code
mov   edx,OFFSET buffer        ; points to buffer
mov   ecx,BUFFER_SIZE          ; max bytes to read
call  ReadFromFile             ; read the file
jc    show_error_message       ; error occurred
mov   bytesRead,eax            ; counts bytes actually read
```

ReadHex   The ReadHex procedure reads a 32-bit hexadecimal integer from the keyboard and returns the value in EAX. No error checking is performed for invalid characters. You can use both uppercase and lowercase letters for the digits A through F. A maximum of eight digits may be entered (additional characters are ignored). Leading spaces are ignored. Sample call:

```
.data
hexVal DWORD ?
.code
call  ReadHex
mov   hexVal,eax
```

ReadInt   The ReadInt procedure reads a 32-bit signed integer from the keyboard and returns the value in EAX. The user can type an optional leading plus or minus sign, and the rest of the number may only consist of digits. ReadInt sets the Overflow flag and display an error message if the value entered cannot be represented as a 32-bit signed integer (range: $-2, 147, 483, 648$ to $+2, 147, 483, 647$). The return value is calculated from all valid digits found until a nondigit character is encountered. For example, if the user enters +123ABC, the value returned is +123. Sample call:

```
.data
intVal SDWORD ?
.code
call  ReadInt
mov   intVal,eax
```

ReadKey   The ReadKey procedure performs a no-wait keyboard check. If no key is found, the Zero flag is set. If a key is found, the Zero flag is clear, and AL contains either zero or an ASCII code. If AL contains zero, the user may have pressed a special key (function key, cursor arrow, etc.) The AH register contains a virtual scan code, DX contains a virtual key code, and EBX contains the keyboard flag bits. The upper halves of EAX and EDX are overwritten. *We will elaborate on ReadKey details in*

Chapter 11. Here's a sample call when Irvine32 library is used and the user presses a standard alphanumeric key:

```
.data
char BYTE ?
.code
L1:  mov   eax,10          ; create 10ms delay
     call  Delay
     call  ReadKey         ; check for key
     jz    L1              ; repeat if no key
     mov   char,AL         ; save the character
```

Notice that we added a 10-millisecond delay to the loop to give MS-Windows time to process event messages. Otherwise, keystrokes can be missed. If you're using the Irvine16 library, you can omit the delay:

```
.data
char BYTE ?
.code
L1:  call  ReadKey         ; check for key
     jz    L1              ; repeat if no key
     mov   char,AL         ; save the character
```

ReadString The ReadString procedure reads a string from the keyboard, stopping when the user presses the Enter key. Pass the offset of a buffer in EDX and set ECX to the maximum number of characters the user can enter, plus 1 (to save space for the terminating null byte). The procedure returns the count of the number of characters typed by the user in EAX. Sample call:

```
.data
buffer BYTE 21 DUP(0)     ; input buffer
byteCount DWORD ?          ; holds counter
.code
mov  edx,OFFSET buffer     ; point to the buffer
mov  ecx,SIZEOF buffer     ; specify max characters
call ReadString            ; input the string
mov  byteCount,eax         ; number of characters
```

ReadString automatically inserts a null terminator in memory at the end of the string. The following is a hexadecimal and ASCII dump of the first 8 bytes of **buffer** after the user has entered the string "ABCDEFG":

41 42 43 44 45 46 47 00	ABCDEFG

The variable **byteCount** equals 7.

SetTextColor The SetTextColor procedure *(Irvine32 library only)* sets the foreground and background colors for text output. When calling SetTextColor, assign a color attribute to AX. The following predefined color constants can be used for both foreground and background:

black = 0	red = 4	gray = 8	lightRed = 12
blue = 1	magenta = 5	lightBlue = 9	lightMagenta = 13
green = 2	brown = 6	lightGreen = 10	yellow = 14
cyan = 3	lightGray = 7	lightCyan = 11	white = 15

Color constants are defined in the include files named *Irvine32.inc* and *Irvine16.inc*. Multiply the background color by 16 and add it to the foreground color.[2] The following constant, for example, indicates yellow characters on a blue background:

```
yellow + (blue * 16)
```

The following statements set the color to white on a blue background:

```
mov  eax,white + (blue * 16)       ; white on blue
call SetTextColor
```

You can find a detailed explanation of video attributes in Section 15.3.2. The Irvine16 version of Set-TextColor clears the console window with the selected colors.

StrLength   The StrLength procedure returns the length of a null-terminated string. Pass the string's offset in EDX. The procedure returns the string's length in EAX. Sample call:

```
.data
buffer BYTE "abcde",0
bufLength DWORD ?
.code
mov  edx,OFFSET buffer              ; point to string
call StrLength                      ; EAX = 5
mov  bufLength,eax                  ; save length
```

WaitMsg   The WaitMsg procedure displays the message "Press any key to continue. . ." and waits for the user to press a key. This procedure is useful when you want to pause the screen display before data scrolls off and disappears. It has no input parameters. Sample call:

```
call WaitMsg
```

WriteBin   The WriteBin procedure writes an integer to the console window in ASCII binary format. Pass the integer in EAX. The binary bits are displayed in groups of four for easy reading. Sample call:

```
mov  eax,12346AF9h
call WriteBin
; displays: "0001 0010 0011 0100 0110 1010 1111 1001"
```

WriteBinB   The WriteBinB procedure writes a 32-bit integer to the console window in ASCII binary format. Pass the value in the EAX register and let EBX indicate the display size in bytes (1, 2, or 4). The bits are displayed in groups of four for easy reading. Sample call:

```
mov  eax,00001234h
mov  ebx,TYPE WORD                  ; 2 bytes
call WriteBinB                      ; displays 0001 0010 0011 0100
```

WriteChar   The WriteChar procedure writes a single character to the console window. Pass the character (or its ASCII code) in AL. Sample call:

```
mov  al,'A'
call WriteChar                      ; displays: "A"
```

WriteDec   The WriteDec procedure writes a 32-bit unsigned integer to the console window in decimal format with no leading zeros. Pass the integer in EAX. Sample call:

```
mov  eax,295
call WriteDec                       ; displays: "295"
```

WriteHex   The WriteHex procedure writes a 32-bit unsigned integer to the console window in 8-digit hexadecimal format. Leading zeros are inserted if necessary. Pass the integer in EAX. Sample call:

```
mov  eax,7FFFh
call WriteHex                          ; displays: "00007FFF"
```

WriteHexB   The WriteHexB procedure writes a 32-bit unsigned integer to the console window in hexadecimal format. Leading zeros are inserted if necessary. Pass the integer in EAX and let EBX indicate the display format in bytes (1, 2, or 4). Sample call:

```
mov  eax,7FFFh
mov  ebx,TYPE WORD                     ; 2 bytes
call WriteHexB                         ; displays: "7FFF"
```

WriteInt   The WriteInt procedure writes a 32-bit signed integer to the console window in decimal format with a leading sign and no leading zeros. Pass the integer in EAX. Sample call:

```
mov  eax,216543
call WriteInt                          ; displays: "+216543"
```

WriteString   The WriteString procedure writes a null-terminated string to the console window. Pass the string's offset in EDX. Sample call:

```
.data
prompt BYTE "Enter your name: ",0
.code
mov  edx,OFFSET prompt
call WriteString
```

WriteToFile   *(Irvine32 only)* The WriteToFile procedure writes the contents of a buffer to an output file. Pass it a valid file handle in EAX, the offset of the buffer in EDX, and the number of bytes to write in ECX. When the procedure returns, EAX contains a count of the number of bytes written. Sample call:

```
BUFFER_SIZE = 5000
.data
fileHandle DWORD ?
buffer BYTE BUFFER_SIZE DUP(?)
bytesWritten DWORD ?
.code
mov  eax,fileHandle
mov  edx,OFFSET buffer
mov  ecx,BUFFER_SIZE
call WriteToFile
mov  bytesWritten,eax                  ; save return value
```

WriteWindowsMsg   *(Irvine32 only)* The WriteWindowsMsg procedure displays a string containing the most recent error generated by MS-Windows. It is most useful when your program is unable to create or open a file. The following example tries to open a file for input, and finding an error, calls WriteWindowsMsg to display the error:

```
mov  edx,OFFSET filename
call OpenInputFile
.IF eax == INVALID_HANDLE_VALUE
call WriteWindowsMsg
.ENDIF
```

The following string is written to the console window:

```
Error 2: The system cannot find the file specified.
```

The Irvine32.inc Include File

The following is a partial listing of the *Irvine32.inc* include file. It contains a prototype for each library procedure, as well as color constants, structures, and symbol definitions. This file will change over time, so download the latest library updates from the book's Web site (www.asmirvine.com):

```
; Include file for Irvine32.lib          (Irvine32.inc)
INCLUDE SmallWin.inc
.NOLIST

Procedure Prototypes
;----------------------------------------
Clrscr PROTO
Crlf PROTO
Delay PROTO
DumpMem PROTO
DumpRegs PROTO
GetCommandTail PROTO
(more procedures...)
.

.
Standard 4-bit color definitions
;----------------------------------------
black         = 0000b
blue          = 0001b
green         = 0010b
cyan          = 0011b
red           = 0100b
magenta       = 0101b
brown         = 0110b
lightGray     = 0111b
gray          = 1000b
lightBlue     = 1001b
lightGreen    = 1010b
lightCyan     = 1011b
lightRed      = 1100b
lightMagenta  = 1101b
yellow        = 1110b
white         = 1111b
.LIST
```

The .NOLIST directive at the top of this file prevents these lines from being shown in source listings created by the assembler. At the end of this file, the .LIST directive enables listing of source lines again. The INCLUDE directive at the beginning of this file causes another include file (SmallWin.inc) to be included in the text stream passed to the assembler.

5.3.3   Library Test Programs

Test Program #1: Integer I/O

Let's take a look at several programs that test the book's link library. Test program #1 changes the text color to yellow characters on a blue background, dumps an array in hexadecimal, prompts the user for a signed integer, and redisplays the integer in decimal, hexadecimal, and binary:

```
TITLE Library Test #1: Integer I/O   (TestLib1.asm)

; Tests the Clrscr, Crlf, DumpMem, ReadInt,
; SetTextColor, WaitMsg, WriteBin, WriteHex,
```

```
; and WriteString procedures.
INCLUDE Irvine32.inc
.data
array    DWORD 1000h,2000h,3000h
prompt1  BYTE "Enter a 32-bit signed integer: ",0
dwordVal DWORD ?

.code
main PROC
; Set text color to yellow text on blue background:
     mov    eax,yellow + (blue * 16)
     call   SetTextColor
     call   Clrscr                    ; clear the screen

; Display the array using DumpMem.
     mov    esi,OFFSET arrayD         ; starting OFFSET
     mov    ecx,LENGTHOF arrayD       ; number of units in dwordVal
     mov    ebx,TYPE arrayD           ; size of a doubleword
     call   DumpMem                   ; display memory
     call   Crlf                      ; new line

; Ask the user to input a signed decimal integer.
     mov    edx,OFFSET prompt1
     call   WriteString
     call   ReadInt                   ; input the integer
     mov    dwordVal,eax              ; save in a variable

; Display the integer in decimal, hexadecimal, and binary.
     call   Crlf                      ; new line
     call   WriteInt                  ; display in signed decimal
     call   Crlf
     call   WriteHex                  ; display in hexadecimal
     call   Crlf
     call   WriteBin                  ; display in binary
     call   Crlf
     call   WaitMsg                   ; "Press any key..."

; Return console window to default colors.
     mov    eax,lightGray + (black * 16)
     call   SetTextColor
     call   Clrscr                    ; clear the screen
     exit
main ENDP
END main
```

Sample Output, Test Program #1   Here is sample output generated by the program (the text is yellow on a blue background):

```
Dump of offset 00405000
-------------------------------
00001000  00002000  00003000
Enter a 32-bit signed integer: 4333
+4333
000010ED
0000 0000 0000 0000 0001 0000 1110 1101
Press any key to continue...
```

Test Program #2: Random Integers

A second library test program demonstrates random-number-generation capabilities of the link library. First, it randomly generates 10 unsigned integers in the range 0 to 4,294,967,294. Next, it generates 10 signed integers in the range −50 to +49:

```
TITLE Link Library Test #2 (TestLib2.asm)

; Testing the Irvine32 Library procedures.

INCLUDE Irvine32.inc

TAB = 9                          ; ASCII code for Tab

.code
main PROC
        call    Randomize        ; init random generator
        call    Rand1
        call    Rand2
        exit
main ENDP

Rand1 PROC
; Generate ten pseudo-random integers.
        mov     ecx,10           ; loop 10 times

L1:     call    Random32         ; generate random int
        call    WriteDec         ; write in unsigned decimal
        mov     al,TAB           ; horizontal tab
        call    WriteChar        ; write the tab
        loop    L1

        call    Crlf
        ret
Rand1 ENDP

Rand2 PROC
; Generate ten pseudo-random integers between -50 and +49
        mov     ecx,10           ; loop 10 times

L1:     mov     eax,100          ; values 0-99
        call    RandomRange      ; generate random int
        sub     eax,50           ; vaues -50 to +49
        call    WriteInt         ; write signed decimal
        mov     al,TAB           ; horizontal tab
        call    WriteChar        ; write the tab
        loop    L1

        call    Crlf
        ret
Rand2 ENDP
END main
```

Here is sample output from the program:

3221236194	2210931702	974700167	367494257	2227888607
926772240	506254858	1769123448	2288603673	736071794
-34 +27 +38 -34 +31 -13 -29 +44 -48 -43				

Test Program #3: Performance Timing

Assembly language is often used to optimize sections of code seen as critical to a program's performance. The **GetMseconds** procedure from the link library returns the number of milliseconds elapsed since midnight. In the third test program, we call GetMseconds and execute a nested loop approximately 17 billion times. After the loop, we call GetMseconds a second time and report the total elapsed time:

```
TITLE Link Library Test #3                  (TestLib3.asm)

; Calculate the elapsed time of executing a nested loop.

INCLUDE Irvine32.inc

OUTER_LOOP_COUNT = 3                    ; adjust for processor speed
.data
startTime DWORD ?
msg1 BYTE "Please wait...",0dh,0ah,0
msg2 BYTE "Elapsed milliseconds: ",0

.code
main PROC
      mov    edx,OFFSET msg1
      call   WriteString
; Save the starting time.
      call   GetMSeconds
      mov    startTime,eax
      mov    ecx,OUTER_LOOP_COUNT

; Perform a busy loop.
L1:   call   innerLoop
      loop   L1

; Display the elapsed time.
      call   GetMSeconds
      sub    eax,startTime
      mov    edx,OFFSET msg2
      call   WriteString
      call   WriteDec
      call   Crlf
      exit
main ENDP

innerLoop PROC
      push   ecx
      mov    ecx,0FFFFFFFFh
L1:   mov    eax,eax
      loop   L1
      pop    ecx
      ret
innerLoop ENDP
END main
```

Here is sample output from the program running on a 3-GHz Pentium 4 processor:

```
Please wait....
Elapsed milliseconds: 9157
```

5.3.4 Section Review

1. Which procedure in the link library generates a random integer within a selected range?
2. Which procedure in the link library displays "Press [Enter] to continue. . ." and waits for the user to press the Enter key?
3. Write statements that cause a program to pause for 700 milliseconds.
4. Which procedure from the link library writes an unsigned integer to the console window in decimal format?
5. Which procedure from the link library places the cursor at a specific console window location?
6. Write the INCLUDE directive that is required when using the Irvine32 library.
7. What types of statements are inside the *Irvine32.inc* file?
8. What are the required input parameters for the DumpMem procedure?
9. What are the required input parameters for the ReadString procedure?
10. Which processor status flags are displayed by the DumpRegs procedure?
11. *Challenge:* Write statements that prompt the user for an identification number and input a string of digits into an array of bytes.

5.4 Stack Operations

If we place 10 pancakes on each other as in the following diagram, the result can be called a *stack*. Ordinarily, we don't pull a pancake from the middle of the stack, but when we load one onto our plate, we remove a pancake from the top of the stack. New pancakes can be added to the top of the stack, but never to the bottom or middle (Figure 5–1):

FIGURE 5–1 Stack of Pancakes.

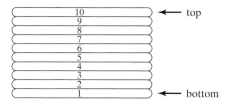

Pancakes have something in common with computer programs. A stack is also called a LIFO structure (*Last-In, First-Out*) because the last value put into the stack is always the first value taken out. (LIFO is a well-known accounting term, but pancakes are much more interesting.)

A *stack data structure* follows the same principle: New values are added to the top of the stack and existing values are removed from the top. Stacks in general are useful structures for a variety of programming applications, and they can easily be implemented using object-oriented programming methods. If you have taken a programming course that used data structures, you have worked with the *stack abstract data type*.

In this chapter, however, we concentrate on what is called the *runtime stack*. It is supported directly by hardware in the CPU, and it is an essential part of the mechanism for calling and returning from procedures. Most of the time, we just call it *the stack*.

5.4.1 Runtime Stack

The *runtime stack* is a memory array managed directly by the CPU, using two registers: SS and ESP. In protected mode, the SS register holds a pointer to a segment descriptor and is not modified by user programs. The ESP register holds a 32-bit offset into some location on the stack. We rarely manipulate ESP directly; instead, it is indirectly modified by instructions such as CALL, RET, PUSH, and POP.

The stack pointer register (ESP) points to the last integer to be added to, or *pushed* on, the stack. To demonstrate, let's begin with a stack containing one value. In the following illustration, the ESP (extended stack pointer) contains hexadecimal 00001000, the offset of the most recently pushed value (00000006):

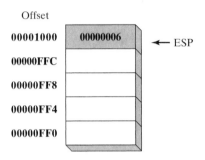

Each stack location in this figure contains 32 bits, which is the case when a program is running in protected mode. In 16-bit real-address mode, the SP register points to the most recently pushed value and stack entries are typically 16 bits long.

> The runtime stack discussed here is not the same as the *stack abstract data type* (ADT) discussed in data structures courses. The runtime stack works at the system level to handle subroutine calls. The stack ADT is a programing construct typically written in a high-level programming language such as C++ or Java. It is used when implementing algorithms that depend on last-in, first-out operations.

Push Operation

A 32-bit *push* operation decrements the stack pointer by 4 and copies a value into the location in the stack pointed to by the stack pointer. In Figure 5–2, we push 000000A5 on the stack. The figure shows the stack ordering opposite to that of the stack of pancakes we saw earlier. The runtime stack always grows downward in memory, following the *last-in, first-out principle*. Before the push, ESP = 00001000h; after the push, ESP = 00000FFCh. Figure 5–3 shows the same stack after pushing two more integers.

Figure 5–2   Pushing Integers on the Stack

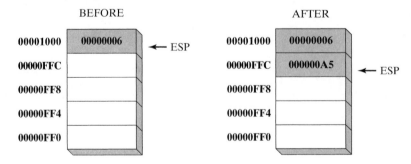

Pop Operation

A *pop* operation removes a value from the stack and copies it to a register or memory location. After the value is popped from the stack, the stack pointer is incremented to point to the next-highest location in the stack. Figure 5–4 shows the stack before and after the value 00000002 is popped from the stack.

FIGURE 5–3 Stack, after Pushing 00000001 and 00000002.

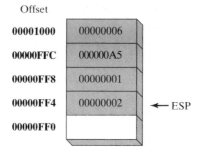

FIGURE 5–4 Popping a Value from the Runtime Stack.

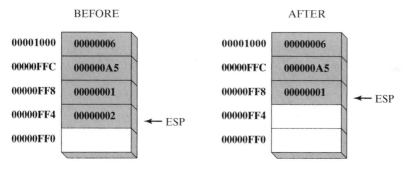

The area of the stack below ESP is *logically empty*, and will be overwritten the next time the current program executes any instruction that pushes a value on the stack.

Stack Applications

There are several important uses of runtime stacks in programs:

- A stack makes a convenient temporary save area for registers when they are used for more than one purpose. After they are modified, they can be restored to their original values.
- When the CALL instruction executes, the CPU saves the current procedure's return address on the stack.
- When calling a procedure, we often pass input values called *arguments* by pushing them on the stack.
- The stack provides temporary storage for local variables inside procedures.

5.4.2 PUSH and POP Instructions

PUSH Instruction

The PUSH instruction first decrements ESP and then copies a 16- or 32-bit source operand into the stack. A 16-bit operand causes ESP to be decremented by 2. A 32-bit operand causes ESP to be decremented by 4. There are three instruction formats:

```
PUSH  r/m16
PUSH  r/m32
PUSH  imm32
```

> If your program calls procedures from the Irvine32 library, you should always push 32-bit values; otherwise, the Win32 Console functions used by this library will not work correctly. If your program calls procedures from the Irvine16 library (in real-address mode), you can push both 16-bit and 32-bit values.

Immediate values are always 32 bits in protected mode. In real-address mode, immediate values default to 16 bits, unless the .386 processor (or higher) directive is used. (The .386 directive was introduced in Section 3.2.1).

POP Instruction

The POP instruction first copies the contents of the stack element pointed to by ESP into a 16- or 32-bit destination operand and then increments ESP. If the operand is 16 bits, ESP is incremented by 2; if the operand is 32 bits, ESP is incremented by 4:

```
POP  r/m16
POP  r/m32
```

PUSHFD and POPFD Instructions

The PUSHFD instruction pushes the 32-bit EFLAGS register on the stack, and POPFD pops the stack into EFLAGS:

```
pushfd
popfd
```

> 16-bit programs use the PUSHF instruction to push the 16-bit FLAGS register on the stack and POPF to pop the stack into FLAGS.

The MOV instruction cannot be used to copy the flags to a variable, so PUSHFD may be the best way to save the flags. There are times when it is useful to make a backup copy of the flags so you can restore them to their former values later. Often, we enclose a block of code within PUSHFD and POPFD:

```
pushfd                              ; save the flags
;
; any sequence of statements here...
;
popfd                               ; restore the flags
```

When using pushes and pops of this type, be sure the program's execution path does not skip over the POPFD instruction. When a program is modified over time, it can be tricky to remember where all the pushes and pops are located. The need for precise documentation is critical!

A less error-prone way to save and restore the flags is to push them on the stack and immediately pop them into a variable:

```
.data
saveFlags DWORD ?
.code
pushfd                              ; push flags on stack
pop  saveFlags                      ; copy into a variable
```

The following statements restore the flags from the same variable:

```
push saveFlags                      ; push saved flag values
popfd                               ; copy into the flags
```

PUSHAD, PUSHA, POPAD, and POPA

The PUSHAD instruction pushes all of the 32-bit general-purpose registers on the stack in the following order: EAX, ECX, EDX, EBX, ESP (value before executing PUSHAD), EBP, ESI, and EDI. The POPAD instruction pops the same registers off the stack in reverse order. Similarly, the PUSHA instruction, introduced with the 80286 processor, pushes the 16-bit general-purpose registers (AX, CX, DX, BX, SP, BP, SI, DI) on the stack in the order listed. The POPA instruction pops the same registers in reverse order.

If you write a procedure that modifies a number of 32-bit registers, use PUSHAD at the beginning of the procedure and POPAD at the end to save and restore the registers. The following code fragment is an example:

```
MySub PROC
      pushad                        ; save general-purpose registers
      .
      .
      mov eax,...
      mov edx,...
      mov ecx,...
      .
      .
      popad                         ; restore general-purpose registers
      ret
MySub ENDP
```

An important exception to the foregoing example must be pointed out: procedures returning results in one or more registers should not use PUSHA and PUSHAD. Suppose the following **ReadValue** procedure returns an integer in EAX; the call to POPAD overwrites the return value from EAX:

```
ReadValue PROC
      pushad                        ; save general-purpose registers
      .
      .
      mov eax,return_value
      .
      .
      popad                         ; overwrites EAX!
      ret
ReadValue ENDP
```

Example: Reversing a String

The *RevStr.asm* program loops through a string and pushes each character on the stack. It then pops the letters from the stack (in reverse order) and stores them back into the same string variable. Because the stack is a LIFO (*last-in, first-out*) structure, the letters in the string are reversed:

```
TITLE Reversing a String          (RevStr.asm)

INCLUDE Irvine32.inc
.data
aName BYTE "Abraham Lincoln",0
nameSize = ($ - aName) - 1

.code
main PROC
; Push the name on the stack.
      mov   ecx,nameSize
      mov   esi,0

L1:   movzx eax,aName[esi]          ; get character
      push  eax                     ; push on stack
      inc   esi
      loop  L1

; Pop the name from the stack, in reverse,
; and store in the aName array.
      mov   ecx,nameSize
      mov   esi,0
```

```
    L2:    pop    eax                    ; get character
           mov    aName[esi],al          ; store in string
           inc    esi
           loop   L2

       ; Display the name.
           mov    edx,OFFSET aName
           call   WriteString
           call   Crlf
           exit
    main ENDP
    END main
```

5.4.3 Section Review

1. Which two registers (in protected mode) manage the stack?

2. How is the runtime stack different from the stack abstract data type?

3. Why is the stack called a LIFO structure?

4. When a 32-bit value is pushed on the stack, what happens to ESP?

5. *(True/False)* Only 32-bit values should be pushed on the stack when using the Irvine32 library.

6. *(True/False)* Only 16-bit values should be pushed on the stack when using the Irvine16 library.

7. *(True/False)* Local variables in procedures are created on the stack.

8. *(True/False)* The PUSH instruction cannot have an immediate operand.

9. Which instruction pushes all of the 32-bit general purpose registers on the stack?

10. Which instruction pushes the 32-bit EFLAGS register on the stack?

11. Which instruction pops the stack into the EFLAGS register?

12. *Challenge:* Another assembler (called NASM) permits the PUSH instruction to list multiple specific registers. Why might this approach be better than the PUSHAD instruction in MASM? Here is an NASM example:

    ```
    PUSH EAX EBX ECX
    ```

13. *Challenge:* Suppose there were no PUSH instruction. Write a sequence of two other instructions that would accomplish the same as PUSH EAX.

5.5   Defining and Using Procedures

If you've already studied a high-level programming language, you know how useful it can be to divide programs into *subroutines*. A complicated problem is usually divided into separate tasks before it can be understood, implemented, and tested effectively. In assembly language, we typically use the term *procedure* to mean a subroutine. In other languages, subroutines are called methods or functions.

In terms of object-oriented programming, the functions or methods in a single class are roughly equivalent to the collection of procedures and data encapsulated in an assembly language module. Assembly language was created long before object-oriented programming, so it doesn't have the formal structure found in object-oriented languages. Assembly programmers must impose their own formal structure on programs.

5.5.1   PROC Directive

Defining a Procedure

Informally, we can define a *procedure* as a named block of statements that ends in a return statement. A procedure is declared using the PROC and ENDP directives. It must be assigned a name (a valid identifier). Each program we've written so far contains a procedure named **main**, for example,

```
main PROC
    .
    .
main ENDP
```

When you create a procedure other than your program's startup procedure, end it with a RET instruction. RET forces the CPU to return to the location from where the procedure was called:

```
sample PROC
    .
    .
    ret
sample ENDP
```

The startup procedure (**main**) is a special case because it ends with the **exit** statement. When you use the INCLUDE *Irvine32.inc* statement, **exit** is an alias for a call to **ExitProcess**, a system procedure that terminates the program:

```
INVOKE ExitProcess,0
```

(In Section 8.5.1 we introduce the INVOKE directive, which can call a procedure and pass arguments.)

If you use the INCLUDE *Irvine16.inc* statement, **exit** is translated to the **.EXIT** assembler directive. The latter causes the assembler to generate the following two instructions:

```
mov ah,4C00h      ; call MS-DOS function 4Ch
int 21h           ; terminate program
```

Example: Sum of Three Integers

Let's create a procedure named **SumOf** that calculates the sum of three 32-bit integers. We will assume that relevant integers are assigned to EAX, EBX, and ECX before the procedure is called. The procedure returns the sum in EAX:

```
SumOf PROC
    add   eax,ebx
    add   eax,ecx
    ret
SumOf ENDP
```

Documenting Procedures

A good habit to cultivate is that of adding clear and readable documentation to your programs. The following are a few suggestions for information that you can put at the beginning of each procedure:

- A description of all tasks accomplished by the procedure.
- A list of input parameters and their usage, labeled by a word such as **Receives**. If any input parameters have specific requirements for their input values, list them here.
- A description of any values returned by the procedure, labeled by a word such as **Returns**.
- A list of any special requirements, called *preconditions,* that must be satisfied before the procedure is called. These can be labeled by the word **Requires**. For example, for a procedure that draws a graphics line, a useful precondition would be that the video display adapter must already be in graphics mode.

The descriptive labels we've chosen, such as Receives, Returns, and Requires, are not absolutes; other useful names are often used.

With these ideas in mind, let's add appropriate documentation to the **SumOf** procedure:

```
;---------------------------------------------------------
Sumof PROC
;
; Calculates and returns the sum of three 32-bit integers.
; Receives: EAX, EBX, ECX, the three integers. May be
;           signed or unsigned.
; Returns:  EAX = sum
;---------------------------------------------------------
      add   eax,ebx
      add   eax,ecx
      ret
SumOf ENDP
```

Functions written in high-level languages like C and C++ typically return 8-bit values in AL, 16-bit values in AX, and 32-bit values in EAX.

5.5.2 CALL and RET Instructions

The CALL instruction calls a procedure by directing the processor to begin execution at a new memory location. The procedure uses a RET (return from procedure) instruction to bring the processor back to the point in the program where the procedure was called. Mechanically speaking, the CALL instruction pushes its return address on the stack and copies the called procedure's address into the instruction pointer. When the procedure is ready to return, its RET instruction pops the return address from the stack into the instruction pointer. In 32-bit mode, the CPU executes the instruction in memory pointed to by EIP (instruction pointer register). In 16-bit mode, IP points to the instruction.

Call and Return Example

Suppose that in **main**, a CALL statement is located at offset 00000020. Typically, this instruction requires five bytes of machine code, so the next statement (a MOV in this case) is located at offset 00000025:

```
                main PROC
00000020          call MySub
00000025          mov  eax,ebx
```

Next, suppose that the first executable instruction in **MySub** is located at offset 00000040:

```
                MySub PROC
00000040          mov eax,edx
                    .
                    .
                    .
                  ret
                MySub ENDP
```

When the CALL instruction executes (Figure 5–5), the address following the call (00000025) is pushed on the stack and the address of **MySub** is loaded into EIP. All instructions in **MySub** execute up to its RET instruction. When the RET instruction executes, the value in the stack pointed to by ESP is popped into EIP (step 1 in Figure 5–6). In step 2, ESP is decremented so it points to the previous value on the stack (step 2).

Nested Procedure Calls

A *nested procedure call* occurs when a called procedure calls another procedure before the first procedure returns. Suppose that **main** calls a procedure named **Sub1**. While **Sub1** is executing, it calls the **Sub2** procedure. While **Sub2** is executing, it calls the **Sub3** procedure. The process is shown in Figure 5–7.

Figure 5–5   Executing a CALL Instruction.

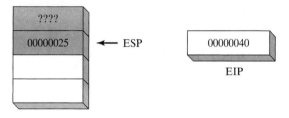

Figure 5–6   Executing the RET Instruction.

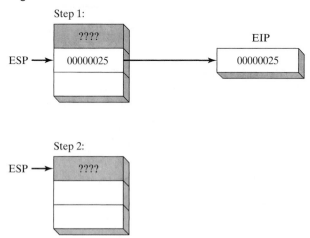

When the RET instruction at the end of **Sub3** executes, it pops the value at stack[ESP] into the instruction pointer. This causes execution to resume at the instruction following the call **Sub3** instruction. The following diagram shows the stack just before the return from **Sub3** is executed:

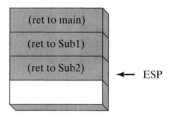

After the return, ESP points to the next-highest stack entry. When the RET instruction at the end of **Sub2** is about to execute, the stack appears as follows:

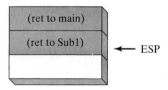

Figure 5–7   Nested Procedure Calls.

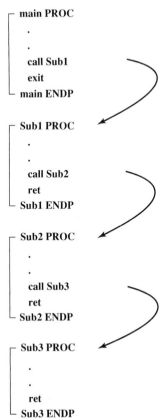

Finally, when **Sub1** returns, stack[ESP] is popped into the instruction pointer, and execution resumes in **main**:

Clearly, the stack proves itself a useful device for remembering information, including nested procedure calls. Stack structures, in general, are used in situations where programs must retrace their steps in a specific order.

Passing Register Arguments to Procedures

If you write a procedure that performs some standard operation such as calculating the sum of an integer array, it's not a good idea to include references to specific variable names inside the procedure. If you did, the procedure could only be used with one array. A better approach is to pass the offset of an array to the procedure and pass an integer specifying the number of array elements. We call these *arguments* (or *input parameters*). In assembly language, it is common to pass arguements inside general-purpose registers.

In the preceding section we created a simple procedure named **SumOf** that added the integers in the EAX, EBX, and ECX registers. In **main**, before calling **SumOf**, we assign values to EAX, EBX, and ECX:

```
.data
theSum   DWORD   ?
.code
main PROC
        mov     eax,10000h                      ; argument
        mov     ebx,20000h                      ; argument
        mov     ecx,30000h                      ; argument
        call    Sumof                           ; EAX = (EAX + EBX + ECX)
        mov     theSum,eax                      ; save the sum
```

After the CALL statement, we have the option of copying the sum in EAX to a variable.

5.5.3   Example: Summing an Integer Array

A very common type of loop that you may have already coded in C++ or Java is one that calculates the sum of an integer array. This is very easy to implement in assembly language, and it can be coded in such a way that it will run as fast as possible. For example, one can use registers rather than variables inside a loop.

Let's create a procedure named **ArraySum** that receives two parameters from a calling program: a pointer to an array of 32-bit integers, and a count of the number of array values. It calculates and returns the sum of the array in EAX:

```
;-----------------------------------------------------
ArraySum PROC
;
; Calculates the sum of an array of 32-bit integers.
; Receives: ESI = the array offset
;           ECX = number of elements in the array
; Returns:  EAX = sum of the array elements
;-----------------------------------------------------
        push    esi                     ; save ESI, ECX
        push    ecx
        mov     eax,0                   ; set the sum to zero

L1:     add     eax,[esi]               ; add each integer to sum
        add     esi,TYPE DWORD          ; point to next integer
        loop    L1                      ; repeat for array size

        pop     ecx                     ; restore ECX, ESI
        pop     esi
        ret                             ; sum is in EAX
ArraySum ENDP
```

Nothing in this procedure is specific to a certain array name or array size. It could be used in any program that needs to sum an array of 32-bit integers. Whenever possible, you should also create procedures that are flexible and adaptable.

Calling ArraySum   Following is an example of calling **ArraySum**, passing the address of **array** in ESI and the array count in ECX. After the call, we copy the sum in EAX to a variable:

```
.data
array   DWORD   10000h,20000h,30000h,40000h,50000h
theSum DWORD    ?
.code
```

```
main PROC
        mov     esi,OFFSET array        ; ESI points to array
        mov     ecx,LENGTHOF array      ; ECX = array count
        call    ArraySum                ; calculate the sum
        mov     theSum,eax              ; returned in EAX
```

5.5.4 Flowcharts

A *flowchart* is a well-established way of diagramming program logic[3]. Each shape in a flowchart represents a single logical step, and lines with arrows connecting the shapes show the ordering of the logical steps. Figure 5–8 shows the most common flowchart shapes. The same shape is used for begin/end connectors, as well as labels that are the targets of jump instructions.

FIGURE 5–8   Basic Flowchart Shapes.

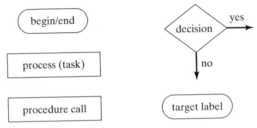

Text notations such as *yes* and *no* are added next to *decision* symbols to show branching directions. There is no required position for each arrow connected to a decision symbol. Each process symbol can contain one or more closely related instructions. The instructions need not be syntactically correct. For example, we could add 1 to CX using either of the following process symbols:

```
cx = cx + 1          add cx, 1
```

Let's use the **ArraySum** procedure from the preceding section to design a simple flowchart, shown in Figure 5–9. It uses a decision symbol for the LOOP instruction because LOOP must determine whether or not to transfer control to a label (based on the value of CX). A code insert shows the original procedure listing.

5.5.5 Saving and Restoring Registers

In the **ArraySum** example, ECX and ESI were pushed on the stack at the beginning of the procedure and popped at the end. This action is typical of most procedures that modify registers. Always save and restore registers that are modified by a procedure so the calling program can be sure that none of its own register values will be overwritten. The exception to this rule pertains to registers used as return values, usually EAX. Do not push and pop them.

USES Operator

The USES operator, coupled with the PROC directive, lets you list the names of all registers modified within a procedure. USES tells the assembler to do two things: First, generate PUSH instructions that save the registers on the stack at the beginning of the procedure. Second, generate POP instructions that restore the register values at the end of the procedure. The USES operator immediately follows PROC, and is itself followed by a list of registers on the same line separated by spaces or tabs (not commas).

Figure 5–9   Flowchart for the **ArraySum** Procedure.

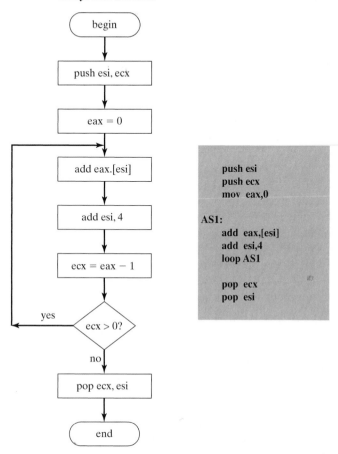

ArraySum Procedure

The **ArraySum** procedure from Section 5.5.3 used PUSH and POP instructions to save and restore ESI and ECX. The USES operator can more easily do the same:

```
ArraySum PROC USES esi ecx
     mov    eax,0                  ; set the sum to zero
L1:
     add    eax,[esi]             ; add each integer to sum
     add    esi,4                 ; point to next integer
     loop   L1                    ; repeat for array size

     ret                          ; sum is in EAX
ArraySum ENDP
```

The corresponding code generated by the assembler shows the effect of USES:

```
ArraySum PROC
     push   esi
     push   ecx
     mov    eax,0                  ; set the sum to zero
```

```
      L1:
              add     eax,[esi]              ; add each integer to sum
              add     esi,4                  ; point to next integer
              loop    L1                     ; repeat for array size

              pop     ecx
              pop     esi
              ret
      ArraySum ENDP
```

Debugging Tip: When using the Microsoft Visual Studio debugger, you can view the hidden machine instructions generated by MASM's advanced operators and directives. Select *Debug Windows* from the *View* menu, and select *Dissassembly*. This window displays your program's source code along with hidden machine instructions generated by the assembler.

Exception There is an important exception to our standing rule about saving registers that applies when a procedure returns a value in a register (usually EAX). In this case, the return register should not be pushed and popped. For example, in the **SumOf** procedure, if we were to push and pop EAX, the procedure's return value would be lost:

```
      SumOf PROC                         ; sum of three integers
              push    eax                ; save EAX
              add     eax,ebx            ; calculate the sum
              add     eax,ecx            ; of EAX, EBX, ECX
              pop     eax                ; lost the sum!
              ret
      SumOf ENDP
```

5.5.6 Section Review

1. *(True/False):* The PROC directive begins a procedure and the ENDP directive ends a procedure.

2. *(True/False):* It is possible to define a procedure inside an existing procedure.

3. What would happen if the RET instruction was omitted from a procedure?

4. How are the words *Receives* and *Returns* used in the suggested procedure documentation?

5. *(True/False):* The CALL instruction pushes the offset of the CALL instruction on the stack.

6. *(True/False):* The CALL instruction pushes the offset of the instruction following the CALL on the stack.

7. *(True/False):* The RET instruction pops the top of the stack into the instruction pointer.

8. *(True/False):* Nested procedure calls are not permitted by the Microsoft assembler unless the NESTED operator is used in the procedure definition.

9. *(True/False):* In protected mode, each procedure call uses a minimum of 4 bytes of stack space.

10. *(True/False):* The ESI and EDI registers cannot be used when passing parameters to procedures.

11. *(True/False):* The **ArraySum** procedure (Section 5.5.3) receives a pointer to any array of doublewords.

12. *(True/False):* The USES operator lets you name all registers that are modified within a procedure.

13. *(True/False):* The USES operator only generates PUSH instructions, so you must code POP instructions yourself.

14. *(True/False):* The register list in the USES directive must use commas to separate the register names.

15. Which statement(s) in the **ArraySum** procedure (Section 5.5.3) would have to be modified so it could accumulate an array of 16-bit words? Create such a version of ArraySum and test it.

5.6   Program Design Using Procedures

Any programming application beyond the trivial tends to involve a number of different tasks. One could code all tasks in a single procedure, but the program would be difficult to read and maintain. Instead, it's best to dedicate a separate procedure for each task.

When creating a program, create a set of specifications that list exactly what the program is supposed to do. The specifications should be the result of careful analysis of the problem you're trying to solve. Then design the program based on the specifications. A standard design approach is to divide an overall problem into discrete tasks, a process known as *functional decomposition, or top-down design*. It relies on some basic principles:

- A large problem may be more easily divided into small tasks.
- A program is easier to maintain if each procedure is tested separately.
- A top-down design lets you see how procedures are related to each other.
- When you are sure of the overall design, you can more easily concentrate on details, writing code that implements each procedure.

In the next section, we demonstrate the top-down design approach for a program that inputs integers and calculates their sum. Although the program is simple, the same approach can be applied to programs of almost any size.

5.6.1   Integer Summation Program (Design)

The following are specifications for a simple program that we will call **Integer Summation**:

> Write a program that prompts the user for three 32-bit integers, stores them in an array, calculates the sum of the array, and displays the sum on the screen.

The following pseudocode shows how we might divide the specifications into tasks:

```
Integer Summation Program
      Prompt user for three integers
      Calculate the sum of the array
      Display the sum
```

In preparation for writing a program, let's assign a procedure name to each task:

```
Main
      PromptForIntegers
      ArraySum
      DisplaySum
```

In assembly language, input-output tasks often require detailed code to implement. To reduce some of this detail, we can call procedures that clear the screen, display a string, input an integer, and display an integer:

```
Main
      Clrscr                          ; clear screen
      PromptForIntegers
         WriteString                  ; display string
         ReadInt                      ; input integer
      ArraySum                        ; sum the integers
      DisplaySum
         WriteString                  ; display string
         WriteInt                     ; display integer
```

Structure Chart   The diagram in Figure 5–10, called a *structure chart*, describes the program's structure. Procedures from the link library are shaded.

FIGURE 5–10   Structure Chart for the Summation Program.

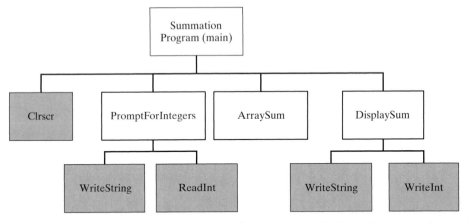

Stub Program   Let's create a minimal version of the program called a *stub program*. It contains only empty (or nearly empty) procedures. The program assembles and runs, but does not actually do anything useful:

```
TITLE Integer Summation Program        (Sum1.asm)

; This program prompts the user for three integers,
; stores them in an array, calculates the sum of the
; array, and displays the sum.

INCLUDE Irvine32.inc
.code
main PROC
; Main program control procedure.
; Calls: Clrscr, PromptForIntegers,
;        ArraySum, DisplaySum

    exit
main ENDP

;------------------------------------------------------
PromptForIntegers PROC
;
; Prompts the user for three integers, inserts
; them in an array.
; Receives: ESI points to an array of
;   doubleword integers, ECX = array size.
; Returns: nothing
; Calls: ReadInt, WriteString
;------------------------------------------------------
    ret
PromptForIntegers ENDP

;------------------------------------------------------
ArraySum PROC
;
; Calculates the sum of an array of 32-bit integers.
```

```
; Receives: ESI points to the array, ECX = array size
; Returns:  EAX = sum of the array elements
;----------------------------------------------------
      ret
ArraySum ENDP

;----------------------------------------------------
DisplaySum PROC
;
; Displays the sum on the screen.
; Receives: EAX = the sum
; Returns: nothing
; Calls: WriteString, WriteInt
;----------------------------------------------------
      ret
DisplaySum ENDP
END main
```

A stub program gives you the chance to map out all procedure calls, study the dependencies between procedures, and possibly improve the structural design before coding the details. Use comments in each procedure to explain its purpose and parameter requirements.

5.6.2   Integer Summation Implementation

Let's complete the summation program. We will declare an array of three integers and use a defined constant for the array size in case we want to change it later:

```
INTEGER_COUNT = 3
array DWORD  INTEGER_COUNT DUP(?)
```

A couple of strings are used as screen prompts:

```
str1  BYTE  "Enter a signed integer: ",0
str2  BYTE  "The sum of the integers is: ",0
```

The **main** procedure clears the screen, passes an array pointer to the **PromptForIntegers** procedure, calls **ArraySum**, and calls **DisplaySum**:

```
call Clrscr
mov  esi,OFFSET array
mov  ecx,INTEGER_COUNT
call PromptForIntegers
call ArraySum
call DisplaySum
```

- **PromptForIntegers** calls **WriteString** to prompt the user for an integer. It then calls ReadInt to input the integer from the user, and stores the integer in the array pointed to by ESI. A loop executes these steps multiple times.
- **ArraySum** calculates and returns the sum of an array of integers.
- **DisplaySum** displays a message on the screen ("The sum of the integers is:") and calls WriteInt to display the integer in EAX.

Finished Program Listing   The following listing shows the completed Summation program:

```
TITLE Integer Summation Program    (Sum2.asm)

; This program prompts the user for three integers,
; stores them in an array, calculates the sum of the
; array, and displays the sum.
```

```
        INCLUDE Irvine32.inc

        INTEGER_COUNT = 3

        .data
        str1  BYTE  "Enter a signed integer: ",0
        str2  BYTE  "The sum of the integers is: ",0
        array DWORD  INTEGER_COUNT DUP(?)

        .code
        main PROC
             call  Clrscr
             mov   esi,OFFSET array
             mov   ecx,INTEGER_COUNT
             call  PromptForIntegers
             call  ArraySum
             call  DisplaySum
             exit
        main ENDP

        ;------------------------------------------------------
        PromptForIntegers PROC USES ecx edx esi
        ;
        ; Prompts the user for an arbitrary number of integers
        ; and inserts the integers into an array.
        ; Receives: ESI points to the array, ECX = array size
        ; Returns:  nothing
        ;------------------------------------------------------
             mov   edx,OFFSET str1       ; "Enter a signed integer"
        L1:  call  WriteString           ; display string
             call  ReadInt               ; read integer into EAX
             call  Crlf                  ; go to next output line
             mov   [esi],eax             ; store in array
             add   esi,TYPE DWORD        ; next integer
             loop  L1
             ret
        PromptForIntegers ENDP

        ;------------------------------------------------------
        ArraySum PROC USES esi ecx
        ;
        ; Calculates the sum of an array of 32-bit integers.
        ; Receives: ESI points to the array, ECX = number
        ;   of array elements
        ; Returns:  EAX = sum of the array elements
        ;------------------------------------------------------
             mov   eax,0                 ; set the sum to zero
        L1:  add   eax,[esi]             ; add each integer to sum
             add   esi,TYPE DWORD        ; point to next integer
             loop  L1                    ; repeat for array size
             ret                         ; sum is in EAX
        ArraySum ENDP

        ;------------------------------------------------------
        DisplaySum PROC USES edx
        ;
        ; Displays the sum on the screen
        ; Receives: EAX = the sum
```

```
    ; Returns:  nothing
    ;---------------------------------------------------
        mov    edx,OFFSET str2          ; "The sum of the..."
        call   WriteString
        call   WriteInt                 ; display EAX
        call   Crlf
        ret
    DisplaySum ENDP
    END main
```

5.6.3   Section Review

1.   What is the name given to the process of dividing up large tasks into smaller ones?

2.   Which procedures in the Summation program design (Section 5.6.1) are located in the Irvine32 library?

3.   What is a *stub program*?

4.   *(True/False):* The **ArraySum** procedure of the Summation program (Section 5.6.1) directly references the name of an array variable.

5.   Which lines in the **PromptForIntegers** procedure of the Summation program (Section 5.6.1) would have to be modified so it could handle an array of 16-bit words? Create such a version and test it.

6.   Draw a flowchart for the **PromptForIntegers** procedure of the Summation program (flowcharts were introduced in Section 5.5.4).

5.7   Chapter Summary

This chapter introduces the book's link library to make it easier for you to process input-output in assembly language applications.

Table 5–1 lists most of the procedures from the Irvine32 link library. The most up-to-date listing of all procedures is available on the book's Web site (www.asmirvine.com).

The *library test program* in Section 5.3.3 demonstrates a number of input-output functions from the Irvine32 library. It generates and displays a list of random numbers, a register dump, and a memory dump. It displays integers in various formats and demonstrates string input/output.

The *runtime stack* is a special array that is used as a temporary holding area for addresses and data. The ESP register holds a 32-bit OFFSET into some location on the stack. The stack is called a LIFO structure (*last-in, first-out*) because the last value placed in the stack is the first value taken out. A *push* operation copies a value into the stack. A *pop* operation removes a value from the stack and copies it to a register or variable. Stacks often hold procedure return addresses, procedure parameters, local variables, and registers used internally by procedures.

The PUSH instruction first decrements the stack pointer and then copies a source operand into the stack. The POP instruction first copies the contents of the stack pointed to by ESP into a 16- or 32-bit destination operand and then increments ESP.

The PUSHAD instruction pushes the 32-bit general-purpose registers on the stack, and the PUSHA instruction does the same for the 16-bit general-purpose registers. The POPAD instruction pops the stack into the 32-bit general-purpose registers, and the POPA instruction does the same for the 16-bit general-purpose registers.

The PUSHFD instruction pushes the 32-bit EFLAGS register on the stack, and POPFD pops the stack into EFLAGS. PUSHF and POPF do the same for the 16-bit FLAGS register.

The *RevStr* program (Section 5.4.2) uses the stack to reverse a string of characters.

A *procedure* is a named block of code declared using the PROC and ENDP directives. A procedure's execution ends with the RET instruction. The **SumOf** procedure, shown in Section 5.5.1, calculates the sum of three integers. The CALL instruction executes a procedure by inserting the procedure's address into the instruction pointer register. When the procedure finishes, the RET (return from procedure) instruction brings the processor back to the point in the program from where the procedure was called. A *nested procedure call* occurs when a called procedure calls another procedure before it returns.

Acode label followed by a single colon is local to its enclosing procedure. A code label followed by :: is a global label, making it accessible from any statement in the same source code file.

The **ArraySum** procedure, shown in Section 5.5.3, calculates and returns the sum of the elements in an array.

The USES operator, coupled with the PROC directive, lets you list all registers modified by a procedure. The assembler generates code that pushes the registers at the beginning of the procedure and pops the registers before returning.

A program of any size should be carefully designed from a set of clear specifications. A standard approach is to use functional decomposition (top-down design) to divide the program into procedures (functions). First, determine the ordering and connections between procedures, and later fill in the procedure details.

5.8   Programming Exercises

When you write programs to solve the programming exercises, use multiple procedures when possible. Follow the style and naming conventions used in this book, unless instructed otherwise by your instructor. Use explanatory comments in your programs at the beginning of each procedure and next to nontrivial statements. As a bonus, your instructor may ask you to provide flowcharts and/or pseudocode for solution programs.

1.   Draw Text Colors

Write a program that displays the same string in four different colors, using a loop. Call the **SetTextColor** procedure from the book's link library. Any colors may be chosen, but you may find it easiest to change the foreground color.

2.   File of Fibonacci Numbers

Challenge: Using Programming Exercise 6 in Chapter 4 as a starting point, write a program that generates the first 47 values in the *Fibonacci* series, stores them in an array of doublewords, and writes the doubleword array to a disk file. You need not perform any error checking on the file I/O because conditional processing has not been covered yet. Your output file size should be 188 bytes because each doubleword is 4 bytes. Use debug.exe or Visual Studio to open and inspect the file contents, shown here in hexadecimal:

```
00000000  01 00 00 00 01 00 00 00   02 00 00 00 03 00 00 00
00000010  05 00 00 00 08 00 00 00   0D 00 00 00 15 00 00 00
00000020  22 00 00 00 37 00 00 00   59 00 00 00 90 00 00 00
00000030  E9 00 00 00 79 01 00 00   62 02 00 00 DB 03 00 00
00000040  3D 06 00 00 18 0A 00 00   55 10 00 00 6D 1A 00 00
00000050  C2 2A 00 00 2F 45 00 00   F1 6F 00 00 20 B5 00 00
00000060  11 25 01 00 31 DA 01 00   42 FF 02 00 73 D9 04 00
00000070  B5 D8 07 00 28 B2 0C 00   DD 8A 14 00 05 3D 21 00
00000080  E2 C7 35 00 E7 04 57 00   C9 CC 8C 00 B0 D1 E3 00
00000090  79 9E 70 01 29 70 54 02   A2 0E C5 03 CB 7E 19 06
000000a0  6D 8D DE 09 38 0C F8 0F   A5 99 D6 19 DD A5 CE 29
000000b0  82 3F A5 43 5F E5 73 6D   E1 24 19 B1
```

3. Simple Addition (1)

Write a program that clears the screen, locates the cursor near the middle of the screen, prompts the user for two integers, adds the integers, and displays their sum.

4. Simple Addition (2)

Use the solution program from the preceding exercise as a starting point. Let this new program repeat the same steps three times, using a loop. Clear the screen after each loop iteration.

5. Random Integers

Write a program that generates and displays 50 random integers between -20 and $+20$.

6. Random Strings

Write a program that generates and displays 20 random strings, each consisting of 10 capital letters {A..Z}.

7. Random Screen Locations

Write a program that displays a single character at 100 random screen locations, using a timing delay of 100 milliseconds. *Hint:* Use the GetMaxXY procedure to determine the current size of the console window.

8. Color Matrix

Write a program that displays a single character in all possible combinations of foreground and background colors ($16 \times 16 = 256$). The colors are numbered from 0 to 15, so you can use a nested loop to generate all possible combinations.

9. Summation Program

Modify the Summation program in Section 5.6.1 as follows: Select an array size using a constant:

```
ARRAY_SIZE = 20
array DWORD  ARRAY_SIZE DUP(?)
```

Write a new procedure that prompts the user for the number of integers to be processed. Pass the same value to the PromptForIntegers procedure. If the user enters a value larger than ARRAY_SIZE, display an error message and halt further processing of the array. For example,

```
How many integers wil be added? 21
The array cannot be larger than 20
```

Design the program in such a way that changing ARRAY_SIZE automatically updates the error message just shown.

End Notes

1. If you would like to read more about random number generators, see Donald Knuth, *The Art of Computer Programming*, Vol. 2, Addison-Wesley, 1997.
2. This amounts to shifting the bits left four positions, which you will read about in Chapter 7.
3. Flowcharts have disappeared from most introductory programming textbooks because they are not suited to object-oriented programming. In assembly language, they still prove useful.

6

Conditional Processing

6.1 Introduction

A programming language that permits decision making lets you alter the flow of control, using a technique known as conditional branching. Every IF statement, switch statement, or conditional loop found in high-level languages has built-in branching logic. Assembly language, as primitive as it is, provides all the tools you need for decision-making logic. In this chapter, we will see how the translation works, from high-level conditional statements to low-level implementation code.

Programs that deal with hardware devices must be able to manipulate individual bits in numbers. Individual bits must be tested, cleared, and set. Data encryption and compression also rely on bit manipulation. We will show how to do these operations in assembly language.

This chapter should answer some basic questions:

- How can I use the boolean operations introduced in Chapter 1 (AND, OR, NOT)?
- How do I write an IF statement in assembly language?
- How are nested-IF statements translated by compilers into machine language?
- How can I set and clear individual bits in a binary number?
- How can I perform simple binary data encryption?
- How are signed numbers differentiated from unsigned numbers in boolean expressions?
- What's a finite-state machine?
- Is GOTO really harmful[1]?

   This chapter follows a *bottom-up* approach, starting with the binary foundations behind programming logic. Next, you will see how the CPU compares instruction operands, using the CMP instruction and the processor status flags. Finally, we put it all together and show how to use assembly language to implement logic structures characteristic of high-level languages.

6.2   Boolean and Comparison Instructions

Let's begin our study of conditional processing by working at the binary level, using four basic operations of boolean algebra: AND, OR, XOR, and NOT. These operations are used in the design of computer hardware and software.

   The IA-32 instruction set contains the AND, OR, XOR, NOT, TEST, and BT*op* instructions, which directly implement boolean operations between bytes, words, and doublewords (see Table 6-1).

Table 6-1   Selected Boolean Instructions.

Operation	Description
AND	Boolean AND operation between a source operand and a destination operand.
OR	Boolean OR operation between a source operand and a destination operand.
XOR	Boolean exclusive-OR operation between a source operand and a destination operand.
NOT	Boolean NOT operation on a destination operand.
TEST	Implied boolean AND operation between a source and destination operand, setting the CPU flags appropriately.
BT, BTC, BTR, BTS	Copy bit n from the source operand to the Carry flag and complement/reset/set the same bit in the destination operand (covered in Section 6.3.5).

6.2.1   The CPU Flags

Boolean instructions affect the Zero, Carry, Sign, Overflow, and Parity flags. Here's a quick review of their meanings:

- The Zero flag is set when the result of an operation equals zero.
- The Carry flag is set when an instruction generates a result that is too large (or too small) for the destination operand when viewed as an unsigned integer.
- The Sign flag is a copy of the high bit of the destination operand, indicating that it is negative if *set* and positive if *clear*. (Zero is assumed to be positive.)
- The Overflow flag is set when an instruction generates an invalid signed result.
- The Parity flag is set when an instruction generates an even number of 1 bits in the low byte of the destination operand.

6.2.2 AND Instruction

The AND instruction performs a boolean (bitwise) AND operation between each pair of matching bits in two operands and places the result in the destination operand:

```
AND   destination,source
```

The following operand combinations are permitted:

```
AND  reg,reg
AND  reg,mem
AND  reg,imm
AND  mem,reg
AND  mem,imm
```

The operands can be 8, 16, or 32 bits, and they must be the same size. For each matching bit in the two operands, the following rule applies: If both bits equal 1, the result bit is 1; otherwise, it is 0. The following truth table from Chapter 1 labels the input bits x and y. The third column shows the value of the expression $x \wedge y$:

x	y	$x \wedge y$
0	0	0
0	1	0
1	0	0
1	1	1

The AND instruction is often used to clear selected bits and preserve others. In the following example, the upper four bits are cleared and the lower four bits are unchanged:

```
              00111011
     AND      00001111
                _____
cleared ——— |0 0 0 0|1 0 1 1|——— unchanged
```

The following instructions carry out this operation:

```
mov al,00111011b
and al,00001111b
```

The lower four bits might contain useful information, whereas we don't care about the upper four bits. It is useful to think of this technique as *bit extraction* because the lower four bits are "pulled" from AL.

Flags   The AND instruction always clears the Overflow and Carry flags. It modifies the Sign, Zero, and Parity flags according to the value of the destination operand.

Converting Characters to Upper Case

The AND instruction provides an easy way to translate a letter from lowercase to uppercase. If we compare the ASCII codes of capital **A** and lowercase **a**, it becomes clear that only bit 5 is different:

```
0 1 1 0 0 0 0 1 = 61h ('a')
0 1 0 0 0 0 0 1 = 41h ('A')
```

The rest of the alphabetic characters have the same relationship. If we AND any character with 11011111 binary, all bits are unchanged except for bit 5, which is cleared. In the following example, all characters in an array are converted to uppercase:

```
.data
```

```
      array BYTE 50 DUP(?)
      .code
            mov     ecx,LENGTHOF array
            mov     esi,OFFSET array
      L1:   and     BYTE PTR [esi],11011111b          ; clear bit 5
            inc     esi
            loop    L1
```

6.2.3   OR Instruction

The OR instruction performs a boolean OR operation between each pair of matching bits in two operands and places the result in the destination operand:

      OR   *destination,source*

The OR instruction uses the same operand combinations as the AND instruction:

      OR *reg,reg*
      OR *reg,mem*
      OR *reg,imm*
      OR *mem,reg*
      OR *mem,imm*

The operands can be 8, 16, or 32 bits, and they must be the same size. For each matching bit in the two operands, the output bit is 1 when at least one of the input bits is 1. The following truth table (from Chapter 1) describes the boolean expression **x** ∨ **y**:

x	**y**	**x** ∨ **y**
0	0	0
0	1	1
1	0	1
1	1	1

The OR instruction is often used to set selected bits and preserve others. In the following figure, 3Bh is ORed with 0Fh. The lower four bits of the result are set and the high four bits are unchanged:

```
                        00111011
                  OR    00001111
      unchanged ———— 0011 1111 ———— set
```

The OR instruction can be used to convert a byte containing an integer between 0 and 9 into an ASCII digit. To do this, you must set bits 4 and 5. If, for example, AL = 05h, you can OR it with 30h to convert it to the ASCII code for the digit 5 (35h):

```
                  00000101      05h
            OR    00110000      30h

                  00110101      35h, '5'
```

The assembly language instructions to do this are as follows:

```
      mov   dl,5                         ; binary value
      or    dl,30h                       ; convert to ASCII
```

Flags   The OR instruction always clears the Carry and Overflow flags. It modifies the Sign, Zero, and Parity flags according to the value of the destination operand. For example, you can OR a number with itself (or zero) to obtain certain information about its value:

```
or    al,al
```

The values of the Zero and Sign flags indicate the following about the contents of AL:

Zero Flag	Sign Flag	Value in AL is . . .
Clear	Clear	Greater than zero
Set	Clear	Equal to zero
Clear	Set	Less than zero

6.2.4 XOR Instruction

The XOR instruction performs a boolean exclusive-OR operation between each pair of matching bits in two operands and stores the result in the destination operand:

```
XOR   destination,source
```

The XOR instruction uses the same operand combinations and sizes as the AND and OR instructions. For each matching bit in the two operands, the following applies: If both bits are the same (both 0 or both 1), the result is 0; otherwise, the result is 1. The following truth table describes the boolean expression $x \oplus y$:

x	y	$x \oplus y$
0	0	0
0	1	1
1	0	1
1	1	0

A bit exclusive-ORed with 0 retains its value, and a bit exclusive-ORed with 1 is toggled (complemented). XOR reverses itself when applied twice to the same operand. The following truth table shows that when bit x is exclusive-ORed with bit y twice, it reverts to its original value:

x	y	$x \oplus y$	$(x \oplus y) \oplus y$
0	0	0	0
0	1	1	0
1	0	1	1
1	1	0	1

As you will find out in Section 6.3.4, this "reversible" property of XOR makes it an ideal tool for a simple form of symmetric encryption.

Flags   The XOR instruction always clears the Overflow and Carry flags. It modifies the Sign, Zero, and Parity flags according to the value of the destination operand.

Checking the Parity Flag   The Parity flag indicates whether the *lowest byte* of the result of a bitwise or arithmetic operation has an even or odd number of 1 bits. The flag is set when the parity is

even and it is clear when the parity is odd. One way to check the parity of a number without changing
its value is to exclusive-OR the number with all zeros:

```
mov   al,10110101b                   ; 5 bits = odd parity
xor   al,0                           ; Parity flag clear (PO)
mov   al,11001100b                   ; 4 bits = even parity
xor   al,0                           ; Parity flag set (PE)
```

(Debuggers often use PE to indicate even parity and PO to indicate odd parity.)

16-Bit Parity   You can check the parity of a 16-bit register by performing an exclusive-OR between
the upper and lower bytes:

```
mov   ax,64C1h                       ; 0110 0100 1100 0001
xor   ah,al                          ; Parity flag set (PE)
```

Imagine the set bits (bits equal to 1) in each register as being members of an 8-bit set. The XOR
instruction zeroes all bits belonging to the intersection of the sets. XOR also forms the union between
the remaining bits. The parity of this union will be the same as the parity of the entire 16-bit integer.

What about 32-bit values? If we number the bytes from B_0 through B_3, we can calculate the parity
as B_0 XOR B_1 XOR B_2 XOR B_3.

6.2.5   NOT Instruction

The NOT instruction toggles all bits in an operand. The result is called the *one's complement*. The following operand types are permitted:

```
NOT reg
NOT mem
```

For example, the one's complement of F0h is 0Fh:

```
mov   al,11110000b
not   al                             ; AL = 00001111b
```

Flags   No flags are affected by the NOT instruction.

6.2.6   TEST Instruction

The TEST instruction performs an implied AND operation between each pair of matching bits in two
operands and sets the flags accordingly. The only difference between TEST and AND is that TEST
does not modify the destination operand. The TEST instruction permits the same operand combinations as the AND instruction. TEST is particularly valuable for finding out whether individual bits in
an operand are set.

Example: Testing Multiple Bits   The TEST instruction can check several bits at once. Suppose we
want to know whether bit 0 or bit 3 is set in the AL register. We can use the following instruction to
find this out:

```
test al,00001001b                    ; test bits 0 and 3
```

(The value 00001001 in this example is called a *bit mask*.) From the following example data sets, we
can infer that the Zero flag is set only when all tested bits are clear:

```
0 0 1 0 0 1 0 1  <- input value
0 0 0 0 1 0 0 1  <- test value
0 0 0 0 0 0 0 1  <- result: ZF = 0

0 0 1 0 0 1 0 0  <- input value
0 0 0 0 1 0 0 1  <- test value
0 0 0 0 0 0 0 0  <- result: ZF = 1
```

Flags   The TEST instruction always clears the Overflow and Carry flags. It modifies the Sign, Zero, and Parity flags in the same way as the AND instruction.

6.2.7   CMP Instruction

The CMP (compare) instruction performs an implied subtraction of a source operand from a destination operand. Neither operand is modified:

```
CMP destination,source
```

CMP uses the same operand combinations as the AND instruction.

Flags   The CMP instruction changes the Overflow, Sign, Zero, Carry, Auxiliary Carry, and Parity flags according to the value the destination operand would have had if the SUB instruction had been used. When two unsigned operands are compared, the Zero and Carry flags indicate the following relations between operands:

CMP Results	ZF	CF
Destination < source	0	1
Destination > source	0	0
Destination = source	1	0

When two signed operands are compared, the Sign, Zero, and Overflow flags indicate the following relations between operands:

CMP Results	Flags
Destination < source	$SF \neq OF$
Destination > source	$SF = OF$
Destination = source	$ZF = 1$

CMP is a valuable tool for creating conditional logic structures. When you follow CMP with a conditional jump instruction, the result is the assembly language equivalent of an IF statement.

Examples   Let's look at three code fragments showing how flags are affected by the CMP instruction. When AX equals 5 and is compared to 10, the Carry flag is set because subtracting 10 from 5 requires a borrow:

```
mov   ax,5
cmp   ax,10                          ; ZF = 0 and CF = 1
```

Comparing 1000 to 1000 sets the Zero flag because subtracting the source from the destination produces zero:

```
mov   ax,1000
mov   cx,1000
cmp   cx,ax                          ; ZF = 1 and CF = 0
```

Comparing 105 to 0 clears both the Zero and Carry flags because 105 is greater than 0:

```
mov   si,105
cmp   si,0                           ; ZF = 0 and CF = 0
```

6.2.8 Setting and Clearing Individual CPU Flags

How can you easily set or clear the Zero, Sign, Carry, and Overflow flags? There are several ways, most of which require modifying the destination operand. To set the Zero flag, TEST or AND an operand with Zero; to clear the Zero flag, OR an operand with 1:

```
test  al,0                 ; set Zero flag
and   al,0                 ; set Zero flag
or    al,1                 ; clear Zero flag
```

TEST does not modify the operand, whereas AND does. To set the Sign flag, OR the highest bit of an operand with 1. To clear the sign flag, AND the highest bit with 0:

```
or    al,80h               ; set Sign flag
and   al,7Fh               ; clear Sign flag
```

To set the Carry flag, use the STC instruction; to clear the Carry flag, use CLC:

```
stc                        ; set Carry flag
clc                        ; clear Carry flag
```

To set the Overflow flag, add two positive byte values that produce a negative sum. To clear the Overflow flag, OR an operand with 0:

```
mov   al,7Fh               ; AL = +127
inc   al                   ; AL = 80h (-128), OF=1
or    eax,0                ; clear Overflow flag
```

6.2.9 Section Review

1. In the following instruction sequence, show the changed value of AL where indicated, in binary:

```
mov   al,01101111b
and   al,00101101b         ; a.
mov   al,6Dh
and   al,4Ah               ; b.
mov   al,00001111b
or    al,61h               ; c.
mov   al,94h
xor   al,37h               ; d.
```

2. In the following instruction sequence, show the changed value of AL where indicated, in hexadecimal:

```
mov   al,7Ah
not   al                   ; a.
mov   al,3Dh
and   al,74h               ; b.
mov   al,9Bh
or    al,35h               ; c.
mov   al,72h
xor   al,0DCh              ; d.
```

3. In the following instruction sequence, show the values of the Carry, Zero, and Sign flags where indicated:

```
mov   al,00001111b
test  al,2                 ; a. CF=    ZF=    SF=
mov   al,6
cmp   al,5                 ; b. CF=    ZF=    SF=
mov   al,5
cmp   al,7                 ; c. CF=    ZF=    SF=
```

4. Write a single instruction using 16-bit operands that clears the high 8 bits of AX and does not change the low 8 bits.

5. Write a single instruction using 16-bit operands that sets the high 8 bits of AX and does not change the low 8 bits.

6. Write a single instruction (other than NOT) that reverses all the bits in EAX.

7. Write instructions that set the Zero flag if the 32-bit value in EAX is even and clear the Zero flag if EAX is odd.

8. Write a single instruction that converts an uppercase character in AL to lowercase but does not modify AL if it already contains a lowercase letter.

9. Write a single instruction that converts an ASCII digit in AL to its corresponding binary value. If AL already contains a binary value (00h to 09h), leave it unchanged.

10. *Challenge:* Write instructions that calculate the parity of the 32-bit memory operand. *Hint:* Use the formula presented earlier in this section: B_0 XOR B_1 XOR B_2 XOR B_3

6.3 Conditional Jumps

6.3.1 Conditional Structures

There are no high-level logic structures in the IA-32 instruction set, but you can implement any logic structure, no matter how complex, using a combination of comparisons and jumps. Two steps are involved in executing a conditional statement: First, an operation such as CMP, AND, or SUB modifies the CPU flags. Second, a conditional jump instruction tests the flags and causes a branch to a new address. Let's look at a couple of examples.

Example 1   The CMP instruction in the following example compares AL to Zero. The JZ (jump if Zero) instruction jumps to label **L1** if the Zero flag was set by the CMP instruction:

```
      cmp    al,0
      jz     L1                       ; jump if ZF = 1
         .
         .
   L1:
```

Example 2   The AND instruction in the following example performs a bitwise AND on the DL register, affecting the Zero flag. The JNZ (jump if not Zero) instruction jumps if the Zero flag is clear:

```
      and    dl,10110000b
      jnz    L2                       ; jump if ZF = 0
         .
         .
   L2:
```

6.3.2 *Jcond* Instruction

A conditional jump instruction branches to a destination label when a flag condition is true. If the flag condition is false, the instruction immediately following the conditional jump is executed. The syntax is as follows:

Jcond destination

cond refers to a flag condition identifying the state of one or more flags. For example:

jc	Jump if carry (Carry flag set)
jnc	Jump if not carry (Carry flag clear)
jz	Jump if zero (Zero flag set)
jnz	Jump if not zero (Zero flag clear)

Flags are almost always set by arithmetic, comparison, and boolean instructions. Conditional jump instructions evaluate the flag states, using them to determine whether or not jumps should be taken.

Limitations By default, MASM requries the *destination* of the jump to be a label within the current procedure (we mentioned this with JMP in Chapter 5). To get around this restriction, you can declare a global label (followed by ::):

```
jc   MyLabel
     .
     .
     .
MyLabel::
```

In general, you should avoid jumping outside the current procedure. Doing so makes a program difficult to debug.

Prior to the Intel 386, the jump's range was limited to a 1-byte offset (positive or negative) from the location of the next instruction following the jump. IA-32 processors can jump anywhere within the same memory segment.

Using the CMP Instruction Suppose we want to jump to location **L1** when AX equals 5. In the next example, suppose AX equals 5: Then the CMP instruction sets the Zero flag and the JE instruction jumps because the Zero flag is set:

```
cmp  ax,5
je   L1                          ; jump if equal
```

If AX were not equal to 5, CMP would clear the Zero flag, and the JE instruction would not jump. In the following example, the jump is taken because AX is less than 6:

```
mov  ax,5
cmp  ax,6
jl   L1                          ; jump if less
```

In the following example, the jump is taken because AX is greater than 4:

```
mov  ax,5
cmp  ax,4
jg   L1                          ; jump if greater
```

6.3.3 Types of Conditional Jump Instructions

The IA-32 instruction set has a surprising number of conditional jump instructions. They support a full range of conditional statements for comparing signed and unsigned integers and checking CPU flags. The conditional jump instructions can be divided into four groups:

- Based on specific flag values.
- Based on equality between operands or the value of (E)CX.
- Based on comparisons of unsigned operands.
- Based on comparisons of signed operands.

Table 6-2 shows a list of jumps based on specific CPU flag values: Zero, Carry, Overflow, Parity, and Sign.

Equality Comparisons

Table 6-3 lists jump instructions based on evaluating the equality of two operands or the values of CX and ECX. In the table, the notations *leftOp* and *rightOp* refer to the left (destination) and right (source) operands in a CMP instruction:

```
CMP leftOp,rightOp
```

TABLE 6-2   Jumps Based on Specific Flag Values.

Mnemonic	Description	Flags / Registers
JZ	Jump if zero	ZF = 1
JNZ	Jump if not zero	ZF = 0
JC	Jump if carry	CF = 1
JNC	Jump if not carry	CF = 0
JO	Jump if overflow	OF = 1
JNO	Jump if not overflow	OF = 0
JS	Jump if signed	SF = 1
JNS	Jump if not signed	SF = 0
JP	Jump if parity (even)	PF = 1
JNP	Jump if not parity (odd)	PF = 0

The operand names reflect the ordering of operands for relational operators in algebra. For example, in the expression X < Y, X can be called *leftOp* and Y called *rightOp*.

TABLE 6-3   Jumps Based on Equality.

Mnemonic	Description
JE	Jump if equal (*leftOp* = *rightOp*)
JNE	Jump if not equal (*leftOp* ≠ *rightOp*)
JCXZ	Jump if CX = 0
JECXZ	Jump if ECX = 0

The JE instruction is equivalent to JZ (jump if Zero) and JNE is equivalent to JNZ (jump if not Zero). Let's look at some examples.

Example 1:

```
mov  edx,0A523h
cmp  edx,0A523h
jne  L5                    ; jump not taken
je   L1                    ; jump is taken
```

Example 2:

```
mov  bx,1234h
sub  bx,1234h
jne  L5                    ; jump not taken
je   L1                    ; jump is taken
```

Example 3:

```
mov  cx,0FFFFh
inc  cx
jcxz L2                    ; jump is taken
```

Example 4:

```
xor   ecx,ecx
jecxz L2                   ; jump is taken
```

Unsigned Comparisons

Jumps based specifically on comparisons of unsigned integers are shown in Table 6-4. This type of jump is useful when comparing unsigned values. As 16-bit unsigned integers, for example, 7FFFh is smaller than 8000h. (As 16-bit *signed* integers, 7FFFh would be greater than 8000h.)

Table 6-4   Jumps Based on Unsigned Comparisons.

Mnemonic	Description
JA	Jump if above (if *leftOp* > *rightOp*)
JNBE	Jump if not below or equal (same as JA)
JAE	Jump if above or equal (if *leftOp* ≥ *rightOp*)
JNB	Jump if not below (same as JAE)
JB	Jump if below (if *leftOp* < *rightOp*)
JNAE	Jump if not above or equal (same as JB)
JBE	Jump if below or equal (if *leftOp* ≤ *rightOp*)
JNA	Jump if not above (same as JBE)

Signed Comparisons

Table 6-5 displays a list of jumps based on signed comparisons. The 1-byte signed value 80h (−128d), for example, is less than 7Fh (+127d). The next example shows how JA and JG differ in their comparison of 80h and 7Fh:

```
mov  al,7Fh          ; (7Fh or +127)
cmp  al,80h          ; (80h or -128)
ja   IsAbove         ; no jump, because 7F not > 80h
jg   IsGreater       ; jump, because +127 > -128
```

The JA instruction does not jump because unsigned 7Fh is smaller than unsigned 80h. The JG instruction, on the other hand, jumps because +127 (7Fh) is greater than −128 (80h).

Table 6-5   Jumps Based on Signed Comparisons.

Mnemonic	Description
JG	Jump if greater (if *leftOp* > *rightOp*)
JNLE	Jump if not less than or equal (same as JG)
JGE	Jump if greater than or equal (if *leftOp* ≥ *rightOp*)
JNL	Jump if not less (same as JGE)
JL	Jump if less (if *leftOp* < *rightOp*)
JNGE	Jump if not greater than or equal (same as JL)
JLE	Jump if less than or equal (if *leftOp* ≤ *rightOp*)
JNG	Jump if not greater (same as JLE)

Let's look at some examples of signed comparisons.

Example 1

```
mov  edx,-1
cmp  edx,0
jnl  L5                              ; jump not taken
```

```
        jnle L5                                    ; jump not taken
        jl   L1                                    ; jump is taken
```

Example 2

```
        mov  bx,+34
        cmp  bx,-35
        jng  L5                                    ; jump not taken
        jnge L5                                    ; jump not taken
        jge  L1                                    ; jump is taken
```

Example 3

```
        mov  ecx,0
        cmp  ecx,0
        jg   L5                                    ; jump not taken
        jnl  L1                                    ; jump is taken
```

Example 4

```
        mov  ecx,0
        cmp  ecx,0
        jl   L5                                    ; jump not taken
        jng  L1                                    ; jump is taken
```

Ranges of Conditional Jump Instructions

In 16-bit Real mode, conditional jumps use a single signed byte called a *relative offset* to locate the jump target. The target is limited to a range of -128 to $+127$ bytes from the current location counter. The location counter is the address of the instruction following the current one because the CPU increments the instruction pointer prior to executing the current instruction. The same limitation on ranges applies to the LOOP, LOOPZ, and LOOPNZ instructions (Section 6.4).

The following example lists the bytes generated by the assembler for a JZ instruction when compiled in 16-bit real mode. The JZ instruction at offset 0000 is encoded as **74 03**. The opcode is 74 and the relative offset is 03. (NOP stands for the no-operation instruction.) The address following JZ is 0002, so the CPU adds 3 to 2, producing 5 (the offset of label L2):

```
Offset Encoding        ASM Source Code
-------------------------------------------
0000    74 03          jz L2
0002    90             nop
0003    90             nop
0004    90             nop
0005                   L2:
```

Similarly, the next example shows a backward jump (negative offset). The offset after the jump is 0005, so 0FBh (-5) is added to 5, producing offset 0000 (the offset of label L1):

```
0000                   L1:
0000    90             nop
0001    90             nop
0002    90             nop
0003    74 FB          jz L1
0005
```

Longer Jumps in 16-Bit Mode   If a jump in a 16-bit mode program exceeds the range permitted by a signed byte offset, MASM generates a *relative jump out of range* error. Assuming instructions have an average length of 3 bytes, you can put approximately 40 instructions inside a loop before encountering an error. To get around the error, jump to an unconditional jump instruction (which has a 16-bit range):

```
        jz    L2
        jmp   L3
L2:     jmp   farTarget
L3:
```

Jumps in 32-Bit Mode   In 32-bit mode, MASM generates a 32-bit signed relative offset for jumps to targets outside the 1-byte range. In the following example, label L1 is located 189 bytes (BDh) forward from the location counter, so the target address field is 32 bits:

```
00000000   0F 84 000000BD     jz    L1
```

The opcodes for 32-bit jumps are 2 bytes long, as in the 0Fh, 84h used in our example.

6.3.4 Conditional Jump Applications

Testing Status Bits

Instructions such as AND, OR, NOT, CMP, and TEST are often followed by conditional jump instructions that alter program flow. Conditional jumps usually test the values of CPU status flags. Assume, for example, that an 8-bit memory operand named **status** contains status information about an external device attached to the computer. The following instructions jump to a label if bit 5 is set, indicating that the device is offline:

```
mov  al,status
test al,00100000b          ; test bit 5
jnz  EquipOffline
```

The following statements jump to a label if any of the bits 0, 1, or 4 are set:

```
mov  al,status
test al,00010011b          ; test bits 0,1,4
jnz  InputDataByte
```

Jumping to a label if bits 2, 3, and 7 are all set requires both the AND and CMP instructions:

```
mov  al,status
and  al,10001100b          ; preserve bits 2,3,7
cmp  al,10001100b          ; all bits set?
je   ResetMachine          ; yes: jump to label
```

Larger of Two Integers   The following code compares the unsigned integers in AX and BX and moves the larger of the two to DX:

```
        mov   dx,ax          ; assume AX is larger
        cmp   ax,bx          ; if AX is >= BX then
        jae   L1             ;    jump to L1
        mov   dx,bx          ; else move BX to DX
L1:                          ; DX contains larger integer
```

Smallest of Three Integers   The following instructions compare the unsigned values in the variables V1, V2, and V3 and move the smallest of the three to AX:

```
.data
V1 WORD ?
V2 WORD ?
V3 WORD ?
.code
```

```
        mov     ax,V1               ; assume V1 is smallest
        cmp     ax,V2               ; if AX <= V2 then
        jbe     L1                  ;    jump to L1
        mov     ax,V2               ; else move V2 to AX
L1:     cmp     ax,V3               ; if AX <= V3 then
        jbe     L2                  ;    jump to L2
        mov     ax,V3               ; else move V3 to AX
L2:
```

Application: Sequential Search of an Array

A common task is to search for values in an array meeting some criteria. When the first matching value is found, you can display its value or return a pointer to its location. Let's show how easily this is accomplished using an array of integers. The *ArryScan.asm* program looks for the first nonzero value in an array of 16-bit integers. If it finds one, it displays the value; otherwise, it displays a message stating that a value could not be found:

```
TITLE Scanning an Array                   (ArryScan.asm)
; Scan an array for the first nonzero value.

INCLUDE Irvine32.inc

.data
intArray  SWORD  0,0,0,0,1,20,35,-12,66,4,0
;intArray SWORD  1,0,0,0                         ; alternate test data
;intArray SWORD  0,0,0,0                         ; alternate test data
;intArray SWORD  0,0,0,1                         ; alternate test data
noneMsg   BYTE "A non-zero value was not found",0
```

> This program contains alternate test data that are currently commented out. Uncomment these lines to test the program with different data configurations.

```
.code
main PROC
        mov     ebx,OFFSET intArray     ; point to the array
        mov     ecx,LENGTHOF intArray   ; loop counter

L1:     cmp     WORD PTR [ebx],0        ; compare value to zero
        jnz     found                   ; found a value
        add     ebx,2                   ; point to next
        loop    L1                      ; continue the loop
        jmp     notFound                ; none found

found:                                  ; display the value
        movsx eax,WORD PTR[ebx]
        call  WriteInt
        jmp   quit

notFound:                               ; display "not found" message
        mov     edx,OFFSET noneMsg
        call  WriteString

quit:
        call Crlf
        exit
main ENDP
END main
```

Application: String Encryption

Section 6.2.4 showed that the XOR instruction has an interesting property. If an integer X is XORed with Y and the resulting value is XORed with Y again, the value produced is X:

$$((X \otimes Y) \otimes Y) = X$$

This "reversible" property of XOR provides an easy way to perform data encryption: A *plain text* message entered by the user is transformed into an unintelligible string called *cipher text by* XORing each of its characters with a character from a third string called a *key*. The cipher text can be stored or transmitted to a remote location without unauthorized persons being able to read it. The intended viewer uses the key to decrypt the cipher text and produce the original plain text.

Example Program   The next program uses *symmetric encryption*, a process by which the same key is used for encryption and decryption. The following steps occur, in order:

- The user enters the plain text.
- The program uses a single-character key to encrypt the plain text, producing the cipher text, which is displayed on the screen.
- The program decrypts the cipher text, producing and displaying the original plain text.

Here is sample output from the program:

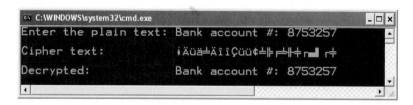

Program Listing   Here is a complete program listing:

```
TITLE Encryption Program              (Encrypt.asm)

INCLUDE Irvine32.inc
KEY = 239                     ; any value between 1-255
BUFMAX = 128                  ; maximum buffer size

.data
sPrompt  BYTE "Enter the plain text: ",0
sEncrypt BYTE "Cipher text:           ",0
sDecrypt BYTE "Decrypted:             ",0
buffer   BYTE    BUFMAX+1 DUP(0)
bufSize  DWORD   ?

.code
main PROC
     call   InputTheString         ; input the plain text
     call   TranslateBuffer        ; encrypt the buffer
     mov    edx,OFFSET sEncrypt     ; display encrypted message
     call   DisplayMessage
     call   TranslateBuffer        ; decrypt the buffer
     mov    edx,OFFSET sDecrypt     ; display decrypted message
     call   DisplayMessage
     exit
main ENDP
```

```
;------------------------------------------------------
InputTheString PROC
;
; Prompts user for a plaintext string. Saves the string
; and its length.
; Receives: nothing
; Returns: nothing
;------------------------------------------------------
     pushad
     mov    edx,OFFSET sPrompt      ; display a prompt
     call   WriteString
     mov    ecx,BUFMAX              ; maximum character count
     mov    edx,OFFSET buffer       ; point to the buffer
     call   ReadString              ; input the string
     mov    bufSize,eax             ; save the length
     call   Crlf
     popad
     ret
InputTheString ENDP

;------------------------------------------------------
DisplayMessage PROC
;
; Displays the encrypted or decrypted message.
; Receives: EDX points to the message
; Returns:  nothing
;------------------------------------------------------
     pushad
     call   WriteString
     mov    edx,OFFSET buffer       ; display the buffer
     call   WriteString
     call   Crlf
     call   Crlf
     popad
     ret
DisplayMessage ENDP

;------------------------------------------------------
TranslateBuffer PROC
;
; Translates the string by exclusive-ORing each
; byte with the encryption key byte.
; Receives: nothing
; Returns: nothing
;------------------------------------------------------
     pushad
     mov    ecx,bufSize             ; loop counter
     mov    esi,0                   ; index 0 in buffer
L1:
     xor    buffer[esi],KEY         ; translate a byte
     inc    esi                     ; point to next byte
     loop   L1
     popad
     ret
TranslateBuffer ENDP
END main
```

The chapter exercises suggest an improvement to this program: Use an encryption key containing multiple characters to encrypt and decrypt the plain text. The key can be entered by the user.

6.3.5   Bit Testing Instructions (Optional)

The BT, BTC, BTR, and BTS instructions are collectively called *bit testing* instructions. They are interesting because they perform multiple steps within a single atomic instruction. This has implications for multithreaded programs, in which it is often very important for flag bits (called *semaphores*) to be tested, cleared, set, and complemented without any danger of interruption by another program thread. See the book's Web site (www.asmirvine.com) for an example that describes a simple multithreading scenario.

BT Instruction

The BT (bit test) instruction selects bit n in the first operand and copies the bit into the Carry flag:

```
BT bitBase,n
```

The first operand, called the *bitBase*, is not changed. BT permits the following types of operands:

```
BT  r/m16,r16
BT  r/m32,r32
BT  r/m16,imm8
BT  r/m32,imm8
```

In the following example, the Carry flag is assigned the value of bit 7 in the variable named **semaphore**:

```
.data
semaphore WORD 10001000b
.code
BT   semaphore,7                 ; CF = 1
```

Before the BT instruction was introduced into the Intel instruction set, we would have had to copy the variable into a register and shift bit 7 into the Carry flag:

```
mov  ax,semaphore
shr  ax,8                        ; CF = 1
```

(The SHR instruction here shifts all bits in AX eight positions to the right. This causes bit 7 to be shifted into the Carry flag. SHR is covered in Chapter 7 in Section 7.2.3.)

BTC Instruction

The BTC (bit test and complement) instruction selects bit n in the first operand, copies the bit into the Carry flag, and complements (toggles) bit n:

```
BTC bitBase,n
```

BTC permits the same types of operands as BT. In the following example, the Carry flag is assigned the value of bit 6 in **semaphore**, and the same bit is complemented:

```
.data
semaphore WORD 10001000b
.code
BTC semaphore,6                  ; CF = 0, semaphore=11001000b
```

BTR Instruction

The BTR (bit test and reset) instruction selects bit n in the first operand, copies the bit into the Carry flag, and resets (clears) bit n:

```
BTR bitBase,n
```

BTR permits the same types of operands as BT and BTC. In the following example, the Carry flag is assigned the value of bit 7 in semaphore, and the same bit is cleared:

```
.data
semaphore WORD 10001000b
.code
BTR  semaphore,7                              ; CF = 1, semaphore=00001000b
```

BTS Instruction

The BTS (bit test and set) instruction selects bit *n* in the first operand, copies the bit into the Carry flag, and sets bit *n*:

```
BTS bitBase,n
```

BTS permits the same types of operands as BT. In the following example, the Carry flag is assigned the value of bit 6 in semaphore, and the same bit is then set:

```
.data
semaphore WORD 10001000b
.code
BTS  semaphore,6                              ; CF = 0, semaphore=11001000b
```

6.3.6 Section Review

1. Which CPU status flags are used in unsigned comparisons?
2. Which CPU status flags are used in signed comparisons?
3. Which conditional jump instruction is based on the contents of ECX?
4. *(Yes/No):* Are the JA and JNBE instructions equivalent? Explain your answer.
5. *(Yes/No):* Are the JB and JL instructions equivalent? Explain your answer.
6. Which jump instruction is equivalent to the JNA instruction?
7. Which jump instruction is equivalent to the JNGE instruction?
8. *(Yes/No):* Will the following code jump to the label named **Target**?

```
mov  ax,8109h
cmp  ax,26h
jg   Target
```

9. *(Yes/No):* Will the following code jump to the label named **Target**?

```
mov  ax,-30
cmp  ax,-50
jg   Target
```

10. *(Yes/No):* Will the following code jump to the label named **Target**?

```
mov  ax,-42
cmp  ax,26
ja   Target
```

11. Write instructions that jump to label L1 when the unsigned integer in DX is less than or equal to the integer in CX.
12. Write instructions that jump to label L2 when the signed integer in AX is greater than the integer in CX.
13. Write instructions that clear bits 0 and 1 in AL. If the destination operand is equal to zero, jump to label L3. Otherwise, jump to label L4.
14. *Challenge:* Given the data

```
semaphore WORD 10001000b
```

describe the difference in the resulting state of the registers and flags between the sequence of instructions

```
mov   ax,semaphore
shr   ax,7
xor   semaphore,01000000b
```

and the instruction

```
BTC semaphore,6
```

6.4 Conditional Loop Instructions

6.4.1 LOOPZ and LOOPE Instructions

The LOOPZ (loop if zero) instruction permits a loop to continue while the Zero flag is set and the unsigned value of ECX is greater than zero. The destination label must be between -128 and $+127$ bytes from the location of the following instruction. The syntax is

```
LOOPZ destination
```

The LOOPE (loop if equal) instruction is equivalent to LOOPZ because they share the same op code. They perform the following tasks:

```
ECX = ECX - 1
if ECX > 0 and ZF = 1, jump to destination
```

Otherwise, no jump occurs, and control passes to the next instruction. LOOPZ and LOOPE do not affect any of the status flags.

> A program running in real-address mode uses CX as the default loop counter in the LOOPZ instruction. If you want to force ECX to be the loop counter, use the LOOPZD instruction instead.

6.4.2 LOOPNZ and LOOPNE Instructions

The LOOPNZ (loop if not zero) instruction is the counterpart of LOOPZ. The loop continues while the unsigned value of ECX is greater than zero and the Zero flag is clear. The syntax is

```
LOOPNZ destination
```

The LOOPNE (loop if not equal) instruction is equivalent to LOOPNZ because they share the same op code. They perform the following tasks:

```
ECX = ECX - 1
if ECX > 0 and ZF = 0, jump to destination
```

Otherwise, nothing happens, and control passes to the next instruction.

Example The following code excerpt (from *Loopnz.asm*) scans each number in an array until a nonnegative number is found (when the sign bit is clear):

```
.data
array   SWORD   -3,-6,-1,-10,10,30,40,4
sentinel SWORD   0
.code
        mov     esi,OFFSET array
        mov     ecx,LENGTHOF array
L1:  test     WORD PTR [esi],8000h        ; test sign bit
        pushfd                              ; push flags on stack
        add     esi,TYPE array
        popfd                               ; pop flags from stack
```

```
        loopnz  L1                          ; continue loop
        jnz     quit                        ; none found
        sub     esi,TYPE array              ; ESI points to value
    quit:
```

If a nonnegative value is found, ESI is left pointing at it. If the loop fails to find a positive number, it stops when ECX equals zero. In that case, the JNZ instruction jumps to label **quit**, and ESI points to the sentinel value (0) just after the array.

6.4.3 Section Review

1. (*True/False*): The LOOPE instruction jumps to a label when (and only when) the Zero flag is clear.

2. (*True/False*): The LOOPNZ instruction jumps to a label when ECX is greater than zero and the Zero flag is clear.

3. (*True/False*): The destination label of a LOOPZ instruction must be no farther than -128 or $+127$ bytes from the instruction immediately following LOOPZ.

4. Modify the LOOPNZ example in Section 6.4.2 so that it scans for the first negative value in the array. Change the data declaration accordingly so it begins with positive values.

5. *Challenge:* The LOOPNZ example in Section 6.4.2 relies on a sentinel value to handle the possibility that a positive value might not be found. What would happen if we removed the sentinel?

6.5 Conditional Structures

In this section we will examine a few of the more common conditional structures used in high-level programming languages. You will see how each structure can easily be translated into assembly language. Let's consider a *conditional structure* to be one or more conditional expressions that trigger a choice between different logical branches. Each branch causes a different sequence of instructions to execute.

> Computer science students often take a course in *compiler construction*, in which they implement a programming language compiler. The code optimization techniques discussed here can be helpful in such a course.

6.5.1 Block-Structured IF Statements

In most high-level languages, an IF structure implies that a boolean expression is followed by two lists of statements: one performed when the expression is true, and another performed when the expression is false:

```
if( expression )
    statement-list-1
else
    statement-list-2
```

The **else** portion of the statement is optional. The flowchart in Figure 6–1 shows the two branching paths in a conditional IF structure, labeled *true* and *false*.

Example 1   Using Java/C++ syntax, two assignment statements are executed if **op1** is equal to **op2**:

```
if( op1 == op2 )
{
    X = 1;
    Y = 2;
}
```

Figure 6–1   Flowchart of an IF Structure.

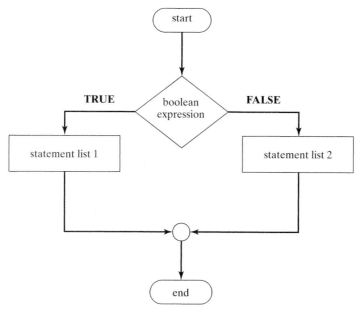

The only way to translate this IF statement into assembly language is to use a CMP instruction followed by one or more conditional jumps. Because **op1** and **op2** are memory operands, one must be moved to a register before executing CMP. The following code implements the IF statement as efficiently as possible by reversing the equality condition and using the JNE instruction:

```
        mov    eax,op1
        cmp    eax,op2          ; op1 == op2?
        jne    L1               ; no: skip next
        mov    X,1              ; yes: assign X and Y
        mov    Y,2
L1:
```

If we implemented the == operator using JE, the resulting code would be less compact (six instructions rather than five):

```
        mov    eax,op1
        cmp    eax,op2          ; op1 == op2?
        je     L1               ; yes: jump to L1
        jmp    L2               ; no: skip assignments
L1:     mov    X,1              ; assign X and Y
        mov    Y,2
L2:
```

> The same high-level language code can be translated into assembly language in multiple ways. When examples of compiled code are shown in this chapter, they represent only what a hypothetical compiler might produce.

Example 2   In the FAT32 file system used under MS-Windows, the size of a disk cluster depends on the disk's overall capacity. In the following pseudocode, we set the cluster size to 4,096 if the disk size (in the variable named **gigabytes**) is less than 8GB. Otherwise, we set the cluster size to 8,192:

```
clusterSize = 8192;
```

```
if gigabytes < 8
  clusterSize = 4096;
```

Here's a good way to implement the same statement in assembly language:

```
mov  clusterSize,8192        ; assume larger cluster
cmp  gigabytes,8             ; larger than 8 GB?
jae  next
mov  clusterSize,4096        ; switch to smaller cluster
next:
```

(Disk clusters are described in Section 14.2.)

Example 3 The following pseudocode IF-ELSE statement has alternative branches:

```
if op1 > op2 then
    call Routine1
else
    call Routine2
end if
```

In the following assembly language translation, we assume op1 and op2 are signed doubleword variables. The > operator is best implemented using JNG, the complement of JG:

```
        mov   eax,op1
        cmp   eax,op2        ; op1 > op2?
        jng   A1             ; no: call Routine2
        call  Routine1       ; yes: call Routine1
        jmp   A2
A1:     call  Routine2
A2:
```

Using White Box Testing

Complex conditional statements in assembly language have multiple execution paths, making them hard to debug by inspection (looking at the code). Good programmers often implement a technique known as *white box testing*, which verifies a subroutine's inputs and corresponding outputs. White box testing requires you to have a copy of the source code. You assign a variety of values to the input variables. For each combination of inputs, you manually trace through the source code and verify the execution path and outputs produced by the subroutine. Let's see how it's done. Suppose we want to translate the following nested-IF statement into assembly language:

```
if op1 == op2 then
  if X > Y then
     call Routine1
  else
     call Routine2
  end if
else
  call Routine3
end if
```

Here is a possible translation to assembly language, with line numbers added for reference. It reverses the initial condition (op1 == op2) and immediately jumps to the ELSE portion. All that is left to translate is the inner IF-ELSE statement:

```
1:        mov   eax,op1
2:        cmp   eax,op2        ; op1 == op2?
3:        jne   L2             ; no: call Routine3
```

```
; process the inner IF-ELSE statement.
4:            mov     eax,X
5:            cmp     eax,Y               ; X > Y?
6:            jg      L1                  ; yes: call Routine1
7:            call    Routine2            ; no: call Routine2
8:            jmp     L3                  ; and exit
9:    L1:     call    Routine1            ; call Routine1
10:           jmp     L3                  ; and exit

11:   L2:     call    Routine3
12:   L3:
```

Table 6-6 shows the results of white box testing of the sample code. Test values have been assigned to op1, op2, X, and Y, and the resulting execution paths are verified.

Table 6-6   Testing the Nested IF Statement.

op1	op2	X	Y	Line Execution Sequence	Calls
10	20	30	40	1, 2, 3, 11, 12	Routine3
10	20	40	30	1, 2, 3, 11, 12	Routine3
10	10	30	40	1, 2, 3, 4, 5, 6, 7, 8, 12	Routine2
10	10	40	30	1, 2, 3, 4, 5, 6, 9, 10, 12	Routine1

6.5.2   Compound Expressions

Logical AND Operator

Assembly language easily implements compound boolean expressions containing AND operators. Consider the following pseudocode, in which the values are assumed to be unsigned integers:

```
if (al > bl) AND (bl > cl)
{
    X = 1
}
```

Short-Circuit Evaluation   The following is a straightforward implementation using *short-circuit* evaluation, in which the second expression is not evaluated if the first expression is false:

```
        cmp     al,bl               ; first expression...
        ja      L1
        jmp     next
L1:     cmp     bl,cl               ; second expression...
        ja      L2
        jmp     next
L2:     mov     X,1                 ; both true: set X to 1
next:
```

We can optimize the code down to five instructions by changing the initial JA instruction to JBE:

```
        cmp     al,bl               ; first expression...
        jbe     next                ; quit if false
        cmp     bl,cl               ; second expression
        jbe     next                ; quit if false
        mov     X,1                 ; both are true
next:
```

The 29% reduction in code size (seven instructions down to five) results from letting the CPU fall through to the second CMP instruction if the first JBE is not taken. High-level language compilers for Java, C, and C++ use short-circuit evaluation, probably for efficiency reasons.

Non–Short-Circuit Evaluation   Some languages (BASIC, for example), do not perform short-circuit evaluation. Implementing such a compound expression in assembly language is tricky because a flag or boolean value is needed to hold the results from the first expression:

```
.data
temp BYTE ?
.code
        mov    temp,0              ; clear temp flag
        cmp    al,bl              ; AL > BL?
        jna    L1                 ; no
        mov    temp,1             ; yes: set flag = true

L1:     cmp    bl,cl              ; BL > CL?
        jna    next               ; no: expression is false
        and    temp,1             ; yes: AND the flag with 1
        jz     next               ; evaluate the flag
        mov    X,1
    next:
```

Coding this example in the most efficient way requires us to take advantage of the way the AND instruction affects the Zero flag. A typical BASIC compiler might not do as well. The resulting eight instructions are still 60% larger than the five instructions we used in the optimized short-circuit evaluation of the same expression.

Logical OR Operator

When multiple expressions occur in a compound expression using the logical OR operator, the expression is automatically true as soon as any one expression is true. Let's use the following pseudocode as an example:

```
if (al > bl) OR (bl > cl)
    X = 1
```

In the following implementation, the code branches to L1 if the first expression is true; otherwise, it falls through to the second CMP instruction. The second expression reverses the > operator and uses JBE instead:

```
        cmp    al,bl              ; 1: compare AL to BL
        ja     L1                 ; if true, skip second expression
        cmp    bl,cl              ; 2: compare BL to CL
        jbe    next               ; false: skip next statement
L1:     mov    X,1                ; true: set X = 1
    next:
```

For a given compound expression, there are at least several ways the expression can be implemented in assembly language.

6.5.3 WHILE Loops

The WHILE structure tests a condition first before performing a block of statements. As long as the loop condition remains true, the statements are repeated. The following loop is written in C++:

```
while( val1 < val2 )
{
    val1++;
    val2--;
}
```

When coding this structure in assembly language, it is convenient to reverse the loop condition and jump to **endwhile** when the condition becomes true. Assuming that **val1** and **val2** are variables, we must move one of them to a register at the beginning and restore the variable at the end:

```
        mov    eax,val1                    ; copy variable to EAX
@@while:
        cmp    eax,val2                    ; if not (val1 < val2)
        jnl    endwhile                    ;    exit the loop
        inc    eax                         ; val1++;
        dec    val2                        ; val2--;
        jmp    @@while                     ; repeat the loop
endwhile:
        mov    val1,eax                    ; save new value for val1
```

EAX is a proxy (substitute) for **val1** inside the loop. References to **val1** must be through EAX. JNL is used, implying that **val1** and **val2** are signed integers.

Example: IF statement Nested in a Loop

High-level structured languages are particularly good at representing nested control structures. In the following C++ example, an IF statement is nested inside a WHILE loop. It calculates the sum of all array elements greater than the value in **sample**:

```
int array[] = {10,60,20,33,72,89,45,65,72,18};
int sample = 50;
int ArraySize = sizeof array / sizeof sample;
int index = 0;
int sum = 0;
while( index < ArraySize )
{
    if( array[index] > sample )
    {
        sum += array[index];
        index++;
    }
}
```

Before we code this loop in assembly language, let's use the flowchart in Figure 6–2 to describe the logic. To simplify the translation and speed up execution by reducing the number of memory accesses, registers have been substituted for variables. EDX = sample, EAX = sum, ESI = index, and ECX = ArraySize (a constant). Label names have been added to the shapes.

Assembly Code   The easiest way to generate assembly code from a flowchart is to implement the code for each shape. Note the direct correlation between the flowchart labels and labels used in the following source code (see *Flowchart.asm*):

```
.data
sum DWORD 0
sample DWORD 50
array DWORD 10,60,20,33,72,89,45,65,72,18
ArraySize = ($ - Array) / TYPE array

.code
main PROC
        mov    eax,0                       ; sum
        mov    edx,sample
        mov    esi,0                       ; index
        mov    ecx,ArraySize
```

```
L1:   cmp    esi,ecx
      jl     L2
      jmp    L5
L2:   cmp    array[esi*4], edx
      jg     L3
      jmp    L4
L3:   add    eax,array[esi*4]
L4:   inc    esi
      jmp    L1
L5:   mov    sum,eax
```

A review question at the end of Section 6.5 will give you a chance to improve this code.

FIGURE 6–2   Loop Containing IF Statement.

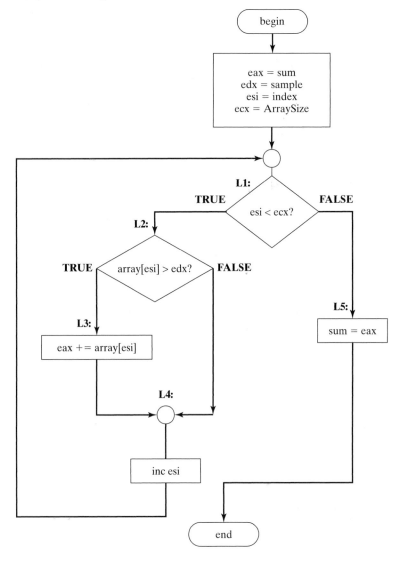

6.5.4 Table-Driven Selection

Table-driven selection is a way of using a table lookup to replace a multiway selection structure. To use it, you must create a table containing lookup values and the offsets of labels or procedures, and use a loop to search the table. This works best when a large number of comparisons are made.

For example, the following is part of a table containing single-character lookup values and addresses of procedures:

```
.data
CaseTable BYTE    'A'                  ; lookup value
    DWORD Process_A                    ; address of procedure
    BYTE  'B'
    DWORD Process_B
    (etc.)
```

Let's assume Process_A, Process_B, Process_C, and Process_D are located at addresses 120h, 130h, 140h, and 150h, respectively. The table would be arranged in memory as shown in Figure 6–3.

FIGURE 6–3   Table of Procedure Offsets.

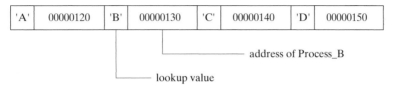

Example Program   In the following example program (*ProcTble.asm*), the user inputs a character from the keyboard. Using a loop, the character is compared to each entry in the table. The first match found in the table causes a call to the procedure offset stored immediately after the lookup value. Each procedure loads EDX with the offset of a different string, which is displayed during the loop:

```
TITLE Table of Procedure Offsets          (ProcTble.asm)

; This program contains a table with offsets of procedures.
; It uses the table to execute indirect procedure calls.

INCLUDE Irvine32.inc
.data
CaseTable   BYTE 'A'                       ; lookup value
            DWORD    Process_A             ; address of procedure
EntrySize = ($ - CaseTable)
            BYTE 'B'
            DWORD    Process_B
            BYTE 'C'
            DWORD    Process_C
            BYTE 'D'
            DWORD    Process_D
NumberOfEntries = ($ - CaseTable) / EntrySize
prompt BYTE "Press capital A,B,C,or D: ",0
```

Define a separate message string for each procedure:

```
msgA BYTE "Process_A",0
msgB BYTE "Process_B",0
msgC BYTE "Process_C",0
msgD BYTE "Process_D",0
```

```
.code
main PROC
        mov     edx,OFFSET prompt           ; ask user for input
        call    WriteString
        call    ReadChar                    ; read character into AL
        mov     ebx,OFFSET CaseTable        ; point EBX to the table
        mov     ecx,NumberOfEntries         ; loop counter
L1:
        cmp     al,[ebx]                    ; match found?
        jne     L2                          ; no: continue
        call    NEAR PTR [ebx + 1]          ; yes: call the procedure
```

This CALL instruction calls the procedure whose address is stored in the memory location referenced by EBX+1. An indirect call such as this requires the NEAR PTR operator.

```
        call    WriteString                 ; display message
        call    Crlf
        jmp     L3                          ; exit the search
L2:
        add     ebx,EntrySize               ; point to the next entry
        loop    L1                          ; repeat until ECX = 0
L3:
        exit
main ENDP
```

Each of the following procedures moves a different string offset to EDX:

```
Process_A PROC
        mov     edx,OFFSET msgA
        ret
Process_A ENDP

Process_B PROC
        mov     edx,OFFSET msgB
        ret
Process_B ENDP

Process_C PROC
        mov     edx,OFFSET msgC
        ret
Process_C ENDP

Process_D PROC
        mov     edx,OFFSET msgD
        ret
Process_D ENDP
END main
```

The table-driven selection method involves some initial overhead, but it can reduce the amount of code you write. A table can handle a large number of comparisons, and it can be more easily modified than a long series of compare, jump, and CALL instructions. A table can even be reconfigured at runtime.

6.5.5 Section Review

Notes: In all compound expressions, use short-circuit evaluation. Assume that **val1**, **val2**, and **val3** are 16-bit variables.

1. Implement the following pseudocode in assembly language:
    ```
    if( bx > cx )
        X = 1;
    ```

2. Implement the following pseudocode in assembly language:
    ```
    if( dx <= cx )
        X = 1;
    else
        X = 2;
    ```

3. Implement the following pseudocode in assembly language:
    ```
    if( val1 > cx AND cx > dx )
        X = 1;
    else
        X = 2;
    ```

4. Implement the following pseudocode in assembly language:
    ```
    if( bx > cx OR bx > val1 )
        X = 1;
    else
        X = 2;
    ```

5. Implement the following pseudocode in assembly language:
    ```
    if( bx > cx AND bx > dx) OR ( dx > ax )
        X = 1;
    else
        X = 2;
    ```

6. In the program from Section 6.5.4, why is it better to let the assembler calculate NumberOfEntries rather than assigning a constant such as NumberOfEnteries = 4?

7. *Challenge:* Rewrite the code from Section 6.5.3 so it is functionally equivalent, but uses fewer instructions.

6.6   Application: Finite-State Machines

A *finite-state machine* (FSM) is a machine or program that changes state based on some input. It is fairly simple to use a graph to represent an FSM, which contains squares (or circles) called *nodes* and lines with arrows between the circles called *edges (or arcs)*.

A simple example is shown in Figure 6–4. Each node represents a program state, and each edge represents a transition from one state to another. One node is designated as the *start state*, shown in our diagram with an incoming arrow. The remaining states can be labeled with numbers or letters. One or more states are designated as *terminal states*, shown by a thick border around the square. A terminal state represents a state in which the program might stop without producing an error. A finite-state machine is a specific instance of a more general type of structure called a *directed graph* (or *digraph*). The latter is a set of nodes connected by edges having specific directions.

FIGURE 6–4   Simple Finite-State Machine.

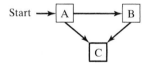

Directed graphs have many useful applications in computer science related to dynamic data structures and advanced searching techniques.

6.6.1 Validating an Input String

Programs that read input streams often must validate their input by performing a certain amount of error checking. A programming language compiler, for instance, can use a finite-state machine to scan source programs and convert words and symbols into *tokens*, which are objects such as keywords, arithmetic operators, and identifiers.

When using a finite-state machine to check the validity of an input string, you usually read the input character by character. Each character is represented by an edge (transition) in the diagram. A finite-state machine detects illegal input sequences in one of two ways:

• The next input character does not correspond to any transitions from the current state.
• The end of input is reached and the current state is a nonterminal state.

Character String Example   Let's check the validity of an input string according to the following two rules:

• The string must begin with the letter 'x' and end with the letter 'z.'
• Between the first and last characters, there can be zero or more letters within the range {'a'..'y'}.

The FSM diagram in Figure 6–5 describes this syntax. Each transition is identified with a particular type of input. For example, the transition from state A to state B can only be accomplished if the letter **x** is read from the input stream. A transition from state B to itself is accomplished by the input of any letter of the alphabet except **z**. A transition from state B to state C occurs only when the letter **z** is read from the input stream.

FIGURE 6–5   FSM for String.

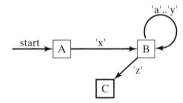

If the end of the input stream is reached while the program is in state A or B, an error condition results because only state C is marked as a terminal state. The following input strings would be recognized by this FSM:

```
xaabcdefgz
xz
xyyqqrrstuvz
```

6.6.2 Validating a Signed Integer

A finite-state machine for parsing a signed integer is shown in Figure 6–6. Input consists of an optional leading sign followed by a sequence of digits. There is no stated maximum number of digits implied by the diagram.

FIGURE 6–6   Signed Decimal Integer FSM.

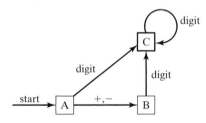

Finite-state machines are very easily translated into assembly language code. Each state in the diagram (A, B, C, . . .) is represented in the program by a label. The following actions are performed at each label:

- A call to an input procedure reads the next character from input.
- If the state is a terminal state, check to see whether the user has pressed the Enter key to end the input.
- One or more compare instructions check for each possible transition leading away from the state. Each comparison is followed by a conditional jump instruction.

For example, at state A, the following code reads the next input character and checks for a possible transition to state B:

```
StateA:
    call    Getnext             ; read next char into AL
    cmp     al,'+'              ; leading + sign?
    je      StateB              ; go to State B
    cmp     al,'-'              ; leading - sign?
    je      StateB              ; go to State B
    call    IsDigit             ; ZF = 1 if AL contains a digit
    jz      StateC              ; go to State C
    call    DisplayErrorMsg     ; invalid input found
    jmp     Quit
```

Also in state A, we call **IsDigit**, a link library procedure that sets the Zero flag when a numeric digit is read from input. This makes it possible to look for a transition to state C. Failing that, the program displays an error message and exits. The flowchart in Figure 6–7 represents the code attached to label **StateA**.

FSM Implementation   The following program implements the finite-state machine from Figure 6–6 describing a signed integer.

```
TITLE Finite State Machine              (Finite.asm)

INCLUDE Irvine32.inc

ENTER_KEY = 13
.data
InvalidInputMsg BYTE "Invalid input",13,10,0

.code
main PROC
    call Clrscr

StateA:
    call    Getnext             ; read next char into AL
    cmp     al,'+'              ; leading + sign?
    je      StateB              ; go to State B
    cmp     al,'-'              ; leading - sign?
    je      StateB              ; go to State B
    call    IsDigit             ; ZF = 1 if AL contains a digit
    jz      StateC              ; go to State C
    call    DisplayErrorMsg     ; invalid input found
    jmp     Quit

StateB:
    call    Getnext             ; read next char into AL
    call    IsDigit             ; ZF = 1 if AL contains a digit
    jz      StateC
    call    DisplayErrorMsg     ; invalid input found
    jmp     Quit

StateC:
    call    Getnext             ; read next char into AL
```

```
        call   IsDigit              ; ZF = 1 if AL contains a digit
        jz     StateC
        cmp    al,ENTER_KEY         ; Enter key pressed?
        je     Quit                 ; yes: quit
        call   DisplayErrorMsg      ; no: invalid input found
        jmp    Quit
Quit:
        call   Crlf
        exit
main ENDP

;---------------------------------------------
Getnext PROC
;
; Reads a character from standard input.
; Receives: nothing
; Returns: AL contains the character
;---------------------------------------------
        call   ReadChar             ; input from keyboard
        call   WriteChar            ; echo on screen
        ret
Getnext ENDP

;---------------------------------------------
DisplayErrorMsg PROC
;
; Displays an error message indicating that
; the input stream contains illegal input.
; Receives: nothing.
; Returns: nothing
;---------------------------------------------
        push   edx
        mov    edx,OFFSET InvalidInputMsg
        call   WriteString
        pop    edx
        ret
DisplayErrorMsg ENDP
END main
```

The **IsDigit** procedure from the book's link library and sets the Zero flag if the character in AL is a valid decimal digit. Otherwise, the Zero flag is cleared:

```
;---------------------------------------------
Isdigit PROC
;
; Determines whether the character in AL is a
; valid decimal digit.
; Receives: AL = character
; Returns: ZF=1 if AL contains a valid decimal
;    digit; otherwise, ZF=0.
;---------------------------------------------
        cmp    al,'0'
        jb     ID1                  ; ZF = 0 when jump taken
        cmp    al,'9'
        ja     ID1                  ; ZF = 0 when jump taken
        test   ax,0                 ; set ZF = 1
ID1: ret
Isdigit ENDP
```

Figure 6–7   Signed Integer FSM Flowchart.

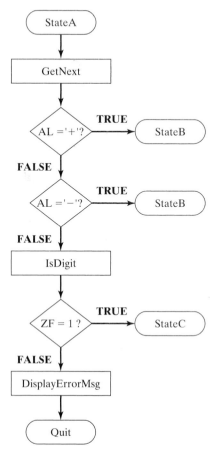

6.6.3 Section Review

1. A finite-state machine is a specific application of what type of data structure?
2. In a finite-state machine diagram, what do the nodes represent?
3. In a finite-state machine diagram, what do the edges represent?
4. In the signed integer finite-state machine (Section 6.6.2), which state is reached when the input consists of "+5"?
5. In the signed integer finite-state machine (Section 6.6.2), how many digits can occur after a minus sign?
6. What happens in a finite-state machine when no more input is available and the current state is a non-terminal state?
7. Would the following simplification of a signed decimal integer finite-state machine work just as well as the one shown in Section 6.6.2? If not, why not?

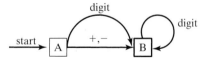

8. *Challenge:* Diagram a finite-state machine that recognizes real numbers without exponents. The decimal point is required. Examples are +3.5, −4.2342, 5., .2.

6.7 Decision Directives

MASM has decision directives (.IF, .ELSE, .ELSEIF, .ENDIF) that make it easy for you to code multiway branching logic. They cause the assembler to generate CMP and conditional jump instructions in the background, which you can see in the output listing file (*progname*.lst). Here is the syntax:

```
.IF condition1
    statements
[.ELSEIF condition2
    statements ]
[.ELSE
    statements ]
.ENDIF
```

The square brackets show that .ELSEIF and .ELSE are optional, whereas .IF and .ENDIF are required. A *condition* is a boolean expression involving the same operators used in C++ and Java (such as $<$, $>$, $==$, and $!=$). The expression is evaluated at runtime. The following are examples of valid conditions, using 32-bit registers and variables:

```
eax > 10000h
val1 <= 100
val2 == eax
val3 != ebx
```

The following are examples of compound conditions:

```
(eax > 0) && (eax > 10000h)
(val1 <= 100) || (val2 <= 100)
(val2 != ebx) && !CARRY?
```

A complete list of relational and logical operators is shown in Table 6-7.

Table 6-7 Runtime Relational and Logical Operators.

Operator	Description
expr1 $==$ *expr2*	Returns true when *expr1* is equal to *expr2*.
expr1 $!=$ *expr2*	Returns true when *expr1* is not equal to *expr2*.
expr1 $>$ *expr2*	Returns true when *expr1* is greater than *expr2*.
expr1 $\geq$ *expr2*	Returns true when *expr1* is greater than or equal to *expr2*.
expr1 $<$ *expr2*	Returns true when *expr1* is less than *expr2*.
expr1 $\leq$ *expr2*	Returns true when *expr1* is less than or equal to *expr2*.
! *expr*	Returns true when *expr* is false.
expr1 && *expr2*	Performs logical AND between *expr1* and *expr2*.
expr1 ‖ *expr2*	Performs logical OR between *expr1* and *expr2*.
expr1 & *expr2*	Performs bitwise AND between *expr1* and *expr2*.
CARRY?	Returns true if the Carry flag is set.
OVERFLOW?	Returns true if the Overflow flag is set.
PARITY?	Returns true if the Parity flag is set.
SIGN?	Returns true if the Sign flag is set.
ZERO?	Returns true if the Zero flag is set.

The use of decision directives is controversial because you can be fooled by their apparent simplicity. Before using them, be sure you thoroughly understand conditional branching instructions. In addition, when a program containing decision directives is assembled, inspect the listing file to make sure the code generated by MASM is what you intended.

Generating ASM Code   When you use high-level directives such as .IF and .ELSE, the assembler takes on the role of code writer for you. For example, let's write an .IF directive that compares EAX to the variable **val1**:

```
mov eax,6
.IF eax > val1
  mov result,1
.ENDIF
```

val1 and **result** are assumed to be 32-bit unsigned integers. When the assembler reads the foregoing lines, it expands them into the following assembly language instructions:

```
        mov     eax,6
        cmp     eax,val1
        jbe     @C0001              ; jump on unsigned comparison
        mov     result,1
@C0001:
```

The label name @C001 was created by the assembler. This is done in a way that guarantees that all labels within same procedure are unique.

6.7.1   Signed and Unsigned Comparisons

When you use the .IF directive to compare values, you must be aware of how MASM generates conditional jumps. If the comparison involves an unsigned variable, an unsigned conditional jump instruction is inserted in the generated code. This is a repeat of a previous example that compares EAX to **val1**, an unsigned doubleword:

```
.data
val1 DWORD    5
result DWORD ?
.code
     mov eax,6
     .IF eax > val1
       mov result,1
     .ENDIF
```

The assembler expands this using the JBE (unsigned jump) instruction:

```
     mov eax,6
     cmp eax,val1
     jbe @C0001                     ; jump on unsigned comparison
     mov result,1
@C0001:
```

Comparing a Signed Integer   Let's try a similar comparison with **val2**, a signed doubleword:

```
.data
val2 SDWORD -1
.code
     mov eax,6
     .IF eax > val2
       mov result,1
     .ENDIF
```

Now the assembler generates code using the JLE instruction, the jump based on signed comparisons:

```
        mov eax,6
        cmp eax,val2
        jle @C0001                          ; jump on signed comparison
        mov result,1
@C0001:
```

Comparing Registers The question we might then ask is, what happens if two registers are compared? Clearly, the assembler cannot determine whether the values are signed or unsigned:

```
        mov eax,6
        mov ebx,val2
        .IF eax > ebx
           mov result,1
        .ENDIF
```

It turns out that the assembler defaults to an unsigned comparison, so the .IF directive comparing two registers is implemented using the JBE instruction.

6.7.2 Compound Expressions

Many compound boolean expressions use the logical OR and AND operators. When using the .IF directive, the ‖ symbol is the logical OR operator:

```
.IF expression1 || expression2
     statements
.ENDIF
```

Similarly, the && symbol is the logical AND operator:

```
.IF expression1 && expression2
     statements
.ENDIF
```

The logical OR operator will be used in the next program example.

SetCursorPosition Example

The **SetCursorPosition** procedure, shown in the next example, performs range checking on its two input parameters, DH and DL (see *SetCur.asm*). The Y-coordinate (DH) must be between 0 and 24. The X-coordinate (DL) must be between 0 and 79. If either is found to be out of range, an error message is displayed:

```
SetCursorPosition PROC
; Sets the cursor position.
; Receives: DL = X-coordinate, DH = Y-coordinate
; Checks the ranges of DL and DH.
; Returns: nothing
;-------------------------------------------------
.data
BadXCoordMsg BYTE "X-Coordinate out of range!",0Dh,0Ah,0
BadYCoordMsg BYTE "Y-Coordinate out of range!",0Dh,0Ah,0
.code
    .IF (dl < 0) || (dl > 79)
        mov  edx,OFFSET BadXCoordMsg
        call WriteString
        jmp  quit
    .ENDIF
    .IF (dh < 0) || (dh > 24)
        mov  edx,OFFSET BadYCoordMsg
```

```
                call WriteString
                jmp  quit
            .ENDIF
            call Gotoxy
    quit:
            ret
    SetCursorPosition ENDP
```

College Registration Example

Suppose a college student wants to register for courses. We will use two criteria to determine whether or not the student can register: The first is the person's grade average, based on a 0 to 400 scale, where 400 is the highest possible grade. The second is the number of credits the person wants to take. A multiway branch structure can be used, involving .IF, .ELSEIF, and .ENDIF. The following shows an example (see *Regist.asm*):

```
    .data
    TRUE = 1
    FALSE = 0
    gradeAverage  WORD 275                ; test value
    credits       WORD 12                 ; test value
    OkToRegister  BYTE ?
    .code
        mov OkToRegister,FALSE
        .IF gradeAverage > 350
           mov OkToRegister,TRUE
        .ELSEIF (gradeAverage > 250) && (credits <= 16)
           mov OkToRegister,TRUE
        .ELSEIF (credits <= 12)
           mov OkToRegister,TRUE
        .ENDIF
```

Table 6-8 lists the corresponding code generated by the assembler, which you can view by looking at the *Disassembly* window of the Microsoft Visual Studio debugger. (It has been cleaned up here a bit to make it easier to read.) MASM-generated code will appear in the source listing file if you use the /Sg command-line option when assembling programs.

Table 6-8   Registration Example, MASM-Generated Code.

```
            mov   byte ptr OkToRegister,FALSE
            cmp   word ptr gradeAverage,350
            jbe   @C0006
            mov   byte ptr OkToRegister,TRUE
            jmp   @C0008
      @C0006:
            cmp   word ptr gradeAverage,250
            jbe   @C0009
            cmp   word ptr credits,16
            ja    @C0009
            mov   byte ptr OkToRegister,TRUE
            jmp   @C0008
      @C0009:
            cmp   word ptr credits,12
            ja    @C0008
            mov   byte ptr OkToRegister,TRUE
      @C0008:
```

6.7.3 .REPEAT and .WHILE Directives

The .REPEAT and .WHILE directives offer alternatives to writing your own loops with CMP and conditional jump instructions. They permit the conditional expressions listed earlier in Table 6-7. The .REPEAT directive executes the loop body before testing the runtime condition following the .UNTIL directive:

```
.REPEAT
    statements
.UNTIL condition
```

The .WHILE directive tests the condition before executing the loop:

```
.WHILE condition
    statements
.ENDW
```

Examples: The following statements display the values 1 through 10 using the .WHILE directive:

```
mov eax,0
.WHILE eax < 10
    inc eax
    call WriteDec
    call Crlf
.ENDW
```

The following statements display the values 1 through 10 using the .REPEAT directive:

```
mov eax,0
.REPEAT
    inc eax
    call WriteDec
    call Crlf
.UNTIL eax == 10
```

Example: Loop Containing an IF Statement

Earlier in this chapter, in Section 6.5.3, we showed how to write assembly language code for an IF statement nested inside a WHILE loop. Here is the pseudocode:

```
while( op1 < op2 )
{
    op1++;
    if( op1 == op3 )
      X = 2;
    else
      X = 3;
}
```

The following is an implementation of the pseudocode using the .WHILE and .IF directives. Because **op1, op2,** and **op3** are variables, they are moved to registers to avoid having two memory operands in any one instruction:

```
.data
X  DWORD 0
op1 DWORD 2                    ; test data
op2 DWORD 4                    ; test data
op3 DWORD 5                    ; test data
.code
    mov eax,op1
    mov ebx,op2
```

```
        mov ecx,op3
        .WHILE eax < ebx
          inc eax
          .IF eax == ecx
              mov X,2
          .ELSE
              mov X,3
          .ENDIF
        .ENDW
```

6.8   Chapter Summary

The AND, OR, XOR, NOT, and TEST instructions are called *bitwise instructions* because they work at the bit level. Each bit in a source operand is matched to a bit in the same position of the destination operand:

- The AND instruction produces 1 when both input bits are 1.
- The OR instruction produces 1 when at least one of the input bits is 1.
- The XOR instruction produces 1 only when the input bits are different.
- The TEST instruction performs an implied AND operation on the destination operand, setting the flags appropriately. The destination operand is not changed.
- The NOT instruction reverses all bits in a destination operand.

The CMP instruction compares a destination operand to a source operand. It performs an implied subtraction of the source from the destination and modifies the CPU status flags accordingly. CMP is usually followed by a conditional jump instruction that may produce a transfer of control to a code label.

Four types of conditional jump instructions are shown in this chapter:

- Table 6-2 contains examples of jumps based on specific flag values, such as JC (jump carry), JZ (jump zero), and JO (jump overflow).
- Table 6-3 contains examples of jumps based on equality, such as JE (jump equal), JNE (jump not equal), and JECXZ (jump if ECX = 0).
- Table 6-4 contains examples of conditional jumps based on comparisons of unsigned integers, such as JA (jump if above), JB (jump if below), and JAE (jump if above or equal).
- Table 6-5 contains examples of jumps based on signed comparisons, such as JL (jump if less) and JG (jump if greater).

The LOOPZ (LOOPE) instruction repeats when the Zero flag is set and ECX is greater than Zero. The LOOPNZ (LOOPNE) instruction repeats when the Zero flag is clear and ECX is greater than zero. (In real-address mode, LOOPZ and LOOPNZ use the CX register.)

Encryption is a process that encodes data, and *decryption* is a process that decodes data. The XOR instruction can be used to perform simple encryption and decryption, one byte at a time.

Flowcharts are an effective tool for visually representing program logic. You can easily write assembly language code, using a flowchart as a model. It is helpful to attach a label to each flowchart symbol and use the same label in your assembly source code.

A *finite-state machine* (FSM) is an effective tool for validating strings containing recognizable characters such as signed integers. It is quite easy to implement a finite-state machine in assembly language if each state is represented by a label.

The .IF, .ELSE, .ELSEIF, and .ENDIF directives evaluate runtime expressions and greatly simplify assembly language coding. They are particularly useful when coding complex compound boolean expressions. You can also create conditional loops, using the .WHILE and .REPEAT directives.

6.9   Programming Exercises

1.   ArrayScan using LOOPZ

Using the ArrayScan program in Section 6.3.4 as a model, implement the search using the LOOPZ instruction. *Optional:* Draw a flowchart of the program.

2.   Loop Implementation

Implement the following C++ code in assembly language, using the block-structured .IF and .WHILE directives. Assume that all variables are 32-bit signed integers:

```
int array[] = {10,60,20,33,72,89,45,65,72,18};
int sample = 50;
int ArraySize = sizeof array / sizeof sample;
int index = 0;
int sum = 0;
while( index < ArraySize )
{
    if( array[index] <= sample )
    {
      sum += array[index];
      index++;
    }
}
```

Optional: Draw a flowchart of your code.

3.   Test Score Evaluation (1)

Using the following table as a guide, write a program that asks the user to enter an integer test score between 0 and 100. The program should display the appropriate letter grade:

Score Range	Letter Grade
90 to 100	A
80 to 89	B
70 to 79	C
60 to 69	D
0 to 59	F

Optional: Draw a flowchart of the program.

4.   Test Score Evaluation (2)

Using the solution program from the preceding exercise as a starting point, add the following features:
  • Run in a loop so that multiple test scores can be entered.
  • Accumulate a counter of the number of test scores.
  • Perform range checking on the user's input: Display an error message if the test score is less than 0 or greater than 100.

Optional: Draw a flowchart of the program.

5.   College Registration (1)

Using the College Registration example from Section 6.7.2 as a starting point, do the following:
  • Recode the logic using CMP and conditional jump instructions (instead of the .IF and .ELSEIF directives).

• Perform range checking on the **credits** value; it cannot be less than 1 or greater than 30. If an invalid entry is discovered, display an appropriate error message.

Optional: Draw a flowchart of the program.

6.   College Registration (2)

Using the solution program from the preceding exercise as a starting point, write a complete program that does the following:

1. Input **gradeAverage** and **credits** from the user. If the user enters zero for either value, halt the program.
2. Perform range checking on both **credits** and **GradeAverage**. Credits must be between 1 and 30. GradeAverage must be between 0 and 400. If either value is out of range, display an appropriate error message.
3. Determine whether or not the person can register (using the existing example) and display an appropriate message.
4. Repeat steps 1 through 3 until the user decides to quit.

Optional: Draw a flowchart of the program.

7.   Boolean Calculator (1)

Create a program that functions as a simple boolean calculator for 32-bit integers. It should display a menu that asks the user to make a selection from the following list:

1. x AND y
2. x OR y
3. NOT x
4. x XOR y
5. Exit program

When the user makes a choice, call a procedure that displays the name of the operation about to be performed. (We will implement the operations in the exercise following this one.)

Optional: Draw a flowchart of the program.

8.   Boolean Calculator (2)

Continue the solution program from the preceding exercise by implementing the following procedures:

• AND_op: Prompt the user for two hexadecimal integers. AND them together and display the result in hexadecimal.
• OR_op: Prompt the user for two hexadecimal integers. OR them together and display the result in hexadecimal.
• NOT_op: Prompt the user for a hexadecimal integer. NOT the integer and display the result in hexadecimal.
• XOR_op: Prompt the user for two hexadecimal integers. Exclusive-OR them together and display the result in hexadecimal.

Optional: Draw a flowchart of the program.

9.   Weighted Probabilities

Write a program that randomly chooses among three different colors for displaying text on the screen. Use a loop to display 20 lines of text, each with a randomly chosen color. The probabilities for each color are to be as follows: white = 30%, blue = 10%, green = 60%. *Hint:* Generate a random integer between 0 and 9. If the resulting integer is in the range 0 to 2, choose white. If the integer equals 3, choose blue. If the integer is in the range 4 to 9, choose green.

10.   Print Fibonacci Until Overflow

Write a program that calculates the Fibonacci number sequence {1, 1, 2, 3, 5, 8, 13, . . .}, stopping only when the Overflow flag is set. Display each unsigned decimal integer value on a separate line.

11. Message Encryption

Revise the encryption program in Section 6.3.4 in the following manner: Let the user enter an encryption key consisting of multiple characters. Use this key to encrypt and decrypt the plain-text by XORing each character of the key against a corresponding byte in the message. Repeat the key as many times as necessary until all plain-text bytes are translated. Suppose, for example the key equals "ABXmv#7". This is how the key would align with the plain-text bytes:

| | | | | | | | | | | | | | | | | | | | | | (etc.) |

Plain text: `T h i s   i s   a   P l a i n t e x t   m e s s a g e`
Key: `A B X m v # 7 A B X m v # 7 A B X m v # 7 A 8 X m v # 7`

(The key repeats until it equals the length of the plain text...)

12. Weighted Probabilities

Create a procedure that receives a value N between 0 and 100. When the procedure is called, there should be a probability of $N/100$ that it clears the Zero flag. Write a program that asks the user to enter a probability value between 0 and 100. The program should call your procedure 30 times, passing it the same probability value and displaying the value of the Zero flag after the procedure returns.

End Note

1. Title of a famous 1968 article by Edsger W. Dijkstra, "Go To Considered Harmful," available at *www.acm.org/ classics/oct95/*.

7

Integer Arithmetic

7.1 Introduction

Every assembly language has instructions that move bits around inside operands. *Shift and rotate* instructions, as they are called, are particularly useful when controlling hardware devices, encrypting data, and implementing high-speed graphics. This chapter explains how to perform shift and rotate operations and how to carry out efficient integer multiplication and division using shift operations.

Next, we explore the integer multiplication and division instructions in the IA-32 instruction set. Intel classifies the instructions according to signed and unsigned operations. Using these instructions, we show how to translate mathematical expressions from C++ into assembly language. Compilers divide compound expressions into discrete sequences of machine instructions. Simulating a compiler helps you to gain a better understanding of how compilers work, and you will be better able to hand optimize assembly language code. You will learn how operator precedence rules and register optimization work at the machine level.

Have you ever wondered how computers add and subtract multiword integers? We will show instructions such as ADC (*add with carry*) and SBB (*subtract with borrow*) that work on integers of any size. Finally, we present Intel's specialized instructions for performing arithmetic on packed decimal integers and integer strings.

7.2   Shift and Rotate Instructions

Along with bitwise instructions introduced in Chapter 6, shift instructions are among the most characteristic of assembly language. *Shifting* means to move bits right and left inside an operand. Intel provides a particularly rich set of instructions in this area (Table 7-1), all affecting the Overflow and Carry flags.

Table 7-1   Shift and Rotate Instructions.

SHL	Shift left
SHR	Shift right
SAL	Shift arithmetic left
SAR	Shift arithmetic right
ROL	Rotate left
ROR	Rotate right
RCL	Rotate carry left
RCR	Rotate carry right
SHLD	Double-precision shift left
SHRD	Double-precision shift right

7.2.1   Logical Shifts and Arithmetic Shifts

There are two ways to shift an operand's bits. The first, *logical shift*, fills the newly created bit position with zero. In the following diagram, a byte is logically shifted one position to the right. Note that bit 7 is assigned 0:

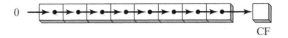

CF

Suppose we execute a single logical right shift on the binary value 11001111, producing 01100111. The lowest bit is shifted into the Carry flag:

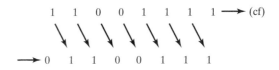

Another type of shift is called an *arithmetic shift*. The newly created bit position is filled with a copy of the original number's sign bit:

Binary 11001111, for example, has a 1 in the sign bit. When shifted arithmetically 1 bit to the right, it becomes 11100111:

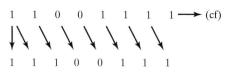

7.2.2   SHL Instruction

The SHL (shift left) instruction performs a logical left shift on the destination operand, filling the lowest bit with 0. The highest bit is moved to the Carry flag, and the bit that was in the Carry flag is lost:

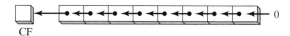

Binary 11001111 shifted left 1 bit becomes 10011110:

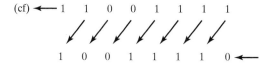

The first operand in SHL is the destination and the second is the shift count:

```
SHL   destination,count
```

The following lists the types of operands permitted by this instruction:

```
SHL   reg,imm8
SHL   mem,imm8
SHL   reg,CL
SHL   mem,CL
```

Intel 8086/8088 processors require *imm8* to be equal to 1. From the Intel 80286 processor onward, *imm8* can be any integer between 0 and 255. On any Intel processor, CL may contain a shift count. Formats shown here also apply to the SHR, SAL, SAR, ROR, ROL, RCR, and RCL instructions.

Examples   In the following instructions, BL is shifted once to the left. The highest bit is copied into the Carry flag and the lowest bit position is assigned zero:

```
mov   bl,8Fh                        ; BL = 10001111b
shl   bl,1                          ; CF,BL = 1,00011110b
```

Multiple Shifts   When a value is shifted multiple times, the Carry flag contains the last bit to be shifted out of the most significant bit (MSB). In the following example, bit 7 does not end up the Carry flag because it is replaced by bit 6 (a zero):

```
mov   al,10000000b
shl   al,2                          ; CF = 0
```

You will find the same to be true when shifting to the right.

Fast Multiplication   SHL can perform high-speed multiplication by powers of 2. Shifting any operand left by n bits multiplies the operand by 2^n. For example, shifting 5 left by 1 bit yields the product 5 * 2:

```
mov   dl,5
shl   dl,1
```

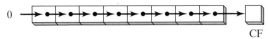

Before: | 0 0 0 0 0 1 0 1 | = 5

After: | 0 0 0 0 1 0 1 0 | = 10

If decimal 10 is shifted left by 2 bits, the result is the same as multiplying 10 by 2^2:

```
mov   dl,10
shl   dl,2                    ; (10 * 4) = 40
```

7.2.3   SHR Instruction

The SHR (shift right) instruction performs a logical right shift on the destination operand, replacing the highest bit with a 0. The lowest bit is copied into the Carry flag, and the bit that was in the Carry flag is lost:

SHR uses the same instruction formats as SHL. In the following example, the 0 from the lowest bit in AL is copied into the Carry flag, and the highest bit in AL is cleared:

```
mov   al,0D0h                 ; AL = 11010000b
shr   al,1                    ; AL = 01101000b, CF = 0
```

Multiple Shifts   In a multiple shift operation, the last bit to be shifted out of position 0 ends up in the Carry flag:

```
mov   al,00000010b
shr   al,2                    ; AL = 00000000b, CF = 1
```

Fast Division   Logically shifting an unsigned integer right by n bits divides the operand by 2^n. Here, for example, we divide 32 by 2^1, producing 16:

```
mov   dl,32
shr   dl,1
```

Before: | 0 0 1 0 0 0 0 0 | = 32

After: | 0 0 0 1 0 0 0 0 | = 16

In the following example, 64 is divided by 2^3:

```
mov   al,01000000b            ; AL = 64
shr   al,3                    ; divide by 8, AL = 00001000b
```

(Division of signed numbers by shifting is accomplished using the SAR instruction because it preserves the number's sign bit.)

7.2.4   SAL and SAR Instructions

SAL (shift arithmetic left) is identical to the SHL instruction. The SAR (shift arithmetic right) instruction performs a right arithmetic shift on its destination operand:

The operands for SAL and SAR are identical to those for SHL and SHR. The shift may be repeated, based on the counter in the second operand:

```
SAR  destination,count
```

The following example shows how SAR duplicates the sign bit. AL is negative before and after it is shifted to the right:

```
mov  al,0F0h                    ; AL = 11110000b (-16)
sar  al,1                       ; AL = 11111000b (-8), CF = 0
```

Signed Division You can divide a signed operand by a power of 2, using the SAR instruction. In the following example, −128 is divided by 2^3. The quotient is −16:

```
mov  dl,-128                    ; DL = 10000000b
sar  dl,3                       ; DL = 11110000b
```

Sign-Extend AX into EAX Suppose AX contains a signed integer and you want to extend its sign into EAX. First shift EAX 16 bits to the left, then shift it arithmetically 16 bits to the right:

```
mov  ax,-128                    ; EAX = ????FF80h
shl  eax,16                     ; EAX = FF800000h
sar  eax,16                     ; EAX = FFFFFF80h
```

7.2.5 ROL Instruction

The ROL (rotate left) instruction shifts each bit to the left. The highest bit is copied into the Carry flag and the lowest bit position. The instruction format is the same as for SHL:

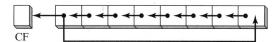

Bit rotation does not lose bits. A bit rotated off one end of a number appears again at the other end. Note in the following example how the high bit is copied into both the Carry flag and bit position 0:

```
mov  al,40h                     ; AL = 01000000b
rol  al,1                       ; AL = 10000000b, CF = 0
rol  al,1                       ; AL = 00000001b, CF = 1
rol  al,1                       ; AL = 00000010b, CF = 0
```

Multiple Rotations When using a rotation count greater than 1, the Carry flag contains the last bit rotated out of the most significant bit position:

```
mov  al,00100000b
rol  al,3                       ; CF = 1, AL = 00000001b
```

Exchanging Groups of Bits You can use ROL to exchange the upper (bits 4–7) and lower (bits 0–3) halves of a byte. For example, 26h rotated four bits in either direction becomes 62h:

```
mov  al,26h
rol  al,4                       ; AL = 62h
```

When rotating a multibyte integer by 4 bits, the effect is to rotate each hexadecimal digit one position to the right or left. Here, for example, we repeatedly rotate 6A4Bh left 4 bits, eventually ending up with the original value:

```
mov  ax,6A4Bh
rol  ax,4                       ; AX = A4B6h
rol  ax,4                       ; AX = 4B6Ah
rol  ax,4                       ; AX = B6A4h
rol  ax,4                       ; AX = 6A4Bh
```

7.2.6 ROR Instruction

The ROR (rotate right) instruction shifts each bit to the right and copies the lowest bit into the Carry flag and the highest bit position. The instruction format is the same as for SHL:

In the following examples, note how the lowest bit is copied into both the Carry flag and the highest bit position of the result:

```
mov  al,01h                      ; AL = 00000001b
ror  al,1                        ; AL = 10000000b, CF = 1
ror  al,1                        ; AL = 01000000b, CF = 0
```

Multiple Rotations   When using a rotation count greater than 1, the Carry flag contains the last bit rotated out of the least significant bit position:

```
mov  al,00000100b
ror  al,3                        ; AL = 10000000b, CF = 1
```

7.2.7 RCL and RCR Instructions

The RCL (rotate carry left) instruction shifts each bit to the left, copies the Carry flag to the least significant bit (LSB), and copies the most significant bit (MSB) into the Carry flag:

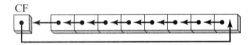

If we imagine the Carry flag as an extra bit added to the high end of the operand, RCL looks like a rotate left operation. In the following example, the CLC instruction clears the Carry flag. The first RCL instruction moves the high bit of BL into the Carry flag and shifts the other bits left. The second RCL instruction moves the Carry flag into the lowest bit position and shifts the other bits left:

```
clc                              ; CF = 0
mov  bl,88h                      ; CF,BL = 0 10001000b
rcl  bl,1                        ; CF,BL = 1 00010000b
rcl  bl,1                        ; CF,BL = 0 00100001b
```

Recover a Bit from the Carry Flag   RCL can recover a bit that was previously shifted into the Carry flag. The following example checks the lowest bit of **testval** by shifting its lowest bit into the Carry flag. If the lowest bit of testval is 1, a jump is taken; if the lowest bit is 0, RCL restores the number to its original value:

```
.data
testval BYTE   01101010b
.code
shr  testval,1                   ; shift LSB into Carry flag
jc   exit                        ; exit if Carry flag set
rcl  testval,1                   ; else restore the number
```

RCR Instruction.   The RCR (rotate carry right) instruction shifts each bit to the right, copies the Carry flag into the most significant bit, and copies the least significant bit into the Carry flag:

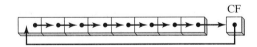

As in the case of RCL, it helps to visualize the integer in this figure as a 9-bit value, with the Carry flag to the right of the least significant bit.

In the following example, STC sets the Carry flag before rotating the Carry flag into the MSB, and rotating the LSB into the Carry flag:

```
stc                     ; CF = 1
mov   ah,10h            ; AH, CF = 00010000 1
rcr   ah,1             ; AH, CF = 10001000 0
```

7.2.8   Signed Overflow

The Overflow flag is set when shifting or rotating a signed integer by one bit position generates a value outside the signed integer range for the operand. To put it another way, the number's sign is reversed. In the following example, a positive integer ($+127$) becomes negative (-2) when rotated left:

```
mov   al,+127           ; AL = 01111111b
rol   al,1             ; OF = 1, AL = 11111110b
```

Similarly, when -128 is shifted one position to the right, the Overflow flag is set. The result in AL ($+64$) has the opposite sign:

```
mov   al,-128           ; AL = 10000000b
shr   al,1             ; OF = 1, AL = 01000000b
```

The value of the Overflow flag is undefined when the shift or rotation count is greater than 1.

7.2.9   SHLD/SHRD Instructions

The SHLD and SHRD instructions were introduced with the Intel386. The SHLD (shift left double) instruction shifts a destination operand a given number of bits to the left. The bit positions opened up by the shift are filled by the most significant bits of the source operand. The source operand is not affected, but the Sign, Zero, Auxiliary, Parity, and Carry flags are affected:

```
SHLD destination, source, count
```

The SHRD (shift right double) instruction shifts a destination operand a given number of bits to the right. The bit positions opened up by the shift are filled by the least significant bits of the source operand:

```
SHRD destination, source, count
```

The following instruction formats apply to both SHLD and SHRD. The *destination* operand can be a register or memory operand, and the *source* operand must be a register. The *count* operand can be the CL register or an 8-bit immediate operand:

```
SHLD reg16,reg16,CL/imm8
SHLD mem16,reg16,CL/imm8
SHLD reg32,reg32,CL/imm8
SHLD mem32,reg32,CL/imm8
```

Example 1   The following statements shift **wval** to the left 4 bits and insert the high 4 bits of AX into the low 4 bit positions of **wval**:

```
.data
wval WORD 9BA6h
.code
mov   ax,0AC36h
shld  wval,ax,4              ; wval = BA6Ah
```

The data movement is shown in the following figure:

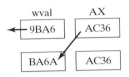

Example 2   In the following example, AX is shifted to the right 4 bits, and the low 4 bits of DX are shifted into the high 4 positions of AX:

```
mov   ax,234Bh
mov   dx,7654h
shrd  ax,dx,4                    ; AX = 4234h
```

SHLD and SHRD can be used to manipulate bit-mapped images, when groups of bits must be shifted left and right to reposition images on the screen. Another potential application is data encryption, in which the encryption algorithm involves the shifting of bits. Finally, the two instructions can be used when performing fast multiplication and division with very long integers.

7.2.10 Section Review

1. Which instruction moves each bit in an operand to the left and copies the highest bit into both the Carry flag and the lowest bit position?

2. Which instruction moves each bit to the right, copies the lowest bit into the Carry flag, and copies the Carry flag into the highest bit position?

3. Which instruction shifts each bit to the right and replicates the sign bit?

4. Which instruction performs the following operation (CF = Carry flag)?
```
Before:   CF,AL = 1 11010101
After:    CF,AL = 1 10101011
```

5. Suppose there were no rotate instructions. Show how we might use SHR and a conditional jump instruction to rotate AL one position to the right.

6. What happens to the Carry flag when the SHR AX,1 instruction is executed?

7. Write a logical shift instruction that multiplies the contents of EAX by 16.

8. Write a logical shift instruction that divides EBX by 4.

9. Write a single rotate instruction that exchanges the high and low halves of the DL register.

10. Write a SHLD instruction that shifts the highest bit in the AX register into the lowest bit position of DX and shifts DX one bit to the left.

11. In the following code sequence, show the value of AL after each shift or rotate instruction has executed:
```
mov   al,0D4h
shr   al,1                       ; a.
mov   al,0D4h
sar   al,1                       ; b.
mov   al,0D4h
sar   al,4                       ; c.
mov   al,0D4h
rol   al,1                       ; d.
```

12. In the following code sequence, show the value of AL after each shift or rotate instruction has executed:

```
mov  al,0D4h
ror  al,3                      ; a.
mov  al,0D4h
rol  al,7                      ; b.
stc
mov  al,0D4h
rcl  al,1                      ; c.
stc
mov  al,0D4h
rcr  al,3                      ; d.
```

13. *Challenge:* Write a series of instructions that shift the lowest bit of AX into the highest bit of BX without using the SHRD instruction. Next, perform the same operation using SHRD.

14. *Challenge:* One way to calculate the parity of a 32-bit number in EAX is to use a loop that shifts each bit into the Carry flag and accumulates a count of the number of times the Carry flag was set. Write a code that does this, and set the Parity flag accordingly.

7.3   Shift and Rotate Applications

7.3.1   Shifting Multiple Doublewords

You can shift an extended-precision integer by dividing it into an array of bytes, words, or doublewords. A common way to store the number in memory is with the low-order value at the lowest address (called *little-endian order*). The following steps show how to shift such an array one bit to the right, using an array of doublewords as an example:

```
ArraySize = 3
.data
array DWORD ArraySize DUP(?)
```

1. Set ESI to the offset of array.
2. Shift the high-order doubleword **at [ESI + 8]** to the right, automatically copying its lowest bit into the Carry flag.
3. Shift the value at **[ESI + 4]** to the right. Its highest bit is automatically filled from the Carry flag and its lowest bit is copied into the new Carry flag.
4. Shift the low-order doubleword at **[ESI + 0]** to the right. Its highest bit is filled from the Carry flag and its lowest bit is copied into the new Carry flag.

The following figure shows the array contents and indirect references:

99999999	99999999	99999999
[esi]	[esi + 4]	[esi + 8]

The program named *MultiShf.asm* implements the following code. We use RCR in this example, but one could use the SHRD instruction instead:

```
.data
ArraySize = 3
array DWORD ArraySize DUP(99999999h)     ; 1001 1001...
.code
mov  esi,0
shr  array[esi + 8],1              ; high dword
rcr  array[esi + 4],1              ; middle dword, include Carry
rcr  array[esi],1                  ; low dword, include Carry
```

The program output shows the numbers in binary before and after the shift:

```
1001 1001 1001 1001 1001 1001 1001 1001 1001 1001 ...(etc.)
0100 1100 1100 1100 1100 1100 1100 1100 1100 1100 ...(etc.)
```

7.3.2 Binary Multiplication

The IA-32's binary multiplication instructions (MUL and IMUL) are considered slow relative to other machine instructions. Assembly programmers often look for better ways to perform binary multiplication, and bit shifting is clearly superior. The SHL instruction performs unsigned multiplication efficiently when the multiplier is a power of 2. Shifting an unsigned integer n bits to the left multiplies it by 2^n. Any other multiplier can be expressed as the sum of powers of 2. For example, to multiply unsigned EAX by 36, we can write 36 as $2^5 + 2^2$ and use the distributive property of multiplication:

```
EAX * 36 = EAX * (32 + 4)
         = (EAX * 32) + (EAX * 4)
```

The following figure shows the multiplication 123 * 36, producing 4428, the product:

$$
\begin{array}{rll}
 01111011 & 123 \\
\times \quad 00100100 & 36 \\
\hline
 01111011 & 123\ \text{SHL}\ 2 \\
+ \quad 01111011 \quad\ \ & 123\ \text{SHL}\ 5 \\
\hline
0001000101001100 & 4428 \\
\end{array}
$$

Bits 2 and 5 are set in the multiplier (36) and they are also the required shift counters. The following code implements this multiplication using 32-bit registers:

```
.code
mov   eax,123
mov   ebx,eax
shl   eax,5          ; mult by 2^5
shl   ebx,2          ; mult by 2^2
add   eax,ebx        ; add the products
```

As a chapter exercise, you will be asked to generalize this example and create a procedure that multiplies any two 32-bit unsigned integers using shifting and addition.

7.3.3 Displaying Binary Bits

A common programming task is converting a binary integer to an ASCII binary string so it can be displayed. The SHL instruction is useful in this regard because it copies the highest bit of an operand into the Carry flag each time the operand is shifted left. The following BinToAsc procedure is a simple implementation:

```
;------------------------------------------------------------
BinToAsc PROC
;
; Converts 32-bit binary integer to ASCII binary.
; Receives: EAX = binary integer, ESI points to buffer
; Returns: buffer filled with ASCII binary digits
;------------------------------------------------------------
      push  ecx
      push  esi

      mov   ecx,32          ; number of bits in EAX
L1:   shl   eax,1           ; shift high bit into Carry flag
```

```
        mov   BYTE PTR [esi],'0'        ; choose 0 as default digit
        jnc   L2                        ; if no Carry, jump to L2
        mov   BYTE PTR [esi],'1'        ; else move 1 to buffer
L2:     inc   esi                       ; next buffer position
        loop  L1                        ; shift another bit to left
        pop   esi
        pop   ecx
        ret
BinToAsc ENDP
```

7.3.4   Isolating MS-DOS File Date Fields

Often a byte or word contains more than one field, making it necessary to extract sequences of bits called *bit strings*. For example, in real-address mode, MS-DOS function 57h returns the date stamp of a file in DX. (The date stamp shows the date on which the file was last modified.) Bits 0 through 4 represent a day number between 1 and 31, bits 5 through 8 are the month number, and bits 9 through 15 hold the year number. Suppose a file was last modified on March 10, 1999. The file's date stamp would appear as follows in the DX register (the year number is relative to 1980):

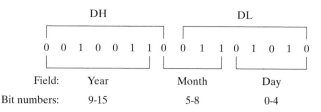

To extract a single field, shift its bits into the lowest part of a register and clear the irrelevant bit positions. The following code example extracts the day number by making a copy of DL and masking off bits not belonging to the field:

```
mov   al,dl                     ; make a copy of DL
and   al,00011111b              ; clear bits 5-7
mov   day,al                    ; save in day
```

To extract the month number, we shift bits 5 through 8 into the low part of AL before masking off all other bits. AL is then copied into a variable:

```
mov   ax,dx                     ; make a copy of DX
shr   ax,5                      ; shift right 5 bits
and   al,00001111b              ; clear bits 4-7
mov   month,al                  ; save in month
```

The year number (bits 9 through 15) is completely within the DH register. We copy it to AL and shift right by 1 bit:

```
mov   al,dh                     ; make a copy of DH
shr   al,1                      ; shift right one position
mov   ah,0                      ; clear AH to zeros
add   ax,1980                   ; year is relative to 1980
mov   year,ax                   ; save in year
```

7.3.5   Section Review

1. Write a sequence of instructions that shift three memory bytes to the right by 1 bit position. Use the following data definition:

    ```
    byteArray BYTE 81h,20h,33h
    ```

2. Write a sequence of instructions that shift three memory words to the left by 1 bit position. Use the following data definition:

    ```
    byteArray WORD 810Dh, 0C064h,93ABh
    ```

3. Write ASM instructions that calculate EAX * 24 using binary multiplication.

4. Write ASM instructions that calculate EAX * 21 using binary multiplication. *Hint:* $21 = 2^4 + 2^2 + 2^0$.

5. What change would be made to the *WriteBin.asm* program in Section 7.3.3 if you wanted to display the binary bits in reverse order?

6. The time stamp of a file uses bits 0 through 4 for the seconds, bits 5 through 10 for the minutes, and bits 11 through 15 for the hours. Write instructions that extract the minutes and copy the value to a byte variable named **bMinutes**.

7.4   Multiplication and Division Instructions

The MUL and IMUL instructions perform unsigned and signed integer multiplication, respectively. The DIV instruction does unsigned integer division, and IDIV performs signed integer division.

7.4.1   MUL Instruction

The MUL (unsigned multiply) instruction comes in three versions: the first multiplies an 8-bit operand by AL, the second multiplies a 16-bit operand by AX, and the third multiplies a 32-bit operand by EAX. The multiplier and multiplicand are the same size, and the product is twice their size. The three formats accept register and memory operands, but not immediate operands:

```
MUL   r/m8
MUL   r/m16
MUL   r/m32
```

The single operand is the multiplier. Table 7-2 shows the default multiplicand and product, depending on the size of the multiplier. Because the destination operand is twice the size of the multiplicand and multiplier, overflow cannot occur. MUL sets the Carry and Overflow flags if the upper half of the product is not equal to zero. The Carry flag is ordinarily used for unsigned arithmetic, so we'll focus on it here. When AX is multiplied by a 16-bit operand, for example, the product is stored in DX:AX. The Carry flag is set if DX is not equal to zero.

Table 7-2   MUL Operands.

Multiplicand	Multiplier	Product
AL	r/m8	AX
AX	r/m16	DX:AX
EAX	r/m32	EDX:EAX

> A good reason for checking the Carry flag after executing MUL is to know whether the upper half of the product can safely be ignored.

MUL Examples

The following statements multiply AL by BL, storing the product in AX. The Carry flag is clear (CF = 0) because AH (the upper half of the product) equals zero:

```
mov   al,5h
mov   bl,10h
mul   bl                          ; AX = 50h, CF = 0
```

The following statements multiply the 16-bit value 2000h by 100h. CF = 1 because the upper part of the product in DX is not equal to zero:

```
.data
val1  WORD  2000h
val2  WORD  0100h
.code
mov  ax,val1                      ; AX = 2000h
mul  val2                         ; DX:AX = 00200000h, CF = 1
```

The following statements multiply 12345h by 1000h, producing a 64-bit product. CF = 0 because EDX equals zero:

```
mov  eax,12345h
mov  ebx,1000h
mul  ebx                          ; EDX:EAX = 0000000012345000h, CF = 0
```

7.4.2   IMUL Instruction

The IMUL (signed multiply) instruction performs signed integer multiplication by preserving the sign of the product. The IA-32 instruction set supports three formats for the instruction: one-operand, two-operand, and three-operand formats. In the one-operand format, the multiplier and multiplicand are the same size and the product is twice their size. (The 8086/8088 processors only support the one-operand format.)

One-Operand Formats   The one-operand formats store the product in the accumulator (AX, DX:AX, or EDX:EAX):

```
IMUL  r/m8                        ; AX = AL * r/m byte
IMUL  r/m16                       ; DX:AX = AX * r/m word
IMUL  r/m32                       ; EDX:EAX = EAX * r/m doubleword
```

As in the case of MUL, the storage size of the product makes overflow impossible in the one-operand IMUL instruction. The Carry and Overflow flags are set if the upper half of the product is not a sign extension of the lower half. You can use this information to decide whether to ignore the upper half of the product.

Two-Operand Formats   The two-operand version of this instruction stores the product in the first operand. The first operand must be a register. The second operand can be a register, memory operand, or immediate value. Following are the 16-bit formats:

```
IMUL  r16,r/m16
IMUL  r16,imm8
IMUL  r16,imm16
```

Following are the 32-bit formats, showing that the multiplier can be a 32-bit register, 32-bit memory operand, or immediate value (8 or 32 bits):

```
IMUL  r32,r/m32
IMUL  r32,imm8
IMUL  r32,imm32
```

The two-operand formats truncate the product to the length of the destination. If significant digits are lost, the Overflow and Carry flags are set. Be sure to check one of these flags after performing an IMUL operation with two operands.

Three-Operand Formats   The three-operand formats store the product in the first operand. A 16-bit register or memory operand can be multipied by an 8- or 16-bit immediate value:

```
IMUL  r16,r/m16,imm8
IMUL  r16,r/m16,imm16
```

A 32-bit register or memory operand can be multiplied by an 8- or 32-bit immediate value:

```
IMUL r32,r/m32,imm8
IMUL r32,r/m32,imm32
```

If significant digits are lost, the Overflow and Carry flags are set. Be sure to check one of these flags after performing an IMUL operation with three operands.

Unsigned Multiplication The two-operand and three-operand IMUL formats may also be used for unsigned multiplication because the lower half of the product is the same for signed and unsigned numbers. There is a small disadvantage to doing so: The Carry and Overflow flags will not indicate whether the upper half of the product is Zero.

IMUL Examples

The following instructions multiply 48 by 4, producing +192 in AX. In the product, AH is not a sign extension of AL, so signed overflow occurs:

```
mov   al,48
mov   bl,4
imul  bl                          ; AX = 00C0h, OF = 1
```

The following instructions multiply −4 by 4, producing −16 in AX. AH is a sign extension of AL in the product, so the Overflow flag is clear:

```
mov   al,-4
mov   bl,4
imul  bl                          ; AX = FFF0h, OF = 0
```

The following instructions multiply 48 by 4, producing +192 in DX:AX. DX is a sign extension of AX, so there is no signed overflow:

```
mov   ax,48
mov   bx,4
imul  bx                          ; DX:AX = 000000C0h, OF = 0
```

The following instructions perform 32-bit signed multiplication (4823424 * −423), producing −2,040,308,352 in EDX:EAX. EDX is a sign extension of EAX, so the Overflow flag is clear:

```
mov   eax,+4823424
mov   ebx,-423
imul  ebx                         ; EDX:EAX = FFFFFFFF86635D80h, OF = 0
```

The following instructions demonstrate two-operand formats:

```
.data
word1   SWORD 4
dword1  SDWORD 4
.code
mov   ax,-16                       ; AX = -16
mov   bx,2                         ; BX = 2
imul  bx,ax                        ; BX = -32
imul  bx,2                         ; BX = -64
imul  bx,word1                     ; BX = -256
mov   eax,-16                      ; EAX = -16
mov   ebx,2                        ; EBX = 2
imul  ebx,eax                      ; EBX = -32
imul  ebx,2                        ; EBX = -64
imul  ebx,dword1                   ; EBX = -256
```

The following two-operand instructions demonstrate signed overflow because −64000 cannot fit within a 16-bit destination operand:

```
mov  ax,-32000
imul ax,2                            ; OF = 1
```

The following instructions demonstrate three-operand formats, including an example of signed overflow:

```
.data
word1  SWORD 4
dword1 SDWORD 4
.code
imul bx,word1,-16                    ; BX = -64
imul ebx,dword1,-16                  ; EBX = -64
imul ebx,dword1,-2000000000         ; OF = 1
```

7.4.3 Benchmarking Multiplication Operations

Now that you have seen multiplication performed by bit shifting and by the standard MUL and IMUL instructions, it is interesting to compare their relative performance. The following procedures multiply EAX by 36 using the two approaches:

```
mult_by_shifting PROC
;
; Multiplies EAX by 36 using SHL, LOOP_COUNT times.

        mov    ecx,LOOP_COUNT
L1:     push   eax                   ; save original EAX
        mov    ebx,eax
        shl    eax,5
        shl    ebx,2
        add    eax,ebx
        pop    eax                   ; restore EAX
        loop   L1

        ret
mult_by_shifting ENDP

mult_by_MUL PROC
;
; Multiplies EAX by 36 using MUL, LOOP_COUNT times.

        mov    ecx,LOOP_COUNT
L1:     push   eax                   ; save original EAX
        mov    ebx,36
        mul    ebx
        pop    eax                   ; restore EAX
        loop   L1

        ret
mult_by_MUL ENDP
```

Lets call **mult_by_shifting** a large number of times and record the execution time:

```
.data
LOOP_COUNT = 0FFFFFFFFh
.data
intval DWORD 5
startTime DWORD ?
.code
```

```
call  GetMseconds                    ; get start time
mov   startTime,eax

mov   eax,intval                     ; multiply now
call  mult_by_shifting

call  GetMseconds                    ; get stop time
sub   eax,startTime
call  WriteDec                       ; display elapsed time
```

Assuming we call **mult_by_MUL** in the same manner, the resulting timings on a 4-GHz Pentium 4 are clear: The SHL approach executes in 6.078 seconds and the MUL approach executes in 20.718 seconds. In other words, using the MUL instruction causes the calculation to be 241 percent slower! (See the *CompareMult.asm* program.)

7.4.4   DIV Instruction

The DIV (unsigned divide) instruction performs 8-bit, 16-bit, and 32-bit unsigned integer division. The single register or memory operand is the divisor. The formats are

```
DIV   r/m8
DIV   r/m16
DIV   r/m32
```

The following table shows the relationship between the dividend, divisor, quotient, and remainder:

Dividend	Divisor	Quotient	Remainder
AX	r/m8	AL	AH
DX:AX	r/m16	AX	DX
EDX:EAX	r/m32	EAX	EDX

DIV Examples

The following instructions perform 8-bit unsigned division (83h / 2), producing a quotient of 41h and a remainder of 1:

```
mov   ax,0083h                       ; dividend
mov   bl,2                           ; divisor
div   bl                             ; AL = 41h,  AH = 01h
```

The following instructions perform 16-bit unsigned division (8003h / 100h), producing a quotient of 80h and a remainder of 3. DX contains the high part of the dividend, so it must be cleared before the DIV instruction executes:

```
mov   dx,0                           ; clear dividend, high
mov   ax,8003h                       ; dividend, low
mov   cx,100h                        ; divisor
div   cx                             ; AX = 0080h,  DX = 0003h
```

The following instructions perform 32-bit unsigned division using a memory operand as the divisor:

```
.data
dividend QWORD 0000000800300020h
divisor  DWORD 00000100h
.code
mov   edx,DWORD PTR dividend + 4     ; high doubleword
mov   eax,DWORD PTR dividend         ; low doubleword
div   divisor                        ; EAX = 08003000h, EDX = 00000020h
```

7.4.5 Signed Integer Division

Signed integer division is nearly identical to unsigned division, with one important difference: The implied dividend must be fully sign-extended before the division takes place. First we will look at sign extension instructions. Then we will apply them to the signed integer divide instruction, IDIV.

Sign Extension Instructions (CBW, CWD, CDQ)

Dividends of signed integer division instructions must often be sign-extended before the division takes place. (Sign extension was explained in Section 4.1.5.) Intel provides three useful sign extension instructions: CBW, CWD, and CDQ. The CBW instruction (convert byte to word) extends the sign bit of AL into AH, preserving the number's sign. In the next example, 9Bh (in AL) and FF9Bh (in AX) both equal −101:

```
.data
byteVal SBYTE -101          ; 9Bh
.code
mov al,byteVal              ; AL = 9Bh
cbw                         ; AX = FF9Bh
```

The CWD (convert word to doubleword) instruction extends the sign bit of AX into DX:

```
.data
wordVal SWORD -101          ; FF9Bh
.code
mov  ax,wordVal             ; AX = FF9Bh
cwd                         ; DX:AX = FFFFFF9Bh
```

The CDQ (convert doubleword to quadword) instruction extends the sign bit of EAX into EDX:

```
.data
dwordVal SDWORD -101        ; FFFFFF9Bh
.code
mov  eax,dwordVal
cdq                         ; EDX:EAX = FFFFFFFFFFFFFF9Bh
```

The IDIV Instruction

The IDIV (signed divide) instruction performs signed integer division, using the same operands as DIV. Before executing 8-bit division, the dividend (AX) must be completely sign-extended. The remainder always has the same sign as the dividend.

Example 1 The following instructions divide −48 by 5. After IDIV executes, the quotient in AL is −9 and the remainder in AH is −3:

```
.data
byteVal SBYTE -48
.code
mov  al,byteVal             ; dividend
cbw                         ; extend AL into AH
mov  bl,+5                  ; divisor
idiv bl                     ; AL = -9, AH = -3
```

Example 2 16-bit division requires AX to be sign-extended into DX. The next example divides −5000 by 256:

```
.data
wordVal SWORD -5000
.code
mov  ax,wordVal             ; dividend, low
cwd                         ; extend AX into DX
```

```
mov  bx,+256                          ; divisor
idiv bx                              ; quotient AX = -19, rem DX = -136
```

Example 3   32-bit division requires EAX to be sign-extended into EDX. The next example divides
–50000 by 256:

```
.data
dwordVal SDWORD +50000
.code
mov  eax,dwordVal                     ; dividend, low
cdq                                   ; extend EAX into EDX
mov  ebx,-256                         ; divisor
idiv ebx                              ; quotient EAX = -195, rem EDX = +80
```

All arithmetic status flag values are undefined after executing DIV and IDIV.

Divide Overflow

If a division operand produces a quotient that will not fit into the destination operand, a *divide overflow*
condition results. This causes a CPU interrupt, and the current program halts. The following instructions,
for example, generate a divide overflow because the quotient (100h) will not fit into the AL register:

```
mov  ax,1000h
mov  bl,10h
div  bl                              ; AL cannot hold 100h
```

When this code executes under MS-Windows, Figure 7–1 shows the resulting error dialog produced
by MS-Windows:

FIGURE 7–1   Divide Overflow Error Example.

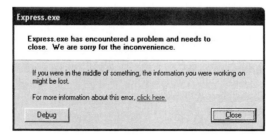

A similar dialog window appears when you write instructions that attempt to divide by zero:

```
mov  ax,dividend
mov  bl,0
div  bl
```

Use a 32-bit divisor to reduce the probability of a divide overflow condition. For example,

```
mov  eax,1000h
cdq
mov  ebx,10h
div  ebx                             ; EAX = 00000100h
```

To prevent division by zero, test the divisor before dividing:

```
mov  ax,dividend
mov  bl,divisor
```

```
cmp  bl,0                          ; check the divisor
je   NoDivideZero                  ; zero? display error
div  bl                            ; not zero: continue
  .
  .
NoDivideZero:                      ;(display "Attempt to divide by zero")
```

7.4.6 Implementing Arithmetic Expressions

Section 4.2.5 showed how to implement arithmetic expressions using addition and subtraction. We can now include multiplication and division. Implementing arithmetic expressions at first seems to be an activity best left for compiler writers, but there is much to be gained by hands-on study. You can learn how compilers optimize code. Also, you can implement better error checking than a typical compiler by checking the size of the product following multiplication operations. Most high-level language compilers ignore the upper 32 bits of the product when multiplying two 32-bit operands. In assembly language, however, you can use the Carry and Overflow flags to tell you when the product does not fit into 32 bits. The use of these flags was explained in Sections 7.4.1 and 7.4.2.

There are two easy ways to view assembly code generated by a C++ compiler: Open a disassembly window while debugging a C++ program or generate an assembly language listing file. In Microsoft Visual C++, for example, the /FA command-line switch generates an assembly language listing file.

Example 1   Implement the following C++ statement in assembly language, using unsigned 32-bit integers:

```
var4 = (var1 + var2) * var3;
```

This is a straightforward problem because we can work from left to right (addition, then multiplication). After the second instruction, EAX contains the sum of **var1** and **var2**. In the third instruction, EAX is multiplied by **var3** and the product is stored in EAX:

```
        mov   eax,var1
        add   eax,var2
        mul   var3                 ; EAX = EAX * var3
        jc    tooBig               ; unsigned overflow?
        mov   var4,eax
        jmp   next
tooBig:                            ; display error message
```

If the MUL instruction generates a product larger than 32 bits, the JC instruction jumps to a label that handles the error.

Example 2   Implement the following C++ statement, using unsigned 32-bit integers:

```
var4 = (var1 * 5) / (var2 - 3);
```

In this example, there are two subexpressions within parentheses. The left side can be assigned to EDX:EAX, so it is not necessary to check for overflow. The right side is assigned to EBX, and the final division completes the expression:

```
        mov   eax,var1             ; left side
        mov   ebx,5
        mul   ebx                  ; EDX:EAX = product
        mov   ebx,var2             ; right side
        sub   ebx,3
        div   ebx                  ; final division
        mov   var4,eax
```

Example 3   Implement the following C++ statement, using signed 32-bit integers:

```
var4 = (var1 * -5) / (-var2 % var3);
```

This example is a little trickier than the previous ones. We can begin with the expression on the right side and store its value in EBX. Because the operands are signed, it is important to sign-extend the dividend into EDX and use the IDIV instruction:

```
mov   eax,var2               ; begin right side
neg   eax
cdq                          ; sign-extend dividend
idiv var3                    ; EDX = remainder
mov   ebx,edx                ; EBX = right side
```

Next, we calculate the expression on the left side, storing the product in EDX:EAX:

```
mov   eax,-5                 ; begin left side
imul var1                    ; EDX:EAX = left side
```

Finally, the left side (EDX:EAX) is divided by the right side (EBX):

```
idiv ebx                     ; final division
mov   var4,eax               ; quotient
```

7.4.7   Section Review

1. Explain why overflow cannot occur when the MUL and one-operand IMUL instructions execute.
2. How is the one-operand IMUL instruction different from MUL in the way it generates a multiplication product?
3. What has to happen in order for the one-operand IMUL to set the Carry and Overflow flags?
4. When EBX is the operand in a DIV instruction, which register holds the quotient?
5. When BX is the operand in a DIV instruction, which register holds the quotient?
6. When BL is the operand in a MUL instruction, which registers hold the product?
7. Show an example of sign extension before calling the IDIV instruction with a 16-bit operand.
8. What will be the contents of AX and DX after the following operation?
   ```
   mov   dx,0
   mov   ax,222h
   mov   cx,100h
   mul   cx
   ```
9. What will be the contents of AX after the following operation?
   ```
   mov   ax,63h
   mov   bl,10h
   div   bl
   ```
10. What will be the contents of EAX and EDX after the following operation?
    ```
    mov   eax,123400h
    mov   edx,0
    mov   ebx,10h
    div   ebx
    ```
11. What will be the contents of AX and DX after the following operation?
    ```
    mov   ax,4000h
    mov   dx,500h
    mov   bx,10h
    div   bx
    ```
12. Write instructions that multiply −5 by 3 and store the result in a 16-bit variable **val1**.
13. Write instructions that divide −276 by 10 and store the result in a 16-bit variable **val1**.

14. Implement the following C++ expression in assembly language, using 32-bit unsigned operands:
     val1 = (val2 * val3) / (val4 − 3)

15. Implement the following C++ expression in assembly language, using 32-bit signed operands: val1 =
     (val2/val3) * (val1 + val2)

7.5   Extended Addition and Subtraction

Extended precision addition and subtraction is adding and subtracting numbers having an almost
unlimited size. Suppose you were asked to write a C++ program that adds two 1024-bit integers. The
solution would not be easy! But in assembly language, the ADC (add with carry) and SBB (subtract
with borrow) instructions are well suited to this type of problem.

7.5.1   ADC Instruction

The ADC (add with carry) instruction adds both a source operand and the contents of the Carry flag to
a destination operand. The instruction formats are the same as for the ADD instruction:

```
ADC    reg,reg
ADC    mem,reg
ADC    reg,mem
ADC    mem,imm
ADC    reg,imm
```

For example, the following instructions add two 8-bit integers (FFh + FFh), producing a 16-bit
sum in DL:AL, which is 01FEh:

```
mov    dl,0
mov    al,0FFh
add    al,0FFh                    ; AL = FE
adc    dl,0                       ; DL = 01
```

Similarly, the following instructions add two 32-bit integers (FFFFFFFFh + FFFFFFFFh), producing a 64-bit sum in EDX:EAX: 00000001FFFFFFFEh:

```
mov    edx,0
mov    eax,0FFFFFFFFh
add    eax,0FFFFFFFFh
adc    edx,0
```

7.5.2   Extended Addition Example

The following **Extended_Add** procedure adds two extended integers of the same size. It uses a loop
to add each pair of doublewords, save the Carry flag, and include the carry with each subsequent pair
of doublewords:

```
;-------------------------------------------------------
Extended_Add PROC
;
; Calculates the sum of two extended integers stored
; as arrays of doublewords.
; Receives: ESI and EDI point to the two integers,
; EBX points to a variable that will hold the sum, and
; ECX indicates the number of doublewords to be added.
; The sum must be one doubleword longer than the
; input operands.
;-------------------------------------------------------
    pushad
    clc                          ; clear the Carry flag
L1: mov    eax,[esi]             ; get the first integer
```

```
        adc     eax,[edi]          ; add the second integer
        pushfd                     ; save the Carry flag
        mov     [ebx],eax          ; store partial sum
        add     esi,4              ; advance all 3 pointers
        add     edi,4
        add     ebx,4
        popfd                      ; restore the Carry flag
        loop    L1                 ; repeat the loop

        mov     dword ptr [ebx],0  ; clear high dword of sum
        adc     dword ptr [ebx],0  ; add any leftover carry
        popad
        ret
Extended_Add ENDP
```

The following excerpt from ExtAdd.asm calls **Extended_Add**, passing it two 64-bit integers. We are careful to allocate an extra doubleword for the sum:

```
    .data
    op1 QWORD 0A2B2A40674981234h
    op2 QWORD 08010870000234502h
    sum DWORD 3 dup(0FFFFFFFFh)     ; = 0000000122C32B0674BB5736

    .code
    main PROC
        mov     esi,OFFSET op1     ; first operand
        mov     edi,OFFSET op2     ; second operand
        mov     ebx,OFFSET sum     ; sum operand
        mov     ecx,2              ; number of doublewords
        call    Extended_Add

    ; Display the sum.
        mov     eax,sum + 8        ; display high-order dword
        call    WriteHex
        mov     eax,sum + 4        ; display middle dword
        call    WriteHex
        mov     eax,sum            ; display low-order dword
        call    WriteHex
        call    Crlf
        exit
    main ENDP
```

The following output is produced by the program. The addition produces a carry:

```
    0000000122C32B0674BB5736
```

7.5.3 SBB Instruction

The SBB (subtract with borrow) instruction subtracts both a source operand and the value of the Carry flag from a destination operand. The possible operands are the same as for the ADC instruction.

The following example code performs 64-bit subtraction. It sets EDX:EAX to 0000000100000000h and subtracts 1 from this value. The lower 32 bits are subtracted first, setting the Carry flag. Then the upper 32 bits are subtracted, including the Carry flag:

```
    mov  edx,1              ; upper half
    mov  eax,0              ; lower half
    sub  eax,1              ; subtract 1
    sbb  edx,0              ; subtract upper half
```

The 64-bit difference in EDX:EAX is 00000000FFFFFFFFh.

7.5.4 Section Review

1. Describe the ADC instruction.

2. Describe the SBB instruction.

3. What will be the values of EDX:EAX after the following instructions execute?

```
mov   edx,10h
mov   eax,0A0000000h
add   eax,20000000h
adc   edx,0
```

4. What will be the values of EDX:EAX after the following instructions execute?

```
mov   edx,100h
mov   eax,80000000h
sub   eax,90000000h
sbb   edx,0
```

5. What will be the contents of DX after the following instructions execute (STC sets the Carry flag)?

```
mov   dx,5
stc                           ; set Carry flag
mov   ax,10h
adc   dx,ax
```

6. *Challenge:* The following program is supposed to subtract **val2** from **val1**. Find and correct all logic errors (CLC clears the Carry flag):

```
.data
val1   QWORD   20403004362047A1h
val2   QWORD   055210304A2630B2h
result QWORD   0
.code
       mov   cx,8                  ; loop counter
       mov   esi,val1              ; set index to start
       mov   edi,val2
       clc                         ; clear Carry flag
top:
       mov   al,BYTE PTR[esi]      ; get first number
       sbb   al,BYTE PTR[edi]      ; subtract second
       mov   BYTE PTR[esi],al      ; store the result
       dec   esi
       dec   edi
       loop  top
```

7.6 ASCII and Unpacked Decimal Arithmetic

The integer arithmetic shown so far in this book has dealt only with binary values. The CPU calculates in binary, but is also able to perform arithmetic on ASCII decimal strings. The latter can be conveniently entered by the user and displayed in the console window, without requiring them to be converted to binary. Suppose a program is to input two numbers from the user and add them together. The following is a sample of the output, in which the user has entered 3402 and 1256:

```
Enter first number:    3402
Enter second number:   1256
The sum is:            4658
```

We have two options when calculating and displaying the sum:

1. Convert both operands to binary, add the binary values, and convert the sum from binary to ASCII digit strings.

2. Add the digit strings directly by successively adding each pair of ASCII digits (2 + 6, 0 + 5, 4 + 2, and 3 + 1). The sum is an ASCII digit string, so it can be directly displayed on the screen.

The second option requires the use of specialized instructions that adjust the sum after adding each pair of ASCII digits. Four instructions that deal with ASCII addition, subtraction, multiplication, and division are as follows:

AAA	(ASCII adjust after addition)
AAS	(ASCII adjust after subtraction)
AAM	(ASCII adjust after multiplication)
AAD	(ASCII adjust before division)

ASCII Decimal and Unpacked Decimal   The high 4 bits of an unpacked decimal integer are always zeros, whereas the same bits in an ASCII decimal number are equal to 0011b. In any case, both types of integers store one digit per byte. The following example shows how 3402 would be stored in both formats:

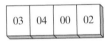

ASCII format: | 33 | 34 | 30 | 32 | Unpacked: | 03 | 04 | 00 | 02 |

(all values are in hexadecimal)

Although ASCII arithmetic executes more slowly than binary arithmetic, it has two distinct advantages:

- Conversion from string format before performing arithmetic is not necessary.
- Using an assumed decimal point permits oprations on real numbers without danger of the roundoff errors that occur with floating-point numbers.

ASCII addition and subtraction permit operands to be in ASCII format or unpacked decimal format. Only unpacked decimal numbers can be used for multiplication and division.

7.6.1   AAA Instruction

The AAA (ASCII adjust after addition) instruction adjusts the binary result of an ADD or ADC instruction. Assuming AX contains a binary value produced by adding two ASCII digits, AAA converts AX to two unpacked decimal digits. Once in unpacked format, AH and AL can easily be converted to ASCII by ORing them with 30h.

The following example shows how to add the ASCII digits 8 and 2 correctly, using the AAA instruction. You must clear AH to zero before performing the addition or it will influence the result returned by AAA. The last instruction converts AH and AL to ASCII digits:

```
mov   ah,0
mov   al,'8'          ; AX = 0038h
add   al,'2'          ; AX = 006Ah
aaa                   ; AX = 0100h (ASCII adjust result)
or    ax,3030h        ; AX = 3130h = '10' (convert to ASCII)
```

Multibyte Addition Using AAA

Let's look at a procedure that adds ASCII decimal values with implied decimal points. The implementation is a bit more complex than one would imagine because the carry from each digit addition must be propagated to the next highest position. In the following pseudocode, the name *acc* refers to an 8-bit accumulator register:

```
esi (index) = length of first_number - 1
edi (index) = length of first_number
ecx = length of first_number
```

```
      set carry value to 0
      Loop
            acc = first_number[esi]
            add previous carry to acc
            save carry in carry1
            acc += second_number[esi]
            OR the carry with carry1
            sum[edi] = acc
            dec edi
      Until ecx == 0
      Store last carry digit in sum
```

The carry digit must always be converted to ASCII. When you add the carry digit to the first operand, you must adjust the result with AAA. Here is the listing:

```
      TITLE ASCII Addition                          (ASCII_add.asm)

      ; Perform ASCII arithmetic on strings having
      ; an implied fixed decimal point.

      INCLUDE Irvine32.inc

      DECIMAL_OFFSET = 5                ; offset from right of string
      .data
      decimal_one BYTE "100123456789765"     ; 1001234567.89765
      decimal_two BYTE "900402076502015"     ; 9004020765.02015
      sum BYTE (SIZEOF decimal_one + 1) DUP(0),0

      .code
      main PROC
      ; Start at the last digit position.
            mov    esi,SIZEOF decimal_one - 1
            mov    edi,SIZEOF decimal_one
            mov    ecx,SIZEOF decimal_one
            mov    bh,0                 ; set carry value to zero

      L1:   mov    ah,0                 ; clear AH before addition
            mov    al,decimal_one[esi]  ; get the first digit
            add    al,bh                ; add the previous carry
            aaa                         ; adjust the sum (AH = carry)
            mov    bh,ah                ; save the carry in carry1
            or     bh,30h               ; convert it to ASCII
            add    al,decimal_two[esi]  ; add the second digit
            aaa                         ; adjust the sum (AH = carry)
            or     bh,ah                ; OR the carry with carry1
            or     bh,30h               ; convert it to ASCII
            or     al,30h               ; convert AL back to ASCII
            mov    sum[edi],al          ; save it in the sum
            dec    esi                  ; back up one digit
            dec    edi
            loop   L1
            mov    sum[edi],bh          ; save last carry digit

      ; Display the sum as a string.
            mov    edx,OFFSET sum
            call   WriteString
            call   Crlf

            exit
      main ENDP
      END main
```

Here is the program's output, showing the sum without a decimal point:

```
1000525533291780
```

7.6.2 AAS Instruction

The AAS (ASCII adjust after subtraction) instruction follows a SUB or SBB instruction that has subtracted one unpacked decimal value from another and stored the result in AL. It makes the result in AL consistent with ASCII digit representation. Adjustment is necessary only when the subtraction generates a negative result. For example, the following statements subtract ASCII 9 from 8:

```
.data
val1 BYTE '8'
val2 BYTE '9'
.code
mov   ah,0
mov   al,val1                  ; AX = 0038h
sub   al,val2                  ; AX = 00FFh
aas                           ; AX = FF09h
pushf                         ; save the Carry flag
or    al,30h                  ; AX = FF39h
popf                          ; restore the Carry flag
```

After the SUB instruction, AX equals 00FFh. The AAS instruction converts AL to 09h and subtracts 1 from AH, setting it to FFh and setting the Carry flag.

7.6.3 AAM Instruction

The AAM (ASCII adjust after multiplication) instruction converts the binary product produced by MUL to unpacked decimal. The multiplication can only use unpacked decimals. In the following example, we multiply 5 by 6 and adjust the result in AX. After adjustment, AX = 0300h, the unpacked decimal representation of 30:

```
.data
AscVal BYTE 05h,06h
.code
mov   bl,ascVal                ; first operand
mov   al,[ascVal+1]            ; second operand
mul   bl                      ; AX = 001Eh
aam                           ; AX = 0300h
```

7.6.4 AAD Instruction

The AAD (ASCII adjust before division) instruction converts an unpacked decimal dividend in AX to binary in preparation for executing the DIV instruction. The following example converts unpacked 0307h to binary, then divides it by 5. DIV produces a quotient of 07h in AL and a remainder of 02h in AH:

```
.data
quotient  BYTE ?
remainder BYTE ?
.code
mov   ax,0307h                 ; dividend
aad                           ; AX = 0025h
mov   bl,5                     ; divisor
div   bl                      ; AX = 0207h
mov   quotient,al
mov   remainder,ah
```

7.6.5   Section Review

1. Write a single instruction that converts a two-digit unpacked decimal integer in AX to ASCII decimal.

2. Write a single instruction that converts a two-digit ASCII decimal integer in AX to unpacked decimal format.

3. Write a two-instruction sequence that converts a two-digit ASCII decimal number in AX to binary.

4. Write a single instruction that converts an unsigned binary integer in AX to unpacked decimal.

5. *Challenge:* Write a procedure that displays an unsigned 8-bit binary value in decimal format. Pass the binary value in AL. The input range is limited 0 to 99, decimal. The only procedure you can call from the book's link library is WriteChar. The procedure should contain no more than eight instructions. Here is a sample call:

```
mov   al,65                          ; range limit: 0 to 99
call showDecimal8
```

6. *Challenge:* Suppose AX contains 0072h and the Auxiliary Carry flag is set as a result of adding two unknown ASCII decimal digits. Use the Intel IA-32 Instruction Set Reference Manual to determine what output the AAA instruction would produce. Explain your answer.

7.7   Packed Decimal Arithmetic

Packed decimal integers store two decimal digits per byte. Each digit is represented by four bits. If there is an odd number of digits, the highest nybble is filled with a zero. Storage sizes may vary:

```
bcd1 QWORD 2345673928737285h         ; 2,345,673,928,737,285 decimal
bcd2 DWORD 12345678h                 ; 12,345,678 decimal
bcd3 DWORD 08723654h                 ; 8,723,654 decimal
bcd4 WORD 9345h                      ; 9,345 decimal
bcd5 WORD 0237h                      ; 237 decimal
bcd6 BYTE 34h                        ; 34 decimal
```

Packed decimal storage has at least two strengths:

• The numbers can have almost any number of significant digits. This makes it possible to perform calculations with a great deal of accuracy.

• Conversion of packed decimal numbers to ASCII (and vice versa) is relatively simple.

Two instructions, DAA (decimal adjust after addition) and DAS (decimal adjust after subtraction), adjust the result of an addition or subtraction operation on packed decimals. Unfortunately, no such instructions exist for multiplication and division. In those cases, the number must be unpacked, multiplied or divided, and repacked.

7.7.1   DAA Instruction

The DAA (decimal adjust after addition) instruction converts a binary sum produced by ADD or ADC in AL to packed decimal format. For example, the following instructions add packed decimals 35 and 48. The binary sum (7Dh) is adjusted to 83h, the packed decimal sum of 35 and 48.

```
mov   al,35h
add   al,48h                         ; AL = 7Dh
daa                                  ; AL = 83h (adjusted result)
```

The internal logic of DAA is documented in the IA-32 Instruction Set Reference Manual.

Example   The following program adds two 16-bit packed decimal integers and stores the sum in a packed doubleword. Addition requires the sum variable to contain space for one more digit than the operands:

```
TITLE Packed Decimal Example         (AddPacked.asm)

; Demonstrate packed decimal addition.
INCLUDE Irvine32.inc
```

```
.data
packed_1 WORD 4536h
packed_2 WORD 7207h
sum DWORD ?

.code
main PROC
; Initialize sum and index.
      mov    sum,0
      mov    esi,0

; Add low bytes.
      mov    al,BYTE PTR packed_1[esi]
      add    al,BYTE PTR packed_2[esi]
      daa
      mov    BYTE PTR sum[esi],al

; Add high bytes, include carry.
      inc    esi
      mov    al,BYTE PTR packed_1[esi]
      adc    al,BYTE PTR packed_2[esi]
      daa
      mov    BYTE PTR sum[esi],al

; Add final carry, if any.
      inc    esi
      mov    al,0
      adc    al,0
      mov    BYTE PTR sum[esi],al

; Display the sum in hexadecimal.
      mov    eax,sum
      call   WriteHex
      call   Crlf
      exit
main ENDP
END main
```

Needless to say, the program contains repetitive code that suggests using a loop. One of the chapter exercises will ask you to create a procedure that adds packed decimal integers of any size.

7.7.2 DAS Instruction

The DAS (decimal adjust after subtraction) instruction converts the binary result of a SUB or SBB instruction in AL to packed decimal format. For example, the following statements subtract packed decimal 48 from 85 and adjust the result:

```
mov   bl,48h
mov   al,85h
sub   al,bl            ; AL = 3Dh
das                    ; AL = 37h  (adjusted result)
```

The internal logic of DAS is documented in the IA-32 Instruction Set Reference Manual.

7.7.3 Section Review

1. Under what circumstances does DAA instruction set the Carry flag? Give an example.
2. Under what circumstances does DAS instruction set the Carry flag? Give an example.
3. When adding two packed decimal integers of length n bytes, how many storage bytes must be reserved for the sum?

4.   *Challenge:* Suppose AL contains 3Dh, AF = 0, and CF = 0. Using the IA-32 Instruction Set Reference Manual as a guide, explain the steps used by the DAS instruction to convert AL to packed decimal (37h).

7.8   Chapter Summary

Along with the bitwise instructions from the preceding chapter, shift instructions are among the most characteristic of assembly language. To *shift* a number means to move its bits right or left.

The SHL (shift left) instruction shifts each bit in a destination operand to the left, filling the lowest bit with 0. One of the best uses of SHL is for performing high-speed multiplication by powers of 2. Shifting any operand left by n bits multiplies the operand by 2^n. The SHR (shift right) instruction shifts each bit to the right, replacing the highest bit with a 0. Shifting any operand right by n bits divides the operand by 2^n.

SAL (shift arithmetic left) and SAR (shift arithmetic right) are shift instructions specifically designed for shifting signed numbers.

The ROL (rotate left) instruction shifts each bit to the left and copies the highest bit to both the Carry flag and the lowest bit position. The ROR (rotate right) instruction shifts each bit to the right and copies the lowest bit to both the Carry flag and the highest bit position.

The RCL (rotate carry left) instruction shifts each bit to the left and copies the highest bit into the Carry flag, which is first copied into the lowest bit of the result. The RCR (rotate carry right) instruction shifts each bit to the right and copies the lowest bit into the Carry flag. The Carry flag is copied into the highest bit of the result.

The SHLD (shift left double) and SHRD (shift right double) instructions, available on IA-32 processors, are particularly effective for shifting bits in large integers.

The MUL instruction multiplies an 8-, 16-, or 32-bit operand by AL, AX, or EAX. The IMUL instruction performs signed integer multiplication. It has three formats: single operand, double operand, and three operand.

The DIV instruction performs 8-bit, 16-bit, and 32-bit division on unsigned integers. The IDIV instruction performs signed integer division, using the same operands as the DIV instruction.

The CBW (convert byte to word) instruction extends the sign bit of AL into the AH register. The CDQ (convert doubleword to quadword) instruction extends the sign bit of EAX into the EDX register. The CWD (convert word to doubleword) instruction extends the sign bit of AX into the DX register.

Extended addition and subtraction refers to adding and subtracting integers of arbitrary size. The ADC and SBB instructions can be used to implement such addition and subtraction. The ADC (add with carry) instruction adds both a source operand and the contents of the Carry flag to a destination operand. The SBB (subtract with borrow) instruction subtracts both a source operand and the value of the Carry flag from a destination operand.

ASCII decimal integers store one digit per byte, encoded as an ASCII digit. The AAA (ASCII adjust after addition) instruction converts the binary result of an ADD or ADC instruction to ASCII decimal. The AAS (ASCII adjust after subtraction) instruction converts the binary result of a SUB or SBB instruction to ASCII decimal.

Unpacked decimal integers store one decimal digit per byte, as a binary value. The AAM (ASCII adjust after multiplication) instruction converts the binary product of a MUL instruction to unpacked decimal. The AAD (ASCII adjust before division) instruction converts an unpacked decimal dividend to binary in preparation for the DIV instruction.

Packed decimal integers store two decimal digits per byte. The DAA (decimal adjust after addition) instruction converts the binary result of an ADD or ADC instruction to packed decimal. The DAS (decimal adjust after subtraction) instruction converts the binary result of a SUB or SBB instruction to packed decimal.

7.9   Programming Exercises

1.   Extended Addition Procedure

Modify the **Extended_Add** procedure in Section 7.5.2 to add two 256-bit (32-byte) integers.

2.   Extended Subtraction Procedure

Create and test a procedure named **Extended_Sub** that subtracts two binary integers of arbitrary size. Restrictions: The storage size of the two integers must be the same, and their size must be a multiple of 32 bits.

3.   ShowFileTime

The time stamp of a MS-DOS file directory entry uses bits 0 through 4 for the number of 2-second increments, bits 5 through 10 for the minutes, and bits 11 through 15 for the hours (24-hour clock). For example, the following binary value indicates a time of 02:16:14, in *hh:mm:ss* format:

```
00010 010000 00111
```

Write a procedure named **ShowFileTime** that receives a binary file time value in the AX register and displays the time in *hh:mm:ss* format.

4.   Shifting Multiple Doublewords

Write a procedure that shifts an array of five 32-bit integers using the SHRD instruction (Section 7.2.9). Write a program that tests your procedure and displays the array.

5.   Fast Multiplication

Write a procedure named **FastMultiply** that multiplies any unsigned 32-bit integer by EAX, using only shifting and addition. Pass the integer to the procedure in the EBX register, and return the product in the EAX register. Write a short test program that calls the procedure and displays the product. (We will assume that the product is never larger than 32 bits.)

6.   Greatest Common Divisor (GCD)

The greatest common divisor of two integers is the largest integer that will evenly divide both integers. The GCD algorithm involves integer division in a loop, described by the following C++ code:

```
int GCD(int x, int y)
{
    x = abs(x);                    // absolute value
    y = abs(y);
    do {
      int n = x % y;
      x = y;
      y = n;
    } while (y > 0);
    return x;
}
```

Implement this function in assembly language and write a test program that calls the function several times, passing it different values. Display all results on the screen.

7.   Prime Number Program

Write a procedure named **IsPrime** that sets the Zero flag if the 32-bit integer passed in the EAX register is prime. Optimize the program's loop to run as efficiently as possible. Write a test program that prompts the user for an integer, calls **IsPrime**, and displays a message indicating whether or not the value is prime. Continue prompting the user for integers and calling **IsPrime** until the user enters −1.

8.   Packed Decimal Conversion

Write a procedure named **PackedToAsc** that converts a 4-byte packed decimal integer to a string of ASCII decimal digits. Pass the packed integer and the address of a buffer holding the ASCII digits to the procedure. Write a short test program that displays several converted integers.

9.   AscAdd Procedure

Convert the code for multidigit ASCII addition presented in Section 7.6.1 to a procedure named **AscAdd** with the following parameters: ESI points to the first number, EDI points to the second number, EDX points to the sum, and ECX contains the number of digits in the operands. Write a program that calls AscAdd and calls WriteString to show that the addition worked correctly.

10.   Display ASCII Decimal

Write a procedure named WriteScaled that outputs a decimal ASCII number with an implied decimal point. Suppose the following number were defined as follows, where DECIMAL_OFFSET indicates that the decimal point must be inserted five positions from the right side of the number:

```
DECIMAL_OFFSET = 5
.data
decimal_one BYTE "100123456789765"
```

WriteScaled would display the number like this:

```
1001234567.89765
```

When calling WriteScaled, pass the number's offset in EDX, the number length in ECX, and the decimal offset in EBX. Write a test program that displays three numbers of different sizes.

11.   Add Packed Integers

Using the code in Section 7.7.1, write a procedure named AddPacked that adds two packed decimal integers of arbitrary size (both must be the same). Write a test program that passes AddPacked several pairs of integers: 4-byte, 8-byte, and 16-byte. Display the sums in hexadecimal. Use the following parameter list:

```
AddPacked PROC,
        pNum1:PTR BYTE,                 ; pointer to first number
        pNum2:PTR BYTE,                 ; pointer to second number
        pSum:PTR BYTE,                  ; pointer to sum
        numSize:DWORD                   ; number of bytes to add
```

8

Advanced Procedures

8.1 Introduction

In this chapter, we focus on the underlying structure of subroutines and subroutine calls. There is a natural tendency to look for universal concepts that make learning easier, so we will use this chapter to show how all procedures work, using assembly language as a low-level programming tool. In other words, what you learn here is often discussed in midlevel programming courses in C++ and Java and in a core computer science course called *programming languages*. The following topics, discussed in this chapter, are basic programming language concepts:

- Stack frames
- Variable scope and lifetime
- Types of stack parameters
- Passing arguments by value and by reference
- Creating and initializing local variables on the stack

• Recursion
• Writing multimodule programs
• Memory models and language specifiers

The following optional topics demonstrate high-level directives included in MASM designed to aid application programmers:

• INVOKE, PROC, and PROTO directives
• USES and ADDR operators

Above all, your knowledge of assembly language makes it possible for you to peek into the mind of the compiler writer as he or she produces the low-level code that makes a program run.

A Note about Terminology   Programming languages use different terms to refer to subroutines. In C and C++, for example, subroutines are called *functions*. In Java, subroutines are called *methods*. In MASM, subroutines are called *procedures*. Our purpose in this chapter is to show low-level implementations of typical subroutine calls as they might appear in C and C++. At the beginning of this chapter, when referring to general principles, we will use the general term *subroutine*. Later in the chapter, when concentrating on specific MASM directives (such as PROC and PROTO), we will use the specific term *procedure*.

8.2   Stack Frames

A *stack frame* (or *activation record*) is the area of the stack set aside for passed arguments, subroutine return address, local variables, and saved registers. The stack frame is created by the following sequential steps:

• Passed arguments, if any, are pushed on the stack.
• The subroutine is called, causing the subroutine return address to be pushed on the stack.
• As the subroutine begins to execute, EBP is pushed on the stack.
• EBP is set equal to ESP. From this point on, EBP acts as a base reference for all of the subroutine parameters.
• If there are local variables, ESP is decremented to reserve space for the variables on the stack.
• If any registers need to be saved, they are pushed on the stack.

The structure of a stack frame is directly affected by a program's memory model and its choice of argument passing convention.

There's a good reason to learn about passing arguments on the stack: Nearly all high-level languages use them. If you want to call functions in the MS-Windows Application Programmer Interface (API), for example, you must pass arguments on the stack.

8.2.1   Stack Parameters

There are two basic types of subroutine parameters: *register parameters* and *stack parameters*. The Irvine32 and Irvine16 libraries use register parameters. In this section, we will show you how to declare and use stack parameters.

> Values passed to a subroutine by a calling program are called *arguments*. When the values are received by the called subroutine, they are called *parameters*.

Arguments pushed on the stack when calling a subroutine are accessed by the called subroutine. Register parameters are optimized for program execution speed. Unfortunately, they tend to create code clutter in calling programs. Existing register contents often must be saved before they can be loaded with argument values. Such is the case when calling **DumpMem**, for example:

```
pushad
mov   esi,OFFSET array          ; starting OFFSET
mov   ecx,LENGTHOF array        ; size, in units
mov   ebx,TYPE array            ; doubleword format
```

```
call DumpMem                         ; display memory
popad
```

Stack parameters offer a more flexible approach. Just before the subroutine call, the arguments are pushed on the stack. For example, if **DumpMem** used stack parameters, we would call it using the following code:

```
push  TYPE array
push  LENGTHOF array
push  OFFSET array
call  DumpMem
```

Two general types of arguments are pushed on the stack during subroutine calls:

- Value arguments (values of variables and constants)
- Reference arguments (addresses of variables)

Passing by Value   When an argument is passed *by value*, a copy of the value is pushed on the stack. Suppose we call a subroutine named **AddTwo**, passing it two 32-bit integers:

```
.data
val1  DWORD 5
val2  DWORD 6
.code
push  val2
push  val1
call  AddTwo
```

Following is a picture of the stack just prior to the CALL instruction:

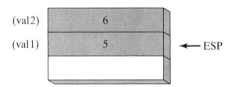

An equivalent function call written in C++ would be

```
int sum = AddTwo( val1, val2 );
```

Observe that the arguments are pushed on the stack in reverse order, which is the norm for the C and C++ languages.

Passing by Reference   An argument passed by reference consists of the address (offset) of an object. The following statements call **Swap**, passing the two arguments by reference:

```
push OFFSET val2
push OFFSET val1
call Swap
```

Following is a picture of the stack just prior to the call to Swap:

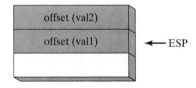

The equivalent function call in C/C++ would pass the addresses of the val1 and val2 arguments:

```
Swap( &val1, &val2 );
```

Passing Arrays   There is one important exception to the rule we just presented regarding passing by value. When passing an array, high-level language programs always pass by reference. It is completely impractical to pass a large amount of data by value because it would entail pushing the data directly on the stack. Doing so would slow the program down and use up precious stack space. The following statements, for example, pass the offset of **array** to a subroutine named **ArrayFill**:

```
.data
array  DWORD 50 DUP(?)
.code
push   OFFSET array
call   ArrayFill
```

Accessing Stack Parameters (C/C++)

C and C++ programs have standard ways of initializing and accessing parameters during function calls. They begin with a *prologue* consisting of statements that save the EBP register, and set EBP to the top of stack. Optionally, they may push certain registers on the stack whose values will be restored when the function returns. The end of the function consists of an *epilogue* in which the EBP register is restored and the RET instruction returns from the function and clears parameters from the stack.

AddTwo Example   The following **AddTwo** function, written in C, receives two integers passed by value and returns their sum:

```
int AddTwo( int x, int y )
{
    return x + y;
}
```

Let's create an equivalent implementation in assembly language. In its prologue, **AddTwo** pushes EBP on the stack to preserve its existing value:

```
AddTwo PROC
       push   ebp
```

Next, EBP is set to the same value as ESP, so EBP can be the base pointer for AddTwo's stack frame:

```
AddTwo PROC
       push  ebp
       mov   ebp,esp
```

After the two instructions execute, the following figure shows the contents of the stack frame. Each entry in the stack is a doubleword:

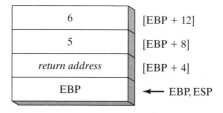

AddTwo could push additional registers on the stack without altering the offsets of the stack parameters from EBP. ESP would change value, but EBP would not.

Accessing Stack Parameters   C and C++ functions use base-offset addressing to access stack parameters. EBP is the base register and the offset is a constant. 32-bit values are usually returned in EAX. The following implementation of AddTwo adds the parameters and returns their sum in EAX:

```
AddTwo PROC
```

```
        push    ebp
        mov     ebp,esp             ; base of stack frame
        mov     eax,[ebp + 12]      ; second parameter
        add     eax,[ebp + 8]       ; first parameter
        pop     ebp
        ret
AddTwo ENDP
```

Cleaning Up the Stack

There must be a way for parameters to be removed from the stack when a subroutine returns. Otherwise, a memory leak results, and the stack becomes corrupted. For example, suppose the following statements in **main** call **AddTwo**:

```
push    5
push    6
call    AddTwo
```

Here is a picture of the stack after return from the call:

Inside main, we can ignore the problem and hope the program terminates normally. If we call AddTwo inside a loop, the stack might overflow because each call eats up 8 bytes of memory. A more serious problem results if we call **Example1** from main, which in turn calls **AddTwo**:

```
main PROC
        call    Example1
        exit
main ENDP

Example1 PROC
        push    5
        push    6
        call    AddTwo
        ret                         ; stack is corrupted!
Example1 ENDP
```

When the RET instruction in Example1 is about to execute, ESP points to the integer 5 rather than the return address that would take us back to main. Needless to say, the program branches to location 5 and crashes:

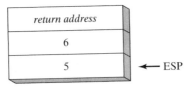

A simple solution to this problem is to add a value to ESP that will point it to the return address. In the current example, we can follow the CALL with an ADD:

```
Example1 PROC
        push    5
        push    6
        call    AddTwo
        add     esp,8               ; remove arguments from stack
```

```
        ret                                     ; stack is ok
    Example1 ENDP
```

This is exactly the action taken by C and C++ programs.

STDCALL Calling Convention   Another common way to handle the stack cleanup problem is to use a convention named STDCALL. We can supply an integer parameter to the RET instruction inside AddSub that fixes ESP. The integer must equal the number of bytes of stack space consumed by the subroutine parameters:

```
AddTwo PROC
    push    ebp
    mov     ebp,esp                     ; base of stack frame
    mov     eax,[ebp + 12]              ; second parameter
    add     eax,[ebp + 8]               ; first parameter
    pop     ebp
    ret     8                           ; clean up the stack
AddTwo ENDP
```

The question then becomes simply, who will be responsible for cleaning up the stack? Code that calls a subroutine, or the subroutine itself? There are tradeoffs. On the one hand, STDCALL reduces the amount of code generated for subroutine calls (by one instruction) and ensures that callers will never forget to clean up the stack. The C calling convention, on the other hand, permits subroutines to declare a variable number of parameters. The caller gets to decide how many arguments it will pass. An example is the **printf** function, whose number of arguments depends on the number of format specifiers in the initial string argument:

```
int x = 5;
float y = 3.2;
char z = 'Z';
printf("Printing values: %d, %f, %c", x, y, z);
```

A C compiler pushes arguments on the stack in reverse order, followed by a count argument indicating the number of actual arguments. The function gets the argument count and accesses the arguments one by one. The function implementation has no convenient way of encoding a constant in the RET instruction to clean up the stack, so the responsibility is left to the caller.

The Irvine32 library uses the STDCALL calling convention in order to be compatible with the MS-Windows API library. The Irvine16 library uses the same convention to be consistent with the Irvine32 library.

> From this point forward, we assume STDCALL is used in all procedure examples, unless explicitly stated otherwise. We will also refer to subroutines as procedures because our examples are written in assembly language.

Passing 8-Bit and 16-Bit Arguments on the Stack

When passing stack arguments procedures in protected mode, it's best to push 32-bit operands. Though you can push 16-bit operands on the stack, doing so prevents ESP from being aligned on a doubleword boundary. A page fault may occur and runtime performance may be degraded. You should expand them to 32 bits before pushing them on the stack.

The following **Uppercase** procedure receives a character argument and returns its uppercase equivalent in AL:

```
Uppercase PROC
    push    ebp
    mov     ebp,esp
    mov     al,[esp+8]                  ; AL = character
    cmp     al,'a'                      ; less than 'a'?
```

```
        jb      L1                      ; yes: do nothing
        cmp     al,'z'                  ; greater than 'z'?
        ja      L1                      ; yes: do nothing
        sub     al,32                   ; no: convert it
L1:     pop     ebp
        ret     4                       ; clean up the stack
Uppercase ENDP
```

If we pass a character literal to Uppercase, the PUSH instruction automatically expands the character to 32 bits:

```
        push    'x'
        call    Uppercase
```

Passing a character variable requires more care because the PUSH instruction does not permit 8-bit operands:

```
.data
charVal BYTE 'x'
.code
        push    charVal                 ; syntax error!
        call    Uppercase
```

Instead, we use MOVZX to expand the character into EAX:

```
        movzx   eax,charVal             ; move with extension
        push    eax
        call    Uppercase
```

16-Bit Argument Example   Suppose we want to pass two 16-bit integers to the AddTwo procedure shown earlier. The procedure expects 32-bit values, so the following call would cause an error:

```
.data
word1 WORD 1234h
word2 WORD 4111h
.code
        push    word1
        push    word2
        call    AddTwo                  ; error!
```

Instead, we can zero-extend each argument before pushing it on the stack. The following code correctly calls AddTwo:

```
        movzx   eax,word1
        push    eax
        movzx   eax,word2
        push    eax
        call    AddTwo                  ; sum is in EAX
```

> The caller of a procedure must ensure the arguments it passes are consistent with the parameters expected by the procedure. In the case of stack parameters, the order and size of the parameters are important!

Passing Multiword Arguments

When passing multiword integers to procedures using the stack, you may want to push the high-order part first, working your way down to the low-order part. Doing so places the integer into the stack in *little endian* order (low-order byte at the lowest address). The following **WriteHex64** procedure receives a 64-bit integer on the stack and displays it in hexadecimal:

```
WriteHex64 PROC
```

```
        push    ebp
        mov     ebp,esp
        mov     eax,[ebp+12]            ; high doubleword
        call    WriteHex
        mov     eax,[ebp+8]             ; low doubleword
        call    WriteHex
        pop     ebp
        ret     8
WriteHex64 ENDP
```

The call to WriteHex64 pushes the upper half of **longVal**, followed by the lower half:

```
.data
longVal DQ 1234567800ABCDEFh
.code
        push    DWORD PTR longVal + 4          ; high doubleword
        push    DWORD PTR longVal              ; low doubleword
        call    WriteHex64
```

Figure 8–1 shows a picture of the stack frame after EBP has been pushed inside WriteHex64.

FIGURE 8–1   Stack Frame after Pushing EBP.

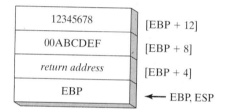

Saving and Restoring Registers

Subroutines often save the current contents of registers on the stack before modifying them so the original values can be restored just before returning. Ideally, the registers in question should be pushed on the stack just after setting EBP to ESP, and just before reserving space for local variables. This helps us to avoid changing offsets of existing stack parameters. For example, assume that the following **MySub** procedure has one stack parameter. It pushes ECX and EDX after setting EBP to the base of the stack frame and loads the stack parameter into EAX:

```
MySub PROC
        push    ebp                     ; save base pointer
        mov     ebp,esp                 ; base of stack frame
        push    ecx
        push    edx                     ; save EDX
        mov     eax,[ebp+8]             ; get the stack parameter
        .
        .
        pop     edx                     ; restore saved registers
        pop     ecx
        pop     ebp                     ; restore base pointer
        ret                             ; clean up the stack
MySub ENDP
```

After it is initialized, EBP's contents remain fixed throughout the subroutine. Pushing ECX and EDX does not affect the displacement from EBP of parameters already on the stack because the stack grows below EBP (see Figure 8–2).

Figure 8–2   Stack Frame for the MySub Procedure.

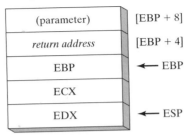

Stack Affected by USES Operator

The USES operator (Chapter 5) lists the names of registers to save at the beginning of a procedure and restore at the procedure's end. MASM automatically generates appropriate PUSH and POP instructions for each named register. *Caution:* **Procedures using explicit stack parameters should avoid the USES operator.** Let's look at an example that shows why. The following **MySub1** procedure employs the USES operator to save and restore ECX and EDX:

```
MySub1 PROC USES ecx edx
      ret
MySub1 ENDP
```

The following code is generated by MASM when it assembles **MySub1**:

```
      push    ecx
      push    edx
      pop     edx
      pop     ecx
      ret
```

Suppose we combine USES with a stack parameter, as does the following **MySub2** procedure. Its parameter is expected to be located on the stack at EBP+8:

```
MySub2 PROC USES ecx edx
      push    ebp                  ; save base pointer
      mov     ebp,esp              ; base of stack frame
      mov     eax,[ebp+8]          ; get the stack parameter
      pop     ebp                  ; restore base pointer
      ret     4                    ; clean up the stack
MySub2 ENDP
```

Here is the corresponding code generated by MASM for **MySub2**:

```
      push    ecx
      push    edx
      push    ebp
      mov     ebp,esp
      mov     eax,dword ptr [ebp+8]   ; wrong location!
      pop     ebp
      pop     edx
      pop     ecx
      ret     4
```

An error results because MASM inserted the PUSH instructions for ECX and EDX at the beginning of the procedure, altering the offset of the stack parameter. Figure 8–3 shows how the stack parameter must now be referenced as [EBP + 16]. USES modifies the stack before saving EBP, going against standard prologue code for subroutines. As we will see in Section 8.5.3, the PROC directive has a high-level syntax for declaring stack parameters. In that context, the USES operator causes no problems.

Procedures using explicit stack parameters should avoid the USES operator.

FIGURE 8–3   Stack Frame of the MySub2 Procedure.

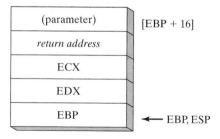

8.2.2   Local Variables

In high-level language programs, variables created, used, and destroyed within a single subroutine are called *local variables*. A local variable has distinct advantages over variables declared outside subroutines:

- Only statements within a local variable's enclosing subroutine can view or modify the variable. This characteristic helps to prevent program bugs caused by modifying variables from many different locations in a program's source code.
- Storage space used by local variables is released when the subroutine ends.
- A local variable can have the same name as a local variable in another subroutine without creating a name clash. This characteristic is useful in large programs when the chance of two variables having the same name is likely.
- Local variables are essential when writing recursive subroutines, as well as subroutines executed by multiple execution threads.

Local variables are created on the runtime stack, usually below the base pointer (EBP). Although they cannot be assigned default values at assembly time, they can be initialized at runtime. We can create local variables in assembly language by using the same techniques as C and C++.

Example   The following C++ function declares local variables X and Y:

```
void MySub()
{
    int X = 10;
    int Y = 20;
}
```

We can use the compiled C++ program as a guide, showing how local variables are allocated by the C++ compiler. Each stack entry defaults to 32 bits, so each variable's storage size is rounded upward to a multiple of 4. A total of 8 bytes is reserved for the two local variables:

Variable	Bytes	Stack Offset
X	4	EBP − 4
Y	4	EBP − 8

The following disassembly (shown by a debugger) of the MySub function shows how a C++ program creates local variables, assigns values, and removes the variables from the stack. It uses the C calling convention:

```
MySub PROC
      push    ebp
      mov     ebp,esp
      sub     esp,8                        ; create locals
```

```
        mov     DWORD PTR [ebp-4],10    ; X
        mov     DWORD PTR [ebp-8],20    ; Y
        mov     esp,ebp                 ; remove locals from stack
        pop     ebp
        ret
    MySub ENDP
```

Figure 8–4 shows the function's stack frame after the local variables are initialized.

Figure 8–4   Stack Frame after Creating Local Variables.

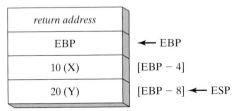

Before finishing, the function resets the stack pointer by assigning it the value of EBP. The effect is to release the local variables from the stack:

```
        mov     esp,ebp                 ; remove locals from stack
```

If this step were omitted, the POP EBP instruction would set EBP to 20 and the RET instruction would branch to memory location 10, causing the program to halt with a processor exception. Such is the case in the following version of MySub:

```
    MySub PROC
        push    ebp
        mov     ebp,esp
        sub     esp,8                   ; create locals
        mov     DWORD PTR [ebp-4],10    ; X
        mov     DWORD PTR [ebp-8],20    ; Y
        pop     ebp
        ret                             ; return to invalid address!
    MySub ENDP
```

Local Variable Symbols   In the interest of making programs easier to read, you can define a symbol for each local variable's offset and use the symbol in your code:

```
    X_local  EQU DWORD PTR [ebp-4]
    Y_local  EQU DWORD PTR [ebp-8]

    MySub PROC
        push    ebp
        mov     ebp,esp
        sub     esp,8                   ; reserve space for locals
        mov     X_local,10              ; X
        mov     Y_local,20              ; Y
        mov     esp,ebp                 ; remove locals from stack
        pop     ebp
        ret
    MySub ENDP
```

Accessing Reference Parameters

Reference parameters are usually accessed by subroutines using base-offset addressing (from EBP). Because each reference parameter is a pointer, it is usually loaded into a register for use as an indirect operand. Suppose, for example, that a pointer to an array is located at stack address [ebp+12]. The following statement copies the pointer into ESI:

```
mov esi,[ebp+12]                    ; points to the array
```

ArrayFill Example   The **ArrayFill** procedure, which we are about to show, fills an array with a pseudorandom sequence of 16-bit integers. It receives two arguments: a pointer to the array and the array length. The first is passed by reference and the second is passed by value. Here is a sample call:

```
.data
count = 100
array WORD count DUP(?)

.code
push    OFFSET array
push    COUNT
call    ArrayFill
```

Inside **ArrayFill**, the following prologue code initializes the stack frame pointer (EBP):

```
ArrayFill PROC
     push   ebp
     mov    ebp,esp
```

Now the stack frame contains the array offset, count, return address, and saved EBP:

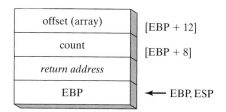

ArrayFill saves the general-purpose registers, retrieves the parameters, and fills the array:

```
ArrayFill PROC
     push   ebp
     mov    ebp,esp
     pushad                         ; save registers
     mov    esi,[ebp+12]            ; offset of array
     mov    ecx,[ebp+8]             ; array size
     cmp    ecx,0                   ; ECX == 0?
     je     L2                      ; yes: skip over loop
L1:
     mov    eax,10000h              ; get random 0 - FFFFh
     call   RandomRange             ; from the link library
     mov    [esi],ax                ; insert value in array
     add    esi,TYPE WORD           ; move to next element
     loop   L1
L2:  popad                          ; restore registers
     pop    ebp
     ret    8                       ; clean up the stack
ArrayFill ENDP
```

LEA Instruction

The LEA instruction returns the offset of an indirect operand. Because indirect operands contain one or more registers, their offsets are calculated at runtime. To show how LEA can be used, let's look at the following C++ program, which declares a local array of char and references **myString** when assigning values:

```
void makeArray( )
{
    char myString[30];
    for( int i = 0; i < 30; i++ )
        myString[i] = '*';
```

The equivalent code in assembly language allocates space for myString on the stack and assigns the address to ESI, an indirect operand. Although the array is only 30 bytes, ESP is decremented by 32 to keep it aligned on a doubleword boundary. Note how LEA is used to assign the array's address to ESI:

```
makeArray PROC
        push    ebp
        mov     ebp,esp
        sub     esp,32              ; myString is at EBP−30
        lea     esi,[ebp−30]        ; load address of myString
        mov     ecx,30              ; loop counter
L1:     mov     BYTE PTR [esi],'*'  ; fill one position
        inc     esi                 ; move to next
        loop    L1                  ; continue until ECX = 0
        add     esp,32              ; remove the array (restore ESP)
        pop     ebp
        ret
makeArray ENDP
```

It is not possible to use OFFSET to get the address of a stack parameter because OFFSET only works with addresses known at compile time. The following statement would not assemble:

```
        mov     esi,OFFSET [ebp−30]             ; error
```

8.2.3 ENTER and LEAVE Instructions

The ENTER instruction automatically creates a stack frame for a called procedure. It reserves stack space for local variables and saves EBP on the stack. Specifically, it performs three actions:

- Pushes EBP on the stack (*push ebp*)
- Sets EBP to the base of the stack frame (*mov ebp, esp*)
- Reserves space for local variables (*sub esp,numbytes*)

ENTER has two operands: The first is a constant specifying the number of bytes of stack space to reserve for local variables and the second specifies the lexical nesting level of the procedure.

```
        ENTER   numbytes, nestinglevel
```

Both operands are immediate values. *Numbytes* is always rounded up to a multiple of 4 to keep ESP on a doubleword boundary. *Nestinglevel* determines the number of stack frame pointers copied into the current stack frame from the stack frame of the calling procedure. In our programs, *nestinglevel* is always zero. The Intel IA-32 manuals explain how the ENTER instruction supports nesting levels in block-structured languages.[1]

Example 1 The following example declares a procedure with no local variables:

```
MySub PROC
    enter 0,0
```

It is equivalent to the following instructions:

```
MySub PROC
        push    ebp
        mov     ebp,esp
```

Example 2   The ENTER instruction reserves 8 bytes of stack space for local variables:

```
MySub PROC
      enter 8,0
```

It is equivalent to the following instructions:

```
MySub PROC
      push   ebp
      mov    ebp,esp
      sub    sp,8
```

Figure 8–5 shows the stack before and after ENTER has executed.

FIGURE 8–5   Stack Frame before and after ENTER Has Executed.

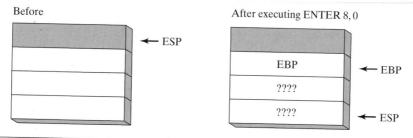

If you use the ENTER instruction, it is strongly advised that you also use the LEAVE instruction at the end of the same procedure. Otherwise, the stack space you create for local variables might not be released. This would cause the RET instruction to pop the wrong return address off the stack.

LEAVE Instruction   The LEAVE instruction terminates the stack frame for a procedure. It reverses the action of a previous ENTER instruction by restoring ESP and EBP to the values they were assigned when the procedure was called. Using the **MySub** procedure example again, we can write the following:

```
MySub PROC
      enter 8,0
      .
      .
      .
      leave
      ret
MySub ENDP
```

The following equivalent set of instructions reserves and discards 8 bytes of space for local variables:

```
MySub PROC
      push   ebp
      mov    ebp,esp
      sub    esp,8
      .
      .
      .
      mov    esp,ebp
      pop    ebp
      ret
MySub ENDP
```

8.2.4   LOCAL Directive

We can guess that Microsoft created the LOCAL directive as a high-level substitute for the ENTER instruction. LOCAL declares one or more local variables by name, assigning them size attributes.

(ENTER, on the other hand, only reserves a single unnamed block of stack space for local variables.) If used, LOCAL must appear on the line immediately following the PROC directive. Its syntax is

```
LOCAL varlist
```

varlist is a list of variable definitions, separated by commas, optionally spanning multiple lines. Each variable definition takes the following form:

```
label:type
```

The label may be any valid identifier, and type can either be a standard type (WORD, DWORD, etc.) or a user-defined type. (Structures and other user-defined types are described in Chapter 10.)

Examples The **MySub** procedure contains a local variable named **var1** of type BYTE:

```
MySub PROC
        LOCAL var1:BYTE
```

The **BubbleSort** procedure contains a doubleword local variable named **temp** and a variable named **SwapFlag** of type BYTE:

```
BubbleSort PROC
        LOCAL temp:DWORD, SwapFlag:BYTE
```

The **Merge** procedure contains a PTR WORD local variable named **pArray**, which is a pointer to a 16-bit integer:

```
Merge PROC
        LOCAL pArray:PTR WORD
```

The local variable **TempArray** is an array of 10 doublewords. Note the use of brackets to show the array size:

```
LOCAL TempArray[10]:DWORD
```

MASM Code Generation

It's a good idea to look at the code generated by MASM when the LOCAL directive is used, by looking at a disassembly. The following **Example1** procedure has a single doubleword local variable:

```
Example1 PROC
        LOCAL temp:DWORD

        mov     eax,temp
        ret
Example1 ENDP
```

MASM generates the following code for Example1, showing how ESP is decremented by 4 to leave space for the doubleword variable:

```
push ebp
mov  ebp,esp
add  esp,0FFFFFFFCh              ; add −4 to ESP
mov  eax,[ebp−4]
leave
ret
```

Here is a diagram of Example1's stack frame:

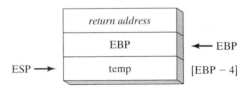

Non-Doubleword Local Variables

The LOCAL directive has interesting behavior when you declare local variables of differing sizes. Each is allocated space according to its size: An 8-bit variable is assigned to the next available byte, a 16-bit variable is assigned to the next even address (word-aligned), and a 32-bit variable is allocated the next doubleword aligned boundary.

Let's look at a few examples. First, the **Example1** procedure contains a local variable named **var1** of type BYTE:

```
Example1 PROC
        LOCAL var1:BYTE

        mov    al,var1                  ; [EBP - 1]
        ret
Example1 ENDP
```

Because stack offsets default to 32 bits, one might expect **var1** to be located at EBP −4. Instead, as shown in Figure 8–6, MASM decrements ESP by 4 and places **var1** at EBP −1, leaving the three bytes below it unused (marked by the letters *nu*).

FIGURE 8–6   Creating Space for Local Variables (Example 1 Procedure).

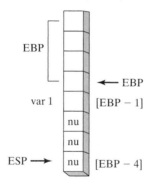

The **Example2** procedure contains a doubleword followed by a byte:

```
Example2 PROC
        LOCAL temp:DWORD, SwapFlag:BYTE
        ;
        ret
Example2 ENDP
```

The following code is generated by MASM for Example2. The ADD instruction adds −8 to ESP, creating an opening in the stack between ESP and EBP for the two local variables:

```
push ebp
mov   ebp,esp
add   esp,0FFFFFFF8h            ; add -8 to ESP
mov   eax,[ebp-4]              ; temp
mov   bl,[ebp-5]              ; SwapFlag
leave
ret
```

Though **SwapFlag** is only a byte, ESP is rounded downward to the next doubleword stack location. A detailed view of the stack, shown as individual bytes in Figure 8–7, shows the exact location of SwapFlag and the unused space below it (labeled *nu*).

FIGURE 8–7   Creating Space in Example 2 for Local Variables.

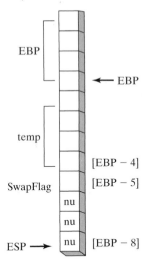

Reserving Extra Stack Space   If you plan to create arrays larger than a few hundred bytes as local variables, be sure to reserve adequate space for the runtime stack, using the STACK directive. In the *Irvine32.inc* library file, for example, we reserve 4096 bytes of stack space:

```
.STACK 4096
```

If procedure calls are nested, the runtime stack must be large enough to hold the sum of all local variables active at any point in the program's execution. For example, suppose **Sub1** calls **Sub2** and **Sub2** calls **Sub3**. Each might have a local array variable:

```
Sub1 PROC
      LOCAL array1[50]:DWORD          ; 200 bytes
   .
   .
Sub2 PROC
      LOCAL array2[80]:WORD           ; 160 bytes
   .
   .
Sub3 PROC
      LOCAL array3[300]:BYTE          ; 300 bytes
```

When the program enters **Sub3,** the runtime stack holds local variables from **Sub1**, **Sub2**, and **Sub3**. The stack will require 660 bytes used by local variables, plus the two procedure return addresses (8 bytes), plus any registers that might have been pushed on the stack within the procedures.

8.2.5   WriteStackFrame Procedure

The book's link library has a useful procedure named **WriteStackFrame** that displays the contents of the current procedure's stack frame. It shows the procedure's stack parameters, return address, local variables, and saved registers. It was generously provided by Professor James Brink of Pacific Lutheran University. Here is the prototype:

```
WriteStackFrame PROTO,
      numParam:DWORD,        ; number of passed parameters
      numLocalVal: DWORD,    ; number of DWordLocal variables
      numSavedReg: DWORD     ; number of saved registers
```

Here's an excerpt from a program that demonstrates WriteStackFrame:

```
main PROC
      mov    eax, 0EAEAEAEAh
      mov    ebx, 0EBEBEBEBh
      INVOKE  aProc, 1111h, 2222h    ; pass two integer arguments
      exit
main ENDP

aProc PROC USES eax ebx,
      x: DWORD, y: DWORD
      LOCAL a:DWORD, b:DWORD
      PARAMS = 2
      LOCALS = 2
      SAVED_REGS = 2
      mov    a,0AAAAh
      mov    b,0BBBBh
      INVOKE WriteStackFrame, PARAMS, LOCALS, SAVED_REGS
```

The following sample output was produced by the call:

```
Stack Frame

00002222   ebp+12 (parameter)
00001111   ebp+8 (parameter)
00401083   ebp+4 (return address)
0012FFF0   ebp+0 (saved ebp) <--- ebp
0000AAAA   ebp-4 (local variable)
0000BBBB   ebp-8 (local variable)
EAEAEAEA   ebp-12 (saved register)
EBEBEBEB   ebp-16 (saved register) <--- esp
```

A second procedure, named **WriteStackFrameName**, has an additional parameter that holds the name of the procedure owning the stack frame:

```
WriteStackFrameName PROTO,
       numParam:DWORD,             ; number of passed parameters
       numLocalVal: DWORD,         ; number of DWordLocal variables
       numSavedReg: DWORD,         ; number of saved registers
       procName: PTR BYTE
```

See the sample program named *Test_WriteStackFrame.asm* for examples and documentation relating to this procedure. In addition, the source code (in *\Lib32\Irvine32.asm*) contains detailed documentation.

8.2.6   Section Review

1. (*True/False*): A subroutine's stack frame always contains the caller's return address and the subroutine's local variables.
2. (*True/False*): Arrays are passed by reference to avoid copying them onto the stack.
3. (*True/False*): A procedure's prologue code always pushes EBP on the stack.
4. (*True/False*): Local variables are created by adding an integer to the stack pointer.
5. (*True/False*): In 32-bit protected mode, the last argument to be pushed on the stack in a procedure call is stored at location ebp+8.
6. (*True/False*): Passing by reference requires popping a parameter's offset from the stack inside the called procedure.
7. What are two common types of stack parameters?

8. Which statements belong in a procedure's epilogue when the procedure has stack parameters and local variables?

9. When a C function returns a 32-bit integer, where is the return value stored?

10. How does a program using the STDCALL calling convention clean up the stack after a procedure call?

11. Here is a calling sequence for a procedure named **AddThree** that adds three doublewords (assume STDCALL):

```
push 10h
push 20h
push 30h
call AddThree
```

Draw a picture of the procedure's stack frame immediately after EBP has been pushed on the stack.

12. How is the LEA instruction more powerful than the OFFSET operator?

13. In the C++ example shown in Section 8.2.2, how much stack space is used by a variable of type *int*?

14. Write statements in the **AddThree** procedure (from the preceding question) that calculate the sum of the three stack parameters.

15. How is an 8-bit character argument passed to a procedure that expects a 32-bit integer parameter?

16. Declare a local variable named **pArray** that is a pointer to an array of doublewords.

17. Declare a local variable named **buffer** that is an array of 20 bytes.

18. Declare a local variable named **pwArray** that points to a 16-bit unsigned integer.

19. Declare a local variable named **myByte** that holds an 8-bit signed integer.

20. Declare a local variable named **myArray** that is an array of 20 doublewords.

21. *Discussion:* What advantages might the C calling convention have over the STDCALL calling convention?

8.3   Recursion

A *recursive* subroutine is one that calls itself, either directly or indirectly. *Recursion*, the practice of calling recursive subroutines, can be a powerful tool when working with data structures that have repeating patterns. Examples are linked lists and various types of connected graphs where a program must retrace its path.

Endless Recursion   The most obvious type of recursion occurs when a subroutine calls itself. The following program, for example, has a procedure named **Endless** that calls itself repeatedly without ever stopping:

```
TITLE Endless Recursion            (Endless.asm)

INCLUDE Irvine32.inc
.data
endlessStr BYTE "This recursion never stops",0
.code
main PROC
     call    Endless
     exit
main ENDP

Endless PROC
     mov     edx,OFFSET endlessStr
     call    WriteString
     call    Endless
     ret                           ; never executes
Endless ENDP
END main
```

Of course, this example doesn't have any practical value. Each time the procedure calls itself, it uses up 4 bytes of stack space when the CALL instruction pushes the return address. The RET instruction is never executed.

> If you have access to a performance-monitoring utility such as the Windows Task manager, open it and click on the Performance dialog. Then run the *Endless.exe* program from this chapter's directory. Memory will slowly fill up and the program will consume 100% of the CPU resources. After a few minutes the program's stack will overflow and cause a processor exception (the program will halt).

8.3.1   Recursively Calculating a Sum

Useful recursive subroutines always contain a terminating condition. When the terminating condition becomes true, the stack unwinds when the program executes all pending RET instructions. To illustrate, let's consider the recursive procedure named **CalcSum**, which sums the integers 1 to n, where n is an input parameter passed in ECX. CalcSum returns the sum in EAX:

```
TITLE Sum of Integers           (CSum.asm)

INCLUDE Irvine32.inc
.code
main PROC
      mov    ecx,5                ; count = 5
      mov    eax,0                ; holds the sum
      call   CalcSum              ; calculate sum
L1:   call   WriteDec             ; display EAX
      call   Crlf                 ; new line
      exit
main ENDP
;----------------------------------------------------
CalcSum PROC
; Calculates the sum of a list of integers
; Receives: ECX = count
; Returns: EAX = sum
;----------------------------------------------------
      cmp    ecx,0                ; check counter value
      jz     L2                   ; quit if zero
      add    eax,ecx              ; otherwise, add to sum
      dec    ecx                  ; decrement counter
      call   CalcSum              ; recursive call
L2:   ret
CalcSum ENDP
end Main
```

The first two lines of **CalcSum** check the counter and exit the procedure when ECX = 0. The code bypasses further recursive calls. When the RET instruction is reached for the first time, it returns to the previous call to CalcSum, which returns to *its* previous call, and so on. Table 8-1 shows the return addresses (as labels) pushed on the stack by the CALL instruction, along with the concurrent values of ECX (counter) and EAX (sum).

Even a simple recursive procedure makes ample use of the stack. At the very minimum, four bytes of stack space are used up each time a procedure call takes place because the return address must be saved on the stack.

8.3.2   Calculating a Factorial

Recursive subroutines often store temporary data in stack parameters. When the recursive calls unwind, the data saved on the stack can be useful. The next example we will look at calculates the

TABLE 8-1   Stack Frame and Registers (CalcSum).

Pushed on Stack	Value in ECX	Value in EAX
L1	5	0
L2	4	5
L2	3	9
L2	2	12
L2	1	14
L2	0	15

factorial of an integer n. The *factorial* algorithm calculates $n!$, where n is an unsigned integer. The first time the **factorial** function is called, the parameter n is the starting number, shown here programmed in C/C++/Java syntax:

```
int function factorial(int n)
{
    if(n == 0)
      return 1;
    else
      return n * factorial(n-1);
}
```

Given any number n, we assume we can calculate the factorial of $n - 1$. If so, we can continue to reduce n until it equals zero. By definition, 0! equals 1. In the process of backing up to the original expression $n!$, we accumulate the product of each multiplication. For example, to calculate 5!, the recursive algorithm descends along the left column of Figure 8–8 and backs up along the right column.

FIGURE 8–8   Recursive Calls to the Factorial Function.

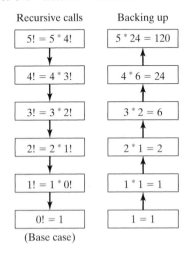

(Base case)

Example Program   The following assembly language program contains a procedure named **Factorial** that uses recursion to calculate a factorial. We pass n (an unsigned integer between 0 and 12) on the stack to the **Factorial** procedure, and a value is returned in EAX. Because a 32-bit register is used, the largest factorial it can hold is 12! (479,001,600).

```
TITLE Calculating a Factorial (Fact.asm)

INCLUDE Irvine32.inc
.code
main PROC
        push   12                      ; calc 12!
        call   Factorial               ; calculate factorial (EAX)
ReturnMain:
        call   WriteDec                ; display it
        call   Crlf
        exit
main ENDP

;-------------------------------------------------------
Factorial PROC
; Calculates a factorial.
; Receives: [ebp+8] = n, the number to calculate
; Returns: eax = the factorial of n
;-------------------------------------------------------
        push   ebp
        mov    ebp,esp
        mov    eax,[ebp+8]             ; get n
        cmp    eax,0                   ; n > 0?
        ja     L1                      ; yes: continue
        mov    eax,1                   ; no: return 1
        jmp    L2

L1:     dec    eax
        push   eax                     ; Factorial(n-1)
        call   Factorial

; Instructions from this point on execute when each
; recursive call returns.

ReturnFact:
        mov    ebx,[ebp+8]             ; get n
        mul    ebx                     ; EDX:EAX = EAX * EBX

L2:     pop    ebp                     ; return EAX
        ret    4                       ; clean up stack
Factorial ENDP
END main
```

When **Factorial** is called, the offset of the next instruction after the call is pushed on the stack. From **main**, this is the offset of the label **ReturnMain**; from **Factorial**, it is the offset of the label **ReturnFact**. In Figure 8–9, the stack is shown after several recursive calls. You can see that new values for *n* and EBP are pushed on the stack each time Factorial calls itself.

Each procedure call in our example uses 12 bytes of stack space. Just before **Factorial** calls itself, *n* − 1 is pushed on the stack as the input argument. The procedure returns its own factorial value in EAX, which is then multiplied by the value pushed on the stack before the call.

8.3.3   Section Review

1. (*True/False*): Given the same task to accomplish, a recursive subroutine usually uses less memory than a nonrecursive one.

2. In the Factorial function, what condition terminates the recursion?

3. Which instructions in the assembly language Factorial procedure execute after each recursive call has finished?

4. What will happen to the Factorial program's output when trying to calculate 13!?

5. *Challenge:* In the Factorial program, how many bytes of stack space are used by the Factorial procedure when calculating 12!?

6. *Challenge:* Write the pseudocode for a recursive algorithm that generates the first 20 integers of the Fibonacci series (1, 1, 2, 3, 5, 8, 13, 21, . . .).

FIGURE 8–9   Partial Stack Frame, Factorial Program.

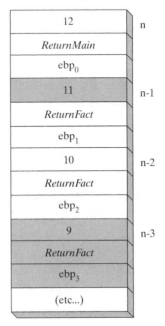

8.4   .MODEL Directive

MASM uses the .MODEL directive to determine several important characteristics of a program: its memory model type, procedure naming scheme, and parameter passing convention. The last two are particularly important when assembly language is called by programs written in other programming languages. The syntax of the .MODEL directive is

```
.MODEL memorymodel [,modeloptions]
```

MemoryModel   The *memorymodel* field can be one of the models described in Table 8-2. All of the modes, with the exception of flat, are used when programming in 16-bit real-address mode.

The real-address mode programs shown so far in this book have all used the small memory model because it keeps all code within a single code segment and all data (including the stack) within a single segment. As a result, we only have to manipulate code and data offsets, and the segments never change.

Protected mode programs use the flat memory model, in which offsets are 32 bits, and the code and data can be as large as 4GB. The *Irvine32.inc* file, for example, contains the following .MODEL directive:

```
.model flat,STDCALL
```

Model Options   The *modeloptions* field in the .MODEL directive can contain both a language specifier and a stack distance. The *language specifier* determines calling and naming conventions for procedures and public symbols. The *stack distance* can be NEARSTACK (the default) or FARSTACK.[2]

Table 8-2   Memory Models.

Model	Description
Tiny	A single segment, containing both code and data. This model is used by programs having a .com extension in their filenames.
Small	One code segment and one data segment. All code and data are near, by default.
Medium	Multiple code segments and a single data segment.
Compact	One code segment and multiple data segments.
Large	Multiple code and data segments.
Huge	Same as the large model, except that individual data items may be larger than a single segment.
Flat	Protected mode. Uses 32-bit offsets for code and data. All data and code (including system resources) are in a single 32-bit segment.

8.4.1   Language Specifiers

Let's take a closer look at the language specifiers used in the .MODEL directive. The options are C, BASIC, FORTRAN, PASCAL, SYSCALL, and STDCALL. The C, BASIC, FORTRAN, and PASCAL specifiers enable assembly language programmers to create procedures that are compatible with these languages. The SYSCALL and STDCALL specifiers are variations on the other language specifiers. In this book, we demonstrate the C and STDCALL specifiers. Each is shown here with the flat memory model:

```
.model flat, C
.model flat, STDCALL
```

STDCALL is used in most of our example programs in this chapter. It is the language specifier used when calling MS-Windows functions. In Chapter 12, we use the C language specifier when linking assembly language code to C and C++ programs.

STDCALL

The STDCALL language specifier causes subroutine arguments to be pushed on the stack in reverse order (last to first). Suppose we write the following function call in a high-level language:

```
AddTwo( 5, 6 );
```

The following assembly language code is equivalent:

```
push 6
push 5
call AddTwo
```

Another important consideration is how arguments are removed from the stack after procedure calls. STDCALL requires a constant operand to be supplied in the RET instruction. The constant indicates the value added to ESP after the return address is popped from the stack by RET:

```
AddTwo PROC
    push    ebp
    mov     ebp,esp
    mov     eax,[ebp + 12]          ; first parameter
    add     eax,[ebp + 8]           ; second parameter
    pop     ebp
    ret     8                       ; clean up the stack
AddTwo ENDPP
```

By adding 8 to the stack pointer, we reset it to the value it had before the arguments were pushed on the stack by the calling program.

Finally, STDCALL modifies exported (public) procedure names by storing them in the following format:

```
_name@nn
```

A leading underscore is added to the procedure name, and an integer follows the @ sign indicating the number of bytes used by the procedure parameters (rounded upward to a multiple of 4). For example, suppose the procedure **AddTwo** has two doubleword parameters. The name passed by the assembler to the linker is **_AddTwo@8**.

The LINK32.EXE utility is case sensitive, so _MYSUB@8 is different from _MySub@8. To view all procedure names inside an OBJ file, use the DUMPBIN utility supplied in Visual Studio with the/SYMBOLS option.

C Specifier

The C language specifier requires procedure arguments to be pushed on the stack from last to first, like STDCALL. Regarding the removal of arguments from the stack after a procedure call, the C language specifier places responsibility on the caller. In the calling program, a constant is added to ESP, resetting it to the value it had before the arguments were pushed:

```
push 6                          ; second argument
push 5                          ; first argument
call AddTwo
add  esp,8                      ; clean up the stack
```

The C language specifier appends a leading underscore character to external procedure names. For example:

```
_AddTwo
```

8.4.2   Section Review

1.   Describe the small memory model.

2.   Describe the flat memory model.

3.   How is the C language option (of the .MODEL directive) different from that of STDCALL in regard to removing arguments from the stack?

8.5   INVOKE, ADDR, PROC, and PROTO (Optional)

The INVOKE, ADDR, PROC, and PROTO directives provide powerful tools for defining and calling procedures. In many ways, they approach the convenience offered by high-level programming languages. From a pedagogical point of view, their use is controversial because they mask the underlying structure of the runtime stack. Students learning computer fundamentals are best served by developing a detailed understanding of the low-level mechanics involved in subroutine calls.

There is a situation in which using advanced procedure directives leads to better programming—when your program executes procedure calls across module boundaries. In such cases, the PROTO directive helps the assembler to validate procedure calls by checking argument lists against procedure declarations. This feature encourages advanced assembly language programmers to take advantage of the convenience offered by advanced MASM directives.

8.5.1   INVOKE Directive

The INVOKE directive pushes arguments on the stack (in the order specified by the MODEL directive's language specifier) and calls a procedure. INVOKE is a convenient replacement for the CALL instruction because it lets you pass multiple arguments using a single line of code. Here is the general syntax:

```
INVOKE procedureName [, argumentList]
```

ArgumentList is an optional comma-delimited list of arguments passed to the procedure. Using the CALL instruction, for example, we could call **DumpMem** after executing several PUSH instructions:

```
push TYPE array
push LENGTHOF array
push OFFSET array
call DumpMem
```

The equivalent statement using INVOKE is reduced to a single line in which the arguments are listed in reverse order (assuming STDCALL is in effect):

```
INVOKE DumpMem, OFFSET array, LENGTHOF array, TYPE array
```

INVOKE permits almost any number of arguments, and individual arguments can appear on separate source code lines. The following INVOKE statement includes helpful comments:

```
INVOKE DumpMem,                     ; displays a block of memory
    OFFSET array,                   ; points to the array
    LENGTHOF array,                 ; the array length
    TYPE array                      ; array component size
```

Argument types are listed in Table 8-3.

Table 8-3   Argument Types Used with INVOKE.

Type	Examples
Immediate value	10, 3000h, OFFSET mylist, TYPE array
Integer expression	(10 * 20), COUNT
Variable	myList, array, myWord, myDword
Address expression	[myList+2], [ebx + esi]
Register	eax, bl, edi
ADDR *name*	ADDR myList
OFFSET *name*	OFFSET myList

EAX, EDX Overwritten   If you pass arguments smaller than 32 bits to a procedure, INVOKE frequently causes the assembler to overwrite EAX and EDX when it widens the arguments before pushing them on the stack. You can avoid this behavior by always passing 32-bit arguments to INVOKE, or you can save and restore EAX and EDX before and after the procedure call.

8.5.2 ADDR Operator

The ADDR operator can be used to pass a pointer argument when calling a procedure using INVOKE. The following INVOKE statement, for example, passes the address of **myArray** to the **FillArray** procedure:

```
INVOKE FillArray, ADDR myArray
```

The argument passed to ADDR must be an assembly time constant. The following is an error:

```
INVOKE mySub, ADDR [ebp+12]         ; error
```

The ADDR operator can only be used in conjunction with INVOKE. The following is an error:

```
mov  esi, ADDR myArray              ; error
```

ADDR passes a near pointer or a far pointer, depending on what is called for by the program's memory model. In protected mode programs, ADDR and OFFSET both pass 32-bit offsets. (The .model directive in *Irvine32.inc* specifies the flat memory model.)

Example   The following INVOKE directive calls **Swap**, passing it the addresses of the first two elements in an array of doublewords:

```
.data
Array DWORD 20 DUP(?)
.code
...
INVOKE Swap,
      ADDR   Array,
      ADDR   [Array+4]
```

Here is the corresponding code generated by the assembler, assuming STDCALL is in effect:

```
push   OFFSET Array+4
push   OFFSET Array
call   Swap
```

8.5.3 PROC Directive

Syntax of the PROC Directive

The PROC directive has the following basic syntax:

```
label PROC [attributes] [USES reglist], parameter_list
```

Label is a user-defined label following the rules for identifiers explained in Chapter 3. *Attributes* refers to any of the following:

```
[distance] [langtype] [visibility] [prologue]
```

Table 8-4 describes each of the attributes.

TABLE 8-4   Attributes Field in the PROC Directive.

Attribute	Description
distance	NEAR or FAR. Indicates the type of RET instruction (RET or RETF) generated by the assembler.
langtype	Specifies the calling convention (parameter passing convention) such as C, PASCAL, or STDCALL. Overrides the language specified in the .MODEL directive.
visibility	Indicates the procedure's visibility to other modules. Choices are PRIVATE, PUBLIC (default), and EXPORT. If the visibility is EXPORT, the linker places the procedure's name in the export table for segmented executables. EXPORT also enables PUBLIC visibility.
prologue	Specifies arguments affecting generation of prologue and epilogue code. See the section entitled "User-Defined Prologue and Epilogue Code" in the MASM 6.1 Programmers Guide, Chapter 7.

Parameter Lists

The PROC directive permits you to declare a procedure with a comma-separated list of named parameters. Your implementation code can refer to the parameters by name rather than by calculated stack offsets such as [ebp+8]:

```
label PROC [attributes] [USES reglist],
      parameter_1,
      parameter_2,
      .
      .
      parameter_n
```

Note the required, but easily missed comma preceding the first parameter. The list of parameters can appear on the same line:

label PROC [*attributes*], *parameter_1, parameter_2, ..., parameter_n*

A single parameter has the following syntax:

paramName:type

ParamName is an arbitrary name you assign to the parameter. Its scope is limited to the current procedure (called *local scope*). The same parameter name can be used in more than one procedure, but it cannot be the name of a global variable or code label. *Type* can be one of the following: BYTE, SBYTE, WORD, SWORD, DWORD, SDWORD, FWORD, QWORD, or TBYTE. It can also be a *qualified type*, which may be a pointer to an existing type. Following are examples of qualified types:

PTR BYTE	PTR SBYTE
PTR WORD	PTR SWORD
PTR DWORD	PTR SDWORD
PTR QWORD	PTR TBYTE

Though it is possible to add NEAR and FAR attributes to these expressions, they are relevant only in more specialized applications. Qualified types can also be created using the TYPEDEF and STRUCT directives, which we explain in Chapter 10.

Example 1   The AddTwo procedure receives two doubleword values and returns their sum in EAX:

```
AddTwo PROC,
     val1:DWORD,
     val2:DWORD
     mov     eax,val1
     add     eax,val2
     ret
AddTwo ENDP
```

The assembly language generated by MASM when assembling AddTwo shows how the parameter names are translated into offsets from EBP. A constant operand is generated for the RET instruction because STDCALL is in effect:

```
AddTwo PROC
     push    ebp
     mov     ebp, esp
     mov     eax,dword ptr [ebp+8]
     add     eax,dword ptr [ebp+0Ch]
     leave
     ret     8
AddTwo ENDP
```

> ***Tip:*** The complete details of MASM-generated procedure code do not appear in listing files (.LST extension). Instead, open your program with a debugger and view the Disassembly window.

Example 2   The FillArray procedure receives a pointer to an array of bytes:

```
FillArray PROC,
     pArray:PTR BYTE
     . . .
FillArray ENDP
```

Example 3   The Swap procedure receives two pointers to doublewords:

```
Swap PROC,
      pValX:PTR DWORD,
      pValY:PTR DWORD
      . . .
Swap ENDP
```

Example 4   The Read_File procedure receives a byte pointer named **pBuffer**. It has a local doubleword variable named **fileHandle**, and it saves two registers on the stack (EAX and EBX):

```
Read_File PROC USES eax ebx,
      pBuffer:PTR BYTE
      LOCAL fileHandle:DWORD

      mov    esi,pBuffer
      mov    fileHandle,eax
      .
      .
      ret
Read_File ENDP
```

The MASM-generated code for Read_File shows how space is reserved on the stack for the local variable (fileHandle) before pushing EAX and EBX (specified in the USES clause):

```
Read_File PROC
      push   ebp
      mov    ebp,esp
      add    esp,0FFFFFFFCh            ; create fileHandle
      push   eax                       ; save EAX
      push   ebx                       ; save EBX
      mov    esi,dword ptr [ebp+8]      ; pBuffer
      mov    dword ptr [ebp-4],eax      ; fileHandle
      pop    ebx
      pop    eax
      leave
      ret    4
Read_File ENDP
```

RET Instruction Modified by PROC   When PROC is used with one or more parameters and STD-CALL is the default protocol, MASM generates the following entry and exit code, assuming PROC has *n* parameters:

```
push ebp
mov  ebp,esp
   .
   .
leave
ret  (n*4)
```

The constant appearing in the RET instruction is the number of parameters multiplied by 4 (because each parameter is a doubleword). The STDCALL convention is the default when you INCLUDE Irvine32.inc, and it is the calling convention used for all Windows API function calls.

Specifying the Parameter Passing Protocol

A program might call Irvine32 library procedures and in turn contain procedures that can be called from C++ programs. To provide this flexibility, the *attributes* field of the PROC directive lets you specify the language convention for passing parameters. It overrides the default language convention specified in the .MODEL directive. The following example declares a procedure with the C calling convention:

```
Example1 PROC C,
    parm1:DWORD, parm2:DWORD
```

If we execute Example1 using INVOKE, the assembler generates code consistent with the C calling convention. Similarly, if we declare Example1 using STDCALL, INVOKE generates consistent with that language convention:

```
Example1 PROC STDCALL,
    parm1:DWORD, parm2:DWORD
```

8.5.4   PROTO Directive

The PROTO directive creates a prototype for an existing procedure. A *prototype* declares a procedure's name and parameter list. It allows you to call a procedure before defining it and to verify that the number and types of arguments match the procedure definition. (The C and C++ languages use function prototypes to validate function calls at compile time.)

MASM requires a prototype for each procedure called by INVOKE. PROTO must appear first before INVOKE. In other words, the standard ordering of these directives is

```
MySub PROTO                        ; procedure prototype

INVOKE MySub                       ; procedure call

MySub PROC                         ; procedure implementation
    .
    .
MySub ENDP
```

An alternative scenario is possible: The procedure implementation can appear in the program prior to the location of the INVOKE statement for that procedure. In that case, PROC acts as its own prototype:

```
MySub PROC                         ; procedure definition
    .
    .
MySub ENDP

INVOKE MySub                       ; procedure call
```

Assuming you have already written a particular procedure, you can easily create its prototype by copying the PROC statement and making the following changes:
• Change the word PROC to PROTO.
• Remove the USES operator if any, along with its register list.

For example, suppose we have already created the **ArraySum** procedure:

```
ArraySum PROC USES esi ecx,
    ptrArray:PTR DWORD,            ; points to the array
    szArray:DWORD                  ; array size
    ; (remaining lines omitted...)
ArraySum ENDP
```

This is a matching PROTO declaration:

```
ArraySum PROTO,
    ptrArray:PTR DWORD,            ; points to the array
    szArray:DWORD                  ; array size
```

The PROTO directive lets you override the default parameter passing protocol in the .MODEL directive. It must be consistent with the procedure's PROC declaration:

```
Example1 PROTO C,
       parm1:DWORD, parm2:DWORD
```

Assembly Time Argument Checking

The PROTO directive helps the assembler compare a list of arguments in a procedure call to the procedure's definition. The quality of error checking is not as good as that of C and C++. Instead, MASM checks for the correct number of parameters, and to a limited extent, matches argument types to parameter types. Suppose, for example, the prototype for **Sub1** is declared thus:

```
Sub1 PROTO, p1:BYTE, p2:WORD, p3:PTR BYTE
```

We will define the following variables:

```
.data
byte_1      BYTE   10h
word_1      WORD   2000h
word_2      WORD   3000h
dword_1     DWORD  12345678h
```

The following is a valid call to Sub1:

```
INVOKE Sub1, byte_1, word_1, ADDR byte_1
```

The code generated by MASM for this INVOKE shows aguments pushed on the stack in reverse order:

```
push   404000h                      ; ptr to byte_1
sub    esp,2                         ; pad stack with 2 bytes
push   word ptr ds:[00404001h]      ; value of word_1
mov    al,byte ptr ds:[00404000h]   ; value of byte_1
push   eax
call   00401071
```

EAX is overwritten, and the **sub esp,2** instruction pads the subsequent stack entry to 32 bits.

Errors Detected by MASM   If an argument exceeds the size of a declared parameter, MASM generates an error:

```
INVOKE Sub1, word_1, word_2, ADDR byte_1          ; arg 1 error
```

MASM generates errors if we invoke Sub1 using too few or too many arguments:

```
INVOKE Sub1, byte_1, word_2          ; error: too few arguments
INVOKE Sub1, byte_1,                 ; error: too many arguments
    word_2, ADDR byte_1, word_2
```

Errors Not Detected by MASM   If an argument's type is smaller than a declared parameter, MASM does not detect an error:

```
INVOKE Sub1, byte_1, byte_1, ADDR byte_1
```

Instead, MASM expands the smaller argument to the size of the declared parameter. In the following code generated by our INVOKE example, the second argument (byte_1) is expanded into EAX before pushing it on the stack:

```
push   404000h                      ; addr of byte_1
mov    al,byte ptr ds:[00404000h]   ; value of byte_1
movzx  eax,al                       ; expand into EAX
push   eax                          ; push on stack
mov    al,byte ptr ds:[00404000h]   ; value of byte_1
```

```
push    eax                         ; push on stack
call    00401071                    ; call Sub1
```

If a doubleword is passed when a pointer was expected, no error is detected. This type of error typically leads to a runtime error when the subroutine tries to use the stack parameter as a pointer:

```
INVOKE Sub1, byte_1, word_2, dword_1      ; no error detected
```

ArraySum Example

Let's review the **ArraySum** procedure from Chapter 5, which calculates the sum of an array of doublewords. Originally, we passed arguments in registers; now we can use the PROC directive to declare stack parameters:

```
ArraySum PROC USES esi ecx,
        ptrArray:PTR DWORD,         ; points to the array
        szArray:DWORD               ; array size

        mov     esi,ptrArray        ; address of the array
        mov     ecx,szArray         ; size of the array
        mov     eax,0               ; set the sum to zero
        cmp     ecx,0               ; length = zero?
        je      L2                  ; yes: quit
L1:     add     eax,[esi]           ; add each integer to sum
        add     esi,4               ; point to next integer
        loop    L1                  ; repeat for array size
L2:     ret                         ; sum is in EAX
ArraySum ENDP
```

The INVOKE statement calls **ArraySum**, passing the address of an array and the number of elements in the array:

```
.data
array DWORD 10000h,20000h,30000h,40000h,50000h
theSum DWORD   ?
.code
main PROC
        INVOKE ArraySum,
           ADDR array,              ; address of the array
           LENGTHOF array           ; number of elements
        mov theSum,eax              ; store the sum
```

8.5.5   Parameter Classifications

Procedure parameters are usually classified according to the direction of data transfer between the calling program and the called procedure:

- *Input:* An input parameter is data passed by a calling program to a procedure. The called procedure is not expected to modify the corresponding parameter variable, and even if it does, the modification is confined to the procedure itself.
- *Output:* An output parameter is created when a calling program passes the address of a variable to a procedure. The procedure uses the address to locate and assign data to the variable. The Win32 Console Library, for example, has a function named **ReadConsole** that reads a string of characters from the keyboard. The calling program passes a pointer to a string buffer, into which ReadConsole stores text typed by the user:

```
.data
buffer BYTE 80 DUP(?)
inputHandle DWORD ?
.code
```

```
INVOKE ReadConsole, inputHandle, ADDR buffer,
    (etc.)
```

- *Input-Output:* An input-output parameter is identical to an output parameter, with one exception: The called procedure expects the variable referenced by the parameter to contain some data. The procedure is also expected to modify the variable via the pointer.

8.5.6 Example: Exchanging Two Integers

The following program exchanges the contents of two 32-bit integers. The Swap procedure has two input-output parameters named **pValX** and **pValY**, which contain the addresses of data to be exchanged:

```
TITLE Swap Procedure Example                    (Swap.asm)

INCLUDE Irvine32.inc
Swap PROTO, pValX:PTR DWORD, pValY:PTR DWORD

.data
Array DWORD 10000h,20000h

.code
main PROC
    ; Display the array before the exchange:
    mov    esi,OFFSET Array
    mov    ecx,2                   ; count = 2
    mov    ebx,TYPE Array
    call   DumpMem                 ; dump the array values

    INVOKE Swap, ADDR Array, ADDR [Array+4]

    ; Display the array after the exchange:
    call   DumpMem
    exit
main ENDP

;-------------------------------------------------------
Swap PROC USES eax esi edi,
        pValX:PTR DWORD,                ; pointer to first integer
        pValY:PTR DWORD                 ; pointer to second integer
;
; Exchange the values of two 32-bit integers
; Returns: nothing
;-------------------------------------------------------
    mov    esi,pValX                ; get pointers
    mov    edi,pValY
    mov    eax,[esi]                ; get first integer
    xchg   eax,[edi]                ; exchange with second
    mov    [esi],eax                ; replace first integer
    ret                             ; PROC generates RET 8 here
Swap ENDP
END main
```

The two parameters in the Swap procedure, **pValX** and **pValY**, are input-output parameters. Their existing values are *input* to the procedure, and their new values are also *output* from the procedure. Because we're using PROC with parameters, the assembler changes the RET instruction at the end of Swap to **RET 8** (assuming STDCALL is the calling convention).

8.5.7 Debugging Tips

In this section, we call attention to a few common errors encountered when passing arguments to procedures in assembly language. We hope you never make these mistakes.

Argument Size Mismatch

Array addresses are based on the sizes of their elements. To address the second element of a double-word array, for example, one adds 4 to the array's starting address. Suppose we call **Swap** from Section 8.5.6, passing pointers to the first two elements of **DoubleArray**. If we incorrectly calculate the address of the second element as **DoubleArray + 1**, the resulting hexadecimal values in **Double-Array** after calling **Swap** are incorrect:

```
.data
DoubleArray DWORD 10000h,20000h
.code
INVOKE Swap, ADDR [DoubleArray + 0], ADDR [DoubleArray + 1]
```

Passing the Wrong Type of Pointer

When using INVOKE, remember that the assembler does not validate the type of pointer you pass to a procedure. For example, the **Swap** procedure from Section 8.5.6 expects to receive two doubleword pointers. Suppose we inadvertently pass it pointers to bytes:

```
.data
ByteArray BYTE 10h,20h,30h,40h,50h,60h,70h,80h
.code
INVOKE Swap, ADDR [ByteArray + 0], ADDR [ByteArray + 1]
```

The program will assemble and run, but when ESI and EDI are dereferenced, 32-bit values are exchanged.

Passing Immediate Values

If a procedure has a reference parameter, do not pass an immediate argument. Consider the following procedure, which has a single reference parameter:

```
Sub2 PROC dataPtr:PTR WORD
     mov  esi,dataPtr            ; get the address
     mov  [esi],0                ; dereference, assign zero
     ret
Sub2 ENDP
```

The following INVOKE statement assembles but causes a runtime error. The **Sub2** procedure receives 1000h as a pointer value and dereferences memory location 1000h:

```
INVOKE  Sub2, 1000h
```

The example is likely to cause a general protection fault, because memory location 1000h is not within the program's data segment.

8.5.8   Section Review

1. (*True/False*): The CALL instruction cannot include procedure arguments.
2. (*True/False*): The INVOKE directive can include up to a maximum of three arguments.
3. (*True/False*): The INVOKE directive can only pass memory operands, but not register values.
4. (*True/False*):The PROC directive can contain a USES operator, but the PROTO directive cannot.
5. (*True/False*): When using the PROC directive, all parameters must be listed on the same line.
6. (*True/False*): If you pass a variable containing the offset of an array of bytes to a procedure that expects a pointer to an array of words, the assembler will not catch your error.
7. (*True/False*): If you pass an immediate value to a procedure that expects a reference parameter, you can generate a general-protection fault (in protected mode).
8. Declare a procedure named **MultArray** that receives two pointers to arrays of doublewords, and a third parameter indicating the number of array elements.

9. Create a PROTO directive for the procedure in the preceding exercise.

10. Did the **Swap** procedure from Section 8.5.6 use input parameters, output parameters, or input-output parameters?

11. In the **ReadConsole** procedure from Section 8.5.5, is **lpBuffer** an input parameter or an output parameter?

8.6 Creating Multimodule Programs

Large source files are hard to manage and slow to assemble. You could break a single file into multiple include files, but a modification to any source file would still require a complete assembly of all the files. A better approach is to divide up a program into *modules* (assembled units). Each module is assembled independently, so a change to one module's source code only requires reassembling the single module. The linker combines all assembled modules (OBJ files) into a single executable file rather quickly. Linking large numbers of object modules requires far less time than assembling the same number of source code files.

There are two general approches to creating multimodule programs: The first is the traditional one, using the EXTERN directive, which is more or less portable across different 80x86 assemblers. The second approach is to use Microsoft's advanced INVOKE and PROTO directives, which simplify procedure calls and hide some low-level details. We will demonstrate both approaches and let you decide which you want to use.

8.6.1 Hiding and Exporting Procedure Names

By default, MASM makes all procedures public, permitting them to be called from any other module in the same program. You can override this behavior using the PRIVATE qualifier:

```
mySub PROC PRIVATE
```

By making procedures private, you use the principle of *encapsulation* to hide procedures inside modules and avoid potential name clashes when procedures in different modules have the same names.

OPTION PROC:PRIVATE Directive   Another way to hide procedures inside a source module is to place the OPTION PROC:PRIVATE directive at the top of the file. All procedures become private by default. Then, you use the PUBLIC directive to identify any procedures you want to export:

```
OPTION PROC:PRIVATE
PUBLIC mySub
```

The PUBLIC directive takes a comma-delimited list of names:

```
PUBLIC sub1, sub2, sub3
```

Alternatively, you can designate individual procedures as public:

```
mySub PROC PUBLIC
  .
mySub ENDP
```

If you use OPTION PROC:PRIVATE in your program's startup module, be sure to designate your startup procedure (usually main) as PUBLIC, or the operating system's loader will not be able to find it. For example,

```
main PROC PUBLIC
```

8.6.2 Calling External Procedures

The EXTERN directive, used when calling a procedure outside the current module, identifies the procedure's name and stack frame size. The following program example calls **sub1**, located in an external module:

```
INCLUDE Irvine32.inc
EXTERN sub1@0:PROC
```

```
.code
main PROC
     call    sub1@0
     exit
main ENDP
END main
```

When the assembler discovers a missing procedure in a source file (identified by a CALL instruction), its default behavior is to issue an error message. Instead, EXTERN tells the assembler to create a blank address for the procedure. The linker resolves the missing address when it creates the program's executable file.

The **@n** suffix at the end of a procedure name identifies the total stack space used by declared parameters (see the extended PROC directive in Section 8.5). If you're using the basic PROC directive with no declared parameters, the suffix on each procedure name in EXTERN will be **@0**. If you declare a procedure using the extended PROC directive, add 4 bytes for every parameter. Suppose we declare **AddTwo** with two doubleword parameters:

```
AddTwo PROC,
    val1:DWORD,
    val2:DWORD
    . . .
AddTwo ENDP
```

The corresponding EXTERN directive is **EXTERN AddTwo@8:PROC**. If you plan to call AddTwo using INVOKE (Section 8.5), use the PROTO directive in place of EXTERN:

```
AddTwo PROTO,
    val1:DWORD,
    val2:DWORD
```

8.6.3 Using Variables and Symbols Across Module Boundaries

Exporting Variables and Symbols

Variables and symbols are, by default, private to their enclosing modules. You can use the PUBLIC directive to export specific names, as in the following example:

```
PUBLIC count, SYM1
SYM1 = 10
.data
count DWORD 0
```

Accessing External Variables and Symbols

You can use the EXTERN directive to access variables and symbols defined in external modules:

```
EXTERN name : type
```

For symbols (defined with EQU and =), *type* should be ABS. For variables, *type* can be a data-definition attribute such as BYTE, WORD, DWORD, and SDWORD, including PTR. Here are examples:

```
EXTERN one:WORD, two:SDWORD, three:PTR BYTE, four:ABS
```

Using an INCLUDE File with EXTERNDEF

MASM has a useful directive named EXTERNDEF that takes the place of both PUBLIC and EXTERN. It can be placed in a text file and copied into each program module using the INCLUDE directive. For example, let's define a file named *vars.inc* containing the following declaration:

```
; vars.inc
EXTERNDEF count:DWORD, SYM1:ABS
```

Next, we create a source file named *sub1.asm* containing **count** and **SYM1**, an INCLUDE statement that copies vars.inc into the compile stream.

```
TITLE sub1.asm
.386
.model flat,STDCALL
INCLUDE vars.inc
SYM1 = 10
.data
count DWORD 0
END
```

Because this is not the program startup module, we omit a program entry point label in the END directive, and we do not need to declare a runtime stack.

Next, we create a startup module named *main.asm* that includes *vars.inc* and makes references to count and SYM1:

```
TITLE main.asm
INCLUDE Irvine32.inc
INCLUDE vars.inc
.code
main PROC
        mov     count,2000h
        mov     eax,SYM1
        exit
main ENDP
END main
```

This module does contain a runtime stack, declared with the .STACK directive inside Irvine32.inc. It also defines the program entry point in the END directive.

8.6.4 Example: ArraySum Program

The *ArraySum* program, first presented in Chapter 5, is an easy program to separate into modules. For a quick review of the program's design, let's review the structure chart (Figure 8–10). Shaded rectangles refer to procedures in the book's link library. The **main** procedure calls **PromptForIntegers**, which in turn calls **WriteString** and **ReadInt**. It's usually easiest to keep track of the various files in a multimodule program by creating a separate disk directory for the files. That's what we did for the *ArraySum* program, to be shown in the next section.

FIGURE 8–10   Structure Chart, ArraySum Program.

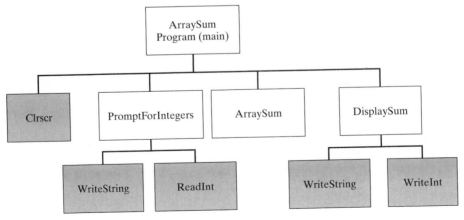

8.6.5 Creating the Modules Using Extern

We will show two versions of the multimodule ArraySum program. This section will use the traditional EXTERN directive to reference functions in separate modules. Later, in Section 8.6.6, we will implement the same program using the advanced capabilities of INVOKE, PROTO, and PROC.

PromptForIntegers *_prompt.asm* contains the source code file for the PromptForIntegers procedure. It displays prompts asking the user to enter three integers, inputs the values by calling ReadInt, and inserts them in an array:

```
TITLE Prompt For Integers        (_prompt.asm)
INCLUDE Irvine32.inc
.code
;-------------------------------------------------------
PromptForIntegers PROC

; Prompts the user for an array of integers and fills
; the array with the user's input.
; Receives:
;     ptrPrompt:PTR BYTE           ; prompt string
;     ptrArray:PTR DWORD           ; pointer to array
;     arraySize:DWORD              ; size of the array
; Returns:  nothing
;-------------------------------------------------------
arraySize   EQU [ebp+16]
ptrArray    EQU [ebp+12]
ptrPrompt   EQU [ebp+8]

    enter 0,0
    pushad                         ; save all registers

    mov   ecx,arraySize
    cmp   ecx,0                    ; array size <= 0?
    jle   L2                       ; yes: quit
    mov   edx,ptrPrompt            ; address of the prompt
    mov   esi,ptrArray

L1: call  WriteString             ; display string
    call  ReadInt                 ; read integer into EAX
    call  Crlf                     ; go to next output line
    mov   [esi],eax               ; store in array
    add   esi,4                   ; next integer
    loop  L1

L2: popad                          ; restore all registers
    leave
    ret   12                       ; restore the stack
PromptForIntegers ENDP
END
```

ArraySum The _arraysum.asm module contains the ArraySum procedure, which calculates the sum of the array elements and returns a result in EAX:

```
TITLE ArraySum Procedure              (_arrysum.asm)

INCLUDE Irvine32.inc
.code
ArraySum PROC
;
; Calculates the sum of an array of 32-bit integers.
; Receives:
```

```
;     ptrArray                        ; pointer to array
;     arraySize                       ; size of array (DWORD)
; Returns:  EAX = sum
;-----------------------------------------------------------
ptrArray EQU [ebp+8]
arraySize EQU [ebp+12]
      enter 0,0
      push  ecx                       ; don't push EAX
      push  esi

      mov   eax,0                     ; set the sum to zero
      mov   esi,ptrArray
      mov   ecx,arraySize
      cmp   ecx,0                     ; array size <= 0?
      jle   L2                        ; yes: quit

L1:   add   eax,[esi]                 ; add each integer to sum
      add   esi,4                     ; point to next integer
      loop  L1                        ; repeat for array size

L2:   pop   esi
      pop   ecx                       ; return sum in EAX
      leave
      ret   8                         ; restore the stack
ArraySum ENDP
END
```

DisplaySum The _display.asm module contains the DisplaySum procedure, which displays a label, followed by the array sum:

```
TITLE DisplaySum Procedure(_display.asm)

INCLUDE Irvine32.inc
.code
;-----------------------------------------------------------
DisplaySum PROC
; Displays the sum on the console.
; Receives:
;     ptrPrompt                       ; offset of prompt string
;     theSum                          ; the array sum (DWORD)
; Returns: nothing
;-----------------------------------------------------------

theSum      EQU [ebp+12]
ptrPrompt   EQU [ebp+8]
      enter 0,0
      push  eax
      push  edx

      mov   edx,ptrPrompt             ; pointer to prompt
      call  WriteString
      mov   eax,theSum
      call  WriteInt                  ; display EAX
      call  Crlf

      pop   edx
      pop   eax
      leave
      ret   8                         ; restore the stack
DisplaySum ENDP
END
```

Startup Module The *Sum_main.asm* module contains the startup procedure (main). It contains EXTERN directives for the three external procedures. To make the source code more user-friendly, the EQU directive redefines the procedure names:

```
ArraySum            EQU ArraySum@0
PromptForIntegers   EQU PromptForIntegers@0
DisplaySum          EQU DisplaySum@0
```

Just before each procedure call, a comment describes the parameter order. This program uses the STDCALL parameter passing convention:

```
TITLE Integer Summation Program (Sum_main.asm)

; Multimodule example:
; This program inputs multiple integers from the user,
; stores them in an array, calculates the sum of the
; array, and displays the sum.

INCLUDE Irvine32.inc

EXTERN PromptForIntegers@0:PROC
EXTERN ArraySum@0:PROC, DisplaySum@0:PROC

; Redefine external symbols for convenience
ArraySum            EQU ArraySum@0
PromptForIntegers   EQU PromptForIntegers@0
DisplaySum          EQU DisplaySum@0

; modify Count to change the size of the array:
Count = 3

.data
prompt1 BYTE "Enter a signed integer: ",0
prompt2 BYTE "The sum of the integers is: ",0
array   DWORD  Count DUP(?)
sum     DWORD  ?

.code
main PROC
     call  Clrscr

; PromptForIntegers( addr prompt1, addr array, Count )
     push  Count
     push  OFFSET array
     push  OFFSET prompt1
     call  PromptForIntegers

; sum = ArraySum( addr array, Count )
     push  Count
     push  OFFSET array
     call  ArraySum
     mov   sum,eax

; DisplaySum( addr prompt2, sum )
     push  sum
     push  OFFSET prompt2
     call  DisplaySum

     call  Crlf
     exit
main ENDP
END main
```

The source files for this program are stored in the example programs directory in a folder named ch08\ModSum32_traditional.

Next, we will see how this program would change if it were built using Microsoft's INVOKE and PROTO directives.

8.6.6 Creating the Modules Using INVOKE and PROTO

Multimodule programs may be created using Microsoft's advanced INVOKE, PROTO, and extended PROC directives (Section 8.5). Their primary advantage over the more traditional use of CALL and EXTERN is their ability to match up argument lists passed by INVOKE to corresponding parameter lists declared by PROC.

Let's recreate the ArraySum program, using the INVOKE, PROTO, and advanced PROC directives. A good first step is to create an include file containing a PROTO directive for each external procedure. Each module will include this file (using the INCLUDE directive) without incurring any code size or runtime overhead. If a module does not call a particular procedure, the corresponding PROTO directive is ignored by the assembler. The source code for this program is located in the \ch08\ModSum32_advanced folder.

The sum.inc Include File   Here is the *sum.inc* include file for our program:

```
; (sum.inc)
INCLUDE Irvine32.inc

PromptForIntegers PROTO,
     ptrPrompt:PTR BYTE,              ; prompt string
     ptrArray:PTR DWORD,              ; points to the array
     arraySize:DWORD                  ; size of the array

ArraySum PROTO,
     ptrArray:PTR DWORD,              ; points to the array
     count:DWORD                      ; size of the array

DisplaySum PROTO,
     ptrPrompt:PTR BYTE,              ; prompt string
     theSum:DWORD                     ; sum of the array
```

The _prompt Module   The *_prompt.asm* file uses the PROC directive to declare parameters for the PromptForIntegers procedure. It uses an INCLUDE to copy *sum.inc* into this file:

```
TITLE Prompt For Integers        (_prompt.asm)

INCLUDE sum.inc                  ; get procedure prototypes
.code
;-----------------------------------------------------
PromptForIntegers PROC,
  ptrPrompt:PTR BYTE,            ; prompt string
  ptrArray:PTR DWORD,            ; pointer to array
  arraySize:DWORD                ; size of the array
;
; Prompts the user for an array of integers and fills
; the array with the user's input.
; Returns:  nothing
;-----------------------------------------------------
     pushad                      ; save all registers

     mov   ecx,arraySize
     cmp   ecx,0                 ; array size <= 0?
```

```
        jle  L2                          ; yes: quit
        mov  edx,ptrPrompt               ; address of the prompt
        mov  esi,ptrArray

L1:     call WriteString                 ; display string
        call ReadInt                     ; read integer into EAX
        call Crlf                        ; go to next output line
        mov  [esi],eax                   ; store in array
        add  esi,4                       ; next integer
        loop L1

L2:     popad                            ; restore all registers
        ret
PromptForIntegers ENDP
END
```

Compared to the previous version of PromptForIntegers, the statements **enter 0, 0** and **leave** are now missing because they will be generated by MASM when it encounters the PROC directive with declared parameters. Also, the RET instruction needs no constant parameter (PROC takes care of that).

The _arraysum Module   Next, the *_arrysum.asm* file contains the ArraySum procedure:

```
TITLE ArraySum Procedure                    (_arrysum.asm)

INCLUDE sum.inc
.code
;----------------------------------------------------
ArraySum PROC,
      ptrArray:PTR DWORD,            ; pointer to array
      arraySize:DWORD                ; size of array
;
; Calculates the sum of an array of 32-bit integers.
; Returns:  EAX = sum
;----------------------------------------------------
        push ecx                     ; don't push EAX
        push esi

        mov  eax,0                    ; set the sum to zero
        mov  esi,ptrArray
        mov  ecx,arraySize
        cmp  ecx,0                    ; array size <= 0?
        jle  L2                       ; yes: quit
L1:     add  eax,[esi]                ; add each integer to sum
        add  esi,4                    ; point to next integer
        loop L1                       ; repeat for array size

L2:     pop  esi
        pop  ecx                      ; return sum in EAX
        ret
ArraySum ENDP
END
```

The _display Module   The *_display.asm* file contains the DisplaySum procedure:

```
TITLE DisplaySum Procedure(_display.asm)

INCLUDE Sum.inc
.code
```

```
;--------------------------------------------------------
DisplaySum PROC,
      ptrPrompt:PTR BYTE,             ; prompt string
      theSum:DWORD                    ; the array sum
;
; Displays the sum on the console.
; Returns: nothing
;--------------------------------------------------------
      push   eax
      push   edx

      mov    edx,ptrPrompt            ; pointer to prompt
      call   WriteString
      mov    eax,theSum
      call   WriteInt                 ; display EAX
      call   Crlf

      pop    edx
      pop    eax
      ret
DisplaySum ENDP
END
```

The Sum_main Module   The *Sum_main.asm* (startup module) contains main and calls each of the other procedures. It uses INCLUDE to copy in the procedure prototypes from *sum.inc*:

```
TITLE Integer Summation Program (Sum_main.asm)

INCLUDE sum.inc
Count = 3
.data
prompt1 BYTE "Enter a signed integer: ",0
prompt2 BYTE "The sum of the integers is: ",0
array   DWORD  Count DUP(?)
sum     DWORD  ?

.code
main PROC
     call Clrscr

     INVOKE PromptForIntegers, ADDR prompt1, ADDR array, Count
     INVOKE ArraySum, ADDR array, Count
     mov    sum,eax
     INVOKE DisplaySum, ADDR prompt2, sum

     call   Crlf
     exit
main ENDP
END main
```

Summary   We have shown two ways of creating multimodule programs—first, using the more conventional EXTERN directive, and second, using the advanced capabilities of INVOKE, PROTO, and PROC. The latter directives simplify many details and are optimized for calling Windows API functions. They also hide a number of details, so you may prefer to use explicit stack parameters along with CALL and EXTERN.

8.6.7   Section Review

1.   (*True/False*): Linking OBJ modules is much faster than assembling ASM source files.

2.   (*True/False*): Separating a large program into short modules makes a program more difficult to maintain.

3. (*True/False*): In a multimodule program, an END statement with a label occurs only once, in the startup module.

4. (*True/False*): PROTO directives use up memory, so you must be careful not to include a PROTO directive for a procedure unless the procedure is actually called.

8.7 Chapter Summary

There are two basic types of procedure parameters: register parameters and stack parameters. The Irvine32 and Irvine16 libraries use register parameters, which are optimized for program execution speed. Unfortunately, they tend to create code clutter in calling programs. Stack parameters are the alternative. The procedure arguments must be pushed on the stack by a calling program.

A stack frame (or activation record) is the area of the stack set aside for a procedure's return address, passed parameters, local variables, and saved registers. The stack frame is created when the running program begins to execute a procedure.

When a copy of a procedure argument is pushed on the stack, it is *passed by value*. When an argument's address is pushed on the stack, it is *passed by reference*; the procedure can modify the variable via its address. Arrays should be passed by reference, to avoid having to push all array elements on the stack.

Procedure parameters can be accessed using indirect addressing with the EBP register. Expressions such as [ebp+8] give you a high level of control over stack parameter addressing. The LEA instruction returns the offset of any type of indirect operand. LEA is ideally suited for use with stack parameters.

The ENTER instruction completes the stack frame by saving EBP on the stack and reserving space for local variables. The LEAVE instruction terminates the stack frame for a procedure by reversing the action of a preceding ENTER instruction.

A recursive procedure is one that calls itself, either directly or indirectly. Recursion, the practice of calling recursive procedures, can be a powerful tool when working with data structures that have repeating patterns.

The LOCAL directive declares one or more local variables inside a procedure. It must be placed on the line immediately following a PROC directive. Local variables have distinct advantages over global variables:

- Access to the name and contents of a local variable can be restricted to its containing procedure. Local variables help when debugging programs because only a limited number of program statements are capable of modifying the local variables.
- A local variable's lifetime is limited to the execution scope of its enclosing procedure. Local variables make efficient use of memory because the same storage space can be used for other variables.
- The same variable name may be used in more than one procedure without causing a naming clash.
- Local variables can be used in recursive procedures to store values on the stack. If global variables were used instead, their values would be overwritten each time the procedure called itself.

The INVOKE directive is a more powerful replacement for Intel's CALL instruction that lets you pass multiple arguments. The ADDR operator can be used to pass a pointer when calling a procedure with the INVOKE directive.

The PROC directive declares a procedure name with a list of named parameters. The PROTO directive creates a prototype for an existing procedure. A prototype declares a procedure's name and parameter list.

MASM uses the .MODEL directive to determine several important characteristics of a program: its memory model type, function naming scheme, and parameter passing convention. The real-address mode programs shown so far in this book have used the small memory model because it keeps all code within a single code segment and all data (including the stack) within a single segment. Protected mode programs use the flat memory model, in which all offsets are 32 bits, and the code and data can be as large as 4GB. The most common language specifiers are C and STDCALL.

An application program of any size is difficult to manage when all of its source code is in the same file. It is more convenient to break the program up into multiple source code files (called modules), making each file easy to view and edit.

8.8 Programming Exercises

The following exercises can be completed in protected or real-address mode.

1. Exchanging Integers

Create an array of randomly ordered integers. Using the **Swap** procedure from Section 8.5.6 as a tool, write a loop that exchanges each consecutive pair of integers in the array.

2. DumpMem Procedure

Write a wrapper procedure for the link library's **DumpMem** procedure, using stack parameters. The name can be slightly different, such as **DumpMemory**. The following is an example of how it should be called:

```
INVOKE DumpMemory,OFFSET array,LENGTHOF array,TYPE array
```

Write a test program that calls your procedure several times, using a variety of data types.

3. Nonrecursive Factorial

Write a nonrecursive version of the **Factorial** procedure (Section 8.3.2) that uses a loop. Write a short program that interactively tests your Factorial procedure. Let the user enter the value of *n*. Display the calculated factorial.

4. Factorial Comparison

Write a program that compares the runtime speeds of both the recursive **Factorial** procedure from Section 8.3.2 and the nonrecursive Factorial procedure written for the preceding programming exercise. Use the **GetMseconds** procedure from the book's link library to measure and display the number of milliseconds required to call each Factorial procedure several thousand times in a row.

5. Greatest Common Divisor

Write a recursive implementation of Euclid's algorithm for finding the greatest common divisor (GCD) of two integers. Descriptions of this algorithm are available in algebra books and on the Web. (Note: A nonrecursive version of the GCD problem was given in the programming exercises for Chapter 7.)

End Notes

1. See Procedure Calls for Block-Structured Languages, Chapter 6, IA-32 Intel Architecture Software Developer's Manual, Volume 1.

2. NEARSTACK combines the program's stack and data into a single physical segment along with data. FARSTACK uses different segments for code and data, so the DS register contains a different value than the SS register.

9

STRiNGS ANd ARRAyS

9.1 Introduction

If you learn to efficiently process strings and arrays, you can master the most common area of code optimization. Studies have shown that most programs spend 90% of their running time executing 10% of their code. No doubt the 10% occurs frequently in loops, and loops are required when processing strings and arrays. In this chapter, we will show techniques for string and array processing, with the goal of writing efficient code.

We will begin with Intel's optimized string primitive instructions designed for moving, comparing, loading, and storing blocks of data. Next, we will introduce several string-handling procedures in Irvine32 (or Irvine16) library. Their implementations are fairly similar to the code you might see in an implementation of the standard C string library. The third part of the chapter shows how to manipulate two-dimensional arrays, using advanced indirect addressing modes: base-index and base-index-displacement. Simple indirect addressing was introduced in Section 4.4.

The last section of the chapter, entitled Searching and Sorting Integer Arrays, is the most interesting. You will see how easy it is to implement two of the most common array processing algorithms in computer science: bubble sort and binary search. It's a great idea to study these algorithms in Java or C++, as well as assembly language.

9.2 String Primitive Instructions

The IA-32 instruction set has five groups of instructions for processing arrays of bytes, words, and doublewords. Although they are called *string primitives*, they are not limited to character arrays. Each instruction in Table 9-1 implicitly uses ESI, EDI, or both registers to address memory. References to the accumulator imply the use of AL, AX, or EAX, depending on the instruction data size. String primitives execute efficently because they automatically repeat and increment array indexes.

Table 9-1   String Primitive Instructions.

Instruction	Description
MOVSB, MOVSW, MOVSD	**Move string data:** Copy data from memory addressed by ESI to memory addressed by EDI.
CMPSB, CMPSW, CMPSD	**Compare strings:** Compare the contents of two memory locations addressed by ESI and EDI.
SCASB, SCASW, SCASD	**Scan string:** Compare the accumulator (AL, AX, or EAX) to the contents of memory addressed by EDI.
STOSB, STOSW, STOSD	**Store string data:** Store the accumulator contents into memory addressed by EDI.
LODSB, LODSW, LODSD	**Load accumulator from string:** Load memory addressed by ESI into the accumulator.

In protected mode programs, ESI is automatically an offset in the segment addressed by DS, and EDI is automatically an offset in the segment addressed by ES. DS and ES are always set to the same value and you cannot change them. (In real-address mode, on the other hand, ES and DS are often manipulated by ASM programmers.)

In real-address mode, string primitives use the SI and DI registers to address memory. SI is an offset from DS, and DI is an offset from ES. Usually you will set ES to the same segment value as DS at the beginning of main:

```
main PROC
     mov   ax,@data     ; get addr of data seg
     mov   ds,ax        ; initialize DS
     mov   es,ax        ; initialize ES
```

Using a Repeat Prefix   By itself, a string primitive instruction processes only a single memory value or pair of values. If you add a *repeat prefix*, the instruction repeats, using ECX as a counter. The repeat prefix permits you to process an entire array using a single instruction. The following repeat prefixes are used:

REP	Repeat while ECX > 0
REPZ, REPE	Repeat while the Zero flag is set and ECX > 0
REPNZ, REPNE	Repeat while the Zero flag is clear and ECX > 0

Example: Copy a String   In the following example, MOVSB moves 10 bytes from **string1** to **string2.** The repeat prefix first tests ECX > 0 before executing the MOVSB instruction. If ECX = 0, the instruction is ignored and control passes to the next line in the program. If ECX > 0, ECX is decremented and the instruction repeats:

```
cld                          ; clear direction flag
mov  esi,OFFSET string1      ; ESI points to source
mov  edi,OFFSET string2      ; EDI points to target
mov  ecx,10                  ; set counter to 10
rep  movsb                   ; move 10 bytes
```

ESI and EDI are automatically incremented when MOVSB repeats. This behavior is controlled by the CPU's Direction flag.

Direction Flag   String primitive instructions increment or decrement ESI and EDI based on the state of the Direction flag (see Table 9-2). The Direction flag can be explicitly modified using the CLD and STD instructions:

```
CLD       ; clear Direction flag (forward direction)
STD       ; set Direction flag (reverse direction)
```

Forgetting to set the Direction flag before a string primitive instruction can be a major headache! The resulting code executes inconsistently based on the arbitrary state of the Direction flag.

Table 9-2   Direction Flag Usage in String Primitive Instructions.

Value of the Direction Flag	Effect on ESI and EDI	Address Sequence
Clear	Incremented	Low-high
Set	Decremented	High-low

9.2.1 MOVSB, MOVSW, and MOVSD

The MOVSB, MOVSW, and MOVSD instructions copy data from the memory location pointed to by ESI to the memory location pointed to by EDI. The two registers are either incremented or decremented automatically (based on the value of the Direction flag):

MOVSB	Move (copy) bytes
MOVSW	Move (copy) words
MOVSD	Move (copy) doublewords

You can use a repeat prefix with MOVSB, MOVSW, and MOVSD. The Direction flag determines whether ESI and EDI will be incremented or decremented. The size of the increment/decrement is shown in the following table:

Instruction	Value Added or Subtracted from ESI and EDI
MOVSB	1
MOVSW	2
MOVSD	4

Example: Copy Doubleword Array   Suppose we want to copy 20 doubleword integers from **source** to **target**. After the array is copied, ESI and EDI point one position (4 bytes) beyond the end of each array:

```
.data
source DWORD 20 DUP(0FFFFFFFFh)
target DWORD 20 DUP(?)
.code
cld                                 ; direction = forward
mov   ecx,LENGTHOF source           ; set REP counter
mov   esi,OFFSET source             ; ESI points to source
mov   edi,OFFSET target             ; EDI points to target
rep   movsd                         ; copy doublewords
```

9.2.2 CMPSB, CMPSW, and CMPSD

The CMPSB, CMPSW, and CMPSD instructions each compare a memory operand pointed to by ESI to a memory operand pointed to by EDI:

CMPSB	Compare bytes
CMPSW	Compare words
CMPSD	Compare doublewords

You can use a repeat prefix with CMPSB, CMPSW, and CMPSD. The Direction flag determines the incrementing or decrementing of ESI and EDI.

CMPS Explicit Form: In another form of the compare string instruction called the *explicit form*, two indirect operands are supplied. The PTR operand clarifies the operand sizes. For example,

```
cmps DWORD PTR [esi],[edi]
```

But CMPS is tricky because the assembler lets you supply misleading operands:

```
cmps DWORD PTR [eax],[ebx]
```

Regardless of which operands are used, CMPS still compares the contents of memory pointed to by ESI to the memory pointed to by EDI. Note that the order of operands in CMPS is opposite to the more familiar CMP instruction:

```
CMP  target,source
CMPS source,target
```

Here's another way to remember the difference: CMP implies subtraction of *source* from *target*. CMPS implies subtraction of *target* from *source*. We think it's best to avoid using CMPS and to use the specific versions (CMPSB, CMPSW, CMPSD) instead.

Example: Comparing Doublewords   Suppose you want to compare a pair of doublewords using CMPSD. In the following example, **source** has a smaller value than **target**. When JA executes, the conditional jump is not taken; the JMP instruction is executed instead:

```
.data
source DWORD 1234h
target DWORD 5678h
.code
mov   esi,OFFSET source
mov   edi,OFFSET target
cmpsd                               ; compare doublewords
ja    L1                            ; jump if source > target
jmp   L2                            ; jump, since source <= target
```

To compare multiple doublewords, clear the Direction flag (forward direction), initialize ECX as a counter, and use a repeat prefix with CMPSD:

```
mov   esi,OFFSET source
mov   edi,OFFSET target
cld                              ; direction = forward
mov   ecx,LENGTHOF source        ; repetition counter
repe cmpsd                       ; repeat while equal
```

The REPE prefix repeats the comparison, incrementing ESI and EDI automatically until ECX equals zero or a pair of doublewords is found to be different.

Example: Comparing Two Strings

Strings are usually compared by matching individual characters in sequence, starting at the beginning of the strings. For example, the first three characters of "AABC" and "AABB" are identical. In the fourth position, the ASCII code for "C" (in the first string) is greater than the ASCII code for "B" (in the second string). Thus, the first string is considered greater than the second string. Similarly, if the strings "AAB" and "AABB" are compared, the second string has a larger value. The first three characters are identical, but one additional character exists in the second string.

The following program uses CMPSB to compare two strings of identical length. The REPE prefix causes CMPSB to continue incrementing ESI and EDI and comparing characters one by one until a difference is found between the two strings:

```
TITLE Comparing Strings(Cmpsb.asm)

; This program uses CMPSB to compare two strings
; of equal length.

INCLUDE Irvine32.inc

.data
source BYTE "MARTIN "
dest   BYTE "MARTINEZ"
str1   BYTE "Source is smaller",0dh,0ah,0
str2   BYTE "Source is not smaller",0dh,0ah,0

.code
main PROC
     cld                         ; direction = forward
     mov   esi,OFFSET source
     mov   edi,OFFSET dest
     mov   ecx,LENGTHOF source
     repe  cmpsb
     jb    source_smaller
     mov   edx,OFFSET str2
     jmp   done
source_smaller:
     mov   edx,OFFSET str1
done:
     call  WriteString
     exit
main ENDP
END main
```

When we use the given test data, the message "Source is smaller" displays. In Figure 9–1, ESI and EDI are left pointing one position beyond the point where the two strings were found to differ. If the strings had been identical, ESI and EDI would have been left pointing one position beyond the ends of their respective strings.

Comparing two strings with CMPSB only works when the strings are of equal length. That is why it was necessary in the preceding example to pad "MARTIN" with trailing spaces to make it the same length as "MARTINEZ". Padding strings with spaces imposes an awkward constraint on string handling, which we eliminate from the **Str_compare** procedure in Section 9.3.1.

Figure 9–1   Comparing Two Strings Using CMPSB.

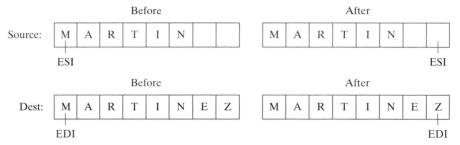

9.2.3   SCASB, SCASW, and SCASD

The SCASB, SCASW, and SCASD instructions compare a value in AL/AX/EAX to a byte, word, or doubleword, respectively, addressed by EDI. The instructions are useful when looking for a single value in a string or array. Combined with the REPE (or REPZ) prefix, the string or array is scanned while ECX > 0 and the value in AL/AX/EAX matches each subsequent value in memory. The REPNE prefix scans until either AL/AX/EAX matches a value in memory or ECX = 0.

Scan for a Matching Character   In the following example we search the string **alpha**, looking for the letter F. If the letter is found, EDI points one position beyond the matching character. If the letter is not found, JNZ exits:

```
.data
alpha BYTE "ABCDEFGH",0
.code
mov    edi,OFFSET alpha          ; EDI points to the string
mov    al,'F'                    ; search for the letter F
mov    ecx,LENGTHOF alpha        ; set the search count
cld                              ; direction = forward
repne  scasb                     ; repeat while not equal
jnz    quit                      ; quit if letter not found
dec    edi   ; found: back up EDI
```

JNZ was added after the loop to test for the possibility that the loop stopped because ECX = 0 and the character in AL was not found.

9.2.4   STOSB, STOSW, and STOSD

The STOSB, STOSW, and STOSD instructions store the contents of AL/AX/EAX, respectively, in memory at the offset pointed to by EDI. EDI is incremented or decremented based on the state of the Direction flag. When used with the REP prefix, these instructions are useful for filling all elements of a string or array with a single value. For example, the following code initializes each byte in **string1** to 0FFh:

```
.data
Count = 100
string1 BYTE Count DUP(?)
.code
```

```
mov    al,0FFh                  ; value to be stored
mov    edi,OFFSET string1       ; EDI points to target
mov    ecx,Count                ; character count
cld                             ; direction = forward
rep    stosb                    ; fill with contents of AL
```

9.2.5 LODSB, LODSW, and LODSD

The LODSB, LODSW, and LODSD instructions load a byte or word from memory at ESI into AL/AX/EAX, respectively. ESI is incremented or decremented based on the state of the Direction flag. The REP prefix is rarely used with LODS because each new value loaded into the accumulator overwrites its previous contents. Instead, LODS is used to load a single value. In the next example, LODSB substitutes for the following two instructions (assuming the Direction flag is clear):

```
mov    al,[esi]                 ; move byte into AL
inc    esi                      ; point to next byte
```

Array Multiplication Example The following program multiplies each element of a doubleword array by a constant value. LODSD and STOSD work together:

```
TITLE Multiply an Array                     (Mult.asm)

; This program multiplies each element of an array
; of 32-bit integers by a constant value.

INCLUDE Irvine32.inc
.data
array DWORD 1,2,3,4,5,6,7,8,9,10            ; test data
multiplier DWORD 10                         ; test data

.code
main PROC
     cld                                    ; direction = forward
     mov    esi,OFFSET array                ; source index
     mov    edi,esi                         ; destination index
     mov    ecx,LENGTHOF array              ; loop counter

L1:  lodsd                                  ; load [ESI] into EAX
     mul    multiplier                      ; multiply by a value
     stosd                                  ; store EAX into [EDI]
     loop   L1

     exit
main ENDP
END main
```

9.2.6 Section Review

1. In reference to string primitives, which 32-bit register is known as the *accumulator*?

2. Which instruction compares a 32-bit integer in the accumulator to the contents of memory, pointed to by EDI?

3. Which index register is used by the STOSD instruction?

4. Which instruction copies data from the memory location addressed by EDI into AX?

5. What does the REPZ prefix do for a CMPSB instruction?

6. Which Direction flag value causes index registers to move backward through memory when executing string primitives?

7. When a repeat prefix is used with STOSW, what value is added to or subtracted from the index register?

8. In what way is the CMPS instruction ambiguous?

9. *Challenge:* When the Direction flag is clear and SCASB has found a matching character, where does EDI point?

10. *Challenge:* When scanning an array for the first occurrence of a particular character, which repeat prefix would be best?

9.3 Selected String Procedures

In this section, we will demonstrate several procedures from the Irvine32 and Irvine16 libraries that manipulate null-terminated strings. The procedures are suspiciously similar to functions in the standard C library:

```
; Copy a source string to a target string.
Str_copy PROTO,
     source:PTR BYTE,
     target:PTR BYTE

; Return the length of a string (excluding the null byte) in EAX.
Str_length PROTO,
     pString:PTR BYTE

; Compare string1 to string2. Set the Zero and
; Carry flags in the same way as the CMP instruction.
Str_compare PROTO,
     string1:PTR BYTE,
     string2:PTR BYTE

; Trim a given trailing character from a string.
; The second argument is the character to trim.
Str_trim PROTO,
     pString:PTR BYTE,
     char:BYTE

; Convert a string to upper case.
Str_ucase PROTO,
     pString:PTR BYTE
```

9.3.1 Str_compare Procedure

The **Str_compare** procedure compares two strings. The calling format is

```
INVOKE Str_compare, ADDR string1, ADDR string2
```

It compares the strings in forward order, starting at the first byte. The comparison is case sensitive because ASCII codes are different for uppercase and lowercase letters. The procedure does not return a value, but the Carry and Zero flags can be interpreted as shown in Table 9-3, using the *string1* and *string2* arguments.

Table 9-3   Flags Affected by the Str_compare Procedure.

Relation	Carry Flag	Zero Flag	Branch If True
string1 < string2	1	0	JB
string1 == string2	0	1	JE
string1 > string2	0	0	JA

See Section 6.2.7 for an explanation of how CMP sets the Carry and Zero flags. The following is a listing of the **Str_compare** procedure. See the *Compare.asm* program for a demonstration:

```
Str_compare PROC USES eax edx esi edi,
        string1:PTR BYTE,
        string2:PTR BYTE
;
; Compare two strings.
; Returns nothing, but the Zero and Carry flags are affected
; exactly as they would be by the CMP instruction.
;----------------------------------------------------
        mov     esi,string1
        mov     edi,string2

L1:     mov     al,[esi]
        mov     dl,[edi]
        cmp     al,0                    ; end of string1?
        jne     L2                      ; no
        cmp     dl,0                    ; yes: end of string2?
        jne     L2                      ; no
        jmp     L3                      ; yes, exit with ZF = 1

L2:     inc     esi                     ; point to next
        inc     edi
        cmp     al,dl                   ; chars equal?
        je      L1                      ; yes: continue loop
                                        ; no: exit with flags set

L3:     ret
Str_compare ENDP
```

We could have used the CMPSB instruction when implementing Str_compare, but it would have required knowing the length of the longer string. Two calls to the **Str_length** procedure would be required. In this particular case, it is easier to check for the null terminators in both strings within the same loop. CMPSB is most effective when dealing with large strings or arrays of known length.

9.3.2 Str_length Procedure

The **Str_length** procedure returns the length of a string in the EAX register. When you call it, pass the string's offset. For example:

```
INVOKE Str_length, ADDR myString
```

Here is the procedure implementation:

```
Str_length PROC USES edi,
        pString:PTR BYTE                ; pointer to string
        mov edi,pString
        mov eax,0                       ; character count

L1:     cmp BYTE PTR[edi],0             ; end of string?
        je  L2                          ; yes: quit
        inc edi                         ; no: point to next
        inc eax                         ; add 1 to count
        jmp L1
L2:     ret
Str_length ENDP
```

See the *Length.asm* program for a demonstration of this procedure.

9.3.3 Str_copy Procedure

The **Str_copy** procedure copies a null-terminated string from a source location to a target location. Before calling this procedure, you must make sure the target operand is large enough to hold the copied string. The syntax for calling Str_copy is

```
INVOKE Str_copy, ADDR source, ADDR target
```

No values are returned by the procedure. Here is the implementation:

```
Str_copy PROC USES eax ecx esi edi,
        source:PTR BYTE,                ; source string
        target:PTR BYTE                 ; target string
    ;
    ; Copy a string from source to target.
    ; Requires: the target string must contain enough
    ;           space to hold a copy of the source string.
    ;-----------------------------------------------------
        INVOKE Str_length,source        ; EAX = length source
        mov    ecx,eax                   ; REP count
        inc    ecx                       ; add 1 for null byte
        mov    esi,source
        mov    edi,target
        cld                              ; direction = forward
        rep    movsb                     ; copy the string
        ret
Str_copy ENDP
```

See the *CopyStr.asm* program for a demonstration of this procedure.

9.3.4 Str_trim Procedure

The **Str_trim** procedure removes all occurrences of a selected trailing character from a null-terminated string. The syntax for calling it is

```
INVOKE Str_trim, ADDR string, char_to_trim
```

The logic for this procedure is interesting because you have to check a number of possible cases (shown here with # as the trailing character):

1. The string is empty.
2. The string contains other characters followed by one or more trailing characters, as in "Hello##".
3. The string contains only one character, the trailing character, as in "#".
4. The string contains no trailing character, as in "Hello" or "H".
5. The string contains one or more trailing characters followed by one or more nontrailing characters, as in "#H" or "###Hello".

You can use Str_trim to remove all spaces (or any other repeated character) from the end of a string. The easiest way to truncate characters from a string is to insert a null byte just after the characters you want to retain. Any characters after the null byte become insignificant. Here is the procedure's source code. The *Trim.asm* program tests **Str_trim**:

```
Str_trim PROC USES eax ecx edi,
        pString:PTR BYTE,               ; points to string
        char:BYTE                       ; char to remove
    ;
    ; Remove all occurrences of a given character from
    ; the end of a string.
    ; Returns: nothing
    ;-----------------------------------------------------
```

```
            mov     edi,pString
            INVOKE Str_length,edi         ; returns length in EAX
            cmp     eax,0                 ; zero-length string?
            je      L2                    ; yes: exit
            mov     ecx,eax               ; no: counter = string length
            dec     eax
            add     edi,eax               ; EDI points to last char
            mov     al,char               ; char to trim
            std                           ; direction = reverse
            repe    scasb                 ; skip past trim character
            jne     L1                    ; removed first character?
            dec     edi                   ; adjust EDI: ZF=1 && ECX=0
    L1:     mov     BYTE PTR [edi+2],0    ; insert null byte
    L2:     ret
    Str_trim ENDP
```

In all cases but one, EDI stops 2 bytes behind the character that we want to replace with null. Table 9-4 shows various test cases for nonempty strings. Based on the first string definition from the foregoing table, Figure 9–2 shows the position of EDI when SCASB stops.

Table 9-4   Testing the Str_trim Procedure.

String Definition	EDI When SCASB Stops	Zero Flag	ECX	Position to Store the Null
str BYTE "Hello##",0	str + 3	0	> 0	[edi + 2]
str BYTE "#",0	str − 1	1	0	[edi + 1]
str BYTE "Hello",0	str + 3	0	> 0	[edi + 2]
str BYTE "H",0	str − 1	0	0	[edi + 2]
str BYTE "#H",0	str + 0	0	> 0	[edi + 2]

Figure 9–2   SCAS Example, after Match Found.

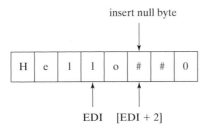

When SCASB ends, a special test is made for the one case in which the string contains a single character and that character is the one to be trimmed. In this case, EDI points only 1 byte ahead of the character to replace with null (because the SCASB stopped because ECX = 0 and not because ZF =1). To compensate, we decrement EDI once before storing a null byte at [edi+2], as shown in Figure 9–3.

9.3.5   Str_ucase Procedure

The **Str_ucase** procedure converts a string to all uppercase characters. It returns no value. When you call it, pass the offset of a string:

```
    INVOKE Str_ucase, ADDR myString
```

Figure 9-3 Inserting a Null Byte after Executing SCAS.

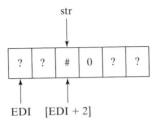

Here is the procedure implementation:

```
Str_ucase PROC USES eax esi,
    pString:PTR BYTE
; Converts a null-terminated string to uppercase.
; Returns: nothing
;------------------------------------------------
    mov    esi,pString
L1:
    mov    al,[esi]                    ; get char
    cmp    al,0                        ; end of string?
    je     L3                          ; yes: quit
    cmp    al,'a'                      ; below "a"?
    jb     L2
    cmp    al,'z'                      ; above "z"?
    ja     L2
    and    BYTE PTR [esi],11011111b    ; convert the char

L2: inc    esi                        ; next char
    jmp    L1

L3: ret
Str_ucase ENDP
```

(See the *Ucase.asm* program for a demonstration of this procedure.)

9.3.6 String Library Demo Program

The following program (StringDemo.asm) shows examples of calling the Str_trim, Str_ucase, Str_compare, and Str_length procedures from the book's library:

```
TITLE String Library Demo          (StringDemo.asm)

; This program demonstrates the string-handling procedures in
; the book's link library.

INCLUDE Irvine32.inc

.data
string_1 BYTE "abcde////",0
string_2 BYTE "ABCDE",0
msg0     BYTE "string_1 in upper case: ",0
msg1     BYTE "string1 and string2 are equal",0
msg2     BYTE "string_1 is less than string_2",0
msg3     BYTE "string_2 is less than string_1",0
msg4     BYTE "Length of string_2 is ",0
msg5     BYTE "string_1 after trimming: ",0

.code
main PROC
```

```
            call    trim_string
            call    upper_case
            call    compare_strings
            call    print_length

            exit
main ENDP

trim_string PROC
; Remove trailing characters from string_1.

            INVOKE Str_trim, ADDR string_1, '/'
            mov     edx,OFFSET msg5
            call    WriteString
            mov     edx,OFFSET string_1
            call    WriteString
            call    Crlf

            ret
trim_string ENDP

upper_case PROC
; Convert string_1 to upper case.

            mov     edx,OFFSET msg0
            call    WriteString
            INVOKE Str_ucase, ADDR string_1
            mov     edx,OFFSET string_1
            call    WriteString
            call    Crlf

            ret
upper_case ENDP

compare_strings PROC
; Compare string_1 to string_2.

            INVOKE Str_compare, ADDR string_1, ADDR string_2
            .IF ZERO?
            mov     edx,OFFSET msg1
            .ELSEIF CARRY?
            mov     edx,OFFSET msg2          ; string 1 is less than...
            .ELSE
            mov     edx,OFFSET msg3          ; string 2 is less than...
            .ENDIF
            call    WriteString
            call    Crlf

            ret
compare_strings  ENDP

print_length PROC
; Display the length of string_2.

            mov     edx,OFFSET msg4
            call    WriteString
            INVOKE Str_length, ADDR string_2
            call    WriteDec
            call    Crlf

            ret
print_length ENDP
END main
```

Trailing characters are removed from string_1 by the call to Str_trim. The string is converted to uppercase by calling the Str_ucase procedure.

Program Output   Here is the String Library Demo program's output:

```
string_1 after trimming: abcde
string_1 in upper case: ABCDE
string1 and string2 are equal
Length of string_2 is 5
```

9.3.7 Section Review

1. (*True/False*): The **Str_compare** procedure stops when the null terminator of the longer string is reached.
2. (*True/False*): The **Str_compare** procedure does not need to use ESI and EDI to access memory.
3. (*True/False*): The **Str_length** procedure uses SCASB to find the null terminator at the end of the string.
4. (*True/False*): The **Str_copy** procedure prevents a string from being copied into too small a memory area.
5. What Direction flag setting is used in the **Str_trim** procedure?
6. Why does the **Str_trim** procedure use the JNE instruction?
7. What happens in the **Str_ucase** procedure if the target string contains a digit?
8. *Challenge:* If the **Str_length** procedure used SCASB, which repeat prefix would be most appropriate?
9. *Challenge:* If the **Str_length** procedure used SCASB, how would it calculate and return the string length?

9.4 Two-Dimensional Arrays

9.4.1 Ordering of Rows and Columns

From an assembly language programmer's perspective, a two-dimensional array is a high-level abstraction of a one-dimensional array. High-level languages select one of two methods of arranging the rows and columns in memory: *row-major order* and *column-major order*. When row-major order (most common) is used, the first row appears at the beginning of the memory block. The last element in the first row is followed in memory by the first element of the second row. When column-major order is used, the elements in the first column appear at the beginning of the memory block. The last element in the first column is followed in memory by the first element of the second column.

FIGURE 9–4   Row-Major and Column-Major Ordering.

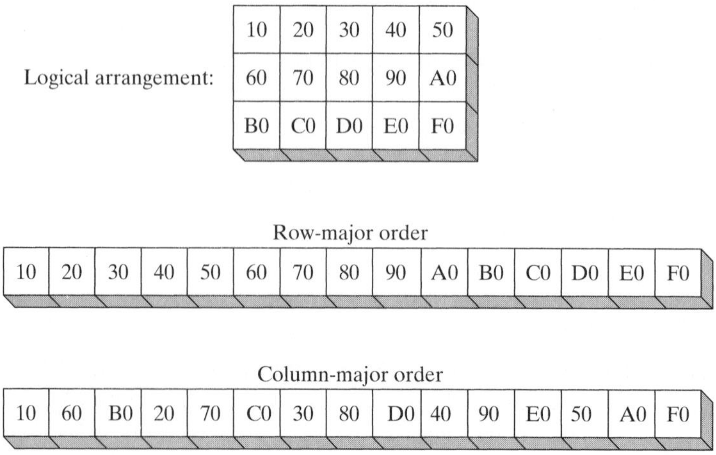

If you implement a two-dimensional array in assembly language, you can choose either ordering method. In this chapter, we will use row-major order. If you write assembly language subroutines for a high-level language, you will follow the ordering specified in their documentation.

The IA-32 instruction set includes two operand types, base-index and base-index-displacement, both suited to array applications. We will examine both and show examples of how they can be used effectively.

9.4.2   Base-Index Operands

A base-index operand adds the values of two registers (called *base* and *index*), producing an offset address:

```
[base + index]
```

The square brackets are required. In 32-bit mode, any 32-bit general-purpose registers may be base and index registers. In 16-bit mode, the base register must be BX or BP. (Avoid using BP or EBP except when addressing the stack.) The index register must be SI or DI. Here are examples of various combinations in 32-bit mode:

```
.data
array WORD 1000h,2000h,3000h
.code
mov   ebx,OFFSET array
mov   esi,2
mov   ax,[ebx+esi]              ; AX = 2000h

mov   edi,OFFSET array
mov   ecx,4
mov   ax,[edi+ecx]             ; AX = 3000h

mov   ebp,OFFSET array
mov   esi,0
mov   ax,[ebp+esi]            ; AX = 1000h
```

Two-Dimensional Array   When accessing a two-dimensional array in row-major order, the row offset is held in the base register and the column offset is in the index register. The following table, for example, has three rows and five columns:

```
tableB   BYTE    10h,  20h,   30h,  40h,  50h
Rowsize = ($ - tableB)
         BYTE    60h,  70h,   80h,  90h,  0A0h
         BYTE    0B0h, 0C0h,  0D0h, 0E0h, 0F0h
```

The table is in row-major order and the constant Rowsize is calculated by the assembler as the number of bytes in each table row. Suppose we want to locate a particular entry in the table using row and column coordinates. Assuming that the coordinates are zero based, the entry at row 1, column 2 contains 80h. We set EBX to the table's offset, add (Rowsize * row_index) to calculate the row offset, and set ESI to the column index:

```
row_index = 1
column_index = 2
mov   ebx,OFFSET tableB         ; table offset
add   ebx,RowSize * row_index   ; row offset
mov   esi,column_index
mov   al,[ebx + esi]            ; AL = 80h
```

Suppose the array is located at offset 0150h. Then the effective address represented by EBX + ESI is 0157h. Figure 9–5 shows how adding EBX and ESI produces the offset of the byte at tableB[1, 2]. If the effective address points outside the program's data region, a general protection fault occurs.

Figure 9–5   Addressing an Array with a Base-Index Operand.

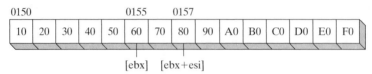

Calculating a Row Sum

Base index addressing simplifies many tasks associated with two-dimensional arrays. We might, for example, want to sum the elements in a row belonging to an integer matrix. The following calc_row_sum procedure (see *RowSum.asm*) calculates the sum of a selected row in a matrix of 8-bit integers:

```
calc_row_sum PROC uses ebx ecx edx esi
;
; Calculates the sum of a row in a byte matrix.
; Receives: EBX = table offset, EAX = row index,
;              ECX = row size, in bytes.
; Returns:  EAX holds the sum.
;-----------------------------------------------------
        mul    ecx                    ; row index * row size
        add    ebx,eax                ; row offset
        mov    eax,0                  ; accumulator
        mov    esi,0                  ; column index

L1:   movzx  edx,BYTE PTR[ebx + esi]  ; get a byte
        add    eax,edx                ; add to accumulator
        inc    esi                    ; next byte in row
        loop   L1

        ret
calc_row_sum ENDP
```

BYTE PTR was needed to clarify the operand size in the MOVZX instruction.

Scale Factors

If you're writing code for an array of WORD, multiply the index operand by a scale factor of 2. The following example locates the value at row 1, column 2:

```
tableW  WORD   10h,  20h,   30h,   40h,   50h
RowsizeW = ($ - tableW)
        WORD   60h,  70h,   80h,   90h,  0A0h
        WORD  0B0h, 0C0h,  0D0h,  0E0h,  0F0h
.code
row_index = 1
column_index = 2
mov   ebx,OFFSET tableW                 ; table offset
add   ebx,RowSizeW * row_index          ; row offset
mov   esi,column_index
mov   ax,[ebx + esi*TYPE tableW]        ; AX = 0080h
```

The scale factor used in this example (TYPE tableW) is equal to 2. Similarly, you must use a scale factor of 4 if the array contains doublewords:

```
tableD DWORD 10h, 20h, ...etc.
.code
mov   eax,[ebx + esi*TYPE tableD]
```

9.4.3 Base-Index-Displacement Operands

A base-index-displacement operand combines a displacement, a base register, an index register, and an optional scale factor to produce an effective address. Here are the formats:

```
[base + index + displacement]
displacement[base + index]
```

Displacement can be the name of a variable or a constant expression. In 32-bit mode, any general-purpose 32-bit registers may be used for the base and index. In 16-bit mode, the base operand may be BX or BP and the index operand may be SI or DI. Base-index-displacement operands are well suited to processing two-dimensional arrays. The displacement can be an array name, the base operand can hold the row offset, and the index operand can hold the column offset.

Doubleword Array Example The following two-dimensional array holds three rows of five doublewords:

```
tableD DWORD   10h,  20h,  30h,  40h,  50h
Rowsize = ($ - tableD)
       DWORD   60h,  70h,  80h,  90h,  0A0h
       DWORD   0B0h, 0C0h, 0D0h, 0E0h, 0F0h
```

Rowsize is equal to 20 (14h). Assuming that the coordinates are zero based, the entry at row 1, column 2 contains 80h. To access this entry, we set EBX to the row index and ESI to the column index:

```
mov   ebx,Rowsize                ; row index
mov   esi,2                      ; column index
mov   eax,tableD[ebx + esi*TYPE tableD]
```

Suppose **tableD** begins at offset 0150h. Figure 9–6 shows the positions of EBX and ESI relative to the array. Offsets are in hexadecimal.

FIGURE 9–6 Base-Index-Displacement Example.

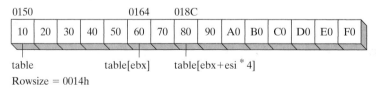

Rowsize = 0014h

9.4.4 Section Review

1. In 32-bit mode, which registers can be used in a base-index operand?
2. Show an example of a base-index operand in 32-bit mode.
3. Show an example of a base-index-displacement operand in 32-bit mode.
4. Suppose a two-dimensional array of doublewords has three logical rows and four logical columns. If ESI is used as the row index, what value would be added to ESI to move from one row to the next?
5. Suppose a two-dimensional array of doublewords has three logical rows and four logical columns. Write an expression using ESI and EDI that addresses the third column in the second row. (Numbering for rows and columns starts at zero.)
6. In real-address mode, should you use BP to address an array?
7. In protected mode, should you use EBP to address an array?

9.5 Searching and Sorting Integer Arrays

A great deal of time and energy has been expended by computer scientists in finding better ways to search and sort massive data sets. It has been proven that choosing the best algorithm for a particular application is far more useful than buying a faster computer. Most students study searching and sorting using high-level languages such as C++ and Java. Assembly language lends a different perspective to the study of algorithms by letting you see low-level implementation details. It's interesting to note that one of the most noted algorithm authors of the twentieth century, Donald Knuth, used assembly language for his published program examples.[1]

Searching and sorting gives you a chance to try out the addressing modes introduced in this chapter. In particular, base-indexed addressing turns out to be useful because you can point one register (such as EBX) to the base of an array and use another register (such as ESI) to index into any other array location.

9.5.1 Bubble Sort

A bubble sort compares pairs of array values, beginning in positions 0 and 1. If the compared values are in reverse order, they are exchanged. Figure 9–7 shows the progress of one pass through an integer array.

Figure 9–7   First Pass through an Array (Bubble Sort).

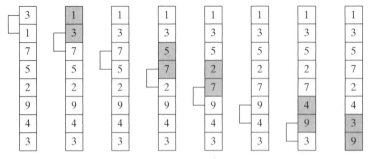

(shaded values have been exchanged)

After one pass, the array is still not sorted, but the largest value is now in the highest index position. The outer loop starts another pass through the array. After $n - 1$ passes, the array is guaranteed to be sorted.

The bubble sort works well for small arrays, but it becomes tremendously inefficient for larger ones. It is an $O(n^2)$ algorithm, meaning that the sort time increases quadratically in relation to the number of array elements (n). Suppose, for example, that it takes 0.1 second to sort 1000 elements. As the number of elements increases by a factor of 10, the time required to sort the array increases by a factor of 10^2 (100). The following table shows sort times for various array sizes, assuming that 1000 array elements can be sorted in 0.1 second:

Array Size	Time (seconds)
1,000	0.1
10,000	10.0
100,000	1000
1,000,000	100,000 (27.78 hours)

A bubble sort would not be a good sort for an array of 1 million integers because it would take more than 27 hours to finish! But it is fine for a few hundred integers.

Pseudocode   It's useful to create a simplified version of the bubble sort, using pseudocode that is similar to assembly language. We will use **N** to represent the size of the array, **cx1** to represent the outer loop counter, and **cx2** to represent the inner loop counter:

```
cx1 = N - 1
while( cx1 > 0 )
{
  esi = addr(array)
  cx2 = cx1
  while( cx2 > 0 )
  {
    if( array[esi] < array[esi+4] )
      exchange( array[esi], array[esi+4] )
    add esi,4
    dec cx2
  }
  dec cx1
}
```

Mechanical concerns, such as saving and restoring the outer loop counter, have purposely been left out. Note that the inner loop count (**cx2**) is based on the current value of the outer loop count (**cx1**), which in turn decreases with each pass through the array.

Assembly Language   From pseudocode, we can easily generate a matching implementation in assembly language, placing it in a procedure with parameters and local variables:

```
;-----------------------------------------------------------
BubbleSort PROC USES eax ecx esi,
      pArray:PTR DWORD,            ; pointer to array
      Count:DWORD                  ; array size
;
; Sort an array of 32-bit signed integers in ascending
; order, using the bubble sort algorithm.
; Receives: pointer to array, array size
; Returns: nothing
;-----------------------------------------------------------
      mov     ecx,Count
      dec     ecx                  ; decrement count by 1

L1:   push    ecx                  ; save outer loop count
      mov     esi,pArray           ; point to first value

L2:   mov     eax,[esi]            ; get array value
      cmp     [esi+4],eax          ; compare a pair of values
      jge     L3                   ; if [ESI] <= [EDI], no exchange
      xchg    eax,[esi+4]          ; exchange the pair
      mov     [esi],eax

L3:   add     esi,4                ; move both pointers forward
      loop    L2                   ; inner loop

      pop     ecx                  ; retrieve outer loop count
      loop    L1                   ; else repeat outer loop

L4:   ret
BubbleSort ENDP
```

9.5.2   Binary Search

Array searches are some of the most common operations in everyday programming. For a small array (1000 elements or less), it's easy to do a *sequential search*, where you start at the beginning of the array and examine each element in sequence until a matching one is found. For any array of *n* elements, a sequential search requires an average of *n*/2 comparisons. If a small array is searched, the execution time is minimal. On the other hand, searching an array of 1 million elements can require a more significant amount of processing time.

The *binary search* algorithm is particularly effective when searching for a single item in a large array. It has one important precondition: The array elements must be arranged in ascending or descending order. Here's an informal description of the algorithm:

Before beginning the search, ask the user to enter an integer, which we will call *searchVal*.

1. The range of the array to be searched is indicated by the subscripts named *first* and *last*. If *first* > *last*, exit the search, indicating failure to find a match.
2. Calculate the midpoint of the array between array subscripts *first* and *last*.
3. Compare *searchVal* to the integer at the midpoint of the array:
   - If the values are equal, return from the procedure with the midpoint in EAX. This return value indicates that a match has been found in the array.
   - On the other hand, if *searchVal* is larger than the number at the midpoint, reset *first* to one position higher than the midpoint.
   - Or, if *searchVal* is smaller than the number at the midpoint, reset *last* to one position below the midpoint.
4. Return to Step 1.

The binary search is spectacularly efficient because it uses a *divide and conquer* strategy. The range of values is divided in half with each iteration of the loop. In general, it is described as an O(log *n*) algorithm, meaning that as the number of array elements increases by a factor of *n*, the average search time increases by only a factor of log *n*. Because the actual number of comparisons may vary, the following table records the maximum number of comparisons required for various array sizes:

Array Size (*n*)	Maximum Comparisons
64	6
1,024	10
65,536	17
1,048,576	21
4,294,967,296	33

The maximum number of comparisons is calculated as $\log_2(n + 1)$, rounded up to the next largest integer. Following is a C++ implementation of a binary search function designed to work with an array of signed integers:

```cpp
int BinSearch( int values[], const int searchVal, int count )
{
  int first = 0;
  int last = count - 1;
  while( first <= last )
  {
    int mid = (last + first) / 2;
    if( values[mid] < searchVal )
      first = mid + 1;
    else if( values[mid] > searchVal )
```

```
         last = mid - 1;
      else
         return mid;        // success
   }
   return -1;               // not found
}
```

Following is an assembly language implementation of the sample C++ code:

```
;------------------------------------------------------------
BinarySearch PROC USES ebx edx esi edi,
     pArray:PTR DWORD,           ; pointer to array
     Count:DWORD,                ; array size
     searchVal:DWORD,            ; search value
LOCAL first:DWORD,               ; first position
     last:DWORD,                 ; last position
     mid:DWORD                   ; midpoint
;
; Searches an array of signed integers for a single value.
; Receives: Pointer to array, array size, search value.
; Returns: If a match is found, EAX = the array position of the
; matching element; otherwise, EAX = -1.
;------------------------------------------------------------
     mov    first,0              ; first = 0
     mov    eax,Count            ; last = (count - 1)
     dec    eax
     mov    last,eax
     mov    edi,searchVal        ; EDI = searchVal
     mov    ebx,pArray           ; EBX points to the array

L1:  ; while first <= last
     mov    eax,first
     cmp    eax,last
     jg     L5                   ; exit search
; mid = (last + first) / 2
     mov    eax,last
     add    eax,first
     shr    eax,1
     mov    mid,eax

; EDX = values[mid]
     mov    esi,mid
     shl    esi,2                ; scale mid value by 4
     mov    edx,[ebx+esi]        ; EDX = values[mid]
; if ( EDX < searchval(EDI) )
     cmp    edx,edi
     jge    L2
;    first = mid + 1
     mov    eax,mid
     inc    eax
     mov    first,eax
     jmp    L4

; else if( EDX > searchVal(EDI) )
L2:  cmp    edx,edi              ; optional
     jle    L3
;    last = mid - 1
```

```
          mov     eax,mid
          dec     eax
          mov     last,eax
          jmp     L4

; else return mid
L3:   mov     eax,mid                 ; value found
      jmp     L9                      ; return (mid)

L4:   jmp     L1                      ; continue the loop

L5:   mov     eax,-1                  ; search failed
L9:   ret
BinarySearch ENDP
```

Test Program

To demonstrate the bubble sort and binary search functions presented in this chapter, let's write a short test program that performs the following steps, in sequence:

- Fills an array with random integers
- Displays the array
- Sorts the array using a bubble sort
- Redisplays the array
- Asks the user to enter an integer
- Performs a binary search for the user's integer (in the array)
- Displays the results of the binary search

The individual procedures have been placed in separate source files to make it easier to locate and edit source code. Table 9-5 lists each module and its contents. Most professionally written programs are divided into separate code modules.

Table 9-5   Modules in the Bubble Sort/Binary Search Program.

Module	Contents
B_main.asm	Main module: Contains the main, **ShowResults**, and **AskForSearchVal** procedures. Contains the program entry point and manages the overall sequence of tasks.
Bsort.asm	**BubbleSort** procedure: Performs a bubble sort on a 32-bit signed integer array.
Bsearch.asm	**BinarySearch** procedure: Performs a binary search on a 32-bit signed integer array.
FillArry.asm	**FillArray** procedure: Fills a 32-bit signed integer array with a range of random values.
PrtArry.asm	**PrintArray** procedure: Writes the contents of a 32-bit signed integer array to standard output.

The procedures in all modules except *B_main* are written in such a way that it would be easy to use them in other programs without making any modifications. This is highly desirable because we might save time in the future by reusing existing code. The same approach is used in the Irvine32 and Irvine16 link libraries. Following is an include file (*Bsearch.inc*) containing prototypes of the procedures called from the main module:

```
; Bsearch.inc - prototypes for procedures used in
; the BubbleSort / BinarySearch program.

; Searches for an integer in an array of 32-bit signed
; integers.
BinarySearch PROTO,
```

```
            pArray:PTR DWORD,                 ; pointer to array
            Count:DWORD,                      ; array size
            searchVal:DWORD                   ; search value

    ; Fills an array with 32-bit signed random integers
    FillArray PROTO,
            pArray:PTR DWORD,                 ; pointer to array
            Count:DWORD,                      ; number of elements
            LowerRange:SDWORD,                ; lower range
            UpperRange:SDWORD                 ; upper range

    ; Writes a 32-bit signed integer array to standard output
    PrintArray PROTO,
            pArray:PTR DWORD,
            Count:DWORD

    ; Sorts the array in ascending order
    BubbleSort PROTO,
            pArray:PTR DWORD,
            Count:DWORD
```

Following is a listing of *B_main.asm*, the main module:

```
    TITLE Bubble Sort and Binary Search        B_main.asm)

    ; Bubble sort an array of signed integers, and perform
    ; a binary search.
    ; Main module, calls Bsearch.asm, Bsort.asm, FillArry.asm,
    ; and PrtArry.asm

    INCLUDE Irvine32.inc
    INCLUDE Bsearch.inc                  ; procedure prototypes

    LOWVAL = -5000                       ; minimum value
    HIGHVAL = +5000                      ; maximum value
    ARRAY_SIZE = 50                      ; size of the array

    .data
    array DWORD ARRAY_SIZE DUP(?)

    .code
    main PROC
        call Randomize

        ; Fill an array with random signed integers
        INVOKE FillArray, ADDR array, ARRAY_SIZE, LOWVAL, HIGHVAL

        ; Display the array
        INVOKE PrintArray, ADDR array, ARRAY_SIZE
        call WaitMsg

        ; Perform a bubble sort and redisplay the array
        INVOKE BubbleSort, ADDR array, ARRAY_SIZE
        INVOKE PrintArray, ADDR array, ARRAY_SIZE

        ; Demonstrate a binary search
        call AskForSearchVal             ; returned in EAX
        INVOKE BinarySearch,
           ADDR array, ARRAY_SIZE, eax
        call ShowResults

        exit
    main ENDP
```

```
;----------------------------------------------------------
AskForSearchVal PROC
;
; Prompt the user for a signed integer.
; Receives: nothing
; Returns: EAX = value input by user
;----------------------------------------------------------
.data
prompt BYTE "Enter a signed decimal integer "
       BYTE "in the range of -5000 to +5000 "
       BYTE "to find in the array: ",0
.code
     call   Crlf
     mov    edx,OFFSET prompt
     call   WriteString
     call   ReadInt
     ret
AskForSearchVal ENDP

;----------------------------------------------------------
ShowResults PROC
;
; Display the resulting value from the binary search.
; Receives: EAX = position number to be displayed
; Returns: nothing
;----------------------------------------------------------
.data
msg1 BYTE "The value was not found.",0
msg2 BYTE "The value was found at position ",0
.code
.IF eax == -1
     mov    edx,OFFSET msg1
     call   WriteString
.ELSE
     mov    edx,OFFSET msg2
     call   WriteString
     call   WriteDec
.ENDIF
     call   Crlf
     call   Crlf
     ret
ShowResults ENDP
END main
```

PrintArray   Following is a listing of the module containing the PrintArray procedure:

```
TITLE PrintArray Procedure (PrtArry.asm)

INCLUDE Irvine32.inc

.code
;----------------------------------------------------------
PrintArray PROC USES eax ecx edx esi,
     pArray:PTR DWORD,; pointer to array
     Count:DWORD; number of elements
;
; Writes an array of 32-bit signed decimal integers to
```

```
        ; standard output, separated by commas
        ; Receives: pointer to array, array size
        ; Returns: nothing
        ;------------------------------------------------------------
        .data
        comma BYTE ", ",0
        .code
            mov    esi,pArray
            mov    ecx,Count
            cld                        ; direction = forward
        L1: lodsd                      ; load [ESI] into EAX
            call   WriteInt            ; send to output
            mov    edx,OFFSET comma
            call   Writestring         ; display comma
            loop   L1

            call   Crlf
            ret
        PrintArray ENDP
        END
```

FillArray   Following is a listing of the module containing the FillArray procedure:

```
        TITLE FillArray Procedure            (FillArry.asm)

        INCLUDE Irvine32.inc

        .code
        ;------------------------------------------------------------
        FillArray PROC USES eax edi ecx edx,
            pArray:PTR DWORD,          ; pointer to array
            Count:DWORD,               ; number of elements
            LowerRange:SDWORD,         ; lower range
            UpperRange:SDWORD          ; upper range
        ;
        ; Fills an array with a random sequence of 32-bit signed
        ; integers between LowerRange and (UpperRange - 1).
        ; Returns: nothing
        ;------------------------------------------------------------
            mov    edi,pArray          ; EDI points to the array
            mov    ecx,Count           ; loop counter
            mov    edx,UpperRange
            sub    edx,LowerRange      ; EDX = absolute range (0..n)
        L1: mov    eax,edx             ; get absolute range
            call   RandomRange
            add    eax,LowerRange      ; bias the result
            stosd                      ; store EAX into [edi]
            loop   L1

            ret
        FillArray ENDP
        END
```

9.5.3 Section Review

1. If an array were already in sequential order, how many times would the outer loop of the **BubbleSort** procedure Section 9.5.1 execute?

2. In the **BubbleSort** procedure, how many times does the inner loop execute on the first pass through the array?

3. In the **BubbleSort** procedure, does the inner loop always execute the same number of times?

4. If it were found (through testing) that an array of 500 integers could be sorted in 0.5 seconds, how many seconds would it take to bubble sort an array of 5000 integers?

5. What is the maximum number of comparisons needed by the binary search algorithm when an array contains 127 elements?

6. Given an array of *n* elements, what is the maximum number of comparisons needed by the binary search algorithm?

7. *Challenge:* In the **BinarySearch** procedure (Section 9.5.2), why could the statement at label **L2** be removed without affecting the outcome?

8. *Challenge:* In the **BinarySearch** procedure, how might the statement at label **L4** be eliminated?

9.6 Chapter Summary

String primitive instructions are unusual in that they require no register operands and are optimized for high-speed memory access. They are

- MOVS: Move string data
- CMPS: Compare strings
- SCAS: Scan string
- STOS: Store string data
- LODS: Load accumulator from string

Each string primitive instruction has a suffix of B, W, or D when mainpulating bytes, words, and doublewords, respectively.

The repeat prefix REP repeats a string primitive instruction with automatic incrementing or decrementing of index registers. For example, when REPNE is used with SCASB, it scans memory bytes until a value in memory pointed to by EDI matches the contents of the AL register. The Direction flag determines whether the index register is incremented or decremented during each iteration of a string primitive instruction.

Strings and arrays are practically the same. Traditionally, a string consisted of an array of single-byte ASCII values, but now strings can contain 16-bit Unicode characters. The only important difference between a string and an array is that a string is usually terminated by a single null byte (containing zero).

Array manipulation is computationally intensive because it usually involves a looping algorithm. Most programs spend 80 to 90 percent of their running time executing small fraction of their code. As a result, you can speed up your software by reducing the number and complexity of instructions inside loops. Assembly language is a great tool for code optimization because you can control every detail. You might optimize a block of code, for example, by substituting registers for memory variables. Or you might use one of the string-processing instructions shown in this chapter rather than MOV and CMP instructions.

Several useful string-processing procedures were introduced in this chapter: The **Str_copy** procedure copies one string to another. **Str_length** returns the length of a string. **Str_compare** compares two strings. **Str_trim** removes a selected character from the end of a string. **Str_ucase** converts a string to uppercase letters.

Base-index operands assist in manipulating two-dimensional arrays (tables). You can set a base register to the address of a table row, and point an index register to the offset of a column within the selected row. In 32-bit mode, any general-purpose 32-bit registers can be used as base and index registers. In 16-bit mode, base registers must be BX and BP; index registers must be SI and DI. Base-index-displacement operands are similar to base-index operands, except that they also include the name of the array:

```
[ebx + esi]                         ; base-index
array[ebx + esi]                    ; base-index-displacement
```

We presented assembly language implementations of a bubble sort and a binary search. A bubble sort orders the elements of an array in ascending or descending order. It is effective for arrays having no more than a few hundred elements, but inefficient for larger arrays. A binary search permits rapid searching for a single value in an ordered array. It is easy to implement in assembly language.

9.7 Programming Exercises

The following exercises can be done in either 32-bit mode or 16-bit mode. Each string-handling procedure assumes the use of null-terminated strings. Even when not explicitly requested, write a short driver program for each exercise solution that tests your new procedure.

1. Improved Str_copy Procedure

The **Str_copy** procedure shown in this chapter does not limit the number of characters to be copied. Create a new version (named **Str_copyN**) that receives an additional input parameter indicating the maximum number of characters to be copied.

2. Str_concat Procedure

Write a procedure named **Str_concat** that concatenates a source string to the end of a target string. Sufficient space must exist in the target string to accommodate the new characters. Pass pointers to the source and target strings. Here is a sample call:

```
.data
targetStr BYTE "ABCDE",10 DUP(0)
sourceStr BYTE "FGH",0
.code
INVOKE Str_concat, ADDR targetStr, ADDR sourceStr
```

3. Str_remove Procedure

Write a procedure named **Str_remove** that removes *n* characters from a string. Pass a pointer to the position in the string where the characters are to be removed. Pass an integer specifying the number of characters to remove. The following code, for example, shows how to remove "xxxx" from **target**:

```
.data
target BYTE "abcxxxxdefghijklmop",0
.code
INVOKE Str_remove, ADDR [target+3], 4
```

4. Str_find Procedure

Write a procedure named **Str_find** that searches for the first matching occurrence of a source string inside a target string and returns the matching position. The input parameters should be a pointer to the source string and a pointer to the target string. If a match is found, the procedure sets the Zero flag and EAX points to the matching position in the target string. Otherwise, the Zero flag is clear and EAX is undefined. The following code, for example, searches for "ABC" and returns with EAX pointing to the "A" in the target string:

```
.data
target BYTE "123ABC342432",0
source BYTE "ABC",0
```

```
pos     DWORD ?
.code
INVOKE Str_find, ADDR source, ADDR target
jnz   notFound
mov   pos,eax                          ; store the position value
```

5. Str_nextword Procedure

Write a procedure called **Str_nextword** that scans a string for the first occurrence of a certain delimiter character and replaces the delimiter with a null byte. There are two input parameters: a pointer to the string, and the delimiter character. After the call, if the delimiter was found, the Zero flag is set and EAX contains the offset of the next character beyond the delimiter. Otherwise, the Zero flag is clear and EAX is undefined. The following example code passes the address of **target** and a comma as the delimiter:

```
.data
target BYTE "Johnson,Calvin",0
.code
INVOKE Str_nextword, ADDR target, ','
jnz notFound
```

In Figure 9–8, after calling **Str_nextword**, EAX points to the character following the position where the comma was found (and replaced).

FIGURE 9–8   Str_nextword Example.

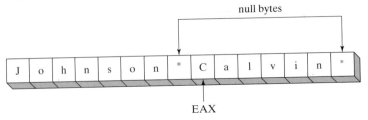

6. Constructing a Frequency Table

Write a procedure named **Get_frequencies** that constructs a character frequency table. Input to the procedure should be a pointer to a string and a pointer to an array of 256 doublewords initialized to all zeros. Each array position is indexed by its corresponding ASCII code. When the procedure returns, each entry in the array contains a count of how many times the corresponding character occurred in the string. For example,

```
.data
target BYTE "AAEBDCFBBC",0
freqTable DWORD 256 DUP(0)
.code
INVOKE Get_frequencies, ADDR target, ADDR freqTable
```

FIGURE 9–9   Sample Character Frequency Table.

Target string:	A	A	E	B	D	C	F	B	B	C	0
ASCII code:	41	41	45	42	44	43	46	42	42	43	0

Frequency table:	2	3	2	1	1	1	0	0	0	0	0
Index:	41	42	43	44	45	46	47	48	49	4A	4B	etc.

Figure 9–9 shows a picture of the string and entries 41 (hexadecimal) through 4B in the frequency table. Position 41 contains the value 2 because the letter A (ASCII code 41h) occurred twice in the string. Similar counts are shown for other characters. Frequency tables are useful in data compression and other applications involving character processing. The *Huffman encoding algorithm*, for example, stores the most frequently occurring characters in fewer bits than other characters that occur less often.

7. Sieve of Eratosthenes

The *Sieve of Eratosthenes,* invented by the Greek mathematician of the same name, provides a quick way to find all prime numbers within a given range. The algorithm involves creating an array of bytes in which positions are "marked" by inserting 1's in the following manner: Beginning with position 2 (which is a prime number), insert a 1 in each array position that is a multiple of 2. Then do the same thing for multiples of 3, the next prime number. Find the next prime number after 3, which is 5, and mark all positions that are multiples of 5. Proceed in this manner until all multiples of primes have been found. The remaining positions of the array that are unmarked indicate which numbers are prime. For this program, create a 65,000-element array and display all primes between 2 and 65,000. Declare the array in an uninitialized data segment (see Section 3.4.11) and use STOSB to fill it with zeros. In 32-bit mode, your array can be much larger.

8. Bubble Sort

Add a variable to the **BubbleSort** procedure in Section 9.5.1 that is set to 1 whenever a pair of values is exchanged within the inner loop. Use this variable to exit the sort before its normal completion if you discover that no exchanges took place during a complete pass through the array. (This variable is commonly known as an *exchange flag*.)

9. Binary Search

Rewrite the binary search procedure shown in this chapter by using registers for mid, first, and last. Add comments to clarify the registers' usage.

10. Letter Matrix

Create a procedure that generates a four-by-four matrix of randomly chosen capital letters. When choosing the letters, there must be a 50% probablility that the chosen letter is a vowel. Write a test program with a loop that calls your procedure five times and displays each matrix in the console window. Following is sample output for the first three matrices:

```
D W A L
S I V W
U I O L
L A I I

K X S V
N U U O
O R Q O
A U U T

P O A Z
A E A U
G K A E
I A G D
```

11. Letter Matrix/Sets with Vowels

Use the letter matrix generated in the previous programming exercise as a starting point for this program. Generate a random four-by-four letter matrix in which each letter has a 50% probability of being a vowel. Traverse each matrix row, column, and diagonal, generating sets of letters. Display only four-letter sets containing exactly two vowels. Suppose, for example, the following matrix was generated:

```
P O A Z
A E A U
G K A E
I A G D
```

Then the four-letter sets displayed by the program would be POAZ, GKAE, IAGD, PAGI, ZUED, PEAD, and ZAKI. The order of letters within each set is unimportant.

12.   Calculating the Sum of an Array Row

Write a procedure named **calc_row_sum** that calculates the sum of a single row in any two-dimensional array of bytes, words, or doublewords. The procedure should have the following stack parameters: array offset, row size, array type, row index. It must return the sum in EAX. Use explicit stack parameters, not INVOKE or extended PROC. Use base-index addressing with scale factors (see Section 4.4.3). Write a program that tests your procedure with arrays of byte, word, and doubleword. Prompt the user for the row index, and display the sum of the selected row.

End Note

1. Donald, Knuth, *The Art of Computer Programming*, Volume I: *Fundamental Algorithms*, Addison-Wesley, 1997.

10

Structures and Macros

10.1   Structures

A *structure* is a template or pattern given to a logically related group of variables. The variables in a structure are called *fields*. Program statements can access the structure as a single entity, or they can access individual fields. Structures often contain fields of different types. A union also groups together multiple identifiers, but the identifiers overlap the same area in memory. Unions will be covered in Section 10.1.7

Structures provide an easy way to cluster data and pass it from one procedure to another. Suppose input parameters for a procedure consisted of 20 different units of data relating to a disk drive. It would not be practical to call the procedure and pass the required arguments correctly. Instead, you could place all of the input data in a structure and pass the address of the structure to the procedure. Minimal stack space would be used (one address), and the called procedure could modify the contents of the structure.

Structures in assembly language are essentially the same as structures in C and C++. With a small effort at translation, you can take any structure from the MS-Windows API library and make it work in assembly language. Most debuggers can display individual structure fields.

COORD Structure   The COORD structure defined in the Windows API identifies X and Y screen coordinates. The field X has an offset of zero relative to the beginning of the structure, and the field Y's offset is 2:

```
COORD STRUCT
    X WORD ?                        ; offset 00
    Y WORD ?                        ; offset 02
COORD ENDS
```

Using a structure involves three sequential steps:

1. Define the structure.
2. Declare one or more variables of the structure type, called *structure variables*.
3. Write runtime instructions that access the structure fields.

10.1.1   Defining Structures

A structure is defined using the STRUCT and ENDS directives. Inside the structure, fields are defined using the same syntax as for ordinary variables. Structures can contain virtually any number of fields:

```
name STRUCT
    field-declarations
name ENDS
```

Field Initializers   When structure fields have initializers, the values are assigned when structure variables are created. You can use various types of field initializers:

• *Undefined:* The ? operator leaves the field contents undefined.
• *String literals:* Character strings enclosed in quotation marks.
• *Integers:* Integer constants and integer expressions.
• *Arrays:* The DUP operator can initialize array elements.

The following **Employee** structure describes employee information, with fields such as ID number, last name, years of service, and an array of salary history values. The following definition must appear prior to the declaration of **Employee** variables:

```
Employee STRUCT
    IdNum     BYTE "000000000"
    LastName BYTE 30 DUP(0)
    Years     WORD 0
    SalaryHistory DWORD 0,0,0,0
Employee ENDS
```

This is a linear representation of the structure's memory layout:

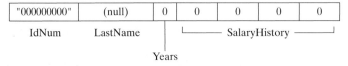

Aligning Structure Fields

For best memory I/O performance, structure members should be aligned to addresses matching their data types. Otherwise, the CPU will require more time to access the members. For example, a doubleword member should be aligned on a doubleword boundary. Table 10-1 lists the alignments used by the Microsoft C and C++ compilers and by Win32 API functions. In assembly language, the ALIGN directive sets the address alignment of the next field or variable:

```
ALIGN datatype
```

The following, for example, aligns **myVar** to a doubleword boundary:

```
.data
ALIGN DWORD
myVar DWORD ?
```

Let's correctly define the Employee structure, using ALIGN to put **Years** on a WORD boundary and **SalaryHistory** on a DWORD boundary. Field sizes appear as comments.

```
Employee STRUCT
        Idnum      BYTE "000000000"             ;  9
        Lastname BYTE 30 DUP(0)                 ; 30
        ALIGN      WORD                         ;  1 byte added
        Years      WORD 0                       ;  2
        ALIGN      DWORD                        ;  2 bytes added
        SalaryHistory DWORD 0,0,0,0             ; 16
Employee ENDS                                   ; 60 total
```

Table 10-1   Alignment of Structure Members

Member Type	Alignment
BYTE, SBYTE	Align on 8-bit (byte) boundary
WORD, SWORD	Align on 16-bit (word) boundary
DWORD, SDWORD	Align on 32-bit (doubleword) boundary
QWORD	Align on 64-bit (quadword) boundary
REAL4	Align on 32-bit (doubleword) boundary
REAL8	Align on 64-bit (quadword) boundary
structure	Largest alignment requirement of any member
union	Alignment requirement of the first member

10.1.2 Declaring Structure Variables

Structure variables can be declared and optionally initialized with specific values. This is the syntax, in which *structureType* has already been defined using the STRUCT directive:

```
identifier structureType < initializer-list >
```

The *identifier* follows the same rules as other variable names in MASM. The *initializer-list* is optional, but if used, is a comma-separated list of assembly-time constants that match the data types of specific structure fields:

```
initializer [, initializer] . . .
```

Empty angle brackets < > cause the structure to contain the default field values from the structure definition. Alternatively, you can insert new values in selected fields. The values are inserted into the structure fields in order from left to right, matching the order of the fields in the structure declaration. Examples of both approaches are shown here, using the **COORD** and **Employee** structures:

```
.data
point1 COORD <5,10>                    ; X = 5, Y = 10
point2 COORD <20>                      ; X = 20, Y = ?
```

```
point2 COORD <>                          ; X = ?, Y = ?
worker Employee <>                       ; (default initializers)
```

It is possible to override only selected field initializers. The following declaration overrides only the **IdNum** field of the **Employee** structure, assigning the remaining fields default values:

```
person1 Employee <"555223333">
```

An alternative notational form uses curly braces {. . .} rather than angle brackets:

```
person2 Employee {"555223333"}
```

When the initializer for a string field is shorter than the field, the remaining positions are padded with spaces. A null byte is not automatically inserted at the end of a string field. You can skip over structure fields by inserting commas as place markers. For example, the following statement skips the **IdNum** field and initializes the **LastName** field:

```
person3 Employee <,"dJones">
```

For an array field, use the DUP operator to initialize some or all of the array elements. If the initializer is shorter than the field, the remaining positions are filled with zeros. In the following, we initialize the first two **SalaryHistory** values and set the rest to zero:

```
person4 Employee <,,,2 DUP(20000)>
```

Array of Structures   Use the DUP operator to create an array of structures. In the following, the X and Y fields of each element in **AllPoints** are initialized to zeros:

```
NumPoints = 3
AllPoints COORD NumPoints DUP(<0,0>)
```

Aligning Structure Variables

For best processor performance, align structure variables on memory boundaries equal to the largest structure member. The Employee structure contains DWORD fields, so the following defintion uses that alignment:

```
.data
ALIGN DWORD
person Employee <>
```

10.1.3   Referencing Structure Variables

References to structure variables and structure names can be made using the TYPE and SIZEOF operators. For example, let's return to the **Employee** structure we saw earlier:

```
Employee STRUCT
     Idnum     BYTE "000000000"          ; 9
     Lastname BYTE 30 DUP(0)             ; 30
     ALIGN    WORD                       ; 1 byte added
     Years    WORD 0                     ; 2
     ALIGN    DWORD                      ; 2 bytes added
     SalaryHistory DWORD 0,0,0,0         ; 16
Employee ENDS                            ; 60 total
```

Given the data definition

```
.data
worker Employee <>
```

each of the following expressions returns the same value:

```
TYPE Employee                            ; 60
SIZEOF Employee                          ; 60
SIZEOF worker                            ; 60
```

The TYPE operator (Section 4.3) returns the number of bytes used by the identifier's storage type (BYTE, WORD, DWORD, etc.) The LENGTHOF operator returns a count of the number of elements in an array. The SIZEOF operator multiplies LENGTHOF by TYPE.

References to Members

References to named structure members require a structure variable as a qualifier. The following constant expressions can be generated at assembly time, using the **Employee** structure:

```
TYPE Employee.SalaryHistory        ; 4
LENGTHOF Employee.SalaryHistory    ; 4
SIZEOF Employee.SalaryHistory      ; 16
TYPE Employee.Years                ; 2
```

The following are runtime references to **worker**, an Employee:

```
.data
worker Employee <>
.code
mov   dx,worker.Years
mov   worker.SalaryHistory,20000         ; first salary
mov   [worker.SalaryHistory+4],30000     ; second salary
```

Using the OFFSET Operator   You can use the OFFSET operator to obtain the address of a field within a structure variable:

```
mov   edx,OFFSET worker.LastName
```

Indirect and Indexed Operands

Indirect operands permit the use of a register (such as ESI) to address structure members. Indirect addressing provides flexibility, particularly when passing a structure address to a procedure or when using an array of structures. The PTR operator is required when referencing indirect operands:

```
mov   esi,OFFSET worker
mov   ax,(Employee PTR [esi]).Years
```

The following statement does not assemble because **Years** by itself does not identify the structure it belongs to:

```
mov   ax,[esi].Years                 ; invalid
```

Indexed Operands   We can use indexed operands to access arrays of structures. Suppose **department** is an array of five Employee objects. The following statements access the **Years** field of the employee in index position 1:

```
.data
department Employee 5 DUP(<>)
.code
mov   esi,TYPE Employee          ; index = 1
mov   department[esi].Years, 4
```

Looping through an Array   A loop can be used with indirect or indexed addressing to manipulate an array of structures. The following program (*AllPoints.asm*) assigns coordinates to the **AllPoints** array:

```
TITLE Loop Through Array              (AllPoints.asm)

INCLUDE Irvine32.inc
NumPoints = 3
.data
ALIGN WORD
AllPoints COORD NumPoints DUP(<0,0>)
```

```
.code
main PROC
        mov     edi,0                           ; array index
        mov     ecx,NumPoints                   ; loop counter
        mov     ax,1                            ; starting X, Y values

L1:     mov     (COORD PTR AllPoints[edi]).X,ax
        mov     (COORD PTR AllPoints[edi]).Y,ax
        add     edi,TYPE COORD
        inc     ax
        loop    L1

        exit
main ENDP
END main
```

Performance of Aligned Structure Members

We have asserted that the processor can more efficiently access properly aligned structure members. How much impact do misaligned fields have on performance? Lets perform a simple test, using the two versions of the Employee structure presented in this chapter. We will rename the first version so both structures may be used in the same program:

```
EmployeeBad STRUCT
        IdNum      BYTE "000000000"
        LastName BYTE 30 DUP(0)
        Years      WORD 0
        SalaryHistory DWORD 0,0,0,0
EmployeeBad ENDS

Employee STRUCT
        Idnum      BYTE "000000000"
        Lastname BYTE 30 DUP(0)
        ALIGN      WORD
        Years      WORD 0
        ALIGN      DWORD
        SalaryHistory DWORD 0,0,0,0
Employee ENDS
```

The following code gets the system time, executes a loop that accesses structure fields, and calculates the elapsed time. The variable emp can be declared as an Employee or EmployeeBad object:

```
.data
ALIGN DWORD
startTime DWORD ?                       ; align startTime
emp Employee <>                         ; or: emp EmployeeBad <>
.code
        call    GetMSeconds             ; get starting time
        mov     startTime,eax

        mov     ecx,0FFFFFFFFh          ; loop counter
L1:     mov     emp.Years,5
        mov     emp.SalaryHistory,35000
        loop    L1

        call    GetMSeconds             ; get starting time
        sub     eax,startTime
        call    WriteDec                ; display elapsed time
```

In our simple test program (*Struct1.asm*), the execution time using the properly aligned Employee structure was 6141 milliseconds. The execution time when using the EmployeeBad structure was

6203 milliseconds. The timing difference was small (62 milliseconds), perhaps because the processor's internal memory cache minimized the alignment problems.

10.1.4   Example: Displaying the System Time

MS-Windows provides console functions that set the screen cursor position and get the system time. To use these functions, create instances of two predefined structures: COORD and SYSTEMTIME:

```
COORD STRUCT
      X WORD ?
      Y WORD ?
COORD ENDS

SYSTEMTIME STRUCT
    wYear WORD ?
    wMonth WORD ?
    wDayOfWeek WORD ?
    wDay WORD ?
    wHour WORD ?
    wMinute WORD ?
    wSecond WORD ?
    wMilliseconds WORD ?
SYSTEMTIME ENDS
```

Both structures are defined in *SmallWin.inc*, a file located in the assembler's INCLUDE directory and referenced by *Irvine32.inc*. To get the system time (adjusted for your local time zone), call the MS-Windows **GetLocalTime** function and pass it the address of a SYSTEMTIME structure:

```
.data
sysTime SYSTEMTIME <>
.code
INVOKE GetLocalTime, ADDR sysTime
```

Next, we retrieve the appropriate values from the SYSTEMTIME structure:

```
movzx eax,sysTime.wYear
call WriteDec
```

> The *SmallWin.inc* file, created by the author, contains structure definitions and function prototypes adapted from the Microsoft Windows header files for C and C++ programmers. It represents a small subset of the possible functions that can be called by application programs.

When a Win32 program produces screen output, it calls the MS-Windows **GetStdHandle** function to retrieve the standard console output handle (an integer):

```
.data
consoleHandle DWORD ?
.code
INVOKE GetStdHandle, STD_OUTPUT_HANDLE
mov consoleHandle,eax
```

(The constant STD_OUTPUT_HANDLE is defined *SmallWin.inc*.)

To set the cursor position, call the MS-Windows **SetConsoleCursorPosition** function, passing it the console output handle and a COORD structure variable containing X, Y character coordinates:

```
.data
XYPos COORD <10,5>
.code
INVOKE SetConsoleCursorPosition, consoleHandle, XYPos
```

Program Listing   The following program (*ShowTime.asm*) retrieves the system time and displays it at a selected screen location. It runs only in protected mode:

```
TITLE Structures                        (ShowTime.ASM)

INCLUDE Irvine32.inc
.data
sysTime SYSTEMTIME <>
XYPos COORD <10,5>
consoleHandle DWORD ?
colonStr BYTE ":",0

.code
main PROC
; Get the standard output handle for the Win32 Console.
    INVOKE GetStdHandle, STD_OUTPUT_HANDLE
    mov consoleHandle,eax

; Set the cursor position and get the system time.
    INVOKE SetConsoleCursorPosition, consoleHandle, XYPos
    INVOKE GetLocalTime, ADDR sysTime

; Display the system time (hh:mm:ss).
    movzx  eax,sysTime.wHour             ; hours
    call   WriteDec
    mov    edx,OFFSET colonStr           ; ":"
    call   WriteString
    movzx  eax,sysTime.wMinute           ; minutes
    call   WriteDec
    call   WriteString
    movzx  eax,sysTime.wSecond           ; seconds
    call   WriteDec
    call   Crlf
    call   WaitMsg                       ; "Press any key..."
    exit
main ENDP
END main
```

The following defintions were used by this program from *SmallWin.inc* (automatically included by *Irvine32.inc*):

```
STD_OUTPUT_HANDLE EQU -11

SYSTEMTIME STRUCT ...

COORD STRUCT ...

GetStdHandle PROTO,
    nStdHandle:DWORD

GetLocalTime PROTO,
    lpSystemTime:PTR SYSTEMTIME

SetConsoleCursorPosition PROTO,
    nStdHandle:DWORD,
    coords:COORD
```

Following is sample program output, taken at 12:16 p.m.:

```
12:16:35
Press any key to continue...
```

10.1.5   Structures Containing Structures

Structures can contain instances of other structures. For example, a **Rectangle** can be defined in terms of its upper-left and lower-right corners, both COORD structures:

```
Rectangle STRUCT
     UpperLeft COORD <>
     LowerRight COORD <>
Rectangle ENDS
```

Rectangle variables can be declared without overrides or by overriding individual COORD fields. Alternative notational forms are shown:

```
rect1 Rectangle < >
rect2 Rectangle { }
rect3 Rectangle { {10,10}, {50,20} }
rect4 Rectangle < <10,10>, <50,20> >
```

The following is a direct reference to a structure field:

```
mov   rect1.UpperLeft.X, 10
```

You can access a structure field using an indirect operand. The following example moves 10 to the Y coordinate of the upper-left corner of the structure pointed to by ESI:

```
mov   esi,OFFSET rect1
mov   (Rectangle PTR [esi]).UpperLeft.Y, 10
```

The OFFSET operator can return pointers to individual structure fields, including nested fields:

```
mov   edi,OFFSET rect2.LowerRight
mov   (COORD PTR [edi]).X, 50
mov   edi,OFFSET rect2.LowerRight.X
mov   WORD PTR [edi], 50
```

10.1.6   Example: Drunkard's Walk

Programming textbooks often contain a version of the "Drunkard's Walk" exercise, in which the program simulates the path taken by a not-too-sober professor on his or her way to class. Using a random number generator, you can choose a direction for each step the professor takes. Usually, you check to make sure the person hasn't veered off into a campus lake, but we won't bother. Suppose the professor begins at the center of an imaginary grid in which each square represents a step in a north, south, east, or west direction. The person follows a random path through the grid (Figure 10–1).

FIGURE 10–1   Drunkard's Walk, Example Path.

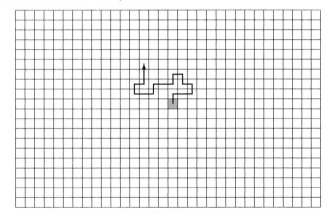

Our program will use a COORD structure to keep track of each step along the path taken by the professor. The steps are stored in an array of COORD objects:

```
WalkMax = 50
DrunkardWalk STRUCT
     path COORD WalkMax DUP(<0,0>)
     pathsUsed WORD 0
DrunkardWalk ENDS
```

Walkmax is a constant that determines the total number of steps taken by the professor in the simulation. The **pathsUsed** field indicates, when the program loop ends, how many steps were taken by the professor. As the professor takes each step, his or her position is stored in a COORD object and inserted in the next available position in the **path** array. The program displays the coordinates on the screen. Here is the complete program listing:

```
TITLE Drunkard's Walk                       (Walk.asm)

; Drunkard's walk program. The professors starts at
; coordinates 50,50 and wanders around the immediate area.

INCLUDE Irvine32.inc
WalkMax = 50
StartX = 25
StartY = 25

DrunkardWalk STRUCT
     path COORD WalkMax DUP(<0,0>)
     pathsUsed WORD 0
DrunkardWalk ENDS

DisplayPosition PROTO currX:WORD, currY:WORD

.data
aWalk DrunkardWalk <>

.code
main PROC
     mov    esi,OFFSET aWalk
     call   TakeDrunkenWalk
     exit
main ENDP

;--------------------------------------------------------
TakeDrunkenWalk PROC
LOCAL currX:WORD, currY:WORD
;
; Take a walk in random directions (north, south, east,
; west).
; Receives: ESI points to a DrunkardWalk structure
; Returns:  the structure is initialized with random values
;--------------------------------------------------------
     pushad

; Use the OFFSET operator to obtain the address of
; path, the array of COORD objects, and copy it to EDI.
     mov    edi,esi
     add    edi,OFFSET DrunkardWalk.path
     mov    ecx,WalkMax               ; loop counter
     mov    currX,StartX             ; current X-location
```

```
        mov    currY,StartY              ; current Y-location
Again:
        ; Insert current location in array.
        mov    ax,currX
        mov    (COORD PTR [edi]).X,ax
        mov    ax,currY
        mov    (COORD PTR [edi]).Y,ax

        INVOKE DisplayPosition, currX, currY

        mov    eax,4                     ; choose a direction (0-3)
        call   RandomRange

        .IF eax == 0                     ; North
          dec currY
        .ELSEIF eax == 1                 ; South
          inc currY
        .ELSEIF eax == 2                 ; West
          dec currX
        .ELSE                            ; East (EAX = 3)
          inc currX
        .ENDIF

        add    edi,TYPE COORD            ; point to next COORD
        loop   Again
Finish:
        mov    (DrunkardWalk PTR [esi]).pathsUsed, WalkMax
        popad
        ret
TakeDrunkenWalk ENDP

;----------------------------------------------------------
DisplayPosition PROC currX:WORD, currY:WORD
; Display the current X and Y positions.
;----------------------------------------------------------
.data
commaStr BYTE ",",0
.code
        pushad
        movzx  eax,currX                 ; current X position
        call   WriteDec
        mov    edx,OFFSET commaStr       ; "," string
        call   WriteString
        movzx  eax,currY                 ; current Y position
        call   WriteDec
        call   Crlf
        popad
        ret
DisplayPosition ENDP
END main
```

TakeDrunkenWalk Procedure   Let's take a closer look at the **TakeDrunkenWalk** procedure. It receives a pointer (ESI) to a **DrunkardWalk** structure. Using the OFFSET operator, it calculates the offset of the **path** array and copies it to EDI:

```
mov  edi,esi
add  edi,OFFSET DrunkardWalk.path
```

The initial X and Y positions (StartX and StartY) of the professor are set to 25, at the center of an imaginary 50-by-50 grid. The loop counter is initialized:

```
mov   ecx, Walkmax          ; loop counter
mov   currX,StartX          ; current X-location
mov   currY,StartY          ; current Y-location
```

At the beginning of the loop, the first two entries in the **path** array are initialized:

```
Again:
      ; Insert current location in array.
      mov   ax,currX
      mov   (COORD PTR [edi]).X,ax
      mov   ax,currY
      mov   (COORD PTR [edi]).Y,ax
```

At the end of the walk, a counter is inserted into the **pathsUsed** field, indicating how many steps were taken:

```
Finish:
      mov (DrunkardWalk PTR [esi]).pathsUsed, WalkMax
```

In the current version of the program, **pathsUsed** is always equal to **WalkMax**, but that could change if we checked for hazards such as lakes and buildings. Then the loop would terminate before **WalMax** was reached.

10.1.7   Declaring and Using Unions

Whereas each field in a structure has an offset relative to the first byte of the structure, all the fields in a *union* start at the same offset. The storage size of a union is equal to the length of its longest field. When not part of a structure, a union is declared using the UNION and ENDS directives:

```
unionname UNION
      union-fields
unionname ENDS
```

If the union is nested inside a structure, the syntax is slightly different:

```
structname STRUCT
      structure-fields
      UNION unionname
          union-fields
      ENDS
structname ENDS
```

The field declarations in a union follow the same rules as for structures, except that each field can have only a single initializer. For example, the **Integer** union has three different size attributes for the same data and initializes all fields to zero:

```
Integer UNION
      D DWORD 0
      W WORD 0
      B BYTE 0
Integer ENDS
```

Be Consistent   Initializers, if used, must have consistent values. Suppose Integer were declared with different initializers

```
Integer UNION
      D DWORD 1
      W WORD  5
      B BYTE  8
Integer ENDS
```

Then we declared an Integer variable named **myInt** using default initializers:

```
.data
myInt Integer <>
```

The values of myInt.D, myInt.W, and myInt.B would all equal 1. The declared initializers for fields W and B would be ignored by the assembler.

Structure Containing a Union   You can nest a union inside a structure by using the union name in a declaration, as we have done here for the **FileID** field inside the **FileInfo** structure,

```
FileInfo STRUCT
    FileID Integer <>
    FileName BYTE 64 DUP(?)
FileInfo ENDS
```

or you can declare a union directly inside the structure, as we have done here for the **FileID** field:

```
FileInfo STRUCT
  UNION FileID
        D DWORD ?
        W WORD ?
        B BYTE ?
  ENDS
  FileName BYTE 64 DUP(?)
FileInfo ENDS
```

Declaring and Using Union Variables   A union variable is declared and initialized in much the same way as a structure variable, with one important difference: No more than one initializer is permitted. The following are examples of Integer-type variables:

```
val1 Integer <12345678h>
val2 Integer <100h>
val3 Integer <>
```

To use a union variable in an executable instruction, you must supply the name of one of the variant fields. In the following example, we assign register values to **Integer** union fields. Note the flexibility we have in being able to use different operand sizes:

```
mov  val3.B, al
mov  val3.W, ax
mov  val3.D, eax
```

Unions can also contain structures. The following INPUT_RECORD structure is used by some MS-Windows console input functions. It contains a union named **Event**, which selects among several predefined structure types. The **EventType** field indicates which type of record appears in the union. Each structure has a different layout and size, but only one is used at a time:

```
INPUT_RECORD STRUCT
    EventType WORD ?
    ALIGN DWORD
    UNION Event
      KEY_EVENT_RECORD <>
      MOUSE_EVENT_RECORD <>
      WINDOW_BUFFER_SIZE_RECORD <>
      MENU_EVENT_RECORD <>
      FOCUS_EVENT_RECORD <>
    ENDS
INPUT_RECORD ENDS
```

The Win32 API often includes the word RECORD when naming structures.[1] This is the definition of a KEY_EVENT_RECORD structure:

```
KEY_EVENT_RECORD STRUCT
        bKeyDown            DWORD ?
        wRepeatCount        WORD  ?
        wVirtualKeyCode     WORD  ?
        wVirtualScanCode    WORD  ?
        UNION uChar
           UnicodeChar      WORD  ?
           AsciiChar        BYTE  ?
        ENDS
        dwControlKeyState DWORD ?
KEY_EVENT_RECORD ENDS
```

The remaining STRUCT definitions from INPUT_RECORD can be found in the SmallWin.inc file.

10.1.8 Section Review

1. What is the purpose of the STRUCT directive?

2. Create a structure named **MyStruct** containing two fields: **field1**, a single word, and **field2**, an array of 20 doublewords. The initial values of the fields may be left undefined.

The structure created in Exercise 2 (MyStruct) will be used in Exercises 3 through 11:

3. Declare a **MyStruct** variable with default values.

4. Declare a **MyStruct** variable that initializes the first field to zero.

5. Declare a **MyStruct** variable and initialize the second field to an array containing all zeros.

6. Declare a variable as an array of 20 **MyStruct** objects.

7. Using the **MyStruct** array from the preceding exercise, move **field1** of the first array element to AX.

8. Using the **MyStruct** array from the preceding exercise, use ESI to index to the third array element and move AX to **field1**. *Hint:* Use the PTR operator.

9. What value does the expression **TYPE MyStruct** return?

10. What value does the expression **SIZEOF MyStruct** return?

11. Write an expression that returns the number of bytes in **field2** of **MyStruct**.

The following exercises are not related to MyStruct:

12. Assume that the following structure has been defined:
```
RentalInvoice STRUCT
   invoiceNum BYTE 5 DUP(' ')
   dailyPrice WORD ?
   daysRented WORD ?
RentalInvoice ENDS
```
State whether or not each of the following declarations is valid:

a. rentals RentalInvoice <>
b. RentalInvoice rentals <>
c. march RentalInvoice <'12345',10,0>
d. RentalInvoice <,10,0>
e. current RentalInvoice <,15,0,0>

13. Write a statement that retrieves the **wHour** field of a SYSTEMTIME structure.

14. Using the following **Triangle** structure, declare a structure variable and initialize its vertices to (0,0), (5, 0), and (7,6):
```
Triangle STRUCT
        Vertex1 COORD <>
```

```
        Vertex2 COORD <>
        Vertex3 COORD <>
   Triangle ENDS
```

15. Declare an array of **Triangle** structures. Write a loop that initializes **Vertex1** of each triangle to random coordinates in the range (0..10, 0..10).

10.2 Macros

10.2.1 Overview

A *macro procedure* is a named block of assembly language statements. Once defined, it can be invoked (called) as many times in a program as you wish. When you *invoke* a macro procedure, a copy of its code is inserted directly into the program at the location where it was invoked. It is customary to refer to *calling* a macro procedure, although technically there is no CALL instruction involved.

> The term *macro procedure* is used in the Microsoft Assembler manual to identify macros that do not return a value. There are also *macro functions* that return a value. Among programmers, the word *macro* is usually understood to mean the same thing as *macro procedure*. From this point on, we will use the shorter form.

Declaring   Macros are defined directly at the beginning of a source program, or they are placed in a separate file and copied into a program by an INCLUDE directive. Macros are expanded during the assembler's *preprocessing* step. In this step, the preprocessor reads a macro definition and scans the remaining source code in the program. At every point where the macro is called, the assembler inserts a copy of the macro's source code into the program. A macro definition must be found by the assembler before trying to assemble any calls of the macro. If a program defines a macro but never calls it, the macro code does not appear in the compiled program.

In the following example, a macro named **PrintX** contains a single statement that calls the **Write-Char** procedure from Irvine32 or Irvine16. This definition would normally be placed just before the data segment:

```
PrintX MACRO
     mov    al,'X'
     call   WriteChar
ENDM
```

Next, in the code segment, we call the macro:

```
.code
PrintX
```

When the preprocessor scans this program and discovers the call to **PrintX**, it replaces the macro call with the following statements:

```
mov  al,'X'
call WriteChar
```

Text substitution has taken place. Although the macro is somewhat inflexible, we will soon show how to pass arguments to macros, making them far more useful.

10.2.2 Defining Macros

A macro is defined using the MACRO and ENDM directives. The syntax is

```
macroname MACRO parameter-1, parameter-2...
   statement-list
ENDM
```

There is no fixed rule regarding indentation, but we recommend that you indent statements between *macroname* and ENDM. You might also want to prefix macro names with the letter m, creating recognizable names such ar **mPutChar, mWriteString,** and **mGotoxy**. The statements between the MACRO and ENDM directives are not assembled until the macro is called. There can be any number of parameters in the macro definition, separated by commas.

Parameters   Macro parameters are named placeholders for text arguments passed to the caller. The arguments may in fact be integers, variable names, or other values, but the preprocessor treats them as text. Parameters are not typed, so the preprocessor does not check argument types to see whether they are correct. If a type mismatch occurs, it is caught by the assembler after the macro has been expanded.

mPutchar Example   The following **mPutchar** macro receives a single input parameter called **char** and displays it on the console by calling **WriteChar** from the book's link library:

```
mPutchar MACRO char
    push    eax
    mov     al,char
    call    WriteChar
    pop     eax
ENDM
```

10.2.3   Invoking Macros

A macro is called (invoked) by inserting its name in the program, possibly followed by macro arguments. The syntax for calling a macro is

```
macroname argument-1, argument-2, ...
```

Macroname must be the name of a macro defined prior to this point in the source code. Each argument is a text value that replaces a parameter in the macro. The order of arguments must correspond to the order of parameters, but the number of arguments does not have to match the number of parameters. If too many arguments are passed, the assembler issues a warning. If too few arguments are passed to a macro, the unfilled parameters are left blank.

Invoking mPutchar   In the previous section, we defined the **mPutChar** macro. When invoking mPutchar, we can pass any character or ASCII code. The following statement invokes mPutchar and passes it the letter A:

```
mPutchar 'A'
```

The assembler's preprocessor expands the statement into the following code, shown in the listing file:

```
1    push eax
1    mov  al,'A'
1    call WriteChar
1    pop  eax
```

The 1 in the left column indicates the macro expansion level, which increases when you call other macros from within a macro. The following loop displays the first 20 letters of the alphabet:

```
    mov al,'A'
    mov ecx,20
L1:
    mPutchar al                    ; macro call
    inc  al
    loop L1
```

Our loop is expanded by the preprocessor into the following code (visible in the source listing file). The macro call is shown just before its expansion:

```
        mov   al,'A'
        mov   ecx,20
L1:
        mPutchar al                    ; macro call
1       push eax
1       mov  al,al
1       call WriteChar
1       pop  eax
        inc  al
        loop L1
```

> In general, macros execute more quickly than procedures because procedures have the extra overhead of CALL and RET instructions. There is, however, one disadvantage to using macros: repeated use of large macros tends to increase a program's size because each call to a macro inserts a new copy of the macro's statements in the program.

Debugging Programs That Contain Macros

Debugging a program that uses macros can be a special challenge. After assembling a program, check its listing file (extension .LST) to make sure each macro is expanded the way you intended. Next, start the program in a debugger (such as Visual Studio .NET). Trace the program in a disassembly window, using the *show source code* option if it is supported by the debugger. Each macro call will be followed by the code generated by the macro. Here is an example:

```
mWriteAt 15,10,"Hi there"
        push  edx
        mov   dh,0Ah
        mov   dl,0Fh
        call  _Gotoxy@0 (401551h)
        pop   edx
        push  edx
        mov   edx,offset ??0000 (405004h)
        call  _WriteString@0 (401D64h)
        pop   edx
```

(The function names begin with underscore (_) because the Irvine32 library uses the STDCALL calling convention. See Section 8.4.1 for details.)

10.2.4 Additional Macro Features

Required Parameters

Using the REQ qualifier, you can specify that a macro parameter is required. If the macro is called without an argument to match the required parameter, the assembler displays an error message. If a macro has multiple required parameters, each one must include the REQ qualifier. In the following **mPutchar** macro, the **char** parameter is required:

```
mPutchar MACRO char:REQ
        push  eax
        mov   al,char
        call  WriteChar
        pop   eax
ENDM
```

Macro Comments

Ordinary comment lines appearing in a macro definition appear each time the macro is expanded. If you want to have comments in the macro that will not appear in macro expansions, begin them with a double semicolon (;;):

```
mPutchar MACRO char:REQ
        push    eax                           ;; reminder: char must 8 bits
        mov     al,char
        call    WriteChar
        pop     eax
ENDM
```

ECHO Directive

The ECHO directive displays a message on the console as the program is assembled. In the following version of **mPutchar**, the message "Expanding the mPutchar macro" appears on the console during assembly:

```
mPutchar MACRO char:REQ
        ECHO Expanding the mPutchar macro
        push    eax
        mov     al,char
        call    WriteChar
        pop     eax
ENDM
```

LOCAL Directive

Macro definitions often contain labels and self-reference those labels in their code. The following **makeString** macro, for example, declares a variable named **string** and initializes it with a character array:

```
makeString MACRO text
        .data
        string BYTE text,0
ENDM
```

Suppose we invoke the macro twice:

```
makeString "Hello"
makeString "Goodbye"
```

An error results because the assembler will not let the **string** label be redefined:

```
        makeString "Hello"
1       .data
1       string BYTE "Hello",0
        makeString "Goodbye"
1       .data
1       string BYTE "Goodbye",0      ; error!
```

Using LOCAL   To avoid problems caused by label redefinitions, you can apply the LOCAL directive to labels inside a macro definition. When a label is marked LOCAL, the preprocessor converts the label's name to a unique identifier each time macro is expanded. Here's a new version of **makeString** that uses LOCAL:

```
makeString MACRO text
        LOCAL string
        .data
        string BYTE text,0
ENDM
```

If we invoke the macro twice as before, the code generated by the preprocessor replaces each occurrence of **string** with a unique identifier:

```
      makeString "Hello"
1     .data
1     ??0000 BYTE "Hello",0
      makeString "Goodbye"
1     .data
1     ??0001 BYTE "Goodbye",0
```

The label names produced by the assembler take the form *??nnnn*, where *nnnn* is a unique integer. The LOCAL directive should also be used for code labels in macros.

Macros Containing Code and Data

Macros often contain both code and data. The following **mWrite** macro, for example, displays a literal string on the console:

```
mWrite MACRO text
      LOCAL string               ;; local label
      .data
      string BYTE text,0         ;; define the string
      .code
      push    edx
      mov     edx,OFFSET string
      call    WriteString
      pop     edx
ENDM
```

The following statements invoke the macro twice, passing it different string literals:

```
mWrite "Please enter your first name"
mWrite "Please enter your last name"
```

The expansion of the two statements by the assembler shows that each string is assigned a unique label, and the **mov** instructions are adjusted accordingly:

```
      mWrite "Please enter your first name"
1     .data
1     ??0000 BYTE "Please enter your first name",0
1     .code
1     push edx
1     mov  edx,OFFSET ??0000
1     call WriteString
1     pop  edx
      mWrite "Please enter your last name"
1     .data
1     ??0001 BYTE "Please enter your last name",0
1     .code
1     push edx
1     mov  edx,OFFSET ??0001
1     call WriteString
1     pop  edx
```

Nested Macros

A macro invoked from another macro is called a *nested macro*. When the assembler's preprocessor encounters a call to a nested macro, it expands the macro in place. Parameters passed to an enclosing macro are passed directly to its nested macros.

Use a modular approach when creating macros. Keep them short and simple so they can be combined into more complex macros. Doing this helps to reduce the amount of duplicate code in your programs.

mWriteln Example   The following **mWriteln** macro writes a string literal to the console and appends an end of line. It invokes the **mWrite** macro and calls the **Crlf** procedure:

```
mWriteln MACRO text
        mWrite  text
        call    Crlf
ENDM
```

The **text** parameter is passed directly to **mWrite**. Suppose the following statement invokes mWriteln:

```
mWriteln "My Sample Macro Program"
```

In the resulting code expansion, the nesting level (2) next to the statements indicates a nested macro has been invoked:

```
          mWriteln "My Sample Macro Program"
2         .data
2         ??0002 BYTE "My Sample Macro Program",0
2         .code
2         push edx
2         mov  edx,OFFSET ??0002
2         call WriteString
2         pop  edx
1         call Crlf
```

10.2.5   Using the Book's Macro Library

The sample programs supplied with this book include a small but useful macro library, which you can enable simply by adding the following line to your programs just after the INCLUDE you already have:

```
INCLUDE Macros.inc
```

Some of the macros are wrappers around existing procedures in the Irvine32 and Irvine16 libraries, making it easier to pass parameters. Other macros provide new functionality. Table 10–2 describes each macro in detail. The example code can be found in *MacroTest.asm*.

Table 10-2   Macros in the Macros.inc Library

Macro Name	Parameters	Description
mDump	varName, useLabel	Displays a variable, using its name and default attributes.
mDumpMem	address, itemCount, componentSize	Displays a range of memory.
mGotoxy	X, Y	Sets the cursor position in the console window buffer.
mReadString	varName	Reads a string from the keyboard.
mShow	itsName, format	Displays a variable or register in various formats.
mShowRegister	regName, regValue	Displays a 32-bit register's name and contents in hexadecimal.
mWrite	text	Writes a string literal to the console window.
mWriteSpace	count	Writes one or more spaces to the console window.
mWriteString	buffer	Writes a string variable's contents to the console window.

mDumpMem

The mDumpMem macro displays a block of memory in the console window. Pass it a constant, register, or variable containing the offset of the memory you want displayed. The second argument should be the number of memory components to be displayed, and the third argument is the size of each memory component. (The macro calls the DumpMem library procedure, assigning the three arguments to ESI, ECX, and EBX, respectively.) Let's assume the following data definition:

```
.data
array DWORD 1000h,2000h,3000h,4000h
```

The following statement displays the array using its default attributes:

```
mDumpMem OFFSET array, LENGTHOF array, TYPE array
```

Output:

```
Dump of offset 00405004
-------------------------------
00001000   00002000   00003000   00004000
```

The following displays the same array as a byte sequence:

```
mDumpMem OFFSET array, SIZEOF array, TYPE BYTE
```

Output:

```
Dump of offset 00405004
-------------------------------
00 10 00 00 00 20 00 00 00 30 00 00 00 40 00 00
```

The following code pushes three values on the stack, sets the values of EBX, ECX, and ESI, and uses mDumpMem to display the stack:

```
mov   eax,0AAAAAAAAh
push  eax
mov   eax,0BBBBBBBBh
push  eax
mov   eax,0CCCCCCCCh
push  eax
mov   ebx,1
mov   ecx,2
mov   esi,3
mDumpMem esp, 8, TYPE DWORD
```

The resulting stack dump shows the macro has pushed EBX, ECX, and ESI on the stack. Following those values are the three integers we pushed on the stack before invoking mDumpMem:

```
Dump of offset 0012FFAC
-------------------------------
00000003   00000002   00000001   CCCCCCCC   BBBBBBBB   AAAAAAAA   7C816D4F
0000001A
```

Implementation   Here is the macro's code listing:

```
mDumpMem MACRO address:REQ, itemCount:REQ, componentSize:REQ
;
; Displays a dump of memory, using the DumpMem procedure.
; Receives: memory offset, count of the number of items
;     to display, and the size of each memory component.
; Avoid passing EBX, ECX, and ESI as arguments.
;-----------------------------------------------------------
```

```
            push  ebx
            push  ecx
            push  esi
            mov   esi,address
            mov   ecx,itemCount
            mov   ebx,componentSize
            call  DumpMem
            pop   esi
            pop   ecx
            pop   ebx
      ENDM
```

mDump

The mDump macro displays the address and contents of a variable in hexadecimal. Pass it the name of a variable and (optionally) a character indicating that a label should be displayed next to the variable. The display format automatically matches the variable's size attribute (BYTE, WORD, or DWORD). The following example shows two calls to mDump:

```
      .data
      diskSize DWORD 12345h
      .code
      mDump        diskSize              ; no label
      mDump        diskSize,Y            ; show label
```

The following output is produced when the code executes:

```
      Dump of offset 00405000
      ------------------------------
      00012345

      Variable name: diskSize
      Dump of offset 00405000
      ------------------------------
      00012345
```

Implementation   Here is a listing of the mDump macro, which in turn calls mDumpMem. It uses a new directive named IFNB (*if not blank*) to find out if the caller has passed an argument into the second parameter (see Section 10.3):

```
      ;------------------------------------------------------
      mDump MACRO varName:REQ, useLabel
      ;
      ; Displays a variable, using its known attributes
      ; Receives: varName, the name of a variable.
      ;    If useLabel is nonblank, the name of the
      ;    variable is displayed.
      ;------------------------------------------------------
            call Crlf
            IFNB <useLabel>
              mWrite "Variable name: &varName"
            ENDIF
            mDumpMem OFFSET varName, LENGTHOF varName, TYPE varName
      ENDM
```

The & in **&varName** is a *substitution operator*, which permits the **varName** parameter's value to be inserted into the string literal. See Section 10.3.7 for more details.

mGotoxy

The **mGotoxy** macro locates the cursor at a specific column and row location in the console window's buffer. You can pass it 8-bit immediate values, memory operands, and register values:

```
mGotoxy   10,20                              ; immediate values
mGotoxy   row,col                            ; memory operands
mGotoxy   ch,cl                              ; register values
```

Implementation   Here is a source listing of the macro:

```
;--------------------------------------------------------
mGotoxy MACRO X:REQ, Y:REQ
;
; Sets the cursor position in the console window.
; Receives: X and Y coordinates (type BYTE). Avoid
;     passing DH and DL as arguments.
;--------------------------------------------------------
      push  edx
      mov   dh,Y
      mov   dl,X
      call  Gotoxy
      pop   edx
ENDM
```

Avoiding Register Conflicts   When macro arguments are registers, they can sometimes conflict with registers used internally by macros. If we call **mGotoxy** using DH and DL, for example, it does not generate correct code. To see why, let's inspect the expanded code after such parameters have been substituted:

```
1     push  edx
2     mov   dh,dl                            ;; row
3     mov   dl,dh                            ;; column
4     call  Gotoxy
5     pop   edx
```

Assuming that DL is passed as the Y value and DH is the X value, line 2 replaces DH before we have a chance to copy the column value to DL on line 3.

> Whenever possible, macro definitions should specify which registers cannot be used as arguments.

mReadString

The **mReadString** macro inputs a string from the keyboard and stores the string in a buffer. Internally, it encapsulates a call to the **ReadString** library procedure. Pass it the name of the buffer:

```
.data
firstName BYTE 30 DUP(?)
.code
mReadString  firstName
```

Here is the macro's source code:

```
;--------------------------------------------------------
mReadString MACRO varName:REQ
;
; Reads from standard input into a buffer.
; Receives: the name of the buffer. Avoid passing
```

```
;      ECX and EDX as arguments.
;----------------------------------------------------
        push    ecx
        push    edx
        mov     edx,OFFSET varName
        mov     ecx,SIZEOF varName
        call    ReadString
        pop     edx
        pop     ecx
ENDM
```

mShow

The mShow macro displays any register or variable's name and contents in a caller-selected format. Pass it the name of the register, followed by an optional sequence of letters identifying the desired format. Use the following codes: H = hexadecimal, D = unsigned decimal, I = signed decimal, B = binary, N = append a newline. Multiple output formats can be combined, and multiple newlines can be specified. The default format is "HIN". mShow is a useful debugging aid, and is used extensively by the DumpRegs library procedure. You can insert calls to mShow in any program, displaying the values of important registers or variables.

Example   The following statements display the AX register in hexadecimal, signed decimal, unsigned decimal, and binary:

```
mov    ax,4096
mShow AX           ; default options: HIN
mShow AX,DBN       ; unsigned decimal, binary, newline
```

Here is the output:

```
AX = 1000h +4096d
AX = 4096d   0001 0000 0000 0000b
```

Example   The following statements display AX, BX, CX, and DX in unsigned decimal, on the same output line:

```
; Insert some test values and show four registers:
mov    ax,1
mov    bx,2
mov    cx,3
mov    dx,4
mShow AX,D
mShow BX,D
mShow CX,D
mShow DX,DN
```

Here is the corresponding output:

```
AX = 1d    BX = 2d    CX = 3d    DX = 4d
```

Example   The following call to mShow displays the contents of **mydword** in unsigned decimal, followed by a newline:

```
.data
mydword DWORD ?
.code
mShow  mydword,DN
```

Implementation   The implementation of mShow is too long to include here, but may be found in the Macros.inc file. When implementing mShow, we had to be careful to show the current register values before they were modified by statements inside the macro itself.

mShowRegister

The mShowRegister macro displays the name and contents of a single 32-bit register in hexadecimal. Pass it the register's name as you want it displayed, followed by the register itself. The following macro invocation specifies the displayed name as EBX:

```
mShowRegister EBX, ebx
```

The following output is produced:

```
EBX=7FFD9000
```

The following invocation uses angle brackets around the label because it contains an embedded space:

```
mShowRegister <Stack Pointer>, esp
```

The following output is produced:

```
Stack Pointer=0012FFC0
```

Implementation   Here is the macro's source code:

```
;--------------------------------------------------
mShowRegister MACRO regName, regValue
LOCAL tempStr
;
; Displays a register's name and contents.
; Receives: the register name, the register value.
;--------------------------------------------------
.data
tempStr BYTE " &regName=",0
.code
      push eax

; Display the register name
      push   edx
      mov    edx,OFFSET tempStr
      call   WriteString
      pop    edx

; Display the register contents
      mov    eax,regValue
      call   WriteHex
      pop    eax
ENDM
```

mWriteSpace

The mWriteSpace macro writes one or more spaces to the console window. You can optionally pass it an integer parameter specifying the number of spaces to write (the default is one). The following statement, for example, writes five spaces:

```
mWriteSpace 5
```

Implementation   Here is the source code for mWriteSpace:

```
;----------------------------------------------------------
mWriteSpace MACRO count:=<1>
;
; Writes one or more spaces to the console window.
; Receives: an integer specifying the number of spaces.
; Default value of count is 1.
;----------------------------------------------------------
LOCAL spaces
```

```
.data
spaces BYTE count DUP(' '),0
.code
     push   edx
     mov    edx,OFFSET spaces
     call   WriteString
     pop    edx
ENDM
```

Section 10.3.2 explains how to use default initializers for macro parameters.

mWriteString

The **mWriteString** macro writes the contents of a string variable to the console window. Internally, it simplifies calls to **WriteString** by letting you pass the name of a string variable on the same statement line. For example:

```
.data
str1 BYTE "Please enter your name: ",0
.code
mWriteString str1
```

Implementation The following **mWriteString** implementation saves EDX on the stack, fills EDX with the string's offset, and pops EDX from the stack after the procedure call:

```
;------------------------------------------------------
mWriteString MACRO buffer:REQ
;
; Writes a string variable to standard output.
; Receives: string variable name.
;------------------------------------------------------
     push   edx
     mov    edx,OFFSET buffer
     call   WriteString
     pop    edx
ENDM
```

10.2.6   Example Program: Wrappers

Let's create a short program named *Wraps.asm* that shows off the macros we've already introduced as procedure wrappers. Because each macro hides a lot of tedious parameter passing, the program is surprisingly compact. We will assume that all of the macros shown so far are located inside the *Macros.inc* file:

```
TITLE Procedure Wrapper Macros          (Wraps.asm)

; This program demonstrates macros as wrappers
; for library procedures. Contents: mGotoxy, mWrite,
; mWriteString, mReadString, and mDumpMem.

INCLUDE Irvine32.inc
INCLUDE Macros.inc                  ; macro definitions

.data
array DWORD 1,2,3,4,5,6,7,8
firstName BYTE 31 DUP(?)
lastName  BYTE 31 DUP(?)

.code
main PROC
     mGotoxy 0,0
     mWrite <"Sample Macro Program",0dh,0ah>
```

```
; Input the user's name.
    mGotoxy 0,5
    mWrite "Please enter your first name: "
    mReadString firstName
    call Crlf

    mWrite "Please enter your last name: "
    mReadString lastName
    call Crlf
; Display the user's name.
    mWrite "Your name is "
    mWriteString firstName
    mWriteSpace
    mWriteString lastName
    call Crlf

; Display the array of integers.
    mDumpMem OFFSET array, LENGTHOF array, TYPE array
    exit
main ENDP
END main
```

Program Output   The following is a sample of the program's output:

```
Sample Macro Program
Please enter your first name: Joe
Please enter your last name: Smith
Your name is Joe Smith
Dump of offset 00404000
------------------------------
00000001  00000002  00000003  00000004  00000005
00000006  00000007  00000008
```

10.2.7 Section Review

1. (*True/False*): When a macro is invoked, the CALL and RET instructions are automatically inserted into the assembled program.

2. (*True/False*): Macro expansion is handled by the assembler's preprocessor.

3. What is the primary advantage to using macros with parameters versus macros without them?

4. (*True/False*): As long as it is in the code segment, a macro definition may appear either before or after statements that invoke the macro.

5. (*True/False*): Replacing a long procedure with a macro containing the procedure's code will typically increase the compiled code size of a program if the macro is invoked multiple times.

6. (*True/False*): A macro cannot contain data definitions.

7. What is the purpose of the LOCAL directive?

8. Which directive displays a message on the console during the assembly step?

9. Write a macro named **mPrintChar** that displays a single character on the screen. It should have two parameters: this first specifies the character to be displayed, the second specifies how many times the character should be repeated. Here is a sample call:

```
    mPrintChar 'X',20
```

10. Write a macro named **mGenRandom** that generates a random integer between 0 and $n - 1$. Let n be the only parameter.

11. Write a macro named **mPromptInteger** that displays a prompt and inputs an integer from the user. Pass it a string literal and the name of a doubleword variable. Sample call:

```
.data
minVal DWORD ?
.code
mPromptInteger "Enter the minimum value", minVal
```

12. Write a macro named **mWriteAt** that locates the cursor and writes a string literal to the console window. *Suggestion:* Invoke the **mGotoxy** and **mWrite** macros.

13. Show the expanded code produced by the following statement that invokes the **mWriteString** macro from Section 10.2.5:

```
mWriteStr namePrompt
```

14. Show the expanded code produced by the following statement that invokes the **mReadString** macro from Section 10.2.5:

```
mReadStr customerName
```

15. *Challenge:* Write a macro named **mDumpMemx** that receives a single parameter, the name of a variable. Your macro must call the **mDumpMem** macro, passing it the variable's offset, number of units, and unit size. Demonstrate a call to the mDumpMemx macro.

10.3   Conditional-Assembly Directives

A number of different conditional-assembly directives can be used in conjunction with macros to make them more flexible. The general syntax for conditional-assembly directives is

```
IF condition
    statements
[ELSE
    statements]
ENDIF
```

> The constant directives shown in this chapter should not be confused with run-time directives such as .IF and .ENDIF introduced in Section 6.7. The latter evaluated expressions based on runtime values stored in registers and variables.

Table 10-3 lists the more common conditional-assembly directives. When the descriptions say that a directive *permits assembly*, it means that any subsequent statements are assembled up to the next ELSE or ENDIF directive. It must be emphasized that the directives listed in the table are evaluated at assembly time, not at run time.

10.3.1   Checking for Missing Arguments

A macro can check to see whether any of its arguments are blank. Often, if a blank argument is received by a macro, invalid instructions result when the macro is expanded by the preprocessor. For example, if we invoke the **mWriteString** macro without passing an argument, the macro expands with an invalid instruction when moving the string offset to EDX. The following are statements generated by the assembler, which detects the missing operand and issues an error message:

```
mWriteString
1    push edx
1    mov  edx,OFFSET
Macro2.asm(18) : error A2081: missing operand after unary operator
1    call WriteString
1    pop  edx
```

Table 10-3   Conditional-Assembly Directives.

Directive	Description
IF *expression*	Permits assembly if the value of *expression* is true (nonzero). Possible relational operators are LT, GT, EQ, NE, LE, and GE.
IFB *<argument>*	Permits assembly if *argument* is blank. The argument name must be enclosed in angle brackets (<>).
IFNB *<argument>*	Permits assembly if *argument* is not blank. The argument name must be enclosed in angle brackets (<>).
IFIDN *<arg1>,<arg2>*	Permits assembly if the two arguments are equal (identical). Uses a case-sensitive comparison.
IFIDNI *<arg1>,<arg2>*	Permits assembly if the two arguments are equal. Uses a case-insensitive comparison.
IFDIF *<arg1>,<arg2>*	Permits assembly if the two arguments are unequal. Uses a case-sensitive comparison.
IFDIFI *<arg1>,<arg2>*	Permits assembly if the two arguments are unequal. Uses a case-insensitive comparison.
IFDEF *name*	Permits assembly if *name* has been defined.
IFNDEF *name*	Permits assembly if *name* has not been defined.
ENDIF	Ends a block that was begun using one of the conditional-assembly directives.
ELSE	Terminates assembly of the previous statements if the condition is True. If the condition is false, ELSE assembles statements up to the next ENDIF.
ELSEIF *expression*	Assembles all statements up to ENDIF if the condition specified by a previous conditional directive is false and the value of the current expression is true.
EXITM	Exits a macro immediately, preventing any following macro statements from being expanded.

To prevent errors caused by missing operands, you can use the IFB (*if blank*) directive, which returns true if a macro argument is blank. Or, you can use the IFNB (*if not blank*) operator, which returns true if a macro argument is not blank. Let's create an alternate version of **mWriteString** that displays an error message during assembly:

```
mWriteString MACRO string
     IFB <string>
        ECHO -----------------------------------------
        ECHO *  Error: parameter missing in mWriteString
        ECHO *  (no code generated)
        ECHO -----------------------------------------
        EXITM
     ENDIF
     push    edx
     mov     edx,OFFSET string
     call    WriteString
     pop     edx
ENDM
```

(Recall from Section 10.2.2 that the ECHO directive writes a message to the console while a program is being assembled.) The EXITM directive tells the preprocessor to exit the macro and to not expand any more statements from the macro. The following shows the screen output when assembling a program with a missing parameter:

```
Assembling: Macro2.asm
-------------------------------------------
*  Error: parameter missing in mWriteString
*  (no code generated)
-------------------------------------------
```

10.3.2   Default Argument Initializers

Macros can have default argument initializers. If a macro argument is missing when the macro is called, the default argument is used instead. The syntax is

```
paramname := < argument >
```

(Spaces before and after the operators are optional.) For example, the **mWriteln** macro can supply a string containing a single space as its default argument. If it is called with no arguments, it still prints a space followed by an end of line:

```
mWriteln MACRO text:=<" ">
        mWrite text
        call Crlf
ENDM
```

The assembler issues an error if a null string (" ") is used as the default argument, so you have to insert at least one space between the quotes.

10.3.3   Boolean Expressions

The assembler permits the following relational operators to be used in constant boolean expressions containing IF and other conditional directives:

```
          LT          Less than
          GT          Greater than
          EQ          Equal to
          NE          Not equal to
          LE          Less than or equal to
          GE          Greater than or equal to
```

10.3.4   IF, ELSE, and ENDIF Directives

The IF directive must be followed by a constant boolean expression. The expression can contain integer constants, symbolic constants, or constant macro arguments, but it cannot contain register or variable names. One syntax format uses just IF and ENDIF:

```
IF expression
    statement-list
ENDIF
```

Another format uses IF, ELSE, and ENDIF:

```
IF expression
    statement-list
ELSE
    statement-list
ENDIF
```

Example: mGotoxyConst Macro   The **mGotoxyConst** macro uses the LT and GT operators to perform range checking on the arguments passed to the macro. The arguments X and Y must be constants. Another constant symbol named ERRS counts the number of errors found. Depending on the value of X, we may set ERRS to 1. Depending on the value of Y, we may add 1 to ERRS. Finally, if ERRS is greater than zero, the EXITM directive exits the macro:

```
;------------------------------------------------------
mGotoxyConst MACRO X:REQ, Y:REQ
;
; Sets the cursor position at column X, row Y.
; Requires X and Y coordinates to be constant expressions
; in the ranges 0 <= X < 80 and 0 <= Y < 24.
;------------------------------------------------------
    LOCAL ERRS                      ;; local constant
    ERRS = 0
    IF (X LT 0) OR (X GT 79)
        ECHO Warning: First argument to mGotoxy (X) is out of range.
        ECHO ***********************************************************
        ERRS = 1
    ENDIF
    IF (Y LT 0) OR (Y GT 24)
        ECHO Warning: Second argument to mGotoxy (Y) is out of range.
        ECHO ***********************************************************
        ERRS = ERRS + 1
    ENDIF
    IF ERRS GT 0                    ;; if errors found,
      EXITM                         ;; exit the macro
    ENDIF
    push   edx
    mov    dh,Y
    mov    dl,X
    call   Gotoxy
    pop    edx
ENDM
```

10.3.5 The IFIDN and IFIDNI Directives

The IFIDNI directive performs a case-insensitive match between two symbols (including macro parameter names) and returns true if they are equal. The IFIDN directive performs a case-sensitive match. The latter is useful when you want to make sure the caller of your macro has not used a register argument that might conflict with register usage inside the macro. The syntax for IFIDNI is

```
IFIDNI <symbol>, <symbol>
    statements
ENDIF
```

The syntax for IFIDN is identical. In the following **mReadBuf** macro, for example, the second argument cannot be EDX because it will be overwritten when the offset of **buffer** is moved into EDX. The following revised version of the macro displays a warning message if this requirement is not met:

```
;------------------------------------------------------
mReadBuf MACRO bufferPtr, maxChars
;
; Reads from the keyboard into a buffer.
; Receives: offset of the buffer, count of the maximum
;    number of characters that can be entered. The
;    second argument cannot be edx or EDX
;------------------------------------------------------
    IFIDNI <maxChars>,<EDX>
        ECHO Warning: Second argument to mReadBuf cannot be EDX
```

```
            ECHO  ***********************************************
            EXITM
        ENDIF
        push ecx
        push edx
        mov  edx,bufferPtr
        mov  ecx,maxChars
        call ReadString
        pop  edx
        pop  ecx
    ENDM
```

The following statement causes the macro to generate a warning message because EDX is the second argument:

```
    mReadBuf OFFSET buffer,edx
```

10.3.6 Example: Summing a Matrix Row

Section 9.4.2 showed how to calculate the sum of a single row in a byte matrix. A programming exercise in Chapter 9 asked you to generalize the procedure for word and doubleword matrices. Although the solution to that exercise is somewhat lengthly, let us see if we can use a macro to simplify the task. First, here is the original **calc_row_sum** procedure shown in Chapter 9:

```
    calc_row_sum PROC USES ebx ecx esi

    ;
    ; Calculates the sum of a row in a byte matrix.
    ; Receives: EBX = table offset, EAX = row index,
    ;           ECX = row size, in bytes.
    ; Returns:  EAX holds the sum.
    ;-----------------------------------------------------------
            mul     ecx                    ; row index * row size
            add     ebx,eax                ; row offset
            mov     eax,0                  ; accumulator
            mov     esi,0                  ; column index

    L1:     movzx   edx,BYTE PTR[ebx + esi]    ; get a byte
            add     eax,edx                ; add to accumulator
            inc     esi                    ; next byte in row
            loop    L1
            ret
    calc_row_sum ENDP
```

We start by changing PROC to MACRO, remove the RET instruction, and change ENDP to ENDM. There is no macro equivalent to the USES directive, so we insert PUSH and POP instructions:

```
    mCalc_row_sum MACRO
            push    ebx                    ; save changed regs
            push    ecx
            push    esi
            mul     ecx                    ; row index * row size
            add     ebx,eax                ; row offset
            mov     eax,0                  ; accumulator
            mov     esi,0                  ; column index

    L1:     movzx   edx,BYTE PTR[ebx + esi]    ; get a byte
            add     eax,edx                ; add to accumulator
            inc     esi                    ; next byte in row
            loop    L1
            pop     esi                    ; restore changed regs
```

```
                pop    ecx
                pop    ebx
        ENDM
```

Next, we substitute macro parameters for register parameters and initialize the registers inside the macro:

```
        mCalc_row_sum MACRO index, arrayOffset, rowSize
                push   ebx                         ; save changed regs
                push   ecx
                push   esi

        ; set up the required registers
                mov    eax,index
                mov    ebx,arrayOffset
                mov    ecx,rowSize

                mul    ecx                         ; row index * row size
                add    ebx,eax                     ; row offset
                mov    eax,0                       ; accumulator
                mov    esi,0                       ; column index

        L1:     movzx  edx,BYTE PTR[ebx + esi]     ; get a byte
                add    eax,edx                     ; add to accumulator
                inc    esi                         ; next byte in row
                loop   L1
                pop    esi                         ; restore changed regs
                pop    ecx
                pop    ebx
        ENDM
```

We now add a parameter named **eltType** that specifies the array type (BYTE, WORD, or DWORD):

```
        mCalc_row_sum MACRO index, arrayOffset, rowSize, eltType
```

The rowSize parameter, copied into ECX, currently indicates the number of bytes in each row. If we are to use it as a loop counter, it must contain the number of *elements* in each row. Therefore, we divide ECX by 2 for 16-bit arrays and by 4 for doubleword arrays. A fast way to accomplish this is to divide **eltType** by 2 and use it as a shift counter, shifting ECX to the right:

```
        shr ecx,(TYPE eltType / 2)              ; byte=0, word=1, dword=2
```

TYPE eltType becomes the scale factor in the base-index operand of the MOVZX instruction:

```
        movzx edx,eltType PTR[ebx + esi*(TYPE eltType)]
```

MOVZX will not assemble if the right-hand operand is a doubleword, so we must use the IFIDNI operator to create a separate MOV instruction when eltType equals DWORD:

```
        IFIDNI <eltType>,<DWORD>
            mov edx,eltType PTR[ebx + esi*(TYPE eltType)]
        ELSE
            movzx edx,eltType PTR[ebx + esi*(TYPE eltType)]
        ENDIF
```

At last, we have the finished macro, remembering to designate label L1 as LOCAL:

```
        ;-----------------------------------------------------------
        mCalc_row_sum MACRO index, arrayOffset, rowSize, eltType
        ; Calculates the sum of a row in a two-dimensional array.
        ;
        ; Receives: row index, offset of the array, number of bytes
        ; in each table row, and the array type (BYTE, WORD, or DWORD).
```

```
; Returns:   EAX = sum.
;----------------------------------------------------------------
LOCAL L1
      push   ebx                    ; save changed regs
      push   ecx
      push   esi

; set up the required registers
      mov    eax,index
      mov    ebx,arrayOffset
      mov    ecx,rowSize

; calculate the row offset.
      mul    ecx                    ; row index * row size
      add    ebx,eax                ; row offset

; prepare the loop counter.
      shr    ecx,(TYPE eltType / 2) ; byte=0, word=1, dword=2
; initialize the accumulator and column indexes
      mov    eax,0                  ; accumulator
      mov    esi,0                  ; column index

L1:
      IFIDNI <eltType>, <DWORD>
        mov      edx,eltType PTR[ebx + esi*(TYPE eltType)]
      ELSE
        movzx    edx,eltType PTR[ebx + esi*(TYPE eltType)]
      ENDIF
      add    eax,edx                ; add to accumulator
      inc    esi
      loop   L1

      pop    esi                    ; restore changed regs
      pop    ecx
      pop    ebx
ENDM
```

Following are sample calls to the macro, using arrays of byte, word, and doubleword. See the *row-sum.asm* program:

```
.data
tableB   DWORD  10h,  20h,  30h,  40h,  50h
RowSizeB = ($ - tableB)
         DWORD  60h,  70h,  80h,  90h,  0A0h
         DWORD  0B0h, 0C0h, 0D0h, 0E0h, 0F0h

tableW   DWORD  10h,  20h,  30h,  40h,  50h
RowSizeW = ($ - tableW)
         DWORD  60h,  70h,  80h,  90h,  0A0h
         DWORD  0B0h, 0C0h, 0D0h, 0E0h, 0F0h

tableD   DWORD  10h,  20h,  30h,  40h,  50h
RowSizeD = ($ - tableD)
         DWORD  60h,  70h,  80h,  90h,  0A0h
         DWORD  0B0h, 0C0h, 0D0h, 0E0h, 0F0h

index DWORD ?
.code
mCalc_row_sum index, OFFSET tableB, RowSizeB, BYTE
mCalc_row_sum index, OFFSET tableW, RowSizeW, WORD
mCalc_row_sum index, OFFSET tableD, RowSizeD, DWORD
```

10.3.7 Special Operators

There are four assembler operators that make macros more flexible:

&	Substitution operator
<>	Literal-text operator
!	Literal-character operator
%	Expansion operator

Substitution Operator (&)

The *substitution* (&) operator resolves ambiguous references to parameter names within a macro. The **mShowRegister** macro (Section 10.2.5) displays the name and hexadecimal contents of a 32-bit register. The following is a sample call:

```
.code
mShowRegister ECX
```

Following is a sample of the output generated by the call to mShowRegister:

```
ECX=00000101
```

A string variable containing the register name could be defined inside the macro:

```
mShowRegister MACRO regName
.data
tempStr BYTE " regName=",0
```

But the preprocessor would assume **regName** was part of a string literal and would not replace it with the argument value passed to the macro. Instead, if we add the & operator, it forces the preprocessor to insert the macro argument (such as ECX) into the string literal. The following shows how to define **tempStr**:

```
mShowRegister MACRO regName
.data
tempStr BYTE " &regName=",0
```

Expansion Operator (%)

The *expansion* operator (%) expands text macros or converts constant expressions into their text representations. It does this in several different ways. When used with TEXTEQU, the % operator evaluates a constant expression and converts the result to an integer. In the following example, the % operator evaluates the expression (5 + count) and returns the integer 15 (as text):

```
count = 10
sumVal TEXTEQU %(5 + count)          ; = "15"
```

If a macro requires a constant integer argument, the % operator gives you the flexibility of passing an integer expression. The expression is evaluated to its integer value, which is then passed to the macro. For example, when invoking **mGotoxyConst**, the expressions here evaluate to 50 and 7:

```
mGotoxyConst %(5 * 10), %(3 + 4)
```

The preprocessor produces the following statements:

```
1    push  edx
1    mov   dh,7
1    mov   dl,50
1    call  Gotoxy
1    pop   edx
```

% at Beginning of Line   When the expansion operator (%) is the first character on a source code line, it instructs the preprocessor to expand all text macros and macro functions found on the same line. Suppose, for example, we wanted to display the size of an array on the screen during assembly. The following attempts would not produce the intended result:

```
.data
array DWORD 1,2,3,4,5,6,7,8
.code
ECHO The array contains (SIZEOF array) bytes
ECHO The array contains %(SIZEOF array) bytes
```

The screen output would be useless:

```
The array contains (SIZEOF array) bytes
The array contains %(SIZEOF array) bytes
```

Instead, if we use TEXTEQU to create a text macro containing (SIZEOF array), the macro can be expanded on the next line:

```
TempStr TEXTEQU %(SIZEOF array)
%      ECHO The array contains TempStr bytes
```

The following output is produced:

```
The array contains 32 bytes
```

Displaying the Line Number   The following **Mul32** macro multiplies its first two arguments together and returns the product in the third argument. Its parameters can be registers, memory operands, and immediate operands (except for the product):

```
Mul32 MACRO op1, op2, product
      IFIDNI <op2>,<EAX>
        LINENUM TEXTEQU %(@LINE)
        ECHO ---------------------------------------------------
%       ECHO *  Error on line LINENUM: EAX cannot be the second
        ECHO *  argument when invoking the MUL32 macro.
        ECHO ---------------------------------------------------
      EXITM
      ENDIF
      push eax
      mov  eax,op1
      mul  op2
      mov  product,eax
      pop  eax
ENDM
```

Mul32 checks one important requirement: EAX cannot be the second argument. What is interesting about the macro is that it displays the line number from where the macro was called, to make it easier to track down and fix the problem. The Text macro LINENUM is defined first. It references @LINE, a predefined assembler operator that returns the current source code line number:

```
LINENUM TEXTEQU %(@LINE)
```

Next, the expansion operator (%) in the first column of the line containing the ECHO statement causes LINENUM to be expanded:

```
%       ECHO * Error on line LINENUM: EAX cannot be the second
```

Suppose the following macro call occurs in a program on line 40:

```
MUL32 val1,eax,val3
```

Then the following message is displayed during assembly:

```
-------------------------------------------------
*   Error on line 40: EAX cannot be the second
*   argument when invoking the MUL32 macro.
-------------------------------------------------
```

You can view a test of the **Mul32** macro in the program named *Macro3.asm*.

Literal-Text Operator (<>)

The *literal-text* operator (<>) groups one or more characters and symbols into a single text literal. It prevents the preprocessor from interpreting members of the list as separate arguments. This operator is particularly useful when a string contains special characters, such as commas, percent signs (%), ampersands (&), and semicolons (;), that would otherwise be interpreted as delimiters or other operators. For example, the **mWrite** macro presented earlier in this chapter receives a string literal as its only argument. If we were to pass it the following string, the preprocessor would interpret it as three separate macro arguments:

```
mWrite "Line three", 0dh, 0ah
```

Text after the first comma would be discarded because the macro expects only one argument. On the other hand, if we surrounded the string with the literal-text operator, the preprocessor considers all text between the brackets to be a single macro argument:

```
mWrite <"Line three", 0dh, 0ah>
```

Literal-Character Operator (!)

The *literal-character* operator (!) was invented for much the same purpose as the literal-text operator: It forces the preprocessor to treat a predefined operator as an ordinary character. In the following TEXTEQU definition, the ! operator prevents the > symbol from being a text delimiter:

```
BadYValue TEXTEQU <Warning: Y-coordinate is !> 24>
```

Warning Message Example   The following example helps to show how the %, &, and ! operators work together. Let's assume we have defined the **BadYValue** symbol. We can create a macro named **ShowWarning** that receives a text argument, encloses it in quotes, and passes the literal to the **mWrite** macro. Note the use of the substitution (&) operator:

```
ShowWarning MACRO message
    mWrite "&message"
ENDM
```

Next, we invoke **ShowWarning**, passing it the expression %BadYValue. The % operator evaluates (dereferences) **BadYValue** and produces its equivalent string:

```
.code
ShowWarning %BadYValue
```

As you might expect, the program runs and displays the warning message:

```
Warning: Y-coordinate is > 24
```

10.3.8 Macro Functions

A macro function is similar to a macro procedure in that it assigns a name to a list of assembly language statements. It is different in that it always returns a constant (integer or string) via the EXITM directive. In the following example, the **IsDefined** macro returns true (-1) if a given symbol has been defined; otherwise, it returns false (0):

```
IsDefined MACRO symbol
      IFDEF symbol
         EXITM <-1>                    ;; True
      ELSE
         EXITM <0>                     ;; False
      ENDIF
ENDM
```

The EXITM (exit macro) directive halts all further expansion of the macro.

Calling a Macro Function   When you call a macro function, its argument list must be enclosed in parentheses. For example, we can call the **IsDefined** macro, passing it **RealMode**, the name of a symbol which may or may not have been defined:

```
IF IsDefined( RealMode )
      mov     ax,@data
      mov     ds,ax
ENDIF
```

If the assembler has already encountered a definition of **RealMode** before this point in the assembly process, it assembles the two instructions:

```
mov ax,@data
mov ds,ax
```

The same IF directive can be placed inside a macro named **Startup**:

```
Startup MACRO
      IF IsDefined( RealMode )
        mov   ax,@data
        mov   ds,ax
      ENDIF
ENDM
```

A macro such as **IsDefined** can be useful when you design programs for multiple memory models. For example, we can use it to determine which include file to use:

```
IF IsDefined( RealMode )
      INCLUDE Irvine16.inc
ELSE
      INCLUDE Irvine32.inc
ENDIF
```

Defining the RealMode Symbol   All that remains is to find a way to define the **RealMode** symbol. One way is to put the following line at the beginning of a program:

```
RealMode = 1
```

Alternatively, the assembler's command line has an option for defining symbols, using the –D switch. The following ML command defines the RealMode symbol and assigns it a value of 1:

```
ML -c -DRealMode=1 myProg.asm
```

The corresponding ML command for protected mode programs does not define the RealMode symbol:

```
ML -c myProg.asm
```

HelloNew Program   The following program (*HelloNew.asm*) uses the macros we have just described, displaying a message on the screen:

```
TITLE Macro Functions                    (HelloNew.asm)

INCLUDE Macros.inc
IF IsDefined( RealMode )
     INCLUDE Irvine16.inc
ELSE
     INCLUDE Irvine32.inc
ENDIF

.code
main PROC
     Startup
     mWrite <"This program can be assembled to run ",0dh,0ah>
     mWrite <"in both Real mode and Protected mode.",0dh,0ah>
     exit
main ENDP
END main
```

This program can be assembled in real-address mode, using *makeHello16.bat*, or in protected mode, using *make32.bat*.

10.3.9   Section Review

1. What is the purpose of the IFB directive?
2. What is the purpose of the IFIDN directive?
3. Which directive stops all further expansion of a macro?
4. How is IFIDNI different from IFIDN?
5. What is the purpose of the IFDEF directive?
6. Which directive marks the end of a conditional block of statements?
7. Show an example of a macro parameter having a default argument initializer.
8. List all the relational operators that can be used in constant boolean expressions.
9. Write a short example that uses the IF, ELSE, and ENDIF directives.
10. Write a statement using the IF directive that checks the value of the constant macro parameter Z; if Z is less than zero, display a message during assembly indicating that Z is invalid.
11. What is the purpose of the & operator in a macro definition?
12. What is the purpose of the ! operator in a macro definition?
13. What is the purpose of the % operator in a macro definition?
14. Write a short macro that demonstrates the use of the & operator when the macro parameter is embedded in a literal string.
15. Assume the following **mLocate** macro definition:

```
mLocate MACRO xval,yval
     IF xval LT 0                        ;; xval < 0?
       EXITM                             ;; if so, exit
     ENDIF
     IF yval LT 0                        ;; yval < 0?
       EXITM                             ;; if so, exit
     ENDIF
     mov     bx,0                        ;; video page 0
     mov     ah,2                        ;; locate cursor
     mov     dh,yval
```

```
        mov    dl,xval
        int    10h                      ;; call the BIOS
ENDM
```

Show the source code generated by the preprocessor when the macro is expanded by each of the following statements:

```
.data
row BYTE 15
col BYTE 60
.code
mLocate  -2,20
mLocate  10,20
mLocate  col,row
```

10.4   Defining Repeat Blocks

MASM has a number of looping directives for generating repeated blocks of statements: WHILE, REPEAT, FOR, and FORC. Unlike the LOOP instruction, these directives work only at assembly time, using constant values as loop conditions and counters:

  • The WHILE directive repeats a statement block based on a boolean expression.
  • The REPEAT directive repeats a statement block based on the value of a counter.
  • The FOR directive repeats a statement block by iterating over a list of symbols.
  • The FORC directive repeats a statement block by iterating over a string of characters.

Each is demonstrated in an example program named *Repeat.asm*.

10.4.1   WHILE Directive

The WHILE directive repeats a statement block as long as a particular constant expression is true. The syntax is

```
WHILE constExpression
     statements
ENDM
```

The following code shows how to generate Fibonacci numbers between 1 and F0000000h as a series of assembly-time constants:

```
.data
val1  = 1
val2  = 1
DWORD val1                          ; first two values
DWORD val2
val3 = val1 + val2
WHILE val3 LT 0F0000000h
     DWORD val3
     val1 = val2
     val2 = val3
     val3 = val1 + val2
ENDM
```

The values generated by this code can be viewed in a listing (.LST) file.

10.4.2   REPEAT Directive

The REPEAT directive repeats a statement block a fixed number of times at assembly time. The syntax is

```
REPEAT constExpression
  statements
ENDM
```

ConstExpression, an unsigned constant integer expression, determines the number of repetitions.

REPEAT can be used in a similar way as DUP to create an array. In the following example, the WeatherReadings struct contains a location string, followed by an array of rainfall and humidity readings:

```
WEEKS_PER_YEAR = 52

WeatherReadings STRUCT
     location BYTE 50 DUP(0)
     REPEAT WEEKS_PER_YEAR
       LOCAL rainfall, humidity
       rainfall DWORD ?
       humidity DWORD ?
     ENDM
WeatherReadings ENDS
```

The LOCAL directive was used to avoid errors caused by redefining rainfall and humidity when the loop was repeated at assembly time.

10.4.3   FOR Directive

The FOR directive repeats a statement block by iterating over a comma-delimited list of symbols. Each symbol in the list causes one iteration of the loop. The syntax is

```
FOR parameter,<arg1,arg2,arg3,...>
     statements
ENDM
```

On the first loop iteration, *parameter* takes on the value of *arg1*; on the second iteration, *parameter* takes on the value of *arg2*; and so on through the last argument in the list.

Student Enrollment Example   Let's create a student enrollment scenario in which we have a COURSE structure containing a course number and number of credits. A SEMESTER structure contains an array of six courses and a counter named **NumCourses**:

```
COURSE STRUCT
     Number  BYTE 9 DUP(?)
     Credits BYTE ?
COURSE ENDS

; A semester contains an array of courses.
SEMESTER STRUCT
     Courses COURSE 6 DUP(<>)
     NumCourses WORD ?
SEMESTER ENDS
```

We can use a FOR loop to define four SEMESTER objects, each having a different name selected from the list symbols between angle brackets:

```
.data
FOR semName,<Fall1999,Spring2000,Summer2000,Fall2000>
     semName SEMESTER <>
ENDM
```

If we inspect the listing file, we find the following variables:

```
.data
Fall1999 SEMESTER <>
Spring2000 SEMESTER <>
Summer2000 SEMESTER <>
Fall2000 SEMESTER <>
```

10.4.4 FORC Directive

The FORC directive repeats a statement block by iterating over a string of characters. Each character in the string causes one iteration of the loop. The syntax is

```
FORC parameter, <string>
     statements
ENDM
```

On the first loop iteration, *parameter* is equal to the first character in the string; on the second iteration, *parameter* is equal to the second character in the string; and so on, to the end of the string. The following example creates a character lookup table consisting of several nonalphabetic characters. Note that < and > must be preceded by the literal-character (!) operator to prevent them from violating the syntax of the FORC directive:

```
Delimiters LABEL BYTE
FORC code,<@#$%^&*!<!>>
     BYTE "&code"
ENDM
```

The following data table is generated, which you can view in the listing file:

```
00000000   401 BYTE "@"
00000001   231 BYTE "#"
00000002   241 BYTE "$"
00000003   251 BYTE "%"
00000004   5E1 BYTE "^"
00000005   261 BYTE "&"
00000006   2A1 BYTE "*"
00000007   3C1 BYTE "<"
00000008   3E1 BYTE ">"
```

10.4.5 Example: Linked List

It is fairly simple to combine a structure declaration with the REPEAT directive to instruct the assembler to create a linked list data structure. Each node in a linked list contains a data area and a link area:

In the data area, one or more variables can hold data unique to each node. In the link area, a pointer contains the address of the next node in the list. The link part of the final node usually contains a null pointer. Let's create a program that creates and displays a simple linked list. First, the program defines a list node having a single integer (data) and a pointer to the next node:

```
ListNode STRUCT
     NodeData DWORD ?                 ; the node's data
     NextPtr  DWORD ?                 ; pointer to next node
ListNode ENDS
```

Next, the REPEAT directive creates multiple instances of **ListNode** objects. For testing purposes, the **NodeData** field contains an integer constant ranging from 1 to 15. Inside the loop, we increment the counter and insert values into the ListNode fields:

```
TotalNodeCount = 15
NULL = 0
Counter = 0

.data
LinkedList LABEL PTR ListNode
```

```
REPEAT TotalNodeCount
    Counter = Counter + 1
    ListNode <Counter, ($ + Counter * SIZEOF ListNode)>
ENDM
```

The expression ($ + Counter * SIZEOF ListNode) tells the assembler to multiply the counter by the **ListNode** size and add their product to the current location counter. The value is inserted into the **NextPtr** field in the structure. (It's interesting to note that the location counter's value ($) remains fixed at the first node of the list.) The list is given a *tail node* marking its end, in which the **NextPtr** field contains null (0):

```
ListNode <0,0>
```

When the program traverses the list, it uses the following statements to retrieve the **NextPtr** field and compare it to NULL so the end of the list can be detected:

```
mov   eax,(ListNode PTR [esi]).NextPtr
cmp   eax,NULL
```

Program Listing   The following is a complete program listing. In main, a loop traverses the list and displays all the node values. Rather than using a fixed counter for the loop, the program checks for the null pointer in the tail node and stops looping when it is found:

```
TITLE Creating a Linked List              (List.asm)

INCLUDE Irvine32.inc

ListNode STRUCT
  NodeData DWORD ?
  NextPtr  DWORD ?
ListNode ENDS

TotalNodeCount = 15
NULL = 0
Counter = 0

.data
LinkedList LABEL PTR ListNode
REPEAT TotalNodeCount
    Counter = Counter + 1
    ListNode <Counter, ($ + Counter * SIZEOF ListNode)>
ENDM
ListNode <0,0>                       ; tail node

.code
main PROC
    mov    esi,OFFSET LinkedList

; Display the integers in the NodeData fields.
NextNode:
    ; Check for the tail node.
    mov    eax,(ListNode PTR [esi]).NextPtr
    cmp    eax,NULL
    je     quit

    ; Display the node data.
    mov    eax,(ListNode PTR [esi]).NodeData
    call   WriteDec
    call   Crlf

    ; Get pointer to next node.
```

```
        mov    esi,(ListNode PTR [esi]).NextPtr
        jmp    NextNode

quit:
        exit
main ENDP
END main
```

10.4.6 Section Review

1. Briefly describe the WHILE directive.
2. Briefly describe the REPEAT directive.
3. Briefly describe the FOR directive.
4. Briefly describe the FORC directive.
5. Which looping directive would be the best tool to generate a character lookup table?
6. Write the statements generated by the following macro:

   ```
   FOR val,<100,20,30>
       BYTE 0,0,0,val
   ENDM
   ```

7. Assume the following **mRepeat** macro has been defined:

   ```
   mRepeat MACRO char,count
           LOCAL L1
           mov    cx,count
   L1:     mov    ah,2
           mov    dl,char
           int    21h
           loop   L1
   ENDM
   ```

   Write the code generated by the preprocessor when the **mRepeat** macro is expanded by each of the following statements (a, b, and c):

   ```
   mRepeat 'X',50         ; a
   mRepeat AL,20          ; b
   mRepeat byteVal,countVal   ; c
   ```

8. *Challenge:* In the Linked List example program (Section 10.4.5), what would be the result if the REPEAT loop were coded as follows?

   ```
   REPEAT TotalNodeCount
       Counter = Counter + 1
       ListNode <Counter, ($ + SIZEOF ListNode)>
   ENDM
   ```

10.5 Chapter Summary

A *structure* is a template or pattern used when creating user-defined types. Many structures are already defined in the MS-Windows API library and are used for the transfer of data between application programs and the library. Structures can contain a diverse set of field types. Each field declaration may use a field-initializer, which assigns a default value to the field.

Structures themselves take up no memory, but structure variables do. The SIZEOF operator returns the number of bytes used by the variable.

The dot operator (.) references a structure field by using either a structure variable or an indirect operand such as [esi]. When an indirect operand references a structure field, you must use the PTR operator to identify the structure type, as in (COORD PTR [esi]).X.

Structures can contain fields that are also structures. An example was shown in the Drunkard's Walk program (Section 10.1.6), where the **DrunkardWalk** structure contained an array of COORD structures.

Macros are usually defined at the beginning of a program, before the data and code segments. Then, when a macro is called, the preprocessor inserts a copy of the macro's code into the program at the calling location.

Macros can be effectively used as *wrappers* around procedure calls to simplify parameter passing and saving registers on the stack. Macros such as **mGotoxy**, **mDumpMem**, and **mWriteString** are examples of wrappers because they call procedures from the book's link library.

A *macro procedure* (or *macro*) is a named block of assembly language statements. A *macro function* is similar, except that it also returns a constant value.

Conditional-assembly directives such as IF, IFNB, and IFIDNI can be used to detect arguments that are out of range, missing, or of the wrong type. The ECHO directive displays error messsages during assembly, making it possible to alert the programmer to errors in arguments passed to macros.

The substitution operator (&) resolves ambiguous references to parameter names. The expansion operator (%) expands text macros and converts constant expressions to text. The literal-text operator (< >) groups diverse characters and text into a single literal. The literal-character operator (!) forces the preprocessor to treat predefined operators as ordinary characters.

Repeat block directives can reduce the amount of repetitive code in programs. The directives are as follows:

- WHILE repeats a statement block based on a boolean expression.
- REPEAT repeats a statement block based on the value of a counter.
- FOR repeats a statement block by iterating over a list of symbols.
- FORC repeats a statement block by iterating over a string of characters.

10.6 Programming Exercises

1. mReadkey Macro
Create a macro that waits for a keystroke and returns the key that was pressed. The macro should include parameters for the ASCII code and keyboard scan code. *Hint:* Call ReadKey from the book's link library. Write a program that tests your macro. For example, the following code waits for a key; when it returns, the two arguments contain the ASCII code and scan code:

```
.data
ascii BYTE ?
scan BYTE ?
.code
mReadkey ascii, scan
```

2. mWritestringAttr Macro
(Requires reading Section 15.3.3 or Section 11.1.11.) Create a macro that writes a null-terminated string to the console with a given text color. The macro parameters should include the string name and the color. *Hint:* Call SetTextColor from the book's link library. Write a program that tests your macro with several strings in different colors. Sample call:

```
.data
myString db "Here is my string",0
.code
mWritestring myString, white
```

3. mMove32 Macro

Write a macro named **mMove32** that receives two 32-bit memory operands. The macro should move the source operand to the destination operand. Write a program that tests your macro.

4. mMult32 Macro

Create a macro named **mMult32** that multiplies two 32-bit memory operands and produces a 32-bit product. Write a program that tests your macro.

5. mReadInt Macro

Create a macro named **mReadInt** that reads a 16- or 32-bit signed integer from standard input and returns the value in an argument. Use conditional operators to allow the macro to adapt to the size of the desired result. Write a program that calls the macro, passing it operands of various sizes.

6. mWriteInt Macro

Create a macro named **mWriteInt** that writes a signed integer to standard output by calling the **WriteInt** library procedure. The argument passed to the macro can be a byte, word, or doubleword. Use conditional operators in the macro so it adapts to the size of the argument. Write a program that tests the macro, passing it arguments of different sizes.

7. mScroll Macro

(Requires reading Section 15.3.3.) Create a macro named **mScroll** that displays a color rectangle in the console window. Include the following parameters in the macro definition. If **attrib** is blank, assume a color of light gray characters on a black background:

ULrow	Upper-left window row
ULcol	Upper-left window column
LRrow	Lower-right window row
LRcol	Lower-right window column
attrib	Color of scrolled lines

Write a program that tests your macro.

8. Drunkard's Walk

When testing the Drunkard Walk program, you may have noticed that the professor doesn't seem to wander very far from the starting point. This is no doubt caused by an equal probability of the professor moving in any direction. Modify the program so there is a 50% probability the professor will continue to walk in the same direction as he or she did when taking the previous step. There should be a 10% probability that he or she will reverse direction and a 20% probability that he or she will turn either right or left. Assign a default starting direction before the loop begins.

9. Shifting Multiple Doublewords

Use the solution program for Exercise 4 in Section 7.8 as a starting point for this exercise. Create a macro named **mShiftDoubleWords** that shifts the contents in **arrayName** either left or right (based on direction) for a specified number of bits:

```
mShiftDoublewords MACRO,
      arrayName,                    ;; name of array
      direction,                    ;; R or L
      numberOfBits                  ;; shift count
```

10. Three-Operand Instructions

Some computer instruction sets permit arithmetic instructions with three operands. Such operations sometimes appear in simple virtual assemblers used to introduce students to the concept of assembly language or using intermediate language in compilers. In the following macros, assume EAX is reserved for macro operations and is not preserved. Other registers modified by the macro must be preserved. All parameters are memory doublewords. Write macros that simulate the following operations:

```
a. add3    destination, source1, source2
b. sub3    destination, source1, source2    (destination = source1 - source2)
c. mul3    destination, source1, source2
d. div3    destination, source1, source2    (destination = source1 / source2)
```

For example, the following macro calls implement the expression **x = (w + y) * z**:

```
.data
temp DWORD ?
.code
add3 temp, w, y                          ; temp = w + y
mul3 x, temp, z                          ; x = temp * z
```

Write a program that tests your macros by implementing four arthmetic expressions, each involving multiple operations.

End Note

1. Probably because RECORD is the term used in the old COBOL programming language, familar to the designers of Windows NT.

11

MS-Windows Programming

11.1 Win32 Console Programming

Some of the following questions should have been in the back of your mind while reading this book:

- How do 32-bit programs handle text input-output?
- How are colors handled in 32-bit console mode?
- How does the Irvine32 link library work?
- How are times and dates handled in MS-Windows?
- How can I use MS-Windows functions to read and write data files?
- Is it possible to write a graphical Windows application in assembly language?
- How do protected mode programs translate segments and offsets to physical addresses?
- I've heard that virtual memory is good. But why is that so?

This chapter will answer these questions and more, as we show you the basics of 32-bit programming under Microsoft Windows. Most of the information here is oriented toward 32-bit console mode text applications because they are reasonably easy to program, given a knowledge of structures and procedure parameters. The Irvine32 link library is completely built on Win32 console functions, so you can compare its source code to the information in this chapter. Find its source code in the \Examples\Lib32 directory of the sample programs accompanying this book.

Why not write graphical applications for MS-Windows? If written in assembly language or C, graphical programs are long and detailed. For years, C and C++ programmers have labored over technical details such as graphical device handles, message posting, font metrics, device bitmaps, and mapping modes, with the help of excellent authors. There is a devoted group of assembly language programmers with excellent Web sites who do graphical Windows programming. See the link to *Assembly Language Sources* from this book's home page (*www.asmirvine.com*).

To avoid disappointing graphical programmers, Section 11.2 introduces 32-bit graphical programming in a generic sort of way. It's only a start, but you might be inspired to go further into the topic. A list of recommended books for futher study is given in the summary at the end of this chapter.

On the surface, 32-bit console mode programs look and behave like 16-bit MS-DOS programs running in text mode. There are differences, however: The former runs in 32-bit protected mode, whereas MS-DOS programs run in real-address mode. They use different function libraries. Win32 programs call functions from the same library used by graphical Windows applications. MS-DOS programs use BIOS and MS-DOS interrupts that have existed since the introduction of the IBM-PC.

An *Application Programming Interface* (API) is a collection of types, constants, and functions that provide a way to directly manipulate objects through programming. Therefore, the Win32 API lets you tap into the functions in the 32-bit version of MS-Windows.

Win32 Platform SDK   Closely related to the Win32 API is the Microsoft *Platform SDK (Software Development Kit)*, a collection of tools, libraries, sample code, and documentation for creating MS-Windows applications. Complete documentation is available online at Microsoft's Web site. Search for "Platform SDK" at www.msdn.microsoft.com. The Platform SDK is a free download.

Tip: The Irvine32 library is compatible with Win32 API functions, so you can call both from the same program.

11.1.1   Background Information

When a Windows application starts, it creates either a console window or a graphical window. We have been using the following option with the LINK command in the *make32.bat* batch file, which tells the linker to create a console-based application:

```
/SUBSYSTEM:CONSOLE
```

A console program looks and behaves like an MS-DOS window, with some enhancements, which we will see later. The console has a single input buffer and one or more screen buffers:

- The *input buffer* contains a queue of *input records*, each containing data about an input event. Examples of input events are keyboard input, mouse clicks, and the user's resizing of the console window.
- A *screen buffer* is a two-dimensional array of character and color data that affects the appearance of text in the console window.

Win32 API Reference Information

Functions   Throughout this section, we can only introduce you to a number of Win32 API functions and provide a few simple examples. There are many details that cannot be covered here because of space limitations. To find out more, click on Help inside Microsoft Visual C++ Express, or visit the Microsoft MSDN Web site (currently located at www.msdn.microsoft.com). When searching for functions or identifiers, set the *Filtered by* parameter to **Platform SDK**. Also, in the sample programs supplied with this book, the kernel32.txt and user32.txt files provide comprehensive lists of function names in the kernel32.lib and user32.lib libraries.

Constants Often when reading documentation for Win32 API functions, you will come across constant names, such as TIME_ZONE_ID_UNKNOWN. In a few cases, the constant will already be defined in SmallWin.inc. But if you can't find it there, look on our book's Web site. A header file named *WinNT.h*, for example, defines TIME_ZONE_ID_UNKNOWN along with related constants:

```
#define TIME_ZONE_ID_UNKNOWN  0
#define TIME_ZONE_ID_STANDARD 1
#define TIME_ZONE_ID_DAYLIGHT 2
```

Using this information, you would add the following to *SmallWin.h* or your own include file:

```
TIME_ZONE_ID_UNKNOWN  = 0
TIME_ZONE_ID_STANDARD = 1
TIME_ZONE_ID_DAYLIGHT = 2
```

Character Sets and Windows API Functions

Two types of character sets are used when calling functions in the Win32 API: the 8-bit ASCII/ANSI character set and the 16-bit Unicode set (available in Windows NT, 2000, and XP). Win32 functions dealing with text are usually supplied in two versions, one ending in the letter A (for 8-bit ANSI characters) and the other ending in W (for *wide* character sets, including Unicode). One of these is WriteConsole:

- WriteConsoleA
- WriteConsoleW

Function names ending in W are not supported by Windows 95 or 98. In Windows NT, 2000, and XP, on the other hand, Unicode is the native character set. If you call a function such as **WriteConsoleA**, for example, the operating system converts the characters from ANSI to Unicode and calls **WriteConsoleW**.

In the Microsoft MSDN Library documentation for functions such as WriteConsole, the trailing A or W is omitted from the name. In the include file for the programs in this book, we redefine function names such as **WriteConsoleA**:

```
WriteConsole EQU <WriteConsoleA>
```

This definition makes it possible to call WriteConsole using its generic name.

High-Level and Low-Level Access

There are two levels of access to the console, permitting tradeoffs between simplicity and complete control:

- High-level console functions read a stream of characters from the console's input buffer. They write character data to the console's screen buffer. Both input and output can be redirected to read from or write to text files.
- Low-level console functions retrieve detailed information about keyboard and mouse events and user interactions with the console window (dragging, resizing, etc.). These functions also permit detailed control of the window size and position, as well as text colors.

Windows Data Types

Win32 functions are documented using function declarations for C/C++ programmers. In these declarations, the types of all function parameters are based either on standard C types or on one of the MS-Windows predefined types (a partial list is in Table 11-1). It is important to distinguish data values from pointers to values. A type name that begins with the letters LP is a *long pointer* to some other object.

SmallWin.inc Include File

SmallWin.inc, created by the author, is an include file containing constant definitions, text equates, and function prototypes for Win32 API programming. It is automatically included in programs by Irvine32.inc, which we have been using throughout the book. The file is located in the \Examples\Lib32 folder where you installed the sample programs from this book. Most of the constants can be found in Windows.h, a header file used for programming in C and C++. Despite its name, SmallWin.inc is rather large, so we'll just show highlights:

```
DO_NOT_SHARE = 0
NULL = 0
TRUE = 1
FALSE = 0

; Win32 Console handles
STD_INPUT_HANDLE EQU -10
STD_OUTPUT_HANDLE EQU -11
STD_ERROR_HANDLE EQU -12
```

Table 11-1   Translating MS-Windows Types to MASM.

MS-Windows Type	MASM Type	Description
BOOL, BOOLEAN	DWORD	A boolean value (TRUE or FALSE)
BYTE	BYTE	An 8-bit unsigned integer
CHAR	BYTE	An 8-bit Windows ANSI character
COLORREF	DWORD	A 32-bit value used as a color value
DWORD	DWORD	A 32-bit unsigned integer
HANDLE	DWORD	Handle to an object
HFILE	DWORD	Handle to a file opened by OpenFile
INT	SDWORD	A 32-bit signed integer
LONG	SDWORD	A 32-bit signed integer
LPARAM	DWORD	Message parameter, used by window procedures and callback functions
LPCSTR	PTR BYTE	A 32-bit pointer to a constant null-terminated string of 8-bit Windows (ANSI) characters
LPCVOID	DWORD	Pointer to a constant of any type
LPSTR	PTR BYTE	A 32-bit pointer to a null-terminated string of 8-bit Windows (ANSI) characters
LPCTSTR	PTR WORD	A 32-bit pointer to a constant character string that is portable for Unicode and double-byte character sets
LPTSTR	PTR WORD	A 32-bit pointer to a character string that is portable for Unicode and double-byte character sets
LPVOID	DWORD	A 32-bit pointer to an unspecified type
LRESULT	DWORD	A 32-bit value returned from a window procedure or callback function
SIZE_T	DWORD	The maximum number of bytes to which a pointer can point.
UINT	DWORD	A 32-bit unsigned integer
WNDPROC	DWORD	A 32-bit pointer to a window procedure
WORD	WORD	A 16-bit unsigned integer
WPARAM	DWORD	A 32-bit value passed as a parameter to a window procedure or callback function

The HANDLE type, an alias for DWORD, helps our function prototypes to be more consistent with the Microsoft Win32 documentation:

```
HANDLE TEXTEQU <DWORD>
```

SmallWin.inc also includes structure definitions used in Win32 calls. Two are shown here:

```
COORD STRUCT
     X WORD ?
     Y WORD ?
COORD ENDS

SYSTEMTIME STRUCT
     wYear WORD ?
     wMonth WORD ?
     wDayOfWeek WORD ?
     wDay WORD ?
     wHour WORD ?
     wMinute WORD ?
     wSecond WORD ?
     wMilliseconds WORD ?
SYSTEMTIME ENDS
```

Finally, SmallWin.inc contains function prototypes for all Win32 functions documented in this chapter.

Console Handles

Nearly all Win32 console functions require you to pass a handle as the first argument. A *handle* is a 32-bit unsigned integer that uniquely identifies an object such as a bitmap, drawing pen, or any input/output device:

```
STD_INPUT_HANDLE        standard input
STD_OUTPUT_HANDLE       standard output
STD_ERROR_HANDLE        standard error output
```

The latter two handles are used when writing to the console's active screen buffer.

The **GetStdHandle** function returns a handle to a console stream: input, output, or error output. You need a handle in order to do any input/output in a console-based program. Here is the function prototype:

```
GetStdHandle PROTO,
     nStdHandle:HANDLE                 ; handle type
```

nStdHandle can be STD_INPUT_HANDLE, STD_OUTPUT_HANDLE, or STD_ERROR_HANDLE. The function returns the handle in EAX, which should be copied into a variable for safekeeping. Here is a sample call:

```
.data
inputHandle HANDLE ?
.code
     INVOKE GetStdHandle, STD_INPUT_HANDLE
     mov inputHandle,eax
```

11.1.2 Win32 Console Functions

Table 11-2 contains a quick reference to the complete set of Win32 console functions.[1] You can find a complete description of each function in the MSDN library at www.msdn.microsoft.com.

> **Tip:** Win32 API functions do not preserve EAX, EBX, ECX, and EDX, so you should push and pop those registers yourself.

Table 11-2   Win32 Console Functions.

Function	Description
AllocConsole	Allocates a new console for the calling process.
CreateConsoleScreenBuffer	Creates a console screen buffer.
ExitProcess	Ends a process and all its threads.
FillConsoleOutputAttribute	Sets the text and background color attributes for a specified number of character cells.
FillConsoleOutputCharacter	Writes a character to the screen buffer a specified number of times.
FlushConsoleInputBuffer	Flushes the console input buffer.
FreeConsole	Detaches the calling process from its console.
GenerateConsoleCtrlEvent	Sends a specified signal to a console process group that shares the console associated with the calling process.
GetConsoleCP	Retrieves the input code page used by the console associated with the calling process.
GetConsoleCursorInfo	Retrieves information about the size and visibility of the cursor for the specified console screen buffer.
GetConsoleMode	Retrieves the current input mode of a console's input buffer or the current output mode of a console screen buffer.
GetConsoleOutputCP	Retrieves the output code page used by the console associated with the calling process.
GetConsoleScreenBufferInfo	Retrieves information about the specified console screen buffer.
GetConsoleTitle	Retrieves the title bar string for the current console window.
GetConsoleWindow	Retrieves the window handle used by the console associated with the calling process.
GetLargestConsoleWindowSize	Retrieves the size of the largest possible console window.
GetNumberOfConsoleInputEvents	Retrieves the number of unread input records in the console's input buffer.
GetNumberOfConsoleMouseButtons	Retrieves the number of buttons on the mouse used by the current console.
GetStdHandle	Retrieves a handle for the standard input, standard output, or standard error device.
HandlerRoutine	An application-defined function used with the SetConsoleCtrlHandler function.
PeekConsoleInput	Reads data from the specified console input buffer without removing it from the buffer.
ReadConsole	Reads character input from the console input buffer and removes it from the buffer.
ReadConsoleInput	Reads data from a console input buffer and removes it from the buffer.
ReadConsoleOutput	Reads character and color attribute data from a rectangular block of character cells in a console screen buffer.
ReadConsoleOutputAttribute	Copies a specified number of foreground and background color attributes from consecutive cells of a console screen buffer.
ReadConsoleOutputCharacter	Copies a number of characters from consecutive cells of a console screen buffer.
ScrollConsoleScreenBuffer	Moves a block of data in a screen buffer.
SetConsoleActiveScreenBuffer	Sets the specified screen buffer to be the currently displayed console screen buffer.
SetConsoleCP	Sets the input code page used by the console associated with the calling process.

Table 11-2   *(Continued)*

Function	Description
SetConsoleCtrlHandler	Adds or removes an application-defined HandlerRoutine from the list of handler functions for the calling process.
SetConsoleCursorInfo	Sets the size and visibility of the cursor for the specified console screen buffer.
SetConsoleCursorPosition	Sets the cursor position in the specified console screen buffer.
SetConsoleMode	Sets the input mode of a console's input buffer or the output mode of a console screen buffer.
SetConsoleOutputCP	Sets the output code page used by the console associated with the calling process.
SetConsoleScreenBufferSize	Changes the size of the specified console screen buffer.
SetConsoleTextAttribute	Sets the foreground (text) and background color attributes of characters written to the screen buffer.
SetConsoleTitle	Sets the title bar string for the current console window.
SetConsoleWindowInfo	Sets the current size and position of a console screen buffer's window.
SetStdHandle	Sets the handle for the standard input, standard output, or standard error device.
WriteConsole	Writes a character string to a console screen buffer beginning at the current cursor location.
WriteConsoleInput	Writes data directly to the console input buffer.
WriteConsoleOutput	Writes character and color attribute data to a specified rectangular block of character cells in a console screen buffer.
WriteConsoleOutputAttribute	Copies a number of foreground and background color attributes to consecutive cells of a console screen buffer.
WriteConsoleOutputCharacter	Copies a number of characters to consecutive cells of a console screen buffer.

11.1.3 Displaying a Message Box

One of the easiest ways to generate output in a Win32 application is to call the **MessageBoxA** function:

```
MessageBoxA PROTO,
    hWnd:DWORD,              ; handle to window (can be null)
    lpText:PTR BYTE,         ; string, inside of box
    lpCaption:PTR BYTE,      ; string, dialog box title
    uType:DWORD              ; contents and behavior
```

In console-based applications, you can set *hWnd* to NULL, indicating that the message box has no owner. The *lpText* parameter is a pointer to the null-terminated string that you want to put in the message box. The *lpCaption* parameter points to a null-terminated string for the dialog box title. The *uType* parameter specifies the dialog box contents and behavior.

Contents and Behavior   The *uType* parameter holds a bit-mapped integer combining three types of options: buttons to display, icons, and default button choice. Several button combinations are possible:

- MB_OK
- MB_OKCANCEL
- MB_YESNO
- MB_YESNOCANCEL
- MB_RETRYCANCEL
- MB_ABORTRETRYIGNORE
- MB_CANCELTRYCONTINUE

Default Button   You can choose which button will be automatically selected if the user presses the Enter key. The choices are MB_DEFBUTTON1 (the default), MB_DEFBUTTON2, MB_DEFBUTTON3, and MB_DEFBUTTON1. Buttons are numbered from the left, starting with 1.

Icons   Four icon choices are available. Sometimes more than one constant produces the same icon:

• Stop-sign: MB_ICONSTOP, MB_ICONHAND, or MB_ICONERROR
• Question mark (?): MB_ICONQUESTION
• Information symbol (i): MB_ICONINFORMATION, MB_ICONASTERISK
• Exclamation point (!): MB_ICONEXCLAMATION, MB_ICONWARNING

Return Value   If MessageBoxA fails, it returns zero. Otherwise, it returns an integer specifying which button the user clicked when closing the box. The choices are IDABORT, IDCANCEL, IDCONTINUE, IDIGNORE, IDNO, IDOK, IDRETRY, IDTRYAGAIN, and IDYES. All are defined in Smallwin.inc.

SmallWin.inc redefines **MessageBoxA** as **MessageBox**, which seems a more user-friendly name.

Demonstration Program

The following program (*MessageBox.asm*) demonstrates some capabilities of the **MessageBoxA** function. The first function call displays a warning message:

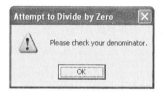

The second function call asks a question. If the user selects the Yes button, the program uses the return value to select a course of action:

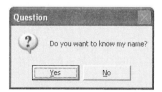

The third function call displays three buttons, and asks what may be safely considered a nonsense question:

Program Listing   Here is the program listing. Because **MessageBox** is an alias for **MessageBoxA**, the simpler name is used here:

```
TITLE Demonstrate MessageBoxA          (MessageBox.asm)
INCLUDE Irvine32.inc
.data
```

```
captionW    BYTE "Attempt to Divide by Zero",0
warningMsg BYTE "Please check your denominator.",0

captionQ    BYTE "Question",0
questionMsg BYTE "Do you want to know my name?",0

showMyName  BYTE "My name is MASM",0dh,0ah,0

captionC  BYTE "Information",0
infoMsg   BYTE "Your file was erased.",0dh,0ah
          BYTE "Notify system admin, or restore backup?",0

.code
main PROC

; Display a warning message.
    INVOKE MessageBox, NULL, ADDR warningMsg,
           ADDR captionW,
           MB_OK + MB_ICONEXCLAMATION

; Ask a question, evaluate the response.
    INVOKE MessageBox, NULL, ADDR questionMsg,
           ADDR captionQ, MB_YESNO + MB_ICONQUESTION

    cmp    eax,IDYES               ; YES button clicked?
    jne    L2                      ; if not, skip
; Write name to console window.
    mov    edx,OFFSET showMyName
    call   WriteString
L2:

; More complex set of buttons. Confuse the user.
    INVOKE MessageBox, NULL, ADDR infoMsg,
       ADDR captionC, MB_YESNOCANCEL + MB_ICONEXCLAMATION \
           + MB_DEFBUTTON2

    exit
main ENDP
END main
```

If you want your message box window to float above all other windows on your desktop, add the MB_SYSTEMMODAL option to the values you pass to the last argument (the *uType* parameter).

11.1.4 Console Input

By now, you have used the **ReadString** and **ReadChar** procedures from the book's link library quite a few times. They were designed to be simple and straightforward, so you could concentrate on other issues. Both procedures are wrappers around **ReadConsole**, a Win32 function. (A *wrapper* procedure hides some of the details of another procedure.)

Console Input Buffer   The Win32 console has an input buffer containing an array of input event records. Each input event, such as a keystroke, mouse movement, or mouse-button click, creates an input record in the console's input buffer. High-level input functions such as **ReadConsole** filter and process the input data, returning only a stream of characters.

ReadConsole Function

The **ReadConsole** function provides a convenient way to read text input and put it in a buffer. Here is the prototype:

```
ReadConsole PROTO,
    hConsoleInput:HANDLE,                   ; input handle
```

```
        lpBuffer:PTR BYTE,                  ; pointer to buffer
        nNumberOfCharsToRead:DWORD,         ; number of chars to read
        lpNumberOfCharsRead:PTR DWORD,      ; ptr to num bytes read
        lpReserved:DWORD                    ; (not used)
```

hConsoleInput is a valid console input handle returned by the **GetStdHandle** function. The *lpBuffer* parameter is the offset of a character array. *nNumberOfCharsToRead* is a 32-bit integer specifying the maximum number of characters to read. *lpNumberOfCharsRead* is a pointer to a doubleword that permits the function to fill in, when it returns, a count of the number of characters placed in the buffer. The last parameter is not used, so pass the value zero.

When calling ReadConsole, include two extra bytes in your input buffer for the end-of-line characters. If you want the input buffer to contain a null-terminated string, replace the byte containing 0Dh with a null byte. This is exactly what is done by the **ReadString** procedure from Irvine32.lib.

Note: Win32 API functions do not preserve the EAX, EBX, ECX, and EDX registers.

Example Program   To read characters entered by the user, call **GetStdHandle** to get the console's standard input handle and call **ReadConsole**, using the same input handle. The following ReadConsole program demonstrates the technique. Notice that Win32 API calls are compatible with the Irvine32 library, so we are able to call DumpRegs at the same time we call Win32 functions:

```
TITLE Read From the Console            (ReadConsole.asm)

INCLUDE Irvine32.inc
BufSize = 80

.data
buffer BYTE BufSize DUP(?),0,0
stdInHandle HANDLE ?
bytesRead   DWORD ?

.code
main PROC
     ; Get handle to standard input
     INVOKE GetStdHandle, STD_INPUT_HANDLE
     mov    stdInHandle,eax

     ; Wait for user input
     INVOKE ReadConsole, stdInHandle, ADDR buffer,
        BufSize - 2, ADDR bytesRead, 0

     ; Display the buffer
     mov    esi,OFFSET buffer
     mov    ecx,bytesRead
     mov    ebx,TYPE buffer
     call   DumpMem

     exit
main ENDP
END main
```

If the user enters "abcdefg", the program generates the following output. Nine bytes are inserted in the buffer: "abcdefg" plus 0Dh and 0Ah, the end-of-line characters inserted when the user pressed the Enter key. **bytesRead** equals 9:

```
Dump of offset 00404000
------------------------------
61 62 63 64 65 66 67 0D 0A
```

Checking for Errors

If a Windows API function returns an error value (such as NULL), you can call the **GetLastError** API function to get more information about the error. It returns a 32-bit integer error code in EAX:

```
.data
messageId DWORD ?
.code
call GetLastError
mov  messageId,eax
```

MS-Windows has thousands of error codes, so you'll probably want to obtain a message string explaining the error. To do that, call the **FormatMessage** function:

```
FormatMessage PROTO,              ; format a message
     dwFlags:DWORD,               ; formatting options
     lpSource:DWORD,              ; location of message def
     dwMsgID:DWORD,               ; message identifier
     dwLanguageID:DWORD,          ; language identifier
     lpBuffer:PTR BYTE,           ; ptr to buffer receiving string
     nSize:DWORD,                 ; buffer size
     va_list:DWORD                ; pointer to list of arguments
```

Its parameters are somewhat complicated, so you will have to read the SDK documentation to get the full picture. Following is a brief listing of the values we find most useful. All are input parameters except *lpBuffer*, an output parameter:

- *dwFlags,* doubleword integer that holds formatting options, including how to interpret the lpSource parameter. It specifies how to handle line breaks, as well as the maximum width of a formatted output line. The recommended values are FORMAT_MESSAGE_ALLOCATE_BUFFER FORMAT_MESSAGE_FROM_SYSTEM
- *lpSource*, a pointer to the location of the message definition. Given the dwFlags setting we recommend, set lpSource to NULL (0).
- *dwMsgID*, the integer doubleword returned by calling GetLastError.
- *dwLanguageID*, a language identifier. If you set it to zero, the message will be language neutral, or it will correspond to the user's default locale.
- *lpBuffer (output parameter)*, a pointer to a buffer that receives the null-terminated message string. Because we use the FORMAT_MESSAGE_ALLOCATE_BUFFER option, the buffer is allocated automatically.
- *nSize*, which can be used to specify a buffer to hold the message string. You can set this parameter to 0 if you use the options for dwFlags suggested above.
- *va_list*, a pointer to an array of values that can be inserted in a formatted message. Because we are not formatting error messages, this parameter can be NULL (0).

Following is a sample call to FormatMessage:

```
.data
messageId DWORD ?
pErrorMsg DWORD ?                        ; points to error message
.code
call GetLastError
mov  messageId,eax
INVOKE FormatMessage, FORMAT_MESSAGE_ALLOCATE_BUFFER + \
     FORMAT_MESSAGE_FROM_SYSTEM, NULL, messageID, 0,
     ADDR pErrorMsg, 0, NULL
```

After calling FormatMessage, call **LocalFree** to release the storage allocated by FormatMessage:

```
INVOKE LocalFree, pErrorMsg
```

WriteWindowsMsg   The book's link library contains the following **WriteWindowsMsg** procedure, which encapsulates the message handling details:

```
;-----------------------------------------------------
WriteWindowsMsg PROC USES eax edx
;
; Displays a string containing the most recent error
; generated by MS-Windows.
; Receives: nothing
; Returns: nothing
;-----------------------------------------------------
.data
WriteWindowsMsg_1 BYTE "Error ",0
WriteWindowsMsg_2 BYTE ": ",0
pErrorMsg DWORD ?                      ; points to error message
messageId DWORD ?
.code
    call    GetLastError
    mov     messageId,eax
```

```
; Display the error number.
    mov     edx,OFFSET WriteWindowsMsg_1
    call    WriteString
    call    WriteDec
    mov     edx,OFFSET WriteWindowsMsg_2
    call    WriteString
```

```
; Get the corresponding message string.
    INVOKE FormatMessage, FORMAT_MESSAGE_ALLOCATE_BUFFER + \
        FORMAT_MESSAGE_FROM_SYSTEM, NULL, messageID, NULL, \
        ADDR pErrorMsg, NULL, NULL
```

```
; Display the error message generated by MS-Windows.
    mov     edx,pErrorMsg
    call    WriteString
```

```
; Free the error message string.
    INVOKE LocalFree, pErrorMsg

    ret
WriteWindowsMsg ENDP
```

Single-Character Input

Single-character input in console mode is a little tricky. MS-Windows provides a device driver for the
currently installed keyboard. When a key is pressed, an 8-bit *scan code* is transmitted to the computer's keyboard port. When the key is released, a second scan code is transmitted. MS-Windows uses
a device driver program to translate the scan code into a 16-bit *virtual-key code*, a device-independent
value defined by MS-Windows that identifies the key's purpose. A message is created by MS-Windows
containing the scan code, the virtual-key code, and other related information. The message is placed
in the MS-Windows message queue, eventually finding its way to the currently executing program
thread (which we identify by the console input handle). If you would like to learn more about the keyboard input process, read the *About Keyboard Input* topic in the Platform SDK documentation. For a
list of virtual key constants, see the *VirtualKeys.inc* file in the book's \Examples\ch11 directory.

Irvine32 Keyboard Procedures   The Irvine32 library has two related procedures:

• **ReadChar** waits for an ASCII character to be typed at the keyboard and returns the character in AL.

• The **ReadKey** procedure performs a no-wait keyboard check. If no key is waiting in the console input buffer, the Zero flag is set. If a key is found, the Zero flag is clear and AL contains either zero or an ASCII code. The upper halves of EAX and EDX are overwritten.

In ReadKey, if AL contains zero, the user may have pressed a special key (function key, cursor arrow, etc.). The AH register contains the keyboard scan code, which you can match to the list of keyboard keys on the facing page inside the front cover of this book. DX contains the virtual-key code, and EBX contains state information about the states of the keyboard control keys. See Table 11-3 for a list of control key values. After calling ReadKey, you can use the TEST instruction to check for various key values. The implementation of ReadKey is somewhat long, so we will not show it here. You can view it in the Irvine32.asm file in the book's \Examples\Lib32 folder.

Table 11-3   Keyboard Control Key State Values.

Value	Meaning
CAPSLOCK_ON	The CAPS LOCK light is on.
ENHANCED_KEY	The key is enhanced.
LEFT_ALT_PRESSED	The left ALT key is pressed.
LEFT_CTRL_PRESSED	The left CTRL key is pressed.
NUMLOCK_ON	The NUM LOCK light is on.
RIGHT_ALT_PRESSED	The right ALT key is pressed.
RIGHT_CTRL_PRESSED	The right CTRL key is pressed.
SCROLLLOCK_ON	The SCROLL LOCK light is on.
SHIFT_PRESSED	The SHIFT key is pressed.

ReadKey Test Program   The following program tests ReadKey by waiting for a keypress and then reporting whether or not the CapsLock key is down. As we mentioned in Chapter 5, you must include a delay factor when calling ReadKey to allow time for MS-Windows to process its message loop:

```
TITLE Testing ReadKey              (TestReadkey.asm)

INCLUDE Irvine32.inc
INCLUDE Macros.inc

.code
main PROC
L1:  mov    eax,10               ; delay for msg processing
     call   Delay
     call   ReadKey              ; wait for a keypress
     jz     L1

     test   ebx,CAPSLOCK_ON
     jz     L2
     mWrite <"CapsLock is ON",0dh,0ah>
     jmp    L3

L2:  mWrite <"CapsLock is OFF",0dh,0ah>

L3:  exit
main ENDP
END main
```

Getting the Keyboard State

You can test the state of individual keyboard keys to find out which are currently pressed. Call the **GetKeyState** API function.

```
GetKeyState PROTO, nVirtKey:DWORD
```

Pass it a virtual key value, such as the ones identified by Table 11-4. Your program must test the value returned in EAX, as indicated by the same table.

Table 11-4   Testing Keys with GetKeyState.

Key	Virtual Key Symbol	Bit to Test in EAX
NumLock	VK_NUMLOCK	0
Scroll Lock	VK_SCROLL	0
Left shift	VK_LSHIFT	15
Right Shift	VK_tRSHIFT	15
Left Ctrl	VK_LCONTROL	15
Right Ctrl	VK_RCONTROL	15
Left Menu	VK_LMENU	15
Right Menu	VK_RMENU	15

The following example program demonstrates GetKeyState by checking the states of the NumLock and Left Shift keys:

```
TITLE Keyboard Toggle Keys            (Keybd.asm)

INCLUDE Irvine32.inc
INCLUDE Macros.inc

; GetKeyState sets bit 0 in EAX if a toggle key is
; currently on (CapsLock, NumLock, ScrollLock).
; Sets bit 15 in EAX if another specified key is
; currently down.

.code
main PROC

    INVOKE GetKeyState, VK_NUMLOCK
    test al,1
    .IF !Zero?
      mWrite <"The NumLock key is ON",0dh,0ah>
    .ENDIF

    INVOKE GetKeyState, VK_LSHIFT
    test al,80h
    .IF !Zero?
      mWrite <"The Left Shift key is currently DOWN",0dh,0ah>
    .ENDIF

    exit
main ENDP
END main
```

11.1.5 Console Output

In earlier chapters we tried to make console output as simple as possible. As far back as Chapter 5, the **WriteString** procedure in the Irvine32 link library required only a single argument, the offset of a string in EDX. It turns out that WriteString is actually a wrapper around a more detailed call to a Win32 function named **WriteConsole**.

In this chapter, however, you learn how to make direct calls to Win32 functions such as **WriteConsole** and **WriteConsoleOutputCharacter**. Direct calls involve more detailed knowledge, but they also offer you more flexibility than the Irvine32 library procedures.

Data Structures

Several of the Win32 console functions use predefined data structures, including COORD and SMALL_RECT. The COORD structure holds the coordinates of a character cell in the console screen buffer. The origin of the coordinate system (0,0) is at the top left cell:

```
COORD STRUCT
      X WORD ?
      Y WORD ?
COORD ENDS
```

The SMALL_RECT structure holds the upper left and lower right corners of a rectangle. It specifies screen buffer character cells in the console window:

```
SMALL_RECT STRUCT
      Left    WORD ?
      Top     WORD ?
      Right   WORD ?
      Bottom  WORD ?
SMALL_RECT ENDS
```

WriteConsole Function

The **WriteConsole** function writes a string to the console window at the current cursor position and leaves the cursor just past the last character written. It acts upon standard ASCII control characters such as *tab*, *carriage return*, and *line feed*. The string does not have to be null-terminated. Here is the function prototype:

```
WriteConsole PROTO,
      hConsoleOutput:HANDLE,
      lpBuffer:PTR BYTE,
      nNumberOfCharsToWrite:DWORD,
      lpNumberOfCharsWritten:PTR DWORD,
      lpReserved:DWORD
```

hConsoleOutput is the console output stream handle; *lpBuffer* is a pointer to the array of characters you want to write; *nNumberOfCharsToWrite* holds the array length; *lpNumberOfCharsWritten* points to an integer assigned the number of bytes actually written when the function returns. The last parameter is not used, so set it to zero.

Example Program: Console1

The following program, *Console1.asm*, demonstrates the **GetStdHandle, ExitProcess,** and **WriteConsole** functions by writing a string to the console window:

```
TITLE Win32 Console Example #1                    (Console1.asm)

; This program calls the following Win32 Console functions:
; GetStdHandle, ExitProcess, WriteConsole

INCLUDE Irvine32.inc

.data
```

```
endl EQU <0dh,0ah>                      ; end of line sequence
message LABEL BYTE
      BYTE "This program is a simple demonstration of"
      BYTE "console mode output, using the GetStdHandle"
      BYTE "and WriteConsole functions.",endl
messageSize = ($-message)

consoleHandle HANDLE 0                   ; handle to standard output device
bytesWritten  DWORD ?                    ; number of bytes written

.code
main PROC
   ; Get the console output handle:
      INVOKE GetStdHandle, STD_OUTPUT_HANDLE
      mov consoleHandle,eax

   ; Write a string to the console:
      INVOKE WriteConsole,
        consoleHandle,                   ; console output handle
        ADDR message,                    ; string pointer
        messageSize,                     ; string length
        ADDR bytesWritten,               ; returns num bytes written
        0                                ; not used

      INVOKE ExitProcess,0
main ENDP
END main
```

The program produces the following output:

```
This program is a simple demonstration of console mode output, using the
GetStdHandle and WriteConsole functions.
```

WriteConsoleOutputCharacter Function

The **WriteConsoleOutputCharacter** function copies an array of characters to consecutive cells of the console screen buffer, beginning at a specified location. Here is the prototype:

```
WriteConsoleOutputCharacter PROTO,
      hConsoleOutput:HANDLE,                  ; console output handle
      lpCharacter:PTR BYTE,                   ; pointer to buffer
      nLength:DWORD,                          ; size of buffer
      dwWriteCoord:COORD,                     ; first cell coordinates
      lpNumberOfCharsWritten:PTR DWORD        ; output count
```

If the text reaches the end of a line, it wraps around. The attribute values in the screen buffer are not changed. If the function cannot write the characters, it returns zero. ASCII control codes such as *tab*, *carriage return*, and *line feed* are ignored.

11.1.6   Reading and Writing Files

CreateFile Function

The **CreateFile** function either creates a new file or opens an existing file. If successful, it returns a handle to the open file; otherwise, it returns a special constant named INVALID_HANDLE_VALUE. Here is the prototype:

```
CreateFile PROTO,                            ; create new file
      lpFilename:PTR BYTE,                   ; ptr to filename
      dwDesiredAccess:DWORD,                 ; access mode
```

```
        dwShareMode:DWORD,                    ; share mode
        lpSecurityAttributes:DWORD,           ; ptr security attrib
        dwCreationDisposition:DWORD,          ; file creation options
        dwFlagsAndAttributes:DWORD,           ; file attributes
        hTemplateFile:DWORD                   ; handle to template file
```

The parameters are described in Table 11-5. The return value is zero if the function fails.

Table 11-5   CreateFile Parameters.

Parameter	Description
lpFileName	Points to a null-terminated string containing either a partial or fully qualified filename (*drive:\path\filename*).
dwDesiredAccess	Specifies how the file will be accessed (reading or writing).
dwShareMode	Controls the ability for multiple programs to access the file while it is open.
lpSecurityAttributes	Points to a security structure controlling security rights.
dwCreationDisposition	Specifies what action to take when a file exists or does not exist.
dwFlagsAndAttributes	Holds bit flags specifying file attributes such as archive, encrypted, hidden, normal, system, and temporary.
hTemplateFile	Contains an optional handle to a template file that supplies file attributes and extended attributes for the file being created; when not using this parameter, set it to zero.

dwDesiredAccess   The *dwDesiredAccess* parameter lets you specify read access, write access, read/write access, or device query access to the file. Choose from the values listed in Table 11-6 or from a large set of specific flag values not listed here. (Search for *CreateFile* in the Platform SDK documentation).

Table 11-6   dwDesiredAccess Parameter Options.

Value	Meaning
0	Specifies device query access to the object. An application can query device attributes without accessing the device, or it can check for the existence of a file.
GENERIC_READ	Specifies read access to the object. Data can be read from the file, and the file pointer can be moved. Combine with GENERIC_WRITE for read/write access.
GENERIC_WRITE	Specifies write access to the object. Data can be written to the file, and the file pointer can be moved. Combine with GENERIC_READ for read/write access.

CreationDisposition   The *dwCreationDisposition* parameter specifies which action to take on files that exist and which action to take when files do not exist. Select one of the values in Table 11-7.

Table 11-8 lists the more commonly used values permitted in the *dwFlagsAndAttributes* parameter. (For a complete list, search for *CreateFile* in the Platform SDK documentation.) Any combination of the attributes is acceptable, except that all other file attributes override FILE_ATTRIBUTE_NORMAL. The values map to powers of 2, so you can use the assembly time OR operator or + operator to combine them into a single argument:

```
        FILE_ATTRIBUTE_HIDDEN OR FILE_ATTRIBUTE_READONLY
        FILE_ATTRIBUTE_HIDDEN + FILE_ATTRIBUTE_READONLY
```

Table 11-7   dwCreationDisposition Parameter Options.

Value	Meaning
CREATE_NEW	Creates a new file. Requires setting the dwDesiredAccess parameter to GENERIC_WRITE. The function fails if the file already exists.
CREATE_ALWAYS	Creates a new file. If the file exists, the function overwrites the file, clears the existing attributes, and combines the file attributes and flags specified by the *attributes* parameter with the predefined constant FILE_ATTRIBUTE_ARCHIVE. Requires setting the dwDesiredAccess parameter to GENERIC_WRITE.
OPEN_EXISTING	Opens the file. The function fails if the file does not exist. May be used for reading from and/or writing to the file.
OPEN_ALWAYS	Opens the file if it exists. If the file does not exist, the function creates the file as if *CreationDisposition* were CREATE_NEW.
TRUNCATE_EXISTING	Opens the file. Once opened, the file is truncated to size zero. Requires setting the dwDesiredAccess parameter to GENERIC_WRITE. This function fails if the file does not exist.

Table 11-8   Selected FlagsAndAttributes Values.

Attribute	Meaning
FILE_ATTRIBUTE_ARCHIVE	The file should be archived. Applications use this attribute to mark files for backup or removal.
FILE_ATTRIBUTE_HIDDEN	The file is hidden. It is not to be included in an ordinary directory listing.
FILE_ATTRIBUTE_NORMAL	The file has no other attributes set. This attribute is valid only if used alone.
FILE_ATTRIBUTE_READONLY	The file is read only. Applications can read the file but cannot write to it or delete it.
FILE_ATTRIBUTE_TEMPORARY	The file is being used for temporary storage.

Examples   The following examples are for illustrative purposes only, to show how you might create and open files. See the online Microsoft MSDN documentation for **CreateFile** to learn about the many available options:

• Open an existing file for reading (input):

```
INVOKE CreateFile,
     ADDR filename,                  ; ptr to filename
     GENERIC_READ,                   ; read from the file
     DO_NOT_SHARE,                   ; share mode
     NULL,                           ; ptr to security attributes
     OPEN_EXISTING,                  ; open an existing file
     FILE_ATTRIBUTE_NORMAL,          ; normal file attribute
     0                               ; not used
```

• Open an existing file for writing (output). Once the file is open, we could write over existing data or append new data to the file by moving the file pointer to the end (see SetFilePointer, Section 11.1.6):

```
INVOKE CreateFile,
     ADDR filename,
```

```
                    GENERIC_WRITE,                  ; write to the file
                    DO_NOT_SHARE,
                    NULL,
                    OPEN_EXISTING,                  ; file must exist
                    FILE_ATTRIBUTE_NORMAL,
                    0
```

• Create a new file with normal attributes, erasing any existing file by the same name:

```
    INVOKE CreateFile,
            ADDR filename,
            GENERIC_WRITE,                  ; write to the file
            DO_NOT_SHARE,
            NULL,
            CREATE_ALWAYS,                  ; overwrite existing file
            FILE_ATTRIBUTE_NORMAL,
            0
```

• Create a new file if the file does not already exist; otherwise, open the existing file for output:

```
    INVOKE CreateFile,
            ADDR filename,
            GENERIC_WRITE,                  ; write to the file
            DO_NOT_SHARE,
            NULL,
            CREATE_NEW,                     ; don't erase existing file
            FILE_ATTRIBUTE_NORMAL,
            0
```

(The constants named DO_NOT_SHARE and NULL are defined in the *SmallWin.inc* include file, which is automatically included by *Irvine32.inc*.)

CloseHandle Function

The **CloseHandle** function closes an open object handle. Its prototype is

```
    CloseHandle PROTO,
        hObject:HANDLE                  ; handle to object
```

You can use CloseHandle to close a currently open file handle. The return value is zero if the function fails.

ReadFile Function

The **ReadFile** function reads text from an input file. Here is the prototype:

```
    ReadFile PROTO,
            hFile:HANDLE,                       ; input handle
            lpBuffer:PTR BYTE,                  ; ptr to buffer
            nNumberOfBytesToRead:DWORD,         ; num bytes to read
            lpNumberOfBytesRead:PTR DWORD,      ; bytes actually read
            lpOverlapped:PTR DWORD              ; ptr to asynch info
```

The *hFile* parameter is an open file handle returned by **CreateFile**; *lpBuffer* points to a buffer that receives data read from the file; *nNumberOfBytesToRead* specifies the maximum number of bytes to read from the file; *lpNumberOfBytesRead* points to an integer indicating the number of bytes actually read when the function returns; *lpOverlapped* should be set to NULL (0) for synchronous reading (which we use). The return value is zero if the function fails.

If called more than once on the same open file handle, ReadFile remembers where it last finished reading and reads from that point on. In other words, it maintains an internal pointer to the current position in the file. ReadFile can also run in asynchronous mode, meaning that the calling program does not wait for the read operation to finish.

WriteFile Function

The **WriteFile** function writes data to a file, using an output handle. The handle can be the screen buffer handle, or it can be one assigned to a text file. The function starts writing data to the file at the position indicated by the file's internal position pointer. After the write operation has been completed, the file's position pointer is adjusted by the number of bytes actually written. Here is the function prototype:

```
WriteFile PROTO,
    hFile:HANDLE,                           ; output handle
    lpBuffer:PTR BYTE,                      ; pointer to buffer
    nNumberOfBytesToWrite:DWORD,            ; size of buffer
    lpNumberOfBytesWritten:PTR DWORD,       ; num bytes written
    lpOverlapped:PTR DWORD                  ; ptr to asynch info
```

hFile is a handle to a previously opened file; *lpBuffer* points to a buffer holding the data written to the file; *nNumberOfBytesToWrite* specifies how many bytes to write to the file; *lpNumberOfBytesWritten* points to an integer that specifies the number of bytes actually written after the function executes; *lpOverlapped* should be set to NULL for synchronous operation. The return value is zero if the function fails.

SetFilePointer Function

The **SetFilePointer** function moves the position pointer of an open file. This function can be used to append data to a file or to perform random-access record processing:

```
SetFilePointer PROTO,
    hFile:HANDLE,                           ; file handle
    lDistanceToMove:SDWORD,                 ; bytes to move pointer
    lpDistanceToMoveHigh:PTR SDWORD,        ; ptr bytes to move, high
    dwMoveMethod:DWORD                      ; starting point
```

The return value is zero if the function fails. *dwMoveMethod* specifies the starting point for moving the file pointer, which is selected from three predefined symbols: FILE_BEGIN, FILE_CURRENT, and FILE_END. The distance itself is a 64-bit signed integer value, divided into two parts:

- *lpDistanceToMove*: the lower 32 bits
- *pDistanceToMoveHigh:* a pointer to a variable containing the upper 32 bits

If *lpDistanceToMoveHigh* is null, only the value in *lpDistanceToMove* is used to move the file pointer. For example, the following code prepares to append to the end of a file:

```
INVOKE SetFilePointer,
    fileHandle,                 ; file handle
    0,                          ; distance low
    0,                          ; distance high
    FILE_END                    ; move method
```

See the *AppendFile.asm* program.

11.1.7   File I/O in the Irvine32 Library

The Irvine32 library contains a few simplified procedures for file input/output, which we documented in Chapter 5. The procedures are wrappers around the Win32 API functions we have described in the current chapter. The following source code lists CreateOutputFile, OpenFile, WriteToFile, Read-FromFile, and CloseFile:

```
;------------------------------------------------------
CreateOutputFile PROC
;
; Creates a new file and opens it in output mode.
; Receives: EDX points to the filename.
```

```
; Returns: If the file was created successfully, EAX
;    contains a valid file handle. Otherwise, EAX
;    equals INVALID_HANDLE_VALUE.
;--------------------------------------------------------
     INVOKE CreateFile,
        edx, GENERIC_WRITE, DO_NOT_SHARE, NULL,
        CREATE_ALWAYS, FILE_ATTRIBUTE_NORMAL, 0
     ret
CreateOutputFile ENDP

;--------------------------------------------------------
OpenFile PROC
;
; Opens a new text file and opens for input.
; Receives: EDX points to the filename.
; Returns: If the file was opened successfully, EAX
; contains a valid file handle. Otherwise, EAX equals
; INVALID_HANDLE_VALUE.
;--------------------------------------------------------
     INVOKE CreateFile,
        edx, GENERIC_READ, DO_NOT_SHARE, NULL,
        OPEN_EXISTING, FILE_ATTRIBUTE_NORMAL, 0
     ret
OpenFile ENDP

;--------------------------------------------------------
WriteToFile PROC
;
; Writes a buffer to an output file.
; Receives: EAX = file handle, EDX = buffer offset,
;    ECX = number of bytes to write
; Returns: EAX = number of bytes written to the file.
; If the value returned in EAX is less than the
; argument passed in ECX, an error likely occurred.
;--------------------------------------------------------
.data
WriteToFile_1 DWORD ?              ; number of bytes written
.code
     INVOKE WriteFile,             ; write buffer to file
            eax,                   ; file handle
            edx,                   ; buffer pointer
            ecx,                   ; number of bytes to write
            ADDR WriteToFile_1,    ; number of bytes written
            0                      ; overlapped execution flag
     mov    eax,WriteToFile_1      ; return value
     ret
WriteToFile ENDP

;--------------------------------------------------------
ReadFromFile PROC
;
; Reads an input file into a buffer.
; Receives: EAX = file handle, EDX = buffer offset,
;    ECX = number of bytes to read
; Returns: If CF = 0, EAX = number of bytes read; if
;    CF = 1, EAX contains the system error code returned
```

```
;      by the GetLastError Win32 API function.
;-----------------------------------------------------------
.data
ReadFromFile_1 DWORD ?                   ; number of bytes read
.code
      INVOKE ReadFile,
            eax,                         ; file handle
            edx,                         ; buffer pointer
            ecx,                         ; max bytes to read
            ADDR ReadFromFile_1,         ; number of bytes read
            0                            ; overlapped execution flag
      mov    eax,ReadFromFile_1
      ret
ReadFromFile ENDP
;-----------------------------------------------------------
CloseFile PROC
;
; Closes a file using its handle as an identifier.
; Receives: EAX = file handle
; Returns: EAX = nonzero if the file is successfully
;    closed.
;-----------------------------------------------------------
      INVOKE CloseHandle, eax
      ret
CloseFile ENDP
```

11.1.8   Testing the File I/O Procedures

CreateFile Program Example

The following program creates a file in output mode, asks the user to enter some text, writes the text to the output file, reports the number of bytes written, and closes the file. It checks for errors after attempting to create the file:

```
TITLE Creating a File              (CreateFile.asm)

INCLUDE Irvine32.inc

BUFFER_SIZE = 501
.data
buffer BYTE BUFFER_SIZE DUP(?)
filename     BYTE "output.txt",0
fileHandle   HANDLE ?
stringLength DWORD ?
bytesWritten DWORD ?
str1 BYTE "Cannot create file",0dh,0ah,0
str2 BYTE "Bytes written to file [output.txt]:",0
str3 BYTE "Enter up to 500 characters and press"
     BYTE "[Enter]: ",0dh,0ah,0

.code
main PROC
; Create a new text file.
      mov    edx,OFFSET filename
      call   CreateOutputFile
      mov    fileHandle,eax

; Check for errors.
```

```
        cmp     eax, INVALID_HANDLE_VALUE      ; error found?
        jne     file_ok                        ; no: skip
        mov     edx,OFFSET str1                ; display error
        call    WriteString
        jmp     quit
file_ok:

; Ask the user to input a string.
        mov     edx,OFFSET str3                ; "Enter up to ...."
        call    WriteString
        mov     ecx,BUFFER_SIZE                ; Input a string
        mov     edx,OFFSET buffer
        call    ReadString
        mov     stringLength,eax               ; counts chars entered

; Write the buffer to the output file.
        mov     eax,fileHandle
        mov     edx,OFFSET buffer
        mov     ecx,stringLength
        call    WriteToFile
        mov     bytesWritten,eax               ; save return value
        call    CloseFile

; Display the return value.
        mov     edx,OFFSET str2                ; "Bytes written"
        call    WriteString
        mov     eax,bytesWritten
        call    WriteDec
        call    Crlf

quit:
        exit
main ENDP
END main
```

ReadFile Program Example

The following program opens a file for input, reads its contents into a buffer, and displays the buffer. All procedures are called from the Irvine32 library:

```
TITLE Reading a File                    (ReadFile.asm)

; Opens, reads, and displays a text file using
; procedures from Irvine32.lib.

INCLUDE Irvine32.inc
INCLUDE macros.inc
BUFFER_SIZE = 5000

.data
buffer BYTE BUFFER_SIZE DUP(?)
filename    BYTE 80 DUP(0)
fileHandle  HANDLE ?

.code
main PROC

; Let user input a filename.
    mWrite "Enter an input filename: "
    mov     edx,OFFSET filename
    mov     ecx,SIZEOF filename
```

```
        call    ReadString
; Open the file for input.
        mov     edx,OFFSET filename
        call    OpenInputFile
        mov     fileHandle,eax
; Check for errors.
        cmp     eax,INVALID_HANDLE_VALUE        ; error opening file?
        jne     file_ok                         ; no: skip
        mWrite  <"Cannot open file",0dh,0ah>
        jmp     quit                            ; and quit
file_ok:

; Read the file into a buffer.
        mov     edx,OFFSET buffer
        mov     ecx,BUFFER_SIZE
        call    ReadFromFile
        jnc     check_buffer_size               ; error reading?
        mWrite  "Error reading file. "          ; yes: show error message
        call    WriteWindowsMsg
        jmp     close_file

check_buffer_size:
        cmp     eax,BUFFER_SIZE                 ; buffer large enough?
        jb      buf_size_ok                     ; yes
        mWrite  <"Error: Buffer too small for the file",0dh,0ah>
        jmp     quit                            ; and quit

buf_size_ok:
        mov     buffer[eax],0                  ; insert null terminator
        mWrite  "File size: "
        call    WriteDec                        ; display file size
        call    Crlf

; Display the buffer.
        mWrite  <"Buffer:",0dh,0ah,0dh,0ah>
        mov     edx,OFFSET buffer               ; display the buffer
        call    WriteString
        call    Crlf

close_file:
        mov     eax,fileHandle
        call    CloseFile

quit:
        exit
main ENDP
END main
```

The program reports an error if the file cannot be opened:

```
Enter an input filename: crazy.txt
Cannot open file
```

It reports an error if it cannot read from the file. Suppose, for example, a bug in the program used the wrong file handle when reading the file:

```
Enter an input filename: infile.txt
Error reading file. Error 6: The handle is invalid.
```

The buffer might be too small to hold the file:

```
Enter an input filename: infile.txt
Error: Buffer too small for the file
```

11.1.9   Console Window Manipulation

The Win32 API provides considerable control over the console window and its buffer. Figure 11–1 shows that the screen buffer can be larger than the number of lines currently displayed in the console window. The console window acts as a "viewport," showing part of the buffer.

FIGURE 11–1   Screen Buffer and Console Window.

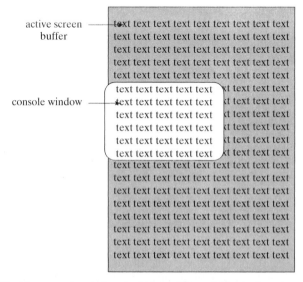

Several functions affect the console window and its position relative to the screen buffer:

- **SetConsoleWindowInfo** sets the size and position of the console window relative to the screen buffer.
- **GetConsoleScreenBufferInfo** returns (among other things) the rectangle coordinates of the console window relative to the screen buffer.
- **SetConsoleCursorPosition** sets the cursor position to any location within the screen buffer; if that area is not visible, the console window is shifted to make the cursor visible.
- **ScrollConsoleScreenBuffer** moves some or all of the text within the screen buffer, which can affect the displayed text in the console window.

SetConsoleTitle

The **SetConsoleTitle** function lets you change the console window's title. An example is

```
.data
titleStr BYTE "Console title",0
.code
INVOKE SetConsoleTitle, ADDR titleStr
```

GetConsoleScreenBufferInfo

The **GetConsoleScreenBufferInfo** function returns information about the current state of the console window. It has two parameters: a handle to the console screen, and a pointer to a structure that is filled in by the function:

```
GetConsoleScreenBufferInfo PROTO,
    hConsoleOutput:HANDLE,
    lpConsoleScreenBufferInfo:PTR CONSOLE_SCREEN_BUFFER_INFO
```

The following is the CONSOLE_SCREEN_BUFFER_INFO structure:

```
CONSOLE_SCREEN_BUFFER_INFO STRUCT
    dwSize                  COORD <>
    dwCursorPosition        COORD <>
    wAttributes             WORD ?
    srWindow                SMALL_RECT <>
    dwMaximumWindowSize     COORD <>
CONSOLE_SCREEN_BUFFER_INFO ENDS
```

dwSize returns the size of the screen buffer, in character columns and rows. *dwCursorPosition* returns the location of the cursor. Both fields are COORD structures. *wAttributes* returns the foreground and background colors of characters written to the console by functions such as **WriteConsole** and **WriteFile**. *srWindow* returns the coordinates of the console window relative to the screen buffer. *drMaximum-WindowSize* returns the maximum size of the console window, based on the current screen buffer size, font, and video display size. The following is a sample call to the function:

```
.data
consoleInfo CONSOLE_SCREEN_BUFFER_INFO <>
outHandle HANDLE ?
.code
INVOKE GetConsoleScreenBufferInfo, outHandle,
    ADDR consoleInfo
```

Figure 11–2 shows a sample of the structure data shown by the Microsoft Visual Studio debugger.

FIGURE 11–2 CONSOLE_SCREEN_BUFFER_INFO Structure.

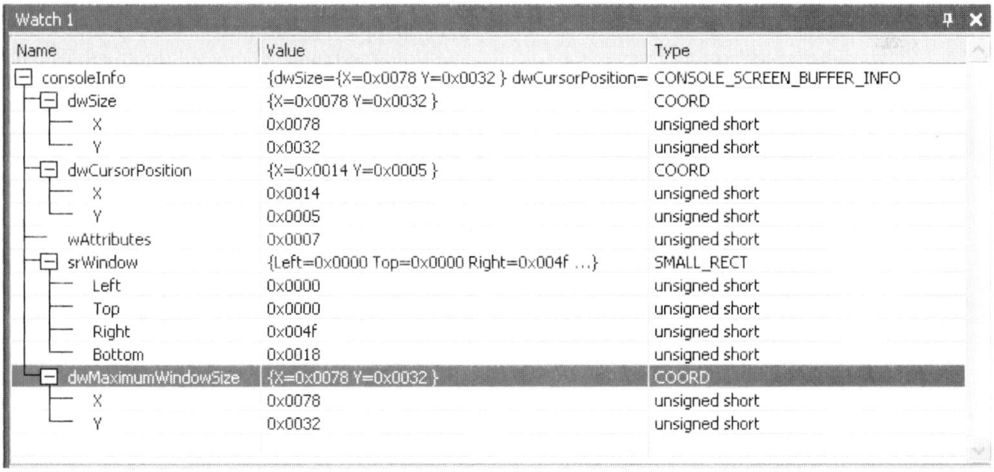

Name	Value	Type
⊟ consoleInfo	{dwSize={X=0x0078 Y=0x0032 } dwCursorPosition=	CONSOLE_SCREEN_BUFFER_INFO
├⊟ dwSize	{X=0x0078 Y=0x0032 }	COORD
│ ├ X	0x0078	unsigned short
│ └ Y	0x0032	unsigned short
├⊟ dwCursorPosition	{X=0x0014 Y=0x0005 }	COORD
│ ├ X	0x0014	unsigned short
│ └ Y	0x0005	unsigned short
├ wAttributes	0x0007	unsigned short
├⊟ srWindow	{Left=0x0000 Top=0x0000 Right=0x004f ...}	SMALL_RECT
│ ├ Left	0x0000	unsigned short
│ ├ Top	0x0000	unsigned short
│ ├ Right	0x004f	unsigned short
│ └ Bottom	0x0018	unsigned short
├⊟ dwMaximumWindowSize	{X=0x0078 Y=0x0032 }	COORD
│ ├ X	0x0078	unsigned short
│ └ Y	0x0032	unsigned short

SetConsoleWindowInfo Function

The **SetConsoleWindowInfo** function lets you set the size and position of the console window relative to its screen buffer. Following is its function prototype:

```
SetConsoleWindowInfo PROTO,
```

```
        hConsoleOutput:HANDLE,                      ; screen buffer handle
        bAbsolute:DWORD,                            ; coordinate type
        lpConsoleWindow:PTR SMALL_RECT              ; ptr to window rectangle
```

bAbsolute indicates how the coordinates in the structure pointed to by *lpConsoleWindow* are to be used. If *bAbsolute* is true, the coordinates specify the new upper left and lower right corners of the console window. If *bAbsolute* is false, the coordinates will be added to the current window coordinates.

The following *Scroll.asm* program writes 50 lines of text to the screen buffer. It then resizes and repositions the console window, effectively scrolling the text backward. It uses the **SetConsoleWindowInfo** function:

```
TITLE Scrolling the Console Window                   (Scroll.asm)

INCLUDE Irvine32.inc

.data
message BYTE ":  This line of text was written "
        BYTE "to the screen buffer",0dh,0ah
messageSize = ($-message)

outHandle       HANDLE 0                    ; standard output handle
bytesWritten    DWORD ?                     ; number of bytes written
lineNum         DWORD 0
windowRect      SMALL_RECT <0,0,60,11>      ; left,top,right,bottom

.code
main PROC
     INVOKE GetStdHandle, STD_OUTPUT_HANDLE
     mov outHandle,eax

.REPEAT
     mov    eax,lineNum
     call   WriteDec                 ; display each line number
     INVOKE WriteConsole,
       outHandle,                    ; console output handle
       ADDR message,                 ; string pointer
       messageSize,                  ; string length
       ADDR bytesWritten,            ; returns num bytes written
       0                             ; not used
     inc    lineNum                  ; next line number
.UNTIL lineNum > 50

; Resize and reposition the console window relative to the
; screen buffer.
     INVOKE SetConsoleWindowInfo,
       outHandle,
       TRUE,
       ADDR windowRect; window rectangle

     call   Readchar                 ; wait for a key
     call   Clrscr                   ; clear the screen buffer
     call   Readchar                 ; wait for a second key

     INVOKE ExitProcess,0
main ENDP
END main
```

It is best to run this program directly from MS-Windows Explorer or a command prompt rather than an integrated editor environment. Otherwise, the editor may affect the behavior and appearance of the console window. You must press a key twice at the end: once to clear the screen buffer and a second time to end the program.

SetConsoleScreenBufferSize Function

The **SetConsoleScreenBufferSize** function lets you set the screen buffer size to X columns by Y rows. Here is the prototype:

```
SetConsoleScreenBufferSize PROTO,
    hConsoleOutput:HANDLE,          ; handle to screen buffer
    dwSize:COORD                    ; new screen buffer size
```

11.1.10   Controlling the Cursor

The Win32 API provides functions to set the cursor size, visibility, and screen location. An important data structure related to these functions is CONSOLE_CURSOR_INFO, which contains information about the console's cursor size and visibility:

```
CONSOLE_CURSOR_INFO STRUCT
    dwSize   DWORD ?
    bVisible DWORD ?
CONSOLE_CURSOR_INFO ENDS
```

dwSize is the percentage (1 to 100) of the character cell filled by the cursor. *bVisible* equals TRUE (1) if the cursor is visible.

GetConsoleCursorInfo Function

The **GetConsoleCursorInfo** function returns the size and visibility of the console cursor. Pass it a pointer to a CONSOLE_CURSOR_INFO structure:

```
GetConsoleCursorInfo PROTO,
    hConsoleOutput:HANDLE,
    lpConsoleCursorInfo:PTR CONSOLE_CURSOR_INFO
```

By default, the cursor size is 25, indicating that the character cell is 25% filled by the cursor.

SetConsoleCursorInfo Function

The **SetConsoleCursorInfo** function sets the size and visibility of the cursor. Pass it a pointer to a CONSOLE_CURSOR_INFO structure:

```
SetConsoleCursorInfo PROTO,
    hConsoleOutput:HANDLE,
    lpConsoleCursorInfo:PTR CONSOLE_CURSOR_INFO
```

SetConsoleCursorPosition

The **SetConsoleCursorPostion** function sets the X, Y position of the cursor. Pass it a COORD structure and the console output handle:

```
SetConsoleCursorPosition PROTO,
    hConsoleOutput:DWORD,           ; input mode handle
    dwCursorPosition:COORD          ; screen X,Y coordinates
```

11.1.11   Controlling the Text Color

There are two ways to control the color of text in a console window. You can change the current text color by calling **SetConsoleTextAttribute**, which affects all subsequent text output to the console. Alternatively, you can set the attributes of specific cells by calling **WriteConsoleOutputAttribute**. The GetConsoleScreenBufferInfo function (Section 11.1.9) returns the current screen colors, along with other console information.

SetConsoleTextAttribute Function

The **SetConsoleTextAttribute** function lets you set the foreground and background colors for all subsequent text output to the console window. Here is its prototype:

```
SetConsoleTextAttribute PROTO,
      hConsoleOutput:HANDLE,            ; console output handle
      wAttributes:WORD                  ; color attribute
```

The color value is stored in the low-order byte of the *wAttributes* parameter. Colors are created using the same method as for the VIDEO BIOS, which is shown in Section 15.3.2.

WriteConsoleOutputAttribute Function

The **WriteConsoleOutputAttribute** function copies an array of attribute values to consecutive cells of the console screen buffer, beginning at a specified location. Here is the prototype:

```
WriteConsoleOutputAttribute PROTO,
      hConsoleOutput:DWORD,             ; output handle
      lpAttribute:PTR WORD,             ; write attributes
      nLength:DWORD,                    ; number of cells
      dwWriteCoord:COORD,               ; first cell coordinates
      lpNumberOfAttrsWritten:PTR DWORD  ; output count
```

lpAttribute points to an array of attributes in which the low-order byte of each contains the color; *nLength* is the length of the array; *dwWriteCoord* is the starting screen cell to receive the attributes; and *lpNuumberOfAttrsWritten* points to a variable that will hold the number of cells written.

Example WriteColors Program

To demonstrate the use of colors and attributes, the *WriteColors.asm* program creates an array of characters and an array of attributes, one for each character. It calls **WriteConsoleOutputAttribute** to copy the attributes to the screen buffer and **WriteConsoleOutputCharacter** to copy the characters to the same screen buffer cells:

```
TITLE Writing Text Colors              (WriteColors.asm)

INCLUDE Irvine32.inc
.data
outHandle     HANDLE ?
cellsWritten DWORD ?
xyPos COORD <10,2>

; Array of character codes:
buffer BYTE 1,2,3,4,5,6,7,8,9,10,11,12,13,14,15
       BYTE 16,17,18,19,20
BufSize = ($ - buffer)
; Array of attributes:
attributes WORD 0Fh,0Eh,0Dh,0Ch,0Bh,0Ah,9,8,7,6
           WORD 5,4,3,2,1,0F0h,0E0h,0D0h,0C0h,0B0h

.code
main PROC
; Get the Console standard output handle:
      INVOKE GetStdHandle,STD_OUTPUT_HANDLE
      mov outHandle,eax

; Set the colors of adjacent cells:
      INVOKE WriteConsoleOutputAttribute,
          outHandle, ADDR attributes,
```

```
            BufSize, xyPos,
            ADDR cellsWritten

    ; Write character codes 1 through 20:
            INVOKE WriteConsoleOutputCharacter,
            outHandle, ADDR buffer, BufSize,
            xyPos, ADDR cellsWritten

            INVOKE ExitProcess,0              ; end program
    main ENDP
    END main
```

Figure 11–3 shows a snapshot of the program's output, in which character codes 1 through 20 are displayed as graphic characters. Each character is in a different color, although the colors do not appear on the printed page.

FIGURE 11–3   Output from the WriteColors Program.

11.1.12   Time and Date Functions

The Win32 API provides a fairly large selection of time and date functions. For starters, you can get and set the current date and time. We can only discuss a small subset of the functions here, but you can look up the Platform SDK documentation for the Win32 functions listed in Table 11-9.

SYSTEMTIME Structure   The SYSTEMTIME structure is used by date- and time-related Windows API functions:

```
    SYSTEMTIME STRUCT
        wYear WORD ?                    ; year (4 digits)
        wMonth WORD ?                   ; month (1-12)
        wDayOfWeek WORD ?               ; day of week (0-6)
        wDay WORD ?                     ; day (1-31)
        wHour WORD ?                    ; hours (0-23)
        wMinute WORD ?                  ; minutes (0-59)
        wSecond WORD ?                  ; seconds (0-59)
        wMilliseconds WORD ?            ; milliseconds (0-999)
    SYSTEMTIME ENDS
```

The *wDayOfWeek* field value begins with Sunday = 0, Monday = 1, and so on. The value in *wMilliseconds* is not exact because the system can periodically refresh the time by synchronizing with a time source.

GetLocalTime and SetLocalTime

The **GetLocalTime** function returns the date and current time of day, according to the system clock. The time is adjusted for the local time zone. When calling it, pass a pointer to a SYSTEMTIME structure:

```
    GetLocalTime PROTO,
      lpSystemTime:PTR SYSTEMTIME
```

Table 11-9   Win32 DateTime Functions.

Function	Description
CompareFileTime	Compares two 64-bit file times.
DosDateTimeToFileTime	Converts MS-DOS date and time values to a 64-bit file time.
FileTimeToDosDateTime	Converts a 64-bit file time to MS-DOS date and time values.
FileTimeToLocalFileTime	Converts a UTC (*universal coordinated time*) file time to a local file time.
FileTimeToSystemTime	Converts a 64-bit file time to system time format.
GetFileTime	Retrieves the date and time that a file was created, last accessed, and last modified.
GetLocalTime	Retrieves the current local date and time.
GetSystemTime	Retrieves the current system date and time in UTC format.
GetSystemTimeAdjustment	Determines whether the system is applying periodic time adjustments to its time-of-day clock.
GetSystemTimeAsFileTime	Retrieves the current system date and time in UTC format.
GetTickCount	Retrieves the number of milliseconds that have elapsed since the system was started.
GetTimeZoneInformation	Retrieves the current time-zone parameters.
LocalFileTimeToFileTime	Converts a local file time to a file time based on UTC.
SetFileTime	Sets the date and time that a file was created, last accessed, or last modified.
SetLocalTime	Sets the current local time and date.
SetSystemTime	Sets the current system time and date.
SetSystemTimeAdjustment	Enables or disables periodic time adjustments to the system's time-of-day clock.
SetTimeZoneInformation	Sets the current time-zone parameters.
SystemTimeToFileTime	Converts a system time to a file time.
SystemTimeToTzSpecificLocalTime	Converts a UTC time to a specified time zone's corresponding local time.

Source: Microsoft MSDN Windows SDK documentation.

The following is a sample call to the GetLocalTime function:

```
.data
sysTime SYSTEMTIME <>
.code
INVOKE GetLocalTime, ADDR sysTime
```

The **SetLocalTime** function sets the system's local date and time. When calling it, pass a pointer to a SYSTEMTIME structure containing the desired date and time:

```
SetLocalTime PROTO,
   lpSystemTime:PTR SYSTEMTIME
```

If the function executes successfully, it returns a nonzero integer; if it fails, it returns zero.

GetTickCount Function

The **GetTickCount** function returns the number of milliseconds that have elapsed since the system was started:

```
GetTickCount PROTO                    ; return value in EAX
```

Because the returned value is a doubleword, the time will wrap around to zero if the system is run continuously for 49.7 days. You can use this function to monitor the elapsed time in a loop and break out of the loop when a certain time limit has been reached.

The following *Timer.asm* program measures the elapsed time between two calls to GetTickCount. It verifies that the timer count has not rolled over (beyond 49.7 days). Similar code could be used in a variety of programs:

```
TITLE Calculate Elapsed Time                    (Timer.asm)

; Demonstrate a simple stopwatch timer, using
; the Win32 GetTickCount function.

INCLUDE Irvine32.inc
INCLUDE macros.inc

.data
startTime DWORD ?

.code
main PROC
    INVOKE GetTickCount         ; get starting tick count
    mov    startTime,eax        ; save it

    ; Create a useless calculation loop.
    mov    ecx,10000100h
L1: imul   ebx
    imul   ebx
    imul   ebx
    loop   L1

    INVOKE GetTickCount         ; get new tick count
    cmp    eax,startTime        ; lower than starting one?
    jb     error                ; it wrapped around

    sub    eax,startTime        ; get elapsed milliseconds
    call   WriteDec             ; display it
    mWrite <" milliseconds have elapsed",0dh,0ah>
    jmp    quit

error:
    mWrite "Error: GetTickCount invalid--system has"
    mWrite <"been active for more than 49.7 days",0dh,0ah>
quit:
    exit
main ENDP
END main
```

Sleep Function

Programs sometimes need to pause or delay for short periods of time. Although one could construct a calculation loop or busy loop that keeps the processor busy, the loop's execution time would vary from one processor to the next. In addition, the busy loop would needlessly tie up the processor, slowing down other programs executing at the same time. The Win32 **Sleep** function suspends the currently executing thread for a specified number of milliseconds:

```
Sleep PROTO,
      dwMilliseconds:DWORD
```

(Because our assembly language programs are single-threaded, we will assume a thread is the same as a program.) A thread uses no processor time while it is sleeping.

GetDateTime Procedure

The **GetDateTime** procedure in the Irvine32 library returns the number of 100-nanosecond time intervals that have elapsed since January 1, 1601. This may seem a little odd, in that computers were completely unknown at the time. In any event, Microsoft uses this value to keep track of file dates and times. The following steps are recommended by the Win32 SDK when you want to prepare a system date/time value for date arithmetic:

1. Call a function such as **GetLocalTime** that fills in a SYSTEMTIME structure.
2. Convert the SYSTEMTIME structure to a FILETIME structure by calling the **SystemTimeToFileTime** function.
3. Copy the resulting FILETIME structure to a 64-bit quadword.

A FILETIME structure divides a 64-bit quadword into two doublewords:

```
FILETIME STRUCT
      loDateTime DWORD ?
      hiDateTime DWORD ?
FILETIME ENDS
```

The following **GetDateTime** procedure receives a pointer to a 64-bit quadword variable. It stores the current date and time in the variable, in Win32 FILETIME format:

```
;-------------------------------------------------------
GetDateTime PROC,
      pStartTime:PTR QWORD
      LOCAL sysTime:SYSTEMTIME, flTime:FILETIME
;
; Gets and saves the current local date/time as a
; 64-bit integer (in the Win32 FILETIME format).
;-------------------------------------------------------
; Get the system local time
      INVOKE GetLocalTime,
        ADDR sysTime

; Convert the SYSTEMTIME to FILETIME
      INVOKE SystemTimeToFileTime,
        ADDR sysTime,
        ADDR flTime

; Copy the FILETIME to a 64-bit integer
      mov     esi,pStartTime
      mov     eax,flTime.loDateTime
      mov     DWORD PTR [esi],eax
      mov     eax,flTime.hiDateTime
      mov     DWORD PTR [esi+4],eax
      ret
GetDateTime ENDP
```

Because a SYSTEMTIME is a 64-bit integer, you can use the extended precision arithmetic techniques shown in Section 7.5 to perform date arithmetic.

11.1.13   Section Review

1. What is the linker command that specifies that the target program is for the Win32 console?

2. *(True/False):* A function ending with the letter W (such as WriteConsoleW) is designed to work with a wide (16-bit) character set such as Unicode.

3. *(True/False):* Unicode is the native character set for Windows 98.

4. *(True/False):* The **ReadConsole** function reads mouse information from the input buffer.

5. *(True/False):* Win32 console input functions can detect when the user has resized the console window.

6. Name the MASM data type that matches each of the following standard MS-Windows types:

    BOOL
    COLORREF
    HANDLE
    LPSTR
    WPARAM

7. Which Win32 function returns a handle to standard input?

8. Which Win32 function reads a string of text from the keyboard and places the string in a buffer?

9. Show an example call to the **ReadConsole** function.

10. Describe the COORD structure.

11. Show an example call to the **WriteConsole** function.

12. Show an example call to the **CreateFile** function that will open an existing file for reading.

13. Show an example call to the **CreateFile** function that will create a new file with normal attributes, erasing any existing file by the same name.

14. Show an example call to the **ReadFile** function.

15. Show an example call to the **WriteFile** function.

16. Which Win32 function moves the file pointer to a specified offset relative to the beginning of a file?

17. Which Win32 function changes the title of the console window?

18. Which Win32 function lets you change the dimensions of the screen buffer?

19. Which Win32 function lets you change the size of the cursor?

20. Which Win32 function lets you change the color of subsequent text output?

21. Which Win32 function lets you copy an array of attribute values to consecutive cells of the console screen buffer?

22. Which Win32 function lets you pause a program for a specified number of milliseconds?

11.2   Writing a Graphical Windows Application

In this section, we will show how to write a simple graphical application for Microsoft Windows. The program creates and displays a main window, displays message boxes, and responds to mouse events. The information provided here is only a brief introduction; it would require at least an entire chapter to describe the workings of even the simplest MS-Windows application. If you want more information, see the Platform SDK documentation. Another great source is Charles Petzold's book, *Programming in Windows: The Definitive Guide to the Win32 API*.

Table 11-10 lists the various libraries and includes files used when building this program. Use the Visual Studio project file located in the book's Examples\Ch11\WinApp folder to build and run the program.

/SUBSYSTEM:WINDOWS replaces the /SUBSYSTEM:CONSOLE we used in previous chapters. The program calls functions from two standard MS-Windows libraries: kernel32.lib and user32.lib.

TABLE 11-10   Files Required When Building the WinApp Program.

Filename	Description
WinApp.asm	Program source code
GraphWin.inc	Include file containing structures, constants, and function prototypes used by the program
kernel32.lib	Same MS-Windows API library used earlier in this chapter
user32.lib	Additional MS-Windows API functions

Main Window The program displays a main window which fills the screen. It is reduced in size here to make it fit on the printed page (Figure 11–4).

FIGURE 11–4   Main Startup Window, WinApp Program.

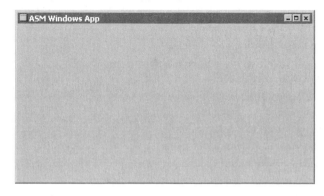

11.2.1 Necessary Structures

The **POINT** structure specifies the X and Y coordinates of a point on the screen, measured in pixels. It can be used, for example, to locate graphic objects, windows, and mouse clicks:

```
POINT STRUCT
     ptX   DWORD ?
     ptY   DWORD ?
POINT ENDS
```

The **RECT** structure defines the boundaries of a rectangle. The **left** member contains the X-coordinate of the left side of the rectangle. The **top** member contains the Y-coordinate of the top of the rectangle. Similar values are stored in the **right** and **bottom** members:

```
RECT STRUCT
     left          DWORD ?
     top           DWORD ?
     right         DWORD ?
     bottom        DWORD ?
RECT ENDS
```

The **MSGStruct** structure defines the data needed for a MS-Windows message:

```
MSGStruct STRUCT
     msgWnd        DWORD ?
     msgMessage    DWORD ?
     msgWparam     DWORD ?
```

```
        msgLparam     DWORD ?
        msgTime       DWORD ?
        msgPt         POINT <>
MSGStruct ENDS
```

The **WNDCLASS** structure defines a window class. Each window in a program must belong to a class, and each program must define a window class for its main window. This class is registered with the operating system before the main window can be shown:

```
WNDCLASS STRUC
    style             DWORD ?       ; window style options
    lpfnWndProc       DWORD ?       ; pointer to WinProc function
    cbClsExtra        DWORD ?       ; shared memory
    cbWndExtra        DWORD ?       ; number of extra bytes
    hInstance         DWORD ?       ; handle to current program
    hIcon             DWORD ?       ; handle to icon
    hCursor           DWORD ?       ; handle to cursor
    hbrBackground     DWORD ?       ; handle to background brush
    lpszMenuName      DWORD ?       ; pointer to menu name
    lpszClassName     DWORD ?       ; pointer to WinClass name
WNDCLASS ENDS
```

Here's a quick summary of the parameters:

- *style* is a conglomerate of different style options, such as WS_CAPTION and WS_BORDER, that control the window's appearance and behavior.
- *lpfnWndProc* is a pointer to a function (in our program) that receives and processes event messages triggered by the user.
- *cbClsExtra* refers to shared memory used by all windows belonging to the class. Can be null.
- *cbWndExtra* specifies the number of extra bytes to allocate following the window instance.
- *hInstance* holds a handle to the current program instance.
- *hIcon* and *hCursor* hold handles to icon and cursor resources for the current program.
- *hbrBackground* holds a background (color) brush.
- *lpszMenuName* points to a menu name.
- *lpszClassName* points to a null-terminated string containing the window's class name.

11.2.2 The MessageBox Function

The easiest way for a program to display text is to put it in a message box that pops up and waits for the user to click on a button. The **MessageBox** function from the Win32 API library displays a simple message box. Its prototype is shown here:

```
MessageBox PROTO,
        hWnd:DWORD,
        lpText:PTR BYTE,
        lpCaption:PTR BYTE,
        uType:DWORD
```

hWnd is a handle to the current window. *lpText* points to a null-terminated string that will appear inside the box. *lpCaption* points to a null-terminated string that will appear in the box's caption bar. *style* is an integer that describes both the dialog box's icon (optional) and the buttons (required). Buttons are identified by constants such as MB_OK and MB_YESNO. Icons are also identified by constants such as MB_ICONQUESTION. When a message box is displayed, you can add together the constants for the icon and buttons:

```
INVOKE MessageBox, hWnd, ADDR QuestionText,
        ADDR QuestionTitle, MB_OK + MB_ICONQUESTION
```

11.2.3   The WinMain Procedure

Every Windows application needs a startup procedure, usually named **WinMain**, which is responsible for the following tasks:

- Get a handle to the current program.
- Load the program's icon and mouse cursor.
- Register the program's main window class and identify the procedure that will process event messages for the window.
- Create the main window.
- Show and update the main window.
- Begin a loop that receives and dispatches messages. The loop continues until the user closes the application window.

WinMain contains a message processing loop that calls **GetMessage** to retrieve the next available message from the program's message queue. If GetMessage retrieves a WM_QUIT message, it returns zero, telling WinMain that it's time to halt the program. For all other messages, WinMain passes them to the **DispatchMessage** function, which forwards them to the program's WinProc procedure. To read more about messages, search for *Windows Messages* in the Platform SDK documentation.

11.2.4   The WinProc Procedure

The **WinProc** procedure receives and processes all event messages relating to a window. Most events are initiated by the user by clicking and dragging the mouse, pressing keyboard keys, and so on. This procedure's job is to decode each message, and if the message is recognized, to carry out application-oriented tasks relating to the message. Here is the declaration:

```
WinProc PROC,
        hWnd:DWORD,              ; handle to the window
        localMsg:DWORD,          ; message ID
        wParam:DWORD,            ; parameter 1 (varies)
        lParam:DWORD             ; parameter 2 (varies)
```

The content of the third and fourth parameters will vary, depending on the specific message ID. When the mouse is clicked, for example, *lParam* contains the X- and Y-coordinates of the point clicked. In the upcoming example program, the **WinProc** procedure handles three specific messages:

- WM_LBUTTONDOWN, generated when the user presses the left mouse button
- WM_CREATE, indicates that the main window was just created
- WM_CLOSE, indicates that the application's main window is about to close

For example, the following lines (from the procedure) handle the WM_LBUTTONDOWN message by calling **MessageBox** to display a popup message to the user:

```
.IF eax == WM_LBUTTONDOWN
   INVOKE MessageBox, hWnd, ADDR PopupText,
     ADDR PopupTitle, MB_OK
   jmp WinProcExit
```

The resulting message seen by the user is shown in Figure 11–5. Any other messages that we don't wish to handle are passed on to **DefWindowProc**, the default message handler for MS-Windows.

FIGURE 11–5   Popup Window, WinApp Program.

11.2.5   The ErrorHandler Procedure

The **ErrorHandler** procedure, which is optional, is called if the system reports an error during the registration and creation of the program's main window. For example, the **RegisterClass** function returns a nonzero value if the program's main window was successfully registered. But if it returns zero, we call **ErrorHandler** (to display a message) and quit the program:

```
INVOKE RegisterClass, ADDR MainWin
.IF eax == 0
  call ErrorHandler
  jmp Exit_Program
.ENDIF
```

The **ErrorHandler** procedure has several important tasks to perform:

- Call **GetLastError** to retrieve the system error number.
- Call **FormatMessage** to retrieve the appropriate system-formatted error message string.
- Call **MessageBox** to display a popup message box containing the error message string.
- Call **LocalFree** to free the memory used by the error message string.

11.2.6   Program Listing

Don't be distressed by the length of this program. Much of it is code that would be identical in any MS-Windows application:

```
TITLE Windows Application                 (WinApp.asm)

; This program displays a resizable application window and
; several popup message boxes. Special thanks to Tom Joyce
; for the first version of this program.

.386
.model flat,STDCALL
INCLUDE GraphWin.inc

;==================== DATA ======================
.data

AppLoadMsgTitle BYTE "Application Loaded",0
AppLoadMsgText  BYTE "This window displays when the WM_CREATE "
                BYTE "message is received",0

PopupTitle  BYTE "Popup Window",0
PopupText   BYTE "This window was activated by a "
            BYTE "WM_LBUTTONDOWN message",0

GreetTitle  BYTE "Main Window Active",0
GreetText   BYTE "This window is shown immediately after "
            BYTE "CreateWindow and UpdateWindow are called.",0

CloseMsg    BYTE "WM_CLOSE message received",0

ErrorTitle  BYTE "Error",0
WindowName  BYTE "ASM Windows App",0
className   BYTE "ASMWin",0

; Define the Application's Window class structure.
MainWin WNDCLASS <NULL,WinProc,NULL,NULL,NULL,NULL,NULL, \
    COLOR_WINDOW,NULL,className>

msg       MSGStruct <>
winRect   RECT <>
hMainWnd  DWORD ?
hInstance DWORD ?
```

```asm
;==================== CODE =========================
.code
WinMain PROC

; Get a handle to the current process.
    INVOKE GetModuleHandle, NULL
    mov    hInstance, eax
    mov    MainWin.hInstance, eax

; Load the program's icon and cursor.
    INVOKE LoadIcon, NULL, IDI_APPLICATION
    mov    MainWin.hIcon, eax
    INVOKE LoadCursor, NULL, IDC_ARROW
    mov    MainWin.hCursor, eax

; Register the window class.
    INVOKE RegisterClass, ADDR MainWin
    .IF eax == 0
      call ErrorHandler
      jmp Exit_Program
    .ENDIF

; Create the application's main window.
    INVOKE CreateWindowEx, 0, ADDR className,
      ADDR WindowName,MAIN_WINDOW_STYLE,
      CW_USEDEFAULT,CW_USEDEFAULT,CW_USEDEFAULT,
      CW_USEDEFAULT,NULL,NULL,hInstance,NULL

; If CreateWindowEx failed, display a message and exit.
    .IF eax == 0
      call ErrorHandler
      jmp  Exit_Program
    .ENDIF

; Save the window handle, show and draw the window.
    mov hMainWnd,eax
    INVOKE ShowWindow, hMainWnd, SW_SHOW
    INVOKE UpdateWindow, hMainWnd

; Display a greeting message.
    INVOKE MessageBox, hMainWnd, ADDR GreetText,
      ADDR GreetTitle, MB_OK

; Begin the program's continuous message-handling loop.
Message_Loop:
    ; Get next message from the queue.
    INVOKE GetMessage, ADDR msg, NULL,NULL,NULL

    ; Quit if no more messages.
    .IF eax == 0
      jmp Exit_Program
    .ENDIF

    ; Relay the message to the program's WinProc.
    INVOKE DispatchMessage, ADDR msg
    jmp Message_Loop

Exit_Program:
    INVOKE ExitProcess,0
WinMain ENDP
```

In the previous loop, the **msg** structure is passed to the **GetMessage** function. It fills in the structure, which is then passed to the MS-Windows **DispatchMessage** function.

```
;----------------------------------------------------
WinProc PROC,
     hWnd:DWORD, localMsg:DWORD, wParam:DWORD, lParam:DWORD
;
; The application's message handler, which handles
; application-specific messages. All other messages
; are forwarded to the default Windows message
; handler.
;----------------------------------------------------
     mov eax, localMsg

     .IF eax == WM_LBUTTONDOWN            ; mouse button?
       INVOKE MessageBox, hWnd, ADDR PopupText,
         ADDR PopupTitle, MB_OK
       jmp WinProcExit
     .ELSEIF eax == WM_CREATE            ; create window?
       INVOKE MessageBox, hWnd, ADDR AppLoadMsgText,
         ADDR AppLoadMsgTitle, MB_OK
       jmp WinProcExit
     .ELSEIF eax == WM_CLOSE             ; close window?
       INVOKE MessageBox, hWnd, ADDR CloseMsg,
         ADDR WindowName, MB_OK
       INVOKE PostQuitMessage,0
       jmp WinProcExit
     .ELSE                               ; other message?
       INVOKE DefWindowProc, hWnd, localMsg, wParam, lParam
       jmp WinProcExit
     .ENDIF

WinProcExit:
     ret
WinProc ENDP

;----------------------------------------------------
ErrorHandler PROC
; Display the appropriate system error message.
;----------------------------------------------------
.data
pErrorMsg  DWORD ?                  ; ptr to error message
messageID  DWORD ?
.code
     INVOKE GetLastError            ; Returns message ID in EAX
     mov    messageID,eax

     ; Get the corresponding message string.
     INVOKE FormatMessage, FORMAT_MESSAGE_ALLOCATE_BUFFER + \
       FORMAT_MESSAGE_FROM_SYSTEM,NULL,messageID,NULL,
       ADDR pErrorMsg,NULL,NULL

     ; Display the error message.
     INVOKE MessageBox,NULL, pErrorMsg, ADDR ErrorTitle,
       MB_ICONERROR+MB_OK

     ; Free the error message string.
```

```
        INVOKE LocalFree, pErrorMsg
        ret
ErrorHandler ENDP
END WinMain
```

Running the Program

When the program first loads, the following message box displays:

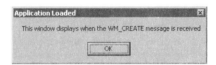

When the user clicks on OK to close the **Application Loaded** message box, another message box displays:

When the user closes the **Main Window Active** message box, the program's main window displays:

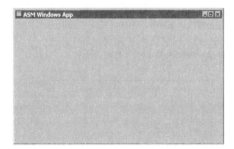

When the user clicks the mouse anywhere inside the main window, the following message box displays:

When the user closes this message box and then clicks on the X in the upper-right corner of the main window, the following message displays just before the window closes:

When the user closes this message box, the program ends.

11.2.7   Section Review

1. Describe a **POINT** structure.
2. How is the **WNDCLASS** structure used?

3. In a **WNDCLASS** structure, what is the meaning of the *lpfnWndProc* field?

4. In a **WNDCLASS** structure, what is the meaning of the *style* field?

5. In a **WNDCLASS** structure, what is the meaning of the *hInstance* field?

6. When **CreateWindowEx** is called, how is the window's appearance information transmitted to the function?

7. Show an example of calling the **MessageBox** function.

8. Name two button constants that can be used when calling the **MessageBox** function.

9. Name two icon constants that can be used when calling the **MessageBox** function.

10. Name at least three tasks performed by the **WinMain** (startup) procedure.

11. Describe the role of the **WinProc** procedure in the example program.

12. Which messages are processed by the **WinProc** procedure in the example program?

13. Describe the role of the **ErrorHandler** procedure in the example program.

14. Does the message box activated immediately after calling **CreateWindow** appear before or after the application's main window?

15. Does the message box activated by WM_CLOSE appear before or after the main window closes?

11.3 Dynamic Memory Allocation

Dynamic memory allocation, also known as *heap allocation*, is a tool programming languages have for reserving memory when objects, arrays, and other structures are created. In Java, for example, a statement such as the following causes memory to be reserved for a String object:

```
String str = new String("abcde");
```

Similarly, in C++ you might want to allocate space for an array of integers, using a size attribute from a variable:

```
int size;
cin >> size;                    // user inputs the size
int array[] = new int[size];
```

C, C++, and Java have built-in runtime heap managers that handle programmatic requests for storage allocation and deallocation. Heap managers generally allocate a large block of memory from the operating system when the program starts up. They create a *free list* of pointers to storage blocks. When an allocation request is received, the heap manager marks an appropriately sized block of memory as reserved and returns a pointer to the block. Later, when a delete request for the same block is received, the heap frees up the block, returning it to the free list. Each time a new allocation request is received, the heap manager scans the free list, looking for the first available block large enough to grant the request.

Assembly language programs can perform dynamic allocation in a couple of ways. First, they can make system calls to get blocks of memory from the operating system. Second, they can implement their own heap managers that serve requests for smaller objects. In this section, we show how to implement the first method. The example program is a 32-bit protected mode application.

You can request multiple blocks of memory of varying sizes from MS-Windows, using several Windows API functions listed in Table 11-11. All of these functions overwrite the general-purpose registers, so you may want to create wrapper procedures that push and pop important registers. To learn more about memory management, search for *Memory Management Reference* in the Platform SDK documentation.

GetProcessHeap GetProcessHeap is suffcent if you're content to use the default heap owned by the current program. It has no parameters, and the return value in EAX is the heap handle:

```
GetProcessHeap PROTO
```

Table 11-11   Heap-Related Functions

Function	Description
GetProcessHeap	Returns a 32-bit integer handle to the program's existing heap area in EAX. If the function succeeds, it returns a handle to the heap in EAX. If it fails, the return value in EAX is NULL.
HeapAlloc	Allocates a block of memory from a heap. If it succeeds, the return value in EAX contains the address of the memory block. If it fails, the returned value in EAX is NULL.
HeapCreate	Creates a new heap and makes it available to the calling program. If the function succeeds, it returns a handle to the newly created heap in EAX. If it fails, the return value in EAX is NULL.
HeapDestroy	Destroys the specified heap object and invalidates its handle. If the function succeeds, the return value in EAX is nonzero.
HeapFree	Frees a block of memory previously allocated from a heap, identified by its address and heap handle. If the block is freed successfully, the return value is nonzero.
HeapReAlloc	Reallocates and resizes a block of memory from a heap. If the function succeeds, the return value is a pointer to the reallocated memory block. If the function fails and you have not specified HEAP_GENERATE_EXCEPTIONS, the return value is NULL.
HeapSize	Returns the size of a memory block previously allocated by a call to HeapAlloc or HeapReAlloc. If the function succeeds, EAX contains the size of the allocated memory block, in bytes. If the function fails, the return value is SIZE_T − 1. (SIZE_T equals the maximum number of bytes to which a pointer can point.)

Sample call:

```
.data
hHeap HANDLE ?
.code
INVOKE GetProcessHeap
.IF eax == NULL              ; cannot get handle
  jmp   quit
.ELSE
  mov   hHeap,eax            ; handle is OK
.ENDIF
```

HeapCreate   HeapCreate lets you create a new private heap for the current program:

```
HeapCreate PROTO,
    flOptions:DWORD,         ; heap allocation options
    dwInitialSize:DWORD,     ; initial heap size, in bytes
    dwMaximumSize:DWORD      ; maximum heap size, in bytes
```

Set *flOptions* to NULL. Set *dwInitialSize* to the initial heap size, in bytes. The value is rounded up to the next page boundary. When calls to HeapAlloc exceed the initial heap size, it will grow as large as the value you specify in the *dwMaximumSize* parameter (rounded up to the next page boundary). After calling it, a null return value in EAX indicates the heap was not created. The following is a sample call to HeapCreate:

```
HEAP_START =   2000000      ;   2 MB
HEAP_MAX   = 400000000      ; 400 MB
.data
hHeap HANDLE ?              ; handle to heap
```

```
.code
INVOKE HeapCreate, 0, HEAP_START, HEAP_MAX
.IF eax == NULL                    ; heap not created
  call WriteWindowsMsg             ; show error message
  jmp   quit
.ELSE
  mov   hHeap,eax                  ; handle is OK
.ENDIF
```

HeapDestroy   HeapDestroy destroys an existing private heap (one created by HeapCreate). Pass it a handle to the heap:

```
HeapDestroy PROTO,
     hHeap:DWORD                          ; heap handle
```

If it fails to destroy the heap, EAX equals NULL. Following is a sample call, using the WriteWindowsMsg procedure described in Section 11.1.4:

```
.data
hHeap HANDLE ?                     ; handle to heap
.code
INVOKE HeapDestroy, hHeap
.IF eax == NULL
  call WriteWindowsMsg             ; show error message
.ENDIF
```

HeapAlloc   HeapAlloc allocates a memory block from an existing heap:

```
HeapAlloc PROTO,
     hHeap:HANDLE,                 ; handle to private heap block
     dwFlags:DWORD,                ; heap allocation control flags
     dwBytes:DWORD                 ; number of bytes to allocate
```

Pass the following arguments:

- *hHeap*, a 32-bit handle to a heap that was initialized by GetProcessHeap or HeapCreate.
- *dwFlags*, a doubleword containing one or more flag values. You can optionally set it to HEAP_ZERO_MEMORY, which sets the memory block to all zeros.
- *dwBytes*, a doubleword indicating the size of the heap, in bytes.

If HeapAlloc fails, the value returned in EAX is NULL. The following statements allocate a 1000-byte array from the heap identified by **hHeap** and set its values to all zeros:

```
.data
hHeap HANDLE ?                     ; heap handle
pArray DWORD ?                     ; pointer to array
.code
INVOKE HeapAlloc, hHeap, HEAP_ZERO_MEMORY, 1000
.IF eax == NULL
  mWrite "HeapAlloc failed"
  jmp   quit
.ELSE
  mov   pArray,eax
.ENDIF
```

HeapFree   The HeapFree function frees a block of memory previously allocated from a heap, identified by its address and heap handle:

```
HeapFree PROTO,
     hHeap:HANDLE,
```

```
        dwFlags:DWORD,
        lpMem:DWORD
```

The first argument is a handle to the heap containing the memory block; the second argument is usually zero; the third argument is a pointer to the block of memory to be freed. If the block is freed successfully, the return value is nonzero. If the block cannot be freed, the function returns zero. Here is a sample call:

```
        INVOKE HeapFree, hHeap, 0, pArray
```

Error Handling   If you encounter an error when calling HeapCreate, HeapDestroy, or GetProcessHeap, you can get details by calling the **GetLastError** API function. Or, you can call the **WriteWindowsMsg** function from the Irvine32 library. Following is an example that calls HeapCreate:

```
        INVOKE HeapCreate, 0,HEAP_START, HEAP_MAX

.IF eax == NULL                      ; failed?
   call   WriteWindowsMsg            ; show error message
.ELSE
   mov    hHeap,eax                  ; success
.ENDIF
```

The **HeapAlloc** function, on the other hand, does not set a system error code when it fails, so you cannot call GetLastError or WriteWindowsMsg.

11.3.1 HeapTest Programs

The following example (*Heaptest1.asm*) uses dynamic memory allocation to create and fill a 1000-byte array:

```
        Title Heap Test #1                        (Heaptest1.asm)

        INCLUDE Irvine32.inc

        ; This program uses dynamic memory allocation to allocate and
        ; fill an array of bytes.

        .data
        ARRAY_SIZE = 1000
        FILL_VAL EQU 0FFh

        hHeap    HANDLE ?                 ; handle to the process heap
        pArray   DWORD ?                  ; pointer to block of memory
        newHeap DWORD ?                   ; handle to new heap
        str1 BYTE "Heap size is: ",0

        .code
        main PROC
            INVOKE GetProcessHeap         ; get handle prog's heap
            .IF eax == NULL               ; failed?
            call   WriteWindowsMsg
            jmp    quit
            .ELSE
            mov    hHeap,eax              ; success
            .ENDIF

            call   allocate_array
            jnc    arrayOk                ; failed (CF = 1)?
            call   WriteWindowsMsg
            call   Crlf
            jmp    quit

        arrayOk:                          ; ok to fill the array
```

```
        call    fill_array
        call    display_array
        call    Crlf

        ; free the array
        INVOKE HeapFree, hHeap, 0, pArray
quit:
        exit
main ENDP

;----------------------------------------------------------
allocate_array PROC USES eax
;
; Dynamically allocates space for the array.
; Receives: nothing
; Returns: CF = 0 if allocation succeeds.
;----------------------------------------------------------
        INVOKE HeapAlloc, hHeap, HEAP_ZERO_MEMORY, ARRAY_SIZE

        .IF eax == NULL
          stc                           ; return with CF = 1
        .ELSE
          mov   pArray,eax              ; save the pointer
          clc                           ; return with CF = 0
        .ENDIF

        ret
allocate_array ENDP

;----------------------------------------------------------
fill_array PROC USES ecx edx esi
;
; Fills all array positions with a single character.
; Receives: nothing
; Returns: nothing
;----------------------------------------------------------
        mov     ecx,ARRAY_SIZE          ; loop counter
        mov     esi,pArray              ; point to the array

L1:     mov     BYTE PTR [esi],FILL_VAL  ; fill each byte
        inc     esi                     ; next location
        loop    L1

        ret
fill_array ENDP

;----------------------------------------------------------
display_array PROC USES eax ebx ecx esi
;
; Displays the array
; Receives: nothing
; Returns: nothing
;----------------------------------------------------------
        mov     ecx,ARRAY_SIZE          ; loop counter
        mov     esi,pArray              ; point to the array

L1:     mov     al,[esi]                ; get a byte
        mov     ebx,TYPE BYTE
        call    WriteHexB               ; display it
```

```
        inc    esi                        ; next location
        loop   L1

        ret
display_array ENDP

END main
```

The following example (*Heaptest2.asm*) uses dynamic memory allocation to create and fill a 1000-byte array:

```
Title Heap Test #2                    (Heaptest2.asm)

INCLUDE Irvine32.inc

; Creates a heap and allocates multiple memory blocks,
; expanding the heap until it fails.

.data
HEAP_START =    2000000               ;   2 MB
HEAP_MAX   =  400000000               ; 400 MB
BLOCK_SIZE =     500000               ;  .5 MB

hHeap HANDLE ?                        ; handle to the heap
pData DWORD ?                         ; pointer to block

str1 BYTE 0dh,0ah,"Memory allocation failed",0dh,0ah,0

.code
main PROC
    INVOKE HeapCreate, 0,HEAP_START, HEAP_MAX

    .IF eax == NULL                  ; failed?
    call   WriteWindowsMsg
    call   Crlf
    jmp    quit
    .ELSE
    mov    hHeap,eax                 ; success
    .ENDIF

    mov    ecx,2000                  ; loop counter

L1: call allocate_block             ; allocate a block
    .IF Carry?                      ; failed?
    mov    edx,OFFSET str1          ; display message
    call   WriteString
    jmp    quit
    .ELSE                           ; no: print a dot to
    mov    al,'.'                   ; show progress
    call   WriteChar
    .ENDIF

    ;call  free_block               ; enable/disable this line
    loop   L1

quit:
    INVOKE HeapDestroy, hHeap        ; destroy the heap
    .IF eax == NULL                  ; failed?
    call   WriteWindowsMsg           ; yes: error message
    call   Crlf
    .ENDIF

    exit
```

```
main ENDP

allocate_block PROC USES ecx

    ; allocate a block and fill with all zeros.
    INVOKE HeapAlloc, hHeap, HEAP_ZERO_MEMORY, BLOCK_SIZE

    .IF eax == NULL
        stc                        ; return with CF = 1
    .ELSE
        mov  pData,eax             ; save the pointer
        clc                        ; return with CF = 0
    .ENDIF

    ret
allocate_block ENDP

free_block PROC USES ecx

    INVOKE HeapFree, hHeap, 0, pData
    ret
free_block ENDP
END main
```

11.3.2   Section Review

1.   What is another term for *heap allocation*, in the context of C, C++, and Java?
2.   Describe the GetProcessHeap function.
3.   Describe the HeapAlloc function.
4.   Show a sample call to the HeapCreate function.
5.   When calling HeapDestroy, how do you identify the memory block being destroyed?

11.4   IA-32 Memory Management

When MS-Windows 3.0 was first released, there was a great deal of interest among programmers about the switch from real-address mode to protected mode. (Anyone who wrote programs for Windows 2.x will recall how difficult it was to stay within 640K in real-address mode!) With Windows protected mode (and soon after, Virtual mode), whole new possibilities seemed to open up. One must not forget that it was the Intel386 processor (the first of the IA-32 family) that made all of this possible. What we now take for granted was a gradual evolution from the unstable Windows 3.0 to the sophisticated (and stable) versions of Windows and Linux offered today.

This section will focus on two primary aspects of memory management:

- Translating logical addresses into linear addresses
- Translating linear addresses into physical addresses (paging)

Let's briefly review some of the IA-32 memory-management terms introduced in Chapter 2, beginning with the following:

- *Multitasking* permits multiple programs (or tasks) to run at the same time. The processor divides its time among all of the running programs.
- *Segments* are variable-sized areas of memory used by a program containing either code or data.
- *Segmentation* provides a way to isolate memory segments from each other. This permits multiple programs to run simultaneously without interfering with each other.
- A *segment descriptor* is a 64-bit value that identifies and describes a single memory segment: It contains information about the segment's base address, access rights, size limit, type, and usage.

Now we will add two new terms to the list:

- A *segment selector* is a 16-bit value stored in a segment register (CS, DS, SS, ES, FS, or GS).
- A *logical address* is a combination of a segment selector and a 32-bit offset.

Segment registers have been ignored throughout this book because they are never modified directly by user programs. We have only been concerned with 32-bit data offsets. From a system programmer's point of view, however, segment registers are important because they contain indirect references to memory segments.

11.4.1   Linear Addresses

Translating Logical Addresses to Linear Addresses

A multitasking operating system allows several programs (tasks) to run in memory at the same time. Each program has its own unique area for data. Suppose three programs each had a variable at offset 200h; how could the three variables be separate from each other without being shared? The answer to this is that the IA-32 processor uses a one- or two-step process to convert each variable's offset into a unique memory location.

The first step combines a segment value with a variable's offset to create a *linear address*. This linear address could be the variable's physical address. But operating systems such as MS-Windows and Linux employ an IA-32 feature called *paging* to permit programs to use more linear memory than is physically available in the computer. They must use a second step called *page translation* to convert a linear address to a physical address. We will explain page translation in Section 11.4.2.

First, let's look at the way the processor uses a segment and offset to determine the linear address of a variable. Each segment selector points to a segment descriptor (in a descriptor table), which contains the base address of a memory segment. The 32-bit offset from the logical address is added to the segment's base address, generating a 32-bit *linear address*, as shown in Figure 11–6.

Linear Address   A *linear address* is a 32-bit integer ranging between 0 and FFFFFFFFh, which refers to a memory location. The linear address may also be the physical address of the target data if a feature called *paging* is disabled.

Paging

Paging is an important feature of the IA-32 processor that makes it possible for a computer to run a combination of programs that would not otherwise fit into memory. The processor does this by initially loading only part of a program in memory while keeping the remaining parts on disk. The memory used by the program is divided into small units called *pages*, typically 4KB each. As each program runs, the processor selectively unloads inactive pages from memory and loads other pages that are immediately required.

The operating system maintains a *page directory* and a set of *page tables* to keep track of the pages used by all programs currently in memory. When a program attempts to access an address somewhere in the linear address space, the processor automatically converts the linear address into a physical address. This conversion is called *page translation*. If the requested page is not currently in memory, the processor interrupts the program and issues a *page fault*. The operating system copies the required page from disk into memory before the program can resume. From the point of view of an application program, page faults and page translation happen automatically.

In Windows 2000, for example, you can activate a utility named *Task Manager* and see the difference between physical memory and virtual memory. Figure 11–7 shows a computer with 256MB of physical memory. The total amount of virtual memory currently in use is in the *Commit Charge* frame of the Task Manager. The virtual memory limit is 633MB, considerably larger than the computer's physical memory size.

FIGURE 11–6   Converting a Logical Address into a Linear Address.

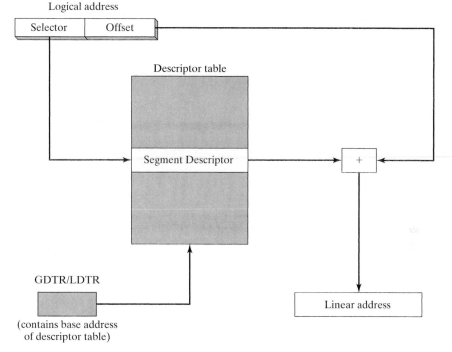

Descriptor Tables

Segment descriptors can be found in two types of tables: *global descriptor tables* (GDT) and *local descriptor tables* (LDT).

Global Descriptor Table (GDT)   A single global descriptor table is created when the operating system switches the processor into protected mode during boot up. Its base address is held in the GDTR (global descriptor table register). The table contains entries (called *segment descriptors*) that point to segments. The operating system has the option of storing the segments used by all programs in the GDT.

Local Descriptor Tables (LDT)   In a multitasking operating system, each task or program is usually assigned its own table of segment descriptors, called a *local descriptor table* (LDT). The LDTR register contains the address of the program's LDT. Each segment descriptor contains the base address of a segment within the linear address space. This segment is usually distinct from all other segments, as in Figure 11–8. Three different logical addresses are shown, each selecting a different entry in the LDT. In this figure we assume that paging is disabled, so the linear address space is also the physical address space.

Segment Descriptor Details

In addition to the segment's base address, the segment descriptor contains bit-mapped fields specifying the segment limit and segment type. An example of a read-only segment type is the code segment. If a program tries to modify a read-only segment, a processor fault is generated. Segment descriptors can contain protection levels that protect operating system data from access by application programs. The following are descriptions of individual selector fields:

Base address: A 32-bit integer that defines the starting location of the segment in the 4GB linear address space.

Figure 11–7   Windows Task Manager Example.

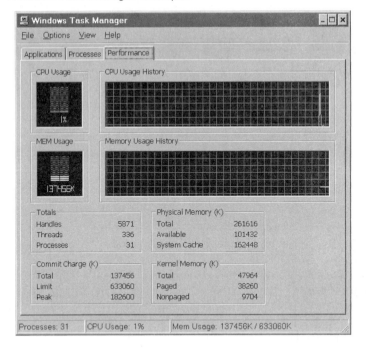

Figure 11–8   Indexing into a Local Descriptor Table.

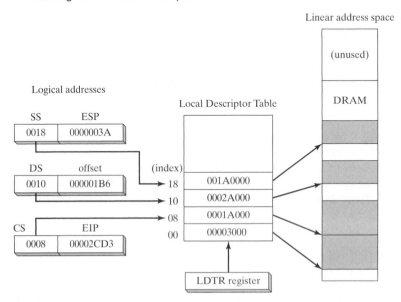

Privilege level: Each segment can be assigned a privilege level between 0 and 3, where 0 is the most privileged, usually for operating system kernel code. If a program with a higher-numbered privilege level tries to access a segment having a lower-numbered privilege level, a processor fault is generated.

Segment type: Indicates the type of segment and specifies the type of access that can be made to the segment and the direction the segment can grow (up or down). Data (including Stack) segments can be read-only or read/write and can grow either up or down. Code segments can be execute-only or execute/read-only.

Segment present flag: This bit indicates whether the segment is currently present in physical memory.

Granularity flag: Determines the interpretation of the Segment limit field. If the bit is clear, the segment limit is interpreted in byte units. If the bit is set, the segment limit is interpreted in 4096-byte units.

Segment limit: This 20-bit integer that specifies the size of the segment. It is interpreted in one of the following two ways, depending on the Granularity flag:

• The number of bytes in the segment, ranging from 1 to 1MB.
• The number of 4096-byte units, permitting the segment size to range from 4KB to 4GB.

11.4.2   Page Translation

When paging is enabled, the processor must translate a 32-bit linear address into a 32-bit physical address.[2] There are three structures used in the process:

• Page directory: An array of up to 1024 32-bit page-directory entries.
• Page table: An array of up to 1024 32-bit page-table entries.
• Page: A 4KB or 4MB address space.

To simplify the following discussion, we will assume that 4KB pages are used:

A linear address is divided into three fields: a pointer to a page directory entry, a pointer to a page table entry, and an offset into a page frame. Control register (CR3) contains the starting address of the page directory. The following steps are carried out by the processor when translating a linear address to a physical address, as shown in Figure 11–9:

1. The *linear address* references a location in the linear address space.
2. The 10-bit *directory* field in the linear address is an index to a page directory entry. The page directory entry contains the base address of a page table.
3. The 10-bit *table* field in the linear address is an index into the page table identified by the page directory entry. The page table entry at that position contains the base location of a *page* in physical memory.
4. The 12-bit *offset* field in the linear address is added to the base address of the page, generating the exact physical address of the operand.

The operating system has the option of using a single page directory for all running programs and tasks, or one page directory per task, or a combination of the two.

MS-Windows Virtual Machine Manager

Now that we have a general idea of how the IA-32 manages memory, it might be interesting to see how memory management is handled by MS-Windows. The following passage is paraphrased from the Platform SDK documentation:

> The Virtual Machine Manager (VMM) is the 32-bit protected mode operating system at the core of MS-Windows. It creates, runs, monitors, and terminates virtual machines. It manages memory, processes, interrupts, and exceptions. It works with *virtual devices*, allowing them to intercept interrupts and faults that control access to hardware and installed software. The VMM and virtual devices run in a single 32-bit flat model address space at privilege level 0. The system creates two global descriptor table entries (segment descriptors), one for code and the other for data. The segments are fixed at linear address 0. The VMM provides multithreaded, preemptive multitasking. It runs multiple applications simultaneously by sharing CPU time between the virtual machines in which the applications run.

FIGURE 11-9   Translating Linear Address to Physical Address.

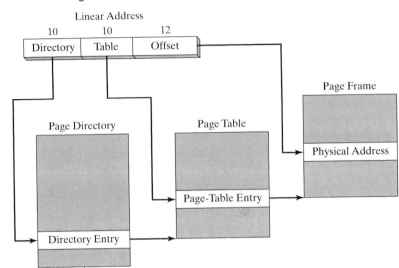

In the foregoing passage, we can interpret the term *virtual machine* to be what Intel calls a *process* or *task*. It consists of program code, supporting software, memory, and registers. Each virtual machine is assigned its own address space, I/O port space, interrupt vector table, and local descriptor table. Applications running in virtual-8086 mode run at privilege level 3. In MS-Windows, protected-mode programs run at privilege levels 0 and 3.

11.4.3   Section Review

1. Define the following terms:
   a. Multitasking.
   b. Segmentation.
2. Define the following terms:
   a. Segment selector
   b. Logical address
3. (*True/False*): A segment selector points to an entry in a segment descriptor table.
4. (*True/False*): A segment descriptor contains the base location of a segment.
5. (*True/False*): A segment selector is 32 bits.
6. (*True/False*): A segment descriptor does not contain segment size information.
7. Describe a linear address.
8. How does paging relate to linear memory?
9. If paging is disabled, how does the processor translate a linear address to a physical address?
10. What advantage does paging offer?
11. Which register contains the base location of a local descriptor table?
12. Which register contains the base location of a global descriptor table?
13. How many global descriptor tables can exist?

14. How many local descriptor tables can exist?

15. Name at least four fields in a segment descriptor.

16. Which structures are involved in the paging process?

17. What structure contains the base address of a page table?

18. What structure contains the base address of a page frame?

11.5   Chapter Summary

On the surface, 32-bit console mode programs look and behave like 16-bit MS-DOS programs running in text mode. Both types of programs read from standard input and write to standard output, they support command-line redirection, and they can display text in color. Beneath the surface, however, Win32 consoles and MS-DOS programs are quite different. Win32 runs in 32-bit protected mode, whereas MS-DOS runs in real-address mode. Win32 programs can call functions from the same function library used by graphical Windows applications. MS-DOS programs are limited to a smaller set of BIOS and MS-DOS interrupts that have existed since the introduction of the IBM-PC.

Types of character sets are used in Windows API functions: the 8-bit ASCII/ANSI character set and a 16-bit version of the Unicode character set.

Standard MS-Windows data types used in the API functions must be translated to MASM data types (see Table 11-1).

Console handles are 32-bit integers used for input/output in console windows. The **GetStdHandle** function retrieves a console handle. For high-level console input, call the **ReadConsole** function; for high-level output, call **WriteConsole**. When creating or opening a file, call **CreateFile**. When reading from a file, call **ReadFile**, and when writing, call **WriteFile**. **CloseHandle** closes a file. To move a file pointer, call **SetFilePointer**.

To manipulate the console screen buffer, call **SetConsoleScreenBufferSize**. To change the text color, call **SetConsoleTextAttribute**. The WriteColors program in this chapter demonstrated the **WriteConsoleOutputAttribute** and **WriteConsoleOutputCharacter** functions.

To get the system time, call **GetLocalTime**; to set the time, call **SetLocalTime**. Both functions use the SYSTEMTIME structure. The **GetDateTime** function example in this chapter returns the date and time as a 64-bit integer, specifying the number of 100-nanosecond intervals that have occurred since January 1, 1601. The **TimerStart** and **TimerStop** functions can be used to create a simple stopwatch timer.

When creating a graphical MS-Windows application, fill in a WNDCLASS structure with information about the program's main window class. Create a **WinMain** procedure that gets a handle to the current process, loads the icon and mouse cursor, registers the program's main window, creates the main window, shows and updates the main windows, and begins a message loop that receives and dispatches messages.

The **WinProc** procedure is responsible for handling incoming Windows messages, often activated by user actions such as a mouse click or keystroke. Our example program processes a WM_LBUTTONDOWN message, a WM_CREATE message, and a WM_CLOSE message. It displays popup messages when these events are detected.

Dynamic memory allocation, or heap allocation, is a tool you can use to reserve memory and free memory for use by your program. Assembly language programs can perform dynamic allocation in a couple of ways. First, they can make system calls to get blocks of memory from the operating system. Second, they can implement their own heap managers that serve requests for smaller objects. Following are the most important Win32 API calls for dynamic memory allocation:

• GetProcessHeap returns a 32-bit integer handle to the program's existing heap area.

• HeapAlloc allocates a block of memory from a heap.

- HeapCreate creates a new heap.
- HeapDestroy destroys a heap.
- HeapFree frees a block of memory previously allocated from a heap.
- HeapReAlloc reallocates and resizes a block of memory from a heap.
- HeapSize returns the size of a previously allocated memory block.

The memory management section of this chapter focuses on two main topics: translating logical addresses into linear addresses and translating linear addresses into physical addresses.

The selector in a logical address points to an entry in a segment descriptor table, which in turn points to a segment in linear memory. The segment descriptor contains information about the segment, including its size and type of access. There are two types of descriptor tables: a single global descriptor table (GDT) and one or more local descriptor tables (LDT).

Paging is an important feature of the IA-32 processor that makes it possible for a computer to run a combination of programs that would not otherwise fit into memory. The processor does this by initially loading only part of a program in memory, while keeping the remaining parts on disk. The processor uses a page directory, page table, and page frame to generate the physical location of data. A page directory contains pointers to page tables. A page table contains pointers to pages.

Reading   For further reading about Windows programming, the following books may be helpful:

- Mark Russinovich and David Solomon, *Microsoft Windows Internals 4th Ed.*, Microsoft Press, 2004.
- Barry Kauler, *Windows Assembly Language and System Programming*, CMP Books, 1997.
- Charles Petzold, *Programming Windows, 5th Ed.*, Microsoft Press, 1998.

11.6 Programming Exercises

1. ReadString

Implement your own version of the **ReadString** procedure, using stack parameters. Pass it a pointer to a string and an integer indicating the maximum number of characters to be entered. Return a count (in EAX) of the number of characters actually entered. The procedure must input a string from the console and insert a null byte at the end of the string (in the position occupied by 0Dh). See Section 11.1.4 for details on the Win32 **ReadConsole** function. Write a short program that tests your procedure.

2. String Input/Output

Write a program that inputs the following information from the user, using the Win32 **ReadConsole** function: first name, last name, age, phone number. Redisplay the same information with labels and attractive formatting, using the Win32 **WriteConsole** function. Do not use any procedures from the Irvine32 library.

3. Clearing the Screen

Write your own version of the link library's **Clrscr** procedure that clears the screen.

4. Random Screen Fill

Write a program that fills each screen cell with a random character in a random color. *Extra:* Assign a 50% probability that the color of any character will be red.

5. DrawBox

Draw a box on the screen using line-drawing characters from the character set listed on the inside back cover of the book. *Hint:* Use the **WriteConsoleOutputCharacter** function.

6. Student Records

Write a program that creates a new text file. Prompt the user for a student identification number, last name, first name, and date of birth. Write this information to the file. Input several more records in the same manner and close the file.

7.   Scrolling Text Window

Write a program that writes 50 lines of text to the console screen buffer. Number each line. Move the console window to the top of the buffer, and begin scrolling the text upward at a steady rate (two lines per second). Stop scrolling when the console window reaches the end of the buffer.

8.   Block Animation

Write a program that draws a small square on the screen using several blocks (ASCII code DBh) in color. Move the square around the screen in randomly generated directions. Use a fixed delay value of 50 milliseconds. *Extra:* Use a randomly generated delay value between 10 and 100 milliseconds.

9.   Last Access Date of a File

Write a procedure named **LastAccessDate** that fills a SYSTEMTIME structure with the date and time stamp information of a file. Pass the offset of a filename in EDX, and pass the offset of a SYSTEMTIME structure in ESI. If the function fails to find the file, set the Carry flag. When you implement this function, you will need to open the file, get its handle, pass the handle to **GetFileTime**, pass its output to **FileTimeToSystemTime**, and close the file. Write a test program that calls your procedure and prints out the date when a particular file was last accessed. Sample:

```
ch11_09.asm was last accessed on: 6/16/2005
```

10.   Reading a Large File

Modify the ReadFile.asm program in Section 11.1.8 so that it can read files larger than its input buffer. Reduce the buffer size to 1024 bytes. Use a loop to continue reading and displaying the file until it can read no more data. If you plan to display the buffer with WriteString, remember to insert a null byte at the end of the buffer data.

11.   Linked List

Advanced: Implement a singly linked list, using the dynamic memory allocation functions presented in this chapter. Each link should be a structure named Node (see Chapter 10) containing an integer value and a pointer to the next link in the list. Using a loop, prompt the user for as many integers as they want to enter. As each integer is entered, allocate a Node object, insert the integer in the Node, and append the Node to the linked list. When a value of 0 is entered, stop the loop. Finally, display the entire list from beginning to end. *This project should only be attempted if you have previously created linked lists in a high-level language.*

End Notes

1. Source: Microsoft MSDN Documentation.
2. The Pentium Pro and later processors permit a 36-bit address option, but it will not be covered here.

12

High-Level Language Interface

12.1 Introduction

Most programmers do not write large-scale applications in assembly language, doing so would require too much time. Instead, high-level languages hide details that would otherwise slow down a project's development. Assembly language is still used widely, however, to configure hardware devices and optimize both the speed and code size of programs.

In this chapter, we focus on the *interface*, or connection, between assembly language and high-level programming languages. In the first section, we will show how to write inline assembly code in C++. In the next section, we will link separate assembly language modules to C++ programs. Examples are shown for both protected mode and real-address mode. Finally, we will show how to call C and C++ functions from assembly language.

12.1.1 General Conventions

There are a number of general considerations that must be addressed when calling assembly language procedures from high-level languages.

First, the *naming convention* used by a language refers to the rules or characteristics regarding the naming of variables and procedures. For example, we have to answer an important question: Does the assembler or compiler alter the names of identifiers placed in object files, and if so, how?

Second, *segment names* must be compatible with those used by the high-level language.

Third, the *memory model* used by a program (tiny, small, compact, medium, large, huge, or flat) determines the segment size (16 or 32 bits), and whether calls and references will be near (within the same segment) or far (between different segments).

Calling Convention   The *calling convention* refers to the low-level details about how procedures are called. The following details must be considered:

- Which registers must be preserved by called procedures.
- The method used to pass arguments: in registers, on the stack, in shared memory, or by some other method.
- The order in which arguments are passed by calling programs to procedures.
- Whether arguments are passed by value or by reference.
- How the stack pointer is restored after a procedure call.
- How functions return values to calling programs.

External Identifiers   When calling an assembly language procedure from a program written in another language, external identifiers must have compatible naming conventions. *External identifiers* are names that have been placed in a module's object file in such a way that the linker can make the names available to other program modules. The linker resolves references to external identifiers, but can only do so if the naming conventions being used are consistent.

For example, suppose a C program named *Main.c* calls an external procedure named **ArraySum**. As illustrated in the following diagram, the C compiler automatically preserves case and appends a leading underscore to the external name, changing it to **_ArraySum**:

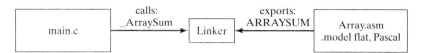

The *Array.asm* module, written in assembly language, exports the **ArraySum** procedure name as ARRAYSUM because the module uses the Pascal language option in its .MODEL directive. The linker fails to produce an executable program because the two exported names are different.

Compilers for older programming languages such as COBOL and PASCAL usually convert identifiers to all uppercase letters. More recent languages such as C, C++, and Java preserve the case of identifiers. In addition, languages that support function overloading (such as C++) use a technique known as *name decoration* that adds additional characters to function names. A function named *MySub(int n, double b)*, for example, might be exported as *MySub#int#double*.

In an assembly language module, you can control case sensitivity by choosing one of the language specifiers in the .MODEL directive (see Section 8.4.1 for details).

Segment Names   When linking an assembly language procedure to a program written in a high-level language, segment names must be compatible. In this chapter, we use the Microsoft simplified segment directives .CODE, .STACK, and .DATA because they are compatible with segment names produced by Microsoft C++ compilers.

Memory Models   A calling program and a called procedure must both use the same memory model. In real-address mode, for example, you can choose from the small, medium, compact, large, and huge models. In protected mode, you must use the flat model. We show examples of both modes in this chapter.

12.1.2   Section Review

1.   What is meant by the *naming convention* used by a language?

2.   Which memory models are available in real-address mode?

3.   Will an assembly language procedure that uses the *Pascal* language specifier link to a C++ program?

4.   When a procedure written in assembly language is called by a high-level language program, must the calling program and the procedure use the same memory model?

5.   Why is case sensitivity important when calling assembly language procedures from C and C++ programs?

6.   Does a language's calling convention include the preserving of certain registers by procedures?

12.2   Inline Assembly Code

12.2.1   __asm Directive in Microsoft Visual C++

Inline assembly code is assembly language source code that is inserted directly into high-level language programs. Most C/C++ compilers support this feature, as do Borland C++, Pascal, and Delphi.

In this section, we demonstrate how to write inline assembly code for Microsoft Visual C++ running in 32-bit protected mode with the flat memory model. Other high-level language compilers support inline assembly code, but the exact syntax varies.

Inline assembly code is a straightforward alternative to writing assembly code in external modules. The primary advantage to writing inline code is simplicity because there are no external linking issues, naming problems, and parameter passing protocols to worry about.

The primary disadvantage to using inline assembly code is its lack of portability. This is an issue when a high-level language program must be compiled for different target platforms. Inline assembly code that runs on an Intel Pentium processor will not run on a RISC processor, for example. To some extent, the problem can be solved by inserting conditional definitions in the program's source code to enable different versions of functions for different target systems. It is easy to see, however, that maintenance is still a problem. A link library of external assembly language procedures, on the other hand, could easily be replaced by a similar link library designed for a different target machine.

The __asm Directive   In Visual C++, the __**asm** directive can be placed at the beginning of a single statement, or it can mark the beginning of a block of assembly language statements (called an *asm block*). The syntax is

```
__asm  statement

__asm {
  statement-1
  statement-2
  ...
  statement-n
}
```

(There are two underline characters before "asm.")

Comments   Comments can be placed after any statements in the asm block, using either assembly language syntax or C/C++ syntax. The Visual C++ manual suggests that you avoid assembler-style comments because they might interfere with C macros, which expand on a single logical line. Here are examples of permissible comments:

```
mov  esi,buf     ; initialize index register
mov  esi,buf     // initialize index register
mov  esi,buf     /* initialize index register */
```

Features   Here is what you can do when writing inline assembly code:
• Use any instruction from the Intel instruction set.
• Use register names as operands.

- Reference function parameters by name.
- Reference code labels and variables that were declared outside the *asm* block. (This is important because local function variables must be declared outside the asm block.)
- Use numeric literals that incorporate either assembler-style or C-style radix notation. For example, 0A26h and 0xA26 are equivalent and can both be used.
- Use the PTR operator in statements such as **inc BYTE PTR [esi]**.
- Use the EVEN and ALIGN directives.

Limitations   You cannot do the following when writing inline assembly code:

- Use data definition directives such as DB (BYTE) and DW (WORD).
- Use assembler operators (other than PTR).
- Use STRUCT, RECORD, WIDTH, and MASK.
- Use macro directives, including MACRO, REPT, IRC, IRP, and ENDM, or macro operators (<>, !, &, %, and .TYPE).
- Reference segments by name. (You can, however, use segment register names as operands.)

Register Values   You cannot make any assumptions about register values at the beginning of an asm block. The registers may have been modified by code that executed just before the asm block. The **__fastcall** keyword in Microsoft Visual C++ causes the compiler to use registers to pass parameters. To avoid register conflicts, do not use **__fastcall** and **__asm** together.

In general, you can modify EAX, EBX, ECX, and EDX in your inline code because the compiler does not expect these values to be preserved between statements. If you modify too many registers, however, you may make it impossible for the compiler to fully optimize the C++ code in the same procedure because optimization requires the use of registers.

Although you cannot use the OFFSET operator, you can retrieve the offset of a variable using the LEA instruction. For example, the following instruction moves the offset of **buffer** to ESI:

```
lea esi,buffer
```

Length, Type, and Size   You can use the LENGTH, SIZE, and TYPE operators with the inline assembler. The LENGTH operator returns the number of elements in an array. The TYPE operator returns one of the following, depending on its target:

- The number of bytes used by a C or C++ type or scalar variable
- The number of bytes used by a structure
- For an array, the size of a single array element

The SIZE operator returns LENGTH * TYPE. The following program excerpt demonstrates the values returned by the inline assembler for various C++ types.

> Microsoft Visual C++ inline assembler does not support the SIZEOF and LENGTHOF operators.

Using the LENGTH, TYPE, and SIZE Operators

The following program contains inline assembly code that uses the LENGTH, TYPE, and SIZE operators to evaluate C++ variables. The value returned by each expression is shown as a comment on the same line:

```
struct Package {
    long originZip;              // 4
    long destinationZip;         // 4
    float shippingPrice;         // 4
};

    char myChar;
    bool myBool;
```

```
        short myShort;
        int myInt;
        long myLong;
        float myFloat;
        double myDouble;
        Package myPackage;

        long double myLongDouble;
        long myLongArray[10];

__asm {
        mov eax,myPackage.destinationZip;

        mov eax,LENGTH myInt;          // 1
        mov eax,LENGTH myLongArray;    // 10

        mov eax,TYPE myChar;           // 1
        mov eax,TYPE myBool;           // 1
        mov eax,TYPE myShort;          // 2
        mov eax,TYPE myInt;            // 4
        mov eax,TYPE myLong;           // 4
        mov eax,TYPE myFloat;          // 4
        mov eax,TYPE myDouble;         // 8
        mov eax,TYPE myPackage;        // 12
        mov eax,TYPE myLongDouble;     // 8
        mov eax,TYPE myLongArray;      // 4

        mov eax,SIZE myLong;           // 4
        mov eax,SIZE myPackage;        // 12
        mov eax,SIZE myLongArray;      // 40
}
```

12.2.2 File Encryption Example

Let's write a short program that reads a file, encrypts it, and writes the output to another file. The **TranslateBuffer** function uses an **__asm** block to define statements that loop through a character array and XOR each character with a predefined value. The inline statements can refer to function parameters, local variables, and code labels. Because this example was compiled under Microsoft Visual C++ as a Win32 Console application, the unsigned integer data type is 32 bits:

```
void TranslateBuffer( char * buf,
     unsigned count, unsigned char eChar )
{
     __asm {
            mov esi,buf
            mov ecx,count
            mov al,eChar
     L1:
            xor [esi],al
            inc esi
            loop L1
     }     // asm
}
```

C++ Module The C++ startup program reads the names of the input and output files from the command line. It calls TranslateBuffer from a loop that reads blocks of data from a file, encrypts it, and writes the translated buffer to a new file:

```
// ENCODE.CPP - Copy and encrypt a file.
```

```
#include <iostream>
#include <fstream>
#include "translat.h"

using namespace std;

int main( int argcount, char * args[] )
{
    // Read input and output files from the command line.
    if( argcount < 3 ) {
        cout << "Usage: encode infile outfile" << endl;
        return -1;
    }

    const int BUFSIZE = 2000;
    char buffer[BUFSIZE];
    unsigned int count;                 // character count

    unsigned char encryptCode;
    cout << "Encryption code [0-255]? ";
    cin >> encryptCode;

    ifstream infile( args[1], ios::binary );
    ofstream outfile( args[2], ios::binary );

    cout << "Reading" << args[1] << "and creating"
         << args[2] << endl;

    while (!infile.eof() )
    {
        infile.read(buffer, BUFSIZE);
        count = infile.gcount();
        TranslateBuffer(buffer, count, encryptCode);
        outfile.write(buffer, count);
    }
    return 0;
}
```

It's easiest to run this program from a command prompt, passing the names of the input and output files. For example, the following command line reads infile.txt and produces encoded.txt:

```
encode infile.txt encoded.txt
```

Header File   The *translat.h* header file contains a single function prototype for **TranslateBuffer**:

```
void TranslateBuffer(char * buf, unsigned count,
                     unsigned char eChar);
```

You can view this program in the book's *Examples\ch12\VisualCPP\Encode* folder.

Procedure Call Overhead

If you view the Disassembly window while debugging this program in a debugger, it is interesting to see exactly how much overhead can be involved in calling and returning from a procedure. The following statements push three arguments on the stack and call **TranslateBuffer**. In the Visual C++ Disassembly window, we activated the Show Source Code and Show Symbol Names options:

```
; TranslateBuffer(buffer, count, encryptCode)
mov   al,byte ptr [encryptCode]
push eax
mov   ecx,dword ptr [count]
push ecx
```

```
lea   edx,[buffer]
push  edx
call  TranslateBuffer (4159BFh)
add   esp,0Ch
```

The following is a disassembly of **TranslateBuffer**. A number of statements were automatically inserted by the compiler to set up EBP and save a standard set of registers that are always preserved whether or not they are actually modified by the procedure:

```
push  ebp
mov   ebp,esp
sub   esp,40h
push  ebx
push  esi
push  edi

; Inline code begins here.
mov   esi,dword ptr [buf]
mov   ecx,dword ptr [count]
mov   al,byte ptr [eChar]
L1:
  xor byte ptr [esi],al
  inc esi
  loop L1 (41D762h)
; End of inline code.

pop   edi
pop   esi
pop   ebx
mov   esp,ebp
pop   ebp
ret
```

If we turn off the *Display Symbol Names* option in the debugger's Disassembly window, the three statements that move parameters to registers appear as

```
mov   esi,dword ptr [ebp+8]
mov   ecx,dword ptr [ebp+0Ch]
mov   al,byte ptr [ebp+10h]
```

The compiler was instructed to generate a *Debug* target, which is nonoptimized code suitable for interactive debugging. If we had selected a *Release* target, the compiler would have generated more efficient (but harder to read) code. In Section 12.3.1 we will show optimized compiler-generated code.

Omit the Procedure Call   The six inline instructions in the **TranslateBuffer** function shown at the beginning of this section required a total of 18 instructions to execute. If the function were called thousands of times, the required execution time might be measurable. To avoid this overhead, let's insert the inline code into the loop that called TranslateBuffer, creating a more efficient program:

```
while (!infile.eof() )
{
    infile.read(buffer, BUFSIZE );
    count = infile.gcount();
    __asm {
        lea esi,buffer
        mov ecx,count
        mov al,encryptCode
    L1:
        xor [esi],al
```

```
        inc  esi
        Loop L1
    } // asm
      outfile.write(buffer, count);
}
```

You can view this program in the book's *Examples\ch12\VisualCPP\Encode_Inline* folder.

12.2.3   Section Review

1.   How is inline assembly code different from an inline C++ procedure?

2.   What advantage does inline assembly code offer over the use of external assembly language procedures?

3.   Show at least two ways of placing comments in inline assembly code.

4.   (*Yes/no*): Can an inline statement refer to code labels outside the __asm block?

5.   (*Yes/no*): Can both the EVEN and ALIGN directives be used in inline assembly code?

6.   (*Yes/no*): Can the OFFSET operator be used in inline assembly code?

7.   (*Yes/no*): Can variables be defined with both DW and the DUP operator in inline assembly code?

8.   When using the **__fastcall** calling convention, what might happen if your inline assembly code modifies registers?

9.   Rather than using the OFFSET operator, is there another way to move a variable's offset into an index register?

10. What value is returned by the LENGTH operator when applied to an array of 32-bit integers?

11. What value is returned by the SIZE operator when applied to an array of long integers?

12.3   Linking to C/C++ in Protected Mode

Programs written for IA-32 processors running in Protected mode can sometimes have bottlenecks that must be optimized for runtime efficiency. If they are embedded systems, they may have stringent memory size limitations. With such goals in mind, we will show how to write external procedures in assembly language that can be called from C and C++ programs running in Protected mode. Such programs consist of at least two modules: The first, written in assembly language, contains the external procedure; the second module contains the C/C++ code that starts and ends the program. There are a few specific requirements and features of C/C++ that affect the way you write assembly code.

Arguments   Arguments are passed by C/C++ programs from right to left, as they appear in the argument list. After the procedure returns, the calling program is responsible for cleaning up the stack. This can be done by either adding a value to the stack pointer equal to the size of the arguments or popping an adequate number of values from the stack.

External Names   In the assembly language source, specify the C calling convention in the .MODEL directive and create a prototype for each procedure called from an external C/C++ program:

```
.586
.model flat,C
AsmFindArray PROTO,
     srchVal:DWORD, arrayPtr:PTR DWORD, count:DWORD
```

Declaring the Function   In a C program, use the **extern** qualifier when declaring an external assembly language procedure. For example, this is how to declare **AsmFindArray**:

```
extern bool AsmFindArray( long n, long array[], long count );
```

If the procedure will be called from a C++ program, add a "C" qualifier to prevent C++ name decoration:

```
extern "C" bool AsmFindArray( long n, long array[], long count );
```

Name decoration is a standard C++ compiler technique that involves modifying a function name with extra characters that indicate the exact type of each function parameter. It is required in any language that supports function overloading (two functions having the same name, with different parameter lists). From the assembly language programmer's point of view, the problem with name decoration is that the C++ compiler tells the linker to look for the decorated name rather than the original one when producing the executable file.

12.3.1 Using Assembly Language to Optimize C++ Code

One of the ways you can use assembly language to optimize programs written in other languages is to look for speed bottlenecks. Loops are good candidates for optimization because any extra statements in a loop may be repeated enough times to have a noticeable effect on your program's performance.

Most C/C++ compilers have a command-line option that automatically generates an assembly language listing of the C/C++ program. In Microsoft Visual C++, for example, the listing file can contain any combination of C++ source code, assembly code, and machine code, shown by the options in Table 12-1. Perhaps the most useful is **/FAs**, which shows how C++ statements are translated into assembly language.

Table 12-1   Visual C++ Command-Line Options for ASM Code Generation.

Command Line	Contents of Listing File
/FA	Assembly-only listing
/FAc	Assembly with machine code
/FAs	Assembly with source code
/FAcs	Assembly, machine code, and source

FindArray Example

Let's create a program that shows how a sample C++ compiler generates code for a function named **FindArray**. Later, we will write an assembly language version of the function, attempting to write more efficient code than the C++ compiler. The following **FindArray** function (in C++) searches for a single value in an array of long integers:

```
bool FindArray( long searchVal, long array[], long count )
{
    for(int i = 0; i < count; i++)
    array[i] *= searchVal;

    return false;
}
```

FindArray Code Generated by Visual C++

Let's look at the assembly language source code generated by Visual C++ for the **FindArray** function, alongside the function's C++ source code. This procedure was compiled to a *Release* target with no code optimization in effect:

```
_i$282 = -4                  ; size = 4
_searchVal$ = 8              ; size = 4
_array$ = 12                 ; size = 4
_count$ = 16                 ; size = 4

_FindArray PROC NEAR
; 9    : {
```

```
        push    ebp
        mov     ebp, esp
        push    ecx
; 10    : for(int i = 0; i < count; i++)
        mov     DWORD PTR _i$282[ebp], 0
        jmp     SHORT $L283
$L284:
        mov     eax, DWORD PTR _i$282[ebp]
        add     eax, 1
        mov     DWORD PTR _i$282[ebp], eax
$L283:
        mov     ecx, DWORD PTR _i$282[ebp]
        cmp     ecx, DWORD PTR _count$[ebp]
        jge     SHORT $L285
; 11    :    array[i] *= searchVal;
        mov     edx, DWORD PTR _i$282[ebp]
        mov     eax, DWORD PTR _array$[ebp]
        mov     ecx, DWORD PTR [eax+edx*4]
        imul    ecx, DWORD PTR _searchVal$[ebp]
        mov     edx, DWORD PTR _i$282[ebp]
        mov     eax, DWORD PTR _array$[ebp]
        mov     DWORD PTR [eax+edx*4], ecx
        jmp     SHORT $L284
$L285:
; 12    :
; 13    :    return false;
        xor     al, al
; 14    : }
        mov     esp, ebp
        pop     ebp
        ret     0
_FindArray ENDP
```

Three 32-bit arguments were pushed on the stack in the following order: **count, array,** and **searchVal**. Of these three, **array** is the only one passed by reference because in C/C++, an array name is an implicit pointer to the array's first element. The procedure saves EBP on the stack and creates space for the local variable **i** by pushing an extra doubleword on the stack (Figure 12–1).

Figure 12–1   Stack Frame for the FindArray Function.

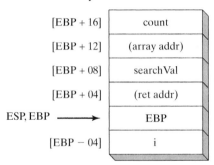

Inside the procedure, the compiler reserves local stack space for the variable **i** by pushing ECX (line 9). The same storage is released at the end when EBP is copied back into ESP (line 14). There are 14 instructions between the labels $L284 and $L285, which constitute the main body of the loop. We can easily write an assembly language procedure that is more efficient than the code shown here.

Linking MASM to Visual C++

Let's create a hand-optimized assembly language version of FindArray, named **AsmFindArray**. A few basic principles are applied to the code optimization:

- Move as much processing out of the loop as possible.
- Move stack parameters and local variables to registers.
- Take advantage of specialized string/array processing instructions (in this case, SCASD).

We will use Microsoft Visual C++ (Visual Studio) to compile the calling C++ program and Microsoft MASM to assemble the called procedure. Visual C++ generates 32-bit applications that run only in protected mode. We choose Win32 Console as the target application type for the examples shown here, although there is no reason why the same procedures would not work in ordinary MS-Windows applications. In Visual C++, functions return 8-bit values in AL, 16-bit values in AX, 32-bit values in EAX, and 64-bit values in EDX:EAX. Larger data structures (structure values, arrays, etc.) are stored in a static data location, and a pointer to the data is returned in EAX.

Our assembly language code is slightly more readable than the code generated by the C++ compiler because we can use meaningful label names and define constants that simplify the use of stack parameters. Here is the complete module listing:

```
TITLE AsmFindArray Procedure        (AsmFindArray.asm)

.586
.model flat,C

AsmFindArray PROTO,
    srchVal:DWORD, arrayPtr:PTR DWORD, count:DWORD

.code
;------------------------------------------------
AsmFindArray PROC USES edi,
    srchVal:DWORD, arrayPtr:PTR DWORD, count:DWORD
;
; Performs a linear search for a 32-bit integer
; in an array of integers. Returns a boolean
; value in AL indicating if the integer was found.
;------------------------------------------------
    true = 1
    false = 0

    mov     eax,srchVal             ; search value
    mov     ecx,count               ; number of items
    mov     edi,arrayPtr            ; pointer to array

    repne scasd                     ; do the search
    jz      returnTrue              ; ZF = 1 if found
returnFalse:
    mov     al,false
    jmp     short exit

returnTrue:
    mov     al, true

exit:
    ret
AsmFindArray ENDP
END
```

Checking the Performance of FindArray

Test Program   It is interesting to check the performance of any assembly language code you write against similar code written in C++. To that end, the following C++ test program inputs a search value and gets the system time before and after executing a loop that calls FindArray one million times. The same test is performed on AsmFindArray. Here is a listing of the *findarr.h* header file, with function prototypes for the assembly language procedure and the C++ function:

```
// findarr.h

extern "C" {
    bool AsmFindArray( long n, long array[], long count );
    // Assembly language version

    bool FindArray( long n, long array[], long count );
    // C++ version
}
```

Main C++ Module   Here is a listing of *main.cpp*, the startup program that calls FindArray and AsmFindArray:

```
// main.cpp - Testing FindArray and AsmFindArray.

#include <iostream>
#include <time.h>
#include "findarr.h"
using namespace std;

int main()
{
    // Fill an array with pseudorandom integers.
    const unsigned ARRAY_SIZE = 10000;
    const unsigned LOOP_SIZE = 1000000;

    long array[ARRAY_SIZE];
    for(unsigned i = 0; i < ARRAY_SIZE; i++)
       array[i] = rand();

    long searchVal;
    time_t startTime, endTime;
    cout << "Enter value to find: ";
    cin >> searchVal;
    cout << "Please wait. This will take between 10 and 30 seconds...\n";

// Test the C++ function:
    time( &startTime );
    bool found = false;

    for( int n = 0; n < LOOP_SIZE; n++)
       found = FindArray( searchVal, array, ARRAY_SIZE );

    time( &endTime );
    cout << "Elapsed CPP time: " << long(endTime - startTime)
           << " seconds. Found = " << found << endl;

// Test the Assembly language procedure:
    time( &startTime );
    found = false;

    for( int n = 0; n < LOOP_SIZE; n++)
       found = AsmFindArray( searchVal, array, ARRAY_SIZE );

    time( &endTime );
```

```
        cout << "Elapsed ASM time: " << long(endTime - startTime)
                << " seconds. Found = " << found << endl;

    return 0;
}
```

Assembly Code versus Nonoptimized C++ Code   We compiled the C++ program to a Release (non-debug) target with code optimization turned off. Here is the output, showing the worst case (value not found):

```
Enter value to find: 55
Elapsed CPP time: 53 seconds. Found = 0
Elapsed ASM time: 14 seconds. Found = 0
```

Assembly Code versus Compiler Optimization   Next, we set the compiler to optimize the executable program for speed and ran the test program again. Here are the results, showing the assembly code is noticeably faster than the compiler-optimized C++ code:

```
Enter value to find: 55
Elapsed CPP time: 20 seconds. Found = 0
Elapsed ASM time: 14 seconds. Found = 0
```

Pointers versus Subscripts

Programmers using older C compilers observed that processing arrays with pointers was more efficient than using subscripts. For example, the following version of **FindArray** uses this approach:

```
bool FindArray( long searchVal, long array[], long count )
{
  long * p = array;
  for(i = 0; i < count; i++, p++)
    if( searchVal == *p )
      return true;
  return false;
}
```

Running this version of **FindArray** through the Visual C++ compiler produced virtually the same assembly language code as the earlier version using subscripts. Because modern compilers are good at code optimization, using a pointer variable is no more efficient than using a subscript. Here is the loop from the **FindArray** target code that was produced by the C++ compiler:

```
$L176:
    cmp   esi, DWORD PTR [ecx]
    je    SHORT $L184
    inc   eax
    add   ecx, 4
    cmp   eax, edx
    jl    SHORT $L176
```

Your time would be well spent studying the output produced by a C++ compiler to learn about optimization techniques, parameter passing, and object code implementation. In fact, many computer science students take a compiler-writing course that includes such topics. It is also important to realize that compilers take the general case because they usually have no specific knowledge about individual applications or installed hardware. Some compilers provide specialized optimization for a particular processor such as the Pentium, which can significantly improve the speed of compiled programs. Hand-coded assembly language can take advantage of IA-32 string primitive instructions, as well as specialized hardware features of video cards, sound cards, and data acquisition boards.

12.3.2 Calling C and C++ Functions

You can write assembly language programs that call C++ functions. There are at least a couple of reasons for doing so:

- Input-output is more flexible under C++, with its rich iostream library. This is particularly useful when working with floating-point numbers.
- C++ has extensive math libraries.

When calling functions from the standard C library (or C++ library), you must start the program from a C or C++ main( ) procedure to allow library initialization code to run.

Function Prototypes

C++ functions called from assembly language code must be defined with the "**C**" and **extern** keywords. Here's the basic syntax:

```
extern "C" funcName( paramlist )
{ . . . }
```

Here's an example:

```
extern "C" int askForInteger( )
{
    cout << "Please enter an integer:";
    //...
}
```

Rather than modifying every function definition, it's easier to group multiple function prototypes inside a block. Then you can omit **extern** and "**C**" from the function implementations:

```
extern "C" {
    int askForInteger();
    int showInt( int value, unsigned outWidth );
    etc.
}
```

Assembly Language Module

Using the Irvine32's Link Library If your assembly language module will be calling procedures from the Irvine32 link library, be aware that it uses the following .MODEL directive:

```
.model flat, STDCALL
```

Although STDCALL is compatible with the Win32 API, it does not match the calling convention used by C programs. Therefore, you must add the C qualifier to the PROTO directive when declaring external C or C++ functions to be called by the assembly module:

```
INCLUDE Irvine32.inc
askForInteger PROTO C
showInt PROTO C, value:SDWORD, outWidth:DWORD
```

The C qualifier is required because the linker must match up the function names and parameter lists to functions exported by the C++ module. In addition, the assembler must generate the right code to clean up the stack after the function calls, using the C calling convention (see Section 8.4.1).

Assembly language procedures called by the C++ program must use also the C qualifier so the assembler will use a naming convention the linker can recognize. The following **SetTextColor** procedure, for example, has a single doubleword parameter:

```
SetTextOutColor PROC C,
    color:DWORD
```

```
          .
          .
     SetTextOutColor ENDP
```

Finally, if your assembly code calls other assembly language procedures, the C calling convention requires you to remove parameters from the stack after each procedure call.

Using the .MODEL Directive   If your assembly language code does not call Irvine32 procedures, you can tell the .MODEL directive to use the C calling convention:

```
; (do not INCLUDE Irvine32.inc)
.586
.model flat,C
```

Now you no longer have to add the C qualifier to the PROTO and PROC directives:

```
askForInteger PROTO
showInt PROTO, value:SDWORD, outWidth:DWORD

SetTextOutColor PROC,
     color:DWORD
     .
     .
SetTextOutColor ENDP
```

Function Return Values

The C++ language specification says nothing about code implementation details, so there is no standardized way for C++ functions to return values. When you write assembly language code that calls C++ functions, check your compiler's documentation to find out how their functions return values. The following list contains several, but by no means all, possibilities:

- Integers can be returned in a single register or combination of registers.
- Space for function return values can be reserved on the stack by the calling program. The function can insert the return values into the stack before returning.
- Floating-point values are usually pushed on the processor's floating-point stack before returning from the function.

The following list shows how Microsoft Visual C++ functions return values:

- **bool** and **char** values are returned in AL.
- **short int** values are returned in AX.
- **int** and **long int** values are returned in EAX.
- Pointers are returned in EAX.
- **float, double**, and **long double** values are pushed on the floating-point stack as 4-, 8-, and 10-byte values, respectively.

12.3.3   Multiplication Table Example

Let's write a simple application that prompts the user for an integer, multiplies it by ascending powers of 2 (from 2^1 to 2^{10}) using bit shifting, and redisplays each product with leading padded spaces. We will use C++ for the input-output. The assembly language module will contain calls to three functions written in C++. The program will be launched from C++.

Assembly Language Module

The assembly language module contains one function, named **DisplayTable**. It calls a C++ function named **askForInteger** that inputs an integer from the user. It uses a loop to repeatedly shift an integer named **intVal** to the left and display it by calling **showInt**.

```
; ASM function called from C++

INCLUDE Irvine32.inc

; External C++ functions:
askForInteger PROTO C
showInt PROTO C, value:SDWORD, outWidth:DWORD
newLine PROTO C

OUT_WIDTH = 8
ENDING_POWER = 10

.data
intVal DWORD ?

.code
;---------------------------------------------
SetTextOutColor PROC C,
     color:DWORD
;
; Sets the text colors and clears the console
; window. Calls Irvine32 library functions.
;---------------------------------------------
     mov    eax,color
     call   SetTextColor
     call   Clrscr
     ret
SetTextOutColor ENDP

;---------------------------------------------
DisplayTable PROC C
;
; Inputs an integer n and displays a
; multiplication table ranging from n * 2^1
; to n * 2^10.
;---------------------------------------------
     INVOKE askForInteger              ; call C++ function
     mov    intVal,eax                 ; save the integer
     mov    ecx,ENDING_POWER           ; loop counter

L1:  push   ecx                        ; save loop counter
     shl    intVal,1                   ; multiply by 2
     INVOKE showInt,intVal,OUT_WIDTH
     INVOKE newLine                    ; output CR/LF
     pop    ecx                        ; restore loop counter
     loop   L1

     ret
DisplayTable ENDP
END
```

In DisplayTable, ECX must be pushed and popped before calling **showInt** and **newLine** because Visual C++ functions do not save and restore general-purpose registers. The **askForInteger** function returns its result in the EAX register.

DisplayTable is not required to use INVOKE when calling the C++ functions. The same result could be achieved using PUSH and CALL instructions. This is how the call to **showInt** would look:

```
push   OUT_WIDTH                  ; push last argument first
push   intVal
```

```
        call    showInt                     ; call the function
        add     esp,8                       ; clean up stack
```

You must follow the C language calling convention, in which arguments are pushed on the stack in reverse order and the caller is responsible for removing arguments from the stack after the call.

C++ Startup Program

Let's look at the C++ module that starts the program. Its entry point is **main( )**, ensuring the execution of required C++ language initialization code. It contains function prototypes for the external assembly language procedure and the three exported functions:

```
// main.cpp

// Demonstrates function calls between a C++ program
// and an external assembly language module.

#include <iostream>
#include <iomanip>
using namespace std;

extern "C" {
    // external ASM procedures:
    void DisplayTable();
    void SetTextOutColor(unsigned color);

    // local C++ functions:
    int askForInteger();
    void showInt(int value, int width);
}

// program entry point
int main()
{
    SetTextOutColor( 0x1E );                 // yellow on blue
    DisplayTable();                          // call ASM procedure
    return 0;
}

// Prompt the user for an integer.

int askForInteger()
{
    int n;
    cout << "Enter an integer between 1 and 90,000:";
    cin >> n;
    return n;
}

// Display a signed integer with a specified width.

void showInt( int value, int width )
{
    cout << setw(width) << value;
}
```

Building the Project   Our Web site (*www.asmirvine.com*) has a tutorial for building combined C++/ Assembly Language projects in Visual Studio.

Program Output   Here is sample output generated by the Multiplication Table program when the user enters 90,000:

```
Enter an integer between 1 and 90,000: 90000
   180000
   360000
   720000
  1440000
  2880000
  5760000
 11520000
 23040000
 46080000
 92160000
```

Visual Studio Project Properties

If you're using Visual Studio to build programs that integrate C++ and assembly language and make calls to the Irvine32 library, you need to alter some project settings. We'll use the Multiplication_Table program as an example. Select *Properties* from the Project menu. In the *Configuration* dropdown list, select *All Configurations*. Under *Configuration Properties*, double-click on *Linker* and select *Command Line*. Add **C:\Irvine\Irvine32.lib** to the *Additional Options* entry (Figure 12–2). Click on OK to close the Property Pages window. Now Visual Studio can find the Irvine32 library.

FIGURE 12–2   Linker Command-Line Property.

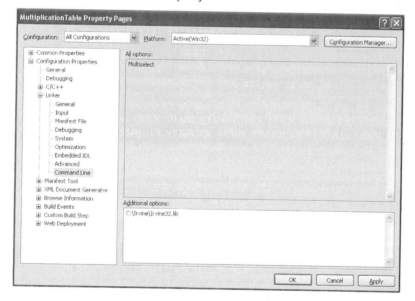

The information here was tested in Visual Studio 2005, but is subject to change. Please see our Web site (www.asmirvine.com) for updates.

12.3.4   Calling C Library Functions

The C language has a standardized collection of functions named the *Standard C Library*. The same functions are available to C++ programs, and therefore to assembly language modules attached to C and C++ programs. Assembly language modules must contain a prototype for each C function they call. You can usually find C function prototypes by accessing the help system supplied with your C++

compiler. You must translate C function prototypes into assembly language prototypes before calling them from your program.

printf Function   The following is the C/C++ language prototype for the **printf** function, showing a pointer to character as its first parameter, followed by a variable number of parameters:

```
int printf(
    const char *format [, argument]...
);
```

(Your C/C++ compiler's help library contains extensive documentation about the printf function.) The equivalent prototype in assembly language changes char * into PTR BYTE, and it changes the variable-length parameter list into the VARARG type:

```
printf PROTO C, pString:PTR BYTE, args:VARARG
```

Another useful function is **scanf**, which inputs characters, numbers, and strings from standard input (the keyboard) and assigns the input values to variables:

```
scanf PROTO C, format:PTR BYTE, args:VARARG
```

Displaying Formatted Reals with the `printf` Function

Writing assembly language functions that format and display floating point values is not easy. Rather than doing it yourself, you can take advantage of the C/C++ language **printf** function. You must create a startup module in C or C++ and link it to your assembly language code. Here's how to set up such a program in Visual C++ .NET:

1. Create a Win32 Console program in Visual C++. Create a file named *main.cpp* and insert a **main** function that calls **asmMain** from C++ **main.** Also in main, insert a declaration of at least one floating-point variable. In the following code, the statement declaring **d** has no effect other than to force Visual C++ to load its floating-point runtime library[1]:

```
extern "C" void asmMain( );

int main( )
{
    double d = 3.5;              // load floating-point library
    asmMain( );
    return 0;
}
```

2. In the same folder as main.cpp, create an assembly language module named *asmMain.asm.* It should contain a procedure named **asmMain**, declared with the C calling convention:

```
TITLE asmMain.asm
.386
.model flat,stdcall
.stack 2000
.code
asmMain PROC C

    ret
asmMain ENDP
END
```

3. Assemble *asmMain.asm* (but do not link), producing *asmMain.obj.*
4. Add *asmMain.obj* to the C++ project.
5. Build and run the project. If you modify *asmMain.asm,* assemble it again and rebuild the project before running it again.

Once your program has been set up properly, you can add code to asmMain.asm that calls C/C++ language functions.

Displaying Double-Precision Values   The following assembly language code in **asmMain** prints a REAL8 by calling printf:

```
.data
double1 REAL8  1234567.890123
formatStr BYTE "%.3f",0dh,0ah,0
.code
INVOKE printf, ADDR formatStr, double1
```

This is the corresponding output:

```
1234567.890
```

The format string passed to **printf** here is a little different than it would be in C++. Rather than embedding escape characters such as \n, you must insert ASCII codes (0dh, 0ah).

> Floating-point arguments passed to printf should be declared type REAL8. Although it is possible to pass values of type REAL4, a fair amount of clever programming is required. You can see how your C++ compiler does it by declaring a variable of type float and passing it to printf. Compile the program and trace the program's disassembled code with a debugger.

Multiple Arguments   The printf function accepts a variable number of arguments, so we can just as easily format and display two numbers in one function call:

```
TAB = 9
.data
formatTwo BYTE "%.2f",TAB,"%.3f",0dh,0ah,0
val1 REAL8 456.789
val2 REAL8 864.231
.code
INVOKE printf, ADDR formatTwo, val1, val2
```

This is the corresponding output:

```
456.79   864.231
```

(See the project named **Printf_Example** in the Examples\ch12\VisualCPP folder on the book's CD-ROM.)

Entering Reals with the `scanf` Function

You can call **scanf** to input floating-point values from the user. The following prototype is defined in SmallWin.inc (included by Irvine32.inc):

```
scanf PROTO C,
      format:PTR BYTE, args:VARARG
```

Pass it the offset of a format string and the offsets of one or more REAL4 or REAL8 variables to hold values entered by the user. Sample calls:

```
.data
strSingle BYTE "%f",0
strDouble BYTE "%lf",0
single1 REAL4 ?
```

```
double1 REAL8 ?
.code
INVOKE scanf, ADDR strSingle, ADDR single1
INVOKE scanf, ADDR strDouble, ADDR double1
```

You must invoke your assembly language code from a C or C++ startup program.

12.3.5   Directory Listing Program

Let's write a short program that clears the screen, displays the current disk directory, and asks the user to enter a filename. (You might want to extend this program so it opens and displays the selected file.)

C++ Stub Module   The C++ module contains only a call to **asm_main**, so we can call it a *stub module*:

```
// main.cpp
// stub module: launches assembly language program

extern "C" void asm_main();          // asm startup proc

void main()
{
     asm_main();
}
```

ASM Module   The assembly language module contains the function prototypes, several strings, and a **fileName** variable. It calls the **system** function twice, passing it "cls" and "dir" commands. Then **printf** is called, displaying a prompt for a filename, and **scanf** is called so the user can input the name. It does not make any calls to the Irvine32 library, so we can set the .MODEL directive to the C language convention:

```
; ASM program launched from C++         (asmMain.asm)

.586
.MODEL flat,C

; Standard C library functions:
system PROTO, pCommand:PTR BYTE
printf PROTO, pString:PTR BYTE, args:VARARG
scanf  PROTO, pFormat:PTR BYTE,pBuffer:PTR BYTE, args:VARARG
fopen  PROTO, mode:PTR BYTE, filename:PTR BYTE
fclose PROTO, pFile:DWORD

BUFFER_SIZE = 5000
.data
str1 BYTE "cls",0
str2 BYTE "dir/w",0
str3 BYTE "Enter the name of a file:",0
str4 BYTE "%s",0
str5 BYTE "cannot open file",0dh,0ah,0
str6 BYTE "The file has been opened",0dh,0ah,0
modeStr BYTE "r",0

fileName BYTE 60 DUP(0)
pBuf  DWORD ?
pFile DWORD ?

.code
asm_main PROC

      ; clear the screen, display disk directory
      INVOKE system,ADDR str1
```

```
        INVOKE system,ADDR str2

        ; ask for a filename
        INVOKE printf,ADDR str3
        INVOKE scanf, ADDR str4, ADDR filename

        ; try to open the file
        INVOKE fopen, ADDR fileName, ADDR modeStr
        mov    pFile,eax

        .IF eax == 0                      ; cannot open file?
        INVOKE printf,ADDR str5
        jmp quit
        .ELSE
        INVOKE printf,ADDR str6
        .ENDIF

        .
        ; Close the file
        INVOKE fclose, pFile

quit:
        ret                               ; return to C++ main
asm_main ENDP
END
```

The **scanf** function requires two arguments: the first is a pointer to a format string ("%s"), and the second is a pointer to the input string variable (**fileName**). We will not take the time to explain standard C functions because there is ample documentation on the Web. An excellent reference is Brian W. Kernighan and Dennis M. Ritchie, The C Programming Language, 2nd Ed., Prentice Hall, 1988.

12.3.6   Section Review

1. Which two C++ keywords must be included in a function definition if the function will be called from an assembly language module?
2. In what way is the calling convention used by the Irvine32 library not compatible with the calling convention used by the C and C++ languages?
3. How do C++ functions usually return floating-point values?
4. How does a Microsoft Visual C++ function return a **short int**?
5. What is a valid assembly language PROTO declaration for the standard C printf( ) function?
6. When the following C language function is called, will the argument **x** be pushed on the stack first or last?
    ```
    void MySub( x, y, z );
    ```
7. What is the purpose of the "C" specifier in the *extern* declaration in procedures called from C++?
8. Why is name decoration important when calling external assembly language procedures from C++?
9. In this chapter, when an optimizing C++ compiler was used, what differences in code generation occurred between the loop coded with array subscripts and the loop coded with pointer variables?

12.4   Linking to C/C++ in Real-Address Mode

Many embedded systems applications continue to be written for 16-bit environments, using the Intel 8086 and 8088 processors. In addition, some applications use 32-bit processors running in real-address mode. It is important, therefore, for us to show examples of assembly language subroutines called from C and C++ in real-mode environments.

The sample programs in this section use the 16-bit version of Borland C++ 5.01 and select Windows 98 (MS-DOS window) as the target operating system with a small memory model. We will use Borland TASM 4.0 as the assembler for these examples because most users of Borland C++ are likely to use Turbo Assembler rather than MASM. We will also create 16-bit real mode applications using Borland C++ 5.01 and demonstrate both small and large memory model programs, showing how to call both near and far procedures.

12.4.1 Linking to Borland C++

Function Return Values   In Borland C++, functions return 16-bit values in AX and 32-bit values in DX:AX. Larger data structures (structure values, arrays, etc.) are stored in a static data location, and a pointer to the data is returned in AX. (In medium, large, and huge memory model programs, a 32-bit pointer is returned in DX:AX.)

Setting Up a Project   In the Borland C++ integrated development environment (IDE), create a new project. Create a source code module (CPP file), and enter the code for the main C++ program. Create the ASM file containing the procedure you plan to call. Use TASM to assemble the program into an object module, either from the DOS command line or from the Borland C++ IDE, using its transfer capability. The filename (minus the extension) must be eight characters or less; otherwise its name will not be recognized by the 16-bit linker.

   If you have assembled the ASM module separately, add the object file created by the assembler to the C++ project. Invoke the MAKE or BUILD command from the menu. It compiles the CPP file, and if there are no errors, it links the two object modules to produce an executable program. Suggestion: Limit the name of the CPP source file to eight characters, otherwise the Turbo Debugger for DOS will not be able to find it when you debug the program.

Debugging   The Borland C++ compiler does not allow the DOS debugger to be run from the IDE. Instead, you need to run Turbo Debugger for DOS either from the DOS prompt or from the Windows desktop. Using the debugger's File/Open menu command, select the executable file created by the C++ linker. The C++ source code file should immediately display, and you can begin tracing and running the program.

Saving Registers   Assembly procedures called by Borland C++ must preserve the values of BP, DS, SS, SI, DI, and the Direction flag.

Storage Sizes   A 16-bit Borland C++ program uses specific storage sizes for all its data types. These are unique to this particular implementation and must be adjusted for every C++ compiler. Refer to Table 12-2.

Table 12-2   Borland C++ Data Types in 16-Bit Applications.

C++ Type	Storage Bytes	ASM Type
char, unsigned char	1	byte
int, unsigned int, short int	2	word
enum	2	word
long, unsigned long	4	dword
float	4	dword
double	8	qword
long double	10	tbyte
near pointer	2	word
far pointer	4	dword

12.4.2 ReadSector Example

(Must be run under MS-DOS, Windows 95, 98, or Millenium.) Let's begin with a Borland C++ program that calls an external assembly language procedure called **ReadSector**. C++ compilers generally do not include library functions for reading disk sectors because such details are too hardware-dependent, and it would be impractical to implement libraries for all possible computers. Assembly language programs can easily read disk sectors by calling INT 21h Function 7305h (see Section 14.4 for details). Our present task, then, is to create the interface between assembly language and C++ that combines the strengths of both languages.

The **ReadSector** example requires the use of a 16-bit compiler because it involves calling MS-DOS interrupts. (Calling 16-bit interrupts from 32-bit programs is possible, but it is beyond the scope of this book.[2]) The last version of Visual C++ to produce 16-bit programs was version 1.5. Other compilers that produce 16-bit code are Turbo C and Turbo Pascal, both by Borland.

Program Execution   First, we will demonstrate the program's execution. When the C++ program starts up, the user selects the drive number, starting sector, and number of sectors to read. For example, this user wants to read sectors 0 to 9 from drive A:

```
Sector display program.
Enter drive number [1=A, 2=B, 3=C, 4=D, 5=E,...]: 1
Starting sector number to read: 0
Number of sectors to read: 20
```

This information is passed to the assembly language procedure, which reads the sectors into a buffer. The C++ program begins to display the buffer, one sector at a time. As each sector is displayed, non-ASCII characters are replaced by dots. For example, the following is the program's display of sector 0 from drive A:

```
Reading sectors 0 - 20 from Drive 1
Sector 0 ------------------------------------------------------
.<.(P3j2IHC........@.................)Y...MYDISK     FAT12   .3.
....{...x..v..V.U."..~..N..........|.E...F..E.8N$}"....w.r...:f..
|f;..W.u.....V....s.3..F...f..F..V..F.....v.`.F..V.. ....^...H...F
..N.a....#.r98-t.`....}..at9Nt... ;.r.....}.......t.<.t.........
..}....}......^.f......}.}..E..N....F..V.....r....p..B.-`fj.RP.Sj
.j...t...3..v...v.B...v.............V$...d.ar.@u.B.^.Iuw....'..I
nvalid system disk...Disk I/O error...Replace the disk, and then
press any key....IOSYSMSDOS   SYS...A....~...@...U.
```

Sectors continue to be displayed, one by one, until the entire buffer has been displayed.

C++ Program Calls ReadSector

We can now show the complete C++ program that calls the **ReadSector** procedure:

```cpp
// main.cpp -  Calls the ReadSector Procedure

#include <iostream.h>
#include <conio.h>
#include <stdlib.h>
const int SECTOR_SIZE = 512;

extern "C" ReadSector( char * buffer, long startSector,
            int driveNum, int numSectors );

void DisplayBuffer( const char * buffer, long startSector,
```

```
        int numSectors )
{
  int n = 0;
  long last = startSector + numSectors;
  for(long sNum = startSector; sNum < last; sNum++)
  {
    cout << "\nSector " << sNum
         << " --------------------------"
         << "--------------------------\n";
    for(int i = 0; i < SECTOR_SIZE; i++)
    {
      char ch = buffer[n++];
      if( unsigned(ch) < 32 || unsigned(ch) > 127)
        cout << '.';
      else
        cout << ch;
    }
    cout << endl;
    getch();            // pause - wait for keypress
  }
}

int main()
{
  char * buffer;
  long startSector;
  int driveNum;
  int numSectors;

  system("CLS");
  cout << "Sector display program.\n\n"
       << "Enter drive number [1=A, 2=B, 3=C, 4=D, 5=E,...]:";
  cin >> driveNum;
  cout << "Starting sector number to read: ";
  cin >> startSector;
  cout << "Number of sectors to read:";
  cin >> numSectors;
  buffer = new char[numSectors * SECTOR_SIZE];

  cout << "\n\nReading sectors" << startSector << " - "
       << (startSector + numSectors) << "from Drive"
       << driveNum << endl;

  ReadSector( buffer, startSector, driveNum, numSectors );
  DisplayBuffer( buffer, startSector, numSectors );
  system("CLS");
  return 0;
}
```

At the top of the listing, we find the declaration, or prototype, of the **ReadSector** function:

```
extern "C" ReadSector( char buffer[], long startSector,
            int driveNum, int numSectors );
```

The first parameter, *buffer*, is a character array holding the sector data after it has been read from the disk. The second parameter, *startSector*, is the starting sector number to read. The third parameter, *driveNum*, is the disk drive number. The fourth parameter, *numSectors*, specifies the number of sectors to read. The first parameter is passed by reference, and all other parameters are passed by value.

In **main**, the user is prompted for the drive number, starting sector, and number of sectors. The program also dynamically allocates storage for the buffer that holds the sector data:

```
cout << "Sector display program.\n\n"
     << "Enter drive number [1=A, 2=B, 3=C, 4=D, 5=E,...]: ";
cin >> driveNum;
cout << "Starting sector number to read:";
cin >> startSector;
cout << "Number of sectors to read:";
cin >> numSectors;
buffer = new char[numSectors * SECTOR_SIZE];
```

This information is passed to the external **ReadSector** procedure, which fills the buffer with sectors from the disk:

```
ReadSector( buffer, startSector, driveNum, numSectors );
```

The buffer is passed to **DisplayBuffer**, a procedure in the C++ program that displays each sector in ASCII text format:

```
DisplayBuffer( buffer, startSector, numSectors );
```

Assembly Language Module

The assembly language module containing the **ReadSector** procedure is shown here. Because this is a real-mode application, the .386 directive must appear after the .MODEL directive to tell the assembler to create 16-bit segments:

```
TITLE Reading Disk Sectors            (ReadSec.asm)

; The ReadSector procedure is called from a 16-bit
; real-mode application written in Borland C++ 5.01.
; It can read FAT12, FAT16, and FAT32 disks under
; MS-DOS, Windows 95, Windows 98, and Windows Me.

Public _ReadSector
.model small
.386

DiskIO STRUC
    strtSector  DD ?            ; starting sector number
    nmSectors   DW 1            ; number of sectors
    bufferOfs   DW ?            ; buffer offset
    bufferSeg   DW ?            ; buffer segment
DiskIO ENDS

.data
diskStruct DiskIO <>

.code
;------------------------------------------------------------
_ReadSector PROC NEAR C
 ARG bufferPtr:WORD, startSector:DWORD, driveNumber:WORD, \
     numSectors:WORD
;
; Read n sectors from a specified disk drive.
; Receives: pointer to buffer that will hold the sector,
;    data, starting sector number, drive number,
;    and number of sectors.
; Returns: nothing
;------------------------------------------------------------
```

```
            enter 0,0
            pusha
            mov  eax,startSector
            mov  diskStruct.strtSector,eax
            mov  ax,numSectors
            mov  diskStruct.nmSectors,ax
            mov  ax,bufferPtr
            mov  diskStruct.bufferOfs,ax
            push ds
            pop  diskStruct.bufferSeg

            mov  ax,7305h                 ; ABSDiskReadWrite
            mov  cx,0FFFFh                ; must be 0FFFFh
            mov  dx,driveNumber           ; drive number
            mov  bx,OFFSET diskStruct     ; sector number
            mov  si,0                     ; read mode
            int  21h                      ; read disk sector
            popa
            leave
            ret
    _ReadSector ENDP
    END
```

Because Borland Turbo Assembler was used to code this example, we use Borland's ARG keyword to specify the procedure arguments. The ARG directive allows you to specify the arguments in the same order as the corresponding C++ function declaration:

```
ASM:        _ReadSector PROC near C
            ARG bufferPtr:word, startSector:dword, \
                driveNumber:word, numSectors:word
C++:        extern "C" ReadSector(char buffer[],
                long startSector, int driveNum,
                int numSectors);
```

The arguments are pushed on the stack in reverse order, following the C calling convention. Farthest away from EBP is **numSectors**, the first parameter pushed on the stack, shown in the stack frame of Figure 12–3. **StartSector** is a 32-bit doubleword and occupies locations [bp+6] through [bp+09] on the stack. The program was compiled for the small memory model, so **buffer** is passed as a 16-bit near pointer.

Figure 12–3   ReadSector Procedure, Stack Frame.

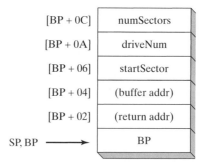

12.4.3   Example: Large Random Integers

To show a useful example of calling an external function from Borland C++, we can call **LongRand**, an assembly language function that returns a pseudorandom unsigned 32-bit integer. This is useful because the standard rand() function in the Borland C++ library only returns an integer between 0 and RAND_MAX (32,767). Our procedure returns an integer between 0 and 4,294,967,295.

This program is compiled in the large memory model, allowing the data to be larger than 64K, and requiring that 32-bit values be used for the return address and data pointer values. The external function declaration in C++ is

```
extern "C" unsigned long LongRandom();
```

The listing of the main program is shown here. The program allocates storage for an array called **rArray**. It uses a loop to call **LongRandom**, inserts each number in the array, and writes the number to standard output:

```cpp
// main.cpp

// Calls the external LongRandom function, written in
// assembly language, that returns an unsigned 32-bit
// random integer. Compile in the Large memory model.

#include <iostream.h>
extern "C" unsigned long LongRandom();
const int ARRAY_SIZE = 500;

int main()
{
  // Allocate array storage, fill with 32-bit
  // unsigned random integers, and display:

  unsigned long * rArray = new unsigned long[ARRAY_SIZE];

  for(unsigned i = 0; i < ARRAY_SIZE; i++)
  {
    rArray[i] = LongRandom();
    cout << rArray[i] << ',';
  }
  cout << endl;
  return 0;
}
```

The LongRandom Function   The assembly language module containing the **LongRandom** function is a simple adaptation of the **Random32** procedure from the book's link library:

```
; LongRandom procedure module                   (longrand.asm)

.model large
.386
Public _LongRandom
.data
seed   DWORD 12345678h

; Return an unsigned pseudo-random 32-bit integer
; in DX:AX,in the range 0 - FFFFFFFFh.
.code
_LongRandom  PROC far, C
        mov    eax, 343FDh
        mul    seed
        xor    edx,edx
        add    eax, 269EC3h
        mov    seed, eax           ; save the seed for next call
        ror    eax,8               ; rotate out the lowest digit
        shld   edx,eax,16          ; copy high 16 bits of EAX to DX
```

```
        ret
_LongRandom   ENDP
end
```

The ROR instruction helps to eliminate recurring patterns when small random integers are generated. Borland C++ expects the 32-bit function return value to be in the DX:AX registers, so we copy the high 16-bits from EAX into DX with the SHLD instruction, which seems conveniently designed for the task.

12.4.4 Section Review

1. Which registers and flags must be preserved by assembly language procedures called from Borland C++?

2. In Borland C++, how many bytes are used by the following types? 1) int, 2) enum, 3) float, 4) double.

3. In the ReadSector module in this section, if the ARG directive were not used, how would you code the following statement?

    ```
    mov   eax,startSector
    ```

4. In the **LongRandom** function shown in this section, what would happen to the output if the ROR instruction were eliminated?

12.5 Chapter Summary

Assembly language is the perfect tool for optimizing selected parts of a large application written in some high-level language. Assembly language is also a good tool for customizing certain procedures for specific hardware. These techniques require one of two approaches:

• Write inline assembly code embedded within high-level language code.
• Link assembly language procedures to high-level language code.

Both approaches have their merits and their limitations. In this chapter, we presented both approaches.

The naming convention used by a language refers to the way segments and modules are named, as well as rules or characteristics regarding the naming of variables and procedures. The memory model used by a program determines whether calls and references will be near (within the same segment) or far (between different segments).

When calling an assembly language procedure from a program written in another language, any identifiers that are shared between the two languages must be compatible. You must also use segment names in the procedure that are compatible with the calling program. The writer of a procedure uses the high-level language's calling convention to determine how to receive parameters. The calling convention affects whether the stack pointer must be restored by the called procedure or by the calling program.

In Visual C++, the __asm directive is used for writing inline assembly code in a C++ source program. In this chapter, a File Encryption program was used to demonstrate inline assembly language.

This chapter showed how to link assembly language procedures to Microsoft Visual C++ programs running in protected mode and Borland C++ programs running in real-address mode.

When calling functions from the Standard C (C++) library, create a stub program in C or C++ containing a main( )function. When main( ) starts, the compiler's runtime library is automatically initialized. From main( ), you can call a startp procedure in the assembly language module. The assembly language module can call any function from the C Standard Library.

A procedure named **FindArray** was written in assembly language and called from a Visual C++ program. We compared the assembly language source file generated by the compiler to hand-assembled code in our efforts to learn more about code optimization techniques. The ReadSector program showed a Borland C++ program running in real-address mode that calls an assembly language procedure to read disk sectors.

12.6 Programming Exercises

1. MultArray Example

Use the FindArray example from Section 12.3.1 as a model for this exercise. Write an assembly language procedure named MultArray that multiplies a doubleword array by an integer. Write the same function in C++. Create a test program that calls both versions of MultArray from loops and compares their execution times.

2. ReadSector, Hexadecimal Display

(Requires a 16-bit real-mode C++ compiler, running under MS-DOS, Windows 95, 98, or Millenium.) Add a new procedure to the C++ program in Section 12.4.2 that calls the **ReadSector** procedure. This new procedure should display each sector in hexadecimal. Use iomanip.setfill( ) to pad each output byte with a leading zero.

3. LongRandomArray Procedure

Using the **LongRandom** procedure in Section 12.4.3 as a starting point, create a procedure called **LongRandomArray** that fills an array with 32-bit unsigned random integers. Pass an array pointer from a C or C++ program, along with a count indicating the number of array elements to be filled:

```
extern "C" void LongRandomArray( unsigned long * buffer,
     unsigned count );
```

4. External TranslateBuffer Procedure

Write an external procedure in assembly language that performs the same type of encryption shown in the inline **TranslateBuffer** procedure from Section 12.2.2. Run the compiled program in the debugger, and judge whether this version runs any faster than the *Encode.cpp* program from Section 12.2.2.

5. Prime Number Program

Write an assembly language procedure that returns a value of 1 if the 32-bit integer passed in the EAX register is prime, and 0 if EAX is nonprime. Call this procedure from a high-level language program. Let the user input some very large numbers, and have your program display a message for each one indicating whether or not it is prime.

6. FindRevArray Procedure

Modify the **FindArray** procedure from Section 12.3.1. Name your function **FindRevArray**, and let it search backward from the end of the array. Return the index of the first matching value, or if no match is found, return –1.

End Notes

1. In the version of visual C++ we tested, you must include at least one statement that uses floating-point values to force Visual C++ to load the floating-point module. Otherwise, a "floating point not loaded" error occurs.

2. See Barry Kauler's, Windows Assembly Language and System Progamming, CMP Books, 1997.

13

16-Bit MS-DOS Programming

13.1 MS-DOS and the IBM-PC

IBM's PC-DOS was the first operating system to implement real-address mode on the IBM Personal Computer, using the Intel 8088 processor. Later, it evolved into Microsoft MS-DOS. Because of this history, it makes sense to use MS-DOS as the environment for explaining real-address mode programming. Real-address mode is also called *16-bit mode* because addresses are constructed from 16-bit values.

In this chapter, you will learn the basic memory organization of MS-DOS, how to activate MS-DOS function calls (called *interrupts*), and how to perform basic input-output operations at the operating system level. All of the programs in this chapter run in real-address mode because they use the INT instruction. Interrupts were originally designed to run under MS-DOS in real-address mode. It is possible to call interrupts in protected mode, but the techniques for doing so are beyond the scope of this book.

Real-address mode programs have the following characteristics:

- They can only address 1 megabyte of memory.
- Only one program can run at once (single tasking) in a single session.
- No memory boundary protection is possible, so any application program can overwrite memory used by the operating system.
- Offsets are 16 bits

When it first appeared, the IBM-PC had a strong appeal because it was affordable and it ran Lotus 1-2-3, the electronic spreadsheet program that was instrumental in the PC's adoption by businesses. Computer hobbyists loved the PC because it was an ideal tool for learning how computers work. It should be noted that Digital Research CP/M, the most popular 8-bit operating system before PC-DOS, was only capable of addressing 64K of RAM. From this point of view, PC-DOS's 640K seemed like a gift from heaven.

Because of the obvious memory and speed limitations of the early Intel microprocessors, the IBM-PC was a single-user computer. There was no built-in protection against memory corruption by application programs. In contrast, the minicomputer systems available at the time could handle multiple users and prevented application programs from overwriting each other's data. Over time, more-robust operating systems for the PC have become available, making it a viable alternative to minicomputer systems, particularly when PCs are networked together.

13.1.1   Memory Organization

In real-address mode, the lowest 640K of memory is used by both the operating system and application programs. Following this is video memory and reserved memory for hardware controllers. Finally, locations F0000 to FFFFF are reserved for system ROM (read-only memory). Figure 13–1 shows a simple memory map. Within the operating system area of memory, the lowest 1024 bytes of memory (addresses 00000 to 003FF) contain a table of 32-bit addresses named the *interrupt vector table*. These addresses, called *interrupt vectors*, are used by the CPU when processing hardware and software interrupts.

Just above the vector table is the *BIOS and MS-DOS data area*. Next is the *software BIOS*, which includes procedures that manage most I/O devices, including the keyboard, disk drive, video display, serial, and printer ports. BIOS procedures are loaded from a hidden system file on an MS-DOS system (boot) disk. The MS-DOS kernel is a collection of procedures (called *services*) that are also loaded from a file on the system disk.

Grouped with the MS-DOS kernel are the file buffers and installable device drivers. Next highest in memory, the resident part of the *command processor* is loaded from an executable file named *command.com*. The command processor interprets commands typed at the MS-DOS prompt and loads and executes programs stored on disk. A second part of the command processor occupies high memory just below location A0000.

Application programs can load into memory at the first address above the resident part of the command processor and can use memory all the way up to address 9FFFF. If the currently running program overwrites the transient command processor area, the latter is reloaded from the boot disk when the program exits.

Video Memory   The video memory area (VRAM) on an IBM-PC begins at location A0000, which is used when the video adapter is switched into graphics mode. When the video is in color text mode, memory location B8000 holds all text currently displayed on the screen. The screen is memory-mapped, so that each row and column on the screen corresponds to a 16-bit word in memory. When a character is copied into video memory, it immediately appears on the screen.

FIGURE 13-1   MS-DOS Memory Map.

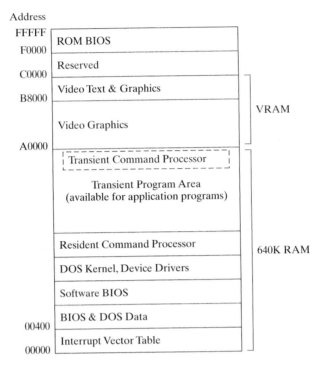

ROM BIOS The *ROM BIOS*, at memory locations F0000 to FFFFF, is an important part of the computer's operating system. It contains system diagnostic and configuration software, as well as low-level input-output procedures used by application programs. The BIOS is stored in a static memory chip on the system board. Most systems follow a standardized BIOS specification modeled after IBM's original BIOS and use the BIOS data area from 00400 to 004FF.

13.1.2   Redirecting Input-Output

Throughout this chapter, references will be made to the *standard input device* and the *standard output device*. Both are collectively called the *console*, which involves the keyboard for input and the video display for output.

When running programs from the command prompt, you can redirect standard input so that it is read from a file or hardware port rather than the keyboard. Standard output can be redirected to a file, printer, or other I/O device. Without this capability, programs would have to be substantially revised before their input-output could be changed. For example, the operating system has a program named *sort.exe* that sorts an input file. The following command sorts a file named *myfile.txt* and displays the output:

```
sort < myfile.txt
```

The following command sorts *myfile.txt* and sends the output to *outfile.txt:*

```
sort < myfile.txt > outfile.txt
```

You can use the pipe (|) symbol to copy the output from the DIR command to the input of the *sort.exe* program. The following command sorts the current disk directory and displays the output on the screen:

```
dir | sort
```

The following command sends the output of the sort program to the default (non-networked) printer (identified by PRN):

```
dir | sort > prn
```

The complete set of device names is shown in Table 13-1.

Table 13-1   Standard MS-DOS Device Names.

Device Name	Description
CON	Console (video display or keyboard)
LPT1 or PRN	First parallel printer
LPT2, LPT3	Parallel ports 2 and 3
COM1, COM2	Serial ports 1 and 2
NUL	Nonexistent or dummy device

13.1.3   Software Interrupts

A *software interrupt* is a call to an operating system procedure. Most of these procedures, called *interrupt handlers*, provide input-output capability to application programs. They are used for such tasks as the following:

- Displaying characters and strings
- Reading characters and strings from the keyboard
- Displaying text in color
- Opening and closing files
- Reading data from files
- Writing data to files
- Setting and retrieving the system time and date

13.1.4   INT Instruction

The INT (*call to interrupt procedure*) instruction calls a system subroutine also known as an *interrupt handler*. Before the INT instruction executes, one or more parameters must be inserted in registers. At the very least, a number identifying the particular procedure must be moved to the AH register. Depending on the function, other values may have to be passed to the interrupt in registers. The syntax is

```
INT number
```

where *number* is an integer in the range 0 to FF hexadecimal.

Interrupt Vectoring

The CPU processes the INT instruction using the interrupt vector table, which, as we've mentioned, is a table of addresses in the lowest 1024 bytes of memory. Each entry in this table is a 32-bit segment-offset address that points to an interrupt handler. The actual addresses in this table vary from one machine to another. Figure 13–2 illustrates the steps taken by the CPU when the INT instruction is invoked by a program:

- **Step 1:** The operand of the INT instruction is multiplied by 4 to locate the matching interrupt vector table entry.
- **Step 2:** The CPU pushes the flags and a 32-bit segment/offset return address on the stack, disables hardware interrupts, and executes a far call to the address stored at location (10h * 4) in the interrupt vector table (F000:F065).
- **Step 3:** The interrupt handler at F000:F065 executes until it reaches an IRET instruction.

- **Step 4:** The IRET (interrupt return) instruction pops the flags and the return address off the stack, causing the processor to resume execution immediately following the INT 10h instruction in the calling program.

Figure 13–2   Interrupt Vectoring Process.

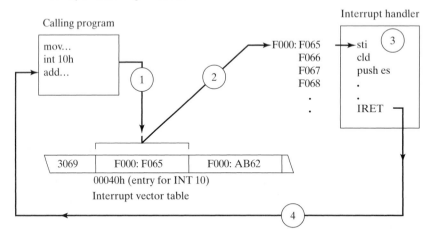

Common Interrupts

Software interrupts call *interrupt service routines* (ISRs) either in the BIOS or in DOS. Some frequently used interrupts are the following:

- ***INT 10h Video Services.*** Procedures that display routines that control the cursor position, write text in color, scroll the screen, and display video graphics.
- ***INT 16h Keyboard Services.*** Procedures that read the keyboard and check its status.
- ***INT 17h Printer Services.*** Procedures that initialize, print, and return the printer status.
- ***INT 1Ah Time of Day.*** Procedure that gets the number of clock ticks since the machine was turned on or sets the counter to a new value.
- ***INT 1Ch User Timer Interrupt.*** An empty procedure that is executed 18.2 times per second.
- ***INT 21h MS-DOS Services.*** Procedures that provide input-output, file handling, and memory management. Also known as *MS-DOS function calls.*

13.1.5   Coding for 16-Bit Programs

Programs designed for MS-DOS must be 16-bit applications running in real-address mode. Real-address mode applications use 16-bit segments and follow the segmented addressing scheme described in Section 2.3.1. If you're using a 32-bit processor, you can use the 32-bit general-purpose registers for data, even in real-address mode. Here is a summary of coding characteristics in 16-bit programs:

- The .MODEL directive specifies which memory model your program will use. We recommend the Small model, which keeps your code in one segment and your stack plus data in another segment:

  ```
  .MODEL small
  ```
- The .STACK directive allocates a small amount of local stack space for your program. Ordinarily, you rarely need more than 256 bytes of stack space. The following is particularly generous, with 512 bytes:

  ```
  .STACK 200h
  ```
- Optionally, you may want to enable the use of 32-bit registers. This can be done with the .386 directive:

  ```
  .386
  ```

- Two instructions are required at the beginning of main if your program references variables. They initialize the DS register to the starting location of the data segment, identified by the predefined MASM constant **@data**:

```
mov   ax,@data
mov   ds,ax
```

- Every program must include a statement that ends the program and returns to the operating system. One way to do this is to use the .EXIT directive:

```
.EXIT
```

Alternatively, you can call INT 21h, Function 4Ch:

```
mov   ah,4ch                    ; terminate process
int   21h                       ; MS-DOS interrupt
```

- You can assign values to segment registers using the MOV instruction, but do so only when assigning the address of a program segment.
- When assembling 16-bit programs, use the *make16.bat* (batch) file. It links to Irvine16.lib and executes the older Microsoft 16-bit linker (version 5.6).
- Real-address mode programs can only access hardware ports, interrupt vectors, and system memory when running under MS-DOS, Windows 95, 98, and Millenium. This type of access is not permitted under Windows NT, 2000, or XP.
- When the **Small** memory model is used, offsets (addresses) of data and code labels are 16 bits. The Irvine16 library uses the Small memory model, in which all code fits in a 16-bit segment and the program's data and stack fit into a 16-bit segment.
- In real-address mode, stack entries are 16 bits by default. You can still place a 32-bit value on the stack (it uses two stack entries).

You can simplify coding of 16-bit programs by including the Irvine16.inc file. It inserts the following statements into the assembly stream, which define the memory mode and calling convention, allocate stack space, enable 32-bit registers, and redefine the .EXIT directive as **exit**:

```
.MODEL small,stdcall
.STACK 200h
.386
exit EQU <.EXIT>
```

13.1.6 Section Review

1. What is the highest memory location into which you can load an application program?
2. What occupies the lowest 1024 bytes of memory?
3. What is the starting location of the BIOS and MS-DOS data area?
4. What is the name of the memory area containing low-level procedures used by the computer for input-output?
5. Show an example of redirecting a program's output to the printer.
6. What is the MS-DOS device name for the first parallel printer?
7. What is an interrupt service routine?
8. When the INT instruction executes, what is the first task carried out by the CPU?
9. What four steps are taken by the CPU when an INT instruction is invoked by a program? *Hint:* See Figure 13–2.
10. When an interrupt service routine finishes, how does an application program resume execution?
11. Which interrupt number is used for video services?
12. Which interrupt number is used for the time of day?
13. What offset within the interrupt vector table contains the address of the INT 21h interrupt handler?

13.2   MS-DOS Function Calls (INT 21h)

MS-DOS provides a lot of easy-to-use functions for displaying text on the console. They are all part of a group typically called *INT 21h MS-DOS Function calls*. There are about 200 different functions supported by this interrupt, identified by a *function number* placed in the AH register. An excellent, if somewhat outdated, source is Ray Duncan's book, *Advanced MS-DOS Programming,* 2nd Ed., Microsoft Press, 1988. A more comprehensive and up-to-date list, named *Ralf Brown's Interupt List*, can be found on the Web. See our Web site for details.

For each INT 21h function described in this chapter, we will list the necessary input parameters and return values, give notes about its use, and include a short code example that calls the function.

A number of functions require that the 32-bit address of an input parameter be stored in the DS:DX registers. DS, the data segment register, is usually set to your program's data area. If for some reason this is not the case, use the SEG operator to set DS to the segment containing the data passed to INT 21h. The following statements do this:

```
.data
inBuffer BYTE 80 DUP(?)
.code
mov   ax,SEG inBuffer
mov   ds,ax
mov   dx,OFFSET inBuffer
```

> The very first Intel assembly language program I wrote (around 1983) displayed a "*" on the screen:
> ```
> mov ah,2
> mov dl,'*'
> int 21h
> ```
> People said assembly language was difficult, but this was encouraging! As it turned out, there were a few more details to learn before writing nontrivial programs.

INT 21h Function 4Ch: Terminate Process   INT 21h Function 4Ch terminates the current program (called a *process*). In the real-address mode programs presented in this book, we have relied on a macro definition in the Irvine16 library named **exit**. It is defined as

```
exit TEXTEQU <.EXIT>
```

In other words, **exit** is an alias, or substitute for .EXIT (the MASM directive that ends a program). The **exit** symbol was created so you could use a single command to terminate 16-bit and 32-bit programs. In 16-bit programs, the code generated by **.EXIT** is

```
mov   ah,4Ch                        ; terminate process
int   21h
```

If you supply an optional return code argument to the .EXIT macro, the assembler generates an additional instruction that moves the return code to AL:

```
.EXIT 0                             ; macro call
```

Generated code:

```
mov   ah,4Ch                        ; terminate process
mov   al,0                          ; return code
int   21h
```

The value in AL, called the *process return code*, is received by the calling process (including a batch file) to indicate the returns status of your program. By convention, a return code of zero is considered successful completion. Other return codes between 1 and 255 can be used to indicate additional outcomes that have specific meaning for your program. For example, ML.EXE, the Microsoft Assembler, returns 0 if a program assembles correctly and a nonzero value if it does not.

> Appendix C contains a fairly extensive list of BIOS and MS-DOS interrupts.

13.2.1   Selected Output Functions

In this section we present some of the most common INT 21h functions for writing characters and text. None of these functions alters the default current screen colors, so output will only be in color if you have previously set the screen color by other means. (For example, you can call video BIOS functions from Chapter 15.)

Filtering Control Characters   All of the functions in this section *filter*, or interpret ASCII control characters. If you write a backspace character to standard output, for example, the cursor moves one column to the left. Table 13-2 contains a list of control characters that you are likely to encounter.

Table 13-2   ASCII Control Characters.

ASCII Code	Description
08h	Backspace (moves one column to the left)
09h	Horizontal tab (skips forward *n* columns)
0Ah	Line feed (moves to next output line)
0Ch	Form feed (moves to next printer page)
0Dh	Carriage return (moves to leftmost output column)
1Bh	Escape character

The next several tables describe the important features of INT 21h Functions 2, 5, 6, 9, and 40h. INT 21h Function 2 writes a single character to standard output. INT 21h Function 5 writes a single character to the printer. INT 21h Function 6 writes a single unfiltered character to standard output. INT 21h Function 9 writes a string (terminated by a $ character) to standard output. INT 21h Function 40h writes an array of bytes to a file or device.

INT 21h Function 2	
Description	Write a single character to standard output and advance the cursor one column forward
Receives	AH = 2 DL = character value
Returns	Nothing

Sample call	```mov ah,2```
	```mov dl,'A'```
	```int 21h```

INT 21h Function 5	
Description	Write a single character to the printer
Receives	AH = 5 DL = character value
Returns	Nothing

Sample call	```mov ah,5 ; select printer output```
	```mov dl,"Z" ; character to be printed```
	```int 21h ; call MS-DOS```

Notes	MS-DOS waits until the printer is ready to accept the character. You can terminate the wait by pressing the Ctrl-Break keys. The default output is to the printer port for LPT1.

INT 21h Function 6	
Description	Write a character to standard output
Receives	AH = 6 DL = character value
Returns	If ZF = 0, AL contains the character's ASCII code

Sample call	```mov ah,6```
	```mov dl,"A"```
	```int 21h```

Notes	Unlike other INT 21h functions, this one does not filter (interpret) ASCII control characters.

INT 21h Function 9	
Description	Write a $-terminated string to standard output
Receives	AH = 9 DS:DX = segment/offset of the string
Returns	Nothing

Sample call	```.data```
	```string BYTE "This is a string$"```
	```.code```
	```mov ah,9```
	```mov dx,OFFSET string```
	```int 21h```

Notes	The string must be terminated by a dollar-sign character ($).

INT 21h Function 40h	
Description	Write an array of bytes to a file or device
Receives	AH = 40h BX = file or device handle (console = 1) CX = number of bytes to write DS:DX = address of array
Returns	AX = number of bytes written
| **Sample call** | ```
.data
message "Hello, world"
.code
mov  ah,40h
mov  bx,1
mov  cx,LENGTHOF message
mov  dx,OFFSET message
int  21h
``` |

13.2.2 Hello World Program Example

The following is a simple program that displays a string on the screen using an MS-DOS function call:

```
TITLE Hello World Program        (Hello.asm)

.MODEL small
.STACK 100h
.386

.data
message BYTE "Hello, world!",0dh,0ah

.code
main PROC
        mov   ax,@data                ; initialize DS
        mov   ds,ax

        mov   ah,40h                  ; write to file/device
        mov   bx,1                    ; output handle
        mov   cx,SIZEOF message       ; number of bytes
        mov   dx,OFFSET message       ; addr of buffer
        int   21h

        .EXIT
main ENDP
END main
```

Alternate Version Another way to write Hello.asm is to use the predefined .STARTUP directive (which initializes the DS register). Doing so requires the removal of the label next to the END directive:

```
TITLE Hello World Program        (Hello2.asm)

.MODEL small
.STACK 100h
.386

.data
message BYTE "Hello, world!",0dh,0ah
```
```

```
.code
main PROC
    .STARTUP
        mov   ah,40h              ; write to file/device
        mov   bx,1                ; output handle
        mov   cx,SIZEOF message   ; number of bytes
        mov   dx,OFFSET message   ; addr of buffer
        int   21h
    .EXIT
main ENDP
END
```

13.2.3 Selected Input Functions

In this section, we describe a few of the most commonly used MS-DOS functions that read from standard input. For a more complete list, see Appendix C. As shown in the following table, INT 21h Function 1 reads a single character from standard input:

INT 21h Function 1	
Description	Read a single character from standard input
Receives	AH = 1
Returns	AL = character (ASCII code)

Sample call	`mov   ah,1`
	`int   21h`
	`mov   char,al`

Notes	If no character is present in the input buffer, the program waits. This function echoes the character to standard output.

INT 21h Function 6 reads a character from standard input if the character is waiting in the input buffer. If the buffer is empty, the function returns with the Zero flag set and no other action is taken:

INT 21h Function 6	
Description	Read a character from standard input without waiting
Receives	AH = 6 DL = FFh
Returns	If ZF = 0, AL contains the character's ASCII code.

Sample call	`mov   ah,6`
	`mov   dl,0FFh`
	`int   21h`
	`jz    skip`
	`mov   char,AL`
	`skip:`

Notes	The interrupt only returns a character if one is already waiting in the input buffer. Does not echo the character to standard output and does not filter control characters.

INT 21h Function 0Ah reads a buffered string from standard input, terminated by the Enter key. When calling this function, pass a pointer to an input structure having the following format (**count** can be between 0 and 128):

```
count = 80
KEYBOARD STRUCT
      maxInput BYTE count          ; max chars to input
      inputCount BYTE ?            ; actual input count
      buffer BYTE count DUP(?)     ; holds input chars
KEYBOARD ENDS
```

The *maxInput* field specifies the maximum number of characters the user can input, including the Enter key. The backspace key can be used to erase characters and back up the cursor. The user terminates the input either by pressing the Enter key or by pressing Ctrl-Break. All non-ASCII keys, such as PageUp and F1, are filtered out and are not stored in the buffer. After the function returns, the *inputCount* field indicates how many characters were input, not counting the Enter key. The following table describes Function 0Ah:

INT 21h Function 0Ah	
Description	Read an array of buffered characters from standard input
Receives	AH = 0Ah DS:DX = address of keyboard input structure
Returns	The structure is initialized with the input characters.

Sample call	```.data
	kybdData KEYBOARD <>
	.code
	      mov ah,0Ah
	      mov dx,OFFSET kybdData
	      int 21h```

INT 21h Function 0Bh gets the status of the standard input buffer:

INT 21h Function 0Bh	
Description	Get the status of the standard input buffer
Receives	AH = 0Bh
Returns	If a character is waiting, AL = 0FFh; otherwise, AL = 0.

Sample Call	``` mov ah,0Bh
	      int 21h
	      cmp al,0
	      je skip
	      ; (input the character)
	skip:```

Notes	Does not remove the character.

Example: String Encryption Program

INT 21h Function 6 has the unique ability to read characters from standard input without pausing the program or filtering control characters. This can be put to good use if we run a program from the command prompt and redirect the input. That is, the input will come from a text file rather than the keyboard.

The following program (*Encrypt.asm*) reads each character from standard input, uses the XOR instruction to alter the character, and writes the altered character to standard output:

```
TITLE Encryption Program                 (Encrypt.asm)

; This program uses MS-DOS function calls to
; read and encrypt a file. Run it from the
; command prompt, using redirection:
;    Encrypt < infile.txt > outfile.txt
; Function 6 is also used for output, to avoid
; filtering ASCII control characters.

INCLUDE Irvine16.inc
XORVAL = 239                      ; any value between 0-255
.code
main PROC
        mov     ax,@data
        mov     ds,ax

L1:
        mov     ah,6              ; direct console input
        mov     dl,0FFh          ; don't wait for character
        int     21h              ; AL = character
        jz      L2               ; quit if ZF = 1 (EOF)
        xor     al,XORVAL
        mov     ah,6             ; write to output
        mov     dl,al
        int     21h
        jmp     L1               ; repeat the loop
L2:     exit
main ENDP
END  main
```

The choice of 239 as the encryption value is completely arbitrary. You can use any value between 0 and 255 in this context, although using 0 will not cause any encryption to occur. The encryption is weak, of course, but it might be enough to discourage the average user from trying to defeat the encryption. When you run the program at the command prompt, indicate the name of the input file (and output file, if any). The following are two examples:

encrypt < infile.txt	Input from file (infile.txt), output to console
encrypt < infile.txt > outfile.txt	Input from file (infile.txt), output to file (outfile.txt)

Int 21h Function 3Fh

INT 21h Function 3Fh, as shown in the following table, reads an array of bytes from a file or device. It can be used for keyboard input when the device handle in BX is equal to zero:

INT 21h Function 3Fh	
Description	Read an array of bytes from a file or device
Receives	AH = 3Fh BX = file/device handle (0 = keyboard) CX = maximum bytes to read DS:DX = address of input buffer
Returns	AX = number of bytes actually read
| **Sample Call** | ```
.data
inputBuffer BYTE 127 dup(0)
bytesRead WORD ?
.code
mov   ah,3Fh
mov   bx,0
mov   cx,127
mov   dx,OFFSET inputBuffer
int   21h
mov   bytesRead,ax
``` |
| **Notes** | If reading from the keyboard, input terminates when the Enter key is pressed, and the 0Dh, 0Ah, characters are appended to the input buffer. |

If the user enters more characters than were requested by the function call, excess characters remain in the MS-DOS input buffer. If the function is called anytime later in the program, execution may not pause and wait for user input because the buffer already contains data (including the 0Dh, 0Ah, marking the end of the line). This can even occur between separate instances of program execution. To be absolutely sure your program works as intended, you need to flush the input buffer, one character at a time, after calling Function 3Fh. The following code does this (see the *Keybd.asm* program for a complete demonstration):

```
;---------------------------------------
FlushBuffer PROC
; Flush the standard input buffer.
; Receives: nothing. Returns: nothing
;---------------------------------------
.data
oneByte BYTE ?
.code
    pusha
L1:
    mov   ah,3Fh             ; read file/device
    mov   bx,0               ; keyboard handle
    mov   cx,1               ; one byte
    mov   dx,OFFSET oneByte  ; save it here
    int   21h               ; call MS-DOS
    cmp   oneByte,0Ah        ; end of line yet?
    jne   L1                 ; no: read another
    popa
    ret
FlushBuffer ENDP
```
```

13.2.4 Date/Time Functions

Many popular software applications display the current date and time. Others retrieve the date and time and use it in their internal logic. A scheduling program, for example, can use the current date to verify that a user is not accidentally scheduling an appointment in the past.

As shown in the next series of tables, INT 21h Function 2Ah gets the system date, and INT 21h Function 2Bh sets the system date. INT 21h Function 2Ch gets the system time, and INT 21h Function 2Dh sets the system time.

INT 21h Function 2Ah	
Description	Get the system date
Receives	AH = 2Ah
Returns	CX = year DH, DL = month, day AL = day of week (Sunday = 0, Monday = 1, etc.)
Sample Call	```mov ah,2Ah
int   21h
mov   year,cx
mov   month,dh
mov   day,dl
mov   dayOfWeek,al```

INT 21h Function 2Bh	
Description	Set the system date
Receives	AH = 2Bh CX = year DH = month DL = day
Returns	If the change was successful, AL = 0; otherwise, AL = FFh.
Sample Call	```mov ah,2Bh
mov   cx,year
mov   dh,month
mov   dl,day
int   21h
cmp   al,0
jne   failed```
Notes	Probably will not work if you are running Windows NT, 2000, or XP with a restricted user profile.

INT 21h Function 2Ch	
Description	Get the system time
Receives	AH = 2Ch
Returns	CH = hours (0 – 23) CL = minutes (0 – 59) DH = seconds (0 – 59) DL = hundredths of seconds (usually not accurate)

Sample Call	```mov ah,2Ch```
	```int 21h```
	```mov hours,ch```
	```mov minutes,cl```
	```mov seconds,dh```

INT 21h Function 2Dh	
Description	Set the system time
Receives	AH = 2Dh CH = hours (0 – 23) CL = minutes (0 – 59) DH = seconds (0 – 59)
Returns	If the change was successful, AL = 0; otherwise, AL = FFh

Sample Call	```mov ah,2Dh```
	```mov ch,hours```
	```mov cl,minutes```
	```mov dh,seconds```
	```int 21h```
	```cmp al,0```
	```jne failed```

Notes	Probably will not work if you are running Windows NT, 2000, or XP with a restricted user profile.

Example: Displaying the Time and Date

The following program (*DateTime.asm*) displays the system date and time. The code is a little longer than one would expect because the program inserts leading zeros before the hours, minutes, and seconds:

```
TITLE Display the Date and Time     (DateTime.asm)

Include Irvine16.inc
Write PROTO char:BYTE
.data
str1 BYTE "Date: ",0
str2 BYTE ",  Time: ",0
```

```
        .code
        main PROC
            mov   ax,@data
            mov   ds,ax

        ; Display the date:
            mov     dx,OFFSET str1
            call    WriteString
            mov     ah,2Ah                  ; get system date
            int     21h
            movzx   eax,dh                  ; month
            call    WriteDec
            INVOKE  Write,'-'
            movzx   eax,dl                  ; day
            call    WriteDec
            INVOKE  Write,'-'
            movzx   eax,cx                  ; year
            call    WriteDec

        ; Display the time:
            mov     dx,OFFSET str2
            call    WriteString
            mov     ah,2Ch                  ; get system time
            int     21h
            movzx   eax,ch                  ; hours
            call    WritePaddedDec
            INVOKE  Write,':'
            movzx   eax,cl                  ; minutes
            call    WritePaddedDec
            INVOKE  Write,':'
            movzx   eax,dh                  ; seconds
            call    WritePaddedDec
            call    Crlf

            exit
        main ENDP

        ;----------------------------------------------
        Write PROC char:BYTE
        ; Display a single character.
        ;----------------------------------------------
            push    eax
            push    edx
            mov     ah,2                    ; character output function
            mov     dl,char
            int     21h
            pop     edx
            pop     eax
            ret
        Write ENDP

        ;----------------------------------------------
        WritePaddedDec PROC
        ; Display unsigned integer in EAX, padding
        ; to two digit positions with a leading zero.
        ;----------------------------------------------
            .IF eax < 10
```

```
        push    eax
        push    edx
        mov     ah,2                    ; display leading zero
        mov     dl,'0'
        int     21h
        pop     edx
        pop     eax
        .ENDIF
        call    WriteDec                ; write unsigned decimal
        ret                             ; using value in EAX
WritePaddedDec ENDP
END main
```

Sample output:

```
Date: 12-8-2006,  Time: 23:01:23
```

13.2.5   Section Review

1. Which register holds the function number when calling INT 21h?

2. Which INT 21h function terminates a program?

3. Which INT 21h function writes a single character to standard output?

4. Which INT 21h function writes a string terminated by a $ character to standard output?

5. Which INT 21h function writes a block of data to a file or device?

6. Which INT 21h function reads a single character from standard input?

7. Which INT 21h function reads a block of data from the standard input device?

8. If you want to get the system date, display it, and then change it, which INT 21h functions are required?

9. Which INT 21h functions shown in this chapter probably will not work under Windows NT, 2000, or XP with a restricted user profile?

10. Which INT 21h function would you use to check the standard input buffer to see if a character is waiting to be processed?

13.3   Standard MS-DOS File I/O Services

INT 21h provides more file and directory I/O services that we can possibly show here. Table 13-3 shows a few of the functions you are likely to use.

Table 13-3   File- and Directory-Related INT 21h Functions.

Function	Description
716Ch	Create or open a file
3Eh	Close file handle
42h	Move file pointer
5706h	Get file creation date and time

File/Device Handles   MS-DOS and MS-Windows use 16-bit integers called *handles* to identify files and I/O devices. There are five predefined device handles. Each, except handle 2 (error output), supports redirection at the command prompt. The following handles are available all the time:

0	Keyboard (standard input)
1	Console (standard output)
2	Error output
3	Auxiliary device (asynchronous)
4	Printer

Each I/O function has a common characteristic: If it fails, the Carry flag is set, and an error code is returned in AX. You can use this error code to display an appropriate message. Table 13-4 contains a list of the error codes and their descriptions.

> Microsoft provides extensive documentation on MS-DOS function calls. Search the Platform SDK documentation for *Windows 9x*.

Table 13-4   MS-DOS Extended Error Codes.

Error Code	Description
01	Invalid function number
02	File not found
03	Path not found
04	Too many open files (no handles left)
05	Access denied
06	Invalid handle
07	Memory control blocks destroyed
08	Insufficient memory
09	Invalid memory block address
0A	Invalid environment
0B	Invalid format
0C	Invalid access code
0D	Invalid data
0E	Reserved
0F	Invalid drive was specified
10	Attempt to remove the current directory
11	Not same device
12	No more files
13	Diskette write-protected
14	Unknown unit
15	Drive not ready
16	Unknown command
17	Data error (CRC)
18	Bad request structure length
19	Seek error
1A	Unknown media type
1B	Sector not found
1C	Printer out of paper
1D	Write fault
1E	Read fault
1F	General failure

13.3.1   Create or Open File (716Ch)

INT 21h Function 716Ch can either create a new file or open an existing file. It permits the use of extended filenames and file sharing. As shown in the following table, the filename may optionally include a directory path.

INT 21h Function 716Ch	
Description	Create new file or open existing file
Receives	AX = 716Ch BX = access mode (0 = read, 1 = write, 2 = read/write) CX = attributes (0 = normal, 1 = read only, 2 = hidden, 3 = system, 8 = volume ID, 20h = archive) DX = action (1 = open, 2 = truncate, 10h = create) DS:SI = segment/offset of filename DI = alias hint (optional)
Returns	If the create/open was successful, CF = 0, AX = file handle, and CX = action taken. If create/open failed, CF = 1.

Sample Call	<pre>mov ax,716Ch ; extended open/create
	mov bx,0 ; read-only
	mov cx,0 ; normal attribute
	mov dx,1 ; open existing file
	mov si,OFFSET Filename
	int 21h
	jc failed
	mov handle,ax ; file handle
	mov actionTaken,cx ; action taken</pre>

Notes	The access mode in BX can optionally be combined with one of the following sharing mode values: OPEN_SHARE_COMPATIBLE, OPEN_SHARE_DENYREADWRITE, OPEN_SHARE_DENYWRITE, OPEN_SHARE_DENYREAD, OPEN_SHARE_DENYNONE. The action taken returned in CX can be one of the following values: ACTION_OPENED, ACTION_CREATED_OPENED, ACTION_REPLACED_OPENED. All are defined in Irvine16.inc.

Additional Examples   The following code either creates a new file or truncates an existing file having the same name:

```
mov   ax,716Ch        ; extended open/create
mov   bx,2            ; read-write
mov   cx,0            ; normal attribute
mov   dx,10h + 02h    ; action: create + truncate
mov   si,OFFSET Filename
int   21h
jc    failed
mov   handle,ax       ; file handle
mov   actionTaken,cx  ; action taken to open file
```

The following code attempts to create a new file. It fails (with the Carry flag set) if the file already exists:

```
mov   ax,716Ch        ; extended open/create
mov   bx,2            ; read-write
mov   cx,0            ; normal attribute
```

```
mov    dx,10h                ; action: create
mov    si,OFFSET Filename
int    21h
jc     failed
mov    handle,ax             ; file handle
mov    actionTaken,cx        ; action taken to open file
```

13.3.2 Close File Handle (3Eh)

INT 21h Function 3Eh closes a file handle. This function flushes the file's write buffer by copying any remaining data to disk, as shown in the following table:

INT 21h Function 3Eh	
Description	Close file handle
Receives	AH = 3Eh BX = file handle
Returns	If the file was closed successfully, CF = 0; otherwise, CF = 1.
Sample Call	```.data
filehandle WORD ?
.code
mov   ah,3Eh
mov   bx,filehandle
int   21h
jc   failed```
Notes	If the file has been modified, its time stamp and date stamp are updated.

13.3.3 Move File Pointer (42h)

INT 21h Function 42h, as can be seen in the following table, moves the position pointer of an open file to a new location. When calling this function, the *method code* in AL identifies how the pointer will be set:

0	Offset from the beginning of the file
1	Offset from the current location
2	Offset from the end of the file

INT 21h Function 42h	
Description	Move file pointer
Receives	AH = 42h AL = method code BX = file handle CX:DX = 32-bit offset value
Returns	If the file pointer was moved successfully, CF = 0 and DX:AX returns the new file pointer offset; otherwise, CF = 1.
Sample Call	```mov ah,42h
mov   al,0   ; method: offset from beginning
mov   bx,handle
mov   cx,offsetHi
mov   dx,offsetLo
int   21h```
Notes	The returned file pointer offset in DX:AX is always relative to the beginning of the file.

13.3.4 Get File Creation Date and Time

INT 21h Function 5706h, shown in the following table, obtains the date and time when a file was created. This is not necessarily the same date and time when the file was last modified or even accessed. To learn about MS-DOS packed date and time formats, see Section 14.3.1. To see an example of extracting date/time fields, see Section 7.3.4.

INT 21h Function 5706h	
Description	Get file creation date and time
Receives	AX = 5706h BX = file handle
Returns	If the function call was successful, CF = 0, DX = date (in MS-DOS packed format), CX = time, and SI = milliseconds. If the function failed, CF = 1.

Sample Call	```mov ax,5706h ; Get creation date/time```
	```mov bx,handle```
	```int 21h```
	```jc error ; quit if failed```
	```mov date,dx```
	```mov time,cx```
	```mov milliseconds,si```

Notes	The file must already be open. The *milliseconds* value indicates the number of 10-millisecond intervals to add to the MS-DOS time. Range is 0 to 199, indicating that the field can add as many as 2 seconds to the overall time.

13.3.5 Selected Library Procedures

Two procedures from the Irvine16 link library are shown here: **ReadString** and **WriteString. ReadString** is the trickiest of the two, since it must read one character at a time until it encounters the end of line sequence (0Dh, 0Ah). It reads these two characters from standard input without copying them to the buffer.

ReadString

The **ReadString** procedure reads a string from standard input and places the characters in an input buffer as a null-terminated string. It terminates when the user presses the Enter key.:

```
;------------------------------------------------------
ReadString PROC
; Receives: DS:DX points to the input buffer,
;           CX = maximum input size
; Returns:  AX = size of the input string
; Comments: Stops when the Enter key (0Dh) is pressed.
;------------------------------------------------------
        push   cx                      ; save registers
        push   si
        push   cx                      ; save digit count again
        mov    si,dx                   ; point to input buffer

L1:     mov    ah,1                    ; function: keyboard input
        int    21h                     ; returns character in AL
        cmp    al,0Dh                  ; end of line?
        je     L2                      ; yes: exit
        mov    [si],al                 ; no: store the character
        inc    si                      ; increment buffer pointer
        loop   L1                      ; loop until CX=0
```

```
L2:   mov  byte ptr [si],0        ; end with a null byte
      pop  ax                     ; original digit count
      sub  ax,cx                  ; AX = size of input string
      pop  si                     ; restore registers
      pop  cx
      ret
ReadString ENDP
```

WriteString

The **WriteString** procedure writes a null-terminated string to standard output. It calls a helper procedure named **Str_length** that returns the number of bytes in a string:

```
;------------------------------------------------------------
WriteString PROC
; Writes a null-terminated string to standard output
; Receives: DS:DX = address of string
; Returns: nothing
;------------------------------------------------------------
      pusha
      push  ds                    ; set ES to DS
      pop   es
      mov   di,dx                 ; ES:DI = string ptr
      call  Str_length            ; AX = string length
      mov   cx,ax                 ; CX = number of bytes
      mov   ah,40h                ; write to file or device
      mov   bx,1                  ; standard output handle
      int   21h                   ; call MS-DOS
      popa
      ret
WriteString ENDP
```

13.3.6 Example: Read and Copy a Text File

We presented INT 21h Function 3Fh earlier in this chapter, in the context of reading from standard input. This function can also be used to read a file if the handle in BX identifies a file that has been opened for input. When Function 3Fh returns, AX indicates the number of bytes actually read from the file. When the end of the file is reached, the value returned in AX is less than the number of bytes requested (in CX).

We also presented INT 21h Function 40h earlier in this chapter in the context of writing to standard output (device handle 1). Instead, the handle in BX can refer to an open file. The function automatically updates the file's position pointer, so the next call to Function 40h begins writing where the previous call left off.

The *Readfile.asm* program we're about to present demonstrates several INT 21h functions presented in this section:

- Function 716Ch: Create new file or open existing file
- Function 3Fh: Read from file or device
- Function 40h: Write to file or device
- Function 3Eh: Close file handle

The following program opens a text file for input, reads no more than 5,000 bytes from the file, displays it on the console, creates a new file, and copies the data to a new file:

```
TITLE Read a text file          (Readfile.asm)

; Read, display, and copy a text file.
INCLUDE Irvine16.inc
```

```
        .data
        BufSize = 5000
        infile      BYTE "my_text_file.txt",0
        outfile     BYTE "my_output_file.txt",0
        inHandle    WORD ?
        outHandle   WORD ?
        buffer      BYTE BufSize DUP(?)
        bytesRead   WORD ?

        .code
        main PROC
            mov     ax,@data
            mov     ds,ax

        ; Open the input file
            mov     ax,716Ch            ; extended create or open
            mov     bx,0                ; mode = read-only
            mov     cx,0                ; normal attribute
            mov     dx,1                ; action: open
            mov     si,OFFSET infile
            int     21h                 ; call MS-DOS
            jc      quit                ; quit if error
            mov     inHandle,ax

        ; Read the input file
            mov     ah,3Fh              ; read file or device
            mov     bx,inHandle         ; file handle
            mov     cx,BufSize          ; max bytes to read
            mov     dx,OFFSET buffer    ; buffer pointer
            int     21h
            jc      quit                ; quit if error
            mov     bytesRead,ax

        ; Display the buffer
            mov     ah,40h              ; write file or device
            mov     bx,1                ; console output handle
            mov     cx,bytesRead        ; number of bytes
            mov     dx,OFFSET buffer    ; buffer pointer
            int     21h
            jc      quit                ; quit if error

        ; Close the file
            mov     ah,3Eh              ; function: close file
            mov     bx,inHandle         ; input file handle
            int     21h                 ; call MS-DOS
            jc      quit                ; quit if error

        ; Create the output file
            mov     ax,716Ch            ; extended create or open
            mov     bx,1                ; mode = write-only
            mov     cx,0                ; normal attribute
            mov     dx,12h              ; action: create/truncate
            mov     si,OFFSET outfile
            int     21h                 ; call MS-DOS
            jc      quit                ; quit if error
            mov     outHandle,ax        ; save handle

        ; Write buffer to new file
            mov     ah,40h              ; write file or device
```

```
        mov     bx,outHandle            ; output file handle
        mov     cx,bytesRead            ; number of bytes
        mov     dx,OFFSET buffer        ; buffer pointer
        int     21h
        jc      quit                    ; quit if error

; Close the file
        mov     ah,3Eh                  ; function: close file
        mov     bx,outHandle            ; output file handle
        int     21h                     ; call MS-DOS

quit:
        call    Crlf
        exit
main ENDP
END main
```

13.3.7 Reading the MS-DOS Command Tail

In the programs that follow, we will often pass information to programs on the command line. Suppose we needed to pass the name *file1.doc* to a program named *attr.exe*. The MS-DOS command line would be

```
    attr file1.doc
```

When a program starts up, any additional text on its command line is automatically stored in the 128-byte *MS-DOS Command Tail* located in memory at offset 80h from the beginning of the segment address specified by the ES register. The memory area is named the *program segment prefix* (PSP). The program segment prefix is discussed in Section 16.3.1. Also see Section 2.3.1 for a discussion of how segmented addressing works in real-address mode.

The first byte contains the length of the command line. If its value is greater than zero, the second byte contains a space character. The remaining bytes contain the text typed on the command line. Using the example command line for the *attr.exe* program, the hexadecimal contents of the command tail would be the following:

Offset:	80	81	82	83	84	85	86	87	88	89	8A	8B
Contents:	0A	20	46	49	4C	45	31	2E	44	4F	43	0D
			F	I	L	E	1	.	D	O	C	

You can see the command tail bytes using the Microsoft CodeView debugger if you load the program and set the command-line arguments before running the program.

> To set command-line parameters in CodeView, choose *Set Runtime Arguments...* from the *Run* menu. Press F10 to execute the first program instruction, open a memory window, select *Memory* from the *Options* menu, and enter ES:0x80 into the *Address Expression* field.

There is one exception to the rule that MS-DOS stores all characters after the command or program name: It doesn't keep the file and device names used when redirecting input-output. For example, MS-DOS does not save any text in the command tail when the following command is typed because both *infile.txt* and PRN are used for redirection:

```
    prog1 < infile.txt > prn
```

GetCommandTail Procedure   The **GetCommandTail** procedure from the Irvine16 library returns a copy of the running program's command tail under MS-DOS. When calling this procedure, set DX to the offset of the buffer where the command tail will be copied. Real-address mode programs often deal directly with segment registers so they can access data in different memory segments. For example, GetCommandTail saves the current value of ES on the stack, obtains the PSP segment using INT 21h Function 62h and copies it to ES:

```
push es
    .
    .
    .
mov   ah,62h                    ; get PSP segment address
int   21h                       ; returned in BX
mov   es,bx                     ; copied to ES
```

Next, it locates a byte inside the PSP. Because ES does not point to the program's default data segment, we must use a *segment override* (es:) to address data inside the program segment prefix:

```
mov   cl,es:[di-1]              ; get length byte
```

GetCommandTail skips over leading spaces with SCASB and sets the Carry flag if the command tail is empty. This makes it easy for the calling program to execute a JC (*jump carry*) instruction if nothing is typed on the command line:

```
        cld                    ; scan in forward direction
        mov   al,20h           ; space character
        repz  scasb            ; scan for non space
        jz    L2               ; all spaces found
        .
        .
L2:     stc                    ; CF=1 means no command tail
```

SCASB automatically scans memory pointed to by the ES segment registers, so we had no choice but to set ES to the PSP segment at the beginning of GetCommandTail. Here's a complete listing:

```
GetCommandTail PROC
;
; Gets a copy of the MS-DOS command tail at PSP:80h.
; Receives: DX contains the offset of the buffer
;     that receives a copy of the command tail.
; Returns: CF=1 if the buffer is empty; otherwise,
;     CF=0.
;-------------------------------------------------------
SPACE = 20h
        push es
        pusha                  ; save general registers

        mov   ah,62h           ; get PSP segment address
        int   21h              ; returned in BX
        mov   es,bx            ; copied to ES

        mov   si,dx            ; point to buffer
        mov   di,81h           ; PSP offset of command tail
        mov   cx,0             ; byte count
        mov   cl,es:[di-1]     ; get length byte
        cmp   cx,0             ; is the tail empty?
        je    L2               ; yes: exit
        cld                    ; scan in forward direction
        mov   al,SPACE         ; space character
        repz  scasb            ; scan for non space
        jz    L2               ; all spaces found
        dec   di               ; non space found
        inc   cx
```

By default, the assembler assumes that DI is an offset from the segment address in DS. The segment override (es:[di]) tells the CPU to use the segment address in ES instead.

```
L1:    mov     al,es:[di]            ; copy tail to buffer
       mov     [si],al              ; pointed to by DS:SI
       inc     si
       inc     di
       loop    L1
       clc                          ; CF=0 means tail found
       jmp     L3

L2:    stc                          ; CF=1 means no command tail
L3:    mov     byte ptr [si],0      ; store null byte
       popa                         ; restore registers
       pop     es
       ret
GetCommandTail ENDP
```

13.3.8 Example: Creating a Binary File

A *binary file* is given its name because the data stored in the file is simply a binary image of program data. Suppose, for example, that your program created and filled an array of doublewords:

```
myArray DWORD 50 DUP(?)
```

If you wanted to write this array to a text file, you would have to convert each integer to a string and write it separately. A more efficient way to store this data would be to just write a binary image of **myArray** to a file. An array of 50 doublewords uses 200 bytes of memory, and that is exactly the amount of disk space the file would use.

The following *Binfile.asm* program fills an array with random integers, displays the integers on the screen, writes the integers to a binary file, and closes the file. It reopens the file, reads the integers, and displays them on the screen:

```
TITLE Binary File Program          (Binfile.asm)

; This program creates a binary file containing
; an array of doublewords. It then reads the file
; back in and displays the values.

INCLUDE Irvine16.inc

.data
myArray DWORD 50 DUP(?)

fileName    BYTE "binary array file.bin",0
fileHandle WORD ?
commaStr    BYTE ", ",0

; Set CreateFile to zero if you just want to
; read and display the existing binary file.
CreateFile = 1

.code
main PROC
       mov     ax,@data
       mov     ds,ax

.IF CreateFile EQ 1
       call    FillTheArray
       call    DisplayTheArray
```

```
                call    CreateTheFile
                call    WaitMsg
                call    Crlf
        .ENDIF
                call    ReadTheFile
                call    DisplayTheArray
        quit:
                call    Crlf
            exit
        main ENDP

        ;------------------------------------------------------------
        ReadTheFile PROC
        ;
        ; Open and read the binary file.
        ; Receives: nothing.
        ; Returns: nothing
        ;------------------------------------------------------------
                mov     ax,716Ch                ; extended file open
                mov     bx,0                    ; mode: read-only
                mov     cx,0                    ; attribute: normal
                mov     dx,1                    ; open existing file
                mov     si,OFFSET fileName      ; filename
                int     21h                     ; call MS-DOS
                jc      quit                    ; quit if error
                mov     fileHandle,ax           ; save handle
        ; Read the input file, then close the file.
                mov     ah,3Fh                  ; read file or device
                mov     bx,fileHandle           ; file handle
                mov     cx,SIZEOF myArray       ; max bytes to read
                mov     dx,OFFSET myArray       ; buffer pointer
                int     21h
                jc      quit                    ; quit if error
                mov     ah,3Eh                  ; function: close file
                mov     bx,fileHandle           ; output file handle
                int     21h                     ; call MS-DOS
        quit:
                ret
        ReadTheFile ENDP

        ;------------------------------------------------------------
        DisplayTheArray PROC
        ;
        ; Display the doubleword array.
        ; Receives: nothing.
        ; Returns: nothing
        ;------------------------------------------------------------
                mov     CX,LENGTHOF myArray
                mov     si,0
        L1:
                mov     eax,myArray[si]         ; get a number
                call    WriteHex                ; display the number
                mov     edx,OFFSET commaStr     ; display a comma
                call    WriteString
                add     si,TYPE myArray         ; next array position
```

```
        loop    L1
        ret
DisplayTheArray ENDP

;-------------------------------------------------------
FillTheArray PROC
;
; Fill the array with random integers.
; Receives: nothing.
; Returns: nothing
;-------------------------------------------------------
        mov     CX,LENGTHOF myArray
        mov     si,0
L1:
        mov     eax,1000            ; generate random integers
        call    RandomRange         ; between 0 - 999 in EAX
        mov     myArray[si],eax     ; store in the array
        add     si,TYPE myArray     ; next array position
        loop    L1
        ret
FillTheArray ENDP

;-------------------------------------------------------
CreateTheFile PROC
;
; Create a file containing binary data.
; Receives: nothing.
; Returns: nothing
;-------------------------------------------------------
        mov     ax,716Ch            ; create file
        mov     bx,1                ; mode: write only
        mov     cx,0                ; normal file
        mov     dx,12h              ; action: create/truncate
        mov     si,OFFSET fileName  ; filename
        int     21h                 ; call MS-DOS
        jc      quit                ; quit if error
        mov     fileHandle,ax       ; save handle

; Write the integer array to the file.
        mov     ah,40h              ; write file or device
        mov     bx,fileHandle       ; output file handle
        mov     cx,SIZEOF myArray   ; number of bytes
        mov     dx,OFFSET myArray   ; buffer pointer
        int     21h
        jc      quit                ; quit if error

; Close the file.
        mov     ah,3Eh              ; function: close file
        mov     bx,fileHandle       ; output file handle
        int     21h                 ; call MS-DOS
quit:
        ret
CreateTheFile ENDP
END main
```

It is worth noting that writing the entire array is done with a single call to INT 21h Function 40h. There is no need for a loop:

```
    mov   ah,40h                          ; write file or device
```

```
mov  bx,fileHandle        ; output file handle
mov  cx,SIZEOF myArray     ; number of bytes
mov  dx,OFFSET myArray     ; buffer pointer
int  21h
```

The same is true when reading the file back into the array. A single call to INT 21h Function 3Fh does the job:

```
mov  ah,3Fh               ; read file or device
mov  bx,fileHandle        ; file handle
mov  cx,SIZEOF myArray     ; max bytes to read
mov  dx,OFFSET myArray     ; buffer pointer
int  21h
```

13.3.9   Section Review

1. Name the five standard MS-DOS device handles.
2. After calling an MS-DOS I/O function, which flag indicates that an error has occurred?
3. When you call Function 716Ch to create a file, what arguments are required?
4. Show an example of opening an existing file for input.
5. When you call Function 716Ch to read a binary array from a file that is already open, what argument values are required?
6. How do you check for end of file when reading an input file using INT 21h Function 3Fh?
7. When calling Function 3Fh, how is reading from a file different from reading from the keyboard?
8. If you wanted to read a random-access file, which INT 21h function would permit you to jump directly to a particular record in the middle of the file?
9. Write a short code segment that positions the file pointer 50 bytes from the beginning of a file. Assume that the file is already open, and BX contains the file handle.

13.4   Chapter Summary

In this chapter, you learned the basic memory organization of MS-DOS, how to activate MS-DOS function calls, and how to perform basic input-output operations at the operating system level.

The standard input device and the standard output device are collectively called the *console*, which involves the keyboard for input and the video display for output.

A *software interrupt* is a call to an operating system procedure. Most of these procedures, called *interrupt handlers*, provide input-output capability to application programs.

The INT (call to interrupt procedure) instruction pushes the CPU flags and 32-bit return address (CS and IP) on the stack, disables other interrupts, and calls an interrupt handler. The CPU processes the INT instruction using the *interrupt vector table*, a table containing 32-bit segment-offset addresses of interrupt handlers.

Programs designed for MS-DOS must be 16-bit applications running in real-address mode. Real-address mode applications use 16-bit segments and use segmented addressing.

The .MODEL directive specifies which memory model your program will use. The .STACK directive allocates a small amount of local stack space for your program. In real-address mode, stack entries are 16 bits by default. Enable the use of 32-bit registers using the .386 directive.

A 16-bit application containing variables must set DS to the location of the data segment before accessing the variables.

Every program must include a statement that ends the program and returns to the operating system. One way to do this is by using the .EXIT directive. Another way is by calling INT 21h Function 4Ch.

Any real-address mode program can access hardware ports, interrupt vectors, and system memory when running under MS-DOS, Windows 95, 98, and Millenium. On the other hand, this type of access is only granted to kernel mode and device driver programs in Windows NT, 2000, and XP

When a program runs, any additional text on its command line is automatically stored in the 128-byte MS-DOS command tail area, at offset 80h in special memory segment named the *program segment prefix* (PSP). The **GetCommandTail** procedure from the Irvine16 library returns a copy of the command tail. The program segment prefix is discussed in Section 16.3.1.

Some frequently used BIOS interrupts are listed here:

- INT 10h Video Services: Procedures that display routines that control the cursor position, write text in color, scroll the screen, and display video graphics.
- INT 16h Keyboard Services: Procedures that read the keyboard and check its status.
- INT 17h Printer Services: Procedures that initialize, print, and return the printer status.
- INT 1Ah Time of Day: A procedure that gets the number of clock ticks since the machine was turned on or sets the counter to a new value.
- INT 1Ch User Timer Interrupt: An empty procedure that is executed 18.2 times per second.

A number of important MS-DOS (INT 21h) functions are listed here:

- INT 21h MS-DOS Services. Procedures that provide input-output, file handling, and memory management. Also known as MS-DOS function calls.
- About 200 different functions are supported by INT 21h, identified by a function number placed in the AH register.
- INT 21h Function 4Ch terminates the current program (called a process).
- INT 21h Functions 2 and 6 write a single character to standard output.
- INT 21h Function 5 writes a single character to the printer.
- INT 21h Function 9 writes a string to standard output.
- INT 21h Function 40h writes an array of bytes to a file or device.
- INT 21h Function 1 reads a single character from standard input.
- INT 21h Function 6 reads a character from standard input without waiting.
- INT 21h Function 0Ah reads a buffered string from standard input.
- INT 21h Function 0Bh gets the status of the standard input buffer
- INT 21h Function 3Fh reads an array of bytes from a file or device.
- INT 21h Function 2Ah gets the system date.
- INT 21h Function 2Bh sets the system date.
- INT 21h Function 2Ch gets the system time.
- INT 21h Function 2Dh sets the system time.
- INT 21h Function 716Ch either creates a file or opens an existing file.
- INT 21h Function 3Eh closes a file handle.
- INT 21h Function 42h moves a file's position pointer.
- INT 21h Function 5706h obtains a file's creation date and time.
- INT 21h Function 62h returns the segment portion of the program segment prefix address.

The following sample programs showed how to apply MS-DOS functions:

- The *DateTime.asm* program displays the system date and time.
- The *Readfile.asm* program opens a text file for input, reads the file, displays it on the console, creates a new file, and copies the data to a new file.
- The *Binfile.asm* program fills an array with random integers, displays the integers on the screen, writes the integers to a binary file, and closes the file. It reopens the file, reads the integers, and displays them on the screen.

A binary file is given its name because the data stored in the file is a binary image of program data.

13.5   Chapter Exercises

The following exercises must be done in real-address mode. Do not use any functions from the Irvine16 library. Use INT 21h function calls for all input-output, unless an exercise specifically says to do otherwise.

1.   Read a Text File

Open a file for input, read the file, and display its contents on the screen in hexadecimal. Make the input buffer small—about 256 bytes—so the program uses a loop to repeat the call to Function 3Fh as many times as necessary until the entire file has been processed.

2.   Copy a Text File

Modify the **Readfile** program in Section 13.3.6 so that it can read a file of any size. Assuming that the buffer is smaller than the input file, use a loop to read all data. Use a buffer size of 256 bytes. Display appropriate error messages if the Carry flag is set after any INT 21h function calls.

3.   Setting the Date

Write a program that displays the current date and prompts the user for a new date. If a nonblank date is entered, use it to update the system date.

4.   Uppercase Conversion

Write a program that uses INT 21h to input lowercase letters from the keyboard and convert them to uppercase. Display only the uppercase letters.

5.   File Creation Date

Write a procedure that displays the date when a file was created, along with its filename. Pass a pointer to the filename in the DX register. Write a test program that demonstrates the procedure with several different filenames, including extended filenames. If a file cannot be found, display an appropriate error message.

6.   Text Matching Program

Write a program that opens a text file containing up to 60K bytes and performs a case-insensitive search for a string. The string and the filename can be input by the user. Display each line from the file on which the string appears and prefix each line with a line number. Review the **Str_find** procedure from the programming exercises in Section 9.7. Your program must run in real-address mode.

7.   File Encryption Using XOR

Enhance the file encryption program from Section 6.3.4 as follows:
  • Prompt the user for the name of a plaintext file and a ciphertext file.
  • Open the plaintext file for input, and open the cipher text file for output.
  • Let the user enter a single integer encryption code (1 to 255).
  • Read the plaintext file into a buffer, and exclusive-OR each byte with the encryption code.
  • Write the buffer to the ciphertext file.

The only procedure you may call from the book's link library is **ReadInt**. All other input/output must be performed using INT 21h. The same code you write could also be used to decrypt the ciphertext file, producing the original plaintext file.

8.   CountWords Procedure

Write a program that counts the words in a text file. Prompt the user for a file name, and display the word count on the screen. The only procedure you may call from the book's link library is **WriteDec**. All other input/output must be performed using INT 21h.

14

Disk Fundamentals

14.1 Disk Storage Systems

In this chapter, we introduce the basics of disk storage systems. We also show how disk storage relates to the BIOS-level disk storage on Intel-based computers. Finally, we show how MS-Windows interacts with application programs to provide access to files and directories. The system BIOS was first mentioned in Section 2.5. The interaction between a computer's virtual layers is readily apparent when you consider disk storage (Figure 14–1):

- At the lowest layer is the *disk controller firmware*, which uses intelligent controller chips to map out the disk geometry (physical locations) for specific disk drive brands and models.
- At the next layer is the *system BIOS*, which provides a low-level collection of functions that operating systems use to perform tasks such as sector reads, sector writes, and track formatting.
- At the next highest layer is the *operating system API*, which provides a collection of API functions that provides services such as opening and closing files, setting file properties, reading files, and writing files.

FIGURE 14–1   Virtual Levels of Disk Access.

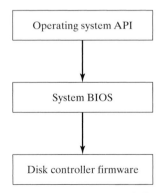

Disk storage systems all have certain common characteristics: They handle physical partitioning of data and access to data at the file level, and they map filenames to physical storage. At the hardware level, disk storage is described in terms of platters, sides, tracks, cylinders, and sectors. At the system BIOS level, disk storage is described in terms of clusters and sectors. At the OS level, disk storage is described in terms of directories and files.

Assembly Language Programs   User-level programs written in assembly language can directly access the system BIOS under MS-DOS, Windows 95, 98, and Millenium. For example, you might want to store and retrieve data stored in an unconventional format, to recover lost data, or to perform diagnostics on disk hardware. In this chapter, we show examples of system-BIOS file and sector functions. As an illustration of typical OS-level access to data, a number of MS-DOS functions for drive and directory manipulation are listed at the end of the chapter.

> If you're using Windows NT, 2000, or XP, user-level programs can only access the disk system using the Win32 API. That rule safeguards system security, and can only be bypassed by device driver programs running at the highest privilege level.

14.1.1   Tracks, Cylinders, and Sectors

A typical hard drive, shown in Figure 14–2, is made up of multiple platters attached to a spindle that rotates at constant speed. Above the surface of each platter is a read/write head that records magnetic pulses. The read/write heads move in toward the center and out toward the rim as a group, in small steps.

FIGURE 14–2   Physical Elements of a Hard Drive.

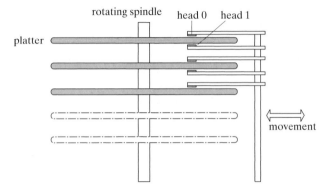

The surface of a disk is formatted into invisible concentric bands called *tracks* on which data is stored magnetically. A typical 3.5" hard drive may contain thousands of tracks. Moving the read/write heads from one track to another is called *seeking*. The *average seek time* is one type of disk speed measurement. Another measurement is RPM (revolutions per minute), typically 7200. The outside track of a disk is track 0, and the track numbers increase as you move toward the center.

A *cylinder* refers to all tracks accessible from a single position of the read/write heads. A file is initially stored on a disk using adjacent cylinders. This reduces the amount of movement by the read/write heads.

A *sector* is a 512-byte portion of a track, as shown in Figure 14–3. Physical sectors are magnetically (invisibly) marked on the disk by the manufacturer, using what is called a *low-level format*. Sector sizes never change, regardless of the installed operating system. A hard disk may have 63 or more sectors per track

FIGURE 14–3   Disk Tracks and Sectors.

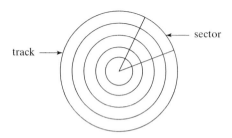

Physical disk geometry is a way of describing the disk's structure to make it readable by the system BIOS. It consists of the number of cylinders per disk, the number of read/write heads per cylinder, and the number of sectors per track. The following relationships exist:

• The number of cylinders per disk equals the number of tracks per surface.
• The total number of tracks equals the number of cylinders times the number of heads per cylinder.

Fragmentation   Over time, as files become more spread out around a disk, they become fragmented. A *fragmented* file is one whose sectors are no longer located in contiguous areas of the disk. When this happens, the read/write heads have to skip across tracks when reading the file's data. This slows down the reading and writing of files.

Translation to Logical Sector Numbers   Hard disk controllers perform a process called *translation*, the conversion of physical disk geometry to a logical structure that is understood by the operating system. The controller is usually embedded in firmware, either on the drive itself or on a separate controller card. After translation, the operating system can work with what are called *logical sector numbers*. Logical sector numbers are always numbered sequentially, starting at zero.

14.1.2   Disk Partitions (Volumes)

Under MS-Windows, a single physical hard drive can be divided into one or more logical units named *partitions*, or *volumes*. Each formatted partition is represented by a separate drive letter such as C, D, or E, and it can be formatted using one of several file systems. A drive may contain two types of partitions: primary and extended.

A primary partition is usually bootable and holds an operating system. An *extended partition* can be divided into an unlimited number of *logical partitions*. Each logical partition is mapped to a drive letter (C, D, E, etc.). Logical partitions cannot be bootable. It is possible to format each system or logical partition with a different file system.

Suppose for example, that a 20GB hard drive was assigned a primary 10GB partition (drive C), and we installed the operating system on it. Its extended partition would be 10GB. Arbitrarily, we could divide the latter into two logical partitions of 2GB and 8GB and format them with various file systems such as FAT16, FAT32, or NTFS. (We will discuss the details of these file systems in the next section of this chapter.) Assuming that no other hard drives were already installed, the two logical partitions would be assigned drive letters D and E.

Multi-Boot Systems   It is quite common to create multiple primary partitions, each capable of booting (loading) a different operating system. This makes it possible to test software in different environments and to take advantage of security features in the more advanced systems. Many software developers use one primary partition to create a test environment for software under development. Then they have another primary partition that holds production software that has already been tested and is ready for use by customers.

Logical partitions, on the other hand, are primarily intended for data. It is possible for different operating systems to share data stored in the same logical partition. For example, all recent versions of MS-Windows and Linux can read FAT32 disks. A computer can boot from any of these operating systems and read the same data files in a shared logical partition.

Tools: You can use the FDISK.EXE program under MS-DOS and Windows 98 to create and remove partitions, but it does not preserve data. Better yet, Windows 2000 and XP have a Disk Manager utility that provides the ability to create, delete, and resize partitions without destroying data. There are also third-party partitioning programs such as *PartitionMagic* by Symantec that permit nondestructive resizing and moving partitions.

Dual-Boot Example   In Figure 14–4, the Windows 2000 *Disk Mangagement* tool displays all six partitions on a single hard drive. The displayed figure is for a system that boots under both Windows 98 and Windows 2000. There are two primary partitions, arbitrarily named SYSTEM 98 and WIN2000-A. Only one primary partition can be active at one time. When active, a primary partition is called the *system partition.*

In the same figure, the system partition is currently WIN2000-A, assigned to drive C. Note that the inactive system partition has no drive letter. If we should restart the computer and boot from SYSTEM 98, it would become drive C, and the WIN2000-A partition would be inactive.

The extended partition, meanwhile, has been divided into four logical partitions, two of which are unformatted, whereas the remaining two, named BACKUP and DATA_1, are formatted using the FAT32 file system.

Figure 14–4   Windows 2000 Disk Management Tool.

Volume	Layout	Type	File System	Status	Capacity	Free Space	% Free
	Partition	Basic		Healthy	5.13 GB	5.13 GB	100 %
	Partition	Basic		Healthy	2.01 GB	2.01 GB	100 %
BACKUP (E:)	Partition	Basic	FAT32	Healthy	7.80 GB	4.84 GB	62 %
DATA_1 (D:)	Partition	Basic	FAT32	Healthy	7.80 GB	2.66 GB	34 %
SYSTEM 98	Partition	Basic	FAT32	Healthy	1.95 GB	1.12 GB	57 %
WIN2000-A (C:)	Partition	Basic	NTFS	Healthy (System)	3.91 GB	1.43 GB	36 %

Master Boot Record   The Master Boot Record (MBR), created when the first partition is created on a hard disk, is located in the drive's first logical sector. The MBR contains the following:

• The disk *partition table*, which describes the sizes and locations of all partitions on the disk.

• A small program that locates the partition's boot sector and transfers control to a program in the sector that loads the operating system.

14.1.3 Section Review

1. (*True/False*): A track is divided into multiple units called *sectors*.

2. (*True/False*): A sector consists of multiple tracks.

3. A _____ consists of all tracks accessible from a single position of the read/write heads of a hard drive.

4. (*True/False*): Physical sectors are always 512 bytes because the sectors are marked on the disk by the manufacturer.

5. Under FAT32, how many bytes are used by a logical sector?

6. Why are files initially stored in adjacent cylinders?

7. When a file's storage becomes fragmented, what does this mean in terms of cylinders and *seek* operations performed by the drive?

8. Another name for a drive partition is a drive _____.

9. What does a drive's *average seek time* measure?

10. What is a *low-level format*?

11. What is contained in the *master boot record*?

12. How many primary partitions can be active at the same time?

13. When a primary partition is active, it is called the _____ partition.

14.2 File Systems

Every operating system has some type of disk management system. At the lowest level, it manages partitions. At the next-highest level, it manages files and directories. A file system must keep track of the location, sizes, and attributes of each disk file. Let's take a look at the FAT-type file system originally created for the IBM-PC, and still used under MS-Windows. A FAT-type file system uses the following structure:

• A mapping of logical sectors to *clusters*, the basic unit of storage for all files and directories.

• A mapping of file and directory names to sequences of clusters.

A *cluster* is the smallest unit of space used by a file; it consists of one or more adjacent disk sectors. A file system stores each file as a linked sequence of clusters. The size of a cluster depends on both the type of file system in use and the size of its disk partition. Figure 14–5 shows a file made up of two 2048-byte clusters, each containing four 512-byte sectors. A chain of clusters is referenced by a *file allocation table* (FAT) that keeps track of all clusters used by a file. A pointer to the first cluster entry in the FAT is stored in each file's directory entry. Section 14.3.3 explains the FAT in greater detail.

FIGURE 14–5   Cluster Chain Example.

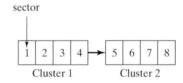

Wasted Space   Even a small file requires at least one cluster of disk storage, which can result in wasted space. Figure 14–6 shows an 8200-byte file, which completely fills two 4096-byte clusters and uses only 8 bytes of a third cluster. This leaves 4088 bytes of wasted disk space in the third cluster. A cluster size of 4096 (4KB) is considered an efficient way to store small files. Imagine what would result if our 8200-byte file were stored on a volume having 32KB clusters. In that case, 24568 bytes (32768 − 8200) would be wasted. On volumes having a large number of small files, small cluster sizes are best.

FIGURE 14–6   Cluster Chain Showing Wasted Space.

Windows 2000/XP Example   Standard cluster sizes and file system types for hard drives used under Windows 2000 and Windows XP are shown in Table 14-1. These values change often with new operating system releases, so the information shown in the table becomes obsolete quickly.

Table 14-1   Partition and Cluster Sizes (Over 1GB).

Volume Size	FAT16 Cluster	FAT32 Cluster	NTFS Cluster[a]
1.25GB–2GB	32KB	4KB	2KB
2GB–4GB	64KB[b]	4KB	4KB
4GB–8GB	ns (*not supported*)	4KB	4KB
8GB–16GB	ns	8KB	4KB
16GB–32GB	ns	16KB	4KB
32GB–2TB	ns	ns[c]	4KB

[a] Default sizes under NTFS. Can be changed when disk is formatted.
[b] 64KB clusters with FAT16 are only supported by Windows 2000 and XP.
[c] A software patch is available that permits Windows 98 to format drives over 32GB.

14.2.1   FAT12

The FAT12 file system was first used on IBM-PC diskettes. It is still supported by all versions of MS-Windows and Linux. The cluster size is only 512 bytes, so it is ideal for storing small files. Each entry in its file allocation table is 12 bits long. A FAT12 volume holds fewer than 4087 clusters.

14.2.2   FAT16

The FAT16 file system is the only available format for hard drives formatted under MS-DOS. It is supported by all versions of MS-Windows and Linux. There are some drawbacks to FAT16:

- Storage is inefficient on volumes over 1GB because FAT16 uses large cluster sizes.
- Each entry in the file allocation table is 16 bits long, limiting the total number of clusters.
- The volume can hold between 4087 and 65,526 clusters.
- The boot sector is not backed up, so a single sector read error can be catastrophic.
- There is no built-in file system security or individual user permissions.

14.2.3   FAT32

The FAT32 file system was introduced with the OEM2 release of Windows 95, and was refined under Windows 98. It has a number of improvements over FAT16:

- A single file can be as large as 4GB minus 2 bytes.
- Each entry in the file allocation table is 32 bits long.

- A volume can hold between 65,526 and 268,435,456 clusters.
- The root folder can be located anywhere on the disk, and it can be almost any size.
- Volumes can hold up to 32GB.
- It uses a smaller cluster size than FAT16 on volumes holding 1GB to 8GB, resulting in less wasted space.
- The boot record includes a backup copy of critical data structures. This means that FAT32 drives are less susceptible to a single point of failure than FAT16 drives.

14.2.4 NTFS

The NTFS file system is supported by Windows NT, 2000, and XP. It has significant improvements over FAT32:

- NTFS handles large volumes, which can be either on a single hard drive or spanned across multiple hard drives.
- The default cluster size is 4KB for disks over 2GB.
- Supports Unicode filenames (non-ANSI characters) up to 255 characters long.
- Allows the setting of permissions on files and folders. Access can be by individual users or groups of users. Different levels of access are possible (read, write, modify, etc.)
- Provides built-in data encryption and compression on files, folders, and volumes.
- Can track individual changes to files over time in a *change journal*.
- Disk quotas can be set for individual users or groups of users.
- Provides robust recovery from data errors. Automatically repairs errors by keeping a transaction log.
- Supports disk mirroring, in which the same data are simultaneously written to multiple drives.

Table 14-2 lists each of the different file systems commonly used on Intel-based computers, showing their support by various operating systems.

Table 14-2   Operating System Support for File Systems.

File System	MS-DOS	Linux	Win 95/ 98	Win NT 4	Win 2000/ XP
FAT12	X	X	X	X	X
FAT16	X	X	X	X	X
FAT32		X	X		X
NTFS				X	X

14.2.5 Primary Disk Areas

FAT12 and FAT16 volumes have specific locations reserved for the boot record, file allocation table, and root directory. (The root directory on a FAT32 drive is not stored in a fixed location.) The size of each area is determined when the volume is formatted. For example, the mapping of sectors on a 3.5-inch, 1.44MB diskette is show in Table 14-3.

Table 14-3   Sector Mapping of a 1.44MB Diskette.

Logical Sector	Contents
0	Boot record
1–18	File allocation table (FAT)
19–32	Root directory
33–2,879	Data area

Boot Record The *boot record* contains a table holding volume information and a short boot program that loads MS-DOS into memory. The boot program checks for the existence of certain operating system files and loads them into memory. Table 14-4 shows a representative list of fields in a typical MS-DOS boot record. The exact arrangement of fields varies among different versions of the operating system.

File Allocation Table (FAT) The file allocation table is fairly complex, so we will discuss it at more length in Section 14.3.3.

Table 14-4   MS-DOS Boot Record Layout.

Offset	Length	Description
00	3	Jump to boot code (JMP instruction)
03	8	Manufacturer name, version number
0B	2	Bytes per sector
0D	1	Sectors per cluster (power of 2)
0E	2	Number of reserved sectors (preceding FAT #1)
10	1	Number of copies of FAT
11	2	Maximum number of root directory entries
13	2	Number of disk sectors for drives under 32MB
15	1	Media descriptor byte
16	2	Size of FAT, in sectors
18	2	Sectors per track
1A	2	Number of drive heads
1C	4	Number of hidden sectors
20	4	Number of disk sectors for drives over 32MB
24	1	Drive number (modified by MS-DOS)
25	1	Reserved
26	1	Extended boot signature (always 29h)
27	4	Volume ID number (binary)
2B	11	Volume label
36	8	File-system type (ASCII)
3E	—	Start of boot program and data

Root Directory The *root directory* is a disk volume's main directory. Directory entries can be other directory names or references to files. A directory entry that refers to a file contains the filename, size, attribute, and starting cluster number used by the file.

Data Area The *data area* of the disk is where files and subdirectories are stored.

14.2.6 Section Review

1. (*True/False*): A file system maps logical sectors to clusters.
2. (*True/False*): The starting cluster number of a file is stored in the *disk parameter table*.
3. (*True/False*): All file systems except NTFS require the use of at least one cluster to store a file.
4. (*True/False*): The FAT32 file system allows the setting of individual user permissions for directories, but not files.
5. (*True/False*): Linux does not support the FAT32 file system.
6. Under Windows 98, what is the largest permitted FAT16 volume?
7. Suppose your disk volume's boot record was corrupted. Which file system(s) would provide support for a backup copy of the boot record?

8. Which MS-Windows file system(s) support 16-bit Unicode filenames?

9. Which MS-Windows file system(s) support *disk mirroring*, where the same data is simultaneously written to multiple drives?

10. Suppose you need to keep a record of the last ten changes to a file. Which file system(s) supports this feature?

11. If you have a 20GB disk volume and you wish to have a cluster size ≤ 8KB (to avoid wasted space), which file system(s) could you use?

12. What is the largest FAT32 disk volume that supports 4KB clusters?

13. Describe the four areas (in order) of a 1.44MB diskette.

14. On a disk drive formatted by MS-DOS, how might you determine the number of sectors used by each cluster?

15. *Challenge:* If a disk has a cluster size of 8KB, how many bytes of wasted space will there be when storing an 8200-byte file?

16. *Challenge:* Explain how NTFS stores sparse files. (To answer this question, you will have to visit the Microsoft MSDN Web site and look for the information.)

14.3   Disk Directory

Every FAT-style and NTFS disk has a *root directory* containing the primary list of files on the disk. The root directory may also contain the names of other directories, called *subdirectories*. A subdirectory may be thought of as a directory whose name appears in some other directory—the latter is known as the *parent directory*. Each subdirectory can contain filenames and additional directory names. The result is a treelike structure with the root directory at the top, branching out to other directories at lower levels (Figure 14–7).

FiGURE 14–7   Disk Directory Tree Example.

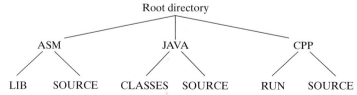

Each directory name and each file within a directory is qualified by the names of the directories above it, called the *path*. For example, the path for the file PROG1.ASM in the SOURCE directory below ASM on drive C is

```
C:\ASM\SOURCE\PROG1.ASM
```

Generally, the drive letter can be omitted from the path when an input-output operation is carried out on the current disk drive. A complete list of the directory names in our sample directory tree follows:

```
C:\
\ASM
\ASM\LIB
\ASM\SOURCE
\JAVA
\JAVA\CLASSES
\JAVA\SOURCE
\CPP
\CPP\RUN
\CPP\SOURCE
```

Thus, a *file specification* can take the form of an individual filename or a directory path followed by a filename. It can also be preceded by a drive specification.

14.3.1   MS-DOS Directory Structure

If we tried to explain all the various directory formats available today on Intel-based computers, we would at least have to include Linux, MS-DOS, and all the versions of MS-Windows. Instead, let's use MS-DOS as a basic example and examine its structure more closely. Then we will follow with a description of the extended filename structure available in MS-Windows.

Each MS-DOS directory entry is 32 bytes long and contains the fields shown in Table 14-5. The *filename* field holds the name of a file, a subdirectory, or the disk volume label. The first byte may indicate the file's status, or it may be the first character of a filename. The possible status values are shown in Table 14-6. The 16-bit *starting cluster number* field refers to the number of the first cluster allocated to the file, as well as its starting entry in the file allocation table (FAT). The *file size* field is a 32-bit number that indicates the file size, in bytes.

Table 14-5   MS-DOS Directory Entry.

Hexadecimal Offset	Field Name	Format
00-07	Filename	ASCII
08-0A	Extension	ASCII
0B	Attribute	8-bit binary
0C-15	Reserved by MS-DOS	
16-17	Time stamp	16-bit binary
18-19	Date stamp	16-bit binary
1A-1B	Starting cluster number	16-bit binary
1C-1F	File size	32-bit binary

Table 14-6   Filename Status Byte.

Status Byte	Description
00h	The entry has never been used.
01h	If the attribute byte = 0Fh and the status byte = 01h, this is the first long filename entry. (Holds the last part of the name, ".", and the filename extension.)
05h	The first character of the filename is actually the E5h character (rare).
E5h	The entry contains a filename, but the file has been erased.
2Eh	The entry (.) is for a directory name. If the second byte is also 2Eh (..), the cluster field contains the cluster number of this directory's parent directory.
4nh	First long filename entry (holds the first part of the name): If the attribute byte = 0Fh, this marks the last of multiple entries containing a single long filename. The digit n indicates the number of entries used by the filename.

Attribute Field

The *attribute* field identifies the type of file. The field is bit-mapped and usually contains a combination of one of the values shown in Figure 14–8. The two *reserved* bits should always be 0. The *archive* bit is set when a file is modified. The *subdirectory* bit is set if the entry contains the name of a subdirectory.

The *volume label* identifies the entry as the name of a disk volume. The *system file* bit indicates that the file is part of the operating system. The *hidden file* bit makes the file hidden; its name does not appear in a display of the directory. The *read-only* bit prevents the file from being deleted or modified in any way. Finally, an attribute value of 0Fh indicates that the current directory entry is for an extended filename.

Figure 14–8 File Attribute Byte Fields.

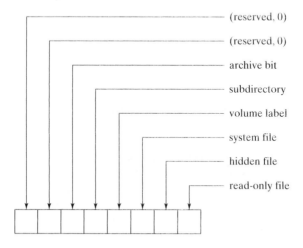

Date and Time

The *date stamp* field (Figure 14–9) indicates the date when the file was created or last changed, expressed as a bit-mapped value. The year value is between 0 and 119, and is automatically added to 1980 (the year the IBM-PC was released). The month value is between 1 and 12, and the day value is between 1 and 31.

Figure 14–9 File Date Stamp Field.

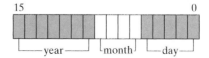

The *time stamp* field (Figure 14–10) indicates the time when the file was created or last changed, expressed as a bit-mapped value. The hours may be 0 to 23, the minutes 0 to 59, and the seconds 0 to 59, stored as a count of 2-second increments. For example, a value of 10100 binary equals 40 seconds. The time stamp in Figure 14–11 indicates a time of 14:02:40.

Figure 14–10 File Time Stamp Field.

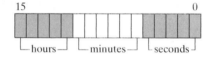

Figure 14–11 Time Stamp Example.

File Directory Entry Example   Let's examine the entry for a file named MAIN.CPP (Figure 14–12). This file has a normal attribute, and its archive bit (20h) has been set, showing that the file was modified. Its starting cluster number is 0020h, its size is 000004EEh bytes, the *Time* field equals 4DBDh (9:45:58), and the *Date* field equals 247Ah (March 26, 1998).

Fɪɢᴜʀᴇ 14–12   Sample File Directory Entry.

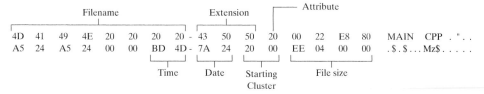

In this figure, the time, date, and starting cluster number are 16-bit values, stored in little endian order (low byte, followed by high byte). The *File size* field is a doubleword, also stored in little endian order.

14.3.2   Long Filenames in MS-Windows

In MS-Windows, a filename longer than 8 + 3 characters or a filename using a combination of uppercase and lowercase letters is assigned multiple disk directory entries. If the attribute byte equals 0Fh, the system looks at the byte at offset 0. If the upper digit equals 4, this entry begins a series of long filename entries. The lower digit indicates the number of directory entries to be used by the long filename. Subsequent entries count downward from $n - 1$ to 1, where n = the number of entries. For example, if a filename requires three entries, the first status byte will be 43h. The subsequent entries will be status bytes equal to 02h and 01h, as may be seen in the following table:

Status Byte	Description
43	Indicates that three entries are used for the long filename, total, and this entry holds the last part of the filename, ".", and a three-character extension.
02	Holds the second part of the filename.
01	Holds the first part of the filename.

Example   To illustrate, let's use a file having the 26-character filename ABCDEFGHIJKLM-NOPQRSTUV.TXT and save it as a text file in the root directory of drive A. Next, we run DEBUG..EXE from the Command prompt and load the directory sectors into memory at offset 100. This is followed by the D (dump command)[1]:

```
L 100 0 13 5          (load sectors 13h - 17h)
D 100                 (dump offset 100 on the screen)
```

Windows creates three directory entries for this file, as shown in Figure 14–13.

Let's start with the entry at 01C0h. The first byte, containing 01, marks this entry as the last of a sequence of long filename entries. It is followed by the first 13 characters of the filename "ABCDEF GHIJKLM". Each Unicode character is 16 bits, stored in little endian order. Note that the attribute byte at offset 0B equals 0F, indicating that this is an extended filename entry (any filename having this attribute is automatically ignored by MS-DOS).

The entry at 01A0h contains the final 13 characters of the long filename, which are "NOPQRSTUV.TXT".

FIGURE 14–13   Directory Entry for a Long Filename.

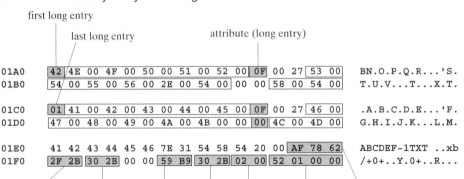

At offset 01E0h, the autogenerated short filename is built from the first six letters of the long filename, followed by ~1, followed by the first three characters after the last period in the original name. These characters are 1-byte ASCII codes. The short filename entry also contains the file creation date and time, the last access date, the last modified date and time, the starting cluster number, and the file size. Figure 14–14 shows the information displayed by the Windows Explorer *Properties* dialog, which matches the raw directory data.

FIGURE 14–14   File Properties Dialog.

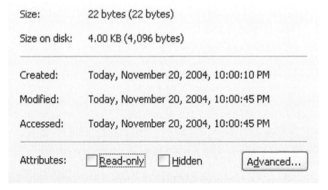

14.3.3   File Allocation Table (FAT)

The FAT12, FAT16, and FAT32 file systems use a table called the *file allocation table* (FAT) to keep track of each file's location on the disk. The FAT maps the disk clusters, showing their ownership by specific files. Each entry corresponds to a cluster number, and each cluster contains one or more sectors. In other words, the 10th FAT entry identifies the 10th cluster on the disk, the 11th entry identifies the 11th cluster, and so on.

Each file is represented in the FAT as a linked list, called a *cluster chain*. Each FAT entry contains an integer that identifies the next entry. Two cluster chains are shown in Figure 14–15, one for **File1** and the other for **File2**. **File1** occupies clusters 1, 2, 3, 4, 8, 9, and 10. **File2** occupies clusters 5, 6, 7, 11, and 12. The **eoc** (*end of chain*) marker in the last FAT entry for a file is a predefined integer value marking the final cluster in the chain.

When a file is created, the operating system looks for the first available cluster entry in the FAT. Gaps occur when not enough contiguous clusters are available to hold the entire file. In the preceding diagram, this happened to both **File1** and **File2**. When a file is modified and saved back to disk, its cluster chain often becomes increasingly fragmented. If many files become fragmented, the disk's performance begins to degrade because the read/write heads must jump between different tracks to locate all of a file's clusters. Most operating systems supply a built-in disk defragmentation utility.

Figure 14–15   Example: Two Cluster Chains.

File1: starting cluster number = 1, size = 7 clusters

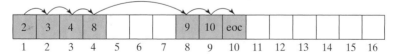

File2: starting cluster number = 5, size = 5 clusters

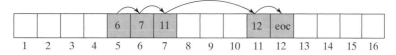

14.3.4   Section Review

1. (*True/False*): A file specification includes both a file path and a file name.
2. (*True/False*): The primary list of files on a disk is called the *base directory*.
3. (*True/False*): A file's directory entry contains the file's starting sector number.
4. (*True/False*): The MS-DOS date field in a directory entry must be added to 1980.
5. How many bytes are used by an MS-DOS directory entry?
6. Name the seven basic fields of an MS-DOS directory entry (do not include the *reserved* field).
7. In an MS-DOS filename entry, identify the six possible status byte values.
8. Show the format of the time stamp field in an MS-DOS directory entry.
9. When a long filename is stored in a volume directory (under MS-Windows), how is the first long filename entry identified?
10. If a filename has 18 characters, how many long filename entries are required?
11. MS-Windows added two new date fields to the original MS-DOS file directory entry. What are their names?
12. *Challenge:* Illustrate the file allocation table links for a file that uses clusters 2, 3, 7, 6, 4, 8, in that order.

14.4   Reading and Writing Disk Sectors (7305h)

INT 21h Function 7305h (absolute disk read and write) lets you read and write logical disk sectors. Like all INT instructions, it is designed to run only in 16-bit real-address mode. We will not atttempt to call INT 21h (or any other interrupt) from protected mode because of the complexities involved.

Function 7305h works on FAT12, FAT16, and FAT32 file systems under Windows 95, 98, and Windows Me. It does not work under Windows NT, 2000, or XP because of their tighter security. Any program permitted to read and write disk sectors could easily bypass file and directory sharing permissions. When calling function 7305h, pass the following arguments:

AX	7305h
DS:BX	Segment/offset of a DISKIO structure variable
CX	0FFFFh
DL	Drive number (0 = default, 1 = A, 2 = B, 3 = C, etc.)
SI	Read/write flag

A DISKIO structure contains the starting sector number, the number of sectors to read or write, and the segment/offset address of the sector buffer:

```
DISKIO STRUCT
      startSector DWORD 0                    ; starting sector number
      numSectors  WORD 1                     ; number of sectors
      bufferOfs   WORD OFFSET buffer         ; buffer offset
      bufferSeg   WORD SEG buffer            ; buffer segment
DISKIO ENDS
```

Following are examples of an input buffer to hold the sector data, along with a DISKIO structure variable:

```
.data
buffer BYTE 512 DUP(?)
diskStruct DISKIO <>
diskStruct2 DiskIO <10,5>          ; sectors 10,11,12,13,14
```

When calling Function 7305h, the argument passed in SI determines whether you want to read or write sectors. To read, clear bit 0; to write, set bit 0. In addition, bits 13, 14, and 15 are configured when writing sectors using the following scheme:

Bits 15–13	Type of Sector
000	Other/unknown
001	FAT data
010	Directory data
011	Normal file data

The remaining bits (1 through 12) must always be clear.

Example 1: The following statements read one or more sectors from drive C:

```
mov   ax,7305h            ; absolute Read/Write
mov   cx,0FFFFh           ; always this value
mov   dl,3                ; drive C
mov   bx,OFFSET diskStruct ; DISKIO structure
mov   si,0                ; read sector
int   21h
```

Example 2: The following statements write one or more sectors to drive A:

```
mov   ax,7305h            ; absolute Read/Write
mov   cx,0FFFFh           ; always this value
mov   dl,1                ; drive A
mov   bx,OFFSET diskStruct ; DISKIO structure
mov   si,6001h            ; write normal sector(s)
int   21h
```

14.4.1 Sector Display Program

Let's put what we've learned about sectors to good use by writing a program that reads and displays individual disk sectors in ASCII format. The pseudocode is listed here:

```
Ask for starting sector number and drive number
do while (keystroke <> ESC)
  Display heading
  Read one sector
  If MS-DOS error then exit
```

```
      Display one sector
      Wait for keystroke
      Increment sector number
   end do
```

Program Listing   Here is a complete listing of the 16-bit *Sector.asm* program. It runs in real-address mode under Windows 95, 98, and Me, but not under Windows NT, 2000, and XP because of their tighter security relating to disk access:

```
TITLE Sector Display Program                    (Sector.asm)

; Demonstrates INT 21h function 7305h (ABSDiskReadWrite)
; This Real-mode program reads and displays disk sectors.
; Works on FAT16 & FAT32 file systems running under Windows
; 95, 98, and Millenium.

INCLUDE Irvine16.inc

Setcursor PROTO, row:BYTE, col:BYTE
EOLN EQU <0dh,0ah>
ESC_KEY = 1Bh
DATA_ROW = 5
DATA_COL = 0
SECTOR_SIZE = 512
READ_MODE = 0                           ; for Function 7505h

DiskIO STRUCT
    startSector DWORD ?                 ; starting sector number
    numSectors  WORD 1                  ; number of sectors
    bufferOfs   WORD buffer             ; buffer offset
    bufferSeg   WORD @DATA              ; buffer segment
DiskIO ENDS

.data
driveNumber BYTE ?
diskStruct DiskIO <>
buffer BYTE SECTOR_SIZE DUP(0),0     ; one sector

curr_row   BYTE   ?
curr_col   BYTE   ?

; String resources
strLine        BYTE   EOLN,79 DUP(0C4h),EOLN,0
strHeading     BYTE   "Sector Display Program (Sector.exe)"
               BYTE   EOLN,EOLN,0
strAskSector   BYTE   "Enter starting sector number: ",0
strAskDrive    BYTE   "Enter drive number (1=A, 2=B, "
               BYTE   "3=C, 4=D, 5=E, 6=F): ",0
strCannotRead  BYTE   EOLN,"*** Cannot read the sector. "
               BYTE   "Press any key...", EOLN, 0
strReadingSector \
    BYTE "Press Esc to quit, or any key to continue..."
    BYTE EOLN,EOLN,"Reading sector: ",0

.code
main PROC
    mov    ax,@data
    mov    ds,ax
    call   Clrscr
    mov    dx,OFFSET strHeading               ; display greeting
```

```
        call    Writestring                 ; ask user for...
        call    AskForSectorNumber

L1:     call    Clrscr
        call    ReadSector                  ; read a sector
        jc      L2                          ; quit if error
        call    DisplaySector
        call    ReadChar
        cmp     al,ESC_KEY                  ; Esc pressed?
        je      L3                          ; yes: quit
        inc     diskStruct.startSector      ; next sector
        jmp     L1                          ; repeat the loop

L2:     mov     dx,OFFSET strCannotRead     ; error message
        call    Writestring
        call    ReadChar

L3:     call    Clrscr
        exit
main ENDP
;----------------------------------------------------
AskForSectorNumber PROC
;
; Prompts the user for the starting sector number
; and drive number. Initializes the startSector
; field of the DiskIO structure, as well as the
; driveNumber variable.
;----------------------------------------------------
        pusha
        mov     dx,OFFSET strAskSector
        call    WriteString
        call    ReadInt
        mov     diskStruct.startSector,eax
        call    Crlf
        mov     dx,OFFSET strAskDrive
        call    WriteString
        call    ReadInt
        mov     driveNumber,al
        call    Crlf
        popa
        ret
AskForSectorNumber ENDP

;----------------------------------------------------
ReadSector PROC
;
; Reads a sector into the input buffer.
; Receives: DL = Drive number
; Requires: DiskIO structure must be initialized.
; Returns:  If CF=0, the operation was successful;
;           otherwise, CF=1 and AX contains an
;           error code.
;----------------------------------------------------
        pusha
        mov     ax,7305h                    ; ABSDiskReadWrite
        mov     cx,-1                       ; always -1
        mov     bx,OFFSET diskStruct        ; sector number
```

```
        mov    si,READ_MODE                 ; read mode
        int    21h                          ; read disk sector
        popa
        ret
ReadSector ENDP

;----------------------------------------------------------
DisplaySector PROC
;
; Display the sector data in <buffer>, using INT 10h
; BIOS function calls. This avoids filtering of ASCII
; control codes.
; Receives: nothing. Returns: nothing.
; Requires: buffer must contain sector data.
;----------------------------------------------------------
        mov    dx,OFFSET strHeading          ; display heading
        call   WriteString
        mov    eax,diskStruct.startSector    ; display sector number
        call   WriteDec
        mov    dx,OFFSET strLine             ; horizontal line
        call   Writestring
        mov    si,OFFSET buffer              ; point to buffer
        mov    curr_row,DATA_ROW             ; set row, column
        mov    curr_col,DATA_COL
        INVOKE SetCursor,curr_row,curr_col

        mov    cx,SECTOR_SIZE                ; loop counter
        mov    bh,0                          ; video page 0
L1:     push   cx                            ; save loop counter
        mov    ah,0Ah                        ; display character
        mov    al,[si]                       ; get byte from buffer
        mov    cx,1                          ; display it
        int    10h
        call   MoveCursor
        inc    si                            ; point to next byte
        pop    cx                            ; restore loop counter
        loop   L1                            ; repeat the loop
        ret
DisplaySector ENDP

;----------------------------------------------------------
MoveCursor PROC
;
; Advance the cursor to the next column,
; check for possible wraparound on screen.
;----------------------------------------------------------
        cmp    curr_col,79                   ; last column?
        jae    L1                            ; yes: go to next row
        inc    curr_col                      ; no: increment column
        jmp    L2
L1:     mov    curr_col,0                    ; next row
        inc    curr_row
L2:     INVOKE Setcursor,curr_row,curr_col
        ret
MoveCursor ENDP

;----------------------------------------------------------
Setcursor PROC USES dx,
```

```
        row:BYTE, col:BYTE
;
; Set the screen cursor position
;----------------------------------------------------
        mov     dh, row
        mov     dl, col
        call    Gotoxy
        ret
Setcursor ENDP
END main
```

The core of the program is the **ReadSector** procedure, which reads each sector from the disk using INT 21h Function 7305h. The sector data is placed in a buffer, and the buffer is displayed by the **DisplaySector** procedure.

Using INT 10h   Most sectors contain binary data, and if INT 21h were used to display them, ASCII control characters would be filtered. Tab and Newline characters, for example, would cause the display to become disjointed. Instead, it's better to use INT 10h Function 9, which displays ASCII codes 0 to 31 as graphics characters. INT 10h is described in Section 15.4. Because Function 9 does not advance the cursor, additional code must be written to move the cursor one column to the right after displaying each character. The **SetCursor** procedure simplifies the implementation of the **Gotoxy** procedure in the Irvine16 library.

Variations   Interesting variations can be created on the Sector Display program. For example, you can prompt the user for a range of sector numbers to be displayed. Each sector can be displayed in hexadecimal. You can let the user scroll forward and backward through the sectors using the PageUp and PageDown keys. Some of these enhancements appear in the chapter exercises.

14.4.2   Section Review

1. (*True/False*): You can read sectors from a hard drive using INT 21h Function 7305h under Windows Me, but not under Windows XP.

2. (*True/False*): INT 21h Function 7305h reads one or more disk sectors only in protected mode.

3. What input parameters are required by INT 21h Function 7305h?

4. In the Sector Display Program (Section 14.4.1), why is Interrupt 10h used to display characters?

5. *Challenge:* In the Sector Display Program (Section 14.4.1), what would happen if the starting sector number was out of range?

14.5   System-Level File Functions

In real-address mode, INT 21h provides system services (Table 14-7) that create and change directories, change file attributes, find matching files, and so forth. These services go beyond what is typically available in high-level programing language libraries. When calling any of these services, the function number is placed in AH or AX. Other registers may contain input parameters. Let's take a detailed look at a few commonly used functions. A more detailed list of MS-DOS interrupts and their descriptions can be found in Appendix C.

Windows 95/98/Me supports all existing MS-DOS INT 21h functions and provides extensions that permit MS-DOS–based applications to take advantage of features such as long filenames and exclusive volume locking. INT 21h Function 7303h (get disk free space) is an example of an enhanced system function that recognizes disks larger than those originally supported in MS-DOS.

Table 14-7   Selected INT 21h Disk Services.

Function Number	Function Name
0Eh	Set default drive
19h	Get default drive
7303h	Get disk free space
39h	Create subdirectory
3Ah	Remove subdirectory
3Bh	Set current directory
41h	Delete file
43h	Get/set file attribute
47h	Get current directory path
4Eh	Find first matching file
4Fh	Find next matching file
56h	Rename file
57h	Get/set file date and time
59h	Get extended error information

14.5.1   Get Disk Free Space (7303h)

INT 21h Function 7303h can be used to find both the size of a disk volume and how much free disk space is available on a FAT16 or FAT32 drive. The information is returned in a standard structure named **ExtGetDskFreSpcStruc**, as follows:

```
ExtGetDskFreSpcStruc STRUC
     StructSize                  WORD  ?
     Level                       WORD  ?
     SectorsPerCluster           DWORD ?
     BytesPerSector              DWORD ?
     AvailableClusters           DWORD ?
     TotalClusters               DWORD ?
     AvailablePhysSectors        DWORD ?
     TotalPhysSectors            DWORD ?
     AvailableAllocationUnits    DWORD ?
     TotalAllocationUnits        DWORD ?
     Rsvd                        DWORD 2 DUP (?)
ExtGetDskFreSpcStruc ENDS
```

(A copy of this structure is in the *Irvine16.inc* file.) The following list contains a short description of each field:

- **StructSize**: A return value that represents the size of the **ExtGetDskFreSpcStruc** structure in bytes. When INT 21h Function 7303h (Get_ExtFreeSpace) executes, it places the structure size in this member.
- **Level**: An input and return level value. This field must be initialized to zero.
- **SectorsPerCluster**: The number of sectors inside each cluster.
- **BytesPerSector**: The number of bytes in each sector.
- **AvailableClusters**: The number of available clusters.
- **TotalClusters**: The total number of clusters on the volume.
- **AvailablePhysSectors**: The number of physical sectors available on the volume, without adjustment for compression.
- **TotalPhysSectors**: The total number of physical sectors on the volume, without adjustment for compression.
- **AvailableAllocationUnits**: The number of available allocation units on the volume, without adjustment for compression.

- **TotalAllocationUnits**: The total number of allocation units on the volume, without adjustment for compression.
- **Rsvd**: Reserved member.

Calling the Function   When calling INT 21h Function 7303h, the following input parameters are required:

- AX must equal 7303h.
- ES:DI must point to a **ExtGetDskFreSpcStruc** variable.
- CX must contain the size of the **ExtGetDskFreSpcStruc** variable.
- DS:DX must point to a null-terminated string containing the drive name. You can use the MS-DOS type of drive specification such as ("C:\"), or you can use a universal naming convention volume specification such as ("\\Server\Share").

If the function executes successfully, it clears the Carry flag and fills in the structure. Otherwise, it sets the Carry flag. After calling the function, the following types of calculations might be useful:

- To find out how large the volume is in kilobytes, use the formula (TotalClusters * SectorsPerCluster * BytesPerSector)/1024.
- To find out how much free space exists in the volume, in kilobytes, the formula is (AvailableClusters * SectorsPerCluster * BytesPerSector)/1024.

Disk Free Space Program

The following program uses INT 21h Function 7303h to get free space information on a FAT-type drive volume. It displays both the volume size and free space. It runs under Windows 95, 98, and Millenium, but not under Windows NT, 2000, and XP:

```
TITLE Disk Free Space                    (DiskSpc.asm)

INCLUDE Irvine16.inc

.data
buffer ExtGetDskFreSpcStruc <>
driveName BYTE "C:\",0
str1 BYTE "Volume size (KB): ",0
str2 BYTE "Free space (KB):  ",0
str3 BYTE "Function call failed.",0dh,0ah,0

.code
main PROC
        mov     ax,@data
        mov     ds,ax
        mov     es,ax

        mov     buffer.Level,0          ; must be zero
        mov     di,OFFSET buffer        ; ES:DI points to buffer
        mov     cx,SIZEOF buffer        ; buffer size
        mov     dx,OFFSET DriveName     ; ptr to drive name
        mov     ax,7303h                ; get disk free space
        int     21h
        jc      error                   ; failed if CF = 1

        mov     dx,OFFSET str1          ; volume size
        call    WriteString
        call    CalcVolumeSize
        call    WriteDec
        call    Crlf

        mov     dx,OFFSET str2          ; free space
        call    WriteString
```

```
        call   CalcVolumeFree
        call   WriteDec
        call   Crlf
        jmp    quit
error:
        mov    dx,OFFSET str3
        call   WriteString
quit:
        exit
main ENDP

;---------------------------------------------------------------
CalcVolumeSize PROC
;
; Calculate and return the disk volume size, in kilobytes.
; Receives: buffer variable, a ExtGetDskFreSpcStruc structure
; Returns:  EAX = volume size
; Remarks:  (SectorsPerCluster * 512 * TotalClusters) / 1024
;---------------------------------------------------------------
        mov    eax,buffer.SectorsPerCluster
        shl    eax,9                       ; mult by 512
        mul    buffer.TotalClusters
        mov    ebx,1024
        div    ebx                         ; return kilobytes
        ret
CalcVolumeSize ENDP

;---------------------------------------------------------------
CalcVolumeFree PROC
;
; Calculate and return the number of available kilobytes
; on the given volume.
; Receives: buffer variable, a ExtGetDskFreSpcStruc structure
; Returns:  EAX = available space, in kilobytes
; Remarks:  (SectorsPerCluster * 512 * AvailableClusters) / 1024
;---------------------------------------------------------------
        mov    eax,buffer.SectorsPerCluster
        shl    eax,9                       ; mult by 512
        mul    buffer.AvailableClusters
        mov    ebx,1024
        div    ebx                         ; return kilobytes
        ret
CalcVolumeFree ENDP
END main
```

14.5.2   Create Subdirectory (39h)

INT 21h Function 39h creates a new subdirectory. It receives a pointer in DS:DX to a null-terminated string containing a path specification. The following example shows how to create a new subdirectory called ASM off the root directory of the default drive:

```
.data
pathname BYTE "\ASM",0
.code
        mov    ah,39h                 ; create subdirectory
        mov    dx,OFFSET pathname
        int    21h
        jc     display_error
```

The Carry flag is set if the function fails. The possible error return codes are 3 and 5. Error 3 (*path not found*) means that some part of the pathname does not exist. Suppose we have asked MS-DOS to create the directory ASM\PROG\NEW, but the path ASM\PROG does not exist. This would generate Error 3. Error 5 (*access denied*) indicates that the proposed subdirectory already exists or the first directory in the path is the root directory and it is already full.

14.5.3 Remove Subdirectory (3Ah)

INT 21h Function 3Ah removes a directory. It receives a pointer to the desired drive and path in DS:DX. If the drive name is left out, the default drive is assumed. The following code removes the \ASM directory from drive C:

```
.data
pathname   BYTE 'C:\ASM',0
.code
mov  ah,3Ah                          ; remove subdirectory
mov  dx,OFFSET pathname
int  21h
jc   display_error
```

The Carry flag is set if the function fails. The possible error codes are 3 (*path not found*), 5 (*access denied: the directory contains files*), 6 (*invalid handle*), and 16 (*attempt to remove the current directory*).

14.5.4 Set Current Directory (3Bh)

INT 21h Function 3Bh sets the current directory. It receives a pointer in DS:DX to a null-terminated string containing the target drive and path. For example, the following statements set the current directory to C:\ASM\PROGS:

```
.data
pathname   BYTE "C:\ASM\PROGS",0
.code
    mov  ah,3Bh                       ; set current directory
    mov  dx,OFFSET pathname
    int  21h
    jc   display_error
```

14.5.5 Get Current Directory (47h)

INT 21h Function 47h returns a string containing the current directory. It receives a drive number in DL (0 = default, 1 = A, 2 = B, etc.) and a pointer in DS:SI to a 64-byte buffer. In this buffer, MS-DOS places a null-terminated string with the full pathname from the root directory to the current directory (the drive letter and leading backslash are omitted). If the Carry flag is set when the function returns, the only possible error return code in AX is 0Fh (*invalid drive specification*).

In the following example, MS-DOS returns the current directory path on the default drive. Assuming that the current directory is C:\ASM\PROGS, the string returned by MS-DOS is "ASM\PROGS":

```
.data
pathname   BYTE 64 dup(0)            ; path stored here by MS-DOS
.code
    mov  ah,47h                       ; get current directory path
    mov  dl,0                         ; on default drive
    mov  si,OFFSET pathname
    int  21h
    jc   display_error
```

14.5.6 Get and Set File Attributes (7143h)

INT 21h Function 7143h retrieves or sets file attributes, among other tasks. (In Windows 9x, it replaces the older MS-DOS INT 21h Function 39.) Pass the offset of a filename in DX. To set the file attributes, assign 1 to BL and set CX to one or more attributes listed in Table 14-8. The _A_NORMAL attribute must be used alone, but the other attributes can be combined using the + operator.

Table 14-8   File Attributes (Defined in *Irvine16.inc*).

Value	Meaning
_A_NORMAL (0000h)	The file can be read from or written to. This value is valid only if used alone.
_A_RDONLY (0001h)	The file can be read from, but not written to.
_A_HIDDEN (0002h)	The file is hidden and does not appear in an ordinary directory listing.
_A_SYSTEM (0004h)	The file is part of the operating system or is used exclusively by it.
_A_ARCH (0020h)	The file is an archive file. Applications use this value to mark files for backup or removal.

The following code sets the attributes of a file to read-only and hidden:

```
mov  ax,7143h
mov  bl,1
mov  cx,_A_HIDDEN + _A_RDONLY
mov  dx,OFFSET filename
int  21h
```

To get the current attributes of a file, set BX to 0 and call the same function. The attribute values are returned in CX as a combination of powers of 2. Use the TEST instruction to evaluate individual attributes. For example,

```
test cx,_A_RDONLY
jnz  readOnlyFile                ; file is read-only
```

The _A_ARCH attribute can appear with any of the other attributes.

14.5.7   Section Review

1. Which INT 21h function would you use to get the cluster size of a disk drive?
2. Which INT 21h function would you use to find out how many clusters are free on drive C?
3. Which INT 21h functions would you call if you wanted to create a directory named D:\apps and make it the current directory?
4. Which INT 21h function would you call if you wanted to make a file read-only?

14.6   Chapter Summary

At the operating system level, it is not useful to know the exact disk geometry (physical locations) or brand-specific disk information. The BIOS, which in this case amounts to disk controller firmware, acts as a broker between the disk hardware and the operating system.

The surface of a disk is formatted into concentric bands called *tracks*, on which data are stored magnetically. The *average seek time* measures the average amount of time spent moving from one track to another. Disk performance can be measured in RPM (revolutions per minute), as well as the *data transfer rate* (amount of data transferred to/from the drive in 1 second).

A *cylinder* refers to all tracks accessible from a single position of the read/write heads. Over time, as files become more spread out around a disk, they become fragmented and are no longer stored on adjacent cylinders.

A *sector* is a 512-byte portion of a track. Physical sectors are magnetically (invisibly) marked on the disk by the manufacturer, using what is called a low-level format.

Physical disk geometry describes a disk's structure to make it readable by the system BIOS. A single physical hard drive is divided into one or more logical units named partitions, or volumes. A drive may have multiple partitions. An extended partition can be subdivided into an unlimited number of logical partitions. Each logical partition appears as a separate drive letter and may have a different file system than other partitions. The primary partitions can each hold a bootable operating system.

The *master boot record* (MBR), created when the first partition is created on a hard disk, is located in the drive's first logical sector. The MBR contains the following:

• The *disk partition table* that describes the sizes and locations of all partitions on the disk.
• A small program that locates the partition's boot sector and transfers control to a program in the boot sector, which in turn loads the operating system.

A file system keeps track of the location, size, and attributes of each disk file. It provides a mapping of logical sectors to clusters, the basic unit of storage for all files and directories, and a mapping of file and directory names to sequences of clusters.

A *cluster* is the smallest unit of space used by a file; it consists of one or more adjacent disk sectors. A chain of clusters is referenced by a file allocation table (FAT) that keeps track of all clusters used by a file.

The following file systems are used in IA-32 Systems:

• The FAT12 file system was first used on IBM-PC diskettes.
• The FAT16 file system is the only available format for hard drives formatted under MS-DOS.
• The FAT32 file system was introduced with the OEM2 release of Windows 95 and was refined under Windows 98.
• The NTFS file system is supported by Windows NT, 2000, and XP.

Every disk in FAT-type and NTFS file systems has a *root directory*, which is the primary list of file's on the disk. The root directory may also contain the names of other directories, called subdirectories.

MS-DOS and Windows use a table called the *file allocation table* (FAT) to keep track of each file's location on the disk. The FAT maps specific disk clusters to files. Each entry corresponds to a cluster number, and each cluster is associated with one or more sectors.

In real-address mode, INT 21h provides functions (Table 14-7) that create and change directories, change file attributes, find matching files, and so forth. These functions tend to be less available in high-level languages.

The Sector Display program reads and displays each sector from the diskette in drive A.

The Disk Free Space program displays both the size of the selected disk volume and the amount of free space.

14.7 Programming Exercises

The following exercises must be compiled and run in real-address mode. Be sure to make a backup copy of any disk affected by these programs, or create a temporary scratch disk to be used while testing them. *Under no circumstances should you run the programs on a fixed disk until you have debugged them carefully!*

1. Set Default Disk Drive

Write a procedure that prompts the user for a disk drive letter (*A, B, C,* or *D*), and then sets the default drive to the user's choice.

2. Disk Space

Write a procedure named **Get_DiskSize** that returns the amount of total data space on a selected disk drive. *Input:* AL = drive number (0 = A, 1 = B, 2 = C, ...). *Output:* DX:AX = data space, in bytes.

3.   Disk Free Space

Write a procedure named **Get_DiskFreespace** that returns the amount of free space on a selected disk drive. *Input:* DS:DX points to a string containing the drive specifier. *Output:* EDX:EAX = disk free space, in bytes. Write a program that tests the procedure and displays the 64-bit result in hexadecimal.

4.   Show File Attributes

Write a procedure named **ShowFileAttributes** that receives the offset of a filename in DX and displays the file's attributes in the console window. Attributes to look for are normal, hidden, read-only, and system. *Hint:* Use INT 21h Function 7143h.

Write a program that calls ShowFileAttributes, passing it the name of a file. Before running your program, set the file attributes from Windows Explorer by right-clicking on the filename, selecting Properties, and checking the Hidden and Read-Only options. Alternatively, you can run the Attrib command from the Windows command prompt. Run your program and verify that the attribute display is correct. Sample output:

```
temp.txt attributes: Hidden Read-only
```

5.   Disk Free Space, in Clusters

Modify the Disk Free Space program from Section 14.5.1 so that it displays the following information:

```
Drive specification:            "C:\"
Bytes per sector:               512
Sectors per cluster:            8
Total Number of clusters:       999999
Number of available clusters:   99999
```

6.   Displaying the Sector Number

Using the Sector Display program (Section 14.4.1) as a starting point, display a string at the top of the screen that indicates the drive specifier and current sector number (in hexadecimal).

7.   Hexadecimal Sector Display

Using the Sector Display program (Section 14.4.1) as a starting point, add code that lets the user press F2 to display the current sector in hexadecimal, with 24 bytes on each line. The offset of the first byte in each line should be displayed at the beginning of the line. The display will be 22 lines high with a partial line at the end. The following is a sample of the first two lines, to show the layout:

```
0000 17311625 25425B75 279A4909 200D0655 D7303825 4B6F9234
0018 273A4655 25324B55 273A4959 293D4655 A732298C FF2323DB

(etc.)
```

End Note

1. See the DEBUG tutorial on the book's Web site.

15

BIOS-Level Programming

15.1 Introduction

Reading this chapter is like taking a step back in history. When the first IBM-PC appeared, droves of programmers (including myself) wanted to know how to get inside the box and work directly with the computer hardware. Peter Norton was quick to discover all sorts of useful and secret information, leading to his landmark book entitled *Inside the IBM-PC*. In a fit of generosity, IBM published all the assembly language source code for the IBM PC/XT BIOS (I still have a copy). Pioneering game designers such as Michael Abrash (author of *Quake* and *Doom*) learned how to optimize graphics and sound software, using their knowledge of PC hardware.[1] Now you can join this esteemed group and work behind the scenes, below MS-DOS and Windows, at the BIOS (*basic input-output system*) level. Is the information obsolete? Absolutely not, if you are working on embedded systems applications or if you would like to learn how a computer BIOS is designed.

All of the programs in this chapter are 16-bit, real-mode applications. You can develop and run the programs shown here in any version of Microsoft Windows. You will learn such useful things as:

• What happens when a keyboard key is pressed, and where all the characters end up.

- How to check the keyboard buffer to see if characters are waiting, and how to clear old keystrokes out of the buffer.
- How to read non-ASCII keyboard keys such as function keys and cursor arrows.
- How to display color text, and why colors are based on the video display's RGB color mixing system.
- How to divide up the screen into color panels and scroll each one separately.
- How to draw bit-mapped graphics in 256 colors.
- How to detect mouse movements and mouse clicks.

15.1.1   BIOS Data Area

The BIOS data area, partially shown in Table 15-1, contains system data used by the ROM BIOS service routines. For example, the keyboard typeahead buffer (at offset 001Eh) contains the ASCII codes and keyboard scan codes of keys waiting to be processed by the BIOS.

Table 15-1   BIOS Data Area, at Segment 0040h.

Hex Offset	Description
0000 – 0007	Port addresses, COM1 – COM4
0008 – 000F	Port addresses, LPT1 – LPT4
0010 – 0011	Installed hardware list
0012	Initialization flag
0013 – 0014	Memory size, in kilobytes
0015 – 0016	Memory in I/O channel
0017 – 0018	Keyboard status flags
0019	Alternate key entry storage
001A – 001B	Keyboard buffer pointer (head)
001C – 001D	Keyboard buffer pointer (tail)
001E – 003D	Keyboard typeahead buffer
003E – 0048	Diskette data area
0049	Current video mode
004A – 004B	Number of screen columns
004C – 004D	Regen (video) buffer length, in bytes
004E – 004F	Regen (video) buffer starting offset
0050 – 005F	Cursor positions, video pages 1 – 8
0060	Cursor end line
0061	Cursor start line
0062	Currently displayed video page number
0063 – 0064	Active display base address
0065	CRT mode register
0066	Register for color graphics adapter
0067 – 006B	Cassette data area
006C – 0070	Timer data area

15.2   Keyboard Input with INT 16h

In Section 2.5 we differentiated the various levels of input-output available to assembly language programs. In this chapter, you are given the opportunity to work directly at the BIOS level by calling functions that were (for the most part) installed by the computer manufacturer. At this level, you are only one level above the hardware, so you have a lot of flexibility and control.

The BIOS handles keyboard input using calls to Interrupt 16h. BIOS routines do not permit redirection, but they make it easy to read extended keyboard keys such as function keys, arrow keys, PgUp, and PgDn. Each extended key generates an 8-bit *scan code*, shown on the inside cover of this book. The scan codes are unique to IBM-compatible computers. All keyboard keys generate scan codes, but we don't usually pay attention to scan codes for ASCII characters because ASCII codes are standardized on nearly all computers. Under MS-Windows, when an extended key is pressed, its ASCII code is either 00h or E0h, shown in the following table:

Keys	ASCII Code
Ins, Del, PageUp, PageDown, Home, End, Up arrow, Down arrow, Left arrow, Right arrow	E0h
Function keys (F1 – F12)	00h

15.2.1   How the Keyboard Works

Keyboard input follows an event path beginning with the keyboard controller chip and ending with characters being placed in an array called the *keyboard typeahead buffer* (see Figure 15–1). Up to 15 keystrokes can be held in the buffer because a keystroke generates 2 bytes (ASCII code + scan code). The following events occur when the user presses a key:

• The keyboard controller chip sends an 8-bit numeric scan code (*sc*) to the PC's keyboard input port.
• The input port is designed so that it triggers an *interrupt*, a predefined signal to the CPU that an input-output device needs attention. The CPU responds by executing the INT 9h service routine.
• The INT 9h service routine retrieves the keyboard scan code (*sc*) from the input port and looks up the corresponding ASCII code (*ac*), if any. It inserts both the scan code and the ASCII code into the keyboard typeahead buffer. (If the scan code has no matching ASCII code, the key's ASCII code in the typeahead buffer equals zero or E0h.)

FIGURE 15–1   Keystroke Processing Sequence.

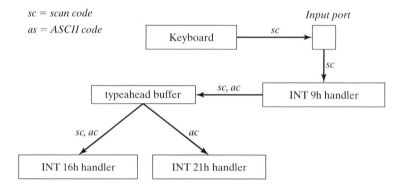

Once the scan code and ASCII code are safely in the typeahead buffer, they stay there until the currently running program retrieves them. There are two ways to do this in real-mode applications:

- Call a BIOS-level function using INT 16h that retrieves both the scan code and ASCII code from the keyboard typeahead buffer. This is useful when processing extended keys such as function keys and cursor arrows, which have no ASCII codes.
- Call an MS-DOS-level function using INT 21h that retrieves the ASCII code from the input buffer. If an extended key has been pressed, INT 21h must be called a second time to retrieve the scan code. INT 21h keyboard input was explained in Section 13.2.3.

15.2.2   INT 16h Functions

INT 16h has some clear advantages over INT 21h when it comes to keyboard handling. First, INT 16h can retrieve both the scan code and ASCII code in a single step. Second, INT 16h has additional operations such as setting the typematic rate and retrieving the state of the keyboard flags. The *typematic rate* is the rate at which a keyboard key repeats when you hold it down. When you don't know whether the user will press an ordinary key or an extended key, INT 16h is usually the best function to call.

Set Typematic Rate (03h)

INT 16h Function 03h lets you set the keyboard typematic repeat rate, as illustrated in the following table. When you hold down a key, there is a delay of 250 to 1000 milliseconds before the key starts to repeat. The repeat rate can be between 1Fh (slowest) and 0 (fastest).

INT 16h Function 03h	
Description	Set typematic repeat rate
Receives	AH = 3 AL = 5 BH = repeat delay (0 = 250 ms; 1 = 500 ms; 2 = 750 ms; 3 = 1000 ms) BL = repeat rate: 0 = fastest (30/sec), 1Fh = slowest (2/sec)
Returns	Nothing

Sample Call	`mov  ax,0305h`
	`mov  bh,1        ; 500 ms repeat delay`
	`mov  bl,0Fh      ; repeat rate`
	`int  16h`

Push Key into Keyboard Buffer (05h)

As shown in the next table, INT 16h Function 05h lets you push a key into the keyboard typeahead buffer. A key consists of two 8-bit integers: the ASCII code and the keyboard scan code.

INT 16h Function 05h	
Description	Push key into keyboard buffer
Receives	AH = 5 CH = scan code CL = ASCII code
Returns	If typeahead buffer is full, CF = 1 and AL = 1; otherwise, CF = 0, AL = 0.

Sample Call	`mov  ah,5`
	`mov  ch,3Bh      ; scan code for F1 key`
	`mov  cl,0        ; ASCII code`
	`int  16h`

Wait for Key (10h)

INT 16h Function 10h removes the next available key from the keyboard typeahead buffer. If none is waiting, the keyboard handler waits for the user to press a key, as shown in the following table:

INT 16h Function 10h	
Description	Wait for key and scan key from keyboard.
Receives	AH = 10h
Returns	AH = keyboard scan code AL = ASCII code

Sample Call	`mov  ah,10h`
	`int  16h`
	`mov  scanCode,ah`
	`mov  ASCIICode,al`

Notes	If no key is already in the buffer, the function waits for a key. Replaces INT 16h Function 00h.

Sample Program

The following keyboard display program uses a loop with INT 16h to input keystrokes and display both the ASCII code and scan code of each key. It terminates when the Esc key is pressed:

```
TITLE Keyboard Display            (Keybd.asm)

; This program displays keyboard scan codes
; and ASCII codes, using INT 16h.

INCLUDE Irvine16.inc
.code
main PROC
        mov   ax,@data
        mov   ds,ax
        call  ClrScr                ; clear screen

L1:     mov   ah,10h                ; keyboard input
        int   16h                   ; using BIOS
        call  DumpRegs              ; AH = scan, AL = ASCII
        cmp   al,1Bh                ; ESC key pressed?
        jne   L1                    ; no: repeat the loop

        call  ClrScr                ; clear screen
        exit
main ENDP
END main
```

The call to **DumpRegs** displays all the registers, but you need only look at AH (scan code) and AL (ASCII code). When the user presses the F1 function key, for example, this is the resulting display (3B00h):

```
EAX=00003B00  EBX=00000000  ECX=000000FF  EDX=000005D6
ESI=00000000  EDI=00002000  EBP=0000091E  ESP=00002000
EIP=0000000F  EFL=00003202  CF=0  SF=0  ZF=0  OF=0  AF=0  PF=0
```

Check Keyboard Buffer (11h)

INT 16h Function 11h lets you peek into the keyboard typeahead buffer to see if any keys are waiting. It returns the ASCII code and scan code of the next available key, if any. You can use this function inside a loop that carries out other program tasks. Note that the function does not remove the key from the typeahead buffer. See the following table for details:

INT 16h Function 11h	
Description	Check keyboard buffer
Receives	AH = 11h
Returns	If a key is waiting, ZF = 0, AH = scan code, AL = ASCII code; otherwise, ZF = 1.

Sample Call	```mov ah,11h```
	```int 16h```
	```jz NoKeyWaiting ; no key in buffer```
	```mov scanCode,ah```
	```mov ASCIICode,al```

Notes	Does not remove the key (if any) from the buffer.

Get Keyboard Flags

INT 16h Function 12h returns valuable information about the current state of the keyboard flags. Perhaps you have noticed that word-processing programs often display flags or notations at the bottom of the screen when keys such as *CapsLock, NumLock,* and *Insert* are pressed. They do this by continually examining the keyboard status flag, watching for any changes.

INT 16h Function 12h	
Description	Get keyboard flags
Receives	AH = 12h
Returns	AX = copy of the keyboard flags

Sample Call	```mov ah,12h```
	```int 16h```
	```mov keyFlags,ax```

Notes	The keyboard flags are located at addresses 00417h – 00418h in the BIOS data area.

The keyboard flags, shown in Table 15-2, are particularly interesting because they tell you a great deal about what the user is doing with the keyboard. Is the user holding down the left shift key or the right shift key? Is he or she also holding down the Alt key? Questions of this type can be answered using INT 16h. Each bit is a 1 when its matching key is either currently held down or is toggled on (Caps lock, Scroll lock, Num lock, and Insert). Under Windows 95 and 98, the keyboard flag bytes can also be obtained by directly reading memory at segment 0040h, offsets 17h 18h.

Clearing the Keyboard Buffer

Programs often have a processing loop that can only be interrupted by prearranged keys. DOS-based game programs, for example, often check the keyboard buffer to see if arrow keys and other special keys have been pressed while at the same time displaying graphic images. The user might press any number of irrelevant keys that only fill up the keyboard typeahead buffer, but when the right key is pressed, the program is expected to immediately respond to the command.

Table 15-2   Keyboard Flag Values.[a]

Bit	Description
0	Right Shift key is down
1	Left Shift key is down
2	Either Ctrl key is down
3	Either Alt key is down
4	Scroll Lock toggle is on
5	Num Lock toggle is on
6	Caps Lock toggle is on
7	Insert toggle is on
8	Left Ctrl key is down
9	Left Alt key is down
10	Right Ctrl key is down
11	Right Alt key is down
12	Scroll key is down
13	Num Lock key is down
14	Caps Lock key is down
15	SysReq key is down

[a]Source: Ray Duncan, *Advanced MS-DOS Programming*, 2nd ed., Microsoft Press, 1988, pp. 586–587.

Using the INT 16h functions, we know how to check the keyboard buffer to see if keys are waiting (Function 11h), and we know how to remove a key from the buffer (Function 10h). The following program demonstrates a procedure named **ClearKeyboard** that uses a loop to clear the keyboard buffer while checking for a particular keyboard scan code. For testing purposes, the program checks for the ESC key, but the procedure can check for any key:

```
TITLE Testing ClearKeyboard        (ClearKbd.asm)

; This program shows how to clear the keyboard
; buffer while waiting for a particular key.
; To test it, rapidly press random keys to fill
; up the buffer. When you press Esc, the program
; ends immediately.

INCLUDE Irvine16.inc
ClearKeyboard PROTO, scanCode:BYTE
ESC_key = 1                                ; scan code

.code
main PROC
L1:
    ; Display a dot, to show program's progress
    mov    ah,2
    mov    dl,'.'
    int    21h
```

```
        mov    eax,300                      ; delay for 300 ms
        call   Delay

        INVOKE ClearKeyboard, ESC_key       ; check for Esc key
        jnz    L1                           ; continue loop if ZF=0
quit:
        call   Clrscr
        exit
main ENDP

;-----------------------------------------------------
ClearKeyboard PROC,
        scanCode:BYTE
;
; Clears the keyboard while checking for a
; particular scan code.
; Receives: keyboard scan code
; Returns: Zero flag set if the ASCII code is
; found; otherwise, Zero flag is clear.
;-----------------------------------------------------
        push   ax
L1:
        mov    ah,11h                       ; check keyboard buffer
        int    16h                          ; any key pressed?
        jz     noKey                        ; no: exit now
        mov    ah,10h                       ; yes: remove from buffer
        int    16h
        cmp    ah,scanCode                  ; was it the exit key?
        je     quit                         ; yes: exit now (ZF=1)
        jmp    L1                           ; no: check buffer again

noKey:                                      ; no key pressed
        or     al,1                         ; clear zero flag
quit:
        pop    ax
        ret
ClearKeyboard ENDP
END main
```

The program displays a dot on the screen every 300 milliseconds. When testing it, press any sequence of random keys, which are ignored and removed from the typeahead buffer. The program stops as soon as ESC is pressed.

15.2.3 Section Review

1. Which interrupt (16h or 21h) is best for reading user input that includes function keys and other extended keys?

2. Where in memory are keyboard input characters kept while waiting to be processed by application programs?

3. What operations are performed by the INT 9h service routine?

4. Which INT 16h function pushes keys into the keyboard buffer?

5. Which INT 16h function removes the next available key from the keyboard buffer?

6. Which INT 16h function examines the keyboard buffer and returns the scan code and ASCII code of the first available input?

7. Does INT 16h function 11h remove a character from the keyboard buffer?

8. Which INT 16h function gives you the value of the keyboard flag byte?

9. Which bit in the keyboard flag byte indicates that the ScrollLock key has been pressed?

10. Write statements that input the keyboard flag byte and repeat a loop until the Ctrl key is pressed.

11. *Challenge:* The **ClearKeyboard** procedure in Section 15.2.2 checks for only a single keyboard scan code. Suppose your program had to check for multiple scan codes (the four cursor arrows, for example). Without writing actual code, suggest modifications you could make to the procedure to make this possible.

15.3   VIDEO Programming with INT 10h

15.3.1   Basic Background

Three Levels of Access

When an application program needs to write characters on the screen in text mode, it can choose among three types of output:

- **MS-DOS-level access:** Any computer running or emulating MS-DOS can use INT 21h to write text to the video display. Input/output can easily be redirected to other devices such as a printer or disk. Output is quite slow, and you cannot control the text color.

- **BIOS-level access:** Characters are output using INT 10h function, known as *BIOS services*. They execute more quickly than INT 21h and let you specify the text color. When filling large screen areas, a slight delay can usually be detected. Output cannot be redirected.

- **Direct video access:** Characters are moved directly to video RAM, so execution is instantaneous. Output cannot be redirected. During the MS-DOS era, word processors and electronic spreadsheet programs all used this method. (Use of this method is restricted to full-screen mode under Windows NT, 2000, and XP.)

Application programs vary in their choice of which level of access to use. Those requiring the highest performance choose direct video access; others choose BIOS-level access. MS-DOS–level access is used when the output may have to be redirected or when the screen is shared with other programs. It should be mentioned that MS-DOS interrupts use BIOS-level routines to do their work, and BIOS routines use direct video access to produce their output.

Running Programs in Full-Screen Mode

Programs that draw graphics using the Video BIOS should be executed in one of the following environments:

- Pure MS-DOS
- A DOS emulator under Linux
- Under MS-Windows in full-screen mode.

In MS-Windows, there are several ways to switch into full-screen mode:

- In Windows XP, create a shortcut to the program's EXE file. Then open the Properties dialog for the shortcut, select Options, and select *Full-screen mode* in the Display Options group.

- Open a Command window from the Start menu, and press Alt-Enter to switch to full screen mode. Using the CD (change directory) command, navigate to your EXE file's directory, and run the program by typing its name. Alt-Enter is a *toggle*, so if you press it again, it will return the program to Window mode.

Understanding Video Text

There are two basic video modes on Intel-based systems, text mode and graphics mode. A program can run in one mode or the other, but not both at the same time:

- In *text mode*, programs write ASCII characters to the screen. The built-in character generator in the BIOS generates a bit-mapped image for each character. A program cannot draw arbitrary lines and shapes in text mode.

- In *graphics mode*, programs control the appearance of each screen pixel. The operation is somewhat primitive because there are no built-in functions for line and shape drawing. You can use built-in functions to write text to the screen in graphics mode, and you can substitute different fonts for the built-in fonts. MS-Windows provides a collection of functions for drawing shapes and lines in graphics mode.

When a computer is booted in MS-DOS, the video controller is set to Video Mode 3 (color text, defaults to 80 columns by 25 rows). In text mode, rows are numbered from the top of the screen, row 0. Each row is the height of a character cell, using the currently active font. Columns are numbered from the left side of the screen, column 0. Each column is the width of a character cell.

Fonts   Characters are generated from a memory-resident table of character fonts. The BIOS permits programs to rewrite the character tables at run time, so custom fonts can be displayed.

Video Text Pages   Text mode video memory is divided into multiple separate video pages, each able to hold a full screen of text. Programs can display one page while writing text to other hidden pages, and they can rapidly flip back and forth between pages. In the days of high-performance MS-DOS applications, it was often necessary to keep several text screens in memory at the same time. With the current popularity of graphical interfaces, this text page feature is no longer important. (INT 10h Function 05h sets the current video page, but we do not cover it in this chapter.) The default video page is page 0.

Attributes   As illustrated in the following diagrams, each screen character is assigned an attribute byte that controls both the color of the character (called the *foreground*) and the screen color behind the character (called the *background*).

Each position on the video display holds a single character, along with its own *attribute* (color). The attribute is stored in a separate byte, following the character in memory. In the following figure, three positions on the screen contain the letters ABC:

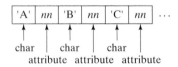

Blinking   Characters on the video display can blink. The video controller does this by reversing the foreground and background colors of a character at a predetermined rate. By default, when a PC boots into MS-DOS mode, blinking is enabled. It is possible to turn blinking off using a video BIOS function. Also, blinking is off by default when you open up an MS-DOS emulation window under MS-Windows.

15.3.2   Controlling the Color

Mixing Primary Colors

Each color pixel on a CRT video display is generated using three separate electron beams: red, green, and blue. A fourth channel controls the overall intensity, or brightness of the pixel. All available text colors can therefore be represented by 4-bit binary values, in the following form (I = intensity, R = red, G = green, B = blue). The following diagram shows the composition of a white pixel:

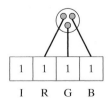

By mixing three primary colors (Table 15-3), new colors can be generated. Furthermore, by turning on the intensity bit, you can make the mixed colors brighter.

Table 15-3   Color Mixing Example.

Mix These Primary Colors . . .	To Get This Color	Add The Intensity Bit
red + green + blue	light gray	white
green + blue	cyan	light cyan
red + blue	magenta	light magenta
red + green	brown	yellow
(no colors)	black	dark gray

The MS-DOS–style primary colors and mixed colors are compiled into a list of all possible 4-bit colors as shown in Table 15-4. Each color in the right-hand column has its intensity bit set.

Table 15-4   Four-Bit Color Text Encoding.

IRGB	Color	IRGB	Color
0000	black	1000	gray
0001	blue	1001	light blue
0010	green	1010	light green
0011	cyan	1011	light cyan
0100	red	1100	light red
0101	magenta	1101	light magenta
0110	brown	1110	yellow
0111	light gray	1111	white

Attribute Byte

In color text mode, each character is assigned an attribute byte, which consists of two 4-bit color codes: background and foreground:

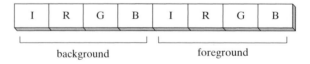

Blinking   There is one complication to this simple color scheme. If the video adapter currently has blinking enabled, the high bit of the background color controls the character blinking. When this bit is set, the character blinks:

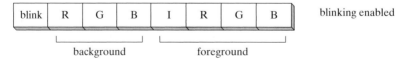

When blinking is enabled, only the low-intensity colors in the left-hand column of Table 15-4 are available as background colors (black, blue, green, cyan, red, magenta, brown, and light gray). The default color when MS-DOS boots is 00000111 binary (light gray on black background).

Constructing Attribute Bytes   To construct a video attribute byte from two colors (foreground and background), use the assembler's SHL operator to shift the background color bits four positions to the left, and OR it with the foreground color. For example, the following statements create an attribute of light gray text on a blue background:

```
blue = 1
lightGray = 111b
mov bh,(blue SHL 4) OR lightGray          ; 00010111
```

The following creates white characters on a red background:

```
white = 1111b
red = 100b
mov bh,(red SHL 4) OR white               ; 01001111
```

The following lines produce blue letters on a brown background:

```
blue = 1
brown = 110b
mov  bh,((brown SHL 4) OR blue)           ; 01100001
```

Fonts and colors may appear slightly different when running the same program under different operating systems. For example, in Windows 2000 and XP, blinking is disabled unless you switch to full-screen mode. The same is true for displaying graphics with INT 10h.

15.3.3   INT 10h Video Functions

Table 15-5 lists the most frequently used INT 10h functions. Each will be discussed separately, with its own short example. The discussion of functions 0Ch and 0Dh will be deferred to the graphics section (Section 15.4).

Table 15-5   Selected INT 10h Functions.

Function Number	Description
0	Set the video display to one of the text or graphics modes.
1	Set cursor lines, controlling the cursor shape and size.
2	Position the cursor on the screen.
3	Get the cursor's screen position and size.
6	Scroll a window on the current video page upward, replacing scrolled lines with blanks.
7	Scroll a window on the current video page downward, replacing scrolled lines with blanks.
8	Read the character and its attribute at the current cursor position.
9	Write a character and its attribute at the current cursor position.
0Ah	Write a character at the current cursor position without changing the color attribute.
0Ch	Write a graphics pixel on the screen in graphics mode (see Appendix C).
0Dh	Read the color of a single graphics pixel at a given location (see Appendix C).
0Fh	Get video mode information.
10h	Set blink/intensity modes.
13h	Write string in teletype mode.
1Eh	Write a string to the screen in teletype mode (see Appendix C).

It's a good idea to preserve the general-purpose registers (using PUSH) before calling INT 10h because the different BIOS versions are not consistent in which registers they preserve.

Set Video Mode (00h)

INT 10h Function 0 lets you set the current video mode to one of the text or graphics modes. Table 15-6 lists the text modes you are most likely to use:

Table 15-6   Video Text Modes Recognized by INT 10h.

Mode	Resolution (columns X rows)	Number of Colors
0	40 × 25	16
1	40 × 25	16
2	80 × 25	16
3	80 × 25	16
7[a]	80 × 25	2
14h	132 × 25	16

[a]Monochrome monitor.

It's a good idea to get the current video mode (INT 10h Function 0Fh) and save it in a variable before setting it to a new value. Then you can restore the original video mode when your program exits. The following table shows how to set the video mode.

INT 10h Function 0	
Description	Set the video mode
Receives	AH = 0 AL = video mode
Returns	Nothing

Sample Call	`mov   ah,0`
	`mov   al,3          ; video mode 3 (color text)`
	`int   10h`

Notes	The screen is cleared automatically unless the high bit in AL is set before calling this function.

Set Cursor Lines (01h)

INT 10h Function 01h, as shown in the next table, sets the text cursor size. The text cursor is displayed using starting and ending scan lines, which make it possible to control its size. Application programs can do this to show the current status of an operation. For example, a text editor might increase the cursor size when the NumLock key is toggled on; when it is pressed again, the cursor returns to its original size.

INT 10h Function 01h	
Description	Set cursor lines
Receives	AH = 01h CH = top line CL = bottom line
Returns	Nothing

Sample Call	`mov   ah,1`
	`mov   cx,0607h       ; default color cursor size`
	`int   10h`

Notes	The color video display uses eight lines for its cursor.

The cursor is described as a sequence of horizontal lines, where line 0 is at the top. The default color cursor starts at line 6 and ends at line 7, as shown in the following figure:

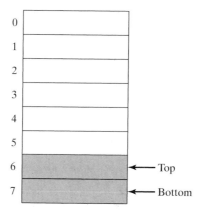

Set Cursor Position (02h)

INT 10h Function 2 locates the cursor at a specific row and column on the video page of your choice, as seen in the following table.

INT 10h Function 02h	
Description	Set cursor position
Receives	AH = 2 DH, DL = row, column values BH = video page
Returns	Nothing

Sample Call	`mov   ah,2`
	 `mov   dh,10        ; row 10`
	 `mov   dl,20        ; column 20`
	 `mov   bh,0         ; video page 0`
	 `int   10h`

Notes	For 80 × 25 modes, DH = 0 to 24, DL = 0 to 79

Get Cursor Position and Size (03h)

INT 10h Function 3, shown in the next table, returns the row/column position of the cursor as well as the starting and ending lines that determine the cursor size. This function can be quite useful in programs where the user is moving the cursor around a menu. Depending on where the cursor is, you know which menu choice has been selected.

INT 10h Function 03h	
Description	Get cursor position and size
Receives	AH = 3 BH = video page
Returns	CH, CL = starting, ending cursor scan lines DH, DL = row, column of cursor's location

Sample Call	`mov   ah,3`
	 `mov   bh,0                  ; video page 0`
	 `int   10h`
	 `mov   cursor,CX`
	 `mov   position,DX`

Showing and Hiding the Cursor   It is useful to be able to temporarily hide the cursor when displaying menus, writing continuously to the screen, or reading mouse input. To hide the cursor, you can set its top line value to an illegal (large) value. To redisplay the cursor, return the cursor lines to their defaults (lines 6 and 7):

```
HideCursor PROC
       mov    ah,3                  ; get cursor size
       int    10h
       or     ch,30h                ; set upper row to illegal value
       mov    ah,1                  ; set cursor size
       int    10h
       ret
HideCursor ENDP

ShowCursor PROC
       mov    ah,3                  ; get cursor size
       int    10h
       mov    ah,1                  ; set cursor size
       mov    cx,0607h              ; default size
       int    10h
       ret
ShowCursor ENDP
```

We're ignoring the possibility that the user might have set the cursor to a different size before hiding the cursor. Here's an alternate version of **ShowCursor** that simply clears the high 4 bits of CH without touching the lower 4 bits where the cursor lines are stored:

```
ShowCursor PROC
       mov    ah,3                  ; get cursor size
       int    10h
       mov    ah,1                  ; set cursor size
       and    ch,0Fh                ; clear high 4 bits
       int    10h
       ret
ShowCursor ENDP
```

Unfortunately, this method of hiding the cursor does not always work. An alternative method is to use INT 10h Function 02h to position the cursor off the edge of the screen (row 25, for example).

Scroll Window Up (06h)

INT 10h Functions 6 scrolls all text within a rectangular area of the screen (called a *window*) upward. A *window* is defined using row and column coordinates for its upper left and lower right corners. The default MS-DOS screen has rows numbered 0 to 24 from the top and columns numbered 0 to 79 from the left. Therefore, a window covering the entire screen would be from 0,0 to 24,79. In Figure 15–2, the CH/CL registers define the row and column of the upper left corner and DH/DL define the row and column of the lower right corner. This function has no predictable effect on the cursor position.

As a window is scrolled up, its bottom line is replaced by a blank line. If all lines are scrolled, the window is cleared (made blank). Lines scrolled off the screen cannot be recovered. The following table describes INT 10h Function 6.

INT 10h Function 06h	
Description	Scroll window up
Receives	AH = 6 AL = number of lines to scroll (0 = all) BH = video attribute for blanked area CH, CL = row, column of upper left window corner DH, DL = row, column of lower right window corner
Returns	Nothing

Sample Call	```mov ah,6 ; scroll window up```
	```mov al,0 ; entire window```
	```mov ch,0 ; upper left row```
	```mov cl,0 ; upper left column```
	```mov dh,24 ; lower right row```
	```mov dl,79 ; lower right column```
	```mov bh,7 ; attribute for blanked area```
	```int 10h ; call BIOS```

Figure 15–2   Defining a Window Using INT 10h.

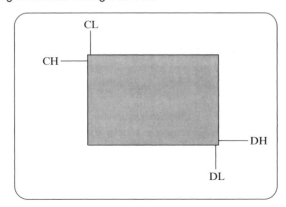

Example: Writing Text to a Window

When INT 10h Function 6 (or 7) scrolls a window, it sets the attributes of the scrolled lines inside the window. If you subsequently write text inside the window using a DOS function call, the text will use the same foreground and background colors. The following program (*TextWin.asm*) demonstrates this technique:

```
TITLE Color Text Window              (TextWin.asm)

; Displays a color window and writes text inside.

INCLUDE Irvine16.inc
.data
message BYTE "Message in Window",0

.code
main PROC
     mov    ax,@data
     mov    ds,ax

; Scroll a window.
```

```
          mov    ax,0600h                    ; scroll window
          mov    bh,(blue SHL 4) OR yellow   ; attribute
          mov    cx,050Ah                    ; upper-left corner
          mov    dx,0A30h                    ; lower-right corner
          int    10h
     ; Position the cursor inside the window.
          mov    ah,2                         ; set cursor position
          mov    dx,0714h                     ; row 7, col 20
          mov    bh,0                         ; video page 0
          int    10h
     ; Write some text in the window.
          mov    dx,OFFSET message
          call   WriteString
     ; Wait for a keypress.
          mov    ah,10h
          int    16h
          exit
main ENDP
END main
```

Scroll Window Down (07h)

The scroll window down function is identical to Function 06h, except that the text inside the window moves downward. It uses the same input parameters.

Read Character and Attribute (08h)

INT 10h Function 8 returns the character and its attribute at the current cursor position. It can be used by programs to read text directly off the screen (a technique known as *screen scraping*). Programs might convert the text to speech for hearing-impaired users.

INT 10h Function 08h	
Description	Read character and attribute at current cursor position.
Receives	AH = 8 BH = video page
Returns	AL = ASCII code of the character AH = attribute of the character

Sample Call	`mov   ah,8`
	`mov   bh,0         ; video page 0`
	`int   10h`
	`mov   char,al     ; save the character`
	`mov   attrib,ah   ; save the attribute`

Write Character and Attribute (09h)

INT 10h Function 9 writes a character in color at the current cursor position. As can be seen in the following table, this function can display any ASCII character, including the special BIOS graphics characters matching ASCII codes 1 to 31.

INT 10h Function 09h	
Description	Write character and attribute
Receives	AH = 9 AL = ASCII code of character BH = video page BL = attribute CX = repetition count
Returns	Nothing

Sample Call	```mov ah,9```
	```mov al,'A' ; ASCII character```
	```mov bh,0 ; video page 0```
	```mov bl,71h ; attribute (blue on light gray)```
	```mov cx,1 ; repetition count```
	```int 10h```

Notes	Does not advance the cursor after writing the character. Can be called in text and graphics modes.

The *repetition count* in CX specifies how many times the character is to be repeated. (The character should not be repeated beyond the end of the current screen line.) After a character is written, you must call INT 10h Function 2 to advance the cursor if more characters will be written on the same line.

Write Character (0Ah)
INT 10h Function 0Ah writes a character to the screen at the current cursor position without changing the current screen attribute. As shown in the next table, it is identical to Function 9, except that the attribute is not specified.

INT 10h Function 0Ah	
Description	Write character
Receives	AH = 0Ah AL = character BH = video page CX = repetition count
Returns	Nothing

Sample Call	```mov ah,0Ah```
	```mov al,'A' ; ASCII character```
	```mov bh,0 ; video page 0```
	```mov cx,1 ; repetition count```
	```int 10h```

Notes	Does not advance the cursor.

Get Video Mode Information (0Fh)

INT 10h Function 0Fh returns information about the current video mode, including the mode number, the number of display columns, and the active video page number, as seen in the following table. This function is useful at the beginning of a program, when you want to save the current video mode and switch to a new mode. When the program ends, you can reset the video mode (with INT 10h Function 0) to the saved value.

INT 10h Function 0Fh	
Description	Get current video mode information
Receives	AH = 0Fh
Returns	AL = current display mode AH = number of columns (characters or pixels) BH = active video page

Sample Call	```mov ah,0Fh```
	```int 10h```
	```mov vmode,al ; save the mode```
	```mov columns,ah ; save the columns```
	```mov page,bh ; save the page```

Notes	Works in both text and graphics modes.

Set Blink/Intensity Mode (10h; 03h)

INT 10h Function 10h has a number of useful subfunctions, including number 03h, which permits the highest bit of a color attribute to either control the color intensity or blink the character. See the following table for details:

INT 10h Function 10h, Subfunction 03h	
Description	Set blink/intensity mode
Receives	AH= 10h AL = 3 BL = blink mode (0 = enable intensity, 1 = enable blinking)
Returns	Nothing

Sample Call	```mov ah,10h```
	```mov al,3```
	```mov bl,1 ; enable blinking```
	```int 10h```

Notes	Switches on-screen text between blinking mode and high-intensity mode. Under MS-Windows, blinking can only occur when running the application in full-screen mode.

Write String in Teletype Mode (13h)

INT 10h Function 13h, shown in the following table, writes a string to the screen at a given row and column location. The string can optionally contain both characters and attribute values. (See the *Colorst2.asm* program in the book's sample programs folder named ch15.) This function can be used in text mode or graphics mode.

INT 10h Function 13h	
Description	Write string in teletype mode
Receives	AH = 13h AL = write mode (see notes) BH = video page BL = attribute (if AL = 00h or 01h) CX = string length (character count) DH, DL = screen row, column ES:BP = segment:offset of string
Returns	Nothing

Sample Call	```
	.data
	colorString BYTE 'A',1Fh,'B',1Ch,'C',1Bh,'D',1Ch
	row BYTE 10
	column BYTE 20
	.code
	mov ax,SEG colorString ; set ES segment
	mov es,ax
	mov ah,13h ; write string
	mov al,2 ; write mode
	mov bh,0 ; video page
	mov cx,(SIZEOF colorString) / 2 ; string length
	mov dh,row ; start row
	mov dl,column ; start column
	mov bp,OFFSET colorString ; string offset
	int 10h
	``

Notes	Can be called when the display adapter is in text mode or graphics mode. Write mode values: • 00h = string contains only character codes; cursor not updated after write, and attribute is in BL. • 01h = string contains only character codes; cursor is updated after write, and attribute is in BL. • 02h = string contains alternating character codes and attribute bytes; cursor position not updated after write. • 03h = string contains alternating character codes and attribute bytes; cursor position is updated after write.

Example: Displaying a Color String

The following program (*ColorStr.asm*) displays a string on the console, using a different color for each character. It must be run in full-screen mode if you want to see characters blink. By default, blinking is enabled, but you can remove the call to **EnableBlinking** and see the same string on a dark gray background:

```
TITLE Color String Example           (ColorStr.asm)

INCLUDE Irvine16.inc
.data
ATTRIB_HI = 10000000b
string BYTE "ABCDEFGHIJKLMOP"
color  BYTE (black SHL 4) OR blue

.code
main PROC
```

```
            mov     ax,@data
            mov     ds,ax

            call    ClrScr
            call    EnableBlinking          ; this is optional
            mov     cx,SIZEOF string
            mov     si,OFFSET string

L1:         push    cx                      ; save loop counter
            mov     ah,9                    ; write character/attribute
            mov     al,[si]                 ; character to display
            mov     bh,0                    ; video page 0
            mov     bl,color                ; attribute
            or      bl,ATTRIB_HI            ; set blink/intensity bit
            mov     cx,1                    ; display it one time
            int     10h
            mov     cx,1                    ; advance cursor to
            call    AdvanceCursor           ; next screen column
            inc     color                   ; next color
            inc     si                      ; next character
            pop     cx                      ; restore loop counter
            loop    L1

            call    Crlf
            exit
main ENDP

;------------------------------------------------------
EnableBlinking PROC
;
; Enable blinking (using the high bit of color
; attributes). In MS-Windows, this only works if
; the program is running in full screen mode.
; Receives: nothing. Returns: nothing
;------------------------------------------------------
            push    ax
            push    bx
            mov     ax,1003h                ; set blink/intensity mode
            mov     bl,1                    ; blinking is enabled
            int     10h
            pop     bx
            pop     ax
            ret
EnableBlinking ENDP
```

The AdvanceCursor procedure can be used in any program that calls INT 10h text functions.

```
;------------------------------------------------------
AdvanceCursor PROC
;
; Advances the cursor n columns to the right.
; (Cursor does not wrap around to the next line.)
; Receives: CX = number of columns
; Returns: nothing
;------------------------------------------------------
            pusha

L1:         push    cx                      ; save loop counter
            mov     ah,3                    ; get cursor position
```

```
        mov    bh,0            ; into DH, DL
        int    10h             ; changes CX register!
        inc    dl              ; increment column
        mov    ah,2            ; set cursor position
        int    10h
        pop    cx              ; restore loop counter
        loop   L1              ; next column

        popa
        ret
AdvanceCursor ENDP
END main
```

15.3.4 Library Procedure Examples

Let's take a look at two useful, but simple procedures from the Irvine16 link library, **Gotoxy** and **Clrscr**.

Gotoxy Procedure

The **Gotoxy** procedure sets the cursor position on video page 0:

```
;----------------------------------------------------
Gotoxy PROC
;
; Sets the cursor position on video page 0.
; Receives: DH,DL = row, column
; Returns: nothing
;----------------------------------------------------
        pusha
        mov    ah,2            ; set cursor position
        mov    bh,0            ; video page 0
        int    10h
        popa
        ret
Gotoxy ENDP
```

Clrscr Procedure

The **Clrscr** procedure clears the screen and locates the cursor at row 0, column 0 on video page 0:

```
;----------------------------------------------------
Clrscr PROC
;
; Clears the screen (video page 0) and locates the
; cursor at row 0, column 0.
; Receives: nothing
; Returns: nothing
;----------------------------------------------------
        pusha
        mov    ax,0600h        ; scroll entire window up
        mov    cx,0            ; upper left corner (0,0)
        mov    dx,184Fh        ; lower right corner (24,79)
        mov    bh,7            ; normal attribute
        int    10h             ; call BIOS
        mov    ah,2            ; locate cursor at 0,0
        mov    bh,0            ; video page 0
        mov    dx,0            ; row 0, column 0
        int    10h
        popa
        ret
Clrscr ENDP
```

15.3.5 Section Review

1. What are the three levels of access to the video display mentioned in the beginning of this section?
2. Which level of access produces the fastest output?
3. How do you run a program in full-screen mode?
4. When a computer is booted in MS-DOS, what is the default video mode?
5. Each position on the video display holds what information for a single character?
6. Which electron beams are required to generate any color on a video display?
7. Show the mapping of foreground and background colors in the video attribute byte.
8. Which INT 10h function positions the cursor on the screen?
9. Which INT 10h function scrolls a rectangular window upward?
10. Which INT 10h function writes a character and attribute at the current cursor position?
11. Which INT 10h function sets the cursor size?
12. Which INT 10h function gets the current video mode?
13. What parameters are required when setting the cursor position with INT 10h?
14. How is it possible to hide the cursor?
15. Which parameters are required when scrolling a window upward?
16. Which parameters are required when writing a character and attribute at the current cursor position?
17. Which INT 10h function sets blink/intensity modes?
18. Which values should be moved to AH and AL when clearing the screen using INT 10h function 6?
19. *Challenge:* If you have a dog, why do you think he or she might be surprised that you spend hours at a time staring at a gray computer screen?

15.4 Drawing Graphics Using INT 10h

INT 10h Function 0Ch draws a single pixel in graphics mode. You could use it to draw complex shapes and lines, but it's unbearably slow. To learn the basics, we will start with this function and later show how to draw graphics by writing data directly to video RAM.

> You can draw text on the screen using INT 10h Function 9h when the video adapter is in graphics mode.

Before drawing pixels, you have to put the video adapter into one of the standard graphics modes, shown in Table 15-7. Each mode can be set using INT 10h function 0 (set video mode).

Table 15-7 Video Graphics Modes Recognized by INT 10h.

Mode	Resolution (Columns X Rows, in Pixels)	Number of Colors
6	640 × 200	2
0Dh	320 × 200	16
0Eh	640 × 200	16
0Fh	640 × 350	2
10h	640 × 350	16
11h	640 × 480	2
12h	640 × 480	16
13h	320 × 200	256
6Ah	800 × 600	16

Coordinates   For each video mode, the resolution is expressed as *horizontal X vertical*, measured in pixels. The screen coordinates range from $x = 0$, $y = 0$ in the upper left corner of the screen, to $x = XMax-1$, $y = YMax-1$ in the lower right corner of the screen.

15.4.1   INT 10h Pixel-Related Functions

Write Graphics Pixel (0Ch)

INT 10h Function 0Ch, as shown in the next table, draws a pixel on the screen when the video controller is in graphics mode. Function 0Ch executes rather slowly, particularly when drawing a lot of pixels. Most graphics applications write directly into video memory after calculating the number of colors per pixel, the horizontal resolution, and so on.

INT 10h Function 0Ch	
Description	Write graphics pixel
Receives	AH = 0Ch AL = pixel value BH = video page CX = x-coordinate DX = y-coordinate
Returns	Nothing

Sample Call	`mov   ah,0Ch`
	`mov   al,pixelValue`
	`mov   bh,videoPage`
	`mov   cx,x_coord`
	`mov   dx,y_coord`
	`int   10h`

Notes	The video display must be in graphics mode. The range of pixel values and the coordinate ranges depend on the current graphics mode. If bit 7 is set in AL, the new pixel will be XORed with the current contents of the pixel (allowing the pixel to be erased).

Read Graphics Pixel (0Dh)

Function 0Dh, shown as follows, reads a graphics pixel from the screen at a given row and column position and returns the pixel value in AL.

INT 10h Function 0Dh	
Description	Read graphics pixel
Receives	AH = 0Dh BH = video page CX = x-coordinate DX = y-coordinate
Returns	AL = pixel value

Sample Call	`mov   ah,0Dh`
	`mov   bh,0              ; video page 0`
	`mov   cx,x_coord`
	`mov   dx,y_coord`
	`int   10h`
	`mov   pixelValue,al`

Notes	The video display must be in graphics mode. The range of pixel values and the coordinate ranges depend on the current graphics mode.

15.4.2 DrawLine Program

The *DrawLine* program switches into graphics mode using INT 10h, writes the name of the program in text, and draws a straight horizontal line. If you run it in MS-Windows, switch the console window to full-screen mode by pressing Alt-Enter.[2] Following is the complete program listing:

```
TITLE DrawLine Program              (DrawLine.asm)

; This program draws text and a straight line in graphics mode.

INCLUDE Irvine16.inc

;------------ Video Mode Constants ------------------
Mode_06 = 6 ; 640 X 200,  2 colors
Mode_0D = 0Dh; 320 X 200, 16 colors
Mode_0E = 0Eh; 640 X 200, 16 colors
Mode_0F = 0Fh; 640 X 350,  2 colors
Mode_10 = 10h; 640 X 350, 16 colors
Mode_11 = 11h; 640 X 480,  2 colors
Mode_12 = 12h; 640 X 480, 16 colors
Mode_13 = 13h; 320 X 200, 256 colors
Mode_6A = 6Ah; 800 X 600, 16 colors

.data
saveMode  BYTE  ?            ; save the current video mode
currentX  WORD 100           ; column number (X-coordinate)
currentY  WORD 100           ; row number (Y-coordinate)
COLOR = 1001b                ; line color (cyan)

progTitle BYTE "DrawLine.asm"
TITLE_ROW = 5
TITLE_COLUMN = 14

; When using a 2-color mode, set COLOR to 1 (white)

.code
main PROC
        mov    ax,@data
        mov    ds,ax

; Save the current video mode.
        mov    ah,0Fh
        int    10h
        mov    saveMode,al

; Switch to a graphics mode.
        mov    ah,0                ; set video mode
        mov    al,Mode_6A
        int    10h

; Write the program name, as text.
        mov    ax,SEG progTitle    ; get segment of progTitle
        mov    es,ax               ; store in ES
        mov    bp,OFFSET progTitle
        mov    ah,13h              ; function: write string
        mov    al,0                ; mode: only character codes
        mov    bh,0                ; video page 0
        mov    bl,7                ; attribute = normal
        mov    cx,SIZEOF progTitle ; string length
        mov    dh,TITLE_ROW        ; row (in character cells)
        mov    dl,TITLE_COLUMN     ; column (in character cells)
        int    10h
```

```
; Draw a straight line.
    LineLength = 100

        mov     dx,currentY
        mov     cx,LineLength           ; loop counter

L1:
        push    cx
        mov     ah,0Ch                  ; write pixel
        mov     al,COLOR                ; pixel color
        mov     bh,0                    ; video page 0
        mov     cx,currentX
        int     10h
        inc     currentX
        ;inc    color                   ; enable to see a multi-color line
        pop     cx
        Loop    L1

; Wait for a keystroke.
        mov     ah,0
        int     16h

; Restore the starting video mode.
        mov     ah,0                    ; set video mode
        mov     al,saveMode             ; saved video mode
        int     10h
        exit
main ENDP
END main
```

Changing the Video Mode   You can try out different graphics modes by modifying a single program statement that currently selects video Mode 6Ah:

```
mov  ah,0                    ; set video mode
mov  al,Mode_6A             ; modify for different modes
int  10h                    ; call BIOS routine
```

15.4.3 Cartesian Coordinates Program

The *Cartesian Coordinates* program draws the X and Y axes of a Cartesian coordinate system, with the intersection point at screen locations X = 400 and Y = 300. There are two important procedures, **DrawHorizLine** and **DrawVerticalLine**, which could easily be inserted in other graphics programs. The program sets the video adapter to Mode 6Ah (800 × 600, 16 colors).

```
TITLE Cartesian Coordinates                    (Pixel2.asm)

; This program switches into 800 X 600 graphics mode and
; draws the X and Y axes of a Cartesian coordinate system.
; Switch to full-screen mode before running this program.
; Color constants are defined in Irvine16.inc.

INCLUDE Irvine16.inc

Mode_6A = 6Ah                        ; 800 X 600, 16 colors
X_axisY = 300
X_axisX = 50
X_axisLen = 700

Y_axisX = 400
Y_axisY = 30
Y_axisLen = 540
```

```
.data
saveMode BYTE ?

.code
main PROC
    mov     ax,@data
    mov     ds,ax

; Save the current video mode
    mov     ah,0Fh                  ; get video mode
    int     10h
    mov     saveMode,al

; Switch to a graphics mode
    mov     ah,0                    ; set video mode
    mov     al,Mode_6A              ; 800 X 600, 16 colors
    int     10h

; Draw the X-axis
    mov     cx,X_axisX              ; X-coord of start of line
    mov     dx,X_axisY              ; Y-coord of start of line
    mov     ax,X_axisLen            ; length of line
    mov     bl,white                ; line color (see IRVINE16.inc)
    call    DrawHorizLine           ; draw the line now

; Draw the Y-axis
    mov     cx,Y_axisX              ; X-coord of start of line
    mov     dx,Y_axisY              ; Y-coord of start of line
    mov     ax,Y_axisLen            ; length of line
    mov     bl,white                ; line color
    call    DrawVerticalLine        ; draw the line now

; Wait for a keystroke
    mov     ah,10h                  ; wait for key
    int     16h

; Restore the starting video mode
    mov     ah,0                    ; set video mode
    mov     al,saveMode             ; saved video mode
    int     10h

    exit
main endp


;-------------------------------------------------------
DrawHorizLine PROC
;
; Draws a horizontal line starting at position X,Y with
; a given length and color.
; Receives: CX = X-coordinate, DX = Y-coordinate,
;           AX = length, and BL = color
; Returns: nothing
;-------------------------------------------------------
.data
currX WORD ?

.code
    pusha
    mov     currX,cx                ; save X-coordinate
    mov     cx,ax                   ; loop counter
```

```
DHL1:
      push  cx                      ; save loop counter
      mov   al,bl                   ; color
      mov   ah,0Ch                  ; draw pixel
      mov   bh,0                    ; video page
      mov   cx,currX                ; retrieve X-coordinate
      int   10h
      inc   currX                   ; move 1 pixel to the right
      pop   cx                      ; restore loop counter
      loop  DHL1

      popa
      ret
DrawHorizLine ENDP

;------------------------------------------------------
DrawVerticalLine PROC
;
; Draws a vertical line starting at position X,Y with
; a given length and color.
; Receives: CX = X-coordinate, DX = Y-coordinate,
;           AX = length, BL = color
; Returns: nothing
;------------------------------------------------------
.data
currY WORD ?

.code
      pusha
      mov   currY,dx                ; save Y-coordinate
      mov   currX,cx                ; save X-coordinate
      mov   cx,ax                   ; loop counter
DVL1:
      push  cx                      ; save loop counter
      mov   al,bl                   ; color
      mov   ah,0Ch                  ; function: draw pixel
      mov   bh,0                    ; set video page
      mov   cx,currX                ; set X-coordinate
      mov   dx,currY                ; set Y-coordinate
      int   10h                     ; draw the pixel
      inc   currY                   ; move down 1 pixel
      pop   cx                      ; restore loop counter
      loop  DVL1

      popa
      ret
DrawVerticalLine ENDP
END main
```

15.4.4 Converting Cartesian Coordinates to Screen Coordinates

Points on a Cartesian graph do not correspond to the absolute coordinates used by the BIOS graphics system. In the preceding two program examples, it was clear that screen coordinates begin at $sx = 0$, $sy = 0$ in the upper left corner of the screen. sx values grow to the right, and sy values grow toward the bottom of the screen. You can use the following formulas to convert Cartesian X, Y to screen coordinates sx, sy:

$$sx = (sOrigX + X) \qquad sy = (sOrigY - Y)$$

where *sOrigX* and *sOrigY* are the screen coordinates of the origin of the Cartesian coordinate system. In the Cartesian Coordinates Program (Section 15.4.3), our lines intersected at *sOrigX* = 400 and *sOrigY* = 300, placing the origin in the middle of the screen. If we use the four points in Figure 15–3 to test the given conversion formulas, Table 15-8 shows the results of the calculations.

Figure 15–3   Test Coordinates for Conversion Formulas.

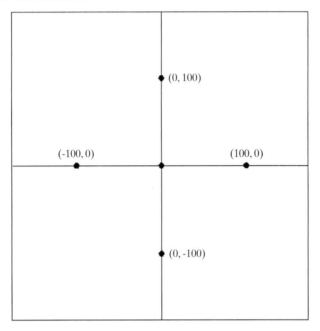

Table 15-8   Testing the Conversion Formulas.

Cartesian (X, Y)	(400 + X, 300 − Y)	Screen (*sx, sy*)
(0, 100)	(400 + 0, 300 − 100)	(400, 200)
(100, 0)	(400 + 100, 300 − 0)	(500, 300)
(0, −100)	(400 + 0, 300 − (−100))	(400, 400)
(−100, 0)	(400 + (−100), 300 − 0)	(300, 300)

15.4.5   Section Review

1. Which INT 10h function draws a single pixel on the video display?
2. When using INT 10h to draw a single pixel, what values must be placed in the AL, BH, CX, and DX registers?
3. What is the main disadvantage to drawing pixels using INT 10h?
4. Write ASM statements that set the video adapter to Mode 11h.
5. Which video mode is 800 × 600 pixels, in 16 colors?
6. What is the formula to convert a Cartesian X-coordinate to screen pixel coordinates? (Use the variable *sx* for the screen column, and use *sOrigX* for the screen column where the Cartesian origin point (0, 0) is located.)
7. If a Cartesian origin point is located at screen coordinates *sy* = 250, *sx* = 350, convert the following Cartesian points in the form (X, Y) into screen coordinates (*sx, sy*):
   a. (0, 100)

b. (25, 25)

c. (−200, −150)

15.5 Memory-Mapped Graphics

We have seen how drawing pixels using INT 10h is unbearably slow except for the most rudimentary graphics output. Quite a lot of code executes each time the BIOS draws a pixel. Now we can show you a more efficient way to draw graphics, as done by professional software. We will write graphics data directly to video RAM (VRAM) via input-output ports.

15.5.1   Mode 13h: 320 X 200, 256 Colors

Video Mode 13h is the easiest mode to use for memory-mapped graphics. Screen pixels are mapped as a two-dimensional array of bytes, 1 byte per pixel. The array begins with the pixel in the upper left corner of the screen and continues across the top line for 320 bytes. The byte at offset 320 maps to the first pixel in the second screen line, which continues sequentially across the screen. The remaining lines are mapped in a similar fashion. The last byte in the array is mapped to the pixel in the lower right corner of the screen. Why use a whole byte for each pixel? Because the byte holds a reference to one of 256 different color values.

OUT Instruction   Pixel and color values are transmitted to the video adapter hardware using the OUT (output to port) instruction. The 16-bit port address is assigned to DX, and the value sent to the port is in AL, AX, or EAX. For example, the video color palette is located at port address 3C8h. The following instructions send the value 20h to the port:

```
mov   dx,3c8h                      ; port address
mov   al,20h                       ; value to be output
out   dx,al                        ; send value to port
```

Color Indexes   The interesting thing about colors in Mode 13h is that each color integer does not directly indicate a color. Instead, it represents an index into a table of colors called a *palette* (Figure 15–4). Each entry in the palette consists of three integer values (0 to 63) known as *RGB* (red, green, blue). Entry 0 in the color palette controls the screen's background color.

You can create 262,144 different colors (64^3) with this scheme. Only 256 different colors can be displayed at a given time, but your program can modify the palette at run time to vary the display colors. Modern operating systems such as Windows and Linux offer (at least) 24-bit color, in which each RGB value has a range of 0 to 255. That scheme offers 256^3 (16.7 million) different colors.

FIGURE 15–4   Converting Pixel Color Indexes to Display Colors.

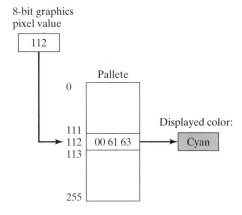

RGB Colors

RGB colors are based on the additive mixing of light, as opposed to the subtractive method one uses when mixing liquid paint. With additive mixing, for example, you create the color black by keeping all color intensity levels at zero. White, on the other hand, is created by setting all color levels at 63 (the maximum). In fact, as the following table demonstrates, when all three levels are equal, you get varying shades of gray:

Red	Green	Blue	Color
0	0	0	black
20	20	20	dark gray
35	35	35	medium gray
50	50	50	light gray
63	63	63	white

Pure colors are created by setting all but one color level to zero. To get a light color, increase the other two colors in equal amounts. Here are variations on the color red:

Red	Green	Blue	Color
63	0	0	bright red
10	0	0	dark red
30	0	0	medium red
63	40	40	pink

Bright blue, dark blue, light blue, bright green, dark green, and light green are created in a similar manner. Of course, you can mix pairs of colors in other amounts to create colors such as magenta and lavender. Following are examples:

Red	Green	Blue	Color
0	30	30	cyan
30	30	0	yellow
30	0	30	magenta
40	0	63	lavender

15.5.2 Memory-Mapped Graphics Program

The *Memory-Mapped Graphics* program introduced next draws a row of 10 pixels on the screen using direct memory mapping in Mode 13h. The main procedure calls procedures that set the video mode to Mode 13h, set the screen's background color, draw some color pixels, and restore the video adapter to its starting mode. Two output ports control the video color palette. The value sent to port 3C8h indicates which video palette entry you plan to change. Then the color values themselves are sent to port 3C9h. Here is the program listing:

```
; Memory Mapped Graphics, Mode 13        (Mode13.asm)

INCLUDE Irvine16.inc

VIDEO_PALLETE_PORT = 3C8h
COLOR_SELECTION_PORT = 3C9h
```

```
        COLOR_INDEX = 1
        PALLETE_INDEX_BACKGROUND = 0
        SET_VIDEO_MODE = 0
        GET_VIDEO_MODE = 0Fh
        VIDEO_SEGMENT = 0A000h
        WAIT_FOR_KEYSTROKE = 10h
        MODE_13 = 13h

        .data
        saveMode BYTE ?                        ; saved video mode
        xVal     WORD ?                        ; x-coordinate
        yVal     WORD ?                        ; y-coordinate
        msg      BYTE "Welcome to Mode 13!",0

        .code
        main PROC
             mov    ax,@data
             mov    ds,ax

             call   SetVideoMode
             call   SetScreenBackground

        ; Display a greeting message.

             mov    edx,OFFSET msg
             call   WriteString

             call   Draw_Some_Pixels
             call   RestoreVideoMode
             exit
        main ENDP

        ;--------------------------------------------------
        SetScreenBackground PROC
        ;
        ; Sets the screen's background color. Video
        ; palette index 0 is the background color.
        ;--------------------------------------------------
             mov   dx,VIDEO_PALLETE_PORT
             mov   al,PALLETE_INDEX_BACKGROUND
             out   dx,al

        ; Set the screen background color to dark blue.

             mov   dx,COLOR_SELECTION_PORT
             mov   al,0                  ; red
             out   dx,al
             mov   al,0                  ; green
             out   dx,al
             mov   al,35                 ; blue (intensity 35/63)
             out   dx,al

             ret
        SetScreenBackground endp

        ;--------------------------------------------------
        SetVideoMode PROC
        ;
        ; Saves the current video mode, switches to a
        ; new mode, and points ES to the video segment.
        ;--------------------------------------------------
```

```
        mov     ah,GET_VIDEO_MODE
        int     10h
        mov     saveMode,al              ; save it

        mov     ah,SET_VIDEO_MODE
        mov     al,MODE_13               ; to mode 13h
        int     10h

        push    VIDEO_SEGMENT            ; video segment address
        pop     es                       ; ES points to video segment

        ret
SetVideoMode ENDP

;-------------------------------------------------
RestoreVideoMode PROC
;
; Waits for a key to be pressed and restores
; the video mode to its original value.
;-------------------------------------------------
        mov     ah,WAIT_FOR_KEYSTROKE
        int     16h
        mov     ah,SET_VIDEO_MODE        ; reset video mode
        mov     al,saveMode              ; to saved mode
        int     10h
        ret
RestoreVideoMode ENDP

;-------------------------------------------------
Draw_Some_Pixels PROC
;
; Sets individual palette colors and draws
; several pixels.
;-------------------------------------------------
; Change the color at index 1 to white (63,63,63).

        mov     dx,VIDEO_PALLETE_PORT
        mov     al,1                     ; set palette index 1
        out     dx,al

        mov     dx,COLOR_SELECTION_PORT
        mov     al,63                    ; red
        out     dx,al
        mov     al,63                    ; green
        out     dx,al
        mov     al,63                    ; blue
        out     dx,al

; Calculate the video buffer offset of the first pixel.
; Method is specific to mode 13h, which is 320 X 200.

        mov     xVal,160                 ; middle of screen
        mov     yVal,100
        mov     ax,320                   ; 320 for video mode 13h
        mul     yVal                     ; y-coordinate
        add     ax,xVAl                  ; x-coordinate

        ; Place the color index into the video buffer.

        mov     cx,10                    ; draw 10 pixels
        mov     di,ax                    ; AX contains buffer offset
```

```
; Draw the pixels now. By default, the assembler assumes
; DI is an offset from the segment address in DS. The
; segment override ES:[DI] tells the CPU to use the segment
; address in ES instead. ES currently points to VRAM.

DP1:
        mov     BYTE PTR es:[di],COLOR_INDEX
        add     di,5                    ; move 5 pixels to the right
        loop    DP1

        ret
Draw_Some_Pixels ENDP
END main
```

This program is fairly easy to implement because the pixels happen to be on the same screen line. To draw a vertical line, on the other hand, you could add 320 to each value of DI to move to the next row of pixels. Or, a diagonal line with slope −1 could be drawn by adding 321 to DI. Drawing arbitrary lines between any two points is best handled by *Bresenham's Algorithm*, which is well-explained on many Web sites.

15.5.3   Section Review

1. (*True/False*): Video mode 13h maps screen pixels as a two-dimensional array of bytes, where each byte corresponds to two pixels.
2. (*True/False*): In video mode 13h, each screen row uses 320 bytes of storage.
3. In one sentence, explain how video mode 13h sets the colors of pixels.
4. How is the color index used in video mode 13h?
5. In video mode 13h, what is contained in each element of the color palette?
6. What are the three RGB values for dark gray?
7. What are the three RGB values for white?
8. What are the three RGB values for bright red?
9. *Challenge:* Show how to set the screen background color in video mode 13h to green.
10. *Challenge:* Show how to set the screen background color in video mode 13h to white.

15.6   Mouse Programming

The mouse is usually connected to the computer's motherboard through a PS-2 mouse port, RS-232 serial port, USB port, or wireless connection. Before detecting the mouse, MS-DOS requires a device driver program to be installed. MS-Windows also has built-in mouse drivers, but for now we will concentrate on functions provided by MS-DOS.

Mouse movements are tracked in a unit of measure called *mickeys* (guess how they came up with that name?). One mickey represents approximately 1/200 inch of physical mouse travel. The mickeys-to-pixels ratio can be set for the mouse, which defaults to 8 mickeys for each 8 horizontal pixels and 16 mickeys for each 8 vertical pixels.[3] There is also a double-speed threshold, which defaults to 64 mickeys per second.

15.6.1   Mouse INT 33h Functions

INT 33h provides information about the mouse, including its current position, last button clicked, speed, and so on. You can also use it to display or hide the mouse cursor. In this section, we cover a few of the more essential mouse functions. INT 33h receives the function number in the AX register rather than AH (which is the norm for BIOS interrupts).

Reset Mouse and Get Status

INT 33h Function 0 resets the mouse and confirms that it is available. The mouse (if found) is centered on the screen, its display page is set to video page 0, its pointer is hidden, and its mickeys-to-pixels ratios and speed are set to default values. The mouse's range of movement is set to the entire screen area. Details are shown in the following table:

INT 33h Function 0	
Description	Reset mouse and get status
Receives	AX = 0
Returns	If mouse support is available AX = FFFFh and BX = number of mouse buttons; otherwise, AX = 0.

Sample Call	```mov ax,0```
	```int 33h```
	```cmp ax,0```
	```je MouseNotAvailable```
	```mov numberOfButtons,bx```

Notes	If the mouse was visible before this call, it is hidden by this function.

Showing and Hiding the Mouse Pointer

INT 33h Functions 1 and 2, shown in the next two tables, display and hide the mouse pointer, respectively. The mouse driver keeps an internal counter, which is incremented (if nonzero) by calls to Function 1 and decremented by calls to Function 2. When the counter is non-negative, the mouse pointer is displayed. Function 0 (reset mouse pointer) sets the counter to −1.

INT 33h Function 1	
Description	Show mouse pointer
Receives	AX = 1
Returns	Nothing
Sample Call	```mov ax,1``` ```int 33h```
Notes	The mouse driver keeps a count of the number of times this function is called. Adds 1 to its internal show/hide counter.

INT 33h Function 2	
Description	Hide mouse pointer
Receives	AX = 2
Returns	Nothing
Sample Call	```mov ax,2``` ```int 33h```
Notes	The mouse driver continues to track the mouse position. Subtracts 1 from its internal show/hide counter.

Get Mouse Position and Status

INT 33h Function 3 gets the mouse position and mouse status, shown in the following table:

INT 33h Function 3	
Description	Get mouse position and status
Receives	AX = 3
Returns	BX = mouse button status CX = X-coordinate (in pixels) DX = Y-coordinate (in pixels)

Sample Call	```mov ax,3```
	```int 33h```
	```test bx,1```
	```jne Left_Button_Down```
	```test bx,2```
	```jne Right_Button_Down```
	```test bx,4```
	```jne Center_Button_Down```
	```mov Xcoord,cx```
	```mov yCoord,dx```

Notes	The mouse button status is returned in BX as follows: If bit 0 is set, the left button is down; if bit 1 is set, the right button is down; if bit 2 is set, the center button is down.

Converting Pixel to Character Coordinates   Standard text fonts in MS-DOS are 8 pixels wide and 16 pixels high, so you can convert pixel coordinates to character coordinates by dividing the former by the character size. Assuming that both pixels and characters start numbering at zero, the following formula converts a pixel coordinate P to a character coordinate C, using character dimension D:

$$C = int(P / D)$$

For example, let's assume that characters are 8 pixels wide. If the X-coordinate returned by INT 33 Function 3 was 100 (pixels), the coordinate would fall within character position 12: $C = int(100 / 8)$.

Set Mouse Position

INT 33h Function 4, shown in the following table, moves the mouse position to specified X and Y pixel coordinates.

INT 33h Function 4	
Description	Set mouse position
Receives	AX = 4 CX = X-coordinate (in pixels) DX = Y-coordinate (in pixels)
Returns	Nothing

Sample Call	```mov ax,4```
	```mov cx,200 ; X-position```
	```mov dx,100 ; Y-position```
	```int 33h```

Notes	If the position lies within an exclusion area, the mouse is not displayed.

Converting Character to Pixel Coordinates   You can convert a screen character coordinate to a pixel coordinate using the following formula, where C = character coordinate, P = pixel coordinate, and D = character dimension:

$$P = C \times D$$

In the horizontal direction, P will be the pixel coordinate of the left side of the character cell. In the vertical direction, P will be the pixel coordinate of the top of the character cell. If characters are 8 pixels wide, and you want to put the mouse in character cell 12, for example, the X-coordinate of the leftmost pixel of that cell is 96.

Get Button Presses and Releases

Function 5 returns the status of all mouse buttons, as well as the position of the last button press. In an event-driven programming environment, a *drag* event always begins with a button press. Once a call is made to this function for a particular button, the button's state is reset, and a second call to the function returns nothing:

INT 33h Function 5	
Description	Get button press information
Receives	AX = 5 BX = button ID (0 = left, 1 = right, 2 = center)
Returns	AX = button status BX = button press counter CX = X-coordinate of last button press DX = Y-coordinate of last button press

Sample Call	```mov ax,5```
	```mov bx,0 ; button ID```
	```int 33h```
	```test ax,1 ; left button down?```
	```jz skip ; no - skip```
	```mov X_coord,cx ; yes: save coordinates```
	```mov Y_coord,dx```

Notes	The mouse button status is returned in AX as follows: If bit 0 is set, the left button is down; if bit 1 is set, the right button is down; if bit 2 is set, the center button is down.

Function 6 gets button release information from the mouse, as shown in the following table. In event-driven programming, a mouse *click* event occurs when a mouse button is released. Similarly, a *drag* event ends when the mouse button is released.

INT 33h Function 6	
Description	Get button release information
Receives	AX = 6 BX = button ID (0 = left, 1 = right, 2 = center)
Returns	AX = button status BX = button release counter CX = X-coordinate of last button release DX = Y-coordinate of last button release

INT 33h Function 6	
Sample Call	``` mov ax,6 mov bx,0 ; button ID int 33h test ax,1 ; left button released? jz skip ; no - skip mov X_coord,cx ; yes: save coordinates mov Y_coord,dx ```
Notes	The mouse button status is returned in AX as follows: If bit 0 is set, the left button was released; if bit 1 is set, the right button was released; if bit 2 is set, the center button was released.

Setting Horizontal and Vertical Limits

INT 33h Functions 7 and 8, as illustrated in the next two tables, let you set limits on where the mouse pointer can go on the screen. You do this by setting minimum and maximum coordinates for the mouse cursor. If necessary, the mouse pointer is moved so it lies within the new limits.

INT 33h Function 7	
Description	Set horizontal limits
Receives	AX = 7 CX = minimum X-coordinate (in pixels) DX = maximum X-coordinate (in pixels)
Returns	Nothing
Sample Call	``` mov ax,7 mov cx,100 ; set X-range to mov dx,700 ; (100,700) int 33h ```

INT 33h Function 8	
Description	Set vertical limits
Receives	AX = 8 CX = minimum Y-coordinate (in pixels) DX = maximum Y-coordinate (in pixels)
Returns	Nothing
Sample Call	``` mov ax,8 int 33h mov cx,100 ; set Y-range to mov dx,500 ; (100,500) int 33h ```

Miscellaneous Mouse Functions

A number of other INT 33h functions are useful for configuring the mouse and controlling its behavior. We don't have the space to elaborate on these functions, but they are listed in Table 15-9.

Table 15-9   Miscellaneous Mouse Functions.

Function	Description	Input/Output Parameters
AX = 0Fh	Sets the number of mickeys per 8 pixels for horizontal and vertical mouse motion.	Receives: CX = horizontal mickeys, DX = vertical mickeys. The defaults are CX = 8, DX = 16.
AX = 10h	Set mouse exclusion area (prevents mouse from entering a rectangle).	Receives: CX, DX = X, Y coordinates of upper left corner. SI, DI = X, Y coordinates of lower right corner
AX = 13h	Set double speed threshold.	Receives: DX = threshold speed in mickeys per second (the default is 64)
AX = 1Ah	Set mouse sensitivity and threshold.	Receives: BX = horizontal speed (mickeys per second), CX = vertical speed (mickeys per second), DX = double speed threshold in mickeys per second
AX = 1Bh	Get mouse sensitivity and threshold.	Returns: BX = horizontal speed, CX = vertical speed, DX = double speed threshold
AX = 1Fh	Disable mouse driver.	Returns: If unsuccessful, AX = FFFFh
AX = 20h	Enable mouse driver.	None
AX = 24h	Get mouse information.	Returns FFFFh on error; otherwise, returns: BH = major version number, BL = minor version number, CH = mouse type (1 = bus, 2 = serial, 3 = InPort, 4 = PS/2, 5 = HP); CL = IRQ number (0 for PS/2 mouse)

15.6.2 Mouse Tracking Program

We've written a simple *mouse tracking* program that tracks the movement of the text mouse cursor. The X and Y coordinates are continually updated in the lower-right corner of the screen, and when the user presses the left button, the mouse's position is displayed in the lower left corner of the screen. Following is the source code:

```
TITLE Tracking the Mouse                     (mouse.asm)

; Demonstrates basic mouse functions available via INT 33h.
; In Standard DOS mode, each character position in the DOS
; window equals 8 mouse units.

INCLUDE Irvine16.inc

GET_MOUSE_STATUS = 0
SHOW_MOUSE_POINTER = 1
HIDE_MOUSE_POINTER = 2
GET_CURSOR_SIZE = 3
GET_BUTTON_PRESS_INFO = 5
GET_MOUSE_POSITION_AND_STATUS = 3
ESCkey = 1Bh

.data
greeting    BYTE "[Mouse.exe] Press Esc to quit",0
statusLine  BYTE "Left button: "
            BYTE "Mouse position: ",0
blanks      BYTE "                    ",0
xCoord WORD 0                         ; current X-coordinate
yCoord WORD 0                         ; current Y-coordinate
```

```
        xPress WORD 0                      ; X-coord of last button press
        yPress WORD 0                      ; Y-coord of last button press

        ; Display coordinates.
        statusRow       BYTE ?
        statusCol       BYTE 15
        buttonPressCol BYTE 20
        statusCol2      BYTE 60
        coordCol        BYTE 65

        .code
        main PROC
                mov     ax,@data
                mov     ds,ax
                call    Clrscr

        ; Get the screen X/Y coordinates.
                call    GetMaxXY           ; DH = rows, DL = columns
                dec     dh                 ; calculate status row value
                mov     statusRow,dh

        ; Hide the text cursor and display the mouse.
                call    HideCursor
                mov     dx,OFFSET greeting
                call    WriteString
                call    ShowMousePointer

        ; Display status information on the bottom screen line.
                mov     dh,statusRow
                mov     dl,0
                call    Gotoxy
                mov     dx,OFFSET statusLine
                call    Writestring

        ; Loop: show mouse coordinates, check for left mouse
        ; button press or keypress (Esc key).

        L1:     call    ShowMousePosition
                call    LeftButtonPress    ; check for button press
                mov     ah,11h             ; key pressed already?
                int     16h
                jz      L2                 ; no, continue the loop
                mov     ah,10h             ; remove key from buffer
                int     16h
                cmp     al,ESCkey          ; yes. Is it the ESC key?
                je      quit               ; yes, quit the program
        L2:     jmp     L1                 ; no, continue the loop

        ; Hide the mouse, restore the text cursor, clear
        ; the screen, and wait for a key press.
        quit:
                call    HideMousePointer
                call    ShowCursor
                call    Clrscr
                call    WaitMsg
                exit
        main ENDP

        ;-------------------------------------------------------------
        GetMousePosition PROC USES ax
        ;
```

```
; Gets the current mouse position and button status.
; Receives: nothing
; Returns:  BX = button status (0 = left button down,
;           (1 = right button down, 2 = center button down)
;           CX = X-coordinate
;           DX = Y-coordinate
;----------------------------------------------------------
      mov   ax,GET_MOUSE_POSITION_AND_STATUS
      int   33h
      ret
GetMousePosition ENDP

;----------------------------------------------------------
HideCursor PROC USES ax cx
;
; Hide the text cursor by setting its top line
; value to an illegal value.
; Receives: nothing. Returns: nothing
;----------------------------------------------------------
      mov   ah,GET_CURSOR_SIZE
      int   10h
      or    ch,30h              ; set upper row to illegal value
      mov   ah,1               ; set cursor size
      int   10h
      ret
HideCursor ENDP

;----------------------------------------------------------
ShowCursor PROC USES ax cx
;
; Show the text cursor by setting size to default.
; Receives: nothing. Returns: nothing
;----------------------------------------------------------
      mov   ah,GET_CURSOR_SIZE
      int   10h
      mov   ah,1               ; set cursor size
      mov   cx,0607h           ; default size
      int   10h
      ret
ShowCursor ENDP

;----------------------------------------------------------
HideMousePointer PROC USES ax
;
; Hides the mouse pointer.
; Receives: nothing. Returns: nothing
;----------------------------------------------------------
      mov   ax,HIDE_MOUSE_POINTER
      int   33h
      ret
HideMousePointer ENDP

;----------------------------------------------------------
ShowMousePointer PROC USES ax
;
; Makes the mouse pointer visible.
; Receives: nothing. Returns: nothing
;----------------------------------------------------------
      mov   ax,SHOW_MOUSE_POINTER ; make mouse cursor visible
```

```
      int    33h
      ret
ShowMousePointer ENDP

;----------------------------------------------------------
LeftButtonPress PROC
;
; Checks for the most recent left mouse button press
; and displays the mouse location.
; Receives: nothing. Returns: nothing
;----------------------------------------------------------
      pusha
      mov    ax,GET_BUTTON_PRESS_INFO
      mov    bx,0                      ; specify the left button
      int    33h

; Exit proc if the coordinates have not changed.
      cmp    cx,xPress                 ; same X coordinate?
      jne    L1                        ; no: continue
      cmp    dx,yPress                 ; same Y coordinate?
      je     L2                        ; yes: exit

; Coordinates have changed, so save them.
L1:   mov    xPress,cx
      mov    yPress,dx

; Position the cursor, clear the old numbers.
      mov    dh,statusRow              ; screen row
      mov    dl,statusCol              ; screen column
      call   Gotoxy
      push   dx
      mov    dx,OFFSET blanks
      call   WriteString
      pop    dx

; Show coordinates where mouse button was pressed.
      call   Gotoxy
      mov    ax,xCoord
      call   WriteDec
      mov    dl,buttonPressCol
      call   Gotoxy
      mov    ax,yCoord
      call   WriteDec

L2:   popa
      ret
LeftButtonPress ENDP

;----------------------------------------------------------
SetMousePosition PROC
;
; Set the mouse's position on the screen.
; Receives: CX = X-coordinate
;           DX = Y-coordinate
; Returns:  nothing
;----------------------------------------------------------
      mov    ax,4
      int    33h
      ret
SetMousePosition ENDP
```

```
;---------------------------------------------------------
ShowMousePosition PROC
;
; Get and show the mouse coordinates at the
; bottom of the screen.
; Receives: nothing
; Returns:  nothing
;---------------------------------------------------------
        pusha
        call   GetMousePosition

; Exit proc if the coordinates have not changed.
        cmp    cx,xCoord              ; same X coordinate?
        jne    L1                     ; no: continue
        cmp    dx,yCoord              ; same Y coordinate?
        je     L2                     ; yes: exit

; Save the new X and Y coordinates.
L1:     mov    xCoord,cx
        mov    yCoord,dx

; Position the cursor, clear the old numbers.
        mov    dh,statusRow           ; screen row
        mov    dl,statusCol2          ; screen column
        call   Gotoxy
        push   dx
        mov    dx,OFFSET blanks
        call   WriteString
        pop    dx

; Show the mouse coordinates.
        call   Gotoxy
        mov    ax,xCoord
        call   WriteDec
        mov    dl,coordCol            ; screen column
        call   Gotoxy
        mov    ax,yCoord
        call   WriteDec

L2:     popa
        ret
ShowMousePosition ENDP
END main
```

Varying Behaviors   The program's behavior changes a bit depending on two factors: (1) which version of MS-Windows you're running, and (2) whether you run it in a console window or full-screen mode. In Windows XP, for example, the console window defaults to 50 vertical text lines. When you run in full-screen mode, the mouse cursor is a solid block; its coordinates appear to change one pixel at a time, whereas the mouse cursor jumps from one character to the next only when you have moved horizontally by 8 pixels or vertically by 16 pixels. In console window mode, the mouse cursor is a pointer; its coordinates change 8 pixels at a time horizontally and 16 pixels at a time vertically.

15.6.3 Section Review

1. Which INT 33h function resets the mouse and gets the mouse status?
2. Write ASM statements that reset the mouse and get the mouse status.
3. Which INT 33h function shows and hides the mouse pointer?

4. Write ASM statements that hide the mouse pointer.

5. Which INT 33h function gets the mouse position and status?

6. Write ASM statements that get the mouse position and store it in the variables **mouseX** and **mouseY**.

7. Which INT 33h function sets the mouse position?

8. Write ASM statements that set the mouse pointer to X = 100 and Y = 400.

9. Which INT 33h function gets mouse button press information?

10. Write ASM statements that jump to label **Button1** when the left mouse button has been pressed.

11. Which INT 33h function gets mouse button release information?

12. Write ASM statements that get the mouse position at the point when the right button was released, and store the position in the variables **mouseX** and **mouseY**.

13. Write ASM statements that set the vertical limits of the mouse to 200 and 400.

14. Write ASM statements that set the horizontal limits of the mouse to 300 and 600.

15. *Challenge:* Suppose you want the mouse pointer to point to the upper left corner of the character cell located at row 10, column 20 in text mode. What X and Y values will you have to pass to INT 33h Function 4, assuming 8 horizontal pixels per character and 16 vertical pixels per character?

16. *Challenge:* Suppose you want the mouse pointer to point to the middle of the character cell located at row 15, column 22 in text mode. What X and Y values will you have to pass to INT 33h Function 4, assuming 8 horizontal pixels per character and 16 vertical pixels per character?

17. *Challenge:* Who invented the computer mouse, in what year, and at what location?

15.7 Chapter Summary

Working at the BIOS level gives you more control over the computer's input-output devices than you would have at the MS-DOS level. This chapter shows how to program the keyboard using INT 16h, the video display using INT 10h, and the mouse, using INT 33h.

INT 16h is particularly useful for reading extended keyboard keys such as function keys and cursor arrow keys.

Keyboard hardware works with the INT 9h, INT 16h, and INT 21h handlers to make keyboard input available to programs. The chapter contains a program that polls the keyboard and breaks out of a loop when the Esc key is pressed.

Colors are produced on the video display using additive synthesis of primary colors. The color bits are mapped to the video attribute byte.

A wide range of useful INT 10h functions can control the video display at the BIOS level. The chapter contains an example program that scrolls a color window and writes text in the middle of it.

You can draw color graphics using INT 10h. The chapter contains two example programs that show how to do this. A simple formula can be used to convert Cartesian coordinates to screen coordinates (pixel locations).

An example program with documentation shows how to draw high-speed color graphics by writing directly to video memory.

Numerous INT 33h functions manipulate and read the mouse. An example program tracks both mouse movements and mouse button clicks.

For More Information   Digging up information on BIOS functions is not easy because many of the good reference books have gone out of print. Here are my favorites:

• Ralf, Brown, and Jim Kyle, *PC Interrupts. A Programmer's Reference to BIOS, DOS, and Third-Party Calls*, Addison-Wesley, 1991.

- Ray, Duncan. *IBM ROM BIOS*, Microsoft Press, 1998.
- Ray, Duncan. *Advanced MS-DOS Programming*, 2nd ed., Microsoft Press, 1988.
- Frank van, Gilluwe. *The Undocumented PC: A Programmer's Guide to I/O, CPUs, and Fixed Memory Areas*, Addison-Wesley, 1996.
- Thom, Hogan. *Programmer's PC Sourcebook: Reference Tables for IBM PCs and Compatibles, Ps/2 Systems, Eisa-Based Systems, Ms-DOS Operating System Through Version*, Microsoft Press, 1991.
- Jim, Kyle. *DOS 6 Developer's Guide*, SAMS, 1993.
- Muhammad Ali, Mazidi, and Janice Gillispie Mazidi, *The 80x86 IBM PC & Compatible Computers*, 4th Ed.,Volumes. I and II, Prentice-Hall, 2002.

This book's Web site (*www.asmirvine.com*) has links to many additional sources of information, including Ralf Brown's current list of MS-DOS and BIOS interrupts.

15.8   Chapter Exercises

The following exercises must be done in real-address mode:

1.   ASCII Table

Using INT 10h, display all 256 characters from the IBM Extended ASCII character set (inside back cover of the book). Display 32 columns per line, with a space following each character.

2.   Scrolling Text Window

Define a text window that is approximately three fourths of the size of the video display. Let the program carry out the following actions, in sequence:

- Draw a string of random characters on the top line of the window. (You can call Random_range from the Irvine16 library.)
- Scroll the window down one line.
- Pause the program for approximately 200 milliseconds. (You can call the **Delay** function from the Irvine16 library.)
- Draw another line of random text.
- Continue scrolling and drawing until 50 lines have been displayed.

> This program and its various enhancements were given a nickname by my assembly language students based on a popular movie in which characters interact in a virtual world. (I can't mention the name of the movie here, but you will probably figure it out by the time you complete the programs.)

3.   Scrolling Color Columns

Using the **Scrolling Text Window** exercise as a starting point, make the following changes:

- The random string should only have characters in columns 0, 3, 6, 9, . . ., 78. The other columns should be blank. This will create the effect of columns as it scrolls downward.
- Each column should be in a different color.

4.   Scrolling Columns in Different Directions

Using the **Scrolling Text Window** exercise as a starting point, make the following change: Before the loop starts, randomly choose each column to scroll either up or down. It should continue in the same direction for the duration of the program. *Hint:* Define each column as a separately scrolling window.

5.   Drawing a Rectangle Using INT 10h

Using the pixel-drawing capabilities of INT 10h, create a procedure named **DrawRectangle** that takes input parameters specifying the location of the upper left corner and the lower right corner, and the color. Write a short test program that draws several rectangles of different sizes and colors.

6. Plotting a Function Using INT 10h

Using the pixel-drawing capabilities of INT 10h, plot the line determined by the equation $Y = 2(X^2)$.

7. Mode 13 Line

Modify the Memory-Mapped Graphics program in Section 15.5.2 so that it draws a single vertical line.

8. Mode 13, Multiple Lines

Modify the Memory-Mapped Graphics program in Section 15.5.2 so that it draws a series of 10 vertical lines, each in a different color.

9. Box-Drawing Program

MS-DOS applications in the 1980s and early 1990s usually displayed boxes and frames using line-drawing characters in text mode. This programming exercise will reproduce those techniques. Write a procedure that draws a single-line frame anywhere on the screen. Use the following extended ASCII codes from the table on the inside back cover of this book: C0h, BFh, B3h, C4h, D9h, and DAh. The procedure's only input parameter should be a pointer to a FRAME structure:

```
FRAME STRUCT
      Left BYTE ?                      ; left side
      Top  BYTE ?                      ; top line
      Right BYTE ?                     ; right side
      Bottom BYTE ?                    ; bottom line
      FrameColor BYTE ?                ; box color
FRAME ENDS
```

Write a program that tests your procedure, passing it pointers to various FRAME objects.

End Notes

1. A prime example is Michael Abrash, *The Zen of Code Optimization*, Coriolis Group Books, 1994.

2. You may have trouble running *Pixel1.asm* and *Pixel2.asm* under MS-Windows on computers having a relatively low amount of video RAM. If this is a problem, switch to another mode or boot into pure MS-DOS mode.

3. From Ray Duncan, *Advanced MS-DOS Programming*, 2nd Ed., Microsoft Press, 1988, p. 601.

16

Expert MS-DOS Programming

16.1   Introduction

This is a good chapter to read if you're planning to be an engineer who works at the hardware level on Intel processors. It's also a good chapter if you want to understand the amazing things MS-DOS experts were able to do with very limited resources a few years ago. It will give you some useful background if you plan to become a systems-level programmer. It is a chapter on MS-DOS system resources and programming. Here's what we're going to do:

- Show you how to get as much flexibility as possible from the .MODEL, .CODE, .STACK, and related directives.
- Show you how to define segments from scratch, using explicit segment directives.
- Demonstrate a large memory model program that has multiple code and data segments.
- Explain the runtime structure of COM and EXE programs, including EXE headers.
- Map out the Program Segment Prefix (PSP) and show how you can find the MS-DOS environment string.
- Show you how to replace existing interrupt handlers with your own. We will demonstrate this by writing a Ctrl-Break interrupt handler (also called an *interrupt service routine*, or ISR).

- Explain how hardware interrupts work and list the various *interrupt request* (IRQ) levels used by the Intel 8259 Programmable Interrupt Controller (PIC).
- Write a *terminate and stay resident* (TSR) program that intercepts the Ctrl-Alt-Del key combination. If you learn to do this, you can join the ranks of MS-DOS experts.
- Show how to write hardware data directly to output ports and how to use ports to monitor the status of hardware, control the behavior of hardware, and read input data from hardware devices.

If you've been around experienced programmers for a few years, you've probably heard a lot of the terms from the foregoing list. Notice how the old-time experts seem to drop terms like IRQ, TSR, PSP, and 8259 into their conversations? Now you can find out what they've been talking about.

16.2   Defining Segments

Programs written for the early versions of MASM had to create rather elaborate definitions for code, data, and stack segments. Instructors all breathed a sigh of relief when simplified segment directives (.code, .stack, .data) came along because they made the first week of class go much more smoothly. It was also clear, however, that expert programmers would probably prefer flexibility over simplicity and would stick with the traditional way of doing things. If you've reached this chapter (and understood all preceding chapters), you are now ready to master the arcane details of explicit segment directives.

First, however, we're going to explore the various ways the simplified directives can be used, just in case they satisfy your needs.

16.2.1   Simplified Segment Directives

When you use the .MODEL directive, the assembler automatically defines DGROUP for your near data segment. The segments in DGROUP form near data, which can normally be accessed directly through DS or SS.

The .DATA and .DATA? directives both create a near data segment, which can be as large as 64Kb when running in real-address mode. It is placed in a special group identified as DGROUP, which is also limited to 64Kb. When .FARDATA and .FARDATA? are used in the small and medium memory models, the assembler creates far data segments named FAR_DATA and FAR_BSS, respectively.

Identifying a Variable's Segment   Some BIOS and DOS functions require you to use a particular segment register when passing argument data. You can assign a segment's address to a segment register using the SEG operator. The following, for example, sets DS to the segment containing **farvar**:

```
mov  ax,SEG farvar
mov  ds,ax
```

Code Segments   Code segments are defined, as you know, by the .CODE directive. In a small memory model program, the .CODE directive causes the assembler to generate a segment named _TEXT. You can see this in the Segments and Groups section of a listing file:

```
_TEXT . . . . .16 Bit 0009        Word Public 'CODE'
```

(This entry indicates that a 16-bit segment named _TEXT is 9 bytes long. It is aligned on an even word boundary, it is a public segment, and its segment class is 'CODE'.)

In medium, large, and huge model programs, each source code module is assigned a different segment name. The name consists of the module name followed by _TEXT. For example, in a program named *MyProg.asm* that uses the .MODEL, LARGE directive, the listing file generates the following code segment entry:

```
MYPROG_TEXT  . . . . .16 Bit 0009   Word Public 'CODE'
```

You can also declare multiple code segments within the same module, regardless of the memory model. Do this by adding an optional segment name to the .CODE directive:

```
.code MyCode
```

Keep this in mind: If you call the book's 16-bit link library procedures, your code must be located inside a segment named **_TEXT**. The following excerpt, for example, would cause the linker to generate a *fixup overflow* message:

```
.code MyCode
      mov    dx,offset msg
      call   Writestring
```

Multiple Code Segment Program   The following *MultCode.asm* program contains two code segments. By not including the *Irvine16.inc* file, we can show you all the MASM directives being used in the program:

```
TITLE Multiple Code Segments        (MultCode.asm)

; This small model program contains multiple
; code segments.

.model small,stdcall
.stack 100h
WriteString PROTO

.data
msg1 db "First Message",0dh,0ah,0
msg2 db "Second Message",0dh,0ah,"$"

.code
main PROC
      mov    ax,@data
      mov    ds,ax

      mov    dx,OFFSET msg1
      call   WriteString           ; NEAR call
      call   Display               ; FAR call
      .exit
main ENDP

.code OtherCode
Display PROC FAR
      mov    ah,9
      mov    dx,offset msg2
      int    21h
      ret
Display ENDP
END main
```

In the foregoing example, the **_TEXT** segment contains the **main** procedure, and the **OtherCode** segment contains the **Display** procedure. Notice that the **Display** procedure must have a FAR modifier to tell the assembler to generate the type of call instruction that saves both the current segment and offset on the stack. For confirmation, we can see the names of the two code segments in the *MultCode.lst* listing file:

```
OtherCode . . . .16 Bit 0008      Word   Public 'CODE'
_TEXT . . . . . .16 Bit 0014      Word   Public 'CODE'
```

16.2.2 Explicit Segment Definitions

There are a few occasions when you may prefer to create explicit segment definitions. You may want to define multiple data segments with extra memory buffers, for instance. Or, you may be linking your program to an object library that uses its own proprietary segment names. Finally, you may be writing a procedure to be called from a high-level language compiler that does not use Microsoft's segment names.

A program with explicit segment definitions has two tasks to perform: First, a segment register (DS, ES, or SS) must be set to the location of each segment before it may be used. Second, the assembler must be told how to calculate the offsets of labels within the correct segments.

The SEGMENT and ENDS directives define the beginning and end of a segment, respectively. A program may contain almost any number of segments, each with a unique name. Segments can also be grouped together (combined). The syntax is

```
name SEGMENT [align] [combine] ['class']
     statement-list
name ENDS
```

- *name* identifies the segment; it can be unique or it can be the name of an existing segment.
- *align* can be BYTE, WORD, DWORD, PARA, or PAGE.
- *combine* can be PRIVATE, PUBLIC, STACK, COMMON, MEMORY, or AT *address*.
- *class* is an identifier enclosed in single quotes that is used when identifying a particular type of segment such as CODE or STACK.

For example, here is how a segment called **ExtraData** could be defined:

```
ExtraData SEGMENT PARA PUBLIC 'DATA'
     var1 BYTE 1
     var2 WORD 2
ExtraData ENDS
```

Align Type

When two or more segments are to be combined, their *align types* tell the linker how to align their starting addresses. The default is PARA, which indicates that the segment must begin on an even 16-byte boundary. Here are examples of 20-bit hexadecimal addresses that fall on paragraph boundaries. Notice that the last digit is always zero:

```
0A150 81B30 07460
```

To create the specified alignment, the assembler inserts bytes at the end of any existing segment until the correct starting address for the new segment is reached. The extra bytes are called *slack bytes*. This only affects segments that are joined to an existing segment because the first segment in a group always begins on a paragraph boundary. (Recall from Chapter 2 that segment addresses always contain four implied low-order zero bits.) The following align types are available:

- The BYTE align type starts the segment on the next byte following the preceding segment.
- The WORD align type starts the segment at the next 16-bit boundary.
- DWORD starts the segment at the next 32-bit boundary.
- PARA starts the segment at the next 16-byte boundary.
- PAGE starts the segment at the next 256-byte boundary.

If a program will likely be run on an 8086 or 80286 processor, a WORD align type (or larger) is best for data segments because the processors have a 16-bit data bus. Such processors always move 2 bytes, the first of which has an even-numbered address. Therefore, a variable on an even boundary requires one memory fetch, whereas a variable on an odd boundary requires two. An IA-32 processor, on the other hand, fetches 32 bits at a time, and should use the DWORD align type.

Combine Type

A segment's *combine type* tells the linker how to combine segments having the same name. The default type is PRIVATE, indicating that such a segment will not be combined with any other segment.

The PUBLIC and MEMORY combine types cause a segment to be combined with all other public or memory segments by the same name; in effect, they become a single segment. The offsets of all labels are adjusted so they are relative to the start of the same segment.

The STACK combine type resembles the PUBLIC type, in that all other stack segments will be combined with it. MS-DOS automatically initializes SS to the start of the first segment that it finds with a combine type of STACK; MS-DOS sets SP to the segment's length (minus 1) when the program is loaded. In an EXE program, there should be at least one segment with a STACK combine type; otherwise, the linker displays a warning message.

The COMMON combine type makes a segment begin at the same address as any other COMMON segments with the same name. In effect, the segments overlay each other. All offsets are calculated from the same starting address, and variables can overlap.

The AT *address* combine type lets you create a segment at an absolute address; it is often used for data whose location is predefined by the hardware or operating system. No variables or data may be initialized, but you can create variable names that refer to specific offsets. For example,

```
bios SEGMENT AT 40h
  ORG 17h
  keyboard_flag  BYTE ?                ; MS-DOS keyboard flag
bios ENDS

.code
    mov    ax,bios                ; point to BIOS segment
    mov    ds,ax
    and    ds:keyboard_flag,7Fh   ; clear high bit
```

In this example, a segment override (DS:) was required because **keyboard_flag** is not in the standard data segment. We will explain segment overrides in Section 16.2.3.

Class Type

A segment's *class type* provides another way of combining segments, in particular, those with different names. The class type is case-sensitive string enclosed in single quotes. Segments with the same class type are loaded together, though they may be in a different order in the original program. One standard type, CODE, is recognized by the linker and should be used for segments containing instructions. You must include this type label if you plan to use a debugger.

ASSUME Directive

The ASSUME directive tells the assembler how to calculate offsets of code and data labels at assembly time. It is usually placed directly after the SEGMENT directive in the code segment. Its syntax requires the name of a segment register, followed by a colon, followed by the name of a segment:

```
ASSUME segreg : segname
```

ASSUME does not actually change the value of a segment register. That must be done at run time, using instructions that assign segment values to segment registers. Your code may contain multiple ASSUME directives. When a new one is encountered, the assembler modifies the way it calculates addresses from that point on.

The following ASSUME tells the assembler to use DS as the default register for the **data1** segment:

```
ASSUME ds:data1
```

The following statement associates CS with **myCode** and SS is associated with **myStack**:

```
ASSUME cs:myCode, ss:myStack
```

Example: Multiple Data Segments

Earlier in this section we showed a program having two code segments. Let's now create a program (*MultData.asm*) containing two data segments named **data1** and **data2**. Both are declared with class name DATA. The ASSUME directive associates DS with **data1** and ES with **data2**:

```
ASSUME cs:cseg, ds:data1, es:data2, ss:mystack
data1 SEGMENT 'DATA'
data2 SEGMENT 'DATA'
```

The following is a complete program listing:

```
TITLE Multiple Data Segments               (MultData.asm)

; This program shows how to explicitly declare
; multiple data segments.

cseg  SEGMENT 'CODE'
      ASSUME cs:cseg, ds:data1, es:data2, ss:mystack

main PROC
      mov    ax,data1            ; point DS to data1 segment
      mov    ds,ax
      mov    ax,SEG val2         ; point ES to data2 segment
      mov    es,ax

      mov    ax,val1             ; data1 segment assumed
      mov    bx,val2             ; data2 segment assumed

      mov    ax,4C00h            ; exit program
      int    21h
main ENDP
cseg  ENDS

data1 SEGMENT 'DATA'
      val1   WORD 1001h
data1 ENDS

data2 SEGMENT 'DATA'
      val2   WORD 1002h
data2 ENDS

mystack SEGMENT para STACK 'STACK'
      BYTE 100h dup('S')
mystack ENDS
END main
```

Two ways of setting segment register values at run time were used. The first used a segment name (**data1**):

```
      mov    ax,data1            ; point DS to data1 segment
      mov    ds,ax
```

The second method was to use the SEG operator to obtain the segment address of **val2**:

```
      mov    ax,SEG val2         ; point ES to data2 segment
      mov    es,ax
```

The listing file created by the assembler shows two variables **val1** and **val2** having the same values (starting offsets) but different segment attributes:

```
Name                          Type  Value Attr
val1 . . . . . . . . . . . . . Word  0000  data1
val2 . . . . . . . . . . . . . Word  0000  data2
```

16.2.3   Segment Overrides

A *segment override* is a one-byte prefix that makes the current instruction use a different segment register from the one specified by the ASSUME directive when calculating the effective address. It can be used, for example, to access a variable in a segment other than the one currently associated with CS or DS:

```
mov   al,cs:var1                   ; segment pointed to by CS
mov   al,es:var2                   ; segment pointed to by ES
```

It should be noted here that in real-address mode, you can place variables in the code segment. You could never get away with that in protected mode!

The following instruction obtains the offset of a variable in a segment not currently ASSUME'd by DS or ES:

```
mov   bx,OFFSET AltSeg:var2
```

Multiple references to variables can be more easily handled by inserting an ASSUME to temporarily change the default segment references:

```
ASSUME ds:AltSeg                   ; use AltSeg for a while
mov   ax,AltSeg
mov   ds,ax
mov   al,var1
   .
   .
ASSUME ds:data                     ; use the default data segment
mov   ax,data
mov   ds,ax
```

16.2.4   Combining Segments

Large programs should be divided into separate modules to simplify editing and debugging. Even source code located in different modules can be combined into the same segment. Just use the same segment name in each module and specify a PUBLIC combine type. That's exactly what happens when you link a 16-bit program with the book's Irvine16 link library, using simplified segment directives.

If you use a BYTE align type, each segment immediately follows the preceding one. If a WORD align type is used, a segment will follow another segment at the next even word boundary. The align type defaults to PARA, in which each segment follows at the next paragraph boundary.

Program Example   Let's look at a two-module program containing one code segment (CSEG), one data segment (DSEG), and one stack segment (SSEG). The main module contains all three segments; CSEG and DSEG have a PUBLIC combine type. A BYTE align type is used for CSEG to avoid creating a gap between code from the two modules.

Main Module:

```
TITLE Segment Example          (main module, Seg2.asm)

EXTRN var2:WORD, subroutine_1:PROC

cseg SEGMENT BYTE PUBLIC 'CODE'
ASSUME cs:cseg,ds:dseg, ss:sseg

main PROC
      mov   ax,dseg              ; initialize DS
      mov   ds,ax

      mov   ax,var1             ; local variable
```

```
        mov    bx,var2              ; external variable
        call   subroutine_1         ; external procedure

        mov    ax,4C00h             ; exit to OS
        int    21h
main ENDP
cseg ENDS

dseg SEGMENT WORD PUBLIC 'DATA'     ; local data segment
        var1 WORD 1000h
dseg ends

sseg SEGMENT STACK 'STACK'          ; stack segment
        BYTE 100h dup('S')
sseg ENDS
END main
```

Submodule:

```
TITLE Segment Example              (submodule, Seg2a.ASM)

PUBLIC subroutine_1, var2

cseg SEGMENT BYTE PUBLIC 'CODE'
ASSUME cs:cseg, ds:dseg

subroutine_1 PROC                  ; called from MAIN
        mov    ah,9
        mov    dx,OFFSET msg
        int    21h
        ret
subroutine_1 ENDP
cseg ENDS

dseg SEGMENT WORD PUBLIC 'DATA'

var2 WORD 2000h                    ; accessed by MAIN
msg  BYTE 'Now in Subroutine_1'
        BYTE 0Dh,0Ah,'$'

dseg ENDS
END
```

The following MAP file was created by the linker, showing one code segment, one data segment, and one stack segment:

```
Start   Stop    Length Name              Class
00000H  0001BH  0001CH CSEG              CODE
0001CH  00035H  0001AH DSEG              DATA
00040H  0013FH  00100H SSEG              STACK

Program entry point at 0000:0000
```

16.2.5 Section Review

1. What is the purpose of the SEGMENT and ENDS directives?
2. What value does the SEG operator return?
3. Explain the function of the ASSUME directive.
4. In a segment definition, what are the possible align types?
5. In a segment definition, what are the possible combine types?
6. Which *align type* is most efficient for an IA-32 processor?

7. What is the purpose of the combine type in a segment definition?

8. How do you define a segment at an absolute address such as 40h?

9. What is the purpose of the class type option in a segment definition?

10. Write an instruction that uses a segment override.

11. In the following example, assume that **segA** begins at address 1A060h. What will be the starting address of the *third* segment, also called **segA**?

```
segA SEGMENT COMMON
  var1  WORD  ?
  var2  BYTE  ?
segA ends

stack SEGMENT STACK
  BYTE 100h dup(0)
stack ends

segA SEGMENT COMMON
  var3  WORD  3000h
  var4  BYTE  40h
segA ends
```

16.3   Runtime Program Structure

An effective assembly language programmer needs to know a lot about MS-DOS. This section describes command.com, the Program Segment Prefix, and the structure of COM and EXE programs. The *command.com* program supplied with MS-DOS and Windows 95 and 98 is called the command processor. In Windows 2000 and XP, it is named *cmd.exe*. It interprets each command typed at a prompt. The following sequence takes place when you type a command:

1. MS-DOS checks to see if the command is internal, such as DIR, REN, or DEL (delete). If it is, the command is immediately executed by a memory-resident MS-DOS routine.

2. MS-DOS looks for a matching file with an extension of COM. If the file is in the current directory, it is executed.

3. MS-DOS looks for a matching file with an extension of EXE. If the file is in the current directory, it is executed.

4. MS-DOS looks for a matching file with an extension of BAT. If the file is in the current directory, it is executed. A file with an extension of BAT is called a batch file, which is a text file containing MS-DOS commands to be executed as if the commands had been typed at the console.

5. If MS-DOS is unable to find a matching COM, EXE, or BAT file in the current directory, it searches the first directory in the current path. If it fails to find a match there, it proceeds to the next directory in the path, and continues this process until either a matching file is found or the path search is exhausted.

Application programs with extensions of COM and EXE are called *transient programs*. In general, they are loaded into memory long enough to be executed; when they finish, the memory they occupy is released. Transient programs can, if needed, leave a portion of their code in memory when they exit; these are called *memory-resident* programs, or TSRs.

16.3.1   Program Segment Prefix

MS-DOS creates a special 256-byte block at the beginning of a program as it is loaded into memory called the *Program Segment Prefix*. The structure of the Program Segment Prefix (PSP) is shown in Table 16-1.

Table 16-1   The Program Segment Prefix (PSP).

Offset	Comments
00–15	MS-DOS pointers and vector addresses
16–2B	Reserved by MS-DOS
2C–2D	Segment address of the current environment string
2E–5B	Reserved by MS-DOS
5C–7F	File control blocks 1 and 2, used mainly by pre–MS-DOS 2.0 programs
80–FF	Default disk transfer area and a copy of the current MS-DOS command tail

16.3.2 COM Programs

There are two types of transient programs, identified by their filename extension (COM or EXE). A COM program is an unmodified binary image of a machine-language program. It is loaded into memory by MS-DOS at the lowest available segment address, and a PSP is created at offset 0. The code, data, and stack are stored in the same physical (and logical) segment. The program may be as large as 64K, minus the size of the PSP and two reserved bytes at the end of the stack. As illustrated in the following diagram, all segment registers are set to the base address of the PSP. The code area begins at offset 100h, and the data area immediately follows the code. The stack area is at the end of the segment because MS-DOS initializes SP to FFFEh:

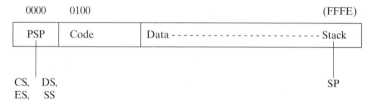

Let's look at a simple program written in COM format. MASM requires a COM program to use the *tiny* memory model. Also, the ORG directive must be used to set the starting location counter for program code to offset 100h. This leaves 100h bytes available for the PSP, which occupies locations 0 through 0FFh:

```
TITLE Hello Program in COM format    (HelloCom.asm)

.model tiny
.code
org 100h                            ; must be before main
main PROC
        mov     ah,9
        mov     dx,OFFSET hello_message
        int     21h
        mov     ax,4C00h
        int     21h
main ENDP

hello_message BYTE 'Hello, world!',0dh,0ah,'$'
END main
```

Variables are usually located after the main procedure because there is no separate segment for data. If we put the data at the top of the program, the CPU would try to execute the data. An alternative is to place a JMP instruction at the beginning that jumps over the data to the first actual instruction:

```
TITLE Hello Program in COM format       (HelloCom.asm)

.model tiny
.code
org 100h                                ; must be before entry point
main proc
    jmp     start                       ; skip over the data
hello_message BYTE 'Hello, world!',0dh,0ah,'$'

start:
    mov     ah,9
    mov     dx,OFFSET hello_message
    int     21h
    mov     ax,4C00h
    int     21h
main ENDP
END main
```

The Microsoft linker requires the /T parameter to tell it to create a COM file rather than an EXE file. COM programs are always smaller than their EXE counterparts—HelloCom.asm, for example, is only 17 bytes long when stored on disk. When in memory, however, a COM program eats up an entire 64K memory segment, whether it needs the space or not. COM programs were not designed to run in a multitasking environment.

16.3.3　EXE Programs

An EXE program is stored on disk with an EXE header followed by a load module containing the program itself. The program header is not actually loaded into memory; instead, it contains information used by MS-DOS to load and execute the program.

When MS-DOS loads an EXE program, a program segment prefix (PSP) is created at the first available address, and the program is placed in memory just above it. As MS-DOS decodes the program header, it sets DS and ES to the program's load address, also known as the *Program Segment Prefix* (PSP). CS and IP are set to the entry point of the program code, from where the program begins executing. SS is set to the beginning of the stack segment, and SP is set to the stack size. Here is a diagram showing overlapping code, data, and stack segments:

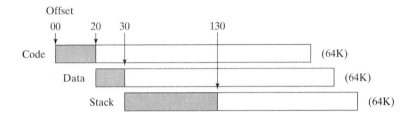

In this program, the code area is 20h bytes, the data area is 10h bytes, and the stack area is 100h bytes.

An EXE program may contain up to 65,535 segments, although it would be unusual to have that many. If a program has multiple data segments, the programmer usually has to manually set DS or ES to each new segment.

Memory Usage

The amount of memory an EXE program uses is specified by its program header—in particular, the values for the minimum and maximum number of paragraphs (16 bytes each) needed in memory following the code area, to handle variables and the stack at run time. By default, the linker sets the maximum value to 65,535 paragraphs, which is more memory than could be available under MS-DOS. When the program is loaded, therefore, MS-DOS automatically allocates whatever memory is available.

The maximum allocation may be set when a program is linked, using the /CP option. This is shown here for a program named *prog1.obj*. The number 1024 refers to the number of 16-byte paragraphs, expressed in decimal:

```
link16 /cp:1024 prog1;
```

The EXE header values can be modified after an EXE program is compiled, using the **exehdr** program supplied with the Microsoft assembler. For example, the command to set the maximum allocation to 400h paragraphs (16,384 bytes) for a program named *prog1.exe* is

```
exehdr prog1 /max 400
```

Exehdr can display important statistics about a program. Sample output is shown here describing the *prog1.exe* program after it was linked with the maximum allocation set at 1024 paragraphs:

PROG1	(Hex)	(Dec)
EXE size (bytes)	876	2166
Minimum load size (bytes)	786	1926
Overlay number	0	0
Initial CS:IP	0000:0010	16
Initial SS:SP	0068:0100	256
Minimum allocation (para)	11	17
Maximum allocation (para)	400	1024
Header size (para)	20	32
Relocation table offset	1E	30
Relocation entries	1	1

EXE Header

The header area of an EXE program is used by MS-DOS to correctly calculate the addresses of segments and other components. The header contains information such as the following:

- A relocation table, containing addresses to be calculated when the program is loaded.
- The file size of the EXE program, measured in 512-byte units.
- Minimum allocation: the minimum number of memory paragraphs to reserve following the program code area. Some of this storage could be used for a runtime heap that holds dynamic data.
- Maximum allocation: the maximum number of paragraphs needed above the program.
- Starting values to be given to the IP and SP registers.
- *Displacement* (measured in 16-byte paragraphs) of the stack and code segments from the beginning of the load module.
- A *checksum* of all words in the file, used in catching data errors when loading the program into memory.

16.3.4   Section Review

1. When a command is typed at the MS-DOS prompt, what happens if the command is not an internal MS-DOS command?
2. Does MS-DOS look for BAT files before EXE files in the current directory when executing a command?
3. What are transient programs?

4. What is the name of the 256-byte area at the beginning of a transient program?

5. Where does a transient program keep the segment address of the current environment string?

6. What is a COM program?

7. Which memory model(s) are used by COM programs?

8. Which linker command-line switch is required when creating a COM program?

9. What is the memory limitation of a COM program?

10. When running, how efficient is a COM program's use of memory?

11. How many program segments can a COM program contain?

12. What are the starting values of all segment registers in a COM program?

13. What is the purpose of the ORG directive?

14. When stored on disk, the two main parts of an EXE program are the *header* and the _____ module.

15. Where do DS and ES point when an EXE program is loaded?

16. What determines the amount of memory allocated to an EXE program?

17. What is the purpose of the **exehdr** program?

18. If you wanted to know the number of relocation entries in an EXE file, where would you look?

16.4   Interrupt Handling

In this section we discuss ways to customize the BIOS and MS-DOS by installing *interrupt handlers* (*interrupt service routines*). As we saw in earlier chapters, the BIOS and MS-DOS contain interrupt handlers that simplify input/output as well as basic system tasks. We saw many of these—the INT 10h routines for video manipulation, the INT 16h keyboard routines, the INT 21h MS-DOS services, and so on. But an equally important part of the operating system is its set of interrupt handlers that respond to hardware interrupts. MS-DOS allows you to replace any of these service routines with one of your own.

> *Limitations:* The interrupt handlers presented in this chapter work only when your computer is booted to MS-DOS mode. You can do this using Windows 95 and 98, but not Windows NT, 2000, and XP. The latter operating systems mask the system hardware from application programs to achieve greater system stability and security. If the OS were to allow two simultaneously running programs to modify internal settings on the same hardware device, the results would be unpredictable at best.

An interrupt handler might be written for a variety of reasons. You might want your program to activate when a *hot* key is pressed, even when the user is running another application. Borland's Side-Kick, for example, was one of the first programs that was able to pop up a notepad or calculator whenever a special combination of hot keys was pressed.

You can replace one of MS-DOS's default interrupt handlers in order to provide more complete services. For example, the *divide by zero* interrupt activates when the CPU tries to divide a number by zero, but there is no standard way for a program to recover.

You can replace the MS-DOS critical error handler or the Ctrl-Break handler with one of your own. MS-DOS's default critical error handler causes a program to abort and return to MS-DOS. Your own handler could recover from an error and let the user continue to run the current application program.

A user-written interrupt service routine can handle hardware interrupts more effectively than MS-DOS. For example, the PC's asynchronous communication handler (INT 14h) performs no input/output buffering. This means that an input character is lost if it is not copied from the port before another character arrives. A memory-resident program can wait for an incoming character to generate a hardware interrupt, input the character from the port, and store it in a circular buffer. This frees an application program from having to take valuable time away from other tasks to repeatedly check the serial port.

Interrupt Vector Table   The key to MS-DOS's flexibility lies in the interrupt vector table located in the first 1024 bytes of RAM (locations 0:0 through 0:03FF). Table 16-2 contains a short sample of vector table entries. Each entry in the table (called an interrupt vector) is a 32-bit segment-offset address that points to one of the existing service routines.

Table 16-2   Interrupt Vector Table Example.

Interrupt Number	Offset	Interrupt Vectors
00–03	0000	02C1:5186 0070:0C67 0DAD:2C1B 0070:0C67
04–07	0010	0070:0C67 F000:FF54 F000:837B F000:837B
08–0B	0020	0D70:022C 0DAD:2BAD 0070:0325 0070:039F
0C–0F	0030	0070:0419 0070:0493 0070:050D 0070:0C67
10–13	0040	C000:0CD7 F000:F84D F000:F841 0070:237D

On any given computer, the vector values will vary because of different versions of the BIOS and MS-DOS. Each interrupt vector corresponds to an interrupt number. In the table, the address of the INT 0 handler (divide by zero) is 02C1:5186h. The offset of any interrupt vector may be found by multiplying its interrupt number by 4. Thus, the offset of the vector for INT 9h is 9 * 4, or 0024 hexadecimal.

Executing Interrupt Handlers   An interrupt handler may be executed in one of two ways: (1) An application program containing an INT instruction could cause a call to the routine, which is called a *software interrupt*; (2) a *hardware interrupt* occurs when a hardware device (asynchronous port, keyboard, timer, and so on) sends a signal to the Programmable Interrupt Controller chip.

16.4.1   Hardware Interrupts

A hardware interrupt is generated by the Intel 8259 *Programmable Interrupt Controller* (PIC), which signals the CPU to suspend execution of the current program and execute an interrupt service routine. For example, a keyboard character waiting at the input port would be lost if not saved by the CPU, or characters received from the serial port would be lost if not for an interrupt-driven routine that stores them in a buffer.

Occasionally, programs must disable hardware interrupts when performing sensitive operations on segment registers and the stack. The CLI (*clear interrupt flag*) instruction disables interrupts, and the STI (*set interrupt flag*) instruction enables interrupts.

IRQ Levels   Interrupts can be triggered by a number of different devices on a PC, including those listed in Table 16-3. Each device has a priority, based on its *interrupt request level* (IRQ). Level 0 has the highest priority, and level 15 has the lowest. A lower-level interrupt cannot interrupt a higher-level one still in progress. For instance, if communications port 1 (COM1) tried to interrupt the keyboard interrupt handler, it would have to wait until the latter was finished. Also, two or more simultaneous interrupt requests are processed according to their priority levels. The scheduling of interrupts is handled by the 8259 PIC.

Let's use the keyboard as an example: When a key is pressed, the 8259 PIC sends an INTR signal to the CPU, passing it the interrupt number; if external interrupts are not currently disabled, the CPU does the following, in sequence:

1. Pushes the Flags register on the stack.
2. Clears the Interrupt flag, preventing any other hardware interrupts.
3. Pushes the current CS and IP on the stack.
4. Locates the interrupt vector table entry for INT 9 and places this address in CS and IP.

TABLE 16-3   IRQ Assignments (ISA Bus).

IRQ	Interrupt Number	Description
0	8	System timer (18.2 times/second)
1	9	Keyboard
2	0Ah	Programmable Interrupt Controller
3	0Bh	COM2 (serial port 2)
4	0Ch	COM1 (serial port 1)
5	0Dh	LPT2 (parallel port 2)
6	0Eh	Floppy disk controller
7	0Fh	LPT1 (parallel port 1)
8	70h	CMOS real-time clock
9	71h	(Redirected to INT 0Ah)
10	72h	(Available) sound card
11	73h	(Available) SCSI card
12	74h	PS/2 mouse
13	75h	Math coprocessor
14	76h	Hard disk controller
15	77h	(Available)

Next, the BIOS routine for INT 9 executes, and it does the following in sequence:

1. Reenables hardware interrupts so the system timer is not affected.
2. Inputs a scan code from the keyboard port, attempts to convert it to an ASCII character, or assigns an ASCII code equal to zero. It then stores the scan code and ASCII code in the keyboard buffer, a 32-byte circular buffer in the BIOS data area.
3. Executes an IRET (interrupt return) instruction, which pops IP, CS, and the Flags register off the stack. Control returns to the program that was executing when the interrupt occurred.

16.4.2   Interrupt Control Instructions

The CPU has a flag called the *Interrupt flag* (IF) that controls the way the CPU responds to external (hardware) interrupts. If the Interrupt flag is set (IF = 1), we say that interrupts are *enabled*; if the flag is clear (IF = 0), then interrupts are *disabled*.

STI Instruction   The STI instruction enables external interrupts. For example, the system responds to keyboard input by suspending a program in process and doing the following: It calls INT 9, which stores the keystroke in a buffer and then returns to the current program. Normally, the Interrupt flag is enabled. Otherwise, the system timer would not calculate the time and date properly, and input keystrokes would be lost.

CLI Instruction   The CLI instruction disables external interrupts. It should be used sparingly—only when a critical operation is about to be performed, one that cannot be interrupted. Suppose, for example, your code was interrupted while in the process of changing the values of SS and SP. Your SS register might point to a new stack segment, whereas your stack pointer has yet to be updated:

```
mov    ax,mystack                      ; reset SS
mov    ss,ax
```

```
; INTERRUPTED HERE!!!
mov    sp,100h                            ; reset SP
```

To be on the safe side, disable interrupts by clearing the Interrupt flag (CLI), and enable interrupts using STI:

```
cli                                       ; disable interrupts
mov    ax,mystack                         ; reset SS
mov    ss,ax
mov    sp,100h                            ; reset SP
sti                                       ; reenable interrupts
```

Interrupts should not be disabled for more than a few milliseconds at a time, or you may lose keystrokes and slow down the system timer. When the CPU responds to an interrupt handler, other interrupts are immediately disabled. MS-DOS and BIOS interrupt service routines reenable interrupts as soon as they begin to execute.

16.4.3   Writing a Custom Interrupt Handler

One might ask why the interrupt vector table exists at all. We could, of course, call specific procedures in ROM to process interrupts. The designers of the IBM-PC wanted to be able to make modifications and corrections to the BIOS routines without having to replace the ROM chips. By having an interrupt vector table, it was possible to replace addresses in the interrupt vector table so they would point to procedures in RAM.

Each address in the interrupt vector table points to a procedure called an *interrupt handler* or *interrupt service routine* (ISR). Application programs can replace an address in the table with a new one that points to a new interrupt handler. For example, one could write a custom keyboard interrupt handler. There would have to be a compelling reason to do so because of the effort involved. A more likely alternative would be for an interrupt handler to directly call the default INT 9 keyboard to read a keystroke from the keyboard port. Once the key was placed in the keyboard typeahead buffer, one could manipulate its contents.

INT 21h Functions 25h and 35h make it possible to install interrupt handlers. Function 35h (get interrupt vector) returns the segment-offset address of an interrupt vector. Call the function with the desired interrupt number in AL. The 32-bit vector is returned by MS-DOS in ES:BX. The following statements would retrieve the INT 9 vector, for example,

```
.data
int9Save LABEL WORD
DWORD ?                                   ; store old INT 9 address here

.code
mov    ah,35h                             ; get interrupt vector
mov    al,9                               ; for INT 9
int    21h                                ; call MS-DOS
mov    int9Save,BX                        ; store the offset
mov    int9Save+2,ES                      ; store the segment
```

INT 21h Function 25h (set interrupt vector) lets you replace an existing interrupt handler with a new handler. Call it with the interrupt number in AL and the segment-offset address of your own interrupt handler in DS:DX. For example,

```
mov    ax,SEG kybd_rtn                    ; keyboard handler
mov    ds,ax                              ; segment
mov    dx,OFFSET kybd_rtn                 ; offset
mov    ah,25h                             ; set Interrupt vector
mov    al,9h                              ; for INT 9h
```

```
        int   21h
        .
        .
        kybd_rtn PROC          ; (new INT 9 interrupt handler begins here)
```

Ctrl-Break Handler Example

If Ctrl-Break is pressed by the user when an MS-DOS program is waiting for input, control passes to the default INT 23h interrupt handler procedure. The default Ctrl-Break handler terminates the currently running program. This can leave the current program in an unstable state because files might be left open, memory not released, and so on. It is possible, however, to substitute your own code into the INT 23h handler and prevent the program from halting. The following program installs a simple Ctrl-Break handler:

```
TITLE Control-Break Handler              (Ctrlbrk.asm)

; This program installs its own Ctrl-Break handler and
; prevents the user from using Ctrl-Break (or Ctrl-C)
; to halt the program. The program inputs and echoes
; keystrokes until the Esc key is pressed.

INCLUDE Irvine16.inc

.data
breakMsg BYTE "BREAK",0
msg   BYTE "Ctrl-Break demonstration."
      BYTE  0dh,0ah
      BYTE "This program disables Ctrl-Break (Ctrl-C). Press any"
      BYTE  0dh,0ah
      BYTE "keys to continue, or press ESC to end the program."
      BYTE  0dh,0ah,0

.code
main PROC
      mov   ax,@data
      mov   ds,ax

      mov   dx,OFFSET msg            ; display greeting message
      call  Writestring

install_handler:
      push  ds                       ; save DS
      mov   ax,@code                 ; initialize DS to code segment
      mov   ds,ax
      mov   ah,25h                   ; set interrupt vector
      mov   al,23h                   ; for interrupt 23h
      mov   dx,OFFSET break_handler
      int   21h
      pop   ds                       ; restore DS

L1:   mov   ah,1                     ; wait for a key, echo it
      int   21h
      cmp   al,1Bh                   ; ESC pressed?
      jnz   L1                       ; no: continue

      exit
main ENDP

; The following procedure executes when Ctrl-Break is
; pressed. All registers must be preserved.

break_handler PROC
```

```
        push    ax
        push    dx
        mov     dx,OFFSET breakMsg
        call    WriteString
        pop     dx
        pop     ax
        iret
break_handler ENDP
END main
```

The **main** procedure initializes the interrupt vector for INT 23h. The required input parameters for INT 21h function 25h are

- AH = 25h
- AL = interrupt vector to be handled (23h)
- DS:DX = segment/offset address of the new Ctrl-Break handler

The program's main loop simply inputs and echoes keystrokes until the Esc key is pressed.

> On some systems, you may have to press Ctrl-C rather than Ctrl-Break to activate the Ctrl-Break handler message.

The **break_handler** procedure executes when Ctrl-Break is pressed; it displays a message by calling WriteString and immediately returns to the calling program. When IRET (return from interrupt) executes at the end of break_handler, control returns to the main program. Whichever MS-DOS function was in progress when Ctrl-Break was pressed is restarted. In general, you can call any MS-DOS interrupts from inside a Ctrl-Break handler. You must preserve all registers in an interrupt handler.

You do not have to restore the INT 23h vector because MS-DOS automatically does it when a program ends. The original vector is stored by MS-DOS at offset 000Eh in the program segment prefix.

16.4.4   Terminate and Stay Resident Programs

A *terminate and stay resident* (TSR) program is installed in memory and stays there until it is either removed by special removal utility software or the computer is rebooted. A TSR remains dormant until activated by some event such as pressing a key.

In the early days of TSRs, compatibility problems would arise when two or more programs replaced the same interrupt vector. Older programs would make the vector point to their own program and provide no forward chain to other programs using the same vector. Later, to remedy this problem, TSR authors would save the existing vector for the interrupt they were replacing, and forward-chain to the original interrupt handler after their own procedure was finished dealing with the interrupt. This, of course, was an improvement over the old method, but it meant that the last TSR to be installed automatically had top priority in handling the interrupt. It meant that users sometimes had to be careful to load TSR programs in a particular order. When MS-DOS applications were widespread, commercial programming tools existed to manage multiple memory-resident programs.

Keyboard Example

Suppose we write an interrupt service routine that can inspect each character typed at the keyboard and store it at location 10B2:0020. To install the ISR, we fetch the current INT 9 vector from the interrupt vector table, save it, and replace the table entry with the address of our ISR.

When a keyboard key is pressed, a single byte is transferred by the keyboard controller to the computer's keyboard port, and a hardware interrupt is triggered. The 8259 PIC passes the interrupt number to the CPU, and the latter jumps to the INT 9 address in the interrupt vector table, the address of our ISR. Our procedure gets an opportunity to inspect the keyboard byte. When our keyboard handler exits, it executes a jump to the original BIOS keyboard handler procedure.

This chaining process is shown in Figure 16–1. The addresses are hypothetical. When the BIOS INT 9h routine finishes, the IRET instruction pops the Flags register from the stack and returns control to the program that was executing when the character was pressed.

FIGURE 16–1   Vectoring an Interrupt.

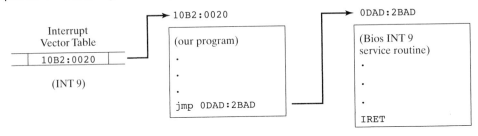

16.4.5   Application: The No_Reset Program

A simple type of memory-resident program is one that prevents the system from being rebooted by the Ctrl-Alt-Delete keys. Once our program is installed in memory, the system may only be rebooted by pressing a special combination of keys: Ctrl-Alt-RightShift-Del. (The only other way to deactivate the program is to turn off and restart the computer.) This program only works if you boot the computer in MS-DOS. Microsoft Windows NT, 2000, and XP prevent a TSR program from intercepting keyboard keys.

The MS-DOS Keyboard Status Byte   One bit of information we need before we start is the location of the keyboard status byte kept by MS-DOS in low memory, shown in Figure 16–2. Our program will inspect this flag to see if the Ctrl, Alt, Del, and RightShift keys are held down. The keyboard status flag is stored in RAM at location 0040:0017h. The label on the right side of the diagram shows what each bit means when it equals 1.

FIGURE 16–2   Keyboard Status Flag Byte.

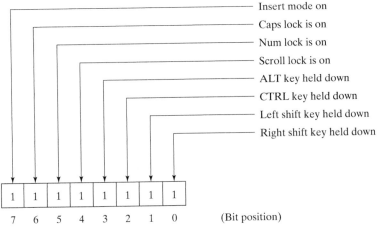

An additional keyboard status byte, located at 0040:0018k, duplicates the preceding flags, except that bit 3 shows when Ctrl-NumLock is currently active.

Installing the Program   The memory-resident code must be installed in memory before it will work. From that point on, all keyboard input is filtered through the program. If the routine has any bugs, the keyboard will probably lock up and require us to cold-start the machine. Keyboard interrupt handlers are particularly hard to debug because we use the keyboard constantly when debugging programs. Professionals who regularly write TSR programs usually invest in hardware-assisted debuggers that maintain a trace buffer in protected memory. Often the most elusive bugs appear only when a program is running in real time, not when you are single-stepping through it. *Note: You must boot the computer in MS-DOS mode before installing this program.*

Program Listing   In the following program listing, the installation code is located at the end because it will not remain resident in memory. The resident portion, beginning with the label **int9_handler**, is left in memory and pointed to by the INT 9h vector:

```
TITLE Reset-Disabling program              (No_Reset.asm)

; This program disables the usual DOS reset command
; (Ctrl-Alt-Del), by intercepting the INT 9 keyboard
; hardware interrupt. It checks the shift status bits
; in the MS-DOS keyboard flag and changes any Ctrl-Alt-Del
; to Alt-Del. The computer can only be rebooted by
; typing Ctrl+Alt+Right shift+Del. Assemble, link,
; and convert to a COM program by including the /T
; command on the Microsoft LINK command line.
; Boot into pure MS-DOS mode before running this program.

.model tiny
.386
.code
        rt_shift    EQU 01h          ; Right shift key: bit 0
        ctrl_key    EQU 04h          ; CTRL key: bit 2
        alt_key     EQU 08h          ; ALT key: bit 3
        del_key     EQU 53h          ; scan code for DEL key
        kybd_port   EQU 60h          ; keyboard input port

        ORG   100h                   ; this is a COM program
start:
        jmp   setup                  ; jump to TSR installation

;    Memory-resident code begins here
int9_handler PROC FAR
        sti                          ; enable hardware interrupts
        pushf                        ; save regs & flags
        push  es
        push  ax
        push  di

;    Point ES:DI to the DOS keyboard flag byte:
L1:   mov   ax,40h                   ; DOS data segment is at 40h
        mov   es,ax
        mov   di,17h                 ; location of keyboard flag
        mov   ah,es:[di]             ; copy keyboard flag into AH

;    Test for the CTRL and ALT keys:
L2:   test  ah,ctrl_key             ; CTRL key held down?
        jz    L5                      ; no: exit
        test  ah,alt_key             ; ALT key held down?
        jz    L5                      ; no: exit

;    Test for the DEL and Right-shift keys:
L3:   in    al,kybd_port            ; read keyboard port
        cmp   al,del_key             ; DEL key pressed?
```

```
        jne     L5                      ; no: exit
        test    ah,rt_shift             ; right shift key pressed?
        jnz     L5                      ; yes: allow system reset
L4:     and     ah,NOT ctrl_key         ; no: turn off bit for CTRL
        mov     es:[di],ah              ; store keyboard_flag
L5:     pop     di                      ; restore regs & flags
        pop     ax
        pop     es
        popf
        jmp     cs:[old_interrupt9]     ; jump to INT 9 routine
old_interrupt9 DWORD ?

int9_handler ENDP
end_ISR label BYTE

; -------------- (end of TSR program) -----------------
;   Save a copy of the original INT 9 vector, and set up
;   the address of our program as the new vector. Terminate
;   this program and leave the int9_handler procedure in memory.

setup:
        mov     ax,3509h                ; get INT 9 vector
        int     21h
        mov     word ptr old_interrupt9,bx   ; save INT 9 vector
        mov     word ptr old_interrupt9+2,es

        mov     ax,2509h                ; set INT 9 vector
        mov     dx,offset int9_handler
        int     21h

        mov     ax,3100h                ; terminate and stay resident
        mov     dx,OFFSET end_ISR       ; point to end of resident code
        shr     dx,4                    ; divide by 16
        inc     dx                      ; round upward to next paragraph
        int     21h                     ; execute MS-DOS function
        END start
```

First let's look at the instructions that install the program. At the label called **setup**, we call INT 21h Function 35h to get the current INT 9h vector, which is then stored in **old_interrupt9**. This is done so the program will be able to forward-chain to the existing keyboard handler procedure. In the same part of the program, INT 21h Function 25h sets interrupt vector 9h to the address of the resident portion of this program. At the end of the program, the call to INT 21h Function 31h exits to MS-DOS, leaving the resident program in memory. The function automatically saves everything from the beginning of the PSP to the offset placed in DX.

The Resident Program The memory-resident interrupt handler begins at the label named **int9_handler**. It is executed every time a keyboard key is pressed. We reenable interrupts as soon as the handler gets control because the 8259 PIC has automatically disabled interrupts:

```
int9_handler PROC far
    sti                     ; enable hardware interrupts
    pushf                   ; save registers and status flags
    (etc...)
```

Bear in mind that a keyboard interrupt often occurs while another program is executing. If we modified the registers or status flags here, we would cause unpredictable results in an application program.

The following statements locate the keyboard flag byte stored at address 0040:0017 and copy it into AH. The byte must be tested to see which keys are currently being held down:

```
L1:   mov    ax,40h              ; MS-DOS data segment is at 40h
      mov    es,ax
      mov    di,17h              ; location of keyboard flag
      mov    ah,es:[di]          ; copy keyboard flag into AH
```

The following statements check for both the Ctrl and Alt keys. If both are not currently held down, we exit:

```
L2:   test   ah,ctrl_key         ; CTRL key held down?
      jz     L5                  ; no: exit
      test   ah,alt_key          ; ALT key held down?
      jz     L5                  ; no: exit
```

If the Ctrl and Alt keys are both held down, someone may be trying to boot the computer. To find out which character was pressed, we input the character from the keyboard port and compare it to the Del key:

```
L3:   in     al,kybd_port        ; read keyboard port
      cmp    al,del_key          ; Del key pressed?
      jne    L5                  ; no: exit
      test   ah,rt_shift         ; Right-Shift key pressed?
      jnz    L5                  ; yes: allow system reset
```

If the user has not pressed the Del key, we simply exit and let INT 9h process the keystroke. If the Del key is held down, we know that Ctrl-Alt-Del was pressed; we only allow the system to be reset if the user is also holding down the Right Shift key. Otherwise, the Ctrl key bit in the keyboard flag byte is cleared, effectively disabling the user's attempt to reboot the computer:

```
L4:   and    ah,NOT ctrl_key     ; no: turn off bit for CTRL
      mov    es:[di],ah          ; store keyboard_flag
```

Finally, we execute a far jump to the existing BIOS INT 9h routine, stored in the variable **old_interrupt9**. This allows all normal keystrokes to be processed, which is vital to the computer's basic operation:

```
      jmp cs:[old_interrupt9]            ; jump to INT 9 routine
```

16.4.6 Section Review

1. What default action is carried out by the *critical error handler*?
2. What is contained in each entry of the interrupt vector table?
3. At which address is the interrupt vector for INT 10h stored?
4. Which controller chip generates hardware interrupts?
5. Which instruction disables hardware interrupts?
6. Which instruction enables hardware interrupts?
7. Which IRQ level has the highest priority, 0 or 15?
8. Based on what you know about IRQ levels, if a program is in the process of creating a disk file and you press a key on the keyboard, when do you think the key will be placed in the keyboard buffer—before or after the file has been created?
9. When a key is pressed on the keyboard, which hardware interrupt is executed?
10. When an interrupt handler finishes, how does the CPU resume execution wherever it was before the interrupt was triggered?

11. Which MS-DOS functions get and set interrupt vectors?

12. Explain the difference between an interrupt handler and a memory-resident program.

13. Describe a TSR program.

14. How can a TSR program be removed from memory?

15. If a memory resident program replaces one of the interrupt vectors, how can it still take advantage of some functions in the interrupt's existing handler?

16. Which MS-DOS function terminates a program and leaves part of the program resident in memory?

17. In the No_reset program, what key combination will actually boot the computer?

16.5   Hardware Control Using I/O Ports

IA-32 systems offer two types of hardware input-output: *memory-mapped* and *port-based*. When *memory-mapped I/O* is used, a program can write data to a particular memory address, and the data is transferred to the output device. Similarly, data can be read from an input device by copying data from a predefined memory address. The text video display is an example of a memory-mapped device. When you place characters in the video segment, they immediately appear on the display.

Port-based I/O requires the IN and OUT instructions to read and write data to specific numbered locations called *ports*. Ports are connections, or gateways, between the CPU and other devices, such as the keyboard, speaker, modem, and sound card.

16.5.1   Input-Output Ports

Each input-output port has a specific number between 0 and FFFFh. A port is used when controlling the speaker, for example, by rapidly toggling the speaker cone in and out. You can communicate directly with the asynchronous adapter through a serial port by setting the port parameters (baud rate, parity, and so on) and by sending data through the port.

The keyboard port is a good example of an input-output port. When a key is pressed, the keyboard controller chip sends an 8-bit scan code to port 60h. The keystroke triggers a hardware interrupt, which prompts the CPU to call INT 9 in the ROM BIOS. INT 9 inputs the scan code from the port, looks up the key's ASCII code, and stores both values in the keyboard input buffer. In fact, it would be possible to bypass the operating system completely and read characters directly from port 60h.

In addition to ports that transfer data, most hardware devices have ports that let you monitor the device status and control the device behavior.

IN and OUT Instructions   The IN instruction inputs a byte, word, or doubleword from a port. Conversely, the OUT instruction outputs a value to a port. The syntax for both instructions is

```
IN    accumulator,port
OUT   port,accumulator
```

Port may be a constant in the range 0 to FFh, or it may be a value in DX between 0 and FFFFh. *Accumulator* must be AL for 8-bit transfers, AX for 16-bit transfers, and EAX for 32-bit transfers. Examples are as follows:

```
in    al,3Ch          ; input byte from port 3Ch
out   3Ch,al          ; output byte to port 3Ch
mov   dx, portNumber  ; DX can contain a port number
in    ax,dx           ; input word from port named in DX
out   dx,ax           ; output word to the same port
in    eax,dx          ; input doubleword from port
out   dx,eax          ; output doubleword to same port
```

16.5.2   PC Sound Program

We can write a program that uses the IN and OUT instructions to generate sound through the PC's built-in speaker. The speaker control port (number 61h) turns the speaker on and off by manipulating the Intel 8255 *Programmable Peripheral Interface* chip. To turn the speaker on, input the current value in port 61h, set the lowest 2 bits, and output the byte back through the port. To turn off the speaker, clear bits 0 and 1 and output the status again.

> Our sound program will not produce sound on a laptop computer if its speaker is directly connected to the sound card rather than the speaker port (61h).

The Intel 8253 Timer chip controls the frequency (pitch) of the sound being generated. To use it, we send a value between 0 and 255 to port 42h. The Speaker Demo program shows how to generate sound by playing a series of ascending notes:

```
TITLE Speaker Demo Program             (Spkr.asm)

; This program plays a series of ascending notes on
; an IBM-PC or compatible computer.

INCLUDE Irvine16.inc

speaker  EQU  61h                  ; address of speaker port
timer    EQU  42h                  ; address of timer port
delay1   EQU  500
delay2   EQU  0D000h               ; delay between notes
.code
main PROC
        in    al,speaker           ; get speaker status
        push  ax                   ; save status
        or    al,00000011b         ; set lowest 2 bits
        out   speaker,al           ; turn speaker on
        mov   al,60                ; starting pitch
L2:     out   timer,al             ; timer port: pulses speaker

        ; Create a delay loop between pitches.

        mov   cx,delay1
L3:     push  cx                   ; outer loop
        mov   cx,delay2
L3a:                               ; inner loop
        loop  L3a
        pop   cx
        loop  L3
        sub   al,1                 ; raise pitch
        jnz   L2                   ; play another note

        pop   ax                   ; get original status
        and   al,11111100b         ; clear lowest 2 bits
        out   speaker,al           ; turn speaker off
        exit
main ENDP
END main
```

First, the program turns the speaker on using port 61h by setting the lowest 2 bits in the speaker status byte:

```
or   al,00000011b                  ; set lowest 2 bits
out  speaker,al                    ; turn speaker on
```

Then it sets the pitch by sending 60 to the timer chip:

```
        mov   al,60                ; starting pitch
L2:     out   timer,al             ; timer port: pulses speaker
```

A delay loop makes the program pause before changing the pitch again. The amount of delay will vary between computers because of differing processor speeds. You may have to adjust the values of **delay1** and **delay2**:

```
        mov    cx,delay1
L3:     push   cx                      ; outer loop
        mov    cx,delay2
L3a:                                    ; inner loop
        loop   L3a
        pop    cx
        loop   L3
```

After the delay, the program subtracts 1 from the period (1/frequency), which raises the pitch. The new frequency is output to the timer when the loop repeats. This process continues until the frequency counter in AL equals 0. Finally, the program pops the original status byte from the speaker port and turns the speaker off by clearing the lowest 2 bits:

```
pop   ax                     ; get original status
and   al,11111100b           ; clear lowest 2 bits
out   speaker,al             ; turn speaker off
```

16.6 Chapter Summary

There are a few occasions when programmers need to create explicit segment definitions, particularly when adapting to existing code libraries that use their own segment names. The SEGMENT and ENDS directives define the beginning and end of a segment, respectively. When the segment being defined is combined with another segment, its *align type* tells the linker how many bytes to skip. The *combine type* tells the linker how to combine segments having the same name. A segment's class type provides yet another way of combining segments. Multiple segments may be combined by giving them the same name and specifying a PUBLIC combine type.

The ASSUME directive makes it possible for the assembler to calculate the offsets of labels and variables at assembly time. A segment override prefix instructs the processor to use a different segment register from the default segment for the current instruction.

The MS-DOS command processor interprets each command typed at a command prompt. Programs with extensions of COM and EXE are called *transient programs*. They are loaded into memory and executed, and then the memory they occupy is released. MS-DOS creates a special 256-byte block at the beginning of a transient program named the *Program Segment Prefix*.

There are two types of transient programs, identified by the extension used: COM and EXE. A COM program is an unmodified binary image of a machine-language program. An EXE program is stored on disk with an EXE header followed by a load module containing the program itself. The header area of an EXE program is used by MS-DOS to correctly calculate the addresses of segments and other components.

Interrupt handlers (interrupt service routines) simplify input/output as well as basic system tasks. You can also replace the default interrupt handlers with your own code to provide more complete or customized services. The interrupt vector table is located in the first 1024 bytes of RAM (locations 0:0 through 0:03FF). Each entry in the table is a 32-bit segment-offset address that points to an interrupt service routine.

A hardware interrupt is generated by the 8259 Programmable Interrupt Controller (PIC), which signals the CPU to suspend execution of the current program and execute an interrupt service routine. Hardware interrupts allow important events in the background to be noticed by the CPU before essential data are lost. Interrupts can be triggered by a number of different devices, each having a priority based on its *interrupt request level* (IRQ).

The Interrupt flag controls the way the CPU responds to external (hardware) interrupts. If the Interrupt flag is set, interrupts are enabled; if the flag is clear, interrupts are disabled. The STI (set interrupt) instruction enables interrupts; the CLI (clear interrupt) instruction disables interrupts.

A *terminate and stay resident* (TSR) program leaves part of itself in memory. The most common use for TSR programs is for installed interrupt handlers that remain in memory until the computer is rebooted or the TSR is removed by a special uninstaller.

The No_reset program presented in this chapter is a TSR program that prevents the system from being rebooted by the usual Ctrl-Alt-Delete keys.

IA-32 systems offer two types of hardware input-output: *memory-mapped* and *port-based*. When *memory-mapped I/O* is used, a program can write data to a particular memory address, and the data is transferred to the output device. *Port-based I/O* requires the IN and OUT instructions to read and write data to specific numbered locations called *ports*.

The speaker control port (number 61h) turns the speaker on and off by manipulating the Intel 8255 *Programmable Peripheral Interface* chip. The Speaker Demo program shows how to generate sound by playing a series of ascending notes.

17

FLOATING-POINT PROCESSING and INSTRUCTION ENCODING

17.1 Floating-Point Binary Representation

A floating-point decimal number contains three components: a sign, a significand, and an exponent. In the number -1.23154×10^5 for example, the sign is negative, the significand is 1.23154, and the exponent is 5.

Finding the Intel IA-32 Documentation. To get the most out of this chapter, get free electronic copies of the Intel *IA-32 Intel Architecture Software Developer's Manual*, Vols. 1 and 2. Point your Web browser to www.intel.com, and search for *IA-32 manuals*.

17.1.1   IEEE Binary Floating-Point Representation

Intel processors use three floating-point binary storage formats specified in the *Standard 754-1985 for Binary Floating-Point Arithmetic* produced by the IEEE organization. Table 17-1 describes their characteristics.[1]

Table 17-1   IEEE Floating-Point Binary Formats.

Single Precision	32 bits: 1 bit for the sign, 8 bits for the exponent, and 23 bits for the fractional part of the significand. Approximate normalized range: 2^{-126} to 2^{127}. Also called a *short real*.
Double Precision	64 bits: 1 bit for the sign, 11 bits for the exponent, and 52 bits for the fractional part of the significand. Approximate normalized range: 2^{-1022} to 2^{1023}. Also called a *long real*.
Double Extended Precision	80 bits: 1 bit for the sign, 16 bits for the exponent, and 63 bits for the fractional part of the significand. Approximate normalized range: 2^{-16382} to 2^{16383}. Also called an *extended real*.

Because the three formats are so similar, we will focus on the single-precision format (Figure 17–1). The 32 bits are arranged with the most significant bit (MSB) on the left. The segment marked *fraction* indicates the fractional part of the significand. As you might expect, the individual bytes are stored in memory in little endian order (LSB at the starting address).

Figure 17–1   Single-Precision Format.

The Sign

If the sign bit is 1, the number is negative; if the bit is 0, the number is positive. Zero is considered positive.

The Significand

In the floating-point number represented by the expression $m * b^e$, m is called the significand, or mantissa; b is the base; and e is the exponent. The *significand* (or mantissa) of a floating-point number consists of the decimal digits to the left and right of the decimal point. In Chapter 1 we introduced the concept of weighted positional notation when explaining the binary, decimal, and hexadecimal numbering systems. The same concept can be extended to include the fractional part of a floating-point number. For example, the decimal value 123.154 is represented by the following sum:

$$123.154 = (1 \times 10^2) + (2 \times 10^1) + (3 \times 10^0) + (1 \times 10^{-1}) + (5 \times 10^{-2}) + (4 \times 10^{-3})$$

All digits to the left of the decimal point have positive exponents, and all digits to the right side have negative exponents.

Binary floating-point numbers also use weighted positional notation. The floating-point binary value 11.1011 is expressed as

$$11.1011 = (1 \times 2^1) + (1 \times 2^0) + (1 \times 2^{-1}) + (0 \times 2^{-2}) + (1 \times 2^{-3}) + (1 \times 2^{-4})$$

Another way to express the values to the right of the binary point is to list them as a sum of fractions whose denominators are powers of 2. In our sample, the sum is 11/16 (or 0.6875):

$$.1011 = 1/2 + 0/4 + 1/8 + 1/16 = 11/16$$

Generating the decimal fraction is fairly intuitive. The decimal numerator (11) represents the binary bit pattern 1011. If e is the number of significant bits to the right of the binary point, the decimal denominator is 2^e. In our example, $e = 4$, so $2^e = 16$. Table 17-2 shows additional examples of translating binary floating-point notation to base-10 fractions. The last entry in the table contains the smallest fraction that can be stored in a 23-bit normalized significand. For quick reference, Table 17-3 lists examples of binary floating-point numbers alongside their equivalent decimal fractions and decimal values.

Table 17-2   Examples: Translating Binary Floating-Point to Fractions.

Binary Floating-Point	Base 10 Fraction
11.11	3 3/4
101.0011	5 3/16
1101.100101	13 37/64
0.00101	5/32
1.011	1 3/8
0.00000000000000000000001	1/8388608

Table 17-3   Binary and Decimal Fractions.

Binary	Decimal Fraction	Decimal Value
.1	1/2	.5
.01	1/4	.25
.001	1/8	.125
.0001	1/16	.0625
.00001	1/32	.03125

The Significand's Precision

The entire continuum of real numbers cannot be represented in any floating-point format having a finite number of bits. Suppose, for example, a simplified floating-point format had 5-bit significands. There would be no way to represent values falling between 1.1111 and 10.0000 binary. The binary value 1.11111, for example, requires a more precise significand. Extending this idea to the IEEE double-precision format, we see that its 53-bit significand cannot represent a binary value requiring 54 or more bits.

17.1.2   The Exponent

Single-precision exponents are stored as 8-bit unsigned integers with a bias of 127. The number's actual exponent must be added to 127. Consider the binary value 1.101×2^5: After the actual exponent (5) is added to 127, the biased exponent (132) is stored in the number's representation. Table 17-4 shows examples of exponents in signed decimal, then biased decimal, and finally unsigned binary. The biased exponent is always positive, between 1 and 254. As stated earlier, the actual exponent range is from −126 to +127. The range was chosen so the smallest possible exponent's reciprocal cannot cause an overflow.

Table 17-4   Sample Exponents Represented in Binary.

Exponent (E)	Biased (E + 127)	Binary
+5	132	10000100
0	127	01111111
−10	117	01110101
+127	254	11111110
−126	1	00000001
−1	126	01111110

17.1.3   Normalized Binary Floating-Point Numbers

Most floating-point binary numbers are stored in *normalized* form so as to maximize the precision of the significand. Given any floating-point binary number, you can normalize it by shifting the binary point until a single "1" appears to the left of the binary point. The exponent expresses the number of positions the binary point is moved left (positive exponent) or right (negative exponent). Here are examples:

Unnormalized	Normalized
1110.1	1.1101×2^3
.000101	1.01×2^{-4}
1010001.	1.010001×2^6

Unnormalized Values   To reverse the normalizing operation might be said to *unnormalize* a binary floating-point number. Shift the binary point until the exponent is zero. If the exponent is positive n, shift the binary point n positions to the right; if the exponent is negative n, shift the binary point n positions to the left, filling leading zeros if necessary.

17.1.4   Creating the IEEE Representation

Real Number Encodings

Once the sign bit, exponent, and significand fields are normalized and encoded, it's easy to generate a complete binary IEEE short real. Using Figure 17–1 as a reference, we can place the sign bit first, the exponent bits next, and the fractional part of the significand last. For example, binary 1.101×2^0 is represented as follows:

- Sign bit: 0
- Exponent: 01111111
- Fraction: 10100000000000000000000

The biased exponent (01111111) is the binary representation of decimal 127. All normalized significands have a 1 to the left of the binary point, so there is no need to explicitly encode the bit. Additional examples are shown in Table 17-5.

The IEEE specification includes several real-number and non-number encodings.

- Positive and negative zero
- Denormalized finite numbers
- Normalized finite numbers
- Positive and negative infinity
- Non-numeric values (NaN, known as *Not a Number*)
- Indefinite numbers

Table 17-5　Examples of Single-Precision Bit Encodings.

Binary Value	Biased Exponent	Sign, Exponent, Fraction		
-1.11	127	1	01111111	11000000000000000000000
+1101.101	130	0	10000010	10110100000000000000000
-.00101	124	1	01111100	01000000000000000000000
+100111.0	132	0	10000100	00111000000000000000000
+.0000001101011	120	0	01111000	10101100000000000000000

Indefinite numbers are used by the Intel floating-point unit as responses to some invalid floating-point operations.

Normalized and Denormalized　*Normalized finite numbers* are all the nonzero finite values that can be encoded in a normalized real number between zero and infinity. Although it would seem that all finite non zero floating-point numbers should be normalized, it is not possible when their values are close to zero. This happens when the FPU cannot shift the binary point to a normalized position, given the limitation posed by the range of the exponent. Suppose the FPU computes a result of $1.0101111 \times 2^{-129}$, which has an exponent that is too small to be stored in a single-precision number. An underflow exception condition is generated, and the number is gradually denormalized by shifting the binary point left 1 bit at a time until the exponent reaches a valid range:

```
1.0101111000000000001111 x 2^-129
0.1010111100000000000111 x 2^-128
0.0101011110000000000011 x 2^-127
0.0010101111000000000001 x 2^-126
```

In this example, some loss of precision occurred in the significand as a result of the shifting of the binary point.

Positive and Negative Infinity　Positive infinity $(+\infty)$ represents the maximum positive real number, and negative infinity $(-\infty)$ represents the maximum negative real number. You can compare infinities to other values: $-\infty$ is less than $+\infty$, $-\infty$ is less than any finite number, and $+\infty$ is greater than any finite number. Either infinity may represent a floating-point overflow condition. The result of a computation cannot be normalized because its exponent would be too large to be represented by the available number of exponent bits.

NaNs　*NaNs* are bit patterns that do not represent any valid real number. The IA-32 architecture includes two types of NaNs: A *quiet NaN* can propagate through most arithmetic operations without causing an exception. A *signalling NaN* can be used to generate a floating-point invalid operation exception. A compiler might fill an uninitialized array with signalling NaN values so that any attempt to perform calculations on the array will generate an exception. A quiet NaN can be used to hold diagnostic information created during debugging sessions. A program is free to encode any information in a NaN it wishes. The floating-point unit does not attempt to perform operations on NaNs. The Intel IA-32 manual details a set of rules that determine instruction results when combinations of the two types of NaNs are used as operands.[2]

Specific Encodings　There are several specific encodings for values often encountered in floating-point operations, listed in Table 17-6. Bit positions marked with the letter x can be either 1 or 0. QNaN is a quiet NaN, and SNaN is a signalling NaN.

Table 17-6   Specific Single-Precision Encodings.

Value	Sign, Exponent, Significand
Positive zero	0 00000000 00000000000000000000000
Negative zero	1 00000000 00000000000000000000000
Positive infinity	0 11111111 00000000000000000000000
Negative infinity	1 11111111 00000000000000000000000
QNaN	x 11111111 1xxxxxxxxxxxxxxxxxxxxxx
SNaN	x 11111111 0xxxxxxxxxxxxxxxxxxxxxx[a]

[a] SNaN significand field begins with 0, but at least one of the remaining bits must be 1.

17.1.5   Converting Decimal Fractions to Binary Reals

When a decimal fraction can be represented as a sum of fractions in the form $(1/2 + 1/4 + 1/8 + ...)$, it is fairly easy for you to discover the corresponding binary real. In Table 17-7, most of the fractions in the left column are not in a form that translates easily to binary. They can, however, be written as in the second column.

Table 17-7   Examples of Decimal Fractions and Binary Reals.

Decimal Fraction	Factored As...	Binary Real
1/2	1/2	.1
1/4	1/4	.01
3/4	1/2 + 1/4	.11
1/8	1/8	.001
7/8	1/2 + 1/4 + 1/8	.111
3/8	1/4 + 1/8	.011
1/16	1/16	.0001
3/16	1/8 + 1/16	.0011
5/16	1/4 + 1/16	.0101

Many real numbers, such as 1/10 (0.1) or 1/100 (.01), cannot be represented by a finite number of binary digits. Such a fraction can only be approximated by a sum of fractions whose denominators are powers of 2. Imagine how currency values such as $39.95 are affected!

Alternate Method, Using Binary Long Division   When small decimal values are involved, an easy way to convert decimal fractions into binary is to first convert the numerator and denominator to binary and then perform long division. For example, decimal 0.5 is represented as the fraction 5/10. Decimal 5 is binary 0101, and decimal 10 is binary 1010. Performing the binary long division, we find that the quotient is 0.1 binary:

$$
\begin{array}{r}
.1 \\
1010\,\overline{)\,0101.0} \\
-1010 \\
\hline
0
\end{array}
$$

When 1010 binary is subtracted from the dividend the remainder is zero, and the division stops. Therefore, the decimal fraction 5/10 equals 0.1 binary. We will call this approach the *binary long division method*.[3]

Representing 0.2 in Binary   Let's convert decimal 0.2 (2/10) to binary using the binary long division method. First, we divide binary 10 by binary 1010 (decimal 10):

$$
\begin{array}{r}
.0\,0\,1\,1\,0\,0\,1\,1 \text{ (etc.)} \\
\hline
1010 \,\big|\, 10.00000000 \\
1010 \\
\hline
1100 \\
1010 \\
\hline
10000 \\
1010 \\
\hline
1100 \\
1010 \\
\hline
\text{etc.}
\end{array}
$$

The first quotient large enough to use is 10000. After dividing 1010 into 10000, the remainder is 110. Appending another zero, the new dividend is 1100. After dividing 1010 into 1100, the remainder is 10. After appending three zeros, the new dividend is 10000. This is the same dividend we started with. From this point on, the sequence of the bits in the quotient repeats (0011. . .), so we know that an exact quotient will not be found and 0.2 cannot be represented by a finite number of bits. The single-precision encoded significand is 00110011001100110011001.

Converting Single-Precision Values to Decimal

Here are suggested steps when converting a IEEE single-precision (SP) value to decimal:

1. If the MSB is 1, the number is negative; otherwise, it is positive.
2. The next 8 bits represent the exponent. Subtract binary 01111111 (decimal 127), producing the unbiased exponent. Convert the unbiased exponent to decimal.
3. The next 23 bits represent the significand. Notate a "1.", followed by the significand bits. Trailing zeros can be ignored. Create a floating-point binary number, using the significand, the sign determined in step 1, and the exponent calculated in step 2.
4. Unnormalize the binary number produced in step 3. (Shift the binary point the number of places equal to the value of the exponent. Shift right if the exponent is positive, or left if the exponent is negative.)
5. From left to right, use weighted positional notation to form the decimal sum of the powers of 2 represented by the floating-point binary number.

Example: **Convert IEEE (0 10000010 01011000000000000000000) to Decimal**

1. The number is positive.
2. The unbiased exponent is binary 00000011, or decimal 3.
3. Combining the sign, exponent, and significand, the binary number is $+1.01011 \times 2^3$.
4. The unnormalized binary number is $+1010.11$.
5. The decimal value is $+10\ 3/4$, or $+10.75$.

17.1.6   Section Review

1. Why doesn't the single-precision real format permit an exponent of -127?
2. Why doesn't the single-precision real format permit an exponent of $+128$?
3. In the IEEE double-precision format, how many bits are reserved for the fractional part of the significand?

4. In the IEEE single-precision format, how many bits are reserved for the exponent?

5. Express the binary floating-point value 1101.01101 as a sum of decimal fractions.

6. Explain why decimal 0.2 cannot be represented exactly by a finite number of bits.

7. Normalize the binary value 11011.01011

8. Normalize the binary value 0000100111101.1

9. Show the IEEE single-precision encoding of binary +1110.011

10. What are the two types of *NaNs*?

11. Convert the fraction 5/8 to a binary real.

12. Convert the fraction 17/32 to a binary real.

13. Convert the decimal value +10.75 to IEEE single-precision real.

14. Convert the decimal value −76.0625 to IEEE single-precision real.

17.2   Floating-Point Unit

The Intel 8086 processor was designed to handle only integer arithmetic. This turned out to be a problem for graphics and calculation-intensive software using floating-point calculations. It was possible to emulate floating-point arithmetic purely through software, but the performance penalty was severe. Programs such as *AutoCad* (by Autodesk) demanded a more powerful way to perform floating-point math. Intel sold a separate floating-point coprocessor chip named the 8087, and upgraded it along with each processor generation. With the advent of the Intel486, floating-point hardware was integrated into the main CPU and called the *Floating-Point Unit* (FPU).

17.2.1   FPU Register Stack

The FPU does not use the general-purpose registers (EAX, EBX, etc.). Instead, it has its own set of registers called a *register stack*. It loads values from memory into the register stack, performs calculations, and stores stack values into memory. FPU instructions evaluate mathematical expressions in *postfix* format, in much the same way as Hewlett-Packard calculators. The following, for example, is called an *infix expression:* (5 * 6) + 4. The postfix equivalent is

    5 6 * 4 +

The infix expression **(A + B) * C** requires parentheses to override the default precedence rules (multiplication before addition). The equivalent postfix expression does not require parentheses:

    A B + C *

Expression Stack   A stack holds intermediate values during the evaluation of postfix expressions. Figure 17–2 shows the steps required to evaluate the postfix expression **5 6 * 4 −**. The stack entries are labeled ST(0) and ST(1), with ST(0) indicating where the stack pointer would normally be pointing.

Commonly used methods for translating infix expressions to postfix are well documented in introductory computer science texts and on the Internet, so we will skip them here. Table 17-8 contains a few examples of equivalent expressions.

Table 17-8   Infix to Postfix Examples.

Infix	Postfix
A + B	A B +
(A − B) / D	A B − D /
(A + B) * (C + D)	A B + C D + *
((A + B) / C) * (E − F)	A B + C / E F − *

FIGURE 17–2   Evaluating the Postfix Expression 5 6 * 4 − .

Left to Right	Stack		Action
5	5	ST (0)	push 5
5 6	5	ST (1)	push 6
	6	ST (0)	
5 6 *	30	ST (0)	Multiply ST(1) by ST(0) and pop ST(0) off the stack.
5 6 * 4	30	ST (1)	push 4
	4	ST (0)	
5 6 * 4 -	26	ST (0)	Subtract ST(0) from ST(1) and pop ST(0) off the stack.

FPU Data Registers

The FPU has eight individually addressable 80-bit data registers named R0 through R7 (see Figure 17–3). Together, they are called a *register stack*. A three-bit field named TOP in the FPU status word identifies the register number that is currently the top of the stack. In Figure 17–3, for example, TOP equals binary 011, identifying R3 as the top of the stack. This stack location is also known as ST(0) (or simply ST) when writing floating-point instructions. The last register is ST(7).

FIGURE 17–3   Floating-Point Data Register Stack.

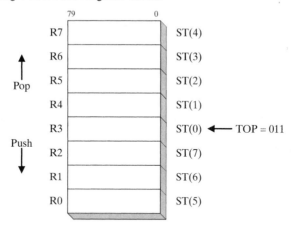

As we might expect, a *push* operation (also called *load*) decrements TOP by 1 and copies an operand into the register indentified as ST(0). If TOP equals 0 before a push, TOP wraps around to register R7. A *pop* operation (also called *store*) copies the data at ST(0) into an operand, then adds 1 to TOP. If TOP equals 7 before the pop, it wraps around to register R0. If loading a value into the stack would result in overwriting existing data in the register stack, a *floating-point exception* is generated. Figure 17–4 shows the same stack after 1.0 and 2.0 have been pushed (loaded) on the stack.

Although it is interesting to understand how the FPU implements the stack using a limited set of registers, we need only focus on the ST(*n*) notation, where ST(0) is always the top of stack. From this point forward, we refer to stack registers as ST(0), ST(1), and so on. Instruction operands cannot refer directly to register numbers.

Figure 17–4   FPU Stack after Pushing 1.0 and 2.0.

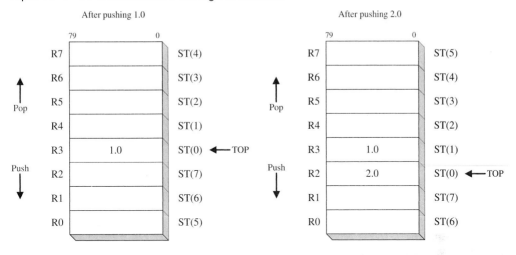

Floating-point values in registers use the IEEE 10-byte *extended real* format (also known as *temporary real*). When the FPU stores the result of an arithmetic operation in memory, it translates the result into one of the following formats: integer, long integer, single precision (short real), double precision (long real), or packed binary-coded decimal.

Special-Purpose Registers

The FPU has six *special-purpose* registers (see Figure 17–5):

- **Opcode register:** stores the opcode of the last noncontrol instruction executed.
- **Control register:** controls the precision and rounding method used by the FPU when performing calculations. You can also use it to mask out (hide) individual floating-point exceptions.
- **Status register:** contains the top-of-stack pointer, condition codes, and warnings about exceptions.
- **Tag register:** indicates the contents of each register in the FPU data-register stack. It uses two bits per register to indicate whether the register contains a valid number, zero, or a special value (NaN, infinity, denormal, or unsupported format) or is empty.
- **Last instruction pointer register:** stores a pointer to the last non-control instruction executed.
- **Last data (operand) pointer register:** stores a pointer to a data operand, if any, used by the last instruction executed.

The special-purpose registers are used by operating systems to preserve state information when switching between tasks. We mentioned state preservation in Chapter 2 when explaining how the CPU performs multitasking.

17.2.2   Rounding

The FPU attempts to generate an infinitely accurate result from a floating-point calculation. In many cases this is impossible because the destination operand may not be able to accurately represent the calculated result. For example, suppose a certain storage format would only permit three fractional bits. It would permit us to store values such as 1.011 or 1.101, but not 1.0101. Suppose the precise result of a calculation produced +1.0111 (decimal 1.4375). We could either round the number up to the next higher value by adding .0001 or round it downward to by subtracting .0001:

```
(a) 1.0111 --> 1.100
(b) 1.0111 --> 1.011
```

If the precise result were negative, adding –.0001 would move the rounded result closer to –∞. Subtracting –.0001 would move the rounded result closer to both zero and +∞:

```
(a) -1.0111 --> -1.100
(b) -1.0111 --> -1.011
```

Figure 17–5   FPU Special-Purpose Registers.

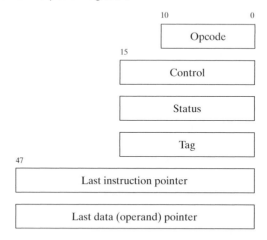

The FPU lets you select one of four rounding methods:

• *Round to nearest even*: The rounded result is the closest to the infinitely precise result. If two values are equally close, the result is an even value (least significant bit = 0).
• *Round down toward* −∞: The rounded result is less than or equal to the infinitely precise result.
• *Round up toward* +∞: The rounded result is greater than or equal to the infinitely precise result.
• *Round toward zero*: Also known as *truncation*: The absolute value of the rounded result is less than or equal to the infinitely precise result.

FPU Control Word   The FPU control word contains two bits named the *RC field* that specify which rounding method to use. The field values are as follows:

• 00 binary: Round to nearest even (default).
• 01 binary: Round down toward negative infinity.
• 10 binary: Round up toward positive infinity.
• 11 binary: Round toward zero (truncate).

Round to nearest even is the default, and is considered to be the most accurate and appropriate for most application programs. Table 17-9 shows how the four rounding methods would be applied to binary +1.0111. Similarly, Table 17-10 shows the possible roundings of binary −1.0111.

Table 17-9   Example: Rounding +1.0111.

Method	Precise Result	Rounded
Round to nearest even	1.0111	1.100
Round down toward −∞	1.0111	1.011
Round toward +∞	1.0111	1.100
Round toward zero	1.0111	1.011

Table 17-10   Example: Rounding –1.0111.

Method	Precise Result	Rounded
Round to nearest (even)	–1.0111	–1.100
Round toward –∞	–1.0111	–1.100
Round toward +∞	–1.0111	–1.011
Round toward zero	–1.0111	–1.011

17.2.3   Floating-Point Exceptions

In every program, things can go wrong, and the FPU has to deal with the results. Consequently, it recognizes and detects six types of exception conditions: Invalid operation (#I), Divide by zero (#Z), Denormalized operand (#D), Numeric overflow (#O), Numeric underflow (#U), and Inexact precision (#P). The first three (#I, #Z, #D) are detected before any arithmetic operation occurs. The latter three (#O, #U, #P) are detected after an operation occurs.

Each exception type has a corresponding flag bit and mask bit. When a floating-point exception is detected, the processor sets the matching flag bit. For each exception flagged by the processor, there are two courses of action:

- If the corresponding mask bit is **set**, the processor handles the exception automatically and lets the program continue.
- If the corresponding mask bit is **clear**, the processor invokes a software exception handler.

The processor's masked (automatic) responses are generally acceptable for most programs. Custom exception handlers can be used in cases where specific responses are required by the application. A single instruction can trigger multiple exceptions, so the processor keeps an ongoing record of all exceptions occurring since the last time exceptions were cleared. After a sequence of calculations completes, you can check to see if any exceptions occurred.

17.2.4   Floating-Point Instruction Set

The FPU instruction set is somewhat complex, so we will attempt here to give you an overview of its capabilities, along with specific examples that demonstrate code typically generated by compilers. In addition, we will see how you can exercise control over the FPU by changing its rounding mode. The instruction set contains the following basic categories of instructions:

- Data transfer
- Basic arithmetic
- Comparison
- Transcendental
- Load constants (specialized predefined constants only)
- x87 FPU control
- x87 FPU and SIMD state management

Floating-point instruction names begin with the letter F to distinguish them from CPU instructions. The second letter of the instruction mnemonic (often B or I) indicates how a memory operand is to be interpreted: B indicates a binary-coded decimal (BCD) operand, and I indicates a binary integer operand. If neither is specified, the memory operand is assumed to be in real-number format. For example, FBLD operates on BCD numbers, FILD operates on integers, and FLD operates on real numbers.

Appendix B contains a reference listing of IA-32 floating-point instructions.

Operands A floating-point instruction can have zero operands, one operand, or two operands. If there are two operands, one must be a floating-point register. There are no immediate operands, but certain predefined constants (such as 0.0, π, and $\log_2 10$) can be loaded into the stack. General-purpose registers such as EAX, EBX, ECX, aand EDX cannot be operands. (The only exception is FSTSW, which stores the FPU status word in AX.) Memory-to-memory operations are not permitted.

Integer operands must be loaded into the FPU from memory (never from CPU registers); they are automatically converted to floating-point format. Similarly, when storing floating-point values into integer memory operands, the values are automatically truncated or rounded into integers.

Initialization (FINIT)

The FINIT instruction initializes the floating-point unit. It sets the FPU control word to 037Fh, which masks (hides) all floating-point exceptions, sets rounding to nearest, and sets the calculation precision to 64 bits. We recommend calling FINIT at the beginning of your programs, so you know the starting state of the processor.

Floating-Point Data Types

Let's quickly review the floating-point data types supported by MASM (QWORD, TBYTE, REAL4, REAL8, and REAL10), listed in Table 17-11. You will need to use these types when defining memory operands for FPU instructions. For example, when loading a floating-point variable into the FPU stack, the variable is defined as REAL4, REAL8, or REAL10:

```
.data
bigVal REAL10 1.212342342234234243E+864
.code
fld  bigVal                          ; load variable into stack
```

Table 17-11   Intrinsic Data Types.

Type	Usage
QWORD	64-bit integer
TBYTE	80-bit (10-byte) integer
REAL4	32-bit (4-byte) IEEE short real
REAL8	64-bit (8-byte) IEEE long real
REAL10	80-bit (10-byte) IEEE extended real

Load Floating-Point Value (FLD)

The FLD (load floating-point value) instruction copies a floating-point operand to the top of the FPU stack (known as ST(0)). The operand can be a 32-bit, 64-bit, or 80-bit memory operand (REAL4, REAL8, REAL10) or another FPU register:

```
FLD  m32fp
FLD  m64fp
FLD  m80fp
FLD  ST(i)
```

Memory Operand Types FLD supports the same memory operand types as MOV. Here are examples:

```
.data
array REAL8 10 DUP(?)
.code
```

```
fld   array                              ; direct
fld   [array+16]                         ; direct-offset
fld   REAL8 PTR[esi]                     ; indrect
fld   array[esi]                         ; indexed
fld   array[esi*8]                       ; indexed, scaled
fld   array[esi*TYPE array]              ; indexed, scaled
fld   REAL8 PTR[ebx+esi]                 ; base-index
fld   array[ebx+esi]                     ; base-index-displacement
fld   array[ebx+esi*TYPE array]          ; base-index-displacement, scaled
```

Example   The following example loads two direct operands on the FPU stack:

```
.data
dblOne    REAL8 234.56
dblTwo    REAL8 10.1
.code
fld   dblOne                             ; ST(0) = dblOne
fld   dblTwo                             ; ST(0) = dblTwo, ST(1) = dblOne
```

The following figure shows the stack contents after executing each instruction:

fld dblOne	ST(0)	234.56

fld dblTwo	ST(1)	234.56
	ST(0)	10.1

When the second FLD executes, TOP is decremented, causing the stack element previously labeled ST(0) to become ST(1).

FILD   The FILD (load integer) instruction coverts a 16-, 32-, or 64-bit signed integer source operand to double-precision floating point and loads it into ST(0). The source operand's sign is preserved. We will demonstrate its use in Section 17.2.10 (Mixed-Mode Arithmetic). FILD supports the same memory operand types as MOV (indirect, indexed, base-indexed, etc.).

Loading Constants   The following instructions load specialized constants on the stack. They have no operands:

- The FLD1 instruction pushes 1.0 onto the register stack.
- The FLDL2T instruction pushes $\log_2 10$ onto the register stack.
- The FLDL2E instruction pushes $\log_2 e$ onto the register stack.
- The FLDPI instruction pushes π onto the register stack.
- The FLDLG2 instruction pushes $\log_{10} 2$ onto the register stack.
- The FLDLN2 instruction pushes $\log_e 2$ onto the register stack.
- The FLDZ (load zero) instruction pushes 0.0 on the FPU stack.

Store Floating-Point Value (FST, FSTP)

The FST (store floating-point value) instruction copies a floating-point operand from the top of the FPU stack into memory. FST supports the same memory operand types as FLD. The operand can be a 32-bit, 64-bit, or 80-bit memory operand (REAL4, REAL8, REAL10) or it can be another FPU register:

```
FST  m32fp
FST  m64fp
FST  ST(i)
```

FST does not pop the stack. The following instructions store ST(0) into memory. Let's assume ST(0) equals 10.1 and ST(1) equals 234.56:

```
fst   dblThree                    ; 10.1
fst   dblFour                     ; 10.1
```

Intuitively, we might have expected dblFour to equal 234.56. But the first FST instruction left 10.1 in ST(0). If our intention is to copy ST(1) into dblFour, we must use the FSTP instruction.

FSTP   The FSTP (store floating-point value and pop) instruction copies the value in ST(0) to memory and pops ST(0) off the stack. Let's assume ST(0) equals 10.1 and ST(1) equals 234.56 before executing the following instructions:

```
fstp   dblThree                   ; 10.1
fstp   dblFour                    ; 234.56
```

After execution, the two values have been logically removed from the stack. Physically, the TOP pointer is incremented each time FSTP executes, changing the location of ST(0).

The FIST (store integer) instruction converts the value in ST(0) to signed integer and stores the result in the destination operand. Values can be stored as words or doublewords. We will demonstrate its use in Section 17.2.10 (Mixed-Mode Arithmetic). FIST supports the same memory operand types as FST.

17.2.5   Arithmetic Instructions

The basic arithmetic operations are listed in Table 17-12. Arithmetic instructions all support the same memory operand types as FLD (load) and FST (store), so operands can be indirect, indexed, base-index, and so on.

Table 17-12   Basic Floating-Point Arithmetic Instructions.

FCHS	Change sign
FADD	Add source to destination
FSUB	Subtract source from destination
FSUBR	Subtract destination from source
FMUL	Multiply source by destination
FDIV	Divide destination by source
FDIVR	Divide source by destination

FCHS and FABS

The FCHS (change sign) instruction reverses the sign of the floating-point value in ST(0). The FABS (absolute value) instruction clears the sign of the number in ST(0) to create its absolute value. Neither instruction has operands:

```
FCHS
FABS
```

FADD, FADDP, FIADD

The FADD (add) instruction has the following formats, where *m32fp* is a REAL4 memory operand, *m64fp* is a REAL8 operand, and *i* is a register number:

```
FADD[4]
FADD m32fp
FADD m64fp
```

```
FADD  ST(0), ST(i)
FADD  ST(i), ST(0)
```

No Operands   If no operands are used with FADD, ST(0) is added to ST(1). The result is temporarily stored in ST(1). ST(0) is then popped from the stack, leaving the result on the top of the stack. The following figure demonstrates FADD, assuming that the stack already contains two values:

fadd   Before: ST(1)   234.56

                        ST(0)   10.1

            After: ST(0)   244.66

Register Operands   Starting with the same stack contents, the following illustration demonstrates adding ST(0) to ST(1):

fadd st(1), st(0)   Before: ST(1)   234.56

                                ST(0)   10.1

                     After: ST(1)   244.66

                                ST(0)   10.1

Memory Operand   When used with a memory operand, FADD adds the operand to ST(0). Here are examples:

```
fadd mySingle                      ; ST(0) += mySingle
fadd REAL8 PTR[esi]                ; ST(0) += [esi]
```

FADDP   The FADDP (add with pop) instruction pops ST(0) from the stack after performing the addition operation. MASM supports the following format:

```
FADDP  ST(i),ST(0
```

The following figure shows how FADDP works:

faddp st(1), st(0)   Before: ST(1)   234.56

                                 ST(0)   10.1

                      After: ST(0)   244.66

FIADD   The FIADD (add integer) instruction converts the source operand to double extended-precision floating-point format before adding the operand to ST(0). It has the following syntax:

```
FIADD   m16int
FIADD   m32int
```

Example:

```
.data
myInteger DWORD 1
```

```
.code
fiadd  myInteger                        ; ST(0) += myInteger
```

FSUB, FSUBP, FISUB

The FSUB instruction subtracts a source operand from a destination operand, storing the difference in the destination operand. The destination is always an FPU register, and the source can be either an FPU register or memory. It accepts the same operands as FADD:

```
FSUB[5]
FSUB m32fp
FSUB m64fp
FSUB ST(0), ST(i)
FSUB ST(i), ST(0)
```

FSUB's operation is similar to that of FADD, except it subtracts rather than adds. For example, the no-operand form of FSUB subtracts ST(0) from ST(1). The result is temporarily stored in ST(1). ST(0) is then popped from the stack, leaving the result on the top of the stack. FSUB with a memory operand subtracts the memory operand from ST(0) and does not pop the stack.

Examples:

```
fsub mySingle                           ; ST(0) -= mySingle
fsub array[edi*8]                       ; ST(0) -= array[edi*8]
```

FSUBP   The FSUBP (subtract with pop) instruction pops ST(0) from the stack after performing the subtraction. MASM supports the following format:

```
FSUBP ST(i),ST(0)
```

FISUB   The FISUB (subtract integer) instruction converts the source operand to double extended-precision floating-point format before subtracting the operand from ST(0):

```
FISUB   m16int
FISUB   m32int
```

FMUL, FMULP, FIMUL

The FMUL instruction multiplies a source operand by a destination operand, storing the product in the destination operand. The destination is always an FPU register, and the source can be a register or memory operand. It uses the same syntax as FADD and FSUB:

```
FMUL[6]
FMUL m32fp
FMUL m64fp
FMUL ST(0), ST(i)
FMUL ST(i), ST(0)
```

FMUL's operation is similar to that of FADD, except it multiplies rather than adds. For example, the no-operand form of FMUL multiplies ST(0) by ST(1). The product is temporarily stored in ST(1). ST(0) is then popped from the stack, leaving the product on the top of the stack. Similarly, FMUL with a memory operand multiplies ST(0) by the memory operand:

```
fmul mySingle                           ; ST(0) *= mySingle
```

FMULP   The FMULP (multiply with pop) instruction pops ST(0) from the stack after performing the multiplication. MASM supports the following format:

```
FMULP ST(i),ST(0)
```

FIMUL is identical to FIADD, except it multiplies rather than adds:

```
FIMUL   m16int
FIMUL   m32int
```

FDIV, FDIVP, FIDIV

The FDIV instruction divides a destination operand by a source operand, storing the dividend in the destination operand. The destination is always a register, and the source operand can be either a register or memory. It has the same syntax as FADD and FSUB:

```
FDIV7
FDIV m32fp
FDIV m64fp
FDIV ST(0), ST(i)
FDIV ST(i), ST(0)
```

FDIV's operation is similar to that of FADD, except it divides rather than adds. For example, the no-operand form of FDIV divides ST(1) by ST(0). ST(0) is popped from the stack, leaving the dividend on the top of the stack. FDIV with a memory operand divides ST(0) by the memory operand. The following code divides **dblOne** by **dblTwo** and stores the quotient in **dblQuot**:

```
.data
dblOne    REAL8   1234.56
dblTwo    REAL8   10.0
dblQuot   REAL8   ?
.code
fld  dblOne                 ; load into ST(0)
fdiv dblTwo                 ; divide ST(0) by dblOne
fstp dblQuot                ; store ST(0) to dblQuot
```

If the source operand is zero, a divide-by-zero exception is generated. A number of special cases apply when operands equal to positive or negative infinity, zero, and *NaN* are divided. For details, see the Intel IA-32 Instruction Set manual.

FIDIV The FIDIV instruction converts an integer source operand to double extended-precision floating-point format before dividing it into ST(0). Syntax:

```
FIDIV  m16int
FIDIV  m32int
```

17.2.6 Comparing Floating-Point Values

Floating-point values cannot be compared using the CMP instruction—the latter uses integer subtraction to perform comparisons. Instead, the FCOM instruction must be used. After executing FCOM, special steps must be taken before using conditional jump instructions (JA, JB, JE, etc.) in logical IF statements.

FCOM, FCOMP, FCOMPP The FCOM (compare floating-point values) instruction compares ST(0) to its source operand. The source can be a memory operand or FPU register. Syntax:

Instruction	Description
FCOM	Compare ST(0) to ST(1)
FCOM m32fp	Compare ST(0) to m32fp
FCOM m64fp	Compare ST(0) to m64fp
FCOM ST(i)	Compare ST(0) to ST(i)

The FCOMP instruction carries out the same operations with the same types of operands, and ends by popping ST(0) from the stack. The FCOMPP instruction is the same as that of FCOMP, except it pops the stack one more time.

Condition Codes   Three FPU condition code flags, C3, C2, and C0, indicate the results of comparing floating-point values (Table 17-13). The column headings show equivalent CPU status flags because C3, C2, and C0 are similar in function to the Zero, Parity, and Carry flags, respectively.

Table 17-13   Condition Codes Set by FCOM, FCOMP, FCOMPP.

Condition	C3 (Zero Flag)	C2 (Parity Flag)	C0 (Carry Flag)	Conditional Jump to Use
ST(0) > SRC	0	0	0	JA, JNBE
ST(0) < SRC	0	0	1	JB, JNAE
ST(0) = SRC	1	0	0	JE, JZ
Unordered[a]	1	1	1	*(None)*

[a] If an invalid arithmetic operand exception is raised (because of invalid operands) and the exception is masked, C3, C2, and C0 are set according to the row marked *Unordered*.

The primary challenge after comparing two values and setting FPU condition codes is to find a way to branch to a label based on the conditions. Two steps are involved:

• Use the FNSTSW instruction to move the FPU status word into AX.
• Use the SAHF instruction to copy AH into the EFLAGS register.

Once the condition codes are in EFLAGS, you can use conditional jumps based the Zero, Parity, and Carry flags. Table 17-13 showed the appropriate conditional jump for each combination of flags. We can infer additional jumps: The JAE instruction causes a transfer of control if CF = 0. JBE causes a transfer of control if CF = 1 or ZF = 1. JNE transfers if ZF = 0.

Example   Assume the following C++ code:

```
double X = 1.2;
double Y = 3.0;
int N = 0;
if( X < Y )
    N = 1;
```

Following is equivalent assembly language code:

```
.data
X REAL8   1.2
Y REAL8   3.0
N DWORD 0
.code
; if( X < Y )
;    N = 1
    fld     X            ; ST(0) = X
    fcomp   Y            ; compare ST(0) to Y
    fnstsw  ax           ; move status word into AX
    sahf                 ; copy AH into EFLAGS
    jnb     L1           ; X not < Y? skip
    mov     N,1          ; N = 1
L1:
```

P6 Improvements   One point to be made about the foregoing example is that floating-point comparisons incur more runtime overhead than integer comparisons. With this in mind, Intel's P6 family introduced the FCOMI instruction. It compares floating-point values and sets the Zero, Parity, and Carry flags directly. (The P6 family started with the Pentium Pro and Pentium II processors.) FCOMI has the following syntax:

```
FCOMI ST(0),ST(i)
```

Let's rewrite our previous code example (comparing X and Y) using FCOMI:

```
.code
; if( X < Y )
;    N = 1
     fld    Y                         ; ST(0) = Y
     fld    X                         ; ST(0)= X, ST(1)= Y
     fcomi  ST(0),ST(1)               ; compare ST(0) to ST(1)
     jnb    L1                        ; ST(0) not < ST(1)? skip
     mov    N,1                       ; N = 1
L1:
```

The FCOMI instruction took the place of three instructions in the previous version, but required one more FLD. The FCOMI instruction does not accept memory operands.

Comparing for Equality

Almost every beginning programming textbook warns readers not to compare floating-point values for equality because of rounding errors that occur during calculations. We can demonstrate the problem by calculating the following expression: (sqrt(2.0) * sqrt(2.0)) − 2.0. Mathematically, it should equal zero, but the results are quite different (approximately 4.4408921E-016). We will use the following data, and show the FPU stack after every step in Table 17-14:

```
val1 REAL8 2.0
```

Table 17-14   Calculating (sqrt(2.0) * sqrt(2.0)) − 2.0.

Instruction	FPU Stack
fld val1	ST(0): +2.0000000E+000
fsqrt	ST(0): +1.4142135E+000
fmul ST(0),ST(0)	ST(0): +2.0000000E+000
fsub val1	ST(0): +4.4408921E-016

The proper way to compare floating-point values x and y is to take the absolute value of their difference, $|x - y|$, and compare it to a small user-defined value called *epsilon*. Here's code in assembly language that does it, using epsilon as the maximum difference they can have and still be considered equal:

```
.data
epsilon REAL8 1.0E-12
val2 REAL8 0.0                        ; value to compare
val3 REAL8 1.001E-13                  ; considered equal to val2

.code
; if( val2 == val3 ), display "Values are equal".
     fld    epsilon
     fld    val2
     fsub   val3
     fabs
     fcomi  ST(0),ST(1)
     ja     skip
     mWrite <"Values are equal",0dh,0ah>
skip:
```

Table 17-15 tracks the program's progress, showing the stack after each of the first four instructions execute.

Table 17-15   Calculating a Dot Product (6.0 * 2.0) + (4.5 * 3.2).

Instruction	FPU Stack
fld epsilon	ST(0): +1.0000000E-012
fld val2	ST(0): +0.0000000E+000 ST(1): +1.0000000E-012
fsub val3	ST(0): -1.0010000E-013 ST(1): +1.0000000E-012
fabs	ST(0): +1.0010000E-013 ST(1): +1.0000000E-012
fcomi ST(0),ST(1)	ST(0) < ST(1), so CF=1, ZF=0

If we redefined val3 as being larger than epsilon, it would not be equal to val2:

```
val3 REAL8 1.001E-12              ; not equal
```

17.2.7   Reading and Writing Floating-Point Values

Included in the book's link libraries are two procedures for floating-point input-output, created by William Barrett of San Jose State University:

- **ReadFloat**: Reads a floating-point value from the keyboard and pushes it on the floating-point stack.
- **WriteFloat**: Writes the floating-point value at ST(0) to the console window in exponential format.

ReadFloat accepts a wide variety of floating-point formats. Here are examples:

```
35
+35.
-3.5
.35
3.5E5
3.5E005
-3.5E+5
3.5E-4
+3.5E-4
```

ShowFPUStack   Another useful procedure, written by James Brink of Pacific Lutheran University, displays the FPU stack. Call it with no parameters:

```
call ShowFPUStack
```

Example Program   The following example program pushes two floating-point values on the FPU stack, displays it, inputs two values from the user, multiplies them, and displays their product:

```
TITLE 32-bit Floating-Point I/O Test   (floatTest32.asm)

INCLUDE Irvine32.inc
INCLUDE macros.inc

.data
first  REAL8 123.456
second REAL8 10.0
third  REAL8 ?

.code
main PROC
     finit                         ; initialize FPU
```

```
; Push two floats and display the FPU stack.
    fld    first
    fld    second
    call   ShowFPUStack

; Input two floats and display their product.
    mWrite "Please enter a real number: "
    call   ReadFloat

    mWrite "Please enter a real number: "
    call   ReadFloat

    fmul   ST(0),ST(1)                    ; multiply

    mWrite "Their product is: "
    call   WriteFloat
    call   Crlf

    exit
main ENDP
END main
```

Sample input/output (user input shown in bold type):

```
------ FPU Stack ------
ST(0): +1.0000000E+001
ST(1): +1.2345600E+002

Please enter a real number: 3.5
Please enter a real number: 4.2
Their product is: +1.4700000E+001
```

17.2.8 Exception Synchronization

The integer (CPU) and FPU are separate units, so floating-point instructions can execute at the same time as integer and system instructions. This capability, named *concurrency*, can be a potential problem when unmasked floating-point exceptions occur. Masked exceptions, on the other hand, are not a problem because the FPU always completes the current operation and stores the result.

When an unmasked exception occurs, the current floating-point instruction is interrupted and the FPU signals the exception event. When the next floating-point instruction or the FWAIT (WAIT) instruction is about to execute, the FPU checks for pending exceptions. If any are found, it invokes the floating-point exception hander (a subroutine).

What if the floating-point instruction causing the exception is followed by an integer or system instruction? Unfortunately, such instructions do not check for pending exceptions—they execute immediately. If the first instruction is supposed to store its output in a memory operand and the second instruction modifies the same memory operand, the exception handler cannot execute properly. Here's an example:

```
.data
intVal DWORD 25
.code
    fild intVal                    ; load integer into ST(0)
    inc  intVal                    ; increment the integer
```

The WAIT and FWAIT instructions were created to force the processor to check for pending, unmasked, floating-point exceptions before proceding to the next instruction. Either one solves our potential synchronization problem, preventing the INC instruction from executing until the exception handler has a chance to finish:

```
fild intVal                    ; load integer into ST(0)
fwait                          ; wait for pending exceptions
inc  intVal                    ; increment the integer
```

17.2.9 Code Examples

In this section, we look at a few short examples that demonstrate floating-point arithmetic instructions. An excellent way to learn is to code expressions in C++, compile them, and inspect the code produced by the compiler.

Expression

Let's code the expression valD = −valA + (valB * valC). A possible step-by-step solution is: Load valA on the stack and negate it. Load valB into ST(0), moving valA down to ST(1). Multiply ST(0 by valC, leaving the product in ST(0). Add ST(1) and ST(0) and store the sum in valD:

```
.data
valA REAL8 1.5
valB REAL8 2.5
valC REAL8 3.0
valD REAL8 ?; +6.0
.code
fld  valA                      ; ST(0) = valA
fchs                           ; change sign of ST(0)
fld  valB                      ; load valB into ST(0)
fmul valC                      ; ST(0) *= valC
fadd                           ; ST(0) += ST(1)
fstp valD                      ; store ST(0) to valD
```

Sum of an Array

The following code calculates and displays the sum of an array of double-precision reals:

```
ARRAY_SIZE = 20
.data
sngArray  REAL8  ARRAY_SIZE DUP(?)
.code
      mov   esi,0              ; array index
      fldz                     ; push 0.0 on stack
      mov   ecx,ARRAY_SIZE

L1:   fld   sngArray[esi]      ; load mem into ST(0)
      fadd                     ; add ST(0), ST(1), pop
      add   esi,TYPE REAL8     ; move to next element
      loop  L1

      call  WriteFloat         ; display the sum in ST(0)
```

Sum of Square Roots

The FSQRT instruction replaces the number in ST(0) with its square root. The following code calculates the sum of two square roots:

```
.data
valA REAL8 25.0
valB REAL8 36.0
.code
fld  valA                      ; push valA
```

```
fsqrt                             ; ST(0) = sqrt(valA)
fld   valB                        ; push valB
fsqrt                             ; ST(0) = sqrt(valB)
fadd                              ; add ST(0), ST(1)
```

Array Dot Product

The following code calculates the expression (array[0] * array[1]) + (array[2] * array[3]). The calculation is sometimes referred to as a *dot product*. Table 17-16 displays the FPU stack after each instruction executes. Here is the input data:

```
.data
array REAL4 6.0, 2.0, 4.5, 3.2
```

Table 17-16   Calculating a Dot Product (6.0 * 2.0) + (4.5 * 3.2).

Instruction	FPU Stack
fld array	ST(0): +6.0000000E+000
fmul [array+4]	ST(0): +1.2000000E+001
fld [array+8]	ST(0): +4.5000000E+000 ST(1): +1.2000000E+001
fmul [array+12]	ST(0): +1.4400000E+001 ST(1): +1.2000000E+001
fadd	ST(0): +2.6400000E+001

17.2.10   Mixed-Mode Arithmetic

Up to this point, we have performed arithmetic operations involving only reals. Applications often perform mixed-mode arithmetic, combining integers and reals. Integer arithmetic instructions such as ADD and MUL cannot handle reals, so our only choice is to use floating-point instructions. The Intel instruction set provides instructions that promote integers to reals and load the values onto the floating-point stack.

Example   The following C++ code adds an integer to a double and stores the sum in a double. C++ automatically promotes the integer to a real before performing the addition:

```
int N = 20;
double X = 3.5;
double Z = N + X;
```

Here is the equivalent assembly language:

```
.data
N SDWORD 20
X REAL8 3.5
Z REAL8 ?
.code
fild N                            ; load integer into ST(0)
fadd X                            ; add mem to ST(0)
fstp Z                            ; store ST(0) to mem
```

Example   The following C++ program promotes N to a double, evaluates a real expression, and stores the result in an integer variable:

```
int N = 20;
double X = 3.5;
int Z = (int) (N + X);
```

The code generated by Visual C++ calls a conversion function (ftol) before storing the truncated result in Z. If we code the expression in assembly language using FIST, we can avoid the function call, but Z is (by default) rounded upward to 24:

```
fild N                          ; load integer into ST(0)
fadd X                          ; add mem to ST(0)
fist Z                          ; store ST(0) to mem int
```

Changing the Rounding Mode   The RC field of the FPU control word lets you specify the type of rounding to be performed. We can use FSTCW to store the control word in a variable, modify the RC field (bits 10 and 11), and use the FLDCW instruction to load the variable back into the control word:

```
fstcw  ctrlWord                 ; store control word
or     ctrlWord,110000000000b   ; set RC = truncate
fldcw  ctrlWord                 ; load control word
```

Then we perform calculations requiring truncation, producing Z = 23:

```
fild N                          ; load integer into ST(0)
fadd X                          ; add mem to ST(0)
fist Z                          ; store ST(0) to mem int
```

Optionally, we reset the rounding mode to its default (*round to nearest even*):

```
fstcw  ctrlWord                 ; store control word
and    ctrlWord,001111111111b   ; reset rounding to default
fldcw  ctrlWord                 ; load control word
```

17.2.11 Masking and Unmasking Exceptions

Exceptions are masked by default (Section 17.2.3), so when a floating-point exception is generated, the processor assigns a default value to the result and continues quietly on its way. For example, dividing a floating-point number by zero produces infinity without halting the program:

```
.data
val1   DWORD 1
val2   REAL8 0.0
.code
fild   val1                     ; load integer into ST(0)
fdiv   val2                     ; ST(0) = positive infinity
```

If you unmask the exception in the FPU control word, the processor tries to execute an appropriate exception handler. Unmasking is accomplished by clearing the appropriate bit in the FPU control word (Table 17-17). Suppose we want to unmask the divide by Zero exception. Here are the required steps:

1. Store the FPU control word in a 16-bit variable.
2. Clear bit 2 (divide by zero flag).
3. Load the variable back into the control word.

The following code unmasks floating-point exceptions:

```
.data
ctrlWord WORD ?
.code
fstcw  ctrlWord                 ; get the control word
and    ctrlWord,1111111111111011b ; unmask divide by zero
fldcw  ctrlWord                 ; load it back into FPU
```

Table 17-17   Fields in the FPU Control Word.

Bit(s)	Description
0	Invalid operation exception mask
1	Denormal operand exception mask
2	Divide by zero exception mask
3	Overflow exception mask
4	Underflow exception mask
5	Precision exception mask
8–9	Precision control
10–11	Rounding control
12	Infinity control

Now, if we execute code that divides by zero, an unmasked exception is generated:

```
fild val1
fdiv val2                          ; divide by zero
fst  val2
```

As soon as the FST instruction begins to execute, MS-Windows displays the following dialog:

Masking Exceptions   To mask an exception, set the appropriate bit in the FPU control word. The following code masks divide by zero exceptions:

```
.data
ctrlWord WORD ?
.code
fstcw   ctrlWord              ; get the control word
or      ctrlWord,100b         ; mask divide by zero
fldcw   ctrlWord              ; load it back into FPU
```

17.2.12   Section Review

1. Write an instruction that loads a duplicate of ST(0) onto the FPU stack.
2. If ST(0) is positioned at absolute register R6 in the register stack, what is the position of ST(2)?
3. Name at least three FPU special-purpose registers.
4. When the second letter of a floating-point instruction is B, what type of operand is indicated?
5. Which instructions accept immediate operands?
6. What is the largest data type permitted by the FLD instruction, and how many bits does it contain?
7. How is the FSTP instruction different from FST?
8. Which instruction changes the sign of a number?

9. What types of operands may be used with the FADD instruction?

10. How is the FISUB instruction different from FSUB?

11. On processors prior to the P6 family, which instruction compares two floating-point values?

12. Write a two-instruction sequence that moves the FPU status flags into the EFLAGS register.

13. Which instruction loads an integer operand into ST(0)?

14. Which field in the FPU control word lets you change the processor's rounding mode?

15. Given a precise result of 1.010101101, round it to an 8-bit significand using the FPU's default rounding method.

16. Given a precise result of −1.010101101, round it to an 8-bit significand using the FPU's default rounding method.

17. Write instructions that implement the following C++ code:
```
double B = 7.8;
double M = 3.6;
double N = 7.1;
double P = -M * (N + B);
```

18. Write instructions that implement the following C++ code:
```
int B = 7;
double N = 7.1;
double P = sqrt(N) + B;
```

17.3   Intel Instruction Encoding

To fully understand assembly language, you need to spend some time looking at the way assembly instructions are translated into machine language. The topic is quite complex because of the rich variety of instructions and addressing modes available in the Intel instruction set. We will begin with the 8086/8088 processor as an illustrative example, running in real-address mode. Later, we will show some of the changes made when Intel introduced 32-bit processors.

As we mentioned in Chapter 2, the Intel 8086 processor was the first in a line of processors using a *Complex Instruction Set Computer* (CISC) design. The instruction set includes a wide variety of memory-addressing, shifting, arithmetic, data movement, and logical operations. Compared to RISC (*Reduced Instruction Set Computer*) instructions, Intel instructions are somewhat tricky to encode and decode. To *encode* an instruction means to convert an assembly language instruction and its operands into machine code. To *decode* an instruction means to convert a machine code instruction into assembly language. If nothing else, our walk-through of the encoding and decoding of Intel instructions will help to give you an appreciation for MASM's authors!

17.3.1   IA-32 Instruction Format

The general IA-32 machine instruction format (Figure 17–6) contains an instruction prefix byte, opcode, Mod R/M byte, scale index byte (SIB), address displacement, and immediate data. Instructions are stored in little endian order, so the prefix byte is located at the instruction's starting address. Every instruction has an opcode, but the remaining fields are optional. Few instructions contain all fields; on average, most instructions are 2 or 3 bytes. Here is a quick summary of the fields:

- The **instruction prefix** overrides default operand sizes.
- The **opcode** (operation code) identifies a specific variant of an instruction. The ADD instruction, for example, has nine different opcodes, depending on the parameter types used.
- The **Mod R/M** field identifies the addressing mode and operands. The notation "R/M" stands for *register* and *mode*. Table 17-18 describes the Mod field, and Table 17-19 describes the R/M field for 16-bit applications when Mod = 10 binary.

- The **scale index byte** (SIB) is used to calculate offsets of array indexes.
- The **address displacement** field holds an operand's offset, or it can be added to base and index registers in addressing modes such as base-displacement or base-index-displacement.
- The **immediate data** field holds constant operands.

Figure 17–6   Intel 8086/8088 Instruction Format.

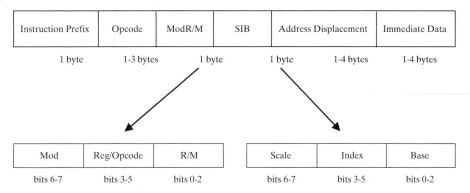

Table 17-18   Mod Field Values.

Mod	Displacement
00	DISP = 0, disp-low and disp-high are absent (unless r/m = 110).
01	DISP = disp-low sign-extended to 16 bits; disp-high is absent.
10	DISP = disp-high and disp-low are used.
11	R/M field contains a register number.

Table 17-19   16-Bit R/M Field Values (for Mod = 10).

R/M	Effective Address
000	[BX + SI] + D16[a]
001	[BX + DI] + D16
010	[BP + SI] + D16
011	[BP + DI] + D16
100	[SI] + D16
101	[DI] + D16
110	[BP] + D16
111	[BX] + D16

[a]D16 indicates a 16-bit displacement.

17.3.2   Single-Byte Instructions

The simplest type of instruction is one with either no operand or an implied operand. Such instructions require only the opcode field, the value of which is predetermined by the processor's instruction set. Table 17-20 lists a few common single-byte instructions. It might appear that the INC DX instruction slipped into the table by mistake, but the designers of the Intel instruction set decided to supply unique opcodes for certain commonly used instructions. As a consequence, register increments are optimized for code size and execution speed.

Table 17-20   Single-Byte Instructions.

Instruction	Opcode
AAA	37
AAS	3F
CBW	98
LODSB	AC
XLAT	D7
INC DX	42

17.3.3   Move Immediate to Register

Immediate operands (constants) are appended to instructions in little endian order (lowest byte first). We will focus first on instructions that move immediate values to registers, avoiding the complications of memory-addressing modes for the moment. The encoding format of a MOV instruction that moves an immediate word into a register is **B8 +*rw* *dw***, where the opcode byte value is **B8 + *rw***, indicating that a register number (0 through 7) is added to B8; *dw* is the immediate word operand, low byte first. (Register numbers used in opcodes are listed in Table 17-21.) All numeric values in the following examples are hexadecimal:

Table 17-21   Register Numbers (8/16 bit).

Register	Code
AX/AL	0
CX/CL	1
DX/DL	2
BX/BL	3
SP/AH	4
BP/CH	5
SI/DH	6
DI/BH	7

Example: *PUSH CX*   The machine instruction is **51**. The encoding steps are as follows:

1. The opcode for PUSH with a 16-bit register operand is **50**.
2. The register number for CX is 1, so add 1 to 50, producing opcode **51**.

Example: *MOV AX,1*   The machine instruction is **B8 01 00** (hexadecimal). Here's how it is encoded:

1. The opcode for moving an immediate value to a 16-bit register is **B8**.
2. The register number for AX is 0, so 0 is added to B8 (refer to Table 17-21).
3. The immediate operand (0001) is appended to the instruction in little endian order (01, 00).

Example: *MOV BX, 1234h*   The machine instruction is **BB 34 12**. The encoding steps are as follows:

1. The opcode for moving an immediate value to a 16-bit register is **B8**.
2. The register number for BX is 3, so add 3 to B8, producing opcode **BB**.
3. The immediate operand bytes are **34 12**.

For practice, we suggest you hand-assemble a few MOV immediate instructions to get the hang of it, and then check your results by inspecting code generated by MASM in a source listing file.

17.3.4   Register-Mode Instructions

In instructions using register operands, the Mod R/M byte contains a 3-bit identifier for each register operand. Table 17-22 lists the bit encodings for registers. The choice of 8-bit or 16-bit register depends on bit 0 of the opcode field: 1 indicates a 16-bit register, and 0 indicates an 8-bit register.

Table 17-22   Identifying Registers in the Mod R/M Field.

R/M	Register	R/M	Register
000	AX or AL	100	SP or AH
001	CX or CL	101	BP or CH
010	DX or DL	110	SI or DH
011	BX or BL	111	DI or BH

For example, the machine language for **MOV AX, BX** is **89 D8**. The Intel encoding of a 16-bit MOV from a register to any other operand is **89/r**, where/r indicates that a Mod R/M byte follows the opcode. The Mod R/M byte is made up of three fields (mod, reg, and r/m). A Mod R/M value of D8, for example, contains the following fields:

mod	reg	r/m
11	011	000

• Bits 6 to 7 are the *mod* field, which identifies the addressing mode. The mod field is 11, indicating that the r/m field contains a register number.
• Bits 3 to 5 are the *reg* field, which identifies the source operand. In our example, BX is register 011.
• Bits 0 to 2 are the *r/m* field, which identifies the destination operand. In our example, AX is register 000.

Table 17-23 lists a few more examples that use 8-bit and 16-bit register operands.

Table 17-23   Sample MOV Instruction Encodings, Register Operands.

Instruction	Opcode	mod	reg	r/m
mov ax,dx	8B	11	000	010
mov al,dl	8A	11	000	010
mov cx,dx	8B	11	001	010
mov cl,dl	8A	11	001	010

17.3.5   IA-32 Processor Operand-Size Prefix

Let us now turn our attention to instruction encoding for 32-bit Intel processors (IA-32). Some machine language instructions generated for IA-32 processors begin with an operand-size prefix (66h) that overrides the default segment attribute for the instruction it modifies. The question is, why have an instruction prefix? When the 8088/8086 instruction set was created, almost all 256 possible opcodes were used to handle instructions using 8- and 16-bit operands. When Intel introduced 32-bit processors, they had to find a way to invent new opcodes to handle 32-bit operands, yet retain compatibility with older processors. For programs targeting 16-bit processors, they added a prefix byte to any instruction that used 32-bit operands. For programs targeting 32-bit processors, 32-bit operands were the default, so a prefix byte was added to any instruction using 16-bit operands. Eight-bit operands need no prefix.

Example: 16-Bit Operands We can see how prefix bytes work in 16-bit mode by assembling the MOV instructions listed earlier in Table 17-23. The .286 directive indicates the target processor for the compiled code, assuring (for one thing) that no 32-bit registers are used. Alongside each MOV instruction, we show its instruction encoding:

```
.model small
.286
.stack 100h
.code
main PROC
        mov     ax,dx                   ; 8B C2
        mov     al,dl                   ; 8A C2
```

(We did not use the *Irvine16.inc* file because it targets the 386 processor.)

Let's assemble the same instructions for a 32-bit processor, using the .386 directive; the default operand size is 32 bits. We will include both 16-bit and 32-bit operands. The first MOV instruction (EAX, EDX) needs no prefix because it uses 32-bit operands. The second MOV (AX, DX) requires an operand-size prefix (66) because it uses 16-bit operands:

```
.model small
.386
.stack 100h
.code
main PROC
        mov     eax,edx                 ; 8B C2
        mov     ax,dx                   ; 66 8B C2
        mov     al,dl                   ; 8A C2
```

17.3.6 Memory-Mode Instructions

If the Mod R/M byte were only used for identifying register operands, Intel instruction encoding would be relatively simple. In fact, Intel assembly language has a wide variety of memory-addressing modes, causing the encoding of the Mod R/M byte to be fairly complex. (The IA-32 instruction set's complexity is a common source of criticism by proponents of reduced instruction set computer designs.)

Exactly 256 different combinations of operands can be specified by the Mod R/M byte. Table 17-24 lists the Mod R/M bytes (in hexadecimal) for Mod 00. (The complete table can be found in the *IA-32 Intel Architecture Software Developer's Manual*, Vol. 2A.) Here's how the encoding of Mod R/M bytes works: The two bits in the **Mod** column indicate groups of addressing modes. Mod 00, for example, has eight possible **R/M** values (000 to 111 binary) that identify operand types listed in the **Effective Address** column.

Suppose we want to encode **MOV AX,[SI]**; the Mod bits are 00, and the R/M bits are 100 binary. We know from Table 17-19 that AX is register number 000 binary, so the complete Mod R/M byte is 00 000 100 binary or 04 hexadecimal:

mod	reg	r/m
00	000	100

The hexadecimal byte 04 appears in the column marked AX, in row 5.

The Mod R/M byte for **MOV [SI],AL** is the same (04h) because register AL is also register number 000. Let's encode the instruction **MOV [SI],AL**. The opcode for a move from an 8-bit register is **88**. The Mod R/M byte is 04h, and the machine instruction is **88 04**.

Table 17-24   Partial List of Mod R/M Bytes (16-bit Segments).

Byte:		AL	CL	DL	BL	AH	CH	DH	BH	
Word:		**AX**	**CX**	**DX**	**BX**	**SP**	**BP**	**SI**	**DI**	
Register ID:		**000**	**001**	**010**	**011**	**100**	**101**	**110**	**111**	
Mod	**R/M**				Mod R/M Value					**Effective Address**
00	000	00	08	10	18	20	28	30	38	[BX + SI]
	001	01	09	11	19	21	29	31	39	[BX + DI]
	010	02	0A	12	1A	22	2A	32	3A	[BP + SI]
	011	03	0B	13	1B	23	2B	33	3B	[BP + DI]
	100	04	0C	14	1C	24	2C	34	3C	[SI]
	101	05	0D	15	1D	25	2D	35	3D	[DI]
	110	06	0E	16	1E	26	2E	36	3E	16-bit displacement
	111	07	0F	17	1F	27	2F	37	3F	[BX]

MOV Instruction Examples

All the instruction formats and opcodes for 8-bit and 16-bit MOV instructions are shown in Table 17-25. Tables 17-26 and 17-27 provide supplemental information about abbreviations used in Table 17-25. Use these tables as references when hand-assembling MOV instructions. (For more details, refer to the *IA-32 Intel Architecture Software Developer's Manual*, Vol. 2A.)

Table 17-25   MOV Instruction Opcodes.

Opcode	Instruction	Description
88/r	MOV eb,rb	Move byte register into EA byte
89/r	MOV ew,rw	Move word register into EA word
8A/r	MOV rb,eb	Move EA byte into byte register
8B/r	MOV rw,ew	Move EA word into word register
8C/0	MOV ew,ES	Move ES into EA word
8C/1	MOV ew,CS	Move CS into EA word
8C/2	MOV ew,SS	Move SS into EA word
8C/3	MOV DS,ew	Move DS into EA word
8E/0	MOV ES,mw	Move memory word into ES
8E/0	MOV ES,rw	Move word register into ES
8E/2	MOV SS,mw	Move memory word into SS

Table 17-25   *(Continued)*

Opcode	Instruction	Description
8E/2	MOV SS,rw	Move register word into SS
8E/3	MOV DS,mw	Move memory word into DS
8E/3	MOV DS,rw	Move word register into DS
A0 dw	MOV AL,xb	Move byte variable (offset dw) into AL
A1 dw	MOV AX,xw	Move word variable (offset dw) into AX
A2 dw	MOV xb,AL	Move AL into byte variable (offset dw)
A3 dw	MOV xw,AX	Move AX into word register (offset dw)
B0 +rb db	MOV rb,db	Move immediate byte into byte register
B8 +rw dw	MOV rw,dw	Move immediate word into word register
C6 /0 db	MOV eb,db	Move immediate byte into EA byte
C7 /0 dw	MOV ew,dw	Move immediate word into EA word

Table 17-26   Key to Instruction Opcodes.

/n:	A Mod R/M byte follows the opcode, possibly followed by immediate and displacement fields. The digit n (0–7) is the value of the reg field of the Mod R/M byte.
/r:	A Mod R/M byte follows the opcode, possibly followed by immediate and displacement fields.
db:	An immediate byte operand follows the opcode and Mod R/M bytes.
dw:	An immediate word operand follows the opcode and Mod R/M bytes.
+rb:	A register code (0–7) for an 8-bit register, which is added to the preceding hexadecimal byte to form an 8-bit opcode.
+rw:	A register code (0–7) for a 16-bit register, which is added to the preceding hexadecimal byte to form an 8-bit opcode.

Table 17-27   Key to Instruction Operands.

db	A signed value between −128 and +127. If combined with a word operand, this value is sign-extended.
dw	An immediate word value that is an operand of the instruction.
eb	A byte-sized operand, either register or memory.
ew	A word-sized operand, either register or memory.
rb	An 8-bit register identified by the value (0–7).
rw	A 16-bit register identified by the value (0–7).
xb	A simple byte memory variable without a base or index register.
xw	A simple word memory variable without a base or index register.

Table 17-28 contains a few additional examples of MOV instructions that you can assemble by hand and compare to the machine code shown in the table. We assume that **myWord** begins at offset 0102h.

Table 17-28   Sample MOV Instructions, with Machine Code.

Instruction	Machine Code	Addressing Mode
mov ax,myWord	A1 02 01	direct (optimized for AX)
mov myWord,bx	89 1E 02 01	direct
mov [di],bx	89 1D	indexed
mov [bx+2],ax	89 47 02	base-disp
mov [bx+si],ax	89 00	base-indexed
mov word ptr [bx+di+2],1234h	C7 41 02 34 12	base-indexed-disp

17.3.7   Section Review

1. Provide opcodes for the following MOV instructions:

```
.data
myByte BYTE ?
myWord WORD ?
.code
mov   ax,@data
mov   ds,ax            ; a.
mov   ax,bx            ; b.
mov   bl,al            ; c.
mov   al,[si]          ; d.
mov   myByte,al        ; e.
mov   myWord,ax        ; f.
```

2. Provide opcodes for the following MOV instructions:

```
.data
myByte BYTE ?
myWord WORD ?
.code
mov   ax,@data
mov   ds,ax
mov   es,ax            ; a.
mov   dl,bl            ; b.
mov   bl,[di]          ; c.
mov   ax,[si+2]        ; d.
mov   al,myByte        ; e.
mov   dx,myWord        ; f.
```

3. Provide Mod R/M bytes for the following MOV instructions:

```
.data
array WORD 5 DUP(?)
.code
mov   ax,@data
mov   ds,ax            ; a.
mov   dl,bl            ; b.
mov   bl,[di]          ; c.
mov   ax,[si+2]        ; d.
mov   ax,array[si]     ; e.
mov   array[di],ax     ; f.
```

4. Provide Mod R/M bytes for the following MOV instructions:

    ```
    .data
    array WORD 5 DUP(?)
    .code
    mov   ax,@data
    mov   ds,ax
    mov   BYTE PTR array,5              ; a.
    mov   dx,[bp+5]                     ; b.
    mov   [di],bx                       ; c.
    mov   [di+2],dx                     ; d.
    mov   array[si+2],ax               ; e.
    mov   array[bx+di],ax             ; f.
    ```

5. Assemble the following instructions by hand and write the hexadecimal machine language bytes for
    each labeled instruction. Assume that **val1** is located at offset 0. Where 16-bit values are used, the
    bytes must appear in little endian order:

    ```
    .data
    val1  BYTE   5
    val2  WORD   256
    .code
    mov   ax,@data
    mov   ds,ax                        ; a.
    mov   al,val1                      ; b.
    mov   cx,val2                      ; c.
    mov   dx,OFFSET val1               ; d.
    mov   dl,2                         ; e.
    mov   bx,1000h                     ; f.
    ```

17.4   Chapter Summary

A binary floating-point number contains three components: a sign, a significand, and an exponent.
Intel processors use three floating-point binary storage formats specified in the Standard 754-1985 for
Binary Floating-Point Arithmetic produced by the IEEE organization:

- A 32-bit single precision value uses 1 bit for the sign, 8 bits for the exponent, and 23 bits for the
  fractional part of the significand.
- A 64-bit double precision value uses 1 bit for the sign, 11 bits for the exponent, and 52 bits for the
  fractional part of the significand.
- An 80-bit double extended precision value uses 1 bit for the sign, 16 bits for the exponent, and 63
  bits for the fractional part of the significand.

If the sign bit equals 1, the number is negative; if the bit is 0, the number is positive.

The significand of a floating-point number consists of the decimal digits to the left and right of the
decimal point.

Not all real numbers between 0 and 1 can be represented by floating-point numbers in a computer
because there are only a finite number of available bits.

Normalized finite numbers are all the nonzero finite values that can be encoded in a normalized
real number between zero and infinity. Positive infinity ($+\infty$) represents the maximum positive real
number, and negative infinity ($-\infty$) represents the maximum negative real number. *NaNs* are bit patterns that do not represent valid floating-point numbers.

The Intel 8086 processor was designed to handle only integer arithmetic, so Intel produced a separate 8087 *floating-point coprocessor* chip that was inserted on the computer's motherboard along with
the 8086. With the advent of the Intel486, floating-point operations were integrated into the main
CPU and renamed the *Floating-Point Unit* (FPU) .

The FPU has eight individually addressable 80-bit registers, named R0 through R7, arranged in the form of a register stack. Floating-point operands are stored in the FPU stack in extended real format while being used in calculations. Memory operands are also used in calculations. When the FPU stores the result of an arithmetic operation in memory, it translates the result into one of the following formats: integer, long integer, single precision, double precision, or binary-coded decimal.

Intel floating-point instruction mnemonics begin with the letter F to distinguish them from CPU instructions. The second letter of an instruction (often B or I) indicates how a memory operand is to be interpreted: B indicates a binary-coded decimal (BCD) operand, and I indicates a binary integer operand. If neither is specified, the memory operand is assumed to be in real-number format.

The Intel 8086 processor was first in a line of processors using a *Complex Instruction Set Computer* (CISC) design. The instruction set is large, and includes a wide variety of memory-addressing, shifting, arithmetic, data movement, and logical operations.

To *encode* an instruction means to convert an assembly language instruction and its operands into machine code. To *decode* an instruction means to convert a machine code instruction into an assembly language instruction and its operands.

The IA-32 machine instruction format contains an optional prefix byte, an opcode, a optional Mod R/M byte, optional immediate bytes, and optional memory displacement bytes. Few instructions contain all of the fields. The prefix byte overrides the default operand size for the target processor. The opcode byte contains the instruction's unique operation code. The Mod R/M field identifies the addressing mode and operands. In instructions using register operands, the Mod R/M byte contains a 3-bit identifier for each register operand.

17.5 Programming Exercises

1. Floating-Point Comparison

Implement the following C++ code in assembly language. Substitute calls to WriteString for the printf() function calls:

```
double X;
double Y;
if( X < Y )
    printf("X is lower\n");
else
    printf("X is not lower\n");
```

(Use Irvine32 library routines for console output, rather than calling the Standard C library's printf function.) Run the program several times, assigning a range of values to X and Y that test your program's logic.

2. Display Floating-Point Binary

Write a procedure that receives a single-precision floating-point binary value and displays it in the following format: sign: display + or −; significand: binary floating-point, prefixed by "**1.**"; exponent: display in decimal, unbiased, preceded by the letter E and the exponent's sign. Sample:

```
.data
sample REAL4 -1.75
```

Displayed output:

```
-1.11000000000000000000000 E+0
```

3. Set Rounding Modes

(Requires knowledge of macros.) Write a macro that sets the FPU rounding mode. The single input parameter is a two-letter code:

- RE: Round to nearest even
- RD: Round down toward negative infinity
- FU: Round up toward positive infinity
- RZ: Round toward zero (truncate)

Sample macro calls (case should not matter):

```
mRound Re
mRound rd
mRound RU
mRound rZ
```

Write a short test program that uses the FIST (store integer) instruction to test each of the possible rounding modes.

4. Expression Evaluation

Write a program that evaluates the following arithmetic expression:

$$((A + B) / C) * ((D - A) + E)$$

Assign test values to the variables and display the resulting value.

5. Area of a Circle

Write a program that prompts the user for the radius of a circle. Calculate and display the circle's area. Use the ReadFloat and WriteFloat procedures from the book's library. Use the FLDPI instruction to load π onto the register stack.

6. Quadratic Formula

Prompt the user for coefficients a, b, and c of a polynomial in the form $ax^2 + bx + c = 0$. Calculate and display the real roots of the polynomial using the *quadratic formula*. If any root is imaginary, display an appropriate message.

7. Showing Register Status Values

The Tag register (Section 17.2.1) indicates the type of contents in each FPU register, using 2 bits for each (Figure 17–7). You can load the Tag word by calling the FSTENV instruction, which fills in the following protected-mode structure (defined in *Irvine32.inc*):

```
FPU_ENVIRON STRUCT
        controlWord     WORD ?
        ALIGN DWORD
        statusWord      WORD ?
        ALIGN DWORD
        tagWord         WORD ?
        ALIGN DWORD
        instrPointerOffset      DWORD ?
        instrPointerSelector    DWORD ?
        operandPointerOffset    DWORD ?
        operandPointerSelector  WORD ?
        WORD ?                          ; not used
    FPU_ENVIRON ENDS
```

(A structure by the same name is defined *Irvine16.inc* with a slightly different format for real-address mode programming.)

Write a program that pushes two or more values on the FPU stack, displays the stack by calling ShowFPUStack, displays the Tag value of each FPU data register, and displays the register number that corresponds to ST(0). (For the latter, call the FSTSW instruction to save the status word in a 16-bit integer variable, and extract the stack TOP indicator from bits 11 through 13.) Use the following sample output as a guide:

```
------ FPU Stack ------
ST(0): +1.5000000E+000
ST(1): +2.0000000E+000

R0  is empty
R1  is empty
R2  is empty
R3  is empty
R4  is empty
R5  is empty
R6  is valid
R7  is valid

ST(0) = R6
```

From the sample output, we can see that ST(0) is R6, and therefore ST(1) is R7. Both contain valid floating-point numbers.

Fɪɢᴜʀᴇ 17–7   Tag Word Values.

15   0

| R7 | R6 | R5 | R4 | R3 | R2 | R1 | R0 |

TAG values:
00 = valid
01 = zero
10 = special (Nan, unsupported, infinity, or denormal)
11 = empty

End Notes

1. *IA-32 Intel Architecture Software Developer's Manual*, Vol. 1, Chapter 4. See also www.grouper.ieee.org/groups/ 754/

2. *IA-32 Intel Architecture Software Developer's Manual*, Vol. 1, Section 4.8.3.

3. From Harvey Nice of DePaul University.

4. MASM uses a no-parameter FADD to perform the same operation as Intel's no-parameter FADDP.

5. MASM uses a no-parameter FSUB to perform the same operation as Intel's no-parameter FSUBP.

6. MASM uses a no-parameter FMUL to perform the same operation as Intel's no-parameter FMULP.

7. MASM uses a no-parameter FDIV to perform the same operation as Intel's no-parameter FDIVP.

A

MASM Reference

A.1   Introduction

The Microsoft MASM 6.11 manuals were last printed in 1992, and consisted of three volumes:

- *Programmers Guide*
- *Reference*
- *Environment and Tools*

Unfortunately, the printed manuals have not been available for many years, but Microsoft supplies electronic copies of the manuals (MS-Word files) in its *Platform SDK* package. The printed manuals are definitely collectors' items.

The information in this chapter was excerpted from Chapters 1 to 3 of the *Reference* manual, with updates from the MASM 6.14 *readme.txt* file. The Microsoft license agreement supplied with this book entitles the reader to a single copy of the software and acompanying documentation, which we have, in part, printed here.

Syntax Notation   Throughout this appendix, a consistent syntax notation is used. Words in all capital letters indicate a MASM reserved word that may appear in your program in either uppercase or lowercase letters. In the following example, DATA is a reserved word:

    .DATA

Words in italics indicate a defined term or category. In the following example, *number* refers to an integer constant:

    ALIGN [[*number*]]

When double brackets ⟦ .. ⟧ surround an item, the item is optional. In the following example, *text* is optional:

   ⟦ *text* ⟧

When a vertical separator | appears between items in a list of two or more items, you must select one of the items. The following example indicates a choice between NEAR and FAR:

   NEAR | FAR

An ellipsis (. . .) indicates repetition of the last item in a list. In the next example, the comma followed by an *initializer* may repeat multiple times:

   ⟦ *name* ⟧ BYTE *initializer* ⟦ , *initializer* ⟧ . . .

A.2   MASM Reserved Words

$	PARITY?
?	PASCAL
@B	QWORD
@F	REAL4
ADDR	REAL8
BASIC	REAL10
BYTE	SBYTE
C	SDWORD
CARRY?	SIGN?
DWORD	STDCALL
FAR	SWORD
FAR16	SYSCALL
FORTRAN	TBYTE
FWORD	VARARG
NEAR	WORD
NEAR16	ZERO?
OVERFLOW?	

A.3   Register Names

AH	CR0	DR1	EBX	SI
AL	CR2	DR2	ECX	SP
AX	CR3	DR3	EDI	SS
BH	CS	DR6	EDX	ST
BL	CX	DR7	ES	TR3
BP	DH	DS	ESI	TR4
BX	DI	DX	ESP	TR5
CH	DL	EAX	FS	TR6
CL	DR0	EBP	GS	TR7

A.4 Microsoft Assembler (ML)

The ML program (*ML.EXE*) assembles and links one or more assembly language source files. The syntax is

ML [[*options*]] *filename* [[[*options*]] *filename*]]... [[**/link** *linkoptions*]]

The only required parameter is at least one *filename*, the name of a source file written in assembly language. The following command, for example, assembles the source file **AddSub.asm** and produces the object file *AddSub.obj*:

```
ML -c AddSub.asm
```

The *options* parameter consists of zero or more command-line options, each starting with a slash (/) or dash (–). Multiple options must be separated by at least one space. Table A-1 lists the complete set of command-line options. The command-line options are case sensitive.

Table A-1   ML Command-Line Options.

Option	Action
/AT	Enables tiny-memory-model support. Enables error messages for code constructs that violate the requirements for .COM format files. Note that this is not equivalent to the .MODEL TINY directive.
/Bl*filename*	Selects an alternate linker.
/c	Assembles only. Does not link.
/coff	Generates an object file in *Microsoft Common Object File Format*.
/Cp	Preserves case of all user identifiers.
/Cu	Maps all identifiers to uppercase.
/Cx	Preserves case in public and external symbols (default).
/D*symbol* [[=*value*]]	Defines a text macro with the given name. If *value* is missing, it is blank. Multiple tokens separated by spaces must be enclosed in quotation marks.
/EP	Generates a preprocessed source listing (sent to STDOUT). See /Sf.
/F*hexnum*	Sets stack size to *hexnum* bytes (this is the same as /link /STACK:*number*). The value must be expressed in hexadecimal notation. There must be a space between /F and *hexnum*.
/Fe*filename*	Names the executable file.
/Fl[[*filename*]]	Generates an assembled code listing. See /Sf.
/Fm[[*filename*]]	Creates a linker map file.
/Fo*filename*	Names an object file.
/FPi	Generates emulator fixups for floating-point arithmetic (mixed-language only).
/Fr[[*filename*]]	Generates a Source Browser .SBR file.
/FR[[*filename*]]	Generates an extended form of a Source Browser .SBR file.
/Gc	Specifies use of FORTRAN- or Pascal-style function calling and naming conventions.
/Gd	Specifies use of C-style function calling and naming conventions.

Option	Action
/Gz	Use STDCALL calling connections.
/H *number*	Restricts external names to *number* significant characters. The default is 31 characters.
/help	Calls QuickHelp for help on ML.
/I *pathname*	Sets path for include file. A maximum of 10 /I options is allowed.
/link	Linker options and libraries.
/nologo	Suppresses messages for successful assembly.
/omf	Generate an OMF (Microsoft Object Module Format) file. This format is required by the older 16-bit Microsoft Linker (LINK16.EXE).
/Sa	Turns on listing of all available information.
/Sc	Adds instruction timings to listing file.
/Sf	Adds first-pass listing to listing file.
/Sg	Causes MASM-generated assembly code to appear in the source listing file. Use this, for example, if you want to see how .IF, and .ELSE directives work.
/Sl *width*	Sets the line width of source listing in characters per line. Range is 60 to 255 or 0. Default is 0. Same as PAGE *width*.
/Sn	Turns off symbol table when producing a listing.
/Sp *length*	Sets the page length of source listing in lines per page. Range is 10 to 255 or 0. Default is 0. Same as PAGE *length*.
/Ss *text*	Specifies text for source listing. Same as SUBTITLE *text*.
/St *text*	Specifies title for source listing. Same as TITLE *text*.
/Sx	Turns on false conditionals in listing.
/Ta *filename*	Assembles source file whose name does not end with the .ASM extension.
/w	Same as /W0.
/W*level*	Sets the warning level, where *level* = 0, 1, 2, or 3.
/WX	Returns an error code if warnings are generated.
/X	Ignore INCLUDE Environment path.
/Zd	Generates line-number information in object file.
/Zf	Makes all symbols public.
/Zi	Generates CodeView information in object file.
/Zm	Enables M510 option for maximum compatibility with MASM 5.1.
/Zp[[*alignment*]]	Packs structures on the specified byte boundary. The *alignment* may be 1, 2, or 4.
/Zs	Performs a syntax check only.
/?	Displays a summary of ML command-line syntax.
/error Report	Report internal assembler errors to Microsoft.

A.5   MASM Directives

name* = *expression

Assigns the numeric value of *expression* to *name*. The symbol may be redefined later.

.186

Enables assembly of instructions for the 80186 processor; disables assembly of instructions introduced with later processors. Also enables 8087 instructions.

.286

Enables assembly of nonprivileged instructions for the 80286 processor; disables assembly of instructions introduced with later processors. Also enables 80287 instructions.

.286P

Enables assembly of all instructions (including privileged) for the 80286 processor; disables assembly of instructions introduced with later processors. Also enables 80287 instructions.

.287

Enables assembly of instructions for the 80287 coprocessor; disables assembly of instructions introduced with later coprocessors.

.386

Enables assembly of nonprivileged instructions for the 80386 processor; disables assembly of instructions introduced with later processors. Also enables 80387 instructions.

.386P

Enables assembly of all instructions (including privileged) for the 80386 processor; disables assembly of instructions introduced with later processors. Also enables 80387 instructions.

.387

Enables assembly of instructions for the 80387 coprocessor.

.486

Enables assembly of nonprivileged instructions for the 80486 processor.

.486P

Enables assembly of all instructions (including privileged) for the 80486 processor.

.586

Enables assembly of nonprivileged instructions for the Pentium processor.

.586P

Enables assembly of all instructions (including privileged) for the Pentium processor.

.686

Enables assembly of nonprivileged instructions for the Pentium Pro processor.

.686P

Enables assembly of all instructions (including privileged) for the Pentium Pro processor.

.8086

Enables assembly of 8086 instructions (and the identical 8088 instructions); disables assembly of instructions introduced with later processors. Also enables 8087 instructions. This is the default mode for processors.

.8087

Enables assembly of 8087 instructions; disables assembly of instructions introduced with later coprocessors. This is the default mode for coprocessors.

ALIAS <alias> = <actual-name>

Maps an old function name to a new name. *Alias* is the alternate or alias name, and *actual-name* is the actual name of the function or procedure. The angle brackets are required. The ALIAS directive can be used for creating libraries that allow the linker (LINK) to map an old function to a new function.

ALIGN [[*number*]]

Aligns the next variable or instruction on a byte that is a multiple of *number*.

.ALPHA

Orders segments alphabetically.

ASSUME *segregister:name* [[*, segregister:name*]]. . .
    ASSUME *dataregister:type* [[*, dataregister:type*]]. . .
    ASSUME *register:***ERROR** [[*, register:***ERROR**]]. . .
    ASSUME [[*register:*]] **NOTHING** [[*, register:***NOTHING**]]. . .

Enables error-checking for register values. After an **ASSUME** is put into effect, the assembler watches for changes to the values of the given registers. **ERROR** generates an error if the register is used. **NOTHING** removes register error-checking. You can combine different kinds of assumptions in one statement.

.BREAK [[**.IF** *condition*]]

Generates code to terminate a **.WHILE** or **.REPEAT** block if *condition* is true.

[[*name*]] **BYTE** *initializer* [[*, initializer*]] . . .

Allocates and optionally initializes a byte of storage for each *initializer*. Can also be used as a type specifier anywhere a type is legal.

name **CATSTR** [[*textitem1* [[*, textitem2*]] . . .]]

Concatenates text items. Each text item can be a literal string, a constant preceded by a %, or the string returned by a macro function.

.CODE [[*name*]]

When used with **.MODEL**, indicates the start of a code segment called *name* (the default segment name is _TEXT for tiny, small, compact, and flat models, or *module*_TEXT for other models).

COMM *definition* [[*, definition*]] . . .

Creates a communal variable with the attributes specified in *definition*. Each *definition* has the following form:

> [[*langtype*]] [[**NEAR | FAR**]] *label:type*[[*:count*]]

The *label* is the name of the variable. The *type* can be any type specifier (**BYTE, WORD,** and so on) or an integer specifying the number of bytes. The *count* specifies the number of data objects (one is the default).

COMMENT *delimiter* [[*text*]]

> [[*text*]]
> [[*text*]] *delimiter* [[*text*]]

Treats all *text* between or on the same line as the delimiters as a comment.

.CONST

When used with **.MODEL**, starts a constant data segment (with segment name CONST). This segment has the read-only attribute.

.CONTINUE [[**.IF** *condition*]]

Generates code to jump to the top of a **.WHILE** or **.REPEAT** block if *condition* is true.

.CREF

Enables listing of symbols in the symbol portion of the symbol table and browser file.

.DATA

When used with **.MODEL**, starts a near data segment for initialized data (segment name _DATA).

.DATA?

When used with **.MODEL**, starts a near data segment for uninitialized data (segment name _BSS).

.DOSSEG

Orders the segments according to the MS-DOS segment convention: CODE first, then segments not in DGROUP, and then segments in DGROUP. The segments in DGROUP follow this order: segments not in BSS or STACK, then BSS segments, and finally STACK segments. Primarily used for ensuring CodeView support in MASM stand-alone programs. Same as **DOSSEG**.

DOSSEG

Identical to **.DOSSEG**, which is the preferred form.

DB

Can be used to define data like **BYTE**.

DD

Can be used to define data like **DWORD**.

DF

Can be used to define data like **FWORD**.

DQ

Can be used to define data like **QWORD**.

DT

Can be used to define data like **TBYTE**.

DW

Can be used to define data like **WORD**.

[[*name*]] DWORD *initializer* [[*, initializer*]]. . .

Allocates and optionally initializes a doubleword (4 bytes) of storage for each *initializer*. Can also be used as a type specifier anywhere a type is legal.

ECHO *message*

Displays *message* to the standard output device (by default, the screen). Same as **%OUT**.

.ELSE

See **.IF**.

ELSE

Marks the beginning of an alternate block within a conditional block. See **IF**.

ELSEIF

Combines **ELSE** and **IF** into one statement. See **IF**.

ELSEIF2

ELSEIF block evaluated on every assembly pass if **OPTION:SETIF2** is **TRUE**.

END [[*address*]]

Marks the end of a module and, optionally, sets the program entry point to *address*.

.ENDIF

See **.IF**.

ENDIF

See **IF**.

ENDM

Terminates a macro or repeat block. See **MACRO, FOR, FORC, REPEAT**, or **WHILE**.

***name* ENDP**

Marks the end of procedure *name* previously begun with **PROC**. See **PROC**.

name **ENDS**

Marks the end of segment, structure, or union *name* previously begun with **SEGMENT, STRUCT, UNION**, or a simplified segment directive.

.ENDW

See **.WHILE**.

name **EQU** *expression*

Assigns numeric value of *expression* to *name*. The *name* cannot be redefined later.

name **EQU** *<text>*

Assigns specified *text* to *name*. The *name* can be assigned a different *text* later. See **TEXTEQU**.

.ERR [[*message*]]

Generates an error.

.ERR2 [[*message*]]

.ERR block evaluated on every assembly pass if **OPTION:SETIF2** is **TRUE**.

.ERRB *<textitem>* [[, *message*]]

Generates an error if *textitem* is blank.

.ERRDEF *name* [[, *message*]]

Generates an error if *name* is a previously defined label, variable, or symbol.

.ERRDIF[[**I**]] *<textitem1>*, *<textitem2>* [[, *message*]]

Generates an error if the text items are different. If **I** is given, the comparison is case insensitive.

.ERRE *expression* [[, *message*]]

Generates an error if *expression* is false (0).

.ERRIDN[[**I**]] *<textitem1>*, *<textitem2>* [[, *message*]]

Generates an error if the text items are identical. If **I** is given, the comparison is case insensitive.

.ERRNB *<textitem>* [[, *message*]]

Generates an error if *textitem* is not blank.

.ERRNDEF *name* [[, *message*]]

Generates an error if *name* has not been defined.

.ERRNZ *expression* [[, *message*]]

Generates an error if *expression* is true (nonzero).

EVEN

Aligns the next variable or instruction on an even byte.

.EXIT [[*expression*]]

Generates termination code. Returns optional *expression* to shell.

EXITM [[*textitem*]]

Terminates expansion of the current repeat or macro block and begins assembly of the next statement outside the block. In a macro function, *textitem* is the value returned.

EXTERN [[*langtype*]] *name* [[(*altid*)]] **:type** [[, [[*langtype*]] *name* [[(*altid*)]] **:type**]]. . .

Defines one or more external variables, labels, or symbols called *name* whose type is *type*. The *type* can be **ABS**, which imports *name* as a constant. Same as **EXTRN**.

EXTERNDEF [[*langtype*]] *name***:type** [[, [[*langtype*]] *name***:type**]]. . .

Defines one or more external variables, labels, or symbols called *name* whose type is *type*. If *name* is defined in the module, it is treated as **PUBLIC**. If *name* is referenced in the module, it is treated as **EXTERN**. If *name* is not referenced, it is ignored. The *type* can be **ABS**, which imports *name* as a constant. Normally used in include files.

EXTRN

See **EXTERN**.

.FARDATA [[*name*]]

When used with **.MODEL**, starts a far data segment for initialized data (segment name FAR_DATA or *name*).

.FARDATA? [[*name*]]

When used with **.MODEL**, starts a far data segment for uninitialized data (segment name FAR_BSS or *name*).

FOR parameter [[**:REQ** | **:=default**]] **, <argument** [[**, argument**]]**. . . >**
  statements
  ENDM

    Marks a block that will be repeated once for each *argument*, with the current *argument* replacing *parameter* on each repetition. Same as **IRP**.

FORC
  parameter, <string> statements
  ENDM

    Marks a block that will be repeated once for each character in *string*, with the current character replacing *parameter* on each repetition. Same as **IRPC**.

[[*name*]] **FWORD** *initializer* [[**,** *initializer*]]**. . .**

    Allocates and optionally initializes 6 bytes of storage for each *initializer*. Also can be used as a type specifier anywhere a type is legal.

GOTO *macrolabel*

    Transfers assembly to the line marked **:***macrolabel*. **GOTO** is permitted only inside **MACRO**, **FOR**, **FORC**, **REPEAT**, and **WHILE** blocks. The label must be the only directive on the line and must be preceded by a leading colon.

name **GROUP** *segment* [[**,** *segment*]]**. . .**

    Add the specified *segments* to the group called *name*. This directive has no effect when used in 32-bit flat-model programming, and will result in error when used with the /coff command-line option.

.IF *condition1*
  statements
  [[**.ELSEIF** condition2
      statements]]
  [[**.ELSE**
      statements]]
  .ENDIF

    Generates code that tests *condition1* (for example, AX > 7) and executes the *statements* if that condition is true. If an **.ELSE** follows, its statements are executed if the original condition was false. Note that the conditions are evaluated at run time.

IF expression1
  ifstatements
  [[**ELSEIF** expression2
      elseifstatements]]
  [[**ELSE**
      elsestatements]]
  ENDIF

    Grants assembly of *ifstatements* if *expression1* is true (nonzero) or *elseifstatements* if *expression1* is false (0) and *expression2* is true. The following directives may be substituted for **ELSEIF: ELSEIFB**,

ELSEIFDEF, ELSEIFDIF, ELSEIFDIFI, ELSEIFE, ELSEIFIDN, ELSEIFIDNI, ELSE-IFNB, and **ELSEIFNDEF**. Optionally, assembles *elsestatements* if the previous expression is false. Note that the expressions are evaluated at assembly time.

IF2 *expression*

> **IF** block is evaluated on every assembly pass if **OPTION:SETIF2** is **TRUE**. See **IF** for complete syntax.

IFB *textitem*

> Grants assembly if *textitem* is blank. See **IF** for complete syntax.

IFDEF *name*

> Grants assembly if *name* is a previously defined label, variable, or symbol. See **IF** for complete syntax.

IFDIF[[I]] *textitem1, textitem2*

> Grants assembly if the text items are different. If **I** is given, the comparison is case insensitive. See **IF** for complete syntax.

IFE *expression*

> Grants assembly if *expression* is false (0). See **IF** for complete syntax.

IFIDN[[I]] *textitem1, textitem2*

> Grants assembly if the text items are identical. If **I** is given, the comparison is case insensitive. See **IF** for complete syntax.

IFNB *textitem*

> Grants assembly if *textitem* is not blank. See **IF** for complete syntax.

IFNDEF *name*

> Grants assembly if *name* has not been defined. See **IF** for complete syntax.

INCLUDE *filename*

> Inserts source code from the source file given by *filename* into the current source file during assembly. The *filename* must be enclosed in angle brackets if it includes a backslash, semicolon, greater-than symbol, less-than symbol, single quotation mark, or double quotation mark.

INCLUDELIB *libraryname*

> Informs the linker that the current module should be linked with *libraryname*. The *libraryname* must be enclosed in angle brackets if it includes a backslash, semicolon, greater-than symbol, less-than symbol, single quotation mark, or double quotation mark.

name **INSTR** [[*position,*]] *textitem1, textitem2*

> Finds the first occurrence of *textitem2* in *textitem1*. The starting *position* is optional. Each text item can be a literal string, a constant preceded by a %, or the string returned by a macro function.

INVOKE *expression* [[*, arguments*]]

> Calls the procedure at the address given by *expression*, passing the arguments on the stack or in registers according to the standard calling conventions of the language type. Each argument passed to the procedure may be an expression, a register pair, or an address expression (an expression preceded by **ADDR**).

IRP

> See **FOR**.

IRPC

> See **FORC**.

name **LABEL** *type*

> Creates a new label by assigning the current location-counter value and the given *type* to *name*.

name **LABEL** [[**NEAR | FAR | PROC**]] **PTR** [[*type*]]

> Creates a new label by assigning the current location-counter value and the given *type* to *name*.

.K3D

Enables assembly of K3D instructions.

.LALL

See **.LISTMACROALL**.

.LFCOND

See **.LISTIF**.

.LIST

Starts listing of statements. This is the default.

.LISTALL

Starts listing of all statements. Equivalent to the combination of **.LIST**, **.LISTIF**, and **.LISTMAC-ROALL**.

.LISTIF

Starts listing of statements in false conditional blocks. Same as **.LFCOND**.

.LISTMACRO

Starts listing of macro expansion statements that generate code or data. This is the default. Same as **.XALL**.

.LISTMACROALL

Starts listing of all statements in macros. Same as **.LALL**.

LOCAL *localname* [[, *localname*]]. . .

Within a macro, **LOCAL** defines labels that are unique to each instance of the macro.

LOCAL *label* [[[*count*]]] [[:*type*]] [[, *label* [[[*count*]]] [[*type*]]]]. . .

Within a procedure definition (**PROC**), **LOCAL** creates stack-based variables that exist for the duration of the procedure. The *label* may be a simple variable or an array containing *count* elements.

name **MACRO** [[*parameter* [[:REQ | :=*default* | :VARARG]]]]. . .

   statements

   ENDM [[*value*]]

      Marks a macro block called *name* and establishes *parameter* placeholders for arguments passed when the macro is called. A macro function returns *value* to the calling statement.

.MMX

Enables assembly of MMX instructions.

.MODEL *memorymodel* [[, *langtype*]] [[, *stackoption*]]

Initializes the program memory model. The *memorymodel* can be **TINY, SMALL, COMPACT, MEDIUM, LARGE, HUGE**, or **FLAT**. The *langtype* can be **C, BASIC, FORTRAN, PASCAL, SYSCALL**, or **STDCALL**. The *stackoption* can be **NEARSTACK** or **FARSTACK**.

NAME *modulename*

Ignored.

.NO87

Disallows assembly of all floating-point instructions.

.NOCREF [[*name*[[, *name*]]. . .]]

Suppresses listing of symbols in the symbol table and browser file. If names are specified, only the given names are suppressed. Same as **.XCREF**.

.NOLIST

Suppresses program listing. Same as **.XLIST**.

.NOLISTIF

Suppresses listing of conditional blocks whose condition evaluates to false (0). This is the default. Same as **.SFCOND**.

.NOLISTMACRO

Suppresses listing of macro expansions. Same as **.SALL**.

OPTION *optionlist*

Enables and disables features of the assembler. Available options include **CASEMAP, DOT-NAME, NODOTNAME, EMULATOR, NOEMULATOR, EPILOGUE, EXPR16, EXPR32, LANGUAGE, LJMP, NOLJMP, M510, NOM510, NOKEYWORD, NOSIGNEXTEND, OFFSET, OLDMACROS, NOOLDMACROS, OLDSTRUCTS, NOOLDSTRUCTS, PROC, PROLOGUE, READONLY, NOREADONLY, SCOPED, NOSCOPED, SEGMENT,** and **SETIF2**.

ORG *expression*

Sets the location counter to *expression*.

%OUT

See **ECHO**.

[[*name*]] **OWORD** *initializer* [[*, initializer*]]. . .

Allocates and optionally initializes an octalword (16 bytes) of storage for each *initializer*. Can also be used as a type specifier anywhere a type is legal. This data type is used primarily by Streaming SIMD instructions; it holds an array of four 4-byte reals.

PAGE [[[[*length*]], *width*]]

Sets line *length* and character *width* of the program listing. If no arguments are given, generates a page break.

PAGE+

Increments the section number and resets the page number to 1.

POPCONTEXT *context*

Restores part or all of the current *context* (saved by the **PUSHCONTEXT** directive). The *context* can be **ASSUMES, RADIX, LISTING, CPU,** or **ALL**.

label **PROC** [[*distance*]] [[*langtype*]] [[*visibility*]] [[*<prologuearg>*]]
    [[**USES** *reglist*]] [[*, parameter* [[*:tag*]]]]. . .
    statements
    label **ENDP**

Marks start and end of a procedure block called *label*. The statements in the block can be called with the **CALL** instruction or **INVOKE** directive.

label **PROTO** [[*distance*]] [[*langtype*]] [[*, * [[*parameter*]]*:tag*]]. . .

Prototypes a function.

PUBLIC [[*langtype*]] *name* [[*, * [[*langtype*]] *name*]]. . .

Makes each variable, label, or absolute symbol specified as *name* available to all other modules in the program.

PURGE *macroname* [[*, macroname*]]. . .

Deletes the specified macros from memory.

PUSHCONTEXT *context*

Saves part or all of the current *context*: segment register assumes, radix value, listing and cref flags, or processor/coprocessor values. The *context* can be **ASSUMES, RADIX, LISTING, CPU,** or **ALL**.

[[*name*]] **QWORD** *initializer* [[*, initializer*]]. . .

Allocates and optionally initializes 8 bytes of storage for each *initializer*. Also can be used as a type specifier anywhere a type is legal.

.RADIX *expression*

Sets the default radix, in the range 2 to 16, to the value of *expression*.

name **REAL4** *initializer* [[, *initializer*]]. . .

  Allocates and optionally initializes a single-precision (4-byte) floating-point number for each *initializer*.

name **REAL8** *initializer* [[, *initializer*]]. . .

  Allocates and optionally initializes a double-precision (8-byte) floating-point number for each *initializer*.

name **REAL10** *initializer* [[, *initializer*]]. . .

  Allocates and optionally initializes a 10-byte floating-point number for each *initializer*.

recordname **RECORD** *fieldname:width* [[= *expression*]]

  [[, *fieldname:width* [[= *expression*]]]]. . .

  Declares a record type consisting of the specified fields. The *fieldname* names the field, *width* specifies the number of bits, and *expression* gives its initial value.

.REPEAT

  statements

  .UNTIL *condition*

  Generates code that repeats execution of the block of *statements* until *condition* becomes true. **.UNTILCXZ**, which becomes true when CX is zero, may be substituted for **.UNTIL**. The *condition* is optional with **.UNTILCXZ**.

REPEAT *expression*

  statements

  ENDM

  Marks a block that is to be repeated *expression* times. Same as **REPT**.

REPT

  See **REPEAT**.

.SALL

  See **.NOLISTMACRO**.

name **SBYTE** *initializer* [[, *initializer*]]. . .

  Allocates and optionally initializes a signed byte of storage for each *initializer*. Can also be used as a type specifier anywhere a type is legal.

name **SDWORD** *initializer* [[, *initializer*]]. . .

  Allocates and optionally initializes a signed doubleword (4 bytes) of storage for each *initializer*. Also can be used as a type specifier anywhere a type is legal.

name **SEGMENT** [[**READONLY**]] [[*align*]] [[*combine*]] [[*use*]] [['*class*']]

  statements

  name **ENDS**

  Defines a program segment called *name* having segment attributes *align* (**BYTE, WORD, DWORD, PARA, PAGE**), *combine* (**PUBLIC, STACK, COMMON, MEMORY, AT** *address*, **PRIVATE**), *use* (**USE16, USE32, FLAT**), and *class*.

.SEQ

  Orders segments sequentially (the default order).

.SFCOND

  See **.NOLISTIF**.

name **SIZESTR** *textitem*

  Finds the size of a text item.

.STACK [[*size*]]

  When used with **.MODEL**, defines a stack segment (with segment name STACK). The optional *size* specifies the number of bytes for the stack (default 1024). The **.STACK** directive automatically closes the stack statement.

.STARTUP

Generates program startup code.

STRUC

See **STRUCT**.

name **STRUCT** [[*alignment*]] [[, **NONUNIQUE**]]
  fielddeclarations
  name **ENDS**

Declares a structure type having the specified *fielddeclarations*. Each field must be a valid data
definition. Same as **STRUC**.

name **SUBSTR** *textitem, position* [[, *length*]]

Returns a substring of *textitem*, starting at *position*. The *textitem* can be a literal string, a constant
preceded by a %, or the string returned by a macro function.

SUBTITLE *text*

Defines the listing subtitle. Same as **SUBTTL**.

SUBTTL

See **SUBTITLE**.

name **SWORD** *initializer* [[, *initializer*]]...

Allocates and optionally initializes a signed word (2 bytes) of storage for each *initializer*. Can also
be used as a type specifier anywhere a type is legal.

[[*name*]] **TBYTE** *initializer* [[, *initializer*]]...

Allocates and optionally initializes 10 bytes of storage for each *initializer*. Can also be used as a
type specifier anywhere a type is legal.

name **TEXTEQU** [[*textitem*]]

Assigns *textitem* to *name*. The *textitem* can be a literal string, a constant preceded by a %, or the
string returned by a macro function.

.TFCOND

Toggles listing of false conditional blocks.

TITLE *text*

Defines the program listing title.

name **TYPEDEF** *type*

Defines a new type called *name*, which is equivalent to *type*.

name **UNION** [[*alignment*]] [[, **NONUNIQUE**]]
  fielddeclarations
[[*name*]] **ENDS**

Declares a union of one or more data types. The *fielddeclarations* must be valid data definitions.
Omit the **ENDS** *name* label on nested **UNION** definitions.

.UNTIL

See **.REPEAT**.

.UNTILCXZ

See **.REPEAT**.

.WHILE *condition*
  statements
  .ENDW

Generates code that executes the block of *statements* while *condition* remains true.

WHILE *expression*
  statements

ENDM

Repeats assembly of block *statements* as long as *expression* remains true.

⟦ *name* ⟧ **WORD initializer** ⟦ , *initializer* ⟧. . .

Allocates and optionally initializes a word (2 bytes) of storage for each *initializer*. Can also be used as a type specifier anywhere a type is legal.

.XALL

See **.LISTMACRO**.

.XCREF

See **.NOCREF**.

.XLIST

See **.NOLIST**.

.XMM

Enables assembly of Internet Streaming SIMD Extension instructions.

A.6   Symbols

$

The current value of the location counter.

?

In data declarations, a value that the assembler allocates but does not initialize.

@@:

Defines a code label recognizable only between *label1* and *label2*, where *label1* is either start of code or the previous **@@:** label, and *label2* is either end of code or the next **@@:** label. See **@B** and **@F**.

@B

The location of the previous **@@:** label.

@CatStr(string1 ⟦, string2. . . ⟧)

Macro function that concatenates one or more strings. Returns a string.

@code

The name of the code segment (text macro).

@CodeSize

0 for **TINY**, **SMALL**, **COMPACT**, and **FLAT** models, and 1 for **MEDIUM**, **LARGE**, and **HUGE** models (numeric equate).

@Cpu

A bit mask specifying the processor mode (numeric equate).

@CurSeg

The name of the current segment (text macro).

@data

The name of the default data group. Evaluates to DGROUP for all models except **FLAT**. Evaluates to **FLAT** under the **FLAT** memory model (text macro).

@DataSize

0 for **TINY**, **SMALL**, **MEDIUM**, and **FLAT** models, 1 for **COMPACT** and **LARGE** models, and 2 for **HUGE** model (numeric equate).

@Date

The system date in the format mm/dd/yy (text macro).

@Environ(envvar)

Value of environment variable *envvar* (macro function).

@F

The location of the next **@@:** label.

@fardata

The name of the segment defined by the **.FARDATA** directive (text macro).

@fardata?

The name of the segment defined by the **.FARDATA?** directive (text macro).

@FileCur

The name of the current file (text macro).

@FileName

The base name of the main file being assembled (text macro).

@InStr([[*position*]]**,** *string1***,** *string2* **)**

Macro function that finds the first occurrence of *string2* in *string1*, beginning at *position* within *string1*. If *position* does not appear, search begins at start of *string1*. Returns a position integer or 0 if *string2* is not found.

@Interface

Information about the language parameters (numeric equate).

@Line

The source line number in the current file (numeric equate).

@Model

1 for **TINY** model, 2 for **SMALL** model, 3 for **COMPACT** model, 4 for **MEDIUM** model, 5 for **LARGE** model, 6 for **HUGE** model, and 7 for **FLAT** model (numeric equate).

@SizeStr(*string* **)**

Macro function that returns the length of the given string. Returns an integer.

@stack

DGROUP for near stacks or STACK for far stacks (text macro).

@SubStr(*string***,** *position* [[**,** *length*]] **)**

Macro function that returns a substring starting at *position*.

@Time

The system time in 24-hour hh:mm:ss format (text macro).

@Version

610 in MASM 6.1 (text macro).

@WordSize

Two for a 16-bit segment or 4 for a 32-bit segment (numeric equate).

A.7 Operators

expression1 **+** *expression2*

Returns *expression1* plus *expression2*.

expression1 **−** *expression2*

Returns *expression1* minus *expression2*.

expression1 * *expression2*

Returns *expression1* times *expression2*.

expression1 **/** *expression2*

Returns *expression1* divided by *expression2*.

−*expression*

Reverses the sign of *expression*.

expression1 [expression2]

Returns *expression1* plus [*expression2*].

segment: expression

Overrides the default segment of *expression* with *segment*. The *segment* can be a segment register, group name, segment name, or segment expression. The *expression* must be a constant.

expression. field ‖ . field ‖ . . .

Returns *expression* plus the offset of *field* within its structure or union.

[register]. field ‖ . field ‖ . . .

Returns value at the location pointed to by *register* plus the offset of *field* within its structure or union.

<text>

Treats *text* as a single literal element.

"text"

Treats "*text*" as a string.

'text'

Treats '*text*' as a string.

!character

Treats *character* as a literal character rather than as an operator or symbol.

;text

Treats *text* as a comment.

;;text

Treats *text* as a comment in a macro that appears only in the macro definition. The listing does not show *text* where the macro is expanded.

%expression

Treats the value of *expression* in a macro argument as text.

&parameter&

Replaces *parameter* with its corresponding argument value.

ABS

See the **EXTERNDEF** directive.

ADDR

See the **INVOKE** directive.

expression1 AND expression2

Returns the result of a bitwise AND operation for *expression1* and *expression2*.

count DUP (initialvalue ‖, initialvalue ‖. . .)

Specifies *count* number of declarations of *initialvalue*.

expression1 EQ expression2

Returns true (-1) if *expression1* equals *expression2* and returns false (0) if it does not.

expression1 GE expression2

Returns true (-1) if *expression1* is greater than or equal to *expression2* and returns false (0) if it is not.

expression1 GT expression2

Returns true (-1) if *expression1* is greater than *expression2* and returns false (0) if it is not.

HIGH expression

Returns the high byte of *expression*.

HIGHWORD expression

Returns the high word of *expression*.

expression1 LE expression2

Returns true (-1) if *expression1* is less than or equal to *expression2* and returns false (0) if it is not.

LENGTH *variable*

Returns the number of data items in *variable* created by the first initializer.

LENGTHOF *variable*

Returns the number of data objects in *variable*.

LOW *expression*

Returns the low byte of *expression*.

LOWWORD *expression*

Returns the low word of *expression*.

LROFFSET *expression*

Returns the offset of *expression*. Same as **OFFSET**, but it generates a loader resolved offset, which allows Windows to relocate code segments.

expression1 **LT** *expression2*

Returns true (−1) if *expression1* is less than *expression2* and returns false (0) if it is not.

MASK { *recordfieldname* | *record* }

Returns a bit mask in which the bits in *recordfieldname* or *record* are set and all other bits are cleared.

expression1 **MOD** *expression2*

Returns the integer value of the remainder (modulo) when dividing *expression1* by *expression2*.

expression1 **NE** *expression2*

Returns true (−1) if *expression1* does not equal *expression2* and returns false (0) if it does.

NOT *expression*

Returns *expression* with all bits reversed.

OFFSET *expression*

Returns the offset of *expression*.

OPATTR *expression*

Returns a word defining the mode and scope of *expression*. The low byte is identical to the byte returned by **.TYPE**. The high byte contains additional information.

expression1 **OR** *expression2*

Returns the result of a bitwise OR operation for *expression1* and *expression2*.

type **PTR** *expression*

Forces the *expression* to be treated as having the specified *type.*

[[*distance*]] **PTR** *type*

Specifies a pointer to *type*.

SEG *expression*

Returns the segment of *expression*.

expression **SHL** *count*

Returns the result of shifting the bits of *expression* left *count* number of bits.

SHORT *label*

Sets the type of *label* to short. All jumps to *label* must be short (within the range −128 to +127 bytes from the jump instruction to *label*).

expression **SHR** *count*

Returns the result of shifting the bits of *expression* right *count* number of bits.

SIZE *variable*

Returns the number of bytes in *variable* allocated by the first initializer.

SIZEOF {*variable* | *type*}

Returns the number of bytes in *variable* or *type*.

THIS *type*

Returns an operand of specified *type* whose offset and segment values are equal to the current location-counter value.

.TYPE *expression*

See **OPATTR**.

TYPE *expression*

Returns the type of *expression*.

WIDTH {*recordfieldname* | *record*}

Returns the width in bits of the current *recordfieldname* or *record*.

expression1 **XOR** *expression2*

Returns the result of a bitwise XOR operation for *expression1* and *expression2*.

A.8   Runtime Operators

The following operators are used only within **.IF, .WHILE,** or **.REPEAT** blocks and are evaluated at run time, not at assembly time:

expression1 **==** *expression2*

Is equal to.

expression1 **!=** *expression2*

Is not equal to.

expression1 **>** *expression2*

Is greater than.

expression1 **>=** *expression2*

Is greater than or equal to.

expression1 **<** *expression2*

Is less than.

expression1 **<=** *expression2*

Is less than or equal to.

expression1 **||** *expression2*

Logical OR.

expression1 **&&** *expression2*

Logical AND.

expression1 **&** *expression2*

Bitwise AND.

!*expression*

Logical negation.

CARRY?

Status of Carry flag.

OVERFLOW?

Status of Overflow flag.

PARITY?

Status of Parity flag.

SIGN?

Status of Sign flag.

ZERO?

Status of Zero flag.

The IA-32 Instruction Set

B.1 Introduction

This appendix is a quick guide to the most commonly used IA-32 instructions. It does not cover system-mode instructions or instructions typically used only in operating system kernel code or protected-mode device drivers.

B.1.1 Flags

Each instruction description contains a series of boxes that describe how the instruction will affect the CPU status flags. Each flag is identified by a single letter:

O	Overflow	S	Sign	P	Parity
D	Direction	Z	Zero	C	Carry
I	Interrupt	A	Auxiliary Carry		

Inside the boxes, the following notation shows how each instruction will affect the flags:

1	Sets the flag.
0	Clears the flag.
?	May change the flag to an undetermined value.
(blank)	The flag is not changed.
*	Changes the flag according to specific rules associated with the flag.

For example, the following diagram of the CPU flags is taken from one of the instruction descriptions:

O	D	I	S	Z	A	P	C
?			?	?	*	?	*

From the diagram, we see that the Overflow, Sign, Zero, and Parity flags will be changed to unknown values. The Auxiliary Carry and Carry flags will be modified according to rules associated with the flags. The Direction and Interrupt flags will not be changed.

B.1.2 Instruction Descriptions and Formats

When a reference to source and destination operands is made, we use the natural order of operands in all Intel 80x86 instructions, in which the first operand is the destination and the second is the source. In the MOV instruction, for example, the destination will be assigned a copy of the data in the source operand:

```
MOV destination, source
```

There may be several formats available for a single instruction. Table B-1 contains a list of symbols used in instruction formats. In the descriptions of individual instructions, we use the notation "(IA-32)" to indicate that an instruction or one of its variants is only available on processors in the IA-32 family (Intel386 onward). Similarly, the notation "(80286)" indicates that at least an 80286 processor must be used.

Register notations such as (E)CX, (E)SI, (E)DI, (E)SP, (E)BP, and (E)IP differentiate between IA-32 processors that use the 32-bit registers and all earlier processors that used 16-bit registers.

Table B-1　　Symbols Used in Instruction Formats.

Symbol	Description
reg	An 8-, 16-, or 32-bit general register from the following list: AH, AL, BH, BL, CH, CL, DH, DL, AX, BX, CX, DX, SI, DI, BP, SP, EAX, EBX, ECX, EDX, ESI, EDI, EBP, and ESP.
reg8, reg16, reg32	A general register, identified by its number of bits.
segreg	A 16-bit segment register (CS, DS, ES, SS, FS, GS).
accum	AL, AX, or EAX.
mem	A memory operand, using any of the standard memory-addressing modes.
mem8, mem16, mem32	A memory operand, identified by its number of bits.
shortlabel	A location in the code segment within -128 to $+127$ bytes of the current location.
nearlabel	A location in the current code segment, identified by a label.
farlabel	A location in an external code segment, identified by a label.
imm	An immediate operand.
imm8, imm16, imm32	An immediate operand, identified by its number of bits.
instruction	An 80x86 assembly language instruction.

B.2 Instruction Set Details (Non Floating-Point)

AAA	**ASCII Adjust After Addition**

O	D	I	S	Z	A	P	C
?			?	?	*	?	*

Adjusts the result in AL after two ASCII digits have been added together. If AL > 9, the high digit of the result is placed in AH, and the Carry and Auxiliary Carry flags are set.
Instruction format:

    AAA

AAD	**ASCII Adjust Before Division**

O	D	I	S	Z	A	P	C
?			*	*	?	*	?

Converts unpacked BCD digits in AH and AL to a single binary value in preparation for the DIV instruction.
Instruction format:

    AAD

AAM	**ASCII Adjust After Multiply**

O	D	I	S	Z	A	P	C
?			*	*	?	*	?

Adjusts the result in AX after two unpacked BCD digits have been multiplied together.
Instruction format:

    AAM

AAS	**ASCII Adjust After Subtraction**

O	D	I	S	Z	A	P	C
?			?	?	*	?	*

Adjusts the result in AX after a subtraction operation. If AL > 9, AAS decrements AH and sets the Carry and Auxiliary Carry flags.
Instruction format:

    AAS

ADC	**Add Carry**

O	D	I	S	Z	A	P	C
*			*	*	*	*	*

Adds both the source operand and the Carry flag to the destination operand. Operands must be the same size.
Instruction formats:

    ADC   reg,reg   ADC   reg,imm
    ADC   mem,reg   ADC   mem,imm
    ADC   reg,mem   ADC   accum,imm

	Add								
ADD		O	D	I	S	Z	A	P	C
		*			*	*	*	*	*

A source operand is added to a destination operand, and the sum is stored in the destination. Operands must be the same size.
Instruction formats:

ADD	reg,reg		ADD	reg,imm
ADD	mem,reg		ADD	mem,imm
ADD	reg,mem		ADD	accum,imm

	Logical AND								
AND		O	D	I	S	Z	A	P	C
		0			*	*	?	*	0

Each bit in the destination operand is ANDed with the corresponding bit in the source operand.
Instruction formats:

AND	reg,reg		AND	reg,imm
AND	mem,reg		AND	mem,imm
AND	reg,mem		AND	accum,imm

	Check Array Bounds (80286)								
BOUND		O	D	I	S	Z	A	P	C

Verifies that a signed index value is within the bounds of an array. On the 80286 processor, the destination operand can be any 16-bit register containing the index to be checked. The source operand must be a 32-bit memory operand in which the high and low words contain the upper and lower bounds of the index value. On the IA-32, the destination can be a 32-bit register and the source can be a 64-bit memory operand.
Instruction formats:

BOUND	reg16,mem32		BOUND	r32,mem64

	Bit Scan (IA-32)								
BSF, BSR		O	D	I	S	Z	A	P	C
		?			?	?	?	?	?

Scans an operand to find the first set bit. If the bit is found, the Zero flag is cleared, and the destination operand is assigned the bit number (index) of the first set bit encountered. If no set bit is found, ZF = 1. BSF scans from bit 0 to the highest bit, and BSR starts at the highest bit and scans toward bit 0.
Instruction formats (apply to both BSF and BSR):

BSF	reg16,r/m16	BSF	reg32,r/m32

BSWAP	**Byte Swap (IA-32)**
	O D I S Z A P C
	Reverses the byte order of a 32-bit destination register. Instruction format: BSWAP *reg32*

BT, BTC, BTR, BTS	**Bit Tests (IA-32)**
	O D I S Z A P C ? ? ? ? ? *

	Copies a specified bit (*n*) into the Carry flag. The destination operand contains the value in which the bit is located, and the source operand indicates the bit's position within the destination. BT copies bit *n* to the Carry flag. BTC copies bit *n* to the Carry flag and complements bit *n* in the destination operand. BTR copies bit *n* to the Carry flag and clears bit *n* in the destination. BTS copies bit *n* to the Carry flag and sets bit *n* in the destination.
	Instruction formats:
	    BT *r/m16,imm8* BT *r/m16,r16*
	    BT *r/m32,imm8* BT *r/m32,r32*

CALL	**Call a Procedure**
	O D I S Z A P C

	Pushes the location of the next instruction on the stack and transfers to the destination location. If the procedure is near (in the same segment), only the offset of the next instruction is pushed; otherwise, both the segment and the offset are pushed.
	Instruction formats:
	    CALL *nearlabel* CALL *mem16*
	    CALL *farlabel* CALL *mem32*
	    CALL *reg*

CBW	**Convert Byte to Word**
	O D I S Z A P C
	Extends the sign bit in AL throughout the AH register. Instruction format: CBW

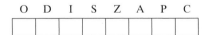

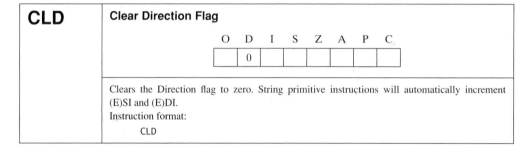

CDQ — **Convert Doubleword to Quadword (IA-32)**

O D I S Z A P C

Extends the sign bit in EAX throughout the EDX register.
Instruction format:
    CDQ

CLC — **Clear Carry Flag**

O D I S Z A P C
                       0

Clears the Carry flag to zero.
Instruction format:
    CLC

CLD — **Clear Direction Flag**

O D I S Z A P C
   0

Clears the Direction flag to zero. String primitive instructions will automatically increment
(E)SI and (E)DI.
Instruction format:
    CLD

CLI — **Clear Interrupt Flag**

O D I S Z A P C
      0

Clears the Interrupt flag to zero. This disables maskable hardware interrupts until an STI instruction is executed.
Instruction format:
    CLI

CMC — **Complement Carry Flag**

O D I S Z A P C
                       *

Toggles the current value of the Carry flag.
Instruction format:
    CMC

CMP — Compare

O	D	I	S	Z	A	P	C
*			*	*	*	*	*

Compares the destination to the source by performing an implied subtraction of the source from the destination.

Instruction formats:

```
CMP    reg,reg               CMP    reg,imm
CMP    mem,reg               CMP    mem,imm
CMP    reg,mem               CMP    accum,imm
```

CMPS, CMPSB, CMPSW, CMPSD — Compare Strings

O	D	I	S	Z	A	P	C
*			*	*	*	*	*

Compares strings in memory addressed by DS:(E)SI and ES:(E)DI. Carries out an implied subtraction of the destination from the source. CMPSB compares bytes, CMPSW compares words, and CMPSD compares doublewords (on IA-32 processors). (E)SI and (E)DI are increased or decreased according to the operand size and the status of the direction flag. If the Direction flag is set, (E)SI and (E)DI are decreased; otherwise (E)SI and (E)DI are increased.

Instruction formats (formats using explicit operands have intentionally been omitted):

```
CMPSB                        CMPSW
CMPSD
```

CMPXCHG — Compare and Exchange

O	D	I	S	Z	A	P	C
*			*	*	*	*	*

Compares the destination to the accumulator (AL, AX, or EAX). If they are equal, the source is copied to the destination. Otherwise, the destination is copied to the accumulator.

Instruction formats:

```
CMPXCHG reg,reg              CMPXCHG mem,reg
```

CWD — Convert Word to Doubleword

O	D	I	S	Z	A	P	C

Extends the sign bit in AX into the DX register.

Instruction format:

```
CWD
```

DAA   Decimal Adjust After Addition

O	D	I	S	Z	A	P	C
?			*	*	*	*	*

Adjusts the binary sum in AL after two packed BCD values have been added. Converts the sum to two BCD digits in AL.
Instruction format:

```
DAA
```

DAS   Decimal Adjust After Subtraction

O	D	I	S	Z	A	P	C
?			*	*	*	*	*

Converts the binary result of a subtraction operation to two packed BCD digits in AL.
Instruction format:

```
DAS
```

DEC   Decrement

O	D	I	S	Z	A	P	C
*			*	*	*	*	

Subtracts 1 from an operand. Does not affect the Carry flag.
Instruction formats:

```
DEC  reg                          DEC  mem
```

DIV   Unsigned Integer Divide

O	D	I	S	Z	A	P	C
?			?	?	?	?	?

Performs either 8-, 16-, or 32-bit unsigned integer division. If the divisor is 8 bits, the dividend is AX, the quotient is AL, and the remainder is AH. If the divisor is 16 bits, the dividend is DX:AX, the quotient is AX, and the remainder is DX. If the divisor is 32 bits, the dividend is EDX:EAX, the quotient is EAX, and the remainder is EDX.
Instruction formats:

```
DIV  reg                          DIV  mem
```

ENTER   Make Stack Frame (80286)

O	D	I	S	Z	A	P	C

Creates a stack frame for a procedure that receives stack parameters and uses local stack variables. The first operand indicates the number of bytes to reserve for local stack variables. The second operand indicates the procedure nesting level (must be set to 0 for C, Basic, and FORTRAN).
Instruction format:

```
ENTER  imm16,imm8
```

HLT	**Halt**

	O	D	I	S	Z	A	P	C

Stops the CPU until a hardware interrupt occurs. (*Note:* The Interrupt flag must be set with the STI instruction before hardware interrupts can occur.)
Instruction format:

```
HLT
```

IDIV	**Signed Integer Divide**

	O	D	I	S	Z	A	P	C
	?			?	?	?	?	?

Performs a signed integer division operation on EDX:EAX, DX:AX, or AX. If the divisor is 8 bits, the dividend is AX, the quotient is AL, and the remainder is AH. If the divisor is 16 bits, the dividend is DX:AX, the quotient is AX, and the remainder is DX. If the divisor is 32 bits, the dividend is EDX:EAX, the quotient is EAX, and the remainder is EDX. Usually the IDIV operation is prefaced by either CBW or CWD to sign-extend the dividend.
Instruction formats:

```
IDIV  reg                         IDIV  mem
```

IMUL	**Signed Integer Multiply**

	O	D	I	S	Z	A	P	C
	*			?	?	?	?	*

Performs a signed integer multiplication on AL, AX, or EAX. If the multiplier is 8 bits, the multiplicand is AL and the product is AX. If the multiplier is 16 bits, the multiplicand is AX and the product is DX:AX. If the multiplier is 32 bits, the mutiplicand is EAX and the product is EDX:EAX. The Carry and Overflow flags are set if a 16-bit product extends into AH, or a 32-bit product extends into DX, or a 64-bit product extends into EDX.
Instruction formats:
Single operand:

```
IMUL  r/m8                        IMUL  r/m16
IMUL  r/m32
```

Two operands:

```
IMUL  r16,r/m16                   IMUL  r16,imm8
IMUL  r32,r/m32                   IMUL  r32,imm8
IMUL  r16,imm16                   IMUL  r32,imm32
```

Three operands:

```
IMUL  r16,r/m16,imm8              IMUL  r16,r/m16,imm16
IMUL  r32,r/m32,imm8              IMUL  r32,r/m32,imm32
```

IN — Input From Port

O	D	I	S	Z	A	P	C

Inputs a byte or word from a port into AL or AX. The source operand is a port address, expressed as either an 8-bit constant or a 16-bit address in DX. On the IA-32, a doubleword can be input from a port into EAX.
Instruction formats:

```
      IN  accum,imm                        IN  accum,DX
```

INC — Increment

O	D	I	S	Z	A	P	C
*			*	*	*	*	

Adds 1 to a register or memory operand.
Instruction formats:

```
      INC  reg                             INC  mem
```

INS, INSB, INSW, INSD — Input from Port to String (80286)

O	D	I	S	Z	A	P	C

Inputs a string pointed to by ES:(E)DI from a port. The port number is specified in DX. For each value received, (E)DI is adjusted in the same way as LODSB and similar string primitive instructions. The REP prefix may be used with this instruction.
Instruction formats:

```
      INS dest,DX                          REP INSB dest,DX
      REP INSW dest,DX                     REP INSD dest,DX
```

INT — Interrupt

O	D	I	S	Z	A	P	C
		0					

Generates a software interrupt, which in turn calls an operating system subroutine. Clears the Interrupt flag and pushes the flags, CS, and IP on the stack before branching to the interrupt routine.
Instruction formats:

```
      INT  imm                             INT  3
```

INTO — Interrupt on Overflow

O	D	I	S	Z	A	P	C
		*	*				

Generates internal CPU Interrupt 4 if the Overflow flag is set. No action is taken by MS-DOS if INT 4 is called, but a user-written routine may be substituted instead.
Instruction format:

```
      INTO
```

IRET	**Interrupt Return**
	O D I S Z A P C
	* | * | * | * | * | * | * | *
	Returns from an interrupt handling routine. Pops the stack into (E)IP, CS, and the flags. Instruction format:
	`IRET`

Jcondition	**Conditional Jump**
	O D I S Z A P C
	(empty flag boxes)
	Jumps to a label if a specified flag condition is true. Prior to the IA-32 processor, the label must be in the range of −128 to +127 bytes from the current location. On IA-32 processors, the label's offset can be a positive or negative 32-bit value. See Table B-2 for a list of mnemonics. Instruction format:
	`Jcondition  label`

Table B-2   Conditional Jump Mnemonics.

Mnemonic	Comment	Mnemonic	Comment
JA	Jump if above	JE	Jump if equal
JNA	Jump if not above	JNE	Jump if not equal
JAE	Jump if above or equal	JZ	Jump if zero
JNAE	Jump if not above or equal	JNZ	Jump if not zero
JB	Jump if below	JS	Jump if sign
JNB	Jump if not below	JNS	Jump if not sign
JBE	Jump if below or equal	JC	Jump if carry
JNBE	Jump if not below or equal	JNC	Jump if no carry
JG	Jump if greater	JO	Jump if overflow
JNG	Jump if not greater	JNO	Jump if no overflow
JGE	Jump if greater or equal	JP	Jump if parity
JNGE	Jump if not greater or equal	JPE	Jump if parity equal
JL	Jump if less	JNP	Jump if no parity
JNL	Jump if not less	JPO	Jump if parity odd
JLE	Jump if less or equal	JNLE	Jump if not less than or equal

JCXZ, JECXZ	Jump If CX Is Zero
	O D I S Z A P C
	Jump to a short label if the CX register is equal to zero. The short label must be in the range −128 to +127 bytes from the next instruction. On the IA-32 processor, JECXZ jumps if ECX equals zero. Instruction formats: JCXZ *shortlabel* JECXZ *shortlabel*

JMP	Jump Unconditionally to Label
	O D I S Z A P C

	Jump to a code label. A short jump is within −128 to +127 bytes from the current location. A near jump is within the same code segment, and a far jump is outside the current segment.
	Instruction formats:
	    JMP *shortlabel* JMP *reg16*
	    JMP *nearlabel* JMP *mem16*
	    JMP *farlabel* JMP *mem32*

LAHF	Load AH from Flags
	O D I S Z A P C
	The following flags are copied to AH: Sign, Zero, Auxiliary Carry, Parity, and Carry. Instruction format: LAHF

LDS, LES, LFS, LGS, LSS	Load Far Pointer
	O D I S Z A P C
	Loads the contents of a doubleword memory operand into a segment register and the specified destination register. Prior to the IA-32 processor, LDS loads into DS, LES loads into ES. On the IA-32 processor, LFS loads into FS, LGS loads into GS, and LSS loads into SS. Instruction format (same for LDS, LES, LFS, LGS, LSS): LDS *reg,mem*

LEA — Load Effective Address

O	D	I	S	Z	A	P	C

Calculates and loads the 16-bit or 32-bit effective address of a memory operand. Similar to MOV..OFFSET, except that only LEA can obtain an address that is calculated at run time.
Instruction format:

```
LEA   reg,mem
```

LEAVE — High-Level Procedure Exit

O	D	I	S	Z	A	P	C

Terminates the stack frame of a procedure. This reverses the action of the ENTER instruction at the beginning of a procedure by restoring (E)SP and (E)BP to their original values.
Instruction format:

```
LEAVE
```

LOCK — Lock the System Bus

O	D	I	S	Z	A	P	C

Prevents other processors from executing during the next instruction. This instruction is used when another processor might modify a memory operand that is currently being accessed by the CPU.
Instruction format:

```
LOCK instruction
```

LODS, LODSB, LODSW, LODSD — Load Accumulator from String

O	D	I	S	Z	A	P	C

Loads a memory byte or word addressed by DS:(E)SI into the accumulator (AL, AX, or EAX). If LODS is used, the memory operand must be specified. LODSB loads a byte into AL, LODSW loads a word into AX, and LODSD on the IA-32 loads a doubleword into EAX. (E)SI is increased or decreased according to the operand size and the status of the direction flag. If the Direction flag (DF) = 1, (E)SI is decreased; if DF = 0, (E)SI is increased.
Instruction formats:

```
LODS   mem                        LODSB
LODS   segreg:mem                 LODSW
LODS
```

LOOP, LOOPW

Loop

O	D	I	S	Z	A	P	C

Decrements (E)CX and jumps to a short label if (E)CX is greater than zero. The destination must be −128 to +127 bytes from the current location. On IA-32 processors, ECX is used as the default loop counter.
Instruction formats:

```
LOOP shortlabel                        LOOPW shortlabel
```

LOOPD

Loop (IA-32)

O	D	I	S	Z	A	P	C

Decrements ECX and jumps to a short label if ECX is greater than Zero. The destination must be −128 to +127 bytes from the current location.
Instruction format:

```
LOOPD shortlabel
```

LOOPE, LOOPZ

Loop If Equal (Zero)

O	D	I	S	Z	A	P	C

Decrements (E)CX and jumps to a short label if (E)CX > 0 and the Zero flag is set.
Instruction formats:

```
LOOPE shortlabel                       LOOPZ shortlabel
```

LOOPNE, LOOPNZ

Loop If Not Equal (Zero)

O	D	I	S	Z	A	P	C

Decrements (E)CX and jumps to a short label if (E)CX > 0 and the Zero flag is clear.
Instruction formats:

```
LOOPNE shortlabel                      LOOPNZ shortlabel
```

MOV

Move

O	D	I	S	Z	A	P	C

Copies a byte or word from a source operand to a destination operand.
Instruction formats:

```
MOV reg,reg                    MOV reg,imm
MOV mem,reg                    MOV mem,imm
MOV reg,mem                    MOV mem16,segreg
MOV reg16,segreg               MOV segreg,mem16
MOV segreg,reg16
```

MOVS, MOVSB, MOVSW, MOVSD	**Move String**

O   D   I   S   Z   A   P   C

Copies a byte or word from memory addressed by DS:(E)SI to memory addressed by ES:(E)DI. MOVS requires both operands to be specified. MOVSB copies a byte, MOVSW copies a word, and on the IA-32, MOVSD copies a doubleword. (E)SI and (E)DI are increased or decreased according to the operand size and the status of the direction flag. If the Direction flag (DF) = 1, (E)SI and (E)DI are decreased; if DF = 0, (E)SI and (E)DI are increased.
Instruction formats:

```
MOVSB
MOVSW
MOVSD
MOVS  dest, source
MOVS  ES:dest, segreg:source
```

MOVSX	**Move with Sign-Extend**

O   D   I   S   Z   A   P   C

Copies a byte or word from a source operand to a destination register and sign-extends into the upper half of the destination. This instruction is used to copy an 8-bit or 16-bit operand into a larger destination.
Instruction formats:

```
MOVSX  reg32,reg16          MOVSX  reg32,mem16
MOVSX  reg16,reg8           MOVSX  reg16,m8
```

MOVZX	**Move with Zero-Extend**

O   D   I   S   Z   A   P   C

Copies a byte or word from a source operand to a destination register and zero-extends into the upper half of the destination. This instruction is used to copy an 8-bit or 16-bit operand into a larger destination.
Instruction formats:

```
MOVSX  reg32,reg16          MOVSX  reg32,mem16
MOVSX  reg16,reg8           MOVSX  reg16,m8
```

MUL	**Unsigned Integer Multiply**

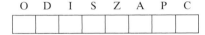

O	D	I	S	Z	A	P	C
*			?	?	?	?	*

Multiplies AL, AX, or EAX by a source operand. If the source is 8 bits, it is multiplied by AL and the product is stored in AX. If the source is 16 bits, it is multiplied by AX and the product is stored in DX:AX. If the source is 32 bits, it is multiplied by EAX and the product is stored in EDX:EAX.
Instruction formats:

```
MUL  reg                    MUL  mem
```

NEG   Negate

O	D	I	S	Z	A	P	C
*			*	*	*	*	*

Calculates the twos complement of the destination operand and stores the result in the destination. Instruction formats:

```
NEG reg                              NEG mem
```

NOP   No Operation

O	D	I	S	Z	A	P	C

This instruction does nothing, but it may be used inside a timing loop or to align a subsequent instruction on a word boundary. Instruction format:

```
NOP
```

NOT   Not

O	D	I	S	Z	A	P	C

Performs a logical NOT operation on an operand by reversing each of its bits. Instruction formats:

```
NOT reg                              NOT mem
```

OR   Inclusive OR

O	D	I	S	Z	A	P	C
0			*	*	?	*	0

Performs a boolean (bitwise) OR operation between each matching bit in the destination operand and each bit in the source operand. Instruction formats:

```
OR  reg,reg                          OR  reg,imm
OR  mem,reg                          OR  mem,imm
OR  reg,mem                          OR  accum,imm
```

OUT   Output to Port

O	D	I	S	Z	A	P	C

Prior to the IA-32, this instruction outputs a byte or word from the accumulator to a port. The port address may be a constant if in the range 0–FFh, or DX may contain a port address between 0 and FFFFh. On an IA-32 processor, a doubleword can be output to a port. Instruction formats:

```
OUT imm8,accum                          OUT DX,accum
```

OUTS, OUTSB, OUTSW, OUTSD	Output String to Port (80286)

O	D	I	S	Z	A	P	C

Outputs a string pointed to by ES:(E)DI to a port. The port number is specified in DX. For each value output, (E)DI is adjusted in the same way as LODSB and similar string primitive instructions. The REP prefix may be used with this instruction.
Instruction formats:

```
OUTS  dest,DX              REP OUTSB dest,DX
REP OUTSW dest,DX          REP OUTSD dest,DX
```

POP	Pop from Stack

O	D	I	S	Z	A	P	C

Copies a word or doubleword at the current stack pointer location into the destination operand and adds 2 (or 4) to (E)SP.
Instruction formats:

```
POP   reg16/r32           POP   segreg
POP   mem16/mem32
```

POPA, POPAD	Pop All

O	D	I	S	Z	A	P	C

Pops 16 bytes from the top of the stack into the eight general-purpose registers, in the following order: DI, SI, BP, SP, BX, DX, CX, AX. The value for SP is discarded, so SP is not reassigned. POPA pops into 16-bit registers, and POPAD on the IA-32 pops into 32-bit registers.
Instruction formats:

```
POPA                      POPAD
```

POPF, POPFD	Pop Flags from Stack

O	D	I	S	Z	A	P	C
*	*	*	*	*	*	*	*

POPF pops the top of the stack into the 16-bit FLAGS register. POPFD on the IA-32 pops the top of the stack into the 32-bit EFLAGS register.
Instruction formats:

```
POPF                      POPFD
```

PUSH	**Push on Stack**

O   D   I   S   Z   A   P   C

Subtracts 2 from (E)SP and copies the source operand into the stack location pointed to by (E)SP. From the 80186 onward, an immediate value can be pushed on the stack.

Instruction formats:

```
PUSH   reg16/reg32                    PUSH   segreg
PUSH   mem16/mem32                    PUSH   imm16/imm32
```

PUSHA, PUSHAD	**Push All (80286)**

O   D   I   S   Z   A   P   C

Pushes the following 16-bit registers on the stack, in order: AX, CX, DX, BX, SP, BP, SI, and DI. The PUSHAD instruction for the IA-32 pushes EAX, ECX, EDX, EBX, ESP, EBP, ESI, and EDI.

Instruction formats:

```
PUSHA                                 PUSHAD
```

PUSHF, PUSHFD	**Push Flags**

O   D   I   S   Z   A   P   C

PUSHF pushes the 16-bit FLAGS register onto the stack. PUSHFD pushes the 32-bit EFLAGS onto the stack (IA-32).

Instruction formats:

```
PUSHF                                 PUSHFD
```

PUSHW, PUSHD	**Push on Stack**

O   D   I   S   Z   A   P   C

PUSHW pushes a 16-bit word on the stack, and on the IA-32, PUSHD pushes a 32-bit doubleword on the stack.

Instruction formats:

```
PUSH   reg16/reg32                    PUSH   segreg
PUSH   mem16/mem32                    PUSH   imm16/imm32
```

RCL — Rotate Carry Left

O	D	I	S	Z	A	P	C
*							*

Rotates the destination operand left, using the source operand to determine the number of rotations. The Carry flag is copied into the lowest bit, and the highest bit is copied into the Carry flag. The *imm8* operand must be a 1 when using the 8086/8088 processor.
Instruction formats:

```
RCL   reg,imm8              RCL   mem,imm8
RCL   reg,CL                RCL   mem,CL
```

RCR — Rotate Carry Right

O	D	I	S	Z	A	P	C
*							*

Rotates the destination operand right, using the source operand to determine the number of rotations. The Carry flag is copied into the highest bit, and the lowest bit is copied into the Carry flag. The *imm8* operand must be a 1 when using the 8086/8088 processor.
Instruction formats:

```
RCR   reg,imm8              RCR   mem,imm8
RCR   reg,CL                RCR   mem,CL
```

REP — Repeat String

O	D	I	S	Z	A	P	C

Repeats a string primitive instruction, using (E)CX as a counter. (E)CX is decremented each time the instruction is repeated, until (E)CX = 0.
Format (shown with MOVS):

```
REP MOVS dest,source
```

REP*condition* — Repeat String Conditionally

O	D	I	S	Z	A	P	C

Repeats a string primitive instruction until (E)CX = 0 and while a flag condition is true. REPZ (REPE) repeats while the Zero flag is set, and REPZ (REPNE) repeats while the Zero flag is clear. Only SCAS and CMPS should be used with REP*condition*, because they are the only string primitives that modify the Zero flag.
Formats used with SCAS:

```
REPZ   SCAS  dest           REPNE   SCAS  dest
REPZ   SCASB                REPNE   SCASB
REPE   SCASW                REPNZ   SCASW
```

RET, RETN, RETF

Return from Procedure

O	D	I	S	Z	A	P	C

Pops a return address from the stack. RETN (return near) pops only the top of the stack into (E)IP. In real-address mode, RETF (return far) pops the stack first into (E)IP and then into CS. RET may be either near or far, depending on the attribute specified or implied by the PROC directive. An optional 8-bit immediate operand tells the CPU to add a value to (E)SP after popping the return address.

Instruction formats:

```
RET                          RET    imm8
RETN                         RETN   imm8
RETF                         RETF   imm8
```

ROL

Rotate Left

O	D	I	S	Z	A	P	C
*							*

Rotates the destination operand left, using the source operand to determine the number of rotations. The highest bit is copied into the Carry flag and moved into the lowest bit position. The *imm8* operand must be a 1 when using the 8086/8088 processor.

Instruction formats:

```
ROL   reg,imm8               ROL    mem,imm8
ROL   reg,CL                 ROL    mem,CL
```

ROR

Rotate Right

O	D	I	S	Z	A	P	C
*							*

Rotates the destination operand right, using the source operand to determine the number of rotations. The lowest bit is copied into both the Carry flag and the highest bit position. The *imm8* operand must be a 1 when using the 8086/8088 processor.

Instruction formats:

```
ROR   reg,imm8               ROR    mem,imm8
ROR   reg,CL                 ROR    mem,CL
```

SAHF

Store AH into Flags

O	D	I	S	Z	A	P	C
			*	*	*	*	*

Copies AH into bits 0 through 7 of the Flags register.

Instruction format:

```
SAHF
```

SAL

Shift Arithmetic Left

O	D	I	S	Z	A	P	C
*			*	*	?	*	*

Shifts each bit in the destination operand to the left, using the source operand to determine the number of shifts. The highest bit is copied into the Carry flag, and the lowest bit is filled with a zero. The *imm8* operand must be a 1 when using the 8086/8088 processor.
Instruction formats:

```
SAL   reg,imm8                SAL   mem,imm8
SAL   reg,CL                  SAL   mem,CL
```

SAR

Shift Arithmetic Right

O	D	I	S	Z	A	P	C
*			*	*	?	*	*

Shifts each bit in the destination operand to the right, using the source operand to determine the number of shifts. The lowest bit is copied into the Carry flag, and the highest bit retains its previous value. This shift is often used with signed operands because it preserves the number's sign. The *imm8* operand must be a 1 when using the 8086/8088 processor.
Instruction formats:

```
SAR   reg,imm8                SAR   mem,imm8
SAR   reg,CL                  SAR   mem,CL
```

SBB

Subtract with Borrow

O	D	I	S	Z	A	P	C
*			*	*	*	*	*

Subtracts the source operand from the destination operand and then subtracts the Carry flag from the destination.
Instruction formats:

```
SBB   reg,reg                 SBB   reg,imm
SBB   mem,reg                 SBB   mem,imm
SBB   reg,mem
```

SCAS, SCASB, SCASW, SCASD

Scan String

O	D	I	S	Z	A	P	C
*			*	*	*	*	*

Scans a string in memory pointed to by ES:(E)DI for a value that matches the accumulator. SCAS requires the operands to be specified. SCASB scans for an 8-bit value matching AL, SCASW scans for a 16-bit value matching AX, and SCASD scans for a 32-bit value matching EAX. (E)DI is increased or decreased according to the operand size and the status of the direction flag. If DF = 1, (E)DI is decreased; if DF = 0, (E)DI is increased.
Instruction formats:

```
SCASB                         SCASW
SCASD
SCAS dest
SCAS ES:dest
```

SET*condition*   Set Conditionally

O	D	I	S	Z	A	P	C

If the given flag condition is true, the byte specified by the destination operand is assigned the value 1. If the flag condition is false, the destination is assigned a value of 0. The possible values for *condition* were listed in Table B-2.
Instruction formats:

   SET*cond reg8*   SET*cond mem8*

SHL   Shift Left

O	D	I	S	Z	A	P	C
*			*	*	?	*	*

Shifts each bit in the destination operand to the left, using the source operand to determine the number of shifts. The highest bit is copied into the Carry flag, and the lowest bit is filled with a zero (identical to SAL). The *imm8* operand must be a 1 when using the 8086/8088 processor.
Instruction formats:

   SHL *reg,imm8*   SHL *mem,imm8*
   SHL *reg*,CL   SHL *mem*,CL

SHLD   Double-Precision Shift Left (IA-32)

O	D	I	S	Z	A	P	C
*			*	*	?	*	*

Shifts the bits of the second operand into the first operand. The third operand indicates the number of bits to be shifted. The positions opened by the shift are filled by the most significant bits of the second operand. The second operand must always be a register, and the third operand may be either an immediate value or the CL register.
Instruction formats:

   SHLD *reg16,reg16,imm8*   SHLD *mem16,reg16,imm8*
   SHLD *reg32,reg32,imm8*   SHLD *mem32,reg32,imm8*
   SHLD *reg16,reg16*,CL   SHLD *mem16,reg16*,CL
   SHLD *reg32,reg32*,CL   SHLD *mem32,reg32*,CL

SHR   Shift Right

O	D	I	S	Z	A	P	C
*			*	*	?	*	*

Shifts each bit in the destination operand to the right, using the source operand to determine the number of shifts. The highest bit is filled with a zero, and the lowest bit is copied into the Carry flag. The *imm8* operand must be a 1 when using the 8086/8088 processor.
Instruction formats:

   SHR *reg,imm8*   SHR *mem,imm8*
   SHR *reg*,CL   SHR *mem*,CL

SHRD — Double-Precision Shift Right (IA-32)

O	D	I	S	Z	A	P	C
*			*	*	?	*	*

Shifts the bits of the second operand into the first operand. The third operand indicates the number of bits to be shifted. The positions opened by the shift are filled by the least significant bits of the second operand. The second operand must always be a register, and the third operand may be either an immediate value or the CL register.

Instruction formats:

```
SHRD reg16,reg16,imm8          SHRD mem16,reg16,imm8
SHRD reg32,reg32,imm8          SHRD mem32,reg32,imm8
SHRD reg16,reg16,CL            SHRD mem16,reg16,CL
SHRD reg32,reg32,CL            SHRD mem32,reg32,CL
```

STC — Set Carry Flag

O	D	I	S	Z	A	P	C
							1

Sets the Carry flag.

Instruction format:

```
STC
```

STD — Set Direction Flag

O	D	I	S	Z	A	P	C
	1						

Sets the Direction flag, causing (E)SI and/or (E)DI to be decremented by string primitive instructions. Thus, string processing will be from high addresses to low addresses.

Instruction format:

```
STD
```

STI — Set Interrupt Flag

O	D	I	S	Z	A	P	C
		1					

Sets the Interrupt flag, which enables maskable interrupts. Interrupts are automatically disabled when an interrupt occurs, so an interrupt handler procedure immediately reenables them, using STI.

Instruction format:

```
STI
```

STOS, STOSB, STOSW, STOSD

Store String Data

O	D	I	S	Z	A	P	C

Stores the accumulator in the memory location addressed by ES:(E)DI. If STOS is used, a destination operand must be specified. STOSB copies AL to memory, STOSW copies AX to memory, and STOSD for the IA-32 copies EAX to memory. (E)DI is increased or decreased according to the operand size and the status of the direction flag. If DF = 1, (E)DI is decreased; if DF = 0, (E)DI is increased.

Instruction formats:

```
STOSB                              STOSW
STOSD
STOS mem
STOS ES:mem
```

SUB

Subtract

O	D	I	S	Z	A	P	C
*			*	*	*	*	*

Subtracts the source operand from the destination operand.

Instruction formats:

```
SUB   reg,reg                      SUB   reg,imm
SUB   mem,reg                      SUB   mem,imm
SUB   reg,mem                      SUB   accum,imm
```

TEST

Test

O	D	I	S	Z	A	P	C
0			*	*	?	*	0

Tests individual bits in the destination operand against those in the source operand. Performs a logical AND operation that affects the flags but not the destination operand.

Instruction formats:

```
TEST   reg,reg                     TEST   reg,imm
TEST   mem,reg                     TEST   mem,imm
TEST   reg,mem                     TEST   accum,imm
```

WAIT

Wait for Coprocessor

O	D	I	S	Z	A	P	C

Suspends CPU execution until the coprocessor finishes the current instruction.

Instruction format:

```
WAIT
```

XADD — Exchange and Add (Intel486)

O	D	I	S	Z	A	P	C
*			*	*	*	*	*

Adds the source operand to the destination operand. At the same time, the original destination value is moved to the source operand.

Instruction formats:

```
XADD   reg,reg                          XADD   mem,reg
```

XCHG — Exchange

O	D	I	S	Z	A	P	C

Exchanges the contents of the source and destination operands.

Instruction formats:

```
XCH    reg,reg                          XCH    mem,reg
XCH    reg,mem
```

XLAT, XLATB — Translate Byte

O	D	I	S	Z	A	P	C

Uses the value in AL to index into a table pointed to by DS:BX. The byte pointed to by the index is moved to AL. An operand may be specified in order to provide a segment override. XLATB may be substituted for XLAT.

Instruction formats:

```
XLAT                                    XLAT   segreg:mem
XLAT   mem                              XLATB
```

XOR — Exclusive OR

O	D	I	S	Z	A	P	C
0			*	*	?	*	0

Each bit in the source operand is exclusive ORed with its corresponding bit in the destination. The destination bit is a 1 only when the original source and destination bits are different.

Instruction formats:

```
XOR    reg,reg                          XOR    reg,imm
XOR    mem,reg                          XOR    mem,imm
XOR    reg,mem                          XOR    accum,imm
```

B.3   Floating-Point Instructions

Table B-3 contains a list of all IA-32 floating-point instructions, with brief descriptions and operand formats. Instructions are usually grouped by function rather than strict alphabetical order. For example, the FIADD instruction immediately follows FADD and FADDP because it performs the same operation with integer conversion.

For complete information about IA-32 floating point instructions, consult the *IA-32 Intel Architecture Software Developer's Manual,* Vol. 2A. The word *stack* in this table refers to the FPU register stack. (Table B-1 lists many of the symbols used when describing the formats and operands of floating-point instructions.)

Table B-3   IA-32 Floating-Point Instructions.

Instruction	Description
F2XM1	**Compute $2^x - 1$.** No operands.
FABS	**Absolute value.** Clears sign bit of ST(0). No operands.
FADD	**Add floating-point.** Adds destination and source operands, stores sum in destination operand. Formats: FADD Add ST(0) to ST(1), and pop stack FADD *m32fp* Add *m32fp* to ST(0) FADD *m64fp* Add *m64fp* to ST(0) FADD ST(0),ST(i) Add ST(i) to ST(0) FADD ST(i),ST(0) Add ST(0) to ST(i)
FADDP	**Add floating-point and pop.** Performs the same operation as FADD, then pops the stack. Format: FADDP ST(i),ST(0) Add ST(0) to ST(i)
FIADD	**Convert integer to floating-point and add.** Adds destination and source operands, stores sum in destination operand. Formats: FIADD *m32int* Add *m32int* to ST(0) FIADD *m16int* Add *m16int* to ST(0)
FBLD	**Load binary-coded decimal.** Converts BCD source operand into double extended-precision floating-point format and pushes it on the stack. Format: FBLD *m80bcd* Push *m80bcd* onto register stack
FBSTP	**Store BCD integer and pop.** Converts the value in the ST(0) register to an 18-digit packed BCD integer, stores the result in the destination operand, and pops the register stack. Format: FBSTP *m80bcd* Store ST(0) into *m80bcd*, and pop stack
FCHS	**Change sign.** Complements the sign of ST(0). No operands.
FCLEX	**Clear exceptions.** Clears the floating-point exception flags (PE, UE, OE, ZE, DE, and IE), the exception summary status flag (ES), the stack fault flag (SF), and the busy flag (B) in the FPU status word. No operands. FNCLEX performs the same operation without checking for pending unmasked floating-point exceptions.
FCMOV*cc*	**Floating-point conditional move.** Tests status flags in EFLAGS, moves source operand (second operand) to the destination operand (first operand) if the given test condition is true. Formats: FCMOVB ST(0),ST(i) Move if below FCMOVE ST(0),ST(i) Move if equal FCMOVBE ST(0),ST(i) Move if below or equal FCMOVU ST(0),ST(i) Move if unordered FCMOVNB ST(0),ST(i) Move if not below FCMOVNE ST(0),ST(i) Move if not equal FCMOVNBE ST(0),ST(i) Move if not below or equal FCMOVNU ST(0),ST(i) Move if not unordered

Instruction	Description

FCOM	**Compare floating-point values.** Compares ST(0) to the source operand and sets condition code flags C0, C2, and C3 in the FPU status word according to the results. Formats:
	
	`FCOM m32fp` `Compare ST(0) to m32fp`
	`FCOM m64fp` `Compare ST(0) to m64fp`
	`FCOM ST(i)` `Compare ST(0) to ST(i)`
	`FCOM` `Compare ST(0) to ST(1)`
	
	FCOMP performs the same operation as FCOM and then pops the stack. FCOMPP does the same task as FCOM and then pops the stack twice. FUCOM, FUCOMP, and FUCOMPP are the same as FCOM, FCOMP, and FCOMPP, respectively, except that they check for unordered values.

FCOMI	**Compare floating-point values and set EFLAGS.** Performs an unordered comparison of registers ST(0) and ST(i) and sets the status flags (ZF, PF, CF) in the EFLAGS register according to the results. Format: `FCOMI ST(0),ST(i)` `Compare ST(0) to ST(i)` FCOMIP does the same task as FCOMI and then pops the stack. FUCOMI and FUCOMIP check for unordered values.
FCOS	**Cosine.** Computes the cosine of ST(0) and stores the result in ST(0). Input must be in radians. No operands.
FDECSTP	**Decrement stack-top pointer.** Subtracts 1 from the TOP field of the FPU status word, effectively rotating the stack. No operands.

FDIV	**Divide floating-point and pop.** Divides the destination operand by the source operand and stores the result in the destination location. Formats:
	
	`FDIV` `ST(1) = ST(1) / ST(0), and pop stack`
	`FDIV m32fp` `ST(0) = ST(0) / m32fp`
	`FDIV m64fp` `ST(0) = ST(0) / m64fp`
	`FDIV ST(0),ST(i)` `ST(0) = ST(0) / ST(i)`
	`FDIV ST(i),ST(0)` `ST(i) = ST(i) / ST(0)`

FDIVP	**Divide floating-point and pop.** Same as FDIV, then pops from the stack. Format: `FDIVP ST(i),ST(0)` `ST(i) = ST(i) / ST(0), and pop stack`

FIDIV	**Convert integer to floating-point and divide.** After converting, performs the same operation as FDIV. Formats:
	
	`FIDIV m32int` `ST(0) = ST(0) / m32int`
	`FIDIV m16int` `ST(0) = ST(0) / m16int`

FDIVR	**Reverse divide.** Divides the source operand by the destination operand and stores the result in the destination location. Formats:
	
	`FDIVR` `ST(0) = ST(0) / ST(1), and pop stack`
	`FDIVR m32fp` `ST(0) = m32fp / ST(0)`
	`FDIVR m64fp` `ST(0) = m64fp / ST(0)`
	`FDIVR ST(0),ST(i)` `ST(0) = ST(i) / ST(0)`
	`FDIVR ST(i),ST(0)` `ST(i) = ST(0) / ST(i)`

FDIVRP	**Reverse divide and pop.** Performs the same operation as FDIVR, then pops from the stack. Format: `FDIVRP ST(i),ST(0)` `ST(i) = ST(0) / ST(i), and pop stack`

FIDIVR	**Convert integer to float and perform reverse divide.** After converting, performs the same operation as FDIVR. Formats:
	
	`FIDIVR m32int` `ST(0) = m32int / ST(0)`
	`FIDIVR m16int` `ST(0) = m16int / ST(0)`

FFREE	**Free floating-point register.** Sets the register to empty, using Tag word. Format: `FFREE ST(i)` `ST(i) = empty`

Table B-3   *(Continued)*

Instruction	Description
FICOM	**Compare integer.** Compares the value in ST(0) with an integer source operand and sets the condition code flags C0, C2, and C3 according to the results. The integer source operand is converted to floating-point before the comparison. Formats: `FICOM m32int` Compare ST(0) to *m32int* `FICOM m16int` Compare ST(0) to *m16int* FICOMP performs the same operation as FICOM, then pops from the stack.
FILD	**Convert integer to float and load onto register stack.** Formats: `FILD m16int` Push *m16int* onto register stack `FILD m32int` Push *m32int* onto register stack `FILD m64int` Push *m64int* onto register stack
FINCSTP	**Increment stack-top pointer.** Adds 1 to the TOP field of the FPU status word. No operands.
FINIT	**Initialize floating-point unit.** Sets the control, status, tag, instruction pointer, and data pointer registers to their default states. The control word is set to 037FH (round to nearest, all exceptions masked, 64-bit precision). The status word is cleared (no exception flags set, TOP = 0). The data registers in the register stack are unchanged, but they are tagged as empty. No operands. FNINIT performs the same operation without checking for pending unmasked floating-point exceptions.
FIST	**Store integer in memory operand.** Stores ST(0) in a signed integer memory operand, rounding according to the RC field in the FPU control word. Formats: `FIST m16int` Store ST(0) in *m16int* `FIST m32int` Store ST(0) in *m32int* FISTP performs the same operation as FIST, then pops the register stack. It has one additional format: `FISTP m64int` Store ST(0) in *m64int*, and pop stack
FISTTP	**Store integer with truncation.** Performs same operation as FIST, but automatically truncates the integer and pops the stack. Formats: `FISTTP m16int` Store ST(0) in *m16int*, and pop stack `FISTTP m32int` Store ST(0) in *m32int*, and pop stack `FISTTP m64int` Store ST(0) in *m64int*, and pop stack
FLD	**Load floating-point value onto register stack.** Formats: `FLD m32fp` Push *m32fp* onto register stack `FLD m64fp` Push *m64fp* onto register stack `FLD m80fp` Push *m80fp* onto register stack `FLD ST(i)` Push ST(i) onto register stack
FLD1	**Load +1.0 onto register stack.** No operands.
FLDL2T	**Load $\log_2 10$ onto register stack.** No operands.
FLDL2E	**Load $\log_2 e$ onto register stack.** No operands.
FLDPI	**Load *pi* onto register stack.** No operands.
FLDLG2	**Load $\log_{10} 2$ onto register stack.** No operands.
FLDLN2	**Load $\log_e 2$ onto register stack.** No operands.
FLDZ	**Load +0.0 onto register stack.** No operands.
FLDCW	**Load FPU control word from 16-bit memory value.** Format: `FLDCW m2byte` Load FPU control word from *m2byte*
FLDENV	**Load FPU environment from memory into the FPU.** Format: `FLDENV m14/28byte` Load FPU environment from memory

Instruction	Description

FMUL	**Multiply floating-point.** Multiplies the destination and source operands and stores the product in the destination location. Formats:
	
	`FMUL` `ST(1) = ST(1) * ST(0), and pop stack`
	`FMUL m32fp` `ST(0) = ST(0) * m32fp`
	`FMUL m64fp` `ST(0) = ST(0) * m64fp`
	`FMUL ST(0),ST(i)` `ST(0) = ST(0) * ST(i)`
	`FMUL ST(i),ST(0)` `ST(i) = ST(i) * ST(0)`

FMULP	**Multiply floating-point and pop.** Performs the same operation as FMUL, then pops the stack. Format: `FMULP ST(i),ST(0)` `ST(i) = ST(i) * ST(0), and pop stack`

FIMUL	**Convert integer and multiply.** Converts the source operand to floating-point, multiplies it by ST(0), and stores the product in ST(0). Formats:
	
	`FIMUL m16int`
	`FIMUL m32int`

FNOP	**No operation.** No operands.
FPATAN	**Partial arctangent.** Replaces ST(1) with arctan(ST(1)/ST(0)) and pops the register stack. No operands.
FPREM	**Partial remainder.** Replaces ST(0) with the remainder obtained from dividing ST(0) by ST(1). No operands. FPREM1 is similar, replacing ST(0) with the IEEE remainder obtained from dividing ST(0) by ST(1).
FPTAN	**Partial tangent.** Replaces ST(0) with its tangent and pushes 1.0 onto the FPU stack. Input must be in radians. No operands.
FRNDINT	**Round to integer.** Rounds ST(0) to the nearest integer value. No operands.
FRSTOR	**Restore x87 FPU State.** Loads the FPU state (operating environment and register stack) from the memory area specified by the source operand. Format: `FRSTOR m94/108byte`
FSAVE	**Store x87 FPU State.** Stores the current FPU state (operating environment and register stack) in memory specified by the destination operand and then reinitializes the FPU. Format: `FSAVE m94/108byte` FNSAVE performs the same operation without checking for pending unmasked floating-point exceptions.
FSCALE	**Scale.** Truncates the value in ST(1) to an integral value and adds that value to the exponent of the destination operand ST(0). No operands.
FSIN	**Sine.** Replaces ST(0) with its sine. Input must be in radians. No operands.
FSINCOS	**Sine and cosine.** Computes the sine and cosine of ST(0). Input must be in radians. Replaces ST(0) with the sine and pushes the cosine on the register stack. No operands.
FSQRT	**Square root.** Replaces ST(0) with its square root. No operands.

FST	**Store floating-point value.** Formats:
	
	`FST m32fp` `Copy ST(0) to m32fp`
	`FST m64fp` `Copy ST(0) to m64fp`
	`FST ST(i)` `Copy ST(0) to ST(i)`
	
	FSTP performs the same operation as FST, then pops the stack. It has one additional format:
	
	`FSTP m80fp` `Copy ST(0) to m80fp, and pop stack`

FSTCW	**Store FPU control word.** Format: `FLDCW m2byte` `Store FPU control word to m2byte` FNSTCW performs the same operation without checking for pending unmasked floating-point exceptions.

Table B-3 *(Continued)*

Instruction	Description
FSTENV	**Store FPU environment.** Stores the FPU environment in a m14byte or m28byte structure, depending on whether the processor is in real mode or protected mode. Format: FSTENV *memop* Store FPU environment to *memop* FNSTENV performs the same operation without checking for pending unmasked floating-point exceptions.

FSTSW	**Store FPU status word.** Formats:
	    FSTSW *m2byte* Store FPU status word to *m2byte*
	    FSTSW AX Store FPU status word to AX register
	FNSTSW performs the same operation without checking for pending unmasked floating-point exceptions.

FSUB	**Subtract floating-point.** Subtracts the source operand from the destination operand and stores the difference in the destination location. Formats:
	    FSUB ST(0) = ST(1) − ST(0), and pop stack
	    FSUB *m32fp* ST(0) = ST(0) − *m32fp*
	    FSUB *m64fp* ST(0) = ST(0) − *m64fp*
	    FSUB ST(0),ST(i) ST(0) = ST(0) − ST(i)
	    FSUB ST(i),ST(0) ST(i) = ST(i) − ST(0)

FSUBP	**Subtract floating-point and pop.** The FSUBP instruction performs the same operation as FSUB, then pops the stack. Format: FSUBP ST(i),ST(0) ST(i) = ST(i) − ST(0), and pop stack

FISUB	**Convert integer to floating-point and subtract.** Converts source operand to floating-point, subtracts it from ST(0), and stores the result in ST(0). Formats:
	    FISUB *m16int* ST(0) = ST(0) − *m16int*
	    FISUB *m32int* ST(0) = ST(0) − *m32int*

FSUBR	**Reverse subtract floating-point.** Subtracts the destination operand from the source operand and stores the difference in the destination location. Formats:
	    FSUBR ST(0) = ST(0) − ST(1), and pop stack
	    FSUBR *m32fp* ST(0) = *m32fp* − ST(0)
	    FSUBR *m64fp* ST(0) = *m64fp* − ST(0)
	    FSUBR ST(0),ST(i) ST(0) = ST(i) − ST(0)
	    FSUBR ST(i),ST(0) ST(i) = ST(0) − ST(i)

FSUBRP	**Reverse subtract floating-point and pop.** The FSUBRP instruction performs the same operation as FSUB, then pops the stack. Format: FSUBRP ST(i),ST(0) ST(i) = ST(0) − ST(i), and pop stack

FISUBR	**Convert integer and reverse subtract floating-point.** After converting to floating-point, performs the same operation as FSUBR. Formats:
	    FISUBR *m16int*
	    FISUBR *m32int*

FTST	**Test.** Compares ST(0) to 0.0 and sets condition code flags in the FPU status word. No operands.
FWAIT	**Wait.** Waits for all pending floating-point exception handlers to complete. No operands.
FXAM	**Examine.** Examines ST(0) and sets condition code flags in the FPU status word. No operands.

FXCH	**Exchange register contents.** Formats:
	    FXCH ST(i) Exchange ST(0) and ST(i)
	    FXCH Exchange ST(0) and ST(1)

Instruction	Description
FXRSTOR	**Restore x87 FPU, MMX Technology, SSE, and SSE2 State.** Reloads the FPU, MMX technology, XMM, and MXCSR registers from the memory image specified in the source operand. Format: FXRSTOR *m512byte*
FXSAVE	**Save x87 FPU, MMX Technology, SSE, and SSE2 State.** Saves the current state of the FPU, MMX technology, XMM, and MXCSR registers to the memory image specified in the destination operand. Format: FXRSAVE *m512byte*
FXTRACT	**Extract exponent and significand.** Separates the source in ST(0) into its exponent and significand, stores the exponent in ST(0), and pushes the significand on the register stack. No operands.
FYL2X	**Compute y * $\log_2 x$.** Register ST(1) holds the value of y, and ST(0) holds the value of x. Stack is popped, so the result is left in ST(0). No operands.
FYL2XP1	**Compute y * $\log_2(x + 1)$.** Register ST(1) holds the value of y, and ST(0) holds the value of x. Stack is popped, so the result is left in ST(0). No operands.

C

BIOS aNd MS-DOS

INTERRUPTS

C.1   Introduction

This appendix lists some of the more commonly used interrupt numbers, in groups:

- General list of PC interrupts, which correspond to the Interrupt vector table stored in the first 1024 bytes of memory.
- INT 21h MS-DOS functions
- INT 10h Video BIOS functions
- INT 16h Keyboard BIOS functions
- INT 33h Mouse functions

Documenting PC interrupts is a huge task, due to the many different versions of MS-DOS, as well as various DOS extenders and PC hardware controllers. The definitive source for interrupts is Ralf Brown's Interrupt List, available in various forms on the Web. My personal favorite is the HTML version, of which one version is currently available at http://www.ctyme.com/rbrown.htm. Web URLs change often, so check our book's Web site for up-to-date links to the Ralf Brown Interrupt List and other assembly language Web sites.

C.2 PC Interrupts

Table C-1   General List of PC Interrupt Numbers.[a]

Number	Description
0	*Divide Error.* CPU-generated: activated when attempting to divide by zero.
1	*Single Step.* CPU-generated: active when the CPU Trap flag is set.
2	*Nonmaskable Interrupt.* External hardware: activated when a memory error occurs.
3	*Breakpoint.* CPU-generated: activated when the 0CCh (INT 3) instruction is executed.
4	*INTO Detected Overflow.* CPU-generated: Activated when the INTO instruction is executed and the Overflow flag is set.
5	*Print Screen.* Activated either by the INT 5 instruction or pressing the Shift-PrtSc keys.
6	*Invalid OpCode* (80286+)
7	*Processor Extension Not Available* (80286+)
8	IRQ0: *System Timer Interrupt.* Updates the BIOS clock 18.2 times per second. For your own programming, see INT 1Ch.
9	IRQ1: *Keyboard Hardware Interrupt.* Activated when a key is pressed. Reads the key from the keyboard port and stores it in the keyboard typeahead buffer.
0A	IRQ2: *Programmable Interrupt Controller*
0B	IRQ3: Serial Communications (COM2)
0C	IRQ4: Serial Communications (COM1)
0D	IRQ5: Fixed Disk
0E	IRQ6: *Diskette Interrupt.* Activated when a disk seek is in progress.
0F	IRQ7: *Parallel Printer*
10	*Video Services.* Routines for manipulating the video display (see the complete list in Table C-3).
11	*Equipment Check.* Return a word showing all the peripherals attached to the system.
12	*Memory Size.* Return the amount of memory (in 1024-byte blocks) in AX.
13	*Floppy Disk Services.* Reset the disk controller, get the status of the most recent disk access, read and write physical sectors, and format a disk.
14	*Asynchronous (Serial) Port Services.* Initialize and read or write the asynchronous communications port, and return the port's status.
15	Cassette Controller.
16	*Keyboard Services.* Read and inspect keyboard input (see the complete list in Table C-4).
17	*Printer Services.* Initialize, print, and return the status of the printer.
18	*ROM BASIC.* Execute cassette BASIC in ROM.

Table C-1   *(Continued)*

Number	Description
19	*Bootstrap Loader.* Reboot MS-DOS.
1A	*Time of Day.* Get the number of timer ticks since the machine was turned on, or set the counter to a new value. Ticks occur 18.2 times per second.
1B	*Keyboard Break.* This interrupt handler is executed by INT 9h when CTRL-BREAK is pressed.
1C	*User Timer Interrupt.* Empty routine, executed 18.2 times per second. May be used by your own program.
1D	*Video Parameters.* Point to a table containing initialization and information for the video controller chip.
1E	*Diskette Parameters.* Point to a table containing initialization information for the diskette controller.
1F	*Graphics Table.* 8 × 8 Graphics font. Table kept in memory of all extended graphics characters with ASCII codes higher than 127.
20	*Terminate Program.* Terminate a COM program (INT 21h Function 4Ch should be used instead).
21	*MS-DOS Services* (see the complete list in Table C-2).
22	*MS-DOS Terminate Address.* Point to the address of the parent program or process. When the current program ends, this will be the return address.
23	*MS-DOS Break Address.* MS-DOS jumps here when CTRL-BREAK is pressed.
24	*MS-DOS Critical Error Address.* DOS jumps to this address when there is a critical error in the current program, such as a disk media error.
25	*Absolute Disk Read* (obsolete).
26	*Absolute Disk Write* (obsolete).
27	*Terminate and Stay Resident* (obsolete).
28–FF	(Reserved)
33	*Microsoft Mouse.* Functions that track and control the mouse.
34–3E	*Floating-Point Emulation.*
3F	*Overlay manager.*
40–41	*Fixed Disk Services.* Fixed disk controller.
42–5F	Reserved: specialized uses
60–6B	Available for application programs to use.
6C–7F	Reserved: specialized uses
80–F0	Reserved: used by ROM BASIC.
F1–FF	Available for application programs.

[a]Sources: Ray Duncan, *Advanced MS-DOS*, 2nd ed., Microsoft Press, 1998. *Ralf Brown's Interrupt List*, available on the Web.

C.3 Interrupt 21H Functions (MS-DOS Services)

There are so many MS-DOS services available through INT 21h that we could not possibly document them all here. Instead, Table C-2 is simply a brief overview of functions that are commonly used.

Table C-2   Interrupt 21h Functions (MS-DOS Services).

Function	Description
1	*Read character from standard input.* If no character is ready, wait for input. Returns: AL = character.
2	*Write character to standard output.* Receives: DL = character.
3	*Read character from standard auxiliary input* (serial port).
4	*Write character to standard auxiliary output* (serial port).
5	*Write character to printer.* Receives: DL = character.
6	*Direct console input/output.* If DL = FFh, read a waiting character from standard input. If DL is any other value, write the character in DL to standard output.
7	*Direct character input without echo.* Wait for a character from standard input. Returns: AL = character.
8	*Character input without echo.* Wait for a character from the standard input device. Returns: AL = character. Character not echoed. May be terminated by Ctrl-Break.
9	*Write string to standard output.* Receives: DS:DX = address of string.
0A	*Buffered keyboard input.* Read a string of characters from the standard input device. Receives: DS:DX points to a predefined keyboard structure.
0B	*Check standard input status.* Check to see if an input character is waiting. Returns: AL = 0FFh if the character is ready; otherwise, AL = 0.
0C	*Clear keyboard buffer and invoke input function.* Clear the console input buffer, and then execute an input function. Receives: AL = desired function (1, 6, 7, 8, or 0Ah).
0E	*Select default drive.* Receives: DL = drive number (0 = A, 1 = B, etc.).
0F–18	FCB file functions (obsolete).
19	*Get current default drive.* Returns: AL = drive number (0 = A, 1 = B, etc.)
1A	*Set disk transfer address.* Receives: DS:DX contains address of disk transfer area.
25	*Set interrupt vector.* Set an entry in the Interrupt Vector Table to a new address. Receives: DS:DX points to the interrupt-handling routine that is inserted in the table; AL = the interrupt number.
26	*Create new program segment prefix.* Receives: DX = segment address for new PSP.
27–29	FCB file functions (obsolete).
2A	*Get system date.* Returns: AL = Day of the week (0–6, where Sunday = 0), CX = year, DH = month, and DL = day.
2B	*Set system date.* Receives: CX = year, DH = month, and DL = day. Returns: AL = 0 if the date is valid.
2C	*Get system time.* Returns: CH = hour, CL = minutes, DH = seconds, and DL = hundredths of seconds.
2D	*Set system time.* Receives: CH = hour, CL = minutes, DH = seconds, and DL = hundredths of seconds. Returns: AL = 0 if the time is valid.
2E	*Set Verify flag.* Receives: AL = new state of MS-DOS Verify flag (0 = off, 1 = on), DL = 00h.

Table C-2   *(Continued)*

Function	Description
2F	*Get disk transfer address* (DTA). Returns: ES:BX = address.
30	*Get MS-DOS version number.* Returns: AL = major version number, AH = minor version number, BH = OEM serial number, BL:CX = 24-bit user serial number.
31	*Terminate and stay resident.* Terminate the current program or process, leaving part of itself in memory. Receives: AL = return code, and DX = requested number of paragraphs.
32	*Get MS-DOS drive parameter block.* Receives: DL = drive number. Returns: AL = status; DS:BX points to drive parameter block.
33	*Extended break checking.* Indicates whether or not MS-DOS is checking for Ctrl-Break.
34	*Get address of INDOS flag.* (Undocumented)
35	*Get interrupt vector.* Receives: AL = interrupt number. Returns: ES:BX = segment/offset of the interrupt handler.
36	*Get disk free space.* (FAT16 only) Receives: DL = drive number (0 = default, 1 = A, etc.). Returns: AX = sectors per cluster, or FFFFh if the drive number is invalid; BX = number of available clusters, CX = bytes per sector, and DX = clusters per drive.
37	*Get switch character.* (Undocumented)
38	*Get or set country information.*[a]
39	*Create subdirectory.* Receives: DS:DX points to an ASCIIZ string with the path and directory name. Returns: AX = error code if the Carry flag is set.
3A	*Remove subdirectory.* Receives: DS:DX points to an ASCIIZ string with the path and directory name. Returns: AX = error code if the Carry flag is set.
3B	*Change current directory.* Receives: DS:DX points to an ASCIIZ string with the new directory path. Returns: AX = error code if the Carry flag is set.
3C	*Create or truncate file.* Create a new file or truncate an old file to zero bytes. Open the file for output. Receives: DS:DX points to an ASCIIZ string with the file name, and CX = file attribute. Returns: AX = error code if the Carry flag is set; otherwise AX = the new file handle.
3D	*Open existing file.* Open a file for input, output, or input-output. Receives: DS:DX points to an ASCIIZ string with the filename, and AL = the access code (0 = read, 1 = write, 2 = read/write). Returns: AX = error code if the Carry flag is set, otherwise AX = the new file handle.
3E	*Close file handle.* Close the file or device specified by a file handle. Receives: BX = file handle from previous open or create. Returns: If the Carry Flag is set, AX = error code.
3F	*Read from file or device.* Read a specified number of bytes from a file or device. Receives: BX = file handle, DS:DX points to an input buffer, and CX = number of bytes to read. Returns: If the Carry flag is set, AX = error code; otherwise, AX = number of bytes read.
40	*Write to file or device.* Write a specified number of bytes to a file or device. Receives: BX = file handle, DS:DX points to an output buffer, and CX = the number of bytes to write. Returns: If the Carry flag is set, AX = error code; otherwise, AX = number of bytes written.
41	*Delete file.* Remove a file from a specified directory. Receives: DS:DX points to an ASCIIZ string with the filename. Returns: AX = error code if the Carry flag is set.

Function	Description
42	*Move file pointer.* Move the file read/write pointer according to a specified method. Receives: CX:DX = distance (bytes) to move the file pointer, AL = method code, BX = file handle. The method codes are as follows: 0 = move from beginning of file, 1 = move to the current location plus an offset, and 2 = move to the end of file plus an offset. Returns: AX = error code if the Carry flag is set.
43	*Get/Set file attribute.* Get or set the attribute of a file. Receives: DS:DX = pointer to an ASCIIZ path and filename, CX = attribute, and AL = function code (1 = set attribute, 0 = get attribute). Returns: AX = error code if the Carry flag is set.
44	*I/O control for devices.* Get or set device information associated with an open device handle, or send a control string to the device handle, or receive a control string from the device handle.
45	*Duplicate file handle.* Return a new file handle for a file that is currently open. Receives: BX = file handle. Returns: AX = error code if the Carry flag is set.
46	*Force duplicate file handle.* Force the handle in CX to refer to the same file at the same position as the handle in BX. Receives: BX = existing file handle and CX = second file handle. Returns: AX = error code if the Carry flag is set.
47	*Get current directory.* Get the full path name of the current directory. Receives: DS:SI points to a 64-byte area to hold the directory path, and DL = drive number. Returns: A buffer at DS:SI is filled with the path, and AX = error code if the Carry flag is set.
48	*Allocate memory.* Allocate a requested number of paragraphs of memory, measured in 16-byte blocks. Receives: BX = number of paragraphs requested. Returns: AX = segment of the allocated block and BX = size of the largest block available (in paragraphs), and AX = error code if the Carry flag is set.
49	*Free allocated memory.* Free memory that was previously allocated by Function 48h. Receives: ES = segment of the block to be freed. Returns: AX = error code if the Carry flag is set.
4A	*Modify memory blocks.* Modify allocated memory blocks to contain a new block size. The block will shrink or grow. Receives: ES = segment of the block and BX = requested number of paragraphs. Returns: AX = error code if the Carry flag is set and BX = maximum number of available blocks.
4B	*Load or execute program.* Create a program segment prefix for another program, load it into memory, and execute it. Receives: DS:DX points to an ASCIIZ string with the drive, path, and filename of the program; ES:BX points to a parameter block and AL = function value. Function values in AL:0 = load and execute the program; 3 = load but do not execute (overlay program). Returns: AX = error code if the Carry flag is set.
4C	*Terminate process.* Usual way to terminate a program and return to either MS-DOS or a calling program. Receives: AL = 8-bit return code, which can be queried by DOS function 4Dh or by the ERRORLEVEL command in a batch file.
4D	*Get return code of process.* Get the return code of a process or program, generated by either function call 31h or function call 4Ch. Returns: AL = 8-bit code returned by the program, AH = type of exit generated: 0 = normal termination, 1 = terminated by CTRLBREAK, 2 = terminated by a critical device error, and 3 = terminated by a call to function call 31h.
4E	*Find first matching file.* Find the first filename that matches a given file specification. Receives: DS:DX points to an ASCIIZ drive, path, and file specification; CX = File attribute to be used when searching. Returns: AX = error code if the Carry flag is set; otherwise, the current DTA is filled with the filename, attribute, time, date, and size. DOS function call 1Ah (set DTA) is usually called before this function.

Table C-2   *(Continued)*

Function	Description
4F	*Find next matching file.* Find the next filename that matches a given file specification. This is always called after DOS function 4Eh. Returns: AX = error code if the Carry flag is set; otherwise, the current DTA is filled with the file's information.
54	*Get Verify flag.* Returns: AH = Verify flag for disk I/O (0 = off; 1 = on).
56	*Rename/move file.* Rename a file or move it to another directory. Receives: DS:DX points to an ASCIIZ string that specifies the current drive, path, and filename; ES:DI points to the new path and filename. Returns: AX = error code if the Carry flag is set.
57	*Get/Set file date/time.* Get or set the date and time stamp for a file. Receives: AL = 0 to get the date/time or AL = 1 to set the date/time; BX = file handle, CX = new file time, and DX = new file date. Returns: AX = error code if the Carry flag is set; otherwise, CX = current file time and DX = current file date.
58	*Get or set memory allocation strategy.*[a]
59	*Get extended error information.* Return additional information about an MS-DOS error, including the error class, locus, and recommended action. Receives: BX = MS-DOS version number (zero for version 3.xx). Returns: AX = extended error code, BH = error class, BL = suggested action, and CH = locus.
5A	*Create temporary file.* Generate a unique filename in a specified directory. Receives: DS:DX points to an ASCIIZ pathname, ending with a backslash (\); CX = desired file attribute. Returns: AX = error code if the Carry flag is set; otherwise, DS:DX points to the path with the new filename appended.
5B	*Create new file.* Try to create a new file, but fail if the filename already exists. This prevents you from overwriting an existing file. Receives: DS:DX points to an ASCIIZ string with the path and filename. Returns: AX = error code if the Carry flag is set.
5C–61	Omitted.
62	*Get program segment prefix (PSP) address.* Returns: BX = the segment value of the current program's PSP.
7303h	*Get disk free space.* Fills a structure containing detailed disk space information. Receives: AX = 7303h, ES:DI points to a ExtGetDskFreSpcStruc structure, CX = size of the ExtGetDskFreSpc-Struc structure, DS:DX points to a null-terminated string containing the drive name. Returns: The ExtGetDskFreSpcStruc is filled in with disk information. See Section 14.5.1 for details.
7305h	*Absolute disk read and write.* Reads individual disk sectors or groups of sectors. Does not work under Windows NT, 2000, and XP. Receives: AX = 7305h, DS:BX = segment/offset of a DISKIO structure variable, CX = 0FFFFh, DL = drive number (0 = default, 1 = A, 2 = B, 3 = C, etc.), SI = Read/write flag. See Section 14.4 for details.

[a]For details see Ray Duncan, *Advanced MS-DOS*, 2nd ed., Microsoft Press, 1998; *Ralf Brown's Interrupt List*, available on the web.

C.4 Interrupt 10H Functions (Video BIOS)

Table C-3   Interrupt 10h Functions (Video BIOS).

Function	Description
0	*Set video mode.* Set the video display to monochrome, text, graphics, or color mode. Receives: AL = display mode.
1	*Set cursor lines.* Identify the starting and ending scan lines for the cursor. Receives: CH = cursor starting line, and CL = cursor ending line.
2	*Set cursor position.* Position the cursor on the screen. Receives: BH = video page, DH = row, and DL = column.
3	*Get cursor position.* Get the cursor's screen position and its size. Receives: BH = video page. Returns: CH = cursor starting line, CL = cursor ending line, DH = cursor row, and DL = cursor column.
4	*Read light pen.* Read the position and status of the light pen. Returns: CH = pixel row, BX = pixel column, DH = character row, and DL = character column.
5	*Set display page.* Select the video page to be displayed. Receives: AL = desired page number.
6	*Scroll window up.* Scroll a window on the current video page upward, replacing scrolled lines with blanks. Receives: AL = number of lines to scroll, BH = attribute for scrolled lines, CX = upper left corner row and column, and DX = lower right row and column.
7	*Scroll window down.* Scroll a window on the current video page downward, replacing scrolled lines with blanks. Receives: AL = number of lines to scroll, BH = attribute for scrolled lines, CX = upper left corner row and column, and DX = lower right row and column.
8	*Read character and attribute.* Read the character and its attribute at the current cursor position. Receives: BH = display page. Returns: AH = attribute byte and AL = ASCII character code.
9	*Write character and attribute.* Write a character and its attribute at the current cursor position. Receives: AL = ASCII character, BH = video page, and CX = repetition factor.
0A	*Write character.* Write a character only (no attribute) at the current cursor position. Receives: AL = ASCII character, BH = video page, BL = attribute, and CX = replication factor.
0B	*Set color palette.* Select a group of available colors for the color or EGA adapter. Receives: AL = display mode and BH = active display page.
0C	*Write graphics pixel.* Write a graphics pixel when in color graphics mode. Receives: Al = pixel value, CX = X-coordinate, and DX = Y-coordinate.
0D	*Read graphics pixel.* Read the color of a single graphics pixel at a given location. Receives: CX = X-coordinate, and DX = Y-coordinate.
0E	*Write character.* Write a character to the screen and advance the cursor. Receives: AL = ASCII character code, BH = video page, BL = attribute or color.
0F	*Get current video mode.* Get the current video mode. Returns: AL = video mode and BH = active video page.
10	*Set video palette.* (EGA only) Set the video palette register, border color, or blink/intensity bit. Receives: AL = function code (00 = set palette register, 01 = set border color, 02 = set palette and border color, 03 = set/reset blink/intensity bit), BH = color, BL = palette register to set. If AL = 2, ES:DX points to a color list.
11	*Character generator.* Select the character size for the EGA display. For example, an 8 by 8 font is used for the 43-line display, and an 8 by 14 font is used for the 25-line display.
12	*Alternate select function.* Return technical information about the EGA display.
13	*Write string.* (PC/AT only) Write a string of text to the video display. Receives: AL = mode, BH = page, BL = attribute, CX = length of string, DH = row, DL = column, and ES:BP points to the string (will not work on the IBM-PC or PC/XT).

C.5   Keyboard BIOS INT 16h Functions

Table C-4   Keyboard BIOS Interrupt 16h Functions.

Function	Description
03h	*Set typematic repeat rate.* Receives: AH = 03h, AL = 5, BH = repeat delay, BL = repeat rate. The delay values in BH are 0 = 250 ms; 1 = 500 ms; 2 = 750 ms; 3 = 1000 ms. The repeat rate in BL varies from 0 (fastest) to 1Fh (slowest). Returns: nothing.
05h	*Push key into buffer.* Pushes a keyboard character and corresponding scan code into the keyboard typeahead buffer. Receives: AH = 05h, CH = scan code, and CL = character code. If the typeahead buffer is already full, the Carry flag will be set, and AL = 1. Returns: nothing
10	*Wait for key.* Wait for an input character and keyboard scan code. Receives: AH = 10h. Returns: AH = scan code, AL = ASCII character. (Function 00h duplicates this function, using an older type of keyboard.)
11	*Check keyboard buffer.* Find out if a character is waiting in the keyboard typeahead buffer. Receives: AH = 01h. Returns: If a key is waiting, its scan code is returned in AH and its ASCII code is returned in AL, and the Zero flag is cleared (the character will remain in the input buffer). If no key is waiting, the Zero flag is set. (Function 01h duplicates this function, using an older type of keyboard.)
12	*Get keyboard flags.* Return the Keyboard Flag byte stored in low RAM. Receives: AH = 12h. Returns: Keyboard flags in AX. (Function 02h duplicates this function, using an older type of keyboard.)

C.6   Mouse Functions (INT 33h)

INT 33h mouse functions receive their function number in the AX register. For more information about these functions, see Section 15.6. For additional mouse functions, see Table 15-9.

Table C-5   INT 33h Mouse Functions.

Function	Description
0000h	*Reset mouse and get status.* Receives: AX = 0000h. Resets the mouse and confirms that it is available. The mouse (if found) is centered on the screen, its display page is set to video page 0, its pointer is hidden, and its mickeys-to-pixels ratios and speed are set to default values. The mouse's range of movement is set to the entire screen area.
0001h	*Show mouse pointer.* Receives: AX = 0001h. Returns: nothing. The mouse driver keeps a count of the number of times this function is called.
0002h	*Hide mouse pointer.* Receives: AX = 0002h. Returns: nothing. The mouse position is still tracked when it is invisible.
0003h	*Get mouse position and status.* Receives: AX = 0003h. Returns: BX = mouse button status, CX = X-coordinate (in pixels), DX = Y-coordinate (in pixels).
0004h	*Set mouse position.* Receives: AX = 0004h, CX = X-coordinate (in pixels), DX = Y-coordinate (in pixels). Returns: nothing.
0005h	*Get button press information.* Receives: AX = 0005h, BX = button ID (0 = left, 1 = right, 2 = center). Returns: AX = button status, BX = button press counter, CX = X-coordinate of last button press, DX = Y-coordinate of last button press.
0006h	*Get button release information.* Receives: AX = 0006h, BX = button ID (0 = left, 1 = right, 2 = center). Returns: AX = button status, BX = button release counter, CX = X-coordinate of last button release, DX = Y-coordinate of last button release.
0007h	*Set horizontal limits.* Receives: AX = 0007h, CX = minimum X-coordinate (in pixels), DX = maximum X-coordinate (in pixels). Returns: nothing.
0008h	*Set vertical limits.* Receives: AX = 0008h, CX = minimum Y-coordinate (in pixels), DX = maximum Y-coordinate (in pixels). Returns: nothing.

D

ANSWERS TO REVIEW QUESTIONS

1 Basic Concepts

1.1 Welcome to Assembly Language

1. An assembler converts source-code programs from assembly language into machine language. A linker combines individual files created by an assembler into a single executable program.

2. Assembly language is a good tool for learning how application programs communicate with the computer's operating system via interrupt handlers, system calls, and common memory areas. Assembly language programming also helps when learning how the operating system loads and executes application programs.

3. In a *one-to-many* relationship, a single statement expands into multiple assembly language or machine instructions.

4. A language whose source programs can be compiled and run on a wide variety of computer systems is said to be *portable*.

5. No. Each assembly language is based on either a processor family or specific computer.

6. Some examples of embedded systems applications are automobile fuel and ignition systems, air-conditioning control systems, security systems, flight control systems, hand-held computers, modems, printers, and other intelligent computer peripherals.

7. *Device drivers* are programs that translate general operating system commands into specific references to hardware details that only the manufacturer knows.

8. C++ does not allow a pointer of one type to be assigned to a pointer of another type. Assembly language has no such restriction regarding pointers.

9. Applications suited to assembly language: hardware device driver and embedded systems and computer games requiring direct hardware access.

10. A high-level language may not provide for direct hardware access. Even if it does, awkward coding techniques must often be used, resulting in possible maintenance problems.

11. Assembly language has minimal formal structure, so structure must be imposed by programmers who have varying levels of experience. This leads to difficulties maintaining existing code.

12. Code for the expression X = (Y * 4) + 3:

```
    mov   eax,Y                    ; move Y to EAX
    mov   ebx,4                    ; move 4 to EBX
```

```
imul ebx        ; EAX = EAX * EBX
add  eax,3      ; add 3 to EAX
mov  X,eax      ; move EAX to X
```

1.2   Virtual Machine Concept

1. Computers are constructed in layers, so that each layer represents a translation layer from a higher-level instruction set to a lower-level instruction set.

2. It is enormously detailed and consists purely of numbers. Hard for humans to understand.

3. True.

4. An entire L1 program is converted into an L0 program by an L0 program specifically designed for this purpose. Then the resulting L0 program is executed directly on the computer hardware.

5. The IA-32's virtual-86 operating mode emulates the architecture of the Intel 8086/8088 processor used in the original IBM-PC.

6. Java byte code is a low-level language that is quickly executed at run time by a program known as a Java virtual machine (JVM).

7. Digital logic, microarchitecture, instruction set architecture, operating system, assembly language, high-level language.

8. The specific microarchitecture commands are often a proprietary secret. Also, microcode programming is impractical because it often requires three or four microinstructions to carry out a single primitive operation.

9. Instruction set architecture

10. Levels 2 and 3.

1.3   Data Representation

1. Least significant bit (bit 0).

2. Most significant bit (the highest numbered bit).

3. (a) 248   (b) 202   (c) 240

4. (a) 53   (b) 150   (c) 204

5. (a) 00010001   (b) 101000000   (c) 00011110

6. (a) 110001010   (b) 110010110   (c) 100100001

7. (a) 2   (b) 4   (c) 8

8. (a) 16   (b) 32   (c) 64

9. (a) 7   (b) 9   (c) 16

10. (a) 12   (b) 16   (c) 22

11. (a) CF57   (b) 5CAD   (c) 93EB

12. (a) 35DA   (b) CEA3   (c) FEDB

13. (a) 1110 0101 1011 0110 1010 1110 1101 0111
    (b) 1011 0110 1001 0111 1100 0111 1010 0001
    (c) 0010 0011 0100 1011 0110 1101 1001 0010

14. (a) 0000 0001 0010 0110 1111 1001 1101 0100
    (b) 0110 1010 1100 1101 1111 1010 1001 0101
    (c) 1111 0110 1001 1011 1101 1100 0010 1010

15. (a) 58   (b) 447   (c) 16534

16. (a) 98   (b) 457   (c) 27227

17. (a) FFE6   (b) FE3C

18. (a) FFE0   (b) FFC2

19. (a) +31915   (b) −16093

20. (a) +32667   (b) −32208

21. (a) −75   (b) +42   (c) −16

22. (a) −128   (b) −52   (c) −73

23. (a) 11111011   (b) 11011100   (c) 11110000

24. (a) 10111000   (b) 10011110   (c) 11100110

25. 58h and 88d.

26. 4Dh and 77d.

27. To handle international character sets that require more than 256 codes.

28. $2^{256} − 1$.

29. $+2^{255} − 1$.

1.4 Boolean Operations

1. (NOT X) OR Y.

2. X AND Y.

3. T.

4. F.

5. T.

6. Truth table:

A	B	A ∨ B	¬(A ∨ B)
F	F	F	T
F	T	T	F
T	F	T	F
T	T	T	F

7. Truth table:

A	B	¬A	¬B	¬A ∧ ¬B
F	F	T	T	T
F	T	T	F	F
T	F	F	T	F
T	T	F	F	F

8. 16, or (2^4).

9. 2 bits, producing the following values: 00, 01, 10, 11.

2   IA-32 Processor Architecture

2.1   General Concepts

1. Control Unit, Arithmetic Logic Unit, and the clock.

2. Data, Address, and Control buses.

3. Conventional memory is outside the CPU and it responds more slowly to access requests. Registers are hard-wired inside the CPU.

4. Fetch, decode, execute.

5. Fetch memory operands, store memory operands.

6. During the fetch step.

7. Executing processor stages in parallel, making possible the overlapped execution of machine instructions.

8. 10 clock cycles.

9. 12 cycles (5 + (8 − 1).

10. A superscalar processor contains two or more execution pipelines.

11. 15 clock cycles (5 + 10).

12. Section 2.1.4 mentions the filename, file size, and starting location on the disk. (Most directories also store the file's last modification date and time.)

13. The OS executes a branch (like a GOTO) to the first machine instruction in the program.

14. The CPU executes multiple tasks (programs) by rapidly switching from one program to the next. This gives the impression that all programs are executing at the same time.

15. The OS scheduler determines how much time to allot to each task, and it switches between tasks.

16. The program counter, the task's variables, and the CPU registers (including the status flags).

17. 3.33×10^{-10}, which is $1.0/3.0 \times 10^9$.

2.2   IA-32 Processor Architecture

1. Real-address mode, Protected mode, and System Managment mode.

2. EAX, EBX, ECX, EDX, ESI, EDI, ESP, EBP.

3. CS, DS, SS, ES, FS, GS.

4. Loop counter.

5. EBP.

6. Most common: Carry, Sign, Zero, Overflow. Less common: Auxiliary Carry, Parity.

7. Carry.

8. Overflow.

9. Sign.

10. Floating-Point Unit.

11. 80 bits.

12. The Intel 80386.

13. The Pentium.

14. The Pentium.

15. CISC means *complex instruction set*: a large collection of instructions, some of which perform sophisticated operations that might be typical of a high-level language.

16. The term RISC stands for *reduced instruction set*: a small set of simple (atomic) instructions that may be combined into more complex operations.

2.3   IA-32 Memory Management

1. 4GB (0 to FFFFFFFFh).
2. 1MB (0 to FFFFFh).
3. Linear (absolute).
4. 09600h.
5. 0CFF0h.
6. 32 bits.
7. SS register.
8. Local descriptor table.
9. Global descriptor table.
10. The total size of all programs loaded into memory can exceed the amount of physical memory installed in the computer.
11. This is an open-ended question, of course. It is a fact that MS-DOS first had to run on the 8086/8088 processors, which only supported Real-address mode. When later processors came out that supported Protected mode, my guess is that Microsoft wanted MS-DOS to continue to run on the older processors. Otherwise, customers with older computers would refuse to upgrade to new versions of MS-DOS.
12. The following segment-offset addresses point to the same linear address: 0640:0100, and 0630:0200.

2.4   Components of an IA-32 Microcomputer

1. SRAM stands for Static RAM, used in CPU cache memory.
2. Pentium.
3. The 8259 is the interrupt controller chip, sometimes called PIC, that schedules hardware interrupts and interrupts the CPU.
4. On either the video board or the motherboard (special memory area).
5. A beam of electrons illuminates phosphorus dots on the screen called pixels. Starting at the top of the screen, the gun fires electrons from the left side to the right in a horizontal row, briefly turns off, and returns to the left side of the screen to begin a new row. Horizontal retrace refers to the time period when the gun is off between rows. When the last row is drawn, the gun turns off (called the vertical retrace) and moves to the upper left corner of the screen to start all over.
6. Dynamic RAM, Static RAM, Video RAM, and CMOS RAM.
7. Static RAM.
8. The computer can query a device connected via USB to find out its name and device type and the type of driver it supports. The computer can also suspend power to individual devices. None of these capabilities is possible with serial and parallel ports.
9. Upstream and downstream
10. 16550 UART (universal asynchronous receiver transmitter).

2.5   Input-Output System

1. The application program level.

2. BIOS functions communicate directly with the system hardware. They are independent of the operating system.

3. New devices are invented all the time with capabilities that were often not anticipated when the BIOS was written.

4. The BIOS level.

5. The operating system, BIOS, and hardware levels.

6. Game programs often try to take advantage of the latest features in specialized sound cards. It should be noted that MS-DOS game applications were more prone to do this than games running under MS-Windows. In fact, Windows-NT, 2000, and XP all prevent applications from directly accessing system hardware.

7. No. The same BIOS would work for both operating systems. Many computer owners install two or three operating systems on the same computer. They would certainly not want to change the system BIOS every time they rebooted the computer!

3 Assembly Language Fundamentals

3.1 Basic Elements of Assembly Language

1. h, q, o, d, b, r, t, y.

2. No (a leading zero is required).

3. No (they have the same precedence).

4. Expression: 10 MOD 3.

5. Real number constant: +3.5E-02.

6. No, they can also be enclosed in double quotes.

7. Directives.

8. 247 characters.

9. True.

10. True.

11. False.

12. True.

13. Label, mnemonic, operand(s), comment.

14. True.

15. True.

16. Code example:
```
Comment !
    This is a comment
    This is also a comment
!
```

17. Because the addresses coded in the instructions would have to be updated whenever new variables were inserted before existing ones.

3.2 Example: Adding Three Integers

1. The INCLUDE directive copies necessary definitions and setup information from the *Irvine32.inc* text file. The data from this file is inserted into the data stream read by the assembler.

2. The .CODE directive marks the beginning of the code segment.

3. code, data, and stack.

4. By calling the **DumpRegs** procedure.

5. The **exit** statement.

6. The PROC directive.

7. The ENDP directive.

8. It marks the last line of the program to be assembled, and the label next to END identifies the program's entry point (where execution begins).

9. PROTO declares the name of a procedure that is called by the current program.

3.3   Assembling, Linking, and Running Programs

1. Object (.OBJ) and listing (.LST) files.

2. True.

3. True.

4. Loader.

5. Executable (.EXE) and map (.MAP).

6. The /Fl option.

7. The /Zi option.

8. It tells the linker to produce a *Win32 Console* application.

9. There are too many to mention here, but you can view their names by opening Kernel32.lib using the TextPad editor supplied on the book's CD-ROM. The file will display in hexadecimal. Scroll down to offset 1840h, and look at the various function names listed from that point on.

10. /ENTRY sets the program's starting address (the entry point). For example, suppose you wanted your program to begining execution at the Startup procedure. The link command line would be

```
link /ENTRY:Startup
```

This is a challenging question because you cannot find the answer in Appendix A. Instead, you can read about the Microsoft 32-bit linker command-line options by visiting the MSDN Web site and searching for *linker reference*.

3.4   Defining Data

1. var1 SWORD ?

2. var2 BYTE ?

3. var3 SBYTE ?

4. var4 QWORD ?

5. SDWORD

6. var5 SDWORD −2147483648

7. wArray WORD 10, 20, 30

8. myColor BYTE "blue", 0

9. dArray DWORD 50 DUP(?)

10. myTestString BYTE 500 DUP("TEST")

11. bArray BYTE 20 DUP(0)

12. 21h, 43h, 65h, 87h

3.5   Symbolic Constants

1. BACKSPACE = 08h
2. SecondsInDay = 24 * 60 * 60
3. ArraySize = ($ − myArray)
4. ArraySize = ($ − myArray) / TYPE DWORD
5. PROCEDURE TEXTEQU <PROC>
6. Code example:
   ```
   Sample TEXTEQU <"This is a string">
   MyString BYTE Sample
   ```
7. SetupESI TEXTEQU <mov esi, OFFSET myArray>

4   Data Transfers, Addressing, and Arithmetic

4.1   Data Transfer Instructions

1. Register, immediate, and memory
2. False
3. False
4. True
5. A 32-bit register or memory operand
6. A 16-bit immediate (constant) operand
7. (a) not valid (b) valid (c) not valid (d) not valid (e) not valid (f) not valid (g) valid (h) not valid
8. (a) FCh (b) 01h
9. (a) 1000h (b) 3000h (c) FFF0h (d) 4000h
10. (a) 00000001h (b) 00001000h (c) 00000002h (d) FFFFFFFCh

4.2   Addition and Subtraction

1. inc val2
2. sub eax,val3
3. Code:
   ```
   mov ax,val4
   sub val2,ax
   ```
4. CF = 0, SF = 1.
5. CF = 1, SF = 1.
6. Write down the following flag values:
   (a) CF = 1, SF = 0, ZF = 1, OF = 0
   (b) CF = 0, SF = 1, ZF = 0, OF = 1
   (c) CF = 0, SF = 1, ZF = 0, OF = 0
7. Code example:
   ```
   mov ax,val2
   neg ax
   add ax,bx
   sub ax,val4
   ```
8. No.

9. Yes.

10. Yes (for example, mov al,–128 . . . followed by . . . neg al).

11. No.

12. Setting the Carry and Overflow flags at the same time:

```
mov al,80h
add al,80h
```

13. Setting the Zero flag after INC and DEC to indicate unsigned overflow:

```
mov al,0FFh
inc al
jz overflow_occurred
mov bl,1
dec bl
jz overflow_occurred
```

14. Subtracting 3 from 4 (unsigned). Carry out of MSB is inverted and placed in the Carry flag:

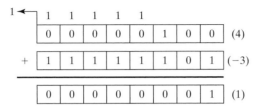

```
mov al,4
sub al,3     ; CF = 0
```

4.3 Data-Related Operators and Directives

1. False.

2. False.

3. True.

4. False.

5. True.

6. Data directive:

```
.data
ALIGN 2
myBytes BYTE 10h, 20h, 30h, 40h
etc.
```

7. (a) 1 (b) 4 (c) 4 (d) 2 (e) 4 (f) 8 (g) 5

8. mov dx, WORD PTR myBytes

9. mov al, BYTE PTR myWords+1

10. mov eax, DWORD PTR myBytes

11. Data directive:

```
myWordsD LABEL DWORD
myWords WORD 3 DUP(?),2000h
.data
mov eax,myWordsD
```

12. Data directive:

```
myBytesW LABEL WORD
myBytes BYTE 10h,20h,30h,40h
.code
mov ax,myBytesW
```

4.4 Indirect Addressing

1. False.
2. True.
3. False.
4. False.
5. True (the PTR operator is required).
6. True.
7. (a) 10h (b) 40h (c) 003Bh (d) 3 (e) 3 (f) 2
8. (a) 2010h (b) 003B008Ah (c) 0 (d) 0 (e) 0044h

4.5 JMP and LOOP Instructions

1. True.
2. False.
3. 4,294,967,296 times.
4. False.
5. True.
6. CX.
7. ECX.
8. False (-128 to $+127$ bytes from the current location).
9. This is a trick! The program does not stop, because the first LOOP instruction decrements ECX to zero. The second LOOP instruction decrements ECX to FFFFFFFFh, causing the outer loop to repeat.
10. Insert the following instruction at label L1: `push ecx`. Also insert the following instruction before the second LOOP instruction: `pop ecx`. (Once you have added these instructions, the final value of eax is 1Ch.)

5 Procedures

5.1 Introduction

No review questions.

5.2 Linking to an External Library

1. False (it contains object code).
2. Code example:
   ```
   MyProc PROTO
   ```
3. Code example:
   ```
   call MyProc
   ```

4. Irvine32.lib.

5. Kernel32.lib.

6. Kernel32.dll is a dynamic link library that is a fundamental part of the MS-Windows operating system.

7. %1.

5.3 The Book's Link Library

1. RandomRange procedure.

2. WaitMsg procedure.

3. Code example:
```
mov   eax,700
call Delay
```

4. WriteDec procedure.

5. Gotoxy procedure.

6. INCLUDE Irvine32.inc.

7. PROTO statements (procedure prototypes) and constant definitions. (There are also text macros, but they are not mentioned in this chapter.)

8. ESI contains the data's starting address, ECX contains the number of data units, and EBX contains the data unit size (byte, word, or doubleword).

9. EDX contains the offset of an array of bytes, and ECX contains the maximum number of characters to read.

10. Carry, Sign, Zero, and Overflow, and EFL displays the flag bits in hexadecimal.

11. Code example:
```
.data
str1 BYTE "Enter identification number: ",0
idStr BYTE 15 DUP(?)
.code
    mov   edx,OFFSET str1
    call WriteString
    mov   edx,OFFSET idStr
    mov   ecx,(SIZEOF idStr) - 1
    call ReadString
```

5.4 Stack Operations

1. SS and ESP.

2. The runtime stack is only type of stack that is managed directly by the CPU. For example, it holds the return addresses of called procedures.

3. LIFO stands for "last in, first out." The last value pushed into the stack is the first value popped out from the stack.

4. ESP is decremented by 4.

5. True.

6. False (you can push both 16-bit and 32-bit values).

7. True.

8. False (yes, it can, from the 80186 processor onward).

9. PUSHAD.

10. PUSHFD.

11. POPFD.

12. NASM's approach permits the programmer to be specific about which registers are to be pushed. PUSHAD, on the other hand, does not have that flexibility. This becomes important when a procedure needs to save several registers and at the same time return a value to its caller in the EAX register. In this type of situation, EAX cannot be pushed and popped because the return value would be lost.

13. Equivalent to PUSH EAX:
```
sub esp,4
mov [esp],eax
```

5.5   Defining and Using Procedures

1. True.

2. False.

3. Execution would contine beyond the end of the procedure, possibly into the beginning of another procedure. This type of programming bug is often difficult to detect!

4. *Receives* indicates the input parameters given to the procedure when it is called. *Returns* indicates what value, if any, the procedure produces when it returns it its caller.

5. False (it pushes the offset of the instruction *following* the call).

6. True.

7. True.

8. False (there is no NESTED operator).

9. True.

10. False.

11. True (it also receives a count of the number of array elements).

12. True.

13. False.

14. False.

15. The following statements would have to be modified:
```
add eax,[esi]    becomes -->   add ax,[esi]
add esi,4        becomes -->   add esi,2
```

5.6   Program Design Using Procedures

1. Functional decomposition, or top-down design.

2. Clrscr, WriteString, ReadInt, and WriteInt.

3. A stub program contains all of its important procedures, but the procedures are either empty or nearly empty.

4. False (it receives a pointer to an array).

5. The following statements would have to be modified:
```
mov [esi],eax    becomes -->   mov [esi],ax
add esi,4        becomes -->   add esi,2
```

6. Flowchart of the PromptForIntegers procedure:

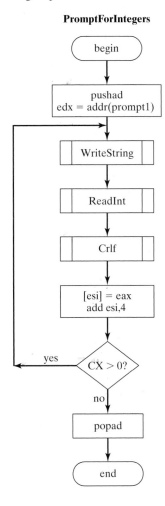

6   Conditional Processing

6.1   Introduction

No review questions.

6.2   Boolean and Comparison Instructions

1. (a) 00101101 (b) 01001000 (c) 01101111 (d) 10100011
2. (a) 85h (b) 34h (c) BFh (d) AEh
3. (a) CF=0, ZF=0, SF=0
   (b) CF=0, ZF=0, SF=0
   (c) CF=1, ZF=0, SF=1

4. and ax,00FFh

5. or ax,0FF00h

6. xor eax,0FFFFFFFFh

7. test eax,1   ; (low bit set if eax is odd)

8. or al,00100000b

9. and al,00001111b

10. Code example:

```
.data
memVal DWORD ?
.code
mov al,BYTE PTR memVal
xor al,BYTE PTR memVal+1
xor al,BYTE PTR memVal+2
xor al,BYTE PTR memVal+3
```

6.3   Conditional Loops

1. JA, JNBE, JAE, JNB, JB, JNAE, JBE, JNA.

2. JG, JNLE, JGE, JNL, JL, JNGE, JLE, JNG.

3. JECXZ.

4. Yes.

5. No (JB uses unsigned operands, whereas JL uses signed operands).

6. JBE.

7. JL.

8. No (8109h is negative and 26h is positive).

9. Yes.

10. Yes (the unsigned representation of -42 is compared to 26).

11. Code:

```
cmp dx,cx
jbe L1
```

12. Code:

```
cmp ax,cx
jg  L2
```

13. Code:

```
and al,11111100b
jz  L3
jmp L4
```

14. The XOR instruction in the three-instruction sequence will always clear the Carry flag. The BTC instruction may or may not clear the Carry flag, depending on the value in sempahore.

6.4   Conditional Loop Instructions

1. False.

2. True.

3. True.

4. Code example:

```
.data
```

```
array SWORD 3,5,14,-3,-6,-1,-10,10,30,40,4
sentinel SWORD 0
.code
main PROC
     mov esi,OFFSET array
     mov ecx,LENGTHOF array
next:
     test WORD PTR [esi],8000h      ; test sign bit
     pushfd                          ; push flags on stack
     add esi,TYPE array
     popfd                           ; pop flags from stack
     loopz next                      ; continue loop while
ZF=1
     jz quit                         ; none found
     sub esi,TYPE array              ; ESI points to value
```

5. If a matching value were not found, ESI would end up pointing beyond the end of the array. This could cause data to be corrupted if ESI were dereferenced and used to modify memory.

6.5 Conditional Structures

We will assume that all values are unsigned in this section.

1. Code example:

```
     cmp bx,cx
     jna next
     mov X,1
next:
```

2. Code example:

```
     cmp  dx,cx
     jnbe L1
     mov  X,1
     jmp  next
L1:  mov  X,2
next:
```

3. Code example:

```
     cmp val1,cx
     jna L1
     cmp cx,dx
     jna L1
     mov X,1
     jmp next
L1:  mov X,2
next:
```

4. Code example:

```
     cmp bx,cx
     ja   L1
     cmp bx,val1
     ja   L1
     mov X,2
     jmp next
L1:  mov X,1
next:
```

5. Code example:

```
     cmp bx,cx                        ; bx > cx?
```

```
        jna L1                      ; no: try condition after OR
        cmp bx,dx                   ; yes: is bx > dx?
        jna L1                      ; no: try condition after OR
        jmp L2                      ; yes: set X to 1
;-----------------OR(dx > ax) -----------------------
L1:     cmp dx,ax                   ; dx > ax?
        jna L3                      ; no: set X to 2
L2:     mov X,1                     ; yes:set X to 1
        jmp next                    ; and quit
L3:     mov X,2                     ; set X to 2
next:
```

6. Future changes to the table will alter the value of NumberOfEntries. We might forget to update the constant manually, but the assembler can correctly adjust a calculated value.

7. Code example:

```
.data
sum DWORD 0
sample DWORD 50
array DWORD 10,60,20,33,72,89,45,65,72,18
ArraySize = ($ - Array) / TYPE array

.code
        mov     eax,0                ; sum
        mov     edx,sample
        mov     esi,0                ; index
        mov     ecx,ArraySize

L1:     cmp     esi,ecx
        jnl     L5
        cmp     array[esi*4],edx
        jng     L4
        add     eax,array[esi*4]
L4:     inc     esi
        jmp     L1

L5:     mov     sum,eax
```

6.6 Application: Finite-State Machines

1. A directed graph (also known as a *diagraph*).

2. Each node is a state.

3. Each edge is a transition from one state to another, caused by some input.

4. State C.

5. An infinite number of digits.

6. The FSM enters an error state.

7. No. The proposed FSM would permit a signed integer to consist of only a plus (+) or minus (−) sign. The FSM in Section 6.6.2 would not permit that.

8. FSM that recognizes real numbers without exponents:

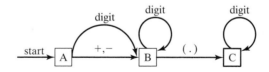

6.7 Decision Directives

No review questions.

7 Integer Arithmetic

7.1 Introduction

No review questions.

7.2 Shift and Rotate Instructions

1. ROL.
2. RCR.
3. SAR.
4. RCL.
5. Code example:

```
    shr al,1             ; shift AL into Carry flag
    jnc next             ; Carry flag set?
    or  al,80h           ; yes: set highest bit
next:                    ; no: do nothing
```

6. The Carry flag receives the lowest bit of AX (before the shift).
7. `shl eax,4`
8. `shr ebx,2`
9. `ror dl,4`   (or: `rol dl,4`)
10. `shld dx,ax,1`
11. (a) 6Ah (b) EAh (c) FDh (d) A9h
12. (a) 9Ah (b) 6Ah (c) 0A9h (d) 3Ah
13. Code example:

```
    shr ax,1             ; shift AX into Carry flag
    rcr bx,1             ; shift Carry flag into BX
  ; Using SHRD:
    shrd bx,ax,1
```

14. Code example:

```
    mov ecx,32           ; loop counter
    mov bl,0             ; counts the '1' bits
L1: shr eax,1            ; shift into Carry flag
    jnc L2               ; Carry flag set?
    inc bl               ; yes: add to bit count
L2: loop L1              ; continue loop

  ; if BL is odd, clear the parity flag
  ; if BL is even, set the parity flag
    shr bl,1
    jc  odd
    mov bh,0
    or  bh,0             ; PF = 1
    jmp next
odd:
    mov bh,1
```

```
          or   bh,1                        ; PF = 0
next:
```

7.3   Shift and Rotate Applications

1. This problem requires us to start with the high-order byte and work our way down to the lowest byte:

```
byteArray BYTE 81h,20h,33h
.code
shr byteArray+2,1
rcr byteArray+1,1
rcr byteArray,1
```

2. This problem requires us to start with the low-order word and work our way up to the highest word:

```
wordArray WORD 810Dh,0C064h,93ABh
.code
shl wordArray,1
rcl wordArray+2,1
rcl wordArray+4,1
```

3. The multiplier (24) can be factored into 16 * 8:

```
mov ebx,eax                        ; save a copy of eax
shl eax,4                          ; multiply by 16
shl ebx,3                          ; multiply by 8
add eax,ebx                        ; add the products
```

4. As the hint explains, the multiplier (21) can be factored into 16 * 4 + 1:

```
mov ebx,eax                        ; save a copy of eax
mov ecx,eax                        ; save another copy of eax
shl eax,4                          ; multiply by 16
shl ebx,2                          ; multiply by 4
add eax,ebx                        ; add the products
add eax,ecx                        ; add original value of eax
```

5. Change the instruction at label L1 to shr eax,1

6. We will assume that the time stamp word is in the DX register:

```
shr dx,5
and dl,00111111b                   ; (leading zeros optional)
mov bMinutes,dl                    ; save in variable
```

7.4   Multiplication and Division Instructions

1. The product is stored in registers that are twice the size of the multiplier and multiplicand. If you multiply 0FFh by 0FFh, for example, the product (FE01h) easily fits within 16 bits.

2. When the product fits completely within the lower register of the product, IMUL sign-extends the product into the upper product register. MUL, on the other hand, zero-extends the product.

3. With IMUL, the Carry and Overflow flags are set when the upper half of the product is not a sign extension of the lower half of the product.

4. EAX.

5. AX.

6. AX.

7. Code example:

```
mov ax,dividendLow
```

```
cwd                                        ; sign-extend dividend
mov bx,divisor
idiv bx
```

8. DX = 0002h, AX = 2200h.

9. AX = 0306h.

10. EDX = 0, EAX = 00012340h.

11. The DIV will cause a divide overflow, so the values of AX and DX cannot be determined.

12. Code example:

```
mov ax,3
mov bx,-5
imul bx
mov val1,ax                                ; product

// alternative solution:
mov al,3
mov bl,-5
imul bl
mov val1,ax                                ; product
```

13. Code example:

```
mov ax,-276
cwd                                        ; sign-extend AX into DX
mov bx,10
idiv bx
mov val1,ax                                ; quotient
```

14. Implement the unsigned expression val1 = (val2 * val3) / (val4 − 3):

```
mov eax,val2
mul val3
mov ebx,val4
sub ebx,3
div ebx
mov val1,eax
```

(You can substitute any 32-bit general-purpose register for EBX in this example.)

15. Implement the signed expression val1 = (val2 / val3) * (val1 + val2):

```
mov eax,val2
cdq                                        ; extend EAX into EDX
idiv val3                                  ; EAX = quotient
mov ebx,val1
add ebx,val2
imul ebx
mov val1,eax                               ; lower 32 bits of product
```

(You can substitute any 32-bit general-purpose register for EBX in this example.)

7.5 Extended Addition and Subtraction

1. The ADC instruction adds both a source operand and the Carry flag to a destination operand.

2. The SBB instruction subtracts both a source operand and the Carry flag from a destination operand.

3. EAX = C0000000h, EDX = 00000010h.

4. EAX = F0000000h, EDX = 000000FFh.

5. DX = 0016h.

6. In correcting this example, it is easiest to reduce the number of instructions. You can use a single register (ESI) to index into all three variables. ESI should be set to zero before the loop because the integers are stored in little endian order with their low-order bytes occurring first:

```
        mov ecx,8                          ; loop counter
        mov esi,0                          ; use the same index reg
        clc                                ; clear Carry flag
top:
        mov al,byte ptr val1[esi]          ; get first number
        sbb al,byte ptr val2[esi]          ; subtract second
        mov byte ptr result[esi],al        ; store the result
        inc esi                            ; move to next pair
        loop top
```

Of course, you could easily reduce the number of loop iterations by adding doublewords rather than bytes.

7.6 ASCII and Unpacked Decimal Arithmetic

1. Code example:
```
    or ax,3030h
```

2. Code example:
```
    and ax,0F0Fh
```

3. Code example:
```
    and ax,0F0Fh                 ; convert to unpacked
    aad
```

4. Code example:
```
    aam
```

5. Code example (displays binary value in AX):
```
out16  PROC
       aam
       or    ax,3030h
       push  eax
       mov   al,ah
       call  WriteChar
       pop   eax
       call  WriteChar
       ret
out16  ENDP
```

6. After AAA, AX would equal 0108h. Intel says: First, if the lower digit of AL is greater than 9 or the AuxCarry flag is set, add 6 to AL and add 1 to AH. Then in all cases, AND AL with 0Fh. Pseudocode:
```
IF ((AL AND 0FH) > 9) OR (AuxCarry = 1) THEN
     add 6 to AL
     add 1 to AH
END IF
AND AL with 0FH;
```

7.7 Packed Decimal Arithmetic

1. When the sum of a packed decimal addition is greater than 99, DAA sets the Carry flag. For example,
```
    mov al,56h
    add al,92h                   ; AL = E8h
    daa                          ; AL = 48h, CF=1
```

2. When a larger packed decimal integer is subtracted from a small one, DAS sets the Carry flag. For example,

```
mov   al,56h
sub   al,92h          ; AL = C4h
das                   ; AL = 64h, CF=1
```

3. $n + 1$ bytes.

4. Suppose AL = 3Dh, AF = 0, and CF = 0. Because the lower digit (D) is > 9, we subtract 6 from D. AL now equals 37h. Because the upper digit (3) is $\leqslant 9$ and CF = 0, no other adjustments are necessary. DAS produces AL = 37h.

8   Advanced Procedures

8.1   Introduction

No review questions.

8.2   Stack Frames

1. True.

2. True.

3. True.

4. False.

5. True.

6. True.

7. Value parameters and Reference parameters.

8. Code example:

```
mov   esp,ebp
pop   ebp
```

9. EAX

10. It passes an integer constant to the RET instruction. This constant is added to the stack pointer right after the RET instruction has popped the procedure's return address off the stack.

11. Stack frame diagram:

10h	[EBP + 16]
20h	[EBP + 12]
30h	[EBP + 8]
(return addr)	[EBP + 4]
EBP	<--ESP

12. LEA can return the offset of an indirect operand; it is particularly useful for obtaining the offset of a stack parameter.

13. Four bytes.

14. Code example:

```
AddThree PROC
; modeled after the AddTwo procedure in Section 8.4.3:
    push ebp
```

```
        mov   ebp,esp
        mov   eax,[ebp + 16]; 10h
        add   eax,[ebp + 12]; 20h
        add   eax,[ebp + 8] ; 30h
        pop   ebp
        ret   12
     AddThree ENDP
```

15. It is zero-extended into EAX and pushed on the stack.

16. Declaration: `LOCAL pArray:PTR DWORD`

17. Declaration: `LOCAL buffer[20]:BYTE`

18. Declaration: `LOCAL pwArray:PTR WORD`

19. Declaration: `LOCAL myByte:SBYTE`

20. Declaration: `LOCAL myArray[20]:DWORD`

21. The C calling convention, because it specifies that arguments must be pushed on the stack in reverse order, makes it possible to create a procedure/function with a variable number of parameters. The last parameter pushed on the stack can be a count specifying the number of parameters already pushed on the stack. In the following diagram, for example, the count value is located at [EBP + 8]:

10h	[EBP + 20]
20h	[EBP + 16]
30h	[EBP + 12]
3	[EBP + 8]
(return addr)	[EBP + 4]
EBP	<--ESP

8.3 Recursion

1. False.

2. It terminates when n equals zero.

3. The following instructions execute after each recursive call has finished:

```
     ReturnFact:
           mov ebx,[ebp+8]
           mul ebx
     L2:   pop ebp
           ret 4
```

4. The calculated value would exceed the range of an unsigned doubleword, and would roll past zero. The output would appear to be smaller than 12 factorial.

5. 12! uses 156 bytes of stack space. *Rationale:* From Figure 8-1, we see that when $n = 0$, 12 stack bytes are used (3 entries). When $n = 1$, 24 bytes are used. When $n = 2$, 36 bytes are used. Therefore, the amount of stack space required for n! is $(n + 1)*12$.

6. A recursive Fibonacci algorithm uses system resources inefficiently because each call to the Fibonacci function with a value of n generates function calls for all Fibonacci numbers between 1 and $n - 1$. Here is the pseudocode to generate the first 20 values:

```
     for(int i = 1; i <= 20; i++)
```

```
    print( fibonacci(i) );
int fibonacci(int n)
{
    if( n == 1 )
        return 1;
    elseif( n == 2 )
        return 2;
    else
        return fibonacci(n-1) + fibonacci(n-2);
}
```

8.4   .MODEL Directive

1. One code segment and one data segment. All code and data are near, which means they can be reached using only 16-bit offsets.
2. Used in Protected mode. All offsets are 32 bits, and both code and data belong to the same segment.
3. The C option preserves the case of identifiers and prepends a leading underscore to external names. The PASCAL option converts all identifiers to upper case.

8.5   INVOKE, ADDR, PROC, and PROTO

1. True.
2. False.
3. False.
4. True.
5. False.
6. True.
7. True.
8. Declaration:

```
MultArray PROC ptr1:PTR DWORD,
    ptr2:PTR DWORD,
    count:DWORD                    ; (may be byte, word, or dword)
```

9. Declaration:

```
MultArray PROTO ptr1:PTR DWORD,
    ptr2:PTR DWORD,
    count:DWORD                    ; (may be byte, word, or dword)
```

10. It uses input-output parameters.
11. It is an output parameter.

8.6   Creating Multimodule Programs

1. True.
2. False.
3. True.
4. False.

9   Strings and Arrays

9.1   Introduction

No review questions.

9.2   String Primitive Instructions

1. EAX.
2. CMPSD.
3. (E)DI.
4. LODSW.
5. Repeat while ZF = 1.
6. 1 (set).
7. 2.
8. Regardless of which operands are used, CMPS still compares the contents of memory pointed to by ESI to the memory pointed to by EDI.
9. 1 byte beyond the matching character.
10. REPNE (REPNZ).

9.3   Selected String Procedures

1. False (it stops when the null terminator of the shorter string is reached).
2. True.
3. False.
4. False.
5. 1 (set).
6. Check for string containing only the character to be trimmed.
7. The digit is unchanged.
8. REPNE (REPNZ).
9. The length would be $(EDI_{final} - EDI_{initial}) - 1$.

9.4   Two-Dimensional Arrays

1. Any general-purpose 32-bit registers.
2. [ebx + esi].
3. array[ebx + esi].
4. 16.
5. Code example:

```
mov esi,2                        ; row
mov edi,3                        ; column
mov eax,[esi*16 + edi*4]
```

6. BP points to the stack segment in Real-address mode.
7. No (the flat memory model uses the same segment for stack and data).

9.5   Searching and Sorting Integer Arrays

1. $n - 1$ times.

2. $n - 1$ times.

3. No: It decreases by 1 each.

4. $T(5000) = 0.5 * 10^2$.

5. $(\log_2 128) + 1 = 8$.

6. $(\log_2 n) + 1$.

7. EDX and EDI were already compared.

8. Change each JMP L4 instruction to JMP L1.

10   Structures and Macros

10.1   Structures

1. Structures are essential whenever you need to pass a large amount of data between procedures. One variable can be used to hold all the data.

2. Structure definition:
```
MyStruct STRUCT
      field1 WORD ?
      field2 DWORD 20 DUP(?)
MyStruct ENDS
```

3. `temp1 MyStruct <>`

4. `temp2 MyStruct <0>`

5. `temp3 MyStruct <, 20 DUP(0)>`

6. `array MyStruct 20 DUP(<>)`

7. `mov ax,array.field1`

8. Code example:
```
mov esi,OFFSET array
add esi,3 * (TYPE myStruct)
mov (MyStruct PTR[esi]).field1.ax
```

9. 82.

10. 82.

11. `TYPE MyStruct.field2 (or: SIZEOF Mystruct.field2)`

12. Multiple answers:
    a. Yes
    b. No
    c. Yes
    d. Yes
    e. No

13. Code example:
```
.data
time SYSTEMTIME <>
.code
mov ax,time.wHour
```

14. Code example:
```
myShape Triangle < <0,0>, <5,0>, <7,6> >
```

15. Code example (initializes an array of Triangle structures):
```
.data
ARRAY_SIZE = 5
```

```
triangles Triangle ARRAY_SIZE DUP(<>)
.code
        mov     ecx,ARRAY_SIZE
        mov     esi,0
L1:     mov     eax,11
        call    RandomRange
        mov     triangles[esi].Vertex1.X, ax
        mov     eax,11
        call    RandomRange
        mov     triangles[esi].Vertex1.Y, ax
        add     esi,TYPE Triangle
        loop    L1
```

10.2 Macros

1. False.

2. True.

3. Macros can have parameters.

4. False.

5. True.

6. False.

7. To permit the use of labels in a macro that is invoked more than once by the same program.

8. ECHO (also, the %OUT operator, which is shown later in the chapter)

9. Code example:

```
mPrintChar MACRO char,count
LOCAL temp
.data
temp BYTE count DUP(&char),0
.code
        push    edx
        mov     edx,OFFSET temp
        call    WriteString
        pop     edx
ENDM
```

10. Code example:

```
mGenRandom MACRO n
        mov   eax,n
        call RandomRange
ENDM
```

11. mPromptInteger:

```
mPromptInteger MACRO prompt,returnVal
        mWrite prompt
        call    ReadInt
        mov     returnVal,eax
ENDM
```

12. Code example:

```
mWriteAt MACRO X,Y,literal
        mGotoxy X,Y
        mWrite literal
ENDM
```

13. Code example:

```
mWriteStr namePrompt
1    push    edx
1    mov     edx,OFFSET namePrompt
1    call    WriteString
1    pop     edx
```

14. Code example:

```
mReadStr customerName
1    push    ecx
1    push    edx
1    mov     edx,OFFSET customerName
1    mov     ecx,(SIZEOF customerName) - 1
1    call    ReadString
1    pop     edx
1    pop     ecx
```

15. Code example:

```
;-----------------------------------------------
mDumpMemx MACRO varName
;
; Displays a variable in hexadecimal, using the
; variable's attributes to determine the number
; of units and unit size.
;-----------------------------------------------
      push  ebx
      push  ecx
      push  esi
      mov   esi,OFFSET varName
      mov   ecx,LENGTHOF varName
      mov   ebx,TYPE varName
      call  DumpMem
      pop   esi
      pop   ecx
      pop   ebx
ENDM
; Sample calls:

.data
array1 BYTE   10h,20h,30h,40h,50h
array2 WORD   10h,20h,30h,40h,50h
array3 DWORD  10h,20h,30h,40h,50h
.code
mDumpMemx array1
mDumpMemx array2
mDumpMemx array3
```

10.3   Conditional-Assembly Directives

1. The IFB directive is used to check for blank macro parameters.

2. The IFIDN directive compares two text values and returns true if they are identical. It performs a case-sensitive comparison.

3. EXITM.

4. IFIDNI is the case-insensitive version of IFIDN.

5. The IFDEF returns true if a symbol has already been defined.

6. ENDIF.

7. Code example:

```
mWriteLn MACRO text:=<" ">
    mWrite text
    call Crlf
ENDM
```

8. List of relational operators:

LT   Less than
GT   Greater than
EQ   Equal to
NE   Not equal to
LE   Less than or equal to
GE   Greater than or equal to

9. Code example:

```
mCopyWord MACRO intVal
    IF (TYPE intVal) EQ 2
      mov ax,intVal
    ELSE
      ECHO Invalid operand size
    ENDIF
ENDM
```

10. Code example:

```
mCheck MACRO Z
    IF Z LT 0
      ECHO **** Operand Z is invalid ****
    ENDIF
ENDM
```

11. The substitution (&) operator resolves ambiguous references to parameter names within a macro.

12. The literal-character operator (!) forces the preprocessor to treat a predefined operator as an ordinary character.

13. The expansion operator (%) expands text macros or converts constant expressions into their text representations.

14. Code example:

```
CreateString MACRO strVal
.data
temp BYTE "Var&strVal",0
.code
ENDM
```

15. Code example:

```
        mLocate -2,20
        ;(no code generated because xval < 0)

        mLocate 10,20
    1   mov bx,0
    1   mov ah,2
    1   mov dh,20
    1   mov dl,10
    1   int 10h
```

```
   mLocate col,row
1    mov bx,0
1    mov ah,2
1    mov dh,row
1    mov dl,col
1    int 10h
```

10.4   Defining Repeat Blocks

1. The WHILE directive repeats a statement block based on a boolean expression.

2. The REPEAT directive repeats a statement block based on the value of a counter.

3. The FOR directive repeats a statement block by iterating over a list of symbols.

4. The FORC directive repeats a statement block by iterating over a string of characters.

5. FORC

6. Code example:
```
   BYTE 0,0,0,100
   BYTE 0,0,0,20
   BYTE 0,0,0,30
```

7. Code example:
```
mRepeat MACRO 'X',50
      mov cx,50
??0000: mov ah,2
      mov dl,'X'
      int 21h
      loop ??0000

mRepeat MACRO AL,20
      mov cx,20
??0001: mov ah,2
      mov dl,AL
      int 21h
      loop ??0001

mRepeat MACRO byteVal,countVal
      mov cx,countVal
??0002: mov ah,2
      mov dl,byteVal
      int 21h
      loop ??0002
```

8. If we examine the linked list data (in the listing file), it is apparent that the **NextPtr** field of each **ListNode** always equals 00000008 (the address of the second node):

```
Offset     ListNode
----------------------------
00000000   00000001   NodeData
           00000008   NextPtr

00000008   00000002   NodeData
           00000008   NextPtr

00000010   00000003   NodeData
           00000008   NextPtr

00000018   00000004   NodeData
           00000008   NextPtr
```

```
00000020   00000005   NodeData
           00000008   NextPtr

00000028   00000006   NodeData
           00000008   NextPtr
```

We hinted at this in the text when we said "the location counter's value ($) remains fixed at the first node of the list."

11   MS-Windows Programming

11.1   Win32 Console Programming

1. /SUBSYSTEM:CONSOLE

2. True.

3. False.

4. False.

5. True.

6. BOOL = byte, COLORREF = DWORD, HANDLE = DWORD, LPSTR = PTR BYTE, WPARAM = DWORD.

7. GetStdHandle.

8. ReadConsole.

9. Example from the *ReadConsole.asm* program in Section 11.1.3:

```
INVOKE ReadConsole, stdInHandle, ADDR buffer,
    BufSize - 2, ADDR bytesRead, 0
```

10. The COORD structure contains X and Y screen coordinates in character measurements.

11. Example from the *Console1.asm* program in Section 11.1.4:

```
INVOKE WriteConsole,
    consoleHandle,          ; console output handle
    ADDR message,           ; string pointer
    messageSize,            ; string length
    ADDR bytesWritten,      ; returns num bytes written
    0                       ; not used
```

12. Calling **CreateFile** when reading an input file:

```
INVOKE CreateFile,
    ADDR filename,          ; ptr to filename
    GENERIC_READ,           ; access mode
    DO_NOT_SHARE,           ; share mode
    NULL,                   ; ptr to security attributes
    OPEN_EXISTING,          ; file creation options
    FILE_ATTRIBUTE_NORMAL,  ; file attributes
    0                       ; handle to template file
```

13. Calling **CreateFile** to create a new file:

```
INVOKE CreateFile,
    ADDR filename,
    GENERIC_WRITE,
    DO_NOT_SHARE,
    NULL,
    CREATE_ALWAYS,
    FILE_ATTRIBUTE_NORMAL,
    0
```

14. Calling **ReadFile**:
```
INVOKE ReadFile,                    ; read file into buffer
     fileHandle,
     ADDR buffer,
     bufSize,
     ADDR byteCount,
     0
```

15. Calling **WriteFile**:
```
INVOKE WriteFile,                   ; write text to file
     fileHandle,                    ; file handle
     ADDR buffer,                   ; buffer pointer
     bufSize,                       ; number of bytes to write
     ADDR bytesWritten,             ; number of bytes written
     0                              ; overlapped execution flag
```

16. SetFilePointer.

17. SetConsoleTitle.

18. SetConsoleScreenBufferSize.

19. SetConsoleCursorInfo.

20. SetConsoleTextAttribute.

21. WriteConsoleOutputAttribute.

22. Sleep.

11.2 Writing a Graphical Windows Application

Note: Most of these questions can be answered by looking in *GraphWin.inc*, the include file supplied with this book's sample programs.

1. A POINT structure contains two fields, ptX and ptY, that describe the X-and Y-coordinates (in pixels) of a point on the screen.

2. The WNDCLASS structure defines a window class. Each window in a program must belong to a class, and each program must define a window class for its main window. This class is registered with the operating system before the main window can be shown.

3. *lpfnWndProc* is a pointer to a function in an application program that receives and processes event messages triggered by the user.

4. The *style* field is a combination of different style options, such as WS_CAPTION and WS_BORDER, that control a window's appearance and behavior.

5. *hInstance* holds a handle to the current program instance. Each programming running under MS-Windows is automatically assigned a handle by the operating system when the program is loaded into memory.

6. (A program that calls CreatewindowEx is shown in Section 11.2.6.)

   The prototype for **CreateWindowEx** is located in the *GraphWin.inc* file:
```
CreateWindowEx PROTO,
     classexWinStyle:DWORD,
     className:PTR BYTE,
     winName:PTR BYTE,
     winStyle:DWORD,
     X:DWORD,
     Y:DWORD,
     rWidth:DWORD,
```

```
rHeight:DWORD,
hWndParent:DWORD,
hMenu:DWORD,
hInstance:DWORD,
lpParam:DWORD
```

The fourth parameter, *winStyle*, determines the window's style characteristics. In the WinApp.asm program in Section 11.2.6, when we call CreateWindowEx, we pass it a combination of predefined style constants:

```
MAIN_WINDOW_STYLE = WS_VISIBLE + WS_DLGFRAME + WS_CAPTION
    + WS_BORDER + WS_SYSMENU + WS_MAXIMIZEBOX + WS_MINIMIZEBOX
    + WS_THICKFRAME
```

The window described here will be visible, and it will have a dialog box frame, a caption bar, a border, a system menu, a maximize icon, a minimize icon, and a thick surrounding frame.

7. Calling MessageBox:

```
INVOKE MessageBox, hMainWnd, ADDR GreetText,
    ADDR GreetTitle, MB_OK
```

8. Choose any two of the following (from *GraphWin.inc*):

```
MB_OK, MB_OKCANCEL, MB_ABORTRETRYIGNORE, MB_YESNOCANCEL, MB_YESNO,
MB_RETRYCANCEL, MB_CANCELTRYCONTINUE
```

9. Icon constants (choose any two):

```
MB_ICONHAND, MB_ICONQUESTION, MB_ICONEXCLAMATION, MB_ICONASTERISK
```

10. Tasks performed by **WinMain** (choose any three):
- Get a handle to the current program.
- Load the program's icon and mouse cursor.
- Register the program's main window class and identify the procedure that will process event messages for the window.
- Create the main window.
- Show and update the main window.
- Begin a loop that receives and dispatches messages.

11. The **WinProc** procedure receives and processes all event messages relating to a window. It decodes each message, and if the message is recognized, carries out application-oriented (or application-specific) tasks relating to the message.

12. The following messages are processed:
- WM_LBUTTONDOWN, generated when the user presses the left mouse button.
- WM_CREATE, indicates that the main window was just created.
- WM_CLOSE, indicates that the application's main window is about to close.

13. The ErrorHandler procedure, which is optional, is called if the system reports an error during the registration and creation of the program's main window.

14. The message box is shown before the application's main window appears.

15. The message box appears before the main window closes.

11.3 Dynamic Memory Allocation

1. Dynamic memory allocation.

2. Returns a 32-bit integer handle to the program's existing heap area in EAX.

3. Allocates a block of memory from a heap.

4. HeapCreate example:

```
HEAP_START =    2000000             ;   2 MB
```

```
HEAP_MAX  =  400000000              ; 400 MB
.data
hHeap HANDLE ?                      ; handle to heap
.code
INVOKE HeapCreate, 0, HEAP_START, HEAP_MAX
```

5. Pass a pointer to the memory block (along with the heap handle).

11.4   IA-32 Memory Management

1. (a) Multitasking permits multiple programs (or tasks) to run at the same time. The processor divides up its time between all of the running programs.
   (b) Segmentation provides a way to isolate memory segments from each other. This permits multiple programs to run simultaneously without interfering with each other.

2. (a) A segment selector is a 16-bit value stored in a segment register (CS, DS, SS, ES, FS, or GS).
   (b) A logical address is a combination of a segment selector and a 32-bit offset.

3. True.

4. True.

5. False.

6. False.

7. A linear address is a 32-bit integer ranging between 0 and FFFFFFFFh, which refers to a memory location. The linear address may also be the physical address of the target data if a feature called paging is disabled.

8. When paging is enabled, the processor translates each 32-bit linear address into a 32-bit physical address. A linear address is divided into three fields: a pointer to a page directory entry, a pointer to a page table entry, and an offset into a page frame.

9. The linear address is automatically a 32-bit physical memory address.

10. Paging makes it possible for a computer to run a combination of programs that would not otherwise fit into memory. The processor does this by initially loading only part of a program in memory while keeping the remaining parts on disk.

11. The LDTR register.

12. The GDTR register.

13. One.

14. Many (each task or program has its own local descriptor table).

15. Choose any four from the following list: base address, privilege level, segment type, segment present flag, granularity flag, segment limit.

16. Page Directory, Page Table, and Page (page frame).

17. The Table field of a linear address (see Figure 11-4).

18. The Offset field of a linear address (see Figure 11-4).

12   High-Level Language Interface

12.1   Introduction

1. The naming convention used by a language refers to the rules or characteristics regarding the naming of variables and procedures.

2. Tiny, small, compact, medium, large, huge.

3. No, because the procedure name will not be found by the linker.

4. The memory model determines whether near or far calls are made. A near call pushes only the 16-bit offset of the return address on the stack. A far call pushes a 32-bit segment/offset address on the stack.

5. C and C++ are case sensitive, so they will only execute calls to procedures that are named in the same fashion.

6. Yes, many languages specify that EBP (BP), ESI (SI), and EDI (DI) must be preserved across procedure calls.

12.2   Inline Assembly Code

1. Inline assembly code is assembly language source code that is inserted directly into high-level language programs. The inline qualifier in C++, on the other hand, asks the C++ compiler to insert the body of a function directly into the program's compiled code to avoid the extra execution time it would take to call and return from the function. (Note: Answering this question requires some knowledge of the C++ language that is not covered in this book.)

2. The primary advantage to writing inline code is simplicity because there are no external linking issues, naming problems, and parameter passing protocols to worry about. Secondarily, inline code can execute more quickly because it avoids the extra execution time typically required by calling and returning from an assembly language procedure.

3. Examples of comments (select any two):

```
mov esi,buf                      ; initialize index register
mov esi,buf                      // initialize index register
mov esi,buf                      /* initialize index register */
```

4. Yes.

5. Yes.

6. No.

7. No.

8. A program bug might result because the __fastcall convention allows the compiler to use general-purpose registers as temporary variables.

9. Use the LEA instruction.

10. The LENGTH operator returns the number of elements in the array specified by the DUP operator. For example, the value placed in EAX by the LENGTH operator is 20:

```
myArray DWORD 20 DUP(?), 10, 20, 30
.code
mov eax,LENGTH myArray            ; 20
```

(Note that the LENGTHOF operator, introduced in Chapter 4, would return 23 when applied to myArray.)

11. The SIZE operator returns the product of TYPE (4) * LENGTH.

12.3   Linking to C++ in Protected Mode

1. The extern and "C" keywords must be used.

2. The Irvine32 library uses STDCALL, which is not the same as the C calling convention used by C and C++. The important difference is in how the stack is cleaned up after a function call.

3. Floating-point values are usually pushed on the processor's floating-point stack before returning from the function.

4. A short int is returned in the AX register.

5. printf PROTO C, pString:PTR BYTE, args:VARARG.

6. X will be pushed last.

7. To prevent the decoration (altering) of external procedure names by the C++ compiler. *Name decoration* (also called *name mangling*) is done by programming languages that permit function overloading, which permits multiple functions to have the same name.

8. If name decoration is in effect, an external function name generated by the C++ compiler will not be the same as the name of the called procedure written in assembly language. Understandably, the assembler does not have any knowledge of the name decoration rules used by C++ compilers.

9. Virtually no changes at all, showing that array subscripts can be just as efficient as pointers when manipulating arrays.

12.4   Linking to C/C++ in Real-Address Mode

1. Assembly procedures called by Borland C++ must preserve the values of BP, DS, SS, SI, DI, and the Direction flag.

2. INT = 2, enum = 1, float = 4, double = 8.

3. mov eax,[bp + 6].

4. The ror eax,8 statement rotates out the lowest digit of EAX, preventing a recurring pattern when generating sequences of small random numbers.

13   16-Bit MS-DOS Programming

13.1   MS-DOS and the IBM-PC

1. 9FFFFh.

2. Interrupt vector table.

3. 00400h.

4. The BIOS.

5. Suppose a program was named myProg.exe. The following would redirect its output to the default printer:

```
myProg > prn
```

6. LPT1.

7. An interrupt service routine (also called an *interrupt handler*) is an operating system procedure that (1) provides basic services to application programs and (2) handles hardware events. For more details, see Section 16.4.

8. Push the flags on the stack.

9. See the four steps in Section 13.1.4.

10. The interrupt handler executes an IRET instruction.

11. 10h.

12. 1Ah.

13. 21h * 4 = 0084h.

13.2   MS-DOS Function Calls (INT 21h)

1. AH.

2. Function 4Ch.

3. Functions 2 and 6 both write a single character.

4. Function 9.

5. Function 40h.

6. Functions 1 and 6.

7. Function 3Fh.

8. Functions 2Ah and 2Bh. To display the time, you would call the **WriteDec** procedure from the book's library. That procedure uses Function 2 to output digits to the console. (Look in the *Irvine16.asm* file for details, located in the \Examples\Lib16 directory.)

9. Functions 2Bh (set system date) and 2Dh (set system time).

10. Function 6.

13.3   Standard MS-DOS File I/O Services

1. Device Handles: 0 = Keyboard (standard input), 1 = Console (standard output), 2 = Error output, 3 = Auxiliary device (asynchronous), 4 = Printer.

2. Carry flag.

3. Parameters for function 716Ch:

```
AX = 716Ch
BX = access mode (0 = read, 1 = write, 2 = read/write)
CX = attributes (0 = normal, 1 = read only, 2 = hidden,
 3 = system, 8 = volume ID, 20h = archive)
DX = action (1 = open, 2 = truncate, 10h = create)
DS:SI = segment/offset of filename
DI = alias hint (optional)
```

4. Opening an existing file for input:

```
.data
infile BYTE "myfile.txt",0
inHandle WORD ?
.code
    mov    ax,716Ch            ; extended create or open
    mov    bx,0                ; mode = read-only
    mov    cx,0                ; normal attribute
    mov    dx,1                ; action: open
    mov    si,OFFSET infile
    int    21h                 ; call MS-DOS
    jc     quit                ; quit if error
    mov    inHandle,ax
```

5. Reading a binary array from a file is best done with INT 21h Function 3Fh. The following parameters are required:

```
AH = 3Fh
BX = open file handle
CX = maximum bytes to read
DS:DX = address of input buffer
```

6. After calling INT 21h, compare the return value in AX to the value that was placed in CX before the function call. If AX is smaller, the end of the file must have been reached.

7. The only difference is the value in BX. When reading from the keyboard, BX is set to the keyboard handle (0). When reading from a file, BX is set to the handle of the open file.

8. Function 42h.

9. Code example (BX already contains the file handle):

```
mov ah,42h              ; move file pointer
mov al,0                ; method: offset from beginning
mov cx,0                ; offsetHi
mov dx,50               ; offsetLo
int 21h
```

14   Disk Fundamentals

14.1   Disk Storage Systems

1. True.
2. False.
3. Cylinder.
4. True.
5. 512.
6. For faster access because the closer are the cylinders, the smaller is distance that the read/write heads must travel.
7. The read/write heads must jump over other cylinders, wasting time and increasing the probablility that errors will occur.
8. Volume.
9. The average amount of time required to move the read/write heads between tracks.
10. The marking of physical sectors on the disk surfaces.
11. The disk partition table and a program that locates a single partition's boot sector and runs another program that loads the operating system.
12. One.
13. System.

14.2   File Systems

1. True.
2. No, it is in the disk directory.
3. False (all systems, including NTFS, require at least one cluster to store a file).
4. False.
5. False.
6. 4GB (shown in Table 14-1)
7. FAT32 and NTFS.
8. NTFS.
9. NTFS.
10. NTFS.
11. NTFS.
12. 8GB.
13. Boot record, file allocation table, root directory, and the data area.
14. This information is at offset 0Dh in the boot record.

15. Two 8KB clusters would be required, for a total of 16,384 bytes. The number of wasted bytes would be (16,384 − 8,200), or 8,184 bytes.

16. (This one is up to you!)

14.3   Disk Directory

1. True.

2. False (it is called the root directory).

3. False (it contains the starting *cluster* number).

4. True.

5. 32.

6. Filename, extension, attribute, time stamp, date stamp, starting cluster number, file size.

7. The status bytes and their descriptions are listed in Table 14-5.

8. Bits 0 to 4 = seconds; bits 5 to 10 = minutes; bits 11 to 15 = hours.

9. The first byte of the entry is 4*x*h, where x indicates the number of long filename entries to be used for the file.

10. Two.

11. Actually, there are three new fields: last access date, create date, and create time.

12. File allocation table links:

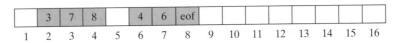

14.4   Reading and Writing Disk Sectors (7305h)

1. True.

2. False (the function runs in Real-address mode).

3. Parameters:
   ```
   AX: 7305h
   DS:BX: Segment/offset of a DISKIO structure variable
   CX: 0FFFFh
   DL: Drive number (0 = default, 1 = A, 2 = B, 3 = C, etc.)
   SI: Read/write flag
   ```

4. INT 10h displays special ASCII graphics characters without trying to interpret them as control codes (such as Tab and Carriage return).

5. The Carry flag is set if function 7305h cannot read the requested sector, and the program displays an error message. (Remember that you cannot test this program under Windows NT, 2000, and XP.)

14.5   System-Level File Functions

1. Function 7303h.

2. Function 7303h.

3. Function 39h (create subdirectory) and Function 3Bh (set current directory).

4. Function 7143h (get and set file attributes).

15   BIOS-Level Programming

15.1   Introduction

No review questions.

15.2   Keyboard Input with INT 16h

1. INT 16h is best.

2. In the keyboard typeahead buffer, at location 0040:001E.

3. INT 9h reads the keyboard input port, retrieves the keyboard scan code, and produces the corresponding ASCII code. It inserts both in the keyboard typeahead buffer.

4. Function 05h.

5. Function 10h.

6. Function 11h examines the buffer and lets you know which key, if any, is waiting.

7. No.

8. Function 12h.

9. Bit 4 (see Table 15-2)

10. Code example:

```
L1:   mov ah,12h                  ; get keyboard flags
      int 16h
      test al1,100h               ; Ctrl key down?
      jz L1                       ; no: repeat the loop
; At this point, the Ctrl key has been pressed
```

11. To check for other keyboard keys, add more CMP and JE instructions after the existing ones currently in the loop. Suppose we wanted to check for the ESC, F1, and Home keys:

```
L1:   .
      .
      cmp ah,1                    ; ESC key's scan code?
      je  quit                    ; yes: quit
      cmp ah,3Bh                  ; F1 function key?
      je  quit                    ; yes: quit
      cmp ah,47h                  ; Home key?
      je  quit                    ; yes: quit
      jmp L1                      ; no: check buffer again
```

15.3   Video Programming with INT 10h

1. MS-DOS level, BIOS level, and Direct video level.

2. Direct video.

3. In MS-Windows, there are two ways to switch into full-screen mode:

   • Create a shortcut to the program's EXE file. Then open the Properties dialog for the shortcut, select the Screen properties, and select Full-screen mode.

   • Open a Command window from the Start menu, then press Alt-Enter to switch to full-screen mode. Using the CD (change directory) command, navigate to your EXE file's directory, and run the program by typing its name. Alt-Enter is a toggle, so if you press it again, it will return the program to Window mode.

4. Mode 3 (color, 80 × 25)

5. ASCII code and attribute (2 bytes)

6. Red, green, blue, and intensity

7. Background: bits 4 to 7. Foreground: bits 0 to 3.

8. Function 02h.

9. Function 06h.

10. Function 09h.

11. Function 01h.

12. Function 00h.

13. AH = 2, DH = row, DL = column, and BH = video page.

14. There are two ways: (1) use INT 10h Function 01h to set the cursor's top line to an illegal value or (2) use INT 10h Function 02h to position the cursor outside the displayable range of rows and columns.

15. AH = 6, AL = number of lines to scroll, BH = attribute of scrolled lines, CH & CL = upper left window corner, and DH & DL = lower right window corner.

16. AH = 9, AL = ASCII code of character, BH = video page, BL = attribute, and CX = repetition count.

17. Function 10h, Subfunction 03h (set AH to 10h and AL to 03h).

18. AH = 06h, and AL = 0.

19. Every pixel on the screen is made of three colors: red, green, and blue. Dogs are color blind, so they cannot see pixels made from colors. I've tried displaying a picture of a cat on the screen, but my dog seems not to notice.

15.4 Drawing Graphics Using INT 10h

1. Function 0Ch

2. AH = 0Ch, AL = pixel value, BH = video page, CX = X-coordinate, and DX = Y-coordinate.

3. It's very slow.

4. Code example:
```
mov ah,0          ; set video mode
mov al,11h        ; to mode 11h
int 10h           ; call the BIOS
```

5. Mode 6Ah.

6. Formula: sx = (sOrigX + X).

7. a. (350,150)   b. (375,225) c. (150,400)

15.5 Memory-Mapped Graphics

1. False (each byte corresponds to 1 pixel).

2. True.

3. Mode 13h maps each pixel's integer value into a table of colors called a palette.

4. The color index of a pixel identifies which color in the palette is to be used when drawing the pixel on the screen.

5. Each entry in the palette consists of three separate integer values (0 to 63) known as RGB (red, green, blue). Entry 0 in the color palette controls the screen's background color.

6. (20,20,20).

7. (63,63,63).

8. (63,0,0).

9. Code example:

```
; Set screen background color to bright green.
mov  dx,3c8h                    ; video paletter port
mov  al,0                       ; index 0 (background color)
out  dx,al
mov  dx,3c9h                    ; colors go to port 3C9h
mov  al,0                       ; red
out  dx,al
mov  al,63                      ; green (intensity = 63)
out  dx,al
mov  al,0                       ; blue
out  dx,al
```

10. Code example:

```
; Set screen background color to white
mov  dx,3c8h                    ; video paletter port
mov  al,0                       ; index 0 (background color)
out  dx,al
mov  dx,3c9h                    ; colors go to port 3C9h
mov  al,63                      ; red = 63
out  dx,al
mov  al,63                      ; green = 63
out  dx,al
mov  al,63                      ; blue = 63
out  dx,al
```

(The last two MOV statements can be eliminated if you want to reduce the amount of code in this example.)

15.6   Mouse Programming

1. Function 0.

2. Code example:

```
mov   ax,0                      ; reset mouse
int   33h                       ; call the BIOS
cmp   ax,0                      ; mouse not available?
je    MouseNotAvailable         ; yes: show error message
```

3. Functions 1 and 2.

4. Code example:

```
mov   ax,2                      ; hide mouse pointer
int   33h
```

5. Function 3.

6. Code example:

```
mov   ax,3                      ; get mouse position and status
int   33h
mov   mouseX,cx
mov   mouseY,dx
```

7. Function 4.

8. Code example:

```
mov   ax,4                      ; set mouse position
```

```
        mov    cx,100                  ; X-value
        mov    dx,400                  ; Y-value
        int    33h
```

9. Function 5.

10. Code example:

```
        mov    ax,5                    ; get button press information
        mov    bx,0                    ; button ID for left button
        int    33h
        test   ax,1                    ; left button currently down?
        jne    Button1                 ; yes: jump to label
```

Implementation note: This function will tell you if a certain button is currently being pressed. But if you just want the coordinates of the last button press, there is no need for the TEST instruction used in our example.

11. Function 6.

12. Code example:

```
        mov    ax,6                    ; get button release information
        mov    bx,1                    ; button ID
        int    33h
        test   ax,2                    ; right button released?
        jz     skip                    ; no – skip
        mov    mouseX,cx               ; yes: save coordinates
        mov    mouseY,dx
skip:
```

13. Code example:

```
        mov    ax,8                    ; set vertical limits
        mov    cx,200                  ; lower limit
        mov    dx,400                  ; upper limit
        int    33h
```

14. Code example:

```
        mov    ax,7                    ; set horizontal limits
        mov    cx,300                  ; lower limit
        mov    dx,600                  ; upper limit
        int    33h
```

15. Assuming that character cells are 8 pixels by 8 pixels, the X, Y-coordinates values would be (8 * 20), (8 * 10). The cell will be at position 160, 80.

16. The upper left corner of the cell will be at (8 * 22), (8 * 15). If we add 4 to each of these values to bring the mouse to the center of the cell, the answer is 180, 124.

17. The mouse was invented by Douglas Engelbart in 1963 at the Stanford Research Institute. (Source: *http://en.wikipedia.org/wiki/Computer_mouse*).

16   Expert MS-DOS Programming

16.1   Introduction

No review questions.

16.2   Defining Segments

1. Declares the beginning of a segment.

2. Returns the segment address of a data label or code label.

3. The ASSUME directive makes it possible for the assembler to calculate the offsets of labels and variables at assembly time. A directive such as

```
assume DS:myData
```

says to the assembler, "assume that from this point on, all references to data labels (via DS) will be located in the segment named **myData**."

4. BYTE, WORD, DWORD, PARA, and PAGE.

5. PRIVATE, PUBLIC, MEMORY, STACK, COMMON, and AT.

6. DWORD.

7. The combine type tells the linker how to combine segments having the same name.

8. Use the AT combine type. The following defines a segment with value 0040h:

```
bios SEGMENT AT 40h
```

9. A segment's class type provides another way of combining segments, in particular, those with different names. Segments having the same class type are loaded together, although they may be listed in a different order in the program source code.

10. Code example:

```
mov al,es:[di]
```

11. The third segment will also begin at address 1A060h.

16.3   Runtime Program Structure

1. The command processor checks to see if there is filename with extension COM in the current directory. If a file is found, it is executed. If a matching file is not found, see Section 16.3 for a description of the subsequent steps.

2. No.

3. Application programs loaded into the lowest 640K of memory. They are transient because when the finish executing, they are automatically unloaded from memory.

4. Program segment prefix

5. At offset 2Ch inside the program segment prefix area.

6. A COM program is a single-segment MS-DOS program. When stored on disk as a COM file, it is simply a binary image of the program when loaded into memory.

7. Tiny.

8. /T.

9. 64 KB.

10. Not efficient because even the smallest COM program uses an entire 64K memory segment.

11. One.

12. All segment registers are set to offset zero within the program. The program, in turn, is loaded into memory at the first available segment location following other programs still in memory.

13. The ORG directive assigns a specific offset to the very next label or instruction following the directive. The addresses of all subsequent labels are calculated from that point onward. COM programs, for example, always have ORG 100h at the beginning of the program code, so the first executable instruction will be located at offset 100h.

14. Load module.

15. DS and ES point to the program segment prefix area of the program.

16. MS-DOS automatically allocates all of available memory to a program when it is first loaded, unless the program's EXE header specificically limits its maximum memory allocation size.

17. The EXEMOD program displays statistics about a program's memory usage, and also permits many settings in the EXE header to be modified.

18. Run the EXEMOD program, passing it the name of the EXE file. The last line of the display will show the number of relocation entries.

16.4 Interrupt Handling

1. It displays a message on the screen "Abort, retry, or ignore?" and terminates the current program.

2. A 32-bit segment/offset address pointing to an interrupt handler

3. At address 0000:0040h because 0040h equals 10h * 4.

4. The 8259 Programmable Interrupt Controller chip.

5. The CLI (clear interrupt flag) instruction.

6. The STI (set interrupt flag) instruction.

7. IRQ 0 has highest priority.

8. Before the file has been created because the keyboard (IRQ 1) is at a higher priority than the disk drive (IRQ 14).

9. INT 9h.

10. An IRET instruction at the end of the interrupt handler returns control to the code that was running when the interrupt occurred.

11. Functions 25h and 35h.

12. An interrupt handler is any procedure that takes over processing an interrupt. It might be loaded when an application starts and then be unloaded when the application ends. A memory-resident program, on the other hand, remains in memory even after the program that installed it has ended. A memory-resident program does not necessarily have to be an interrupt handler.

13. A terminate and stay resident (TSR) program leaves part of itself in memory when it exits. This is accomplished by calling INT 21h function 31h.

14. The computer can be rebooted, or a special utility program can remove the TSR.

15. Rather than executing an IRET instruction when it finishes, it can instead execute a JMP to the address that was previously stored in the interrupt vector.

16. A terminate and stay resident (TSR) program.

17. Ctrl + Alt + Right shift + Del.

17 Floating-Point Processing and Instruction Encoding

17.1 Floating-Point Binary Representation

1. Because the reciprocal of -127 is $+127$, which would generate an overflow.

2. Because adding $+128$ to the exponent bias (127) would generate a negative value.

3. 52 bits.

4. 8 bits.

5. 1101.01101 = 13/1 + 1/4 + 1/8 + 1/32.

6. 0.2 generates an infinitely repeating bit pattern.

7. 11011.01011 = 1.101101011×2^4.

8. 0000100111101.1 = $1.001111011 \times 2^{-8}$.

9. $+1110.011 = 1.110011 \times 2^{-3}$, so the encoding is 0 01111100 11001100000000000000000.

10. Quiet NaN and Signaling NaN.

11. $5/8 = 0.101$ binary.

12. $17/32 = 0.10001$ binary.

13. $+10.75 = +1010.11 = +1.01011 \times 2^3$, encoded as 0 10000010 01011000000000000000000.

14. $-76.0625 = -01001100.0001 = -1.0011000001 \times 2^{-6}$, encoded as:
    1 10000101 00110000010000000000000

15. Positive or negative infinity, depending on the sign of the numerator.

17.2   Floating-Point Unit

1. fld st(0).

2. R0.

3. Choose from opcode, control, status, tag word, last instruction pointer, last data pointer.

4. Binary-coded decimal.

5. None.

6. REAL10 80 bits.

7. It pops ST(0) off the stack.

8. FCHS.

9. None, m32fp, m64fp, stack register.

10. FISUB converts the source operand from integer to floating-point.

11. FCOM, or FCOMP.

12. Code example:
    ```
    fnstsw  ax
    lahf
    ```

13. FILD.

14. RC field.

15. 1.010101101 rounded to nearest even becomes 1.010101110.

16. -1.010101101 rounded to nearest even becomes -1.010101110.

17. Assembly instructions:
    ```
    .data
    B REAL8 7.8
    M REAL8 3.6
    N REAL8 7.1
    P REAL8 ?
    .code
    fld   M
    fchs
    fld   N
    fadd  B
    fmul
    fst   P
    ```

18. Assembly language code:
    ```
    .data
    B DWORD 7
    N REAL8 7.1
    P REAL8 ?
    .code
    ```

```
.id  N
fsqrt
fiadd B
fst  P
```

17.3   Intel Instruction Encoding

1. (a) 8E (b) 8B (c) 8A (d) 8A (e) A2 (f) A3

2. (a) 8E (b) 8A (c) 8A (d) 8B (e) A0 (f) 8B

3. (a) D8 (b) D3 (c) 1D (d) 44 (e) 84 (f) 85

4. (a) 06 (b) 56 (c) 1D (d) 55 (e) 84 (f) 81

5. Machine language bytes:

```
a.    8E D8
b.    A0 00 00
c.    8B 0E 01 00
d.    BA 00 00
e.    B2 02
f.    BB 00 10
```

Index